ISBN 978-0-260-67554-5
PIBN 10963661

I Y

WASHINGTON REPORTS June

VOL. 35

CASES DETERMINED

IN THE

SUPREME COURT

OF

WASHINGTON

APRIL 18, 1904—SEPTEMBER 21, 1904

O

ARTHUR REMINGTON

REPORTER

BANCROFT-WHITNEY CO.
LAW PUBLISHERS AND LAW BOOK SELLERS
SEATTLE AND SAN FRANCISCO
1904

OFFICIAL REPORT

Published pursuant to Laws of Washington, 1895, page 97
(1 Ballinger's Codes and Statutes, 226 et seq.)
Under the personal supervision of the Reporter.

Rec. Dec. 9, 1904.

PRINTED, ELECTROTYPED AND BOUND
BY
THE GRAHAM-HICKMAN COMPANY,
SEATTLE.

JUDGES

OF THE

SUPREME COURT OF WASHINGTON

DURING THE PERIOD COVERED IN THIS VOLUME

Hon. MARK A. FULLERTON, Chief Justice

Hon. THOMAS J. ANDERS

Hon. RALPH O. DUNBAR

Hon. WALLACE MOUNT

Hon. HIRAM E. HADLEY

ATTORNEY GENERAL

Hon. W. B. STRATTON

CLERK - - - - - - C. S. REINHART

JUDGES

OF THE

SUPERIOR COURTS OF WASHINGTON

During the Pendency Therein of the Cases Reported in this Volume.

COUNTIES.	JUDGES.
Spokane and Stevens . . .	Hon. WILLIAM E. RICHARDSON.
Spokane	Hon. GEORGE W. BELT. Hon. LEANDER H. PRATHER.* Hon. HENRY L. KENNAN.†
Whitman	Hon. STEPHEN J. CHADWICK.
Adams and Lincoln . . .	Hon. CHARLES H. NEAL.
Chelan, Douglas, Okanogan and Ferry	Hon. CHARLES VICTOR MARTIN.
Walla Walla	Hon. THOMAS H. BRENTS.
Columbia, Garfield and Asotin .	Hon. CHESTER F. MILLER.
Kittitas, Yakima and Franklin .	Hon. FRANK H. RUDKIN.
Clarke, Skamania, Cowlitz and Klickitat	Hon. ABRAHAM L. MILLER.
Lewis, Pacific and Wahkiakum .	Hon. ALONZO E. RICE.
Chehalis	Hon. MASON IRWIN.
Thurston and Mason . . .	Hon. OLIVER V. LINN.
Pierce	Hon. WILLIAM H. SNELL. Hon. THAD HUSTON. Hon. WILLIAM O. CHAPMAN.
King	Hon. WILLIAM R. BELL. HON. ARTHUR E. GRIFFIN. Hon. BOYD J. TALLMAN. Hon. G. MEADE EMORY.* Hon. GEORGE E. MORRIS.† Hon. ROBERT B. ALBERTSON.
Clallam, Jefferson and Island .	Hon. GEORGE C. HATCH.
Skagit and San Juan . . .	Hon. GEORGE A. JOINER.
Kitsap and Snohomish . . .	Hon. JOHN C. DENNEY.
Whatcom	Hon. JEREMIAH NETERER.

* Term expired January, 1903.
† Term commenced January, 1903.

ROLL OF ATTORNEYS

Admitted to Practice in the Supreme Court of Washington from January 19, 1903, to October 8, 1904. For previous lists, see 30 Wash. v.

Abrams, Curtis E.
Abrams, James B.
Adams, J. Oscar
Alderson, Tom
Allen, Clay
Anderson, Christian J.
Anderson, Christian O.
Anderson, John S.
Anderson, Oliver
Arnold, H. W.
Atkins, Herbert F.
Austin, H. A.
Axtell, Abram
Aylmore, Reeves
Back, Roscius
Bain, Thomas H.
Balleray, Joseph J.
Ballinger, John H.
Barnes, James L.
Barrows, O. P.
Bassett, Thomas W.
Baxter, Charles M.
Baxter, Chauncey L.
Bayley, Frank S.
Beach, Henry C.
Beardslee, Geo. E.
Bell, Ralph C.
Bennett, E. A.
Best, Chas. M.
Bishop, W. E.
Bixby, Frank W.
Blake, J. F.
Blewett, Robert L.
Blockberger, Charles H.
Bluemly, E. F.
Boddy, Marshall V.

Boner, W. W.
Bonney, Wm. W.
Boryer, R. J.
Boyd, Daniel
Bradford, Burton P.
Brewer, Merton E.
Brickey, Willard L.
Bridgman, William B.
Bright, George W.
Brightman, F. E.
Brooks, George I.
Brooks, H. Maxwell
Brown, Edwin J.
Brown, Wm. P.
Buchanan, Hubert D.
Buck, Vernon W.
Burglehaus, Rufus J.
Burnam, John C.
Burr, Eugene Wyllys
Burruss, W. B.
Burson, James P.
Campbell, J. B.
Campbell, J. D.
Campbell, Jos. H.
Campbell, Rolla L.
Carey, Edward J.
Carpenter, C. H.
Carrick, Krickel K.
Carver, Fred J.
Clark, Chas. Allen
Clark, Charles. C.
Clark, Geo. A.
Clements, C. H.
Congdon, Geo. C.
Congdon, Ossian M.
Congleton, Chas. E.

Conway, Fred R.
Corbin, A. W., Jr.
Cosgrove, Howard G.
Cox, John W.
Crawford, Edgar I.
Crow, Denton M.
Curtis, E. A.
Cutts, Russel W.

Dailey, E. C.
Dally, John R.
Dalton, H. W.
Daly, William J.
Davis, Allen Sidney
Davis, Edward A.
Davis, Harold H.
Davis, Horatio S.
Davis, I. F.
Davis, Robert M.
Davison, Geo. M.
Dean, Fay F.
Degrange, McQuilkin
Devecmon, Geo. W.
Devers, Robert A.
Dilley, William A.
Douglas, James H.
Drain, James A.
Driggers, Gettis H.
Drill, Lewis L.
Duff, James
Dykeman, King

Egan, Francis M.
Elsworth, Allen Merton
Eshelman, Carl D.
Evans, Daniel S.
Evans, Linus A.
Evans, Marvin

Falkner, Jesse W.
Farley, Phillip J.
Fenton, B. B.
Ferris, Geo. M.
Fierce, H.
Fink, Albert
Finlay, James
Finn, C. H.

Finnegan, John J.
Fitzpatrick, John L.
Fleming, W. E.
Follmer, E. Sherman
Force, Horton C.
Forsyth, Charles E.
Freedman, H. Y.
Friese, August J.

Gale, Albert W.
Gandy, Lloyd E.
Garber, Wm. A.
Gardner, A. E.
Garrell, Wm. R.
Garrett, Garfield A.
Gill, Edwin S.
Gilman, Fred A.
Glasgow, David R.
Gleason, Jesse W.
Godfrey, James J.
Gosdor, C. A.
Gostorf, Geo. W.
Grant, A. J.
Gray, John P.
Gray, T. S.
Gregory, George W.
Grimshaw, Wm. A.
Guesmer, Arnold L.

Hamlin, Robert D.
Hanson, Howard A.
Harrison, W. A.
Hawkins, C. R.
Hays, Perry C.
Heglar, Will R.
Herriott, George
Hibbard, George J.
Hibschman, H. J.
Hill, Sam B.
Hodge, Edward D.
Hodge, George J.
Hoey, Bernard
Hoppe, Dorsey R.
Horsey, Chas. Lee
Horstman, H. G.
Hubbell, Bert L.

Irwin, L. J.
Jack, A. L.
Jackson, Henry Davis
Jackson, W. H.
Jewett, G. W.
Johnson, John Andrew
Johnston, Wm. T.
Joujon-Roche, J. B.
Kane, James H.
Kane, Morris F.
Keener, John B.
Kellogg, James A.
Kelly, Frederick W.
Kennan, Ralph A.
Kenyon, E. D.
Kidd, Fred G.
Kindall, Joseph W.
King, J. J.
Kirkpatrick, L. E.
Kizer, Donald F.
Klingenberg, T. W.
Kuen, H. J.
Kuykendall, E. V.
Lafferty, Hugh J.
Lane, Gilbert A.
Lane, Warren D.
Lanning, Will
Laube, Wm. T.
Lentz, Theo.
Liddy, Philip M.
Linck, John W.
Little, M. O.
Loeb, Joseph
Longfellow, Mathew L.
Lundy, Charles L.
Lynch, John Henry
McAvoy, Charles E.
McCarthy, Jos.
McFadden, Thomas Lewis
McGee, Eugene H.
McGregor, Bruce E.
McGrew, J. E.
McKenzie, James A.
McMath, G. K.

McMenamin, James H.
McNeill, Angus M.
Maddock, Geo. N.
Mahoney, William J.
Majors, Frank P.
Malmin, Joseph E.
Marshall, J. C.
Martin, Winter S.
Mathis, O. C.
Miller, John W.
Miller, Sinclair
Minor, John B.
Mitten, Frank L.
Moore, H. W.
Morrison, Sam'l
Moser, B. B.
Mulligan, John F.
Mulvihill, Robert
Mundy, Chas I.
Munyon, H.
Murray, Chas. A.
Murray, Herman
Narvestad, Anton C.
Neergard, R. L.
Nelson, Lewis J.
Noethe, J. J.
Norkels, Louis
O'Connor, Wm.
O'Neal, Smith D.
Osbourn, Walter B.
Packer, Ray
Parker, Adella M.
Parker, Alfred E.
Parks, W. J.
Paswater, Geo. W.
Patterson, Theodore H., Jr.
Peightel, I. S.
Pendarvis, Charles Roy
Penfield, Walter Scott
Penrose, C. G.
Perry, John H.
Peters, H. C.
Petrovitsky, Chas. G.
Philbrick, Edgar A.

Phillips, Wm. W.
Pinckney, John J.
Ping, John Roy
Piper, Fred W.
Plater, Sherman
Porter, Marcellus F.
Price, John G.

Ratcliffe, Benjamin W.
Reagan, Francis Charles
Reed, Joseph L.
Reese, Frank
Reeves, Fred
Revelle, J. Plummer
Revelle, W. Roger
Rhodes, Harry A.
Richardson, M. M.
Ridle, William B.
Riley, Michael G.
Roberts, Chas. V.
Roberts, Logan H.
Roberts, T. W.
Roney, Ned
Rosenbaum, L. N.
Rossman, Geo. P.
Roudebush, John W.
Rupp, Otto B.
Rutherford, Frank P.

Samsel, John L.
Sather, Charles A.
Sault, Samuel A.
Saunderson, Jas. T.
Schoff, E. T.
Schneider, C. A.
Schutt, W. D.
Schwager, Lewis
Schwartz, Henry H.
Shackelford, Thos. W.
Shaefer, Geo. W.
Shank, James M.
Shaughnessy, M. P.
Sherfey, J. Hugh
Sherrill, R. L.
Sigrist, Charles F.
Smith, J. P.

Snyder, Edgar C.
Snyder, Fred O.
Spirk, Charles A.
Startzman, Howard H.
Steele, Earl N.
Steffen, C. H.
Stevens, E. B.
Stoddard, J. J.
Stork, A. M.
Stuart, Chas. K.
Sutton, Chas. D.
Swindells, Charles J.

Talbot, Geo. D.
Taylor, F. L.
Tennant, George R.
Tennant, J. K.
Thomas, Percy F.
Thompson, Henry Rice
Thornton, E. L.
Tindall, Philip
Tucker, Orville A.
Turner, C. W.
Turner De Los W.
Turner, Homer E.
Tworoger, Philip

Vaughn, Loren F.
Villa, G. R. F.
Vinsonhaler, Edwin A.
Vollmer, Adrien W.

Wade, Austin M.
Wadham, James E.
Wagner, E. W.
Waldron, F. W.
Ward, J. Lenox
Ward, Nathan L.
Ward, T. H.
Wardall, M. M.
Wardall, Raymar M.
Warner, A. D.
Warner, Robert Tuttle
Waterman, Howard W.
Watkins, Walter H.
Wetherby, Geo.
Wheeler, A. K.

White, Ralph C.
Whitham, John W.
Whiting, Edwin P.
Wilcox, Robert A.
Wilds, Alex G.
Wilkeson, S. R.
Willett, Oscar L.
Williams, Edwin A.
Williams, W. M.
Wills, Chas. S.
Wilson, F. Y.
Wilson, H. S.
Wilson, James G.
Wilson, John R.

Wilson, O. V.
Wilson, Warren N.
Winders, Charles H.
Wingate, Sam'l D.
Woodruff, Chas. A.
Woods, C. E.
Woods, Ralph
Wooten, Dudley G.
Wotton, G. A.
Wright, E. J.
Wright, J. Walter
Wright, R. M.
Wynn, W. H., Jr.
Yale, F. D.

TABLE

OF

CASES REPORTED

	Page
Aberdeen, Northwestern Lumber Co. v.	636
Adams v. Dempsey	80
Alexander v. Tacoma	366
Allen v. Northern Pacific Railway Co.	221
American Bridge Co. of New York v. Wheeler	40
Bailey v. Cascade Timber Co.	295
Baker, O'Connell v.	376
Ball v. O'Keefe	699
Bartlett v. British America Assurance Co.	525
Beebe v. Redward	615
Belfast Manufacturing Co., Matthews v.	662
Bertelson v. Hoffman	459
Bier v. Hosford	544
Bjorklund v. Seattle Electric Co.	439
Bonne v. Security Savings Society	696
Braymer v. Seattle, Renton & Southern Railway Co.	346
British America Assurance Co., Bartlett v.	525
Byrkett v. Gardner	668
Cain, Cooke v.	353
Cannel Coal Co., Seattle & Lake Washington Waterway Co. v.	700
Carstens, Wilcox v.	701
Cascade Timber Co., Bailey v.	295
Casety v. Jamison	478
Chapman, State ex rel. Payson v.	64
Chase v Smith	631

Page

Clark, McConaghy v............................. 689
Clark, Minnesota Sandstone Co. v.................. 466
Cole, Oudin & Bergman Fire Clay Mining & Manufac-
    turing Co. v................................ 647
Colman, Farwell v.............................. 308
Cooke v. Cain................................. 353
Cully v. Northern Pacific Railway Co............... 241

Davis v. Tacoma Railway & Power Co.............. 203
Dempsey, Adams v.............................. 80
Detherage, State v.............................. 326
Dick v. Washington Match Co.................... 700
Dickerson v. Spokane........................... 414
Dickson, Washington State Bank of Ellensburg v.... 641
Dodds v. Gregson.............................. 402
Drasdo, In re Estate of......................... 412

Evans, Templeman v............................ 302

Fair, State v.................................. 127
Farwell v. Colman............................. 308
Foster v. Seattle Electric Co.................... 177
Fraternal Knights & Ladies, State v.............. 338
Frazier v. Wilson.............................. 625
Friend v. Ralston.............................. 422

Gardner, Byrkett v............................. 668
Gardner, Hill v................................ 529
Graves v. Thompson............................ 282
Gregson, Dodds v.............................. 402

Halverson v. Seattle Electric Co................. 600
Hanna, Stewart v.............................. 148
Harvey v. Ivory............................... 397
Henry H. Schott Co. v. Stone, Fisher & Lane........ 252
Henry, Wilcox v............................... 591
Herrick, Jones v............................... 434
Hesser v. Siepmann............................ 14
Hester v. Thomson............................. 119
Hill v. Gardner............................... 529

Page

Hoffman, Bertelson v.............................. 459
Hogan, Smits v................................... 290
Hosford, Bier v.................................. 544

Ide, State v..................................... 576
Independent Telephone Co., Windham v............ 166
Ingersoll v. Rousseau............................ 92
Ingram v. Wishkah Boom Co....................... 191
In re Estate of Drasdo........................... 412
Ivory, Harvey v.................................. 397

James v. James................................... 650
James v. James................................... 655
Jamison, Casety v................................ 478
Jensen-King-Byrd Co. v. Williams................. 161
John Davis & Co., Lough v........................ 449
Johnson v. Seattle Electric Co................... 382
Jones v. Herrick................................. 434
Jones v. Miller.................................. 499

Kane v. Kane..................................... 517
Kennan, State ex rel. Fisher v................... 52
Kent (Town of), Watson v......................... 21
King, Teater v................................... 138

Lamona v. Odessa State Bank...................... 113
Lewis v. Mauerman................................ 156
Lewis, State v................................... 261
Linn, State ex rel. Royal v...................... 116
Loomis, Waring v................................. 85
Lough v. John Davis & Co......................... 449

McCleary v. Willis............................... 676
McConaghy v. Clark............................... 689
McConkey v. Oregon Railroad & Navigation Co...... 55
McInnes v. Sutton................................ 384
McKenzie v. Royal Dairy.......................... 390
McNaught, Washington Iron Works v................ 10
Matthews v. Belfast Manufacturing Co............. 662
Mauerman, Lewis v................................ 156

Page

Maynard, State ex rel. Stratton v................. 168
Menzel, Monroe Mill Co. v........................ 487
Miller, Jones v.................................. 499
Minnesota Sandstone Co. v. Clark................. 466
Monroe Mill Co. v. Menzel....................... 487
Mulholland v. Washington Match Co............... 315

Nathan v. Spokane County........................ 26
Northern Pacific Railway Co., Allen v........... 221
Northern Pacific Railway Co., Cully v........... 241
Northport Smelting & Refining Co., Rowe v....... 101
Northwestern Lumber Co. v. Aberdeen............. 636

O'Connell v. Baker.............................. 376
Odessa State Bank, Lamona v..................... 113
O'Keefe, Ball v................................. 699
Oleson, State v................................. 149
Oregon Railroad & Navigation Co., McConkey v.... 55
O'Sullivan v. O'Sullivan........................ 481
Oudin & Bergman Fire Clay Mining & Manufacturing
     Co. v. Cole................................ 647

Pacific Realty Co., Rice Fisheries Co. v........ 535
Phillips v. Thurston County..................... 187
Pietsch, Riverside Land Co. v................... 210
Pittock, Williams v............................. 271
Post v. Spokane................................. 114

Ralston, Friend v............................... 422
Redward, Beebe v................................ 615
Rice Fisheries Co. v. Pacific Realty Co......... 535
Riverside Land Co. v. Pietsch................... 210
Robe v. Snohomish County........................ 475
Rousseau, Ingersoll v........................... 92
Rowe v. Northport Smelting & Refining Co........ 101
Royal Dairy, McKenzie v......................... 390
Rutledge, Tischner v............................ 285

Schott Co. v. Stone, Fisher & Lane.............. 252
Seattle, Swope v................................ 69

Page

Seattle Dock Co., Seattle & Lake Washington Water-
way Co. v....................................... 503
Seattle Electric Co., Bjorklund v.................... 439
Seattle Electric Co., Foster v...................... 177
Seattle Electric Co., Halverson v................... 600
Seattle Electric Co., Johnson v..................... 382
Seattle & Lake Washington Waterway Co. v. Cannel
Coal Co. 700
Seattle & Lake Washington Waterway Co. v. Seattle
Dock Co. 503
Seattle, Renton & Southern Railway Co., Braymer v.. 346
Security Savings Society, Bonne v.................. 696
Siepmann, Hesser v............................... 14
Smith, Chase v.................................... 631
Smits v. Hogan................................... 290
Snohomish County, Robe v......................... 475
Spokane, Dickerson v.............................. 414
Spokane, Post v................................... 114
Spokane County, Nathan v......................... 26
State v. Detherage................................ 326
State v. Fair...................................... 127
State v. Fraternal Knights & Ladies................ 338
State v. Ide....................................... 576
State v. Lewis..................................... 261
State v. Oleson.................................... 149
State v. Underwood................................ 558
State v. Zenner.................................... 249
State ex rel. Corbin v. Superior Court, Lincoln County 201
State ex rel. Fisher v. Kennan..................... 52
State ex rel. Flaherty v. Superior Court, King County 200
State ex rel. Kent Lumber Co. v. Superior Court, King
County 303
State ex rel. Payson v. Chapman.................. 64
State ex rel. Royal v. Linn........................ 116
State ex rel. Stratton v. Maynard.................. 168
Stewart v. Hanna.................................. 148
Stone, Fisher & Lane, Henry G. Schott Co. v......... 252

CASES REPORTED.

Page

Superior Court, State ex rel. Corbin v............... 201
Superior Court, State ex rel. Flaherty v............. 200
Superior Court, State ex rel. Kent Lumber Co. v...... 303
Suter v. Wenatchee Water Power Co................ 1
Sutton, McInnes v................................. 384
Swope v. Seattle.................................. 69

Tacoma, Alexander v.............................. 366
Tacoma Railway & Power Co., Davis v.............. 203
Teater v. King................................... 138
Templeman v. Evans.............................. 302
Thompson, Graves v.............................. 282
Thomson, Hester v............................... 119
Thurston County, Phillips v....................... 187
Tischner v. Rutledge............................. 285
Town of Kent, Watson v........................... 21

Underwood, State v............................... 558

Waring v. Loomis................................. 85
Washington Iron Works v. McNaught.............. 10
Washington Match Co., Dick v.................... 700
Washington Match Co., Mulholland v.............. 315
Washington Match Co., Woods v................... 699
Washington State Bank of Ellensburg v. Dickson.... 641
Watson v. Town of Kent........................... 21
Wenatchee Water Power Co., Suter v.............. 1
Wheeler, American Bridge Co. of New York v....... 40
Wilcox v. Carstens............................... 701
Wilcox v. Henry................................. 591
Williams, Jensen-King-Byrd Co. v................ 161
Williams v. Pittock.............................. 271
Willis, McCleary v............................... 676
Wilson, Frazier v................................ 625
Windham v. Independent Telephone Co............ 166
Wishkah Boom Co., Ingram v.................... 191
Woods v. Washington Match Co................... 699

Zenner, State v.................................. 249

TABLE

OF

CASES CITED BY THE COURT

		Page
Abernethy v. Medical Lake	9 Wash. 112	45
Adams v. Dempsey	22 Wash. 284	82
Adams v. Dempsey	29 Wash. 155	82
Adrian Furniture Mfg. Co. v. Lane.	92 Mich. 295	67
Ah Doon v. Smith	25 Ore. 89	472
Ahern v. Ahern	31 Wash. 334	660, 662
Albrecht v. Milwaukee etc. R. Co...	87 Wis. 105	446
Aldrich v. McClaine	98 Fed. 378	5
Aldrich v. McClaine	106 Fed. 791	5
Aldrich v. Skinner	98 Fed. 375	5
Allen v. Forrest	8 Wash. 700	513
Allison v. Horning	22 Ohio St. 138	464
American Sug. Ref. Co. v. Louisiana	179 U. S. 89	345
Ames v. Union Pac. R. Co	64 Fed. 165	345
Anderson v. City & Sub. R. Co.	42 Ore. 505	230, 240
Anderson v. Doty	33 Hun. 160	98, 99
Annie Wright Seminary v. Tacoma.	23 Wash. 109	373
Ansonia v. Cooper	64 Conn. 536	147
Armour v. Hahn	111 U. S. 313	247
Association v. McComber	41 Minn. 20	275
Astell v. Phillippi	55 Cal. 265	285
Attorney General v. Forbes	2 Myl. & Cr. 129	96
Aultman & Taylor Co. v. Shelton..	90 Iowa 288	361
Baars v. Hyland	65 Minn. 150	461
Babcock v. Goodrich	47 Cal. 488	45
Bailey v. Cascade Timber Co.	32 Wash. 319	296
Ball v. Gussenhoven	74 Pac. (Mont.) 873	550
Barnes v. German Sav. & L. Soc..	21 Wash. 448	461
Barry v. New York etc. R. Co.	92 N. Y. 289	58
Bell v Riggs	37 La. Ann. 813	78
Bernhardt v West Penn. R. Co.	159 Pa. St. 363	230
Bertelson v. Hoffman	35 Wash 459	685
Blagen v. Smith	34 Ore. 394	99

Page

Blake v. Shriver .... 27 Wash. 593 18
Blakney v. Seattle Electric Co. .... 28 Wash. 607 238
Boston Clothing Co. v. Solberg .... 28 Wash. 262 647
Bowers v. Ledgerwood .... 25 Wash. 14 20
Bringgold v. Spokane .... 19 Wash. 333 114
Brooks v. People .... 49 N. Y. 436 135
Brown v. Calloway .... 34 Wash. 175 657
Brown v. Seattle .... 5 Wash. 35 76
Brown v. Tabor Mill Co .... 22 Wash. 317 556
Buckingham v. Harris .... 10 Colo. 455 465
Bucklin v. Strickler .... 32 Neb. 602 142
Burik v. Dundee Woolen Co....... 66 N. J. L. 420 445
Burns v. Fox ....113 Ind. 205 361
Butler v. Kennard .... 23 Neb. 357 685

Cadwell v. First Nat. Bank .... 3 Wash. 188 524
Cahill v. Chicago etc. R. Co .... 74 Fed. 285 57
Campbell v. Boyd .... 88 N. C. 129 62
Campbell v. Russell ....139 Mass. 278 105
Campbell v. Seaman .... 63 N. Y. 568 598
Carl v. West Aberdeen etc. Co .... 13 Wash. 616 ......97, 497
Carlson v. Exchange Co .... 63 Minn. 428 248
Carstens v. McReavy .... 1 Wash. 359 461
Cassida v. Oregon R. & Nav. Co... 14 Ore. 551 58
Cattano v. Metropolitan St. R. Co.173 N. Y. 565 612
Cattell v. Fergusson .... 3 Wash. 541 523
Central Iowa R. Co. v. Board ..... 67 Iowa 199 345
Chamberlain v. Winn .... 1 Wash. 501 400
Cherry v. Western Wash. etc. Co.. 11 Wash. 586 77
Chevalier & Co. v. Wilson .... 30 Wash. 227 538
Chicago etc. R. Co. v. Belliwith ... 83 Fed. 437 447
Chicago etc. R. Co. v. Champion... 9 Ind. App. 510 110
Chicago etc. R. Co. v. Iowa .... 94 U. S. 155 345
Chicago etc. R. Co. v. Reno ....113 Ill. 39 219
Christianson v. Pacific Bridge Co.. 27 Wash. 582 ..552, 553, 555
City of Fairibault v. Misener ..... 20 Minn. 396 587
Clukey v. Seattle Electric Co...... 27 Wash. 70 384
Cochran v. Yoho .... 34 Wash. 238 484
Coe v. Errol ....116 U. S. 517 33
Coffer v. Territory .... 1 Wash. 325 100
Connecticut Fire Ins. Co. v. Tilley. 88 Va. 1024 ....: 528
Connolly v. Eldredge ....160 Mass. 570 555
Coolidge v. Pierce County .... 28 Wash. 95 274
Coon v. Plymouth Plank Road Co.. 32 Mich. 248 388
Cooper v. Hall .... 5 Ohio 321 8
Coppell v. Hall .... 7 Wall. 558 472

Page

Courtright v. Burnes .... 13 Fed. 317, 320 293
Cowdery v. McChesney ....124 Cal. 363 608
Cowles v. U. S. Fid. & Guar Co.... 32 Wash. 120 .....431, 433
Cowley v. People .... 83 N. Y. 464 572
Cox v. Holmes .... 14 Wash. 255 176
Crawford v. Tyrrell ....128 N. Y. 341 98
Croco v. Oregon etc. R. Co .... 18 Utah 311 294
Crook v. Hewitt .... 4 Wash. 749 496
Crooker v. Pac. Lounge etc. Co... 34 Wash. 191 553
Crowley v. McDonough .... 30 Wash. 57 406
Crowley v. Pacific Mills ....148 Mass. 228 556
Cullen v. Whitham .... 33 Wash. 366 484
Curry v. Catlin .... 9 Wash. 495 533
Cusick v. Adams ....115 N. Y. 55 59

Dale v. Doddridge .... 9 Neb. 138 143
Daneri v. Southern Cal. R. Co.....122 Cal. 507 8
Danuser v. Seller & Co........... 24 Wash. 567 552
Davidson v. Moorman .... 2 Heisk. (Tenn.) 575.. 131
Davis v. Chicago etc. R. Co....... 58 Wis. 646 61
Dawson v. McMillan .... 34 Wash. 269 495
De Wald v. Ingle .... 31 Wash. 616 197
Dickerson v. Spokane .... 26 Wash. 292 .....415, 420
Dickinson County v. Miss. Valley
  Ins. Co .... 41 Iowa 286 454
Doremus v. Root .... 23 Wash. 710 433
Doty v. Krutz .... 13 Wash. 169 284
Douthitt v. MacCulsky .... 11 Wash. 601 433
Downs v. Board of Directors ...... 4 Wash. 309 287
Dubcich v. Grand Lodge A.O.U.W. 33 Wash 651 ....67, 103
Duclos v. Cunningham ....102 N. Y. 678 462

Eighmie v. Taylor .... 98 N. Y. 288 474
Elderkin v. Peterson .... 8 Wash. 674 608
Emerson v. Lowell Gas Light Co.. 3 Allen 410 105
England v. Westchester Fire Ins.
  Co .... 81 Wis. 583 527
Enos v. Wilcox .... 3 Wash. 44 524
Etson v. Ft. Wayne etc. R. Co....110 Mich. 494 230
Excelsior Mfg. Co. v. Boyle....... 46 Kan. 202 362
Ex parte Koser.................. 60 Cal. 177 345
Eyster v. Gaff .... 91 U. S. 521 165

Farrell v. Hennesy.............. 21 Wis. 639 544
Farrell v. New York Steam Co.... 53 N. Y. Supp. 55 598
Farrelly v. Cole................ 60 Kan. 356 ....131, 133
Fearn v. West Jersey Ferry Co....143 Pa. St. 122 229
Fidelity Mut. Life Ass'n v. Mettler185 U. S. 308 345

Page

Fiedelday v. Diserens .... 26 Ohio St. 312 137
Fitch v. Applegate .... 24 Wash. 25 344
Fitzgerald Const. Co. v. Fitzgerald.137, U. S. 98 142
Fleetwood v. Read .... 21 Wash. 548 582
Flint v. Long .... 12 Wash. 342 19
Francis v. Atchison etc. R. Co.... 19 Kans. 303 581
Fredenburg v. Lyon Lake M. E.
  Church .... 37 Mich. 476 220
Frederick v. Seattle .... 13 Wash. 428 375
Freeburger v. Caldwell .... 5 Wash. 769 283
Friedman v. Manley .... 21 Wash. 675 390
Fuller v. Madison Mut. Ins. Co.... 36 Wis. 599 446

Gaffney v. St. Paul City R. Co..... 81 Minn. 459 186
Garneau v. Port Blakely Mill Co.. 8 Wash. 467 654
Gelpcke v. City of Dubuque....... 1 Wall. 221 472
Gilbert v. Guild ....144 Mass. 601 555
Gill v. Sullivan .... 55 Iowa 341 654
Gleeson v. Virginia Midland R. Co.140 U. S. 435 228
Gold v. Bissell .... 1 Wend. 210 331
Golding v. Merchant & Co........ 43 Ala. 705 454
Graham v. McNeill .... 20 Wash. 466 612
Gray v. Washington Water Pr. Co. 27 Wash. 713 225
Gray v. Washington Water Pr. Co. 30 Wash. 665 209
Graves v. Thomas .... 95 Ind. 361 62
Great Northern R. Co. v. Kasischke.104 Fed. 440 444
Greef v. Brown .... 7 Kan. App. 394 551
Greene v. Williams .... 13 Wash. 674 390
Griffith v. Strand .... 19 Wash 686 321
Griggs v. MacLean .... 33 Wash. 244 538
Groth v. Thomann ....110 Wis. 488 554
Gulf etc. R. Co. v Ellis ....165 U. S. 150 586
Gulf etc. R. Co. v. Jackson .... 65 Fed. 48 247
Gulliher v. Chicago etc. R. Co..... 59 Iowa 416 447
Gustin v. Jose .... 11 Wash. 348 607

Hagar v. Reclamation District etc.111 U. S. 701 ....34, 35
Hamar v. Peterson .... 9 Wash. 152 484
Hamilton v. Whitridge .... 11 Md. 128 ....98, 99
Hansen v. Southern Pac. Co......105 Cal. 379 ....57, 58
Hardin v. Mullen .... 16 Wash. 647 25
Harding v. Atlantic Trust Co...... 26 Wash. 536 161
Harriman v. Pittsburg etc. R. Co.. 45 Ohio St. 11 61
Hathaway v. Yakima Water etc. Co. 14 Wash. 469 493
Hawkins v. Front Street Cable R.
  Co........ .... 3 Wash. 592 228
Hawkins v. Hawkins .... 50 Cal. 558 447

Page

Hawks v. Charlemont ....110 Mass. 110 105
Hayes v. Missouri ....120 U. S. 68 345
Healy Lumber Co. v. Morris...... 33 Wash. 490 ......665, 666
Heath v. McCrea .... 20 Wash. 342 372
Hedges v. Roach .... 16 Neb. 673 362
Henck v. Todhunter .... 7 Har. & J. (Md.) 275. 389
Herrin v. Pugh .... 9 Wash. 637 283
Hice v. Orr .... 16 Wash. 163 502
Hicks v. Drew ....117 Cal. 305 6
Higgins v. DeLoach .... 54 Miss. 498 285
Holly v. Boston Gas Light Co..... 8 Gray 123 7
Hooker v. Chicago etc. R. Co...... 76 Wis. 542 57
Hoyt v. Thompson .... 1 Selden 347 293
Hunsaker v. Wright .... 30 Ill. 146 .'........... 589

Indiana etc. R. Co. v. Fowler......201 Ill. 152 445
Indianapolis v. Navin ....151 Ind. 139 345
Ingersoll v. Rosseau .... 35 Wash. 92 597
In re Governor's Proclamation.... 19 Col. 333 131
— Murphy's Estate .... 26 Wash. 222 657
— Nelson .... 69 Fed. 712 251
— Oberg .... 21 Ore. 406 345
International etc. R. Co. v. Harris. 65 S. W. (Tex.) 885.... 444
Ivall v. Willis .... 17 Wash. 647 688

Jacobson v. Poindexter .... 42 Ark. 97 454
Jewett v. Darlington .... 1 Wash. Ter. 601 654
Jones v. State .... 11 Tex. App. 412 269
Johnson v. Campbell .... 39 Tex. 83 44
Johnston v. Whatcom County .... 27 Wash. 95 32
Jones v. Theall .... 3 Nev. 233 131

Kath v. Wisconsin Cent. R. Co.... 99 N. W. (Wis.) 221.... 247
Keeler v. White .... 10 Wash. 420 77
Kelley v. Rhoads .... 7 Wyo. 237 ....33, 34
Kelliher v. Miller .... 97 Mass. 71 105
Kelly v. Wimberly .... 61 Miss. 548 45
Kidder v. Smith .... 34 Vt. 294 464
Kiewit v. Carter .... 25 Neb. 460 430
King v. Dahl .... 82 Minn. 240 473
Kimball v. Grantsville City .... 19 Utah 368 133
Kirby v. Collins .... 6 Wash. 297 524
Klanowski v. Grand Trunk R. Co.. 64 Mich. 279 110
Klepsch v. Donald .... 8 Wash. 164 228
Konnerup v. Frandsen .... 8 Wash. 551 647
Krutz v. Batts .... 18 Wash. 460 160
Kuhn v. Mason .... 24 Wash. 94 390
Kulman v. Erie R. Co............ 65 N. J. L. 241 240

Page

Lancey v. King County .... 15 Wash. 9 512
Lamb v. Davenport .... 18 Wall. 307 90
Lamona v. Cowley .... 31 Wash. 297 406
Lane v. Spokane Falls etc. R. Co.. 21 Wash. 119 240
Lane v. State................... 6 Kan. App. 106 269
Lawshe v. Tacoma R. & P. Co.... 29 Wash. 681 351
Leigh v. Green...................193 U. S. 79 276
Lemon v. Waterman............. 2 Wash. Ter. 485 533
Lewis v. Bishop.................. 19 Wash. 312 36
Lewis v. Seattle................. 28 Wash. 639 .....372, 375
Libby v. Sherman................146 Ill. 540 110
Lillstrom v. Northern Pac. R. Co.. 53 Minn. 464 61
Lincoln v. Taunton Copper Mfg. Co. 91 Mass. 181 105
Litchfield v. Cowley.............. 34 Wash. 566 430
Lloyd v. Matthews.............. 51 N. Y. 124 686
London Sav. Fund Soc. v. Hagers-
town .... 36 Pa. St. 498 454
Loos v. Rondema................. 10 Wash. 164 407
Lough v. John Davis & Co....... 30 Wash, 204 .... 4o0
Lovejoy v. Murray............... 3 Wall. 1 .... **433**
Luebke v. Berlin Machine Works.. 88 Wis. 442 ....551, 552
Lunney v. Healey............... 56 Neb. 313 686
Lynde v. Dibble................. 19 Wash. 328 502
Lytle v. State.................. 17 Ark. 608 294

McAllister v. Tacoma............. 9 Wash. 272 .....368, 375
McCollister v. Yard.............. 90 Iowa 621 654
McConnell v. Poor...............113 Iowa 133 433
McDaniels v. Connelly Shoe Co... 30 Wash. 549 ....345, 586
McDannald v. Washington etc. R.
Co............... .... 31 Wash. 585 552
McGaffin v. City of Cohoes........ 74 N. Y. 387 5
McNamee v. Tacoma.............. 24 Wash. 591 373
McPherson v. Weston............ 85 Cal. 90 362
McQuade v. Jaffray.............. 47 Minn. 326 .....275, 276
McQuesten v. Morrill............ 12 Wash. 335 407
Magoun v. Illinois etc. Bank......170 U. S. 283 ....345, 587
Marsan v. French............... 61 Tex. 173 100
Martin v. Supervisors etc........ 29 N. Y. 645 44
Masterton v. Mayor of Brooklyn... 7 Hill 61 635
Mather v. Walsh................107 Mo. 121 18
Mathewson v. Fitch............. 22 Cal. 86 293
Meier v. Pennsylvania R. Co...... 64 Pa. St. 225 228
Meyer v. Haas..................126 Cal. 560 444
Miller v. Fries.................. 66 N. J. L. 377 430
Miner v. Connecticut etc. R. Co....153 Mass. 398 550

Mississippi Valley Trust Co. v. Hoflus .... 20 Wash. 272 .....513, 516
Missouri Pac. R. Co. v. Mackey...127 U. S. 205 345
Monroe Mill Co. v. Menzel .... 35 Wash. 487 667
Montgomery v. Leavenworth...... 2 Cal. 57 137
Moon Anchor etc. Mines v. Hopkins ....111 Fed. 298 247
Moore v. Brownfield............. 7 Wash. 23 18
Morford v. Unger .... 8 Iowa 82 133
Morgan v. Pennsylvania R. Co.... 7 Fed. 78 60
Mosher v. Bruhn................. 15 Wash. 332 24
Mott v. Small................... 22 Wend. 405 293
Mudgett v. Clay................. 5 Wash. 103 647
Mulholland v. Washington Match Co .... 35 Wash. 315 .....699, 700
Mundle v. Hill Mfg. Co........... 86 Me. 400 551

Nave v. Tucker................. 70 Ind. 15 572
Neaf v. Palmer.................103 Ky. 496 99
Newbold v. Mead................ 57 Pa. St. 487 110
New Whatcom v. Bellingham Bay Imp. Co...................... 16 Wash. 131 .....372, 688
New Whatcom v. Bellingham Bay Imp. Co...................... 18 Wash. 181 372
New Whatcom v. Fairhaven Land Co...... .... 24 Wash. 493 496
New York etc. R. Co. v. Doane....105 Ind. 92 67
New York etc. R. Co. v. New York.165 U. S. 628 345
New York Security & Trust Co. v. Tacoma .... 30 Wash. 661 .....639, 640
Nicholson v. Golden............. 27 Mo. App. 132 454
Nickeus v. Lewis County........ 23 Wash. 125 524
Nicol v. Skagit Boom Co.......... 12 Wash. 230 137
Nicoll v. Amer. Ins. Co........... 3 Woodb. & M. (U. S.) 529 454
North Chicago St. R. Co. v. Williams ....140 Ill. 275 ....232, 240
Northern Pac. R. Co. v. Hess...... 2 Wash. 383 384
Northwestern Lum. Co. v. Chehalis County .... 24 Wash. 626 191
Noyes v. Pugin.................. 2 Wash. 655 635

O'Connor v. Jackson............. 23 Wash. 229 219
Oleson v. McMurray Cedar L. Co.. 9 Wash. 502 555
Olson v. Seattle................. 30 Wash. 687 ....76, 77
Osborne & Co. v. Williams........ 37 Minn. 507 361

Pacific Nat. Bank v. San Fran. Bridge Co........... .... 23 Wash. 425 474

Page

Palmer v. Stacy.................. 44 Iowa 340 46
Patnode v. Warren Cotton Mills ..157 Mass. 283 556
Payne v. Spokane St. R. Co....... 15 Wash. 522 184
Payne v. Still.................... 10 Wash. 433 647
Pederson v. Seattle Consol. St. R.
  Co......... .... 6 Wash. 202 445
Pennsylvania R. Co. v. MacKinney.124 Pa. St. 462 230
Penter v. Straight............... 1 Wash. 365 ......683, 684
People v. Clark..................106 Cal. 32 135
  — v. Draper .... 15 N. Y. 532 133
  — v. Phippin .... 70 Mich. 6 345
  — v. Richmond .... 16 Colo. 274 133
  — v. Sessions ....: 58 Mich. 594 572
  — v. Wickham ....113 Cal. 283 269
People ex rel Dannat v. Comptrol-
  ler .... 77 N. Y. 45 45
Perkins v. Hayward.............132 Ind. 95 142
Perkins v. Delta etc. Co.......... 66 Miss. 378 137
Peters v. Gay..........:......... 9 Wash. 383 654
Peyton v. Robertson............. 9 Wheat. 527 285
Phelan v. Smith................. 22 Wash. 397 191
Philadelphia Mtge. & T. Co. v. Pal-
  mer .... 32 Wash. 455 287
Pioneer Cooperage Co. v. Roman-
  owicz ....186 Ill. 9 444
Porter v. Silver Creek etc. Co..... 84 Wis. 418 247
Post v. Spokane.................. 28 Wash. 701 115
Potter v. Whatcom............... 25 Wash. 207 373
Prichard v. Farrar..............116 Mass. 221 433
Puyallup Light etc. Co. v. Steven-
  son .... 21 Wash. 604 149

Quinn v. Parke & Lacy Mach. Co.. 9 Wash. 136 363

Ralph v. Lomer.................. 3 Wash. 401 280
Ranahan v. Gibbons............. 23 Wash. 255 657
Reardon v. Thompson...........149 Mass. 267 ....59, 60
Redford v. Spokane St. R. Co..... 15 Wash. 419 344
Richardson v. Rowland........... 40 Conn. 565 294
Richmond etc. Co. v. Powers.....149 U. S. 43 240
Rigney v. Tacoma Light & W Co.. 9 Wash. 576 .....493, 496
Rio Grande Irr. Co. v. Gildersleeve.174 U. S. 603 389
Ritchie v. Carpenter............ 2 Wash. 512 479
Rogers v. State .... 79 Ala. 59 269
Ross v. Butler.................... 19 N. J. Eq. 294 597
Roth v. Union Depot Co. .... 13 Wash. 525 58
Roundtree v. Brantley........... 34 Ala. 544 7

St. Louis etc. R. Co. v. Phillips.... 66 Fed. 35 445
Sampson v. Shaw.................101 Mass. 145 472
Sanders v. Stimson Mill Co....... 34 Wash. 357 220
Sanford v. Royal Ins. Co.......... 11 Wash. 653 445
Sargent v. Tacoma............... 10 Wash. 212 4
Sayward v. Carlson............... 1 Wash. 29 142
Schmidt v. North Jersey St. R. Co. 66 N. J. L. 424 230
Schmidt v. North Yakima......... 12 Wash 121 167
Scoland v. Scoland............... 4 Wash. 118 522
Scholpp v. Forrest............... 11 Wash. 640 .....513, 516
Schreiner v. Great Northern R. Co. 86 Minn. 245 59
Schus v. Powers-Simpson Co...... 85 Minn. 447 444
Seanor v. County Com'rs......... 13 Wash. 48 39
Sears v. Seattle Consol. etc. Co... 6 Wash. 227 184
Seattle & Lake Wash. Waterway
Co. v. Seattle Dock Co.......... 35 Wash. 503 ......,... 700
Sedgwick v. Stanton............. 14 N. Y. 289 294
Shearer v. Weaver............... 56 Iowa 578 654
Shephard v. Gove............... 26 Wash. 452 693
Sherman v. Sweeny............... 29 Wash. 331 432
Shine v. Cocheco Mfg. Co.........173 Mass. 558 557
Shinn v. Cummins................ 65 Cal. 97 280
Shuey v. Holmes................. 27 Wash. 489 538
Skeel v. Christenson............. 17 Wash. 649 484
Slauson v. Schwabacher Bros. &
Co........ .... 4 Wash. 783 501
Smith v. Mitchell................. 21 Wash. 536 97
Smith v. White.................. 32 Wash. 414 279
Spitze v. Baltimore etc. Co........ 75 Md. 162 447
State v. Adams .... 58 Kan. 365 135
— v. Austin .... 6 Wis. 203 543
— v. Biles .... 6 Wash. 186 135
— v. Brodie .... 7 Wash. 442 268
— v. Carey .... 4 Wash. 424 344
— v. Clark .... 30 Wash. 439 .....345, 582
— v. Frost .... 25 Wash. 134 629
— v. Gee .... 85 Mo. 647 335
— v. Gifford .... 19 Wash. 464 156
— v. Glindemann .... 34 Wash. 222 251
— v. Greer .... 11 Wash. 244 569
— v. Howard .... 33 Wash. 250 569
— v. Kroenert .... 13 Wash. 644 136
— v. Maldonado .... 21 Wash. 653 136
— v. Mitchell .... 32 Wash. 64 ......136, 333
— v. Nichols .... 28 Wash. 628 344
— v. Pierce .... 52 Kan. 521 ......43, 48, 49

Page

State v. Raby .... 31 Wash. 111 50
— v. Ripley .... 32 Wash 182 ....136, 338
— v. Van Cleve............... 5 Wash. 642 153
State ex rel. Barnard v. Board.... 19 Wash. 8 381
— Chamberlain v. Daniel... 17 Wash. 111 589
— Colner v. Wickersham... 16 Wash. 161 502
— Commercial etc. Co. v.
    Stallcup .... 15 Wash. 263 201
— Craig v. Dougherty...... 45 Mo. 294 45
— Fetterley v. Griffin...... 32 Wash. 67 118
— Foster v. Sup'r Court.... 30 Wash. 156 54
— Heckman v. Sup'r Court. 28 Wash. 35 165
— Hersner v. Arthur....... 7 Wash. 358 118
— Land v. Christopher..... 32 Wash 59 114
— Lewis v. Hogg.......... 22 Wash 646 36
— Murphy v. McBride...... 29 Wash. 335 151
— Nichols v. Cherry........ 22 Utah 1 133
— Payson v. Chapman..... 35 Wash. 64 538
— Post v. Sup'r Court...... 31 Wash 53 115
— Ross v. Headlee......... 22 Wash. 126 45
— Scottish Am. etc. Co. v.
    Meacham .... 17 Wash. 429 114
— Sears v. Wright......... 10 Nev. 167 46
— Sheehan v. Headlee..... 17 Wash 637 45
— Smith v. Sup'r Court.... 26 Wash 278 77
— Strohl v. Sup'r Court ... 20 Wash 545 165
— Taylor v. Cummings..... 27 Wash. 316 502
— Van Name v. Board..... 14 Wash. 222 524
— Van Vliet v. Wilson..... 17 Wis. 709 45
Stearns v. Field.................. 90 N. Y. 640 572
Steffens v. Earl................. 11 Vroom 128 143
Sterger v. Van Sicklen...........132 N. Y. 499 60
Stull v. De Mattos................ 23 Wash. 71 582
Sultan Water & P. Co. v. Weyer-
hauser Timber Co.............. 31 Wash. 558 497
Sussdorff v. Schmidt............. 55 N. Y. 320 465
Sutton v. Snohomish .... 11 Wash 24 26
Swanson v. Great Northern R. Co.. 68 Minn. 184 247

Tacoma v. State.................. 4 Wash. 64 306
Tacoma etc. Paving Co. v. Stern-
berg .... 26 Wash. 84 373
Tarpey v. Madsen................178 U. S. 215 90
Taylor v. Spokane Falls & N. R.
Co. .... 32 Wash. 450 149
Tennessee etc. R. Co. v. Danforth.112 Ala. 80 ....634, 635

Page

Texas & Pacific R. Co. v. Bryant.. 8 Tex. Civ. App. 134.. 550
Thalheimer v. Brinkerhoff .... 3 Cowen 647 293
Thirteenth etc. R. Co. v. Boudrou.. 92 Pa. St. 475 612
Thomas v. Chicago etc. R. Co. ....103 Iowa 649 58
Thomas v. Hartford Fire Ins. Co.. 21 Ky. L. 914 528
Thomas v. Union Pacific R. Co.... 1 Utah 235 5
Thompson v. Robbins .... 32 Wash. 149 279
Tobin v. Portland etc. R. Co...... 59 Me. 183 61
Towle v. Stimson Mill Co......... 33 Wash. 305 227
Traver v. Spokane Street R. Co.... 25 Wash. 225 607
Truntle v. North Star Woolen-Mill
    Co. .... 57 Minn. 52 555
Tumwater v. Pix ...·.............. 18 Wash. 153 374
Turner v. Great Northern R. Co... 15 Wash. 213 608
Tyler v. Reynolds .... 53 Iowa 146 653

United States v. Curry .... 6 How. 106 389

Veasey v. Carson ....177 Mass. 117 461

Wagnitz v. Ritter .... 31 Wash. 343 280
Walker v. McNeill .... 17 Wash. 582 ......550, 608
Walla Walla v. Ferndon .... 21 Wash. 308 582
Wallace v. Chicago etc. R. Co. .... 67 Iowa 547 446
Walsh v. Bushell .... 26 Wash. 576 321
Washington Central Imp. Co. v.
    Newlands .... 11 Wash. 212 321
Washington Dredging etc. Co. v.
    Partridge .... 19 Wash. 62 484
Washington Iron Works v. King
    County .... 20 Wash. 150 629
Washington Timber etc. Co. v.
    Smith .... 34 Wash. 625 274
Watkins v. Dorris .... 24 Wash. 636 .....494, 497
Watkinson v. McCoy .... 23 Wash. 372 .....196, 667
Watson v. Merkle .... 21 Wash. 635 502
Weakley v. Page ....102 Tenn. 178 99
Weaver v. Coumbe .... 15 Neb. 167 147
Webb v. Allington & Anderson .... 27 Mo. App. 570 472
Wells v. Missouri Pac. R. Co......110 Mo. 286 131
West Seattle Land & Imp. Co. v.
    Herren .... 16 Wash. 665 321
Western Loan & Sav. Co. v. Wais-
    man .... 32 Wash. 644 363
Wheeler v. Buck & Co. .... 23 Wash. 688 464
Whitney v. Knowlton .... 33 Wash. 319 281
Whitney etc. Co. v. O'Rourke ....172 Ill. 177 444
Wilcox v. Chicago etc. R. Co. ..... 24 Minn. 269 455

Page

Wilcox v. Henry .... 35 Wash. 591 701
Wildey v. Crane .... 63 Mich. 720 294
Williams v. Clayton .... 6 Utah 86 46
Wilson v. Northern Pac. R. Co. .... 5 Wash. 621 209
Wise v. Ackerman .... 76 Md. 375 110
Wollin v. Smith .... 27 Wash. 349 406
Woodland Lumber Co. v. Link .... 16 Wash. 72 533
Wright v. Stewart .... 19 Wash. 184 474
Wright v. Stinson .... 16 Wash. 368 32
Wright v. Whiting .... 40 Barb. 235 430

Yesler v. Hochstettler .... 4 Wash. 349 533
Yesler v. Seattle .... 1 Wash. 308 43
Yesler Estate v. Orth .... 24 Wash. 483 143
Young v. Clark .... 16 Utah 42 58
Young v. Tacoma .... 31 Wash. 153 375

Zindorf Constr. Co. v. Western
    Amer. Co. .... 27 Wash. 31 406

STATUTES

CITED AND CONSTRUED

		Page
Constitution, article	1, section 3	512
Constitution, article	1, section 12	36, 343, 515
Constitution, article	1, section 16	76
Constitution, article	1, section 22	155
Constitution, article	2, section 1	132
Constitution, article	2, section 19	166, 341
Constitution, article	3, section 7	130
Constitution, article	3, sections 14, 16, 17	173
Constitution, article	3, sections 19, 20	174
Constitution, article	3, section 21	172, 174, 175
Constitution, article	3, section 22	174
Constitution, article	4, section 16	334, 569
Constitution, article	7, section 1	31
Constitution, article	7, section 2	583
Constitution, article	7, section 9	584, 585, 589
Constitution, article	8, section 3	514
Constitution, article	8, section 5	513
Constitution, article	11, section 8	175, 176
Constitution, article	11, section 9	38
Constitution, article	11, section 10	580
Constitution, article	11, section 12	584
Constitution, article	11, section 15	515
Constitution, article	12, section 7	343
Constitution, article	12, section 9	513
Constitution, article	12, section 12	151
Constitution, article	12, section 22	515
Code of 1881, section 829		129
Code of Procedure, section 193		24
Ballinger's Code, section	393	44
Ballinger's Code, section	739	305, 306
Ballinger's Code, section	775	306
Ballinger's Code, section	938	580, 581, 582
Ballinger's Code, section	1699	274
Ballinger's Code, section	1740a	31
Ballinger's Code, section	1751, subdivision 1	274
Ballinger's Code, section	1767, subdivision 6	278, 281

Page

Ballinger's Code, sections 3084, 3085, 3087, 3093............ 595
Ballinger's Code, sections 4080–4089...................... 507
Ballinger's Code, section 4771............................. 387
Ballinger's Code, section 4794............................. 137
Ballinger's Code, sections 4800, 4805...................... 4
Ballinger's Code, section 4869............................. 111
Ballinger's Code, sections 4870, 4872...................... 280
Ballinger's Code, section 4878............................. 279
Ballinger's Code, section 4880............................. 281
Ballinger's Code, section 4930............................. 195
Ballinger's Code, section 4931............................. 684
Ballinger's Code, section 4953...................358, 361, 687
Ballinger's Code, section 4994............................. 81
Ballinger's Code, section 5012............................. 542
Ballinger's Code, section 5020............................. 401
Ballinger's Code, section 5023............................. 480
Ballinger's Code, sections 5029, 5030...................... 66
Ballinger's Code, section 5058.....................118, 407
Ballinger's Code, section 5060............................. 524
Ballinger's Code, section 5062......................65, 406
Ballingér's Code, section 5070............................. 66
Ballinger's Code, sections 5071, 5075..................... 67
Ballinger's Code, section 5115............................. 66
Ballinger's Code, section 5153............................. 115
Ballinger's Code, section 5165............................. 294
Ballinger's Code, section 5185............................. 137
Ballinger's Code, section 5262. . ...530, 534
Ballinger's Code, section 5266...................533, 534
Ballinger's Code, section 5438............................. 77
Ballinger's Code, section 5503............................. 17
Ballinger's Code, section 5504....................17, 438
Ballinger's Code, section 5527...................673, 674
Ballinger's Code, section 5695............................. 501
Ballinger's Code, section 5741....................36, 126
Ballinger's Code, section 5755............................. 45
Ballinger's Code, section 6009..................245, 246, 247
Ballinger's Code, section 6047...................246, 247
Ballinger's Code, section 6048............................. 619
Ballinger's Code, section 6502............................. 67
Ballinger's Code, section 6503............................. 657
Ballinger's Code, section 6506............................. 413
Ballinger's Code, section 6535............................. 267
Ballinger's Code, sections 6845, 6846...................... 154
Ballinger's Code, section 6907............................. 569
Ballinger's Code, section 6910..................267, 268, 270

Page

Ballinger's Code. section 6911................................ 267
Ballinger's Code, section 6941................................ 334
Ballinger's Code, section 6944................................ 134
Ballinger's Code, section 7103................................ 129
Ballinger's Code, section 7121................................ 151
Pierce's Code, section 251................................... 137
Pierce's Code, sections 285, 289a............................. 4
Pierce's Code, section 401................................... 684
Pierce's Code, section 1066.................................. 657
Pierce's Code, section 1122.................................. 137
Pierce's Code, [section 1396] chapter 59.................... 36
Pierce's Code, section 1396.................................. 36
Pierce's Code, section 2016.................................. 134
Pierce's Code, section 8640.................................. 190
Pierce's Code, section 8679.................................. 31
Laws 1887–8, page —, chapter 7, section 8.................... 171
Laws 1890, page 88, section 15............................... 166
Laws 1890, page 361, section 17.............................. 176
Laws 1893, page 226.. 375
Laws 1893, page 241, chapter 99...............507, 508, 509, 511
Laws 1895, page 105.. 32
Laws 1895, page 109, chapter 64, section 7.................. 159
Laws 1895, page 115.. 36
Laws 1897, page 242, section 18.............................. 630
Laws 1899, page 79... 657
Laws 1899, page 287, section 3.............................. 274
Laws 1899, page 295, section 12.......................28, 31
Laws 1899, page 299, section 18.............................. 278
Laws 1901, page 28... 137
Laws 1901, page 194, chapter 94............................. 395
Laws 1901, page 356, chapter 174..........239, 340, 341, 342, 345
Laws 1901, page 383, section 1, subdivision 1................ 274
Laws 1901, pages 383, 384, section 1, subdivision 2.......... 279
Laws Ex. Sess. 1901, page 13................................. 130
Laws 1903, page 5.. 130
Laws 1903, page 68... 294
Laws 1903, page 230, chapter 123, section 2................. 250
Laws 1903, page 285....................................66, 537
Revised Ordinances, City of Seattle, section 446..........122, 124
Revised Ordinances, City of Seattle, sections 449, 452........ 124
Revised Ordinances, City of Seattle, section 451..122, 123, 124, 125
Revised Ordinances, City of Seattle, section 478.............. 121
Ordinance of Seattle, No. 10,723............................ 307
Ordinances, City of Port Townsend, No. 639...578, 579, 580, 581
Ordinances, City of Port Townsend, No. 675........578, 579, 581

CASES

DETERMINED IN THE

SUPREME COURT

OF

WASHINGTON

[No. 4867.   Decided April 18, 1904.]

P. D. SUTER et al., Respondents, v. WENATCHEE WATER POWER COMPANY, Appellant.[1]

LIMITATION OF ACTIONS — THREE-YEAR LIMITATION UPON CONTRACTS NOT IN WRITING—CONSTRUCTION OF STATUTE.   The limitation of Bal. Code, § 4800, subd. 3, for the commencement of actions upon a contract "or liability," express or implied, which is not in writing, refers only to contractual liabilities.

SAME—DAMAGE TO REAL PROPERTY BY OVERFLOW—WHEN NOT A TRESPASS.   An action for damages to real property through an overflow caused by the defendant's negligent construction of an irrigating canal, lawfully built, but without sufficiently providing for carrying off the surplus water or controlling the flow, is not an action for trespass within the purview of the three-year limitation for actions for "trespass upon real property," since the damages are consequential only, and not direct, as required to create trespass at common law; and such action is barred if not commenced within two years from the time the damage accrued.

SAME.   In such a case, even if the water was under control, negligently permitting it to escape would not create a forcible trespass, and the damages would be consequential, recoverable at common law in an action on the case only.

Appeal from a judgment of the superior court for Chelan county, Martin, J., entered June 1, 1903, upon the verdict of a jury rendered in favor of the plaintiff in

1Reported in 76 Pac. 298.

an action for damages to real property by reason of the overflow of an irrigation canal. Reversed.

Will H. Thompson, L. C. Gilman, Danson & Huneke, and *Burt J. Williams,* for appellant.

Dill & Crass, for respondents.

HADLEY, J.—Respondents are husband and wife, and the appellant, a corporation, is the owner and operator of an irrigation canal with lateral connections, in Chelan county, Washington. The canal was constructed prior to 1899. It commences about five miles above the mouth of the Wenatchee river, follows along the bank of said river a distance of about four miles, and thence one branch extends in a northeasterly direction to a point near the Columbia river.

This suit was brought by respondents against appellant, and the complaint alleges, that the said lateral canal was constructed about five feet wide and three feet deep, to the point last mentioned; that, from said point, appellant plowed a furrow across and around the lands of respondents, leading to the Columbia river, which furrow was about twelve inches in width and six inches in depth; that the furrow was not of sufficient capacity to carry away, and around the lands of respondents, the volume of water conveyed to said point as the terminus of the original canal. It is further alleged, that the appellant carelessly and negligently constructed said canal by failing to supply the necessary waste gates and means for the escape of the surplus accumulation of water, before it arrived at respondents' land, and also failed to properly attend to the escape of such surplus accumulation; that on or about June 10, 1900, the appellant permitted the waste and surplus water, which naturally drained from the

country lying above said canal, to accumulate therein
to such an extent as to fill it to its full capacity; that appellant permitted the water to flow along said original
canal to its full capacity, to the point of its terminus
aforesaid; that the aforesaid furrow, leading from said
terminus, was wholly insufficient in capacity to receive
and convey the water which had thus accumulated in the
original canal; that, by reason of the insufficiency of said
furrow for said purpose, the waters overflowed, washed
and cut through the bank of the furrow and the end of
the canal, and thence ran over and across the lands of respondents and down into the Columbia river; that thereby
such deep and wide ditches were washed and cut in said
land as damaged it to the extent of $1,000, and recovery
thereof is demanded.

Appellant demurred to the complaint on the ground
that it appears upon the face thereof that the action was
not commenced within the time prescribed by law. The
demurrer was overruled, to which ruling appellant excepted. Appellant then answered, denying material allegations of the complaint, and, among other things, pleaded
affirmatively that the acts complained of occurred more
than two years prior to the commencement of the action,
and that, if respondents ever had any cause of action whatsoever, on account of said acts, the same had been barred
by the statute of limitations. A demurrer to said affirmative defense was sustained, and appellant excepted thereto.
The cause was thereafter tried before the court and a
jury, and a verdict was returned in favor of respondents
in the sum of $300. Appellant moved for a new trial,
which was denied. Judgment was entered for the amount
of the verdict, and the defendant has appealed.

Respondents have moved to strike from the record
appellant's exceptions to the court's instructions, on the

ground that they were neither included in the statement of facts, nor in any way certified by the trial court. A motion is also made to strike the statement of facts and certain affidavits sent up with the record. We think it unnecessary to discuss these motions, since we believe the case must be determined upon the demurrers heretofore mentioned.

It is assigned that the court erred in overruling the demurrer to the complaint, and in sustaining the demurrer to the affirmative answer, each of which rulings involved the statute of limitations. It will be remembered that the damages sought are alleged to have accrued on the 10th of June, 1900. This action was commenced more than two years thereafter. Unless the acts complained of come within some specific provision of the statute of limitations, the action must be governed by § 289a, Pierce's Code, § 4805, Bal. Code, which limits the time for commencing the action to a period of two years after the cause of action shall have accrued.

Since the cause of action is not based upon a contract in writing, or liability, express or implied, arising out of a written contract, we must therefore refer to § 285, Pierce's Code, § 4800, Bal. Code, to ascertain if any specific provision of the three-year statute of limitations applies here. The action, not being founded upon contract, or liability arising therefrom, is not governed by subd. 3 of said section, which provides as follows: "An action upon a contract or liability, express or implied, which is not in writing, and does not arise out of any written instrument." The term "liability," used in said subdivision, was evidently intended to refer to a contractual liability. Such, in effect, was the decision in *Sargent v. Tacoma*, 10 Wash. 212, 215, 38 Pac. 1048. The same statute was so construed by the United States circuit court, district of Washington, in *Aldrich v. Skinner*, 98 Fed. 375, and also in *Aldrich v. McClaine*, 98 Fed. 378. The last named case was, on appeal to the United States circuit court of appeals, reversed. *Aldrich v. McClaine*, 106 Fed. 791. The reversal was, however, upon the ground that the liability involved was a contractual one, the lower court having held otherwise. The appellate court construed the statute itself as did the lower court. For similar construction, see *McGaffin v. City of Cohoes*, 74 N. Y. 387, 30 Am. Rep. 307, and *Thomas v. Union Pacific R. Co.*, 1 Utah 235.

If any part of the said three-year statute applies here, it must be subdivision 1, which is as follows: "An action for waste or trespass upon real property." Respondents urge that the action is for trespass, and is, therefore, governed by the above quoted subdivision. It is therefore necessary to determine whether the acts complained of constituted a trespass. The construction of the canal by appellant was for a lawful purpose, and it was, therefore, not an unlawful or wrongful act to permit water to flow through it. The complaint, however, charges negligence in the manner of construction, and in permitting an excessive amount of water to flow through the canal. The manner of construction was not in itself wrongful. Appellant had the lawful right to construct as it chose, and to permit the water to flow through the canal to to its full capacity. These things were of no concern to respondents, unless they resulted in some injury to them. Such injury, so resulting, must necessarily have been consequential, and not the direct result of wrongful force applied to the respondents' lands, as must have been true to create a trespass.

"It is not trespass to flow the lands of another with water by erecting a dam below his land, for any one may lawfully build a dam on his land, and the act, being injurious only in its consequences, is to be redressed by an action on the case." Gould, Waters (3d ed.), § 210.

In this state the distinctions between common law actions are abolished, as far as relates to the procedure. We must, however, determine what the legislature meant when it referred to an action for "trespass upon real property." The same was true in *Hicks v. Drew,* 117 Cal. 305, 49 Pac. 189. There it was held that the erection of a bulkhead on one's own land, whereby the lands of another were flooded, was not a trespass, and hence that an action for damages caused by such flooding was not within the statute limiting actions for "trespass upon real property." The court observes as follows:

"While in this state all distinctions between common-law actions are abolished as relating to the procedure. yet it is plain that we are bound to consult the common law, and the classification of common-law actions, for the proper determination as to what the law-making power of this state had in mind when using the phrase, 'trespass upon real property.' It appears that the courts of England often experienced difficulty in determining whether trespass or case was the true remedy to be pursued. This same difficulty often arises in this state, when the statute of limitations is invoked. But in the case at bar, weighed and tested by the rules of the common law, the distinction between these two forms of common law actions is clearly apparent; and that this case upon its facts is one wherein it is sought to recover upon a liability not based upon an instrument of writing, and, therefore, barred in two years, we are satisfied. One of the best tests by which to distinguish trespass is found in the answer to the question, When was the damage done? If the damage does not come directly from the act, but is simply an after result from the act, it is essentially consequential, and no trespass."

Then follows a discussion of authorities, showing the distinction between acts constituting trespass, for which redress was had through the common law action of trespass, and those affecting only consequential results, damages for which were recoverable through an action on the case.

In *Roundtree v. Brantley,* 34 Ala. 544, 73 Am. Dec. 470, the action was for the overflowing of the plaintiff's land, caused by the formation of a sand bank in a stream from the washing of sand through the defendant's ditch. It was held that the acts did not constitute trespass, and that the statute of limitations upon the subject of trespass to real property did not apply.   The court said:

"It is argued that trespass is a comprehensive term, which includes trespass on the case; and that this cause of action is a trespass on the case to real or personal property, which is embraced in the section under the term 'trespass.' It is true that *trespass,* in one sense, means an injury or wrong; and, in that sense, it would include every cause of action, at least in tort.   But trespass has, in the law, a well ascertained and fixed meaning.   It refers to injuries which are immediate, and not consequential.   It is clear that the word is used in that sense in section 2477.   It would be a perversion of language to dominate an act, which produced a consequential injury to real or personal property, a trespass.   It would be a perversion alike of the legal and common acceptation of the words."

In *Holly v. Boston Gas Light Co.,* 8 Gray 123, 69 Am. Dec. 233, the action was for damages arising from negligence in suffering gas pipes to be and remain out of repair.   The court declared that the act complained of was not trespass, and observed as follows:

"The defendants lawfully laid down their pipes in the public street, and filled them with gas.   If they failed to discharge their duty in regard to its distribution, and negligently suffered it to escape, they were liable therefor to other parties for all consequential damages, and might be proceeded against for the recovery of compensation, in an action in the nature of an action of the case, but not as trespassers, in an action of trespass."

The same distinctions are observed in *Cooper v. Hall*, 5 Ohio 321, and *Daneri v. Southern Cal. R. Co.*, 122 Cal. 507, 55 Pac. 243.

Respondents cite cases involving trespasses committed by animals, as analogous to the principle under examination here. Such were, however, expressly held to constitute trespass at common law. Every unwarrantable entry by a person or his cattle on the land of another was a trespass. The act of the animal was classified as though it were the act of the owner. The injury was the direct and immediate result of the wrongful force, and was not consequential. Consequential damages, resulting from such acts as are complained of in the case at bar, were, however, recoverable in an action on the case only, and not in an action for trespass.

We must, therefore, conclude that, when our law makers provided a three-year limitation for actions for "trespass upon real property," they meant to include only such recovery as could have been had through the action of trespass at common law. It follows that actions under our present procedure, through which relief is sought for injuries to land, and which could have been had at common law through an action on the case only, are governed by our two-year statute of limitations, hereinbefore cited.

Respondents argue in their brief that appellant's act was a forcible one, in that they assert it let the waters into the canal through the head gate, and that the injury to their lands was the immediate result of such forcible act. It is asserted that the water was under appellant's absolute control from the time it entered into its

canal from the Wenatchee river until it was let out at
the end of the lateral. Such is, however, not the case
alleged in the complaint. The complaint is based upon
the negligence in the construction of the canal, and upon
its insufficiency to carry the surplus water which accumulated, at the time mentioned, by drainage from above.
If such were true, it is manifest that the water was not
under the immediate and absolute control of appellant,
as respondents now argue. The theory of the complaint
is that the injury resulted from negligent construction,
which occurred long before, and whereby appellant failed
to properly handle the waste and surplus water. The
act was remote from the injury. The latter was purely
consequential, and not the direct or immediate result of
the former.

Moreover, if respondents' present argument were supported by the allegations and theory of the complaint, then,
even though appellant had full control of the water, it
still follows, from the reasoning in the cases cited above,
that it was not doing a thing unlawful in itself when it
permitted the water to run through its canal; and if,
after running through the canal, it was negligently permitted to escape, the appellant was liable for consequential
damages, recoverable at common law in an action on the
case only, and not in an action of trespass. We therefore
think, that, under the cause of action stated in the complaint, our statute of limitations barred the action after
two years. It follows that the court erred in overruling
the demurrer to the complaint.

The judgment is, therefore, reversed, and the cause remanded, with instructions to the lower court to set aside
the verdict and to sustain the demurrer to the complaint.

FULLERTON, C. J., and MOUNT, ANDERS, and DUNBAR,
JJ., concur.

[No. 5013.   Decided April 18, 1904.]

WASHINGTON IRON WORKS, *Respondent*, v. JAMES Mc-
NAUGHT, *Appellant*.[1]

GUARANTY—CONSIDERATION. There is sufficient consideration
for a contract guaranteeing the payment for machinery sold and
delivered on board of one of the purchaser's boats, where one
dollar is the expressed consideration and the vendor refused to
let the boat depart without payment of the balance due, and
gave permission in consideration of the written guaranty.

SALES—DELIVERY—DEMURRAGE ON DELAY. Nothing is due for
delay in delivering machinery sold under a contract providing
for $100 a day demurrage where, shortly before the day fixed, the
contract was modified to include additional machinery and sixty
days was given within which to manufacture the same, and the
machinery was delivered in said time.

GUARANTY—EXTENSION OF TIME—ACCEPTANCE OF DRAFTS. The
acceptance of drafts extending the time for payment does not
operate to discharge a guarantor, when they were drawn at his
request or at the request of his agent, and for his benefit.

EVIDENCE—LETTERS—COMPETENCY—AUTHORITY OF AGENT. Although a letter not shown to be signed by an authorized agent
might not be competent as an independent letter, it is admissible
when referred to in a letter of the duly authorized agent, where
both letters are offered as one.

TRIAL—INSTRUCTIONS. Instructions which are not justified by
any evidence are properly refused.

Appeal from a judgment of the superior court for King
county, Griffin, J., entered September 12, 1903, upon the
verdict of a jury rendered in favor of the plaintiff, in
an action upon a contract of guaranty. Affirmed.

Robert F. Booth and *Root, Palmer & Brown,* for appellant.

L. C. Gilman (*Carr & Preston* and *Everett C. Ellis,*
of counsel), for respondent.

[1]Reported in 76 Pac. 301.

Mount, J.—Plaintiff brought this action to recover
$2,000 upon a written contract of guaranty made by de-
fendant, guaranteeing the payment, by the Boston &
Alaska Transportation Company, of all sums of money
due to the plaintiff. The answer, after denying the allegations in the complaint, alleged three affirmative defenses:
(1) That, at the time the action was brought, plaintiff
was indebted to the Boston & Alaska Transportation
Company for demurrage, in a sum in excess of the amount
sued for; (2) that, after the contract of guaranty, plaintiff agreed to, and did, accept two certain drafts upon the
Boston & Alaska Transportation Company, without the
knowledge or consent of defendant, and thereby extended
the time for the payment of the indebtedness due plaintiff
from said Boston & Alaska Transportation Company; and
(3) that plaintiff, subsequent to said guaranty, accepted
receiver's certificates in satisfaction of the indebtedness
owing from said Boston & Alaska Transportation Company. The reply denied the allegations of new matter
in the answer. The cause was tried to the court and a
jury. A verdict was returned in favor of the plaintiff
for the full amount claimed. Defendant appeals from a
judgment on the verdict.

At the close of the evidence appellant moved the court
for a nonsuit. This motion was denied, and appellant assigns error thereon, and argues, (1) that the contract
of guaranty was without consideration; (2) that the demurrage due the transportation company was more than
the amount of respondent's claim; and (3) that the drafts
drawn by respondent extended the time of payment of
the obligation guaranteed by appellant.

All three of these questions were questions of fact for
the jury. The evidence of the respondent showed that

[No. 5012.   Decided April 18, 1904.]

there was an express consideration of one dollar for the contract of guaranty; and also, that, when the machinery, which was ordered from respondent by the Boston & Alaska Transportation Company, was delivered by the respondent to the said company on board of one of its boats, respondent refused to let the boat depart without payment of the balance of the contract price for the machinery; and that the appellant, in consideration of respondent's permitting the machinery to be taken away, made the written guaranty sued on. This evidence was not disputed, and, aside from the express consideration, was amply sufficient to support the contract of guaranty.

The same is true of the demurrage. The original contract provided that, if the machinery was not delivered on March 31, 1898, respondent should pay the transportation company $100 per day for every day thereafter that the machinery remained undelivered. But, a short time before the machinery was to be delivered, that contract was modified, and other machinery was included, and respondent given sixty days' additional time within which to manufacture the machinery. Within this sixty days, the machinery was delivered to the transportation company. This company, under this evidence, was clearly not entitled to any demurrage.

Upon the question of the drafts, the evidence is conclusive that they were drawn and time given at the request of appellant, or his agent, for the benefit of appellant. Appellant, after that time and with knowledge of the extension, assured respondent that he would pay the obligation. There was sufficient evidence to go to the jury upon each of these questions, and it was therefore not error to deny the motion.

Appellant assigns error upon the ruling of the court admitting two letters in evidence. These letters were

offered in rebuttal to show a change in the original contract between respondent and the transportation company,
and an extension of the time within which the machinery
was to be furnished. They were certainly competent for
the purpose. It is true, the one signed by J. F. McNaught
might not, of itself, have been competent without showing his authority, but it was not offered as an independent
letter. It was referred to in the letter from Lockwood,
who was proven to be the general agent of the transportation company, and was made a part of his letter. The
two letters were offered as one, which, in fact, they were.

Appellant alleges error in the refusal of the court to
give instructions.requested, as follows:

"2. Any statement made by Mr. Ling as to his having authority from the defendant to represent him is incompetent to prove such authority, and you cannot consider such statements made by Mr. Ling to Mr. Frink
or any one else, as proving Mr. Ling's authority from
the defendant, unless such statements were made by Mr.
Ling in the presence of the defendant.

"3. If the defendant told Mr. Frink that Mr. Ling
did look after defendant's business and attended to the
same in his absence, this would not be sufficient authority
to authorize Mr. Ling to bind the defendant by an extension which said Ling as treasurer might agree to do
with the plaintiff.

"4. If you find from the evidence that it was the intention of both parties hereto that the defendant guaranteed the payment of the balance due upon the machinery
manufactured under the contract which has been offered
in evidence, and you further find that the machinery unpaid for was manufactured under some other and different contract or contracts, then your verdict must be for
the defendant.

"5. The court instructs you that only one contract is
mentioned in the pleadings in this case, and if the sum
which is sued for in this action is due upon machinery
which was manufactured, sold or furnished pursuant to

any other contracts or agreements, then your verdict must be for the defendant."

There was no evidence in the case to justify any of these instructions requested, and, if they had been given, they would have been confusing and misleading. It was, therefore, not error to refuse them.

We have examined the instructions which were given, and are satisfied that the cause was fairly and correctly given to the jury, and that the verdict was in accord with the evidence. The judgment is therefore affirmed.

FULLERTON, C. J., and HADLEY, ANDERS, and DUNBAR, JJ., concur.

[No. 4936.   Decided April 18, 1904.]

SARAH HESSER, *Appellant*, v. HENRY SIEPMANN *et al.*, *Respondents*.[1]

ADVERSE POSSESSION—PAYMENT OF TAXES—SEVEN YEAR LIMITATION—COLOR OF TITLE—PAPER TITLE ESSENTIAL. Bal. Code, §§ 5503-5504, providing for the obtaining of title to vacant land by the payment of taxes under color of title for seven years, has no application unless the payment is supported by actual paper title.

ADVERSE POSSESSION—PLEADING—COMPLAINT—HOSTILE CLAIM SHOWN. A complaint alleging actual, open, notorious, and adverse possession, under color of title and claim of right, is not insufficient as failing to show hostile or exclusive possession.

ADVERSE POSSESSION—CLAIM OF RIGHT—SUFFICIENCY WITHOUT COLOR OF TITLE. Where a deed of a lot excepted the west twenty feet thereof, upon the erroneous supposition that said west twenty feet extended into the adjoining street, and the grantee took possession up to the line of the street, including the excepted portion, supposing it to be the land purchased, there was sufficient claim of right to support a title by ten years' adverse possession without any color of title thereto, since such possession under claim of right is sufficient without color of title.

[1]Reported in 76 Pac. 295.

Appeal from a judgment of the superior court for King
county, Tallman, J., entered April 11, 1903, upon findings
in favor of the defendants, dismissing an action to quiet
title, after a trial on the merits before the court without a
jury. Reversed.

Fred H. Peterson, for appellant.

Greene & Griffiths, for respondents.

Dunbar, J.— Appellant brought this action against respondents to quiet her title to the whole of lot 30, in block
72, Gilman Park, situated in Ballard, King county, Washington, and particularly the west twenty feet thereof; also,
to enjoin respondents from entering upon said lot 30, and
particularly the west twenty feet thereof. The appellant
alleged that she and her grantors had been in the actual,
open, notorious, and adverse possession, under color of title
and claim of right, for more than ten years last past, to wit,
since March 6, 1891, and continuously thereafter until the
present time. The deeds through which she deraigned title
are set forth, one conveying an undivided one-third of said
lot 30, excepting twenty feet the full width of the lot on the
west, and the other an undivided two-thirds of said lot 30,
except twenty feet the full width of the lot on the west.

It is alleged that the appellant and her grantors, at the
time of taking possession thereof, on March 6, 1891, made
inquiry as to the lines and corners of said lot, and were
informed, and verily believed, that the land described
in the said two deeds included all the tract of land now
claimed by the respondents; that, at the time of purchas-
ing said lot, said appellant and her grantors went into the
actual, open, and notorious possession of the land described in their deeds, including all of the west twenty
feet of said lot, believing at the said time that the west

twenty feet of said lot was situated west of the east marginal line of what is now known as Fourth avenue west, in the city of Ballard; and that, by reason of the aforesaid acts and actual belief of ownership, under and by virtue of said deeds, appellant and her grantors continued to hold possession of said land, and held said entire lot, as now actually occupied, and particularly said west twenty feet. She also alleged that, for more than seven years last past, appellant had actually paid all the taxes, municipal, county, and state, which were levied against the whole of said lot 30, including the west twenty feet thereof, and that said taxes were paid under claim of right and color of title. The lot in dispute is an irregular lot, and the west twenty feet of the lot reaches the east boundary of Fourth avenue west. The answer was practically a denial of the allegations of the complaint.

At the conclusion of the trial, the court found, that the respondents were the true owners in fee simple of the westerly twenty feet of said lot; that the appellant was not the owner in fee simple, nor in the possession of the property in controversy, to wit, the westerly twenty feet of said lot 30; but that the appellant, and her predecessors in interest, had paid, and caused to be paid, a certain amount of taxes assessed against said lot, including the westerly twenty feet thereof; and decreed a dismissal of the action upon the payment to the appellant by the respondents of said amount of taxes.

Appellant contends that judgment should have been rendered in her favor for two reasons: (1) by reason of actual, open, notorious, and adverse possession for a period of more than ten years prior to the commencement of the action; and (2) by reason of the payment of all taxes legally assessed thereon for more than seven successive

years, under color of title, to wit, by paying all of said
taxes from the year 1891 to the year 1902, inclusive.

It does not seem to us that the appellant's second contention can be sustained. There is no claim here that
there was any actual paper title to the west twenty feet
of lot 30, and § 5504, Bal. Code, upon which appellant
relies, is to the effect that, "every person having color of
title made in good faith to vacant and unoccupied land,
who shall pay all taxes legally assessed thereon for seven
successive years, he or she shall be deemed and adjudged
to be the legal owner of said vacant and unoccupied land
to the extent and according to the purport of his or her
paper title;" and § 5503, in regard to the possession of
lands or tenements, is in practically the same language.
There being no paper title to ascertain the extent of in
this case, it seems to us that the statutes have no application.

But we think that the court erred in finding that appellant was not the owner of the land in controversy, on the
first ground claimed, viz., actual, open, notorious, and
adverse possession for a period of more than ten years.
It was evidently the view of the court that, in order to
obtain title by adverse possession, there must have been some
instrument in writing of record, or some record title. The
court's finding indicates that this was the construction
that it placed upon the law, and it also stated that, notwithstanding the fact asserted by counsel for respondents—that the matters of fact alleged in the complaint
were disputed—the court regarded the contest as one involving a question of law.

It is also contended by the attorney for the respondents that there was neither good faith nor color of title,
such as is required by the statute, shown in this case, and
that the complaint was defective as to the first cause of

action because there was no allegation of any hostile or exclusive possession. The allegation that the appellant "is now, and she and her grantors have been, in the actual, open, notorious, and adverse possession, under color of title and claim of right for more than ten years last past," it seems to us, is a sufficient allegation of adverse possession, if adverse possession will work a bar to the bringing of an action for the recovery of real estate, in the absence of a color of title on the part of the party alleging the adverse possession. The qualification "color of title" is generally coupled with that of claim of right, and adverse possession, either under color of title or claim of right, or both, has been held sufficient by this court, in common with most other courts, without the aid of record title. In *Moore v. Brownfield*, 7 Wash. 23, 34 Pac. 199, it was held that actual, uninterrupted, and notorious possession under a claim of right, but without color of title, was sufficient to entitle the possessor to the benefit of the statute of limitations. The language of the court in that case was:

"Actual, uninterrupted and notorious possession under a claim of right is sufficient, without color of title, and such possession need not be adverse to all the world;"

citing *Mather v. Walsh*, 107 Mo. 121, 17 S. W. 755. In *Blake v. Shriver*, 27 Wash. 593, 68 Pac. 330, it is true that this court held that squatters upon unoccupied land in the city of Spokane did not obtain title to said land by reason of a residence thereon for more than ten years; but it was not the intention in that case to over-rule any of the preceding cases decided by this court. There, there was no pretense of any claim of right or color of title, by record or otherwise. The land was known to the claimants to be land the title of which was in litigation. The court, in speaking of one of the claimants, said:

"The whole testimony convinces us that the claimant, when he went there, simply squatted upon the land for present convenience; that he had neither color of title nor claim of right to it in any sense whatever; that he did not even intend or think of obtaining title to it, by the statute of limitations or in any other way, at the time he settled upon it, or for many years thereafter; that the occupation was purely permissive, by reason of the circumstances which we have above portrayed; and that it was the intention upon the part of these claimants to reap the benefit to which they are not entitled by now claiming an adverse possession for ten years. It is not such strolling, straggling occupancy as is shown by the testimony in this case that constitutes a notice of adverse possession."

In the case at bar the testimony is to the effect that, at the time the deeds were given to this appellant and her husband, it was the understanding that the west twenty feet, excepted by the deed from lot 30, was that portion of the lot which was occupied by Fourth avenue west; that the lot which was purchased reached to the west line of said street or avenue; and that there was no intention to purchase a lot with twenty feet intervening between the west boundary of the lot purchased and the street. This, it seems to us, brings the case squarely within the rule announced in *Flint v. Long,* 12 Wash. 342, 41 Pac. 49, where it was held that, where land had been platted into lots by actually staking it out on the face of the earth, a deed purporting to convey certain of the lots was sufficient to constitute a color of title for a bona fide entry, although the recorded plat of the lands might not include such lots within the bounds of the platted tract as described therein. The court, in dscussing that case, said:

"Conceding the necessity under the provisions of our statute, to show color of title on the part of the respondent in this case,—a question upon which we do not now pass,—it seems to us that such color of title was fairly shown. All that is necessary to be shown is that there was a proof of colorable title under which the entry or claim has been made in good faith. The land in question was purchased by the respondents and the platting on file merely represented the lots as staked out upon the ground, and a deed to certain lots purporting to convey land actually staked out upon the face of the earth to correspond with the deed, would certainly be a purchase and an entry thereunder, if such entry was made in good faith."

While in the case at bar the land was not actually staked out, the principle is the same, if it was the intention, on the one hand, to convey, and on the other, to purchase, the land reaching to the street, although a mistake was made in the description in the deed which was actually executed. We decided in *Bowers v. Ledgerwood,* 25 Wash. 14, 64 Pac. 936, that the inclosure of the lands of another within a fence, built by the adjoining owner under the mistaken impression that such fence constituted the boundary line, and the occupancy, cultivation, and improvement of such inclosed lands for a period beyond the statute of limitations, was sufficient to constitute title thereto by adverse possession. This case, it seems to us, is directly in point, and, while the amount of improvements in the case cited was vastly more than in the case at bar, the principle—so far as the question of mistaken boundary is concerned—is exactly the same.

Without reviewing the testimony, we think there was sufficient to show actual, adverse possession and improvements, under claim of right. Such being the case, the judgment is reversed, and the case remanded, with instructions to the lower court to enter judgment in favor of the appellant.

FULLERTON, C. J., and MOUNT, HADLEY, and ANDERS, JJ., concur.

[No. 4904. Decided April 18, 1904.]

W. W. WATSON et al., Respondents, v. TOWN OF KENT, Appellant.[1]

PLEADING—DEMURRER—WAIVER BY WITHDRAWING—OBJECTION TO ANY EVIDENCE. The objection that the complaint does not state a cause of action, first raised by demurrer, is waived by the withdrawal of the demurrer and answering on the merits, and cannot be subsequently raised by an objection to any evidence.

MUNICIPAL CORPORATIONS—NUISANCE—LIABILITY OF TOWN FOR MAINTENANCE OF PESTHOUSE—RATIFICATION OF ACTS OF OFFICERS. In an action for damages for the establishment and maintenance of a nuisance on plaintiffs' premises, by converting one of their dwellings into a pest house for smallpox patients, a motion for a nonsuit, on the theory that the town was not responsible for the acts of its officers, is properly overruled, where there was sufficient evidence to warrant a finding that the health officer acted with the knowledge and authority of the town council and that his acts were ratified by the town.

MUNICIPAL CORPORATIONS — ACTIONS — PRESENTING CLAIM FOR DAMAGES—WHEN NOT NECESSARY. In an action for damages for the wrongful act of a town through its qualified agents in establishing a nuisance on plaintiffs' premises, the presentation of a claim is not necessary before bringing suit against the town.

J. G. Price (*C. A. Riddle* and *Kirkpatrick, Price & Carver,* of counsel), for appellant, contended, among other things, that a municipal corporation is not liable for tortious or unauthorized acts of its officers. *Spring v. Hyde Park,* 137 Mass. 554, 50 Am. Rep. 334; *Gordon v. Taunton,* 126 Mass. 349; *Lynd v. Rockland,* 66 Me. 309; Dillon, Mun. Corp. (3d ed.), § 972; *Russell v. Tacoma,* 8 Wash. 156, 35 Pac. 605, 40 Am. St. 895. The only liability of a municipal corporation for acts done in a public capacity and for the public good is that imposed by statute. Dillon, Mun. Corp. (3d ed.), §§ 949, 976, 977;

[1]Reported in 76 Pac. 297.

Barrows, Negligence, §§ 177-184; *Russell v. Tacoma,*
supra; Bryant v. St. Paul, 33 Minn. 289, 23 N. W. 220.
There can be no ratification of the act of one who does
not act, or pretend to act, for the principal. *Ferry v.*
Taylor, 33 Mo. 323; *Crowder v. Reed,* 80 Ind. 1; *Puget*
Sound Lumber Co. v. Krug, 89 Cal. 237; *Richardson v.*
Payne, 114 Mass. 429; *Pittsburg and Steubenville R. Co.*
v. Gazzam, 32 Pa. St. 340; *Commercial etc. Bank v.*
Jones, 18 Tex. 811; *Mitchell v. Minnesota Fire Ass.,*
48 Minn. 278, 51 N. W. 608; *Fellows v. Commissioners*
etc., 36 Barb. (N. Y.) 655; *Hammerslough v. Cheatham,*
84 Mo. 13; *Allred v. Bray,* 41 Mo. 44; *McLaren v. Hall,*
26 Iowa 297; *Hamlin v. Sears,* 82 N. Y. 327; *DeBolle v.*
Pa. Ins. Co., 4 Whar. 68. The character of the health
office and of the acts would prevent any liability arising
therefor, even if ratification were attempted. Dillon,
Mun. Corp. (3d ed.), § 975, and notes; *Peters v. City of*
Lindsborg, 40 Kan. 654, 20 Pac. 490; *Lorillard v. Town*
of Monroe, 11 N. Y. 392, 62 Am. Dec. 120, and notes.
It was error to sustain a challenge to jurors who said they
were disgusted with the bringing of damage suits without
merit, but had no prejudice against a suit with merit.
State v. Croney, 31 Wash. 122, 71 Pac. 783; *State v.*
Farris, 26 Wash. 205, 66 Pac. 412.

William C. Keith and *Tucker & Hyland,* for respondents.

Dunbar, J.—This is an action brought in the superior
court for King county, Washington, by the respondents,
to recover from appellant the sum of $1,000, claimed as
damages growing out of the alleged establishment and
maintenance of a nuisance on the premises near the dwelling of respondents. The complaint alleges, in substance,
that, on the 27th day of January, 1902, the plaintiffs

were residents of the town of Kent; that they had two
dwelling houses, furnished, one of which dwelling houses
was occupied by the said plaintiffs, and the other of
which was situated about eighteen feet from the residence
of the plaintiffs; that on said day the dwelling house
situated next to the residence of these plaintiffs contained
a large amount of furniture, wearing apparel, bedding,
household fixtures, carpets, etc., belonging to the plaintiffs; that one room in said house was temporarily occupied by one Samuel Dugar, who about that date became
afflicted with the disease known as the smallpox, and immediately thereafter the plaintiffs notified the council
of the town of Kent, and the authorities, officers, and
agents of said town of Kent, to remove said smallpox
patient from the dwelling house owned by the plaintiffs;
but that, notwithstanding the warning and notice so given
to the authorities, officers, and agents of said town, and
against the express will and desire of these plaintiffs, the
said town of Kent, through its council, officers, agents, and
servants, proceeded to, and did, convert said dwelling
house into a pesthouse, for the housing of other persons
afflicted with said smallpox, and whom the authorities
suspected of being afflicted with smallpox, and quaran-
tined said building, and put a guard upon said dwelling
both day and night, and kept and maintained said house
for a pesthouse for smallpox patients for the period of
sixteen days, and at the end of said time left the said
house in a filthy, dirty, obnoxious, and indecent condition;
whereby it became necessary to destroy a large amount
of personal property, to the damage of the plaintiffs.
And, further, it is alleged that Elizabeth T. Watson, one
of the plaintiffs, at the time of said contagion was in deli-
cate health, and, by reason of said dwelling house being
so converted into a pesthouse, she was subjected to great

physical and mental pain and worry, was troubled and
frightened for fear of the infection, and was made nervous, sick, and hysterical, and was, at the time, rendered
unable to attend to her household duties, necessitating the
hiring of a nurse and other expenses, the damages altogether alleged amounting to the sum of $1,000. The
answer was a denial of all the allegations of the complaint.
A trial was had to a jury, and verdict was rendered in
favor of plaintiffs for $650. Judgment was entered upon
said verdict, and from such judgment this appeal is taken.

It is contended by the appellant that the town, under
the allegations of this complaint, is not responsible to the
respondents for damages that might have resulted from
the action of the officers of the town, and that the complaint does not state a cause of action against the town.
Whether, under the allegations of the complaint, the town
would be liable, we are not called upon to decide, for a
demurrer—to the effect that the complaint did not state
a cause of action—was interposed to the complaint, and
was afterwards waived by the defendant, which answered
and went to trial upon the merits. This being true, the
question of the sufficiency of the complaint cannot be
raised on this appeal, under the rule announced in *Mosher
v. Bruhn,* 15 Wash. 332, 46 Pac. 397, where it was held
that, where the objection that the complaint does not state
a cause of action had been raised in the lower court by demurrer, and the demurrer had been subsequently waived,
the defendant could not raise the objection of insufficiency
of the complaint on appeal, as Code of Procedure, § 193,
permitting the defendant to raise the objection, at any
stage of the proceedings, that the complaint does not state
a cause of action, has no application to cases where the
point has been once raised in the lower court by demurrer,
and then abandoned. This doctrine was again announced

in *Hardin v. Mullen,* 16 Wash. 647, 48 Pac. 349, and we have no disposition to depart from the rule there announced.

It is true that, in the case at bar, practically the same question was raised by the defendant by objecting to any testimony being offered under the complaint, for the reason that it did not state a cause of action. But this objection, having been specially withdrawn by the waiver of the demurrer, which was the proper method of raising the question, must be considered to have been waived for all time. And, if the question could not again be raised in this court, there is no good reason apparent why it should be raised again in the court below. It might be that, if, after the introduction of all the testimony of the plaintiffs, the whole testimony did not show that a case had been made out which would bind the town, this question could be raised by a motion for nonsuit; and a motion for nonsuit was made by the appellant in this case, but not upon the ground that the complaint did not state a cause of action, or that the evidence would not sustain a verdict, so far as the allegations of the complaint were concerned. An examination of the testimony shows that the proof was practically as broad as the allegations.

The questions raised by the motion for nonsuit, we think, were properly decided by the court against the appellant, the principal contention there being that the officers acted without any authority or direction of the appellant, and that there was no sufficient act of ratification on the part of the town. We think the testimony fully sustained the judgment in this respect, and it is clear to our minds, not only that the health officer acted with the knowledge and authority of the town council, but that all his acts were ratified by the town. In any event, there was sufficient testimony offered on this sub-

ject to go to the jury. All the other questions raised by
the motion for nonsuit were questions which were properly
submitted to the consideration of the jury.

We think the court did not abuse its discretion in sustaining challenges to the jurors mentioned in the 1st,
2d, 3d, 4th, and 5th assignments, and that no prejudicial
error was committed by the introduction or rejection of
testimony, or by the giving or refusing to give instructions.

It is contended by the appellant that the presentation
of the claim for damages required by the statute was not
made in this case, the complaint having alleged the presentation of the claim, and the allegation having been
denied by the answer. But, as we view this complaint—it
being for the wrongful act of the town through its qualified
agent—the presentation of a claim was not necessary,
under the rule announced in *Sutton v. Snohomish,* 11
Wash. 24, 39 Pac. 273, 48 Am. St. 847.

The judgment is affirmed.

FULLERTON, C. J., and MOUNT, HADLEY, and ANDERS,
JJ., concur.

[No. 4458.   Decided April 19, 1904.]

A. E. NATHAN, *Appellant,* v. SPOKANE COUNTY *et al.,*
Respondents.[1]

TAXATION—EXPEDIENCY OF METHOD—DISCRETION OF LEGISLATURE.
The power to impose and the method of collecting taxes, rest in
the discretion of the legislature, and the expediency thereof will
not be questioned by the courts.

SAME—MIGRATORY STOCK TAX—UNIFORMITY—DIFFERENT METH-
ODS OF ASSESSMENT. The "migratory stock tax" (Laws 1899, p.
295, § 12) upon goods brought into the state after the time for as-

[1]Reported in 76 Pac. 521.

sessing property, to be sold in a place of business temporarily occupied, is not unconstitutional on account of making distinctions
as to the manner of assessments, since there is uniformity in the
rate and basis of valuation.

SAME — ASSESSMENT OF PROPERTY TAXED IN ANOTHER STATE.
Where property is otherwise taxable it is not exempt because it
may have been taxed for the same year in another state.

SAME—VALUATION—NO PROVISION FOR EQUALIZATION—NOTICE—
DUE PROCESS OF LAW—HEARING BEFORE ASSESSOR—REVIEW BY
COMMON LAW REMEDIES. Laws 1899, p. 295, § 12, providing for a
tax upon stocks of goods temporarily brought into the state for
sale, is not unconstitutional as a taking of property without due
process of law, in that it fails to provide for notice of the tax, or
for any hearing before the board of equalization, since it is made
the duty of the owner to notify the taxing officers, and the law
provides for a hearing before the assessor, who acts in a judicial
capacity in fixing the valuation, and the common law remedies
may be invoked to review his decision.

SAME—PROVISO AUTHORIZING ABATEMENT OF PART OF TAX. The
proviso added to the "migratory stock tax" law of 1899, authorizing an abatement or deduction from the next regular assessment
corresponding to the portion of the year that the goods were in
this state, is unconstitutional, since such discrimination is unequal, the property must be taxed in proportion to its value, and
no person can be released or discharged from any share of his
tax.

SAME—PARTIAL UNCONSTITUTIONALITY OF ACT NOT AFFECTING
OTHER PORTIONS. The unconstitutionality of the proviso added
to the "migratory stock tax" law, authorizing an abatement or deduction of a portion of the tax, does not affect the validity of
other portions of the section, since the balance is distinct and separable and complete in itself.

Appeal from a judgment of the superior court for Spokane county, Belt, J., entered May 24, 1902, upon sustaining a demurrer to the complaint, dismissing an action
to enjoin the collection of a tax. Affirmed.

Robertson, Miller & Rosenhaupt, for appellant, contended, *inter alia,* that a state cannot impose a business or
license tax heavier upon nonresidents than upon residents
doing the same business. *Ward v. Maryland,* 12 Wall.

418; *State v. Wiggin,* 64 N. H. 508; Cooley, Const. Lim.,
pp. 596-598. There must be notice to the taxpayer.
Blackwell, Tax Titles, § 397; Desty, Taxation, 597;
Kuntz v. Sumption, 117 Ind. 1, 19 N. E. 474; *South
Platte Land Co. v. Buffalo County,* 7 Neb. 254; *Patten v.
Green,* 13 Cal. 330; Cooley, Const. Lim., 431. And he
must have the right to a hearing. *Railroad Tax Cases,*
13 Fed. 722; Cooley, Taxation, pp. 52, 361, 364; *Stuart
v. Palmer,* 74 N. Y. 183; *Hagar v. Reclamation District,*
111 U. S. 701; *Darling v. Gunn,* 50 Ill. 424. Property
not in the state at the time of the assessment cannot be
taxed for the year. *People v. Kohl,* 40 Cal. 127; *Wang-
ler Bros. v. Black Hawk County,* 56 Iowa 384, 9 N. W.
314.

Horace Kimball and *Miles Poindexter,* for respondents.

PER CURIAM.—This is an action instituted in the superior court of Spokane county by A. E. Nathan, appellant and plaintiff below, against Spokane county, George
Mudgett as county treasurer, and A. P. Williams, county
assessor of such county, defendants and respondents. The
object of the suit is to enjoin the collection of $750 levied
as taxes upon plaintiff's property for the year 1901. The
court below sustained a general demurrer to the complaint.
The plaintiff elected to stand on his complaint. The action
was thereupon dismissed, and an appeal taken to this court.

The assignments of error present but the one question,
whether the complaint states sufficient facts to entitle appellant to relief. His brief in this court contains the following statement: "The action was presented in the court
below, and is presented now to this court, to determine
the constitutionality of § 12, Session Laws 1899, p. 295."
The transcript discloses that appellant, in order to prevent distraint of his goods and merchandise, deposited

$750 in the hands of the county treasurer, which, by
stipulation, stands in lieu of a levy, if the appellant shall
be adjudged to pay the tax. The complaint, among other
things, alleges, that on or about the 10th day of November, 1901, appellant, A. E. Nathan, brought a stock of
goods and merchandise from the state of Montana to the
city and county of Spokane; that the value placed on
such stock by appellant was $8,000; that appellant, im-
mediately upon his arrival in Spokane, commenced doing
business as a merchant, under the style of A. E. Nathan &
Co., and proceeded, in the regular and ordinary course of
business, to dispose of his merchandise at a place of business in said city temporarily used for that purpose, without
the intention, on the part of appellant, of permanently engaging in trade at such place; that on or about the 12th day
of November, 1901, respondent A. P. Williams, the county
assessor of Spokane county, by himself and deputies, came
into the store of appellant and notified him that he (the
assessor) would forthwith proceed to assess such stock of
goods; that appellant then and there offered to show to said
assessor the value of such stock, and that the same had been
assessed, and taxes paid thereon, in Montana for the then
current year (1901); that such assessor proceeded to assess
such merchandise, and on the 12th day of November, 1901,
the county treasurer, George Mudgett, came to appellant's
said place of business and threatened to distrain appellant's goods, unless such tax were paid; that, in order to
prevent such levy, appellant, under protest, deposited the
sum of $750 in the hands of said Mudgett, not as county
treasurer, but as a private individual, pending the final
determination of this controversy, and that this has been
done with the consent of the prosecuting attorney of Spokane county.

The complaint further alleges that the above statute, under which this tax levy was made, is unconstitutional for the following reasons: (1) the said enactment provides a different mode and manner of the assessment levied against the property of appellant, than is provided for other persons and property similarly situated; (2) that there is no provision made for any board of equalization, or other person, to hear and determine the matter as to the justness of such tax, and the value of the property sought to be assessed; (3) that it provides for a rebate to persons residing permanently in this state, and is a discrimination against persons temporarily residing therein; (4) that this law is special in its character, and unequal in its application.

The provisions of the statute attacked by appellant are as follows:

"Whenever any person, firm or corporation shall, subsequent to the first day of March of any year, bring or send into any county any stock of goods or merchandise to be sold or disposed of in a place of business temporarily occupied for their sale, without the intention of engaging in permanent trade in such place, the owner, consignee or person in charge of the said goods or merchandise shall immediately notify the county assessor, and thereupon the assessor shall at once proceed to value the said stock of goods and merchandise at its true value, and upon such valuation the said owner, consignee or person in charge shall pay to the collector of taxes a tax at the rate assessed for state, county and local purposes in the taxing district in the year then current. And it shall not be lawful to sell or dispose of any such goods or merchandise as aforesaid in such taxing district until the assessor shall have been so notified as aforesaid and the tax assessed thereon paid to the collector. Every person, firm or corporation bringing into any county of this state goods or merchandise after the first day of March shall be deemed subject to the provisions of this section: Provided, That all persons having paid the tax as herein provided for, shall at the time of the regular assessment next succeeding said payment, be allowed by the county assessor in making his assessment a deduction in a sum equal to that part of the entire assessment of the previous year as the number of days of the previous assessment year he was not in such county bears to the whole of such assessment year." Laws of 1899, p. 295, § 12; Pierce's Code, § 8679; 3 Bal. Code, § 1740a.

Article 7, § 1, Constitution, State of Washington, provides: "All property in the state not exempt under the laws of the United States, or under this constitution, shall be taxed in proportion to its value, to be ascertained as provided by law." The object and intent of the framers of the constitution was, that all property not exempt by virtue of the provisions of such instrument should bear a tax in proportion to its value; that the listing, assessment, levy, enforcement, and collection of taxes, subject to certain limitations unnecessary to notice in this connection, should be in the discretion of the legislature. The expediency of such enactments, within the limitations prescribed by this constitution, constitutes a subject-matter with which the courts will not intermeddle. The legislature is a branch of our state government co-ordinate with the executive and judicial. Each department is supreme within its proper sphere. The lawmaking power is vested in the legislature, under the provisions of our fundamental law.

Judge Cooley, in his able treatise on Constitutional Limitations (5th ed.), p. 593, uses the following pertinent language:

"The power to impose taxes is one so unlimited in force and so searching in extent, that the courts scarcely venture to declare that it is subject to any restrictions whatever, except such as rest in the discretion of the authority which exercises it. It reaches to every trade or occupa-

tion; to every object of industry, use, or enjoyment; to
every species of possession; and it imposes a burden which,
in case of failure to discharge it, may be followed by seizure and sale or confiscation of property."

Again, at page 645 of the same treatise, the learned jurist
observes:

"What method shall be devised for the collection of a
tax, the legislature must determine, subject only to such
rules, limitations, and restraints as the constitution of
the state may have imposed. Very summary methods are
sanctioned by practice and precedent."

This court, in the case of *Johnston v. Whatcom County,*
27 Wash. 95, 67 Pac. 569, construed the above statutory
provision as applying to persons, firms, or corporations
bringing their goods and merchandise into this state from
beyond its boundaries, after the first day of March, to
be sold or disposed of in a place of business temporarily
occupied for their sale, without the intention of engaging
in permanent trade at such place; holding that it did not
apply to merchants moving their goods from one county
into another within the state, after the first day of March,
when such goods had already been listed and assessed
for taxes in the county of the situs of the property at that
date for the then current year. It is true that the constitutionality of this statute was not considered in the above
case; but the contention of appellant—that this enactment is unconstitutional because it "provides a different
mode and manner of the assessment levied against the
property of this appellant, than is provided for other persons and other property similarly situated"—is met by
the decision of this court in *Wright v. Stinson,* 16 Wash.
368, 47 Pac. 761. We held in that case, that the "Migratory Stock Act" (Laws 1895, p. 105) was not unconstitutional on account of making distinctions as to the manner

of assessment and collection of taxes levied against the
different kinds of personal property.

The case of *Kelley v. Rhoads,* 7 Wyo. 237, 51 Pac. 593,
39 L. R. A. 594, 75 Am. St. 904, was, in many of its features, similar to the case at bar. The court held, that the
provision of the state constitution of Wyoming, requiring
property to be uniformly assessed for taxation, does not
mean that, in the case of the assessment of all kinds of
taxable property, the same officers shall act, or that the
proceedings touching the assessment shall be the same; that
there is uniformity in the assessment, if the same basis
of valuation is taken as to all property of like character;
that, as long as the rate and method of valuation are the
same as in case of other property, a statute may be enacted affecting the taxation of a peculiar class of property,
to guard against its escape therefrom, without violating
any constitutional provision. This case is also authority
on the proposition presented in this controversy, that,
where personal property is otherwise taxable in the state
of Washington, it is not exempt from taxation because
it may have been returned for taxation for the same year
in another state. See, also, Cooley, Taxation (2nd ed.),
37, 219-221; *Coe v. Errol,* 116 U. S. 517, 524, 6 Sup.
Ct. 475, 29 L. Ed. 715; exhaustive note, 62 Am. St. Rep.
p. 448.

The appellant in his complaint alleges, that the tax in
question was assessed and levied against his property
after the time fixed by law for the equalization of taxes
by the county board, and therefore the proceedings had in
that behalf were invalid, because he had no opportunity,
under the provisions of this statute, to have the valuation
of his goods, as determined by the county assessor for the
purposes of taxation, reviewed in any manner; that the
law in question is also unconstitutional in this: it fails to

provide for the giving of notice to the owner of the property before the assessment and levy of the tax. In the case of *Kelley v. Rhoads, supra*, it would seem, from the opinion of the court, that the party assessed under the provisions of the Wyoming statute, before or after the annual levy, and feeling himself aggrieved, may subsequently appear before the county board, at either a regular or special session, and obtain relief.

The authorities cited by appellant's counsel, on the proposition that a statute authorizing a board of equalization to raise the valuation of the property of an individual taxpayer, listed by him for taxation, without providing for notice to him of the proposed increase in his assessment, is unconstitutional and void, are not applicable to the questions under consideration. This statute provides that the owner, consignee, or person in charge of the goods or merchandise, shall immediately notify the county assessor, who shall thereupon proceed to value the same at their true value; upon which valuation the taxes for the then current year shall be assessed and collected. The party liable to the payment of the tax has the opportunity to submit evidence to the assessor, and to be heard with regard to the valuation of such property. It is presumed that the assessor, being a sworn officer, will do his duty under the law, and that he will not act unfairly and arbitrarily regarding the assessment of property for the purposes of taxation. In *Hagar v. Reclamation District etc.*, 111 U. S. 701, 4 Sup. Ct. 663, 28 L. Ed. 569, the court held that the duties of assessors, in determining the value of property for the purposes of general taxation, are judicial in their nature. Thus, in the case at bar, respondent Williams, the county assessor, acted in a judicial capacity in placing the valuation upon appellant's goods for such purposes. Assessors are usually classified as officials performing both ministerial and judicial functions. We are therefore of the opinion that this statute does not deprive a party of his property without due process of law, as urged by appellant, in that it fails to provide for a hearing in behalf of an aggrieved party whose property is sought to be charged with the tax. *Hagar v. Reclamation District etc., supra.*

The question as to what remedies may be open to a taxpayer under this law, in case of an illegal assessment or overvaluation of his property, is not properly before us on this appeal. The present inquiry, on the face of the record, by the stipulation of the parties to this controversy, is limited to the single proposition regarding the constitutionality of the above statutory provisions. Inasmuch as this law provides that the party charged with the tax has an opportunity to submit his proofs and make his showing to the assessor, in the matter of assessing his property for taxation, we are not justified in concluding that such party is deprived of his property "without due process of law," because he is, by the express terms of the revenue law, given no opportunity to have the assessment reviewed by a board of equalization, or otherwise. Undoubtedly in case the assessor should act arbitrarily, unfairly, or fraudulently in the performance of his duties under this statute, the aggrieved party might, if he saw fit, invoke the common law remedies in the courts to redress the wrongs which he suffers in consequence of such official misfeasance or malfeasance. Moreover, the code provides that,

"A writ of review shall be granted by any court, except a police or justice court, when an inferior tribunal, board or officer, exercising judicial functions, has exceeded the jurisdiction of such tribunal, board or officer, or one acting illegally, or to correct any erroneous or void proceeding, or a proceeding not according to the course of the common law, and there is no appeal, nor in the judgment of the court, any plain, speedy and adequate remedy at law." Laws 1895, p. 115, § 4; Pierce's Code, § 1396; Bal. Code, § 5741.

This court, in *State ex rel. Lewis v. Hogg,* 22 Wash. 646, 62 Pac. 143, held that the above provisions applied to a county treasurer exercising judicial functions, where "there is no appeal, nor in the judgment of the court, any plain, speedy and adequate remedy at law." We see no reason why this remedy may not be invoked in a proper case regarding the acts of a county assessor, or other official exercising judicial functions. Under the provisions of Chap. 59, Pierce's Code, the court issuing the writ is vested with ample powers to inquire into the merits of the controversy and "give judgment, either affirming or annulling or modifying the proceedings below." See further, *Lewis v. Bishop,* 19 Wash. 312, 53 Pac. 165, and authorities cited.

Coming now to the consideration of the constitutionality of the proviso contained in the above statute, we think that the legislature was without power or authority to enact any law providing that, after the payment of such taxes, the person paying them should be allowed certain deductions from the next regular assessment of such property. Article 1, § 12, of the state constitution, provides: "No law shall be passed granting to any citizen, class of citizens, or corporation other than municipal, privileges or immunities which, upon the same terms, shall not equally belong to all citizens or corporations." This law, by the terms of the proviso, not only discriminates between taxpayers of the same class, but grants privileges and immunities to taxpayers who own or possess property at the time of the next regular assessment, which are withheld from and denied to parties similarly situated, who may have paid their taxes levied pursuant to the above statute, and who cease to own or have property on the tax rolls at the time of the next regular assessment. Again, this provision discriminates between taxpayers whose property is listed on rolls of the next regular assessment, after the itinerant shall have paid his tax. He is granted exemptions in the latter instance which are denied to other property owners or taxpayers of the same class, whose property is listed for the regular assessment named in such proviso. The legislature cannot grant such exemptions or immunities directly; neither can it accomplish the same object by indirection. Cooley's Const. Lim. (5th ed.), p. *391·

Absolute equality in matters of taxation is an impossibility. An eminent jurist, the late Mr. Justice Miller, of the supreme court of the United States, in one of his opinions, remarked that such a condition was an "unrealized dream." Moreover, we think that this proviso is repugnant to the purview of the section to which it is appended. This section was evidently enacted for the purpose of reaching a certain class of property that was liable to escape taxation, unless special measures and remedies were provided for the assessment and collection of the tax. While it was competent for the legislature to enact such a law, it was not competent for it to tack on a further provision, allowing a commutation or abatement of the tax, or any portion thereof, either directly or indirectly. The logic of this conclusion is made the more apparent when we read the proviso in the light of the enactments found in our state constitution, above noted. It is provided in our organic law that all property, unless legally exempt, "shall be taxed in proportion to its value to be ascertained as provided by law." It is significant in this connection that there are no exemptions mentioned or provided for in our fundamental law, authorizing the

legislature to make any deductions from the amount of
any tax, after it shall have been assessed, levied, and collected pursuant to law. See, also, art. 11, § 9, state constitution, which provides that "No county, nor the inhabitants thereof, nor the property therein, shall be released or discharged from its or their proportionate share
of taxes to be levied for state purposes, nor shall commutation for such taxes be authorized in any form whatever."
True, this provision only relates to the discharge or release of state taxes. Still, if this proviso were allowed
to stand, it would have the indirect effect to authorize and
permit a release, *pro tanto,* of the state's revenue.

We are fully aware of the rule of law enunciated by
some authors, as well as by courts of high repute, that "a
saving clause which is repugnant to the enacting part of
a statute is void; but a proviso which is repugnant to the
purview of the act will override and control the latter."
Black, Interpretation of Laws, p. 278. This same learned
author, on the next page, says that the distinction drawn
between saving clauses and provisos has been much criticised.   The following language of Chancellor Kent in
Vol. 1 of his Commentaries, p. 463, is quoted by Mr.
Black with approval:

"There is a distinction in some of the books between
a saving clause and a proviso in the statute; though the
reason of the distinction is not very apparent. . . . It
may be remarked that a proviso repugnant to the purview of the statute renders it equally nugatory and void
as a repugnant saving clause, and it is difficult to see why
the act should be destroyed by the one and not by the
other, or why the proviso and the saving clause, when inconsistent with the body of the act, should not both of
them be equally rejected."

Be this rule of construction as it may, the foregoing distinction is without significance, as applied to the facts

in the action at bar, since we have reached the conclusion that the proviso of the above statute is void on constitutional grounds, and must therefore be rejected. Eliminating the proviso from the above section 12 of the act of 1895, such enactment seems to be complete in itself, fully authorizing the assessment, levy, and collection of the tax in question. *Seanor v. County Com'rs,* 13 Wash. 48, 42 Pac. 552. Judge Cooley in his work on Constitutional Limitations, 5th ed., p. *178, uses the following language:

"Where, therefore, a part of a statute is unconstitutional, that fact does not authorize the courts to declare the remainder void also, unless all provisions are connected in subject-matter, depending on each other, operating together for the same purpose, or otherwise so connected together in meaning, that it cannot be presumed the legislature would have passed the one without the other. The constitutional and unconstitutional provisions may even be contained in the same section, and yet be perfectly distinct and separable, so that the first may stand though the last fall."

Testing appellant's complaint in the light of the foregoing propositions of law, we are of the opinion that it fails to state a cause of action against respondents, or either of them, and that there is no error in the record of which appellant has any legal ground for complaint.

The judgment of the superior court is therefore affirmed.

[No. 4797.   Decided April 20, 1904.]

AMERICAN BRIDGE COMPANY OF NEW YORK, *Appellant,*
v. H. H. WHEELER, *as County Auditor, etc., et al.,*
Respondents.[1]

COUNTIES—WARRANTS—ISSUANCE.   A county warrant is not
"issued" until it is actually delivered to the person authorized to
receive it, and the auditor's forgery of the payee's indorsement
and a wrongful delivery do not discharge the duty to issue a warrant to the person entitled thereto (FULLERTON, C. J., dissents).

SAME—DUTY TO ISSUE WARRANT UPON CLAIM ALLOWED BY COM
MISSIONERS—MANDAMUS.   Since the allowance of a claim by the
county commissioners has the force of a judgment, the auditor
has no discretion, and his duty to issue a warrant therefor is ministerial and may be enforced by mandamus.

SAME—MANDAMUS TO COMPEL ISSUANCE OF COUNTY WARRANT—
WRONGFUL DELIVERY BY PREDECESSOR—ACTION ON OFFICIAL BOND—
ADEQUATE REMEDY AT LAW.   Mandamus will lie to compel the
county auditor to issue a warrant, when the former county auditor drew a warrant, forged the payee's name, and drew and misappropriated the funds; and the fact that the relator has a remedy
on the official bond of the auditor will not preclude the remedy by
mandamus, since the remedy on the bond is inadequate to compel
the performance of the officer's duty, and a remedy by ordinary
action will not defeat the right to mandamus, unless it is a remedy against the respondent in the mandamus proceedings (FUL
LERTON, C. J., dissents).

SAME—MANDAMUS—PARTIES—COUNTY COMMISSIONERS PROPER
PARTIES IN ACTION AGAINST AUDITOR.   County commissioners
may be proper but they are not necessary parties to a proceeding
in mandamus against the county auditor to compel him to issue a
warrant upon a claim allowed by the commissioners against the
county, since the county may be affected by the result (ANDERS,
J., dissents).

Appeal from a judgment of the superior court for Whitman county, Chadwick, J., entered June 11, 1903, upon

[1]Reported in 76 Pac. 534.

sustaining demurrers to a petition for a writ of mandate, dismissing the proceeding. Reversed.

Root, Palmer & Brown and *McCloskey & Canfield,* for appellant.

Robert M. Hanna, for respondents, to the point that an unauthorized delivery of the warrant was not within the legal duties of the auditor, and, not having been confirmed, the county is not liable, cited *Mitchell v. Rockland,* 41 Me. 363, 66 Am. Dec. 252; *Wallace v. Muscatine,* 4 G. Greene (Iowa) 373, 61 Am. Dec. 131; *Thayer v. Boston,* 19 Pick. 511, 31 Am. Dec. 157; *Sigmonds v. Clay County,* 71 Ill. 355; *Summers v. Davies County,* 103 Ind. 262, 53 Am. Rep. 512; *Vigo Tp. v. Knox County Com'rs,* 111 Ind. 170, 12 N. E. 305; *Estep v. Keokuk County,* 18 Iowa 199. Raby was plaintiff's agent for the delivery of the warrant. *State v. Raby,* 31 Wash. 111, 71 Pac. 771. Mandamus will not lie to compel the issuance of a second warrant where the first has been illegally paid to a defaulting agent, since the principal has a remedy at law. *State v. Auditor of Hamilton County,* 5 Ohio S. & C. P. Dec. 545; 33 Cent. Dig., Mandamus, col. 2093, § 31; *Crandall v. Amador County,* 20 Cal. 72; *People v. Thompson,* 25 Barb. 73; *State ex rel. Townsend Gas etc. Co. v. Superior Court,* 20 Wash. 502, 55 Pac. 933. Former payment to an unauthorized person is not ground for mandamus compelling issuance of a new warrant. 19 Am. & Eng. Enc. Law (2d ed.), 789; *State v. Lewis,* 6 Ohio Dec. 221, 4 Ohio N. P. 176; *State ex rel. Thayer v. Mish,* 13 Wash. 302, 43 Pac. 40; *Bates v. Porter,* 74 Cal. 224, 15 Pac. 732; *Eyerly v. Board of Supervisors,* 81 Iowa 189, 46 N. W. 986. Mandamus lies only in case of default by respondent. §§ 5755, 5756, Bal. Code; *Northwestern Warehouse Co. v. Oregon R. & Nav. Co.,* 32

Wash. 218, 73 Pac. 388; *Wright v. Kelly* (Idaho), 43
Pac. 565; *People v. Davis,* 93 Ill. 133.   Plaintiff's rem-
edy is by action on the defaulting officer's bond.   § 1519,
Bal. Code; 4 Am. & Eng. Enc. Law, 466.

Hadley, J.—This is a proceeding in mandamus, whereby it is sought to compel the issuance of a county warrant.
On the 8th day of October, 1901, the board of county
commissioners of Whitman county allowed, and ordered
paid, to relator the sum of $1,753, the same being the
balance due for the construction of a steel bridge across
the Palouse river, in the city of Palouse, in said county.
The board at said time directed the then county auditor,
one C. G. Raby, to issue a county warrant to the relator
for said sum, drawn on the treasurer of said county, and
payable from the road and bridge fund.   On the 18th day
of October, 1901, said Raby, as county auditor aforesaid,
did, pursuant to said order of the board, draw a warrant
for said sum, payable to the order of relator from said
fund.   Thereafter, without the authority, knowledge, or
consent of relator, the said Raby indorsed said warrant
as follows: "American Bridge Company, by C. G. Raby,
County Auditor," and then presented the same to the
county treasurer, who paid the amount called for in the
warrant to said Raby, and the latter retained and appropriated the proceeds to his own use.   No part of said sum
of $1,753 has been paid to relator, and, prior to the com-
mencement of this action, the relator demanded of said
Raby, while the latter was county auditor, that he execute
and deliver to it a warrant for said sum, as ordered and
directed, but he neglected and refused to issue to relator
any warrant on account of said indebtedness.   H. H.
Wheeler, one of the respondents in this mandamus proceeding, is the successor of said Raby as county auditor,

and a similar demand was made of him, which was also refused. The above facts appear in relator's petition for a writ of mandate. The said Wheeler, as the present county auditor, and also the present members of the board of county commissioners, were made parties to the proceeding. The several members of the board of county commissioners joined in a separate demurrer to the petition and the said Wheeler, as auditor, also demurred separately thereto. The demurrers were by the court sustained. The relator elected to stand upon its petition, refusing to plead further, and judgment was thereupon entered, dismissing the action. The relator has appealed.

It appears by the petition that the county commissioners regularly allowed appellant's claim, and ordered the county auditor to issue a warrant to appellant in payment of such approved claim. He drew and signed such a warrant, but it was never delivered to appellant, or to any one authorized to receive it. The auditor did not therefore "issue" the warrant. The Century Dictionary defines the word "issue," when used as a verb, as follows: "To send out; deliver for use; deliver authoritatively; emit; put into circulation." Under the above definition, a county warrant is not "issued" until it is actually delivered into the hands of a person authorized to receive it. Such was expressly held in *State v. Pierce*, 52 Kan. 521, 35 Pac. 19. The same principle, in effect, was declared in *Yesler v. Seattle*, 1 Wash. 308, 25 Pac. 1014, in which case the court observed as follows:

"In financial parlance the term 'issue' seems to have two phases of meaning. 'Date of issue,' when applied to notes, bonds, etc., of a series, usually means the arbitrary date fixed as the beginning of the term for which they run, without reference to the precise time when convenience or the state of the market may permit of their sale or delivery, and we see no reason why the act of March

26, 1890, should not have that interpretation. When
the bonds are delivered to the purchaser, they will be
'issued' to him, which is the other meaning of the term."
Section 393, Bal. Code, which enumerates the duties of
county auditors, among other things contains the following:

"For claims allowed by the county commissioners . . .
he shall draw a warrant on the county treasurer made payable to the claimant or his order . . . and when a
warrant is issued, the stub shall be carefully retained
. . ."

His duty is, therefore, manifest. He shall not only
"draw" the warrant, but he shall also "issue" it—that is
to say, *deliver* it; and when he issues it, he shall retain
the stub. Thus, the mere drawing is not an issuance, but
the latter requires the additional act of a subsequent au-
thoritative delivery. When so delivered, the stub shall be
retained, and issuance is then complete.

Appellant is, therefore, in the position of holding a
claim duly approved and allowed by the county commissioners, for which no warrant has ever been issued. The
allowance of the claim by the board of county commissioners had the conclusive effect of a judgment. *Martin
v. Supervisors etc.*, 29 N. Y. 645; *Kelly v. Wimberly*, 61
Miss. 548; *Johnson v. Campbell*, 39 Tex. 83. The auditor, therefore, has no discretion in the premises. His
duty is clearly declared by statute, § 393, *supra.* It was
the duty of the former auditor to issue the warrant, but,
he not having done so, it follows the office, and, inasmuch
as it remains undischarged, it becomes the obligation
of the respondent Wheeler, as the successor of Raby and
present incumbent of the office, to discharge the duty.
The duty involves no discretion, is purely ministerial, and
mandamus is therefore the proper remedy to compel its

performance. Bal. Code, § 5755; *Abernethy v. Medical
Lake*, 9 Wash. 112, 37 Pac. 306, *State ex rel. Sheehan
v. Headlee*, 17 Wash. 637, 50 Pac. 493; *State ex rel.
Ross v. Headlee*, 22 Wash. 126, 60 Pac. 126. The forgery
of appellant's indorsement, and the unauthorized turning
over, to some one else, of a warrant merely drawn but not
issued, although it was all done by the incumbent of the
auditor's office, did not discharge the duty of that office
to appellant, and does not constitute any defense to the
action. It is also immaterial that the appropriation of
the money was made by the predecessor of the present incumbent of the office. *People ex rel. Dannat v. Comptroller*, 77 N. Y. 45.

Respondents urge that appellant has a plain, speedy,
and adequate remedy by suit upon the official bond of the
former county treasurer. We do not think appellant
should be driven to the extremity of litigating with bondsmen concerning an obligation owing to it from the county,
and in respect to which appellant has been in no way at
fault. The county's agents—the two auditors—have
failed to discharge their duty, and that should not be
urged as a reason why appellant, an innocent claimant,
should be required to enter into vexatious litigation with
persons who are entire strangers to its original contract
with the county, out of which its present claim arose.
In *State ex rel. Craig v. Dougherty*, 45 Mo. 294, it was
held that the fact that the relator had a remedy on the
respondent's official bond did not preclude the remedy
by mandamus. The same was held in *Babcock v. Good-
rich*, 47 Cal. 488. To the same effect is *State ex rel. Van
Vliet v. Wilson*, 17 Wis. 709.

"Though corporations and ministerial officers are liable to be sued for neglect of duty, yet the writ of mandamus will go to compel a proper execution of their duties,

such suits not accomplishing the object desired—the fulfillment of the duty." Merrill, Mandamus, § 109.

The same rule is stated by another author as follows:

"Nor will the fact that the party aggrieved by the nonperformance of official duty has a remedy by an action against the officer upon his official bond prevent the courts from lending their aid by mandamus to enforce the duty, the remedy upon the bond being inadequate for the grievance." High, Extr. Leg. Rem. (3d ed.), § 35.

Moreover, the plain, speedy, and adequate remedy by an ordinary action, which will defeat the right to mandamus must be a remedy against the respondent in the mandamus proceedings, and not against third persons. Merrill, Mandamus, § 53, p. 59; *Williams v. Clayton,* 6 Utah 86, 21 Pac. 398; *Palmer v. Stacy,* 44 Iowa 340; *State ex rel. Sears v. Wright,* 10 Nev. 167. Appellant, under its contract with the county, is entitled to receive a warrant. It is the duty of the auditor to issue such warrant, and appellant is entitled to have that duty discharged without being driven to sue the bondsmen of a former county auditor. There is no other plain, speedy, and adequate remedy to compel the respondent auditor to discharge his said duty.

The county commissioners were made parties in this proceeding on the theory that the county will be ultimately affected by the result. Under the circumstances detailed in the allegations of the petition, we think the commissioners were not improperly joined as parties, although they may not have been necessary ones. We therefore believe that the court erred in sustaining each of the demurrers to the petition.

The judgment is reversed, and the cause remanded, with instructions to the lower court to overrule the demurrers.

DUNBAR and MOUNT, JJ., concur.

ANDERS, J.—While I believe the court erred in sustaining the demurrer to the complaint herein, interposed by the county auditor, I am of the opinion that the commissioners were not proper parties to the action, and, for that reason, I think their demurrer was properly sustained.

FULLERTON, C. J. (dissenting).—I am unable to concur in either the opinion or the judgment in this case.   It seems to me the court has not only overlooked the real question presented by the record, but has decided erroneously the question thought to be presented.

Taking up, first, the question decided by the court, it will be observed, from the statement made at the opening of the main opinion, that this is not a case where no warrant has been issued, as a matter of fact, for the appellant's claim.   On the contrary, a warrant has not only been issued in fact for that claim, but it has been actually paid by the county treasurer. Wrongfully issued and paid, it may be, but issued and paid in fact, nevertheless. But the majority, as I understand it, do not rest their decision on the ground that no warrant in fact has been issued, but hold that a warrant is not "issued," as a matter of law, unless it is actually delivered into the hands of a person authorized to receive it.   In other words, a wrongful issuance of a county warrant is not an issuance, within the meaning of that term as used in the statute.

I am frank to say I can find no satisfactory reason for this distinction, nor do I think it is supported by the authorities cited in the opinion of the court.   The statute does not undertake to define the term, and hence must be taken to have used it in its commonly accepted sense.   That sense is sufficiently indicated by the definition quoted in the majority opinion.   It is at once apparent, however, that that definition is as applicable to a warrant wrongfully issued as it is to one delivered to a person authorized to receive it. When it is delivered to a person not authorized to receive it, it is "sent out;" it may be "delivered for use;" it is "emitted;" and may be "put into circulation;" any one of which acts amounts to an "issuance," according to the definition. And this, it seems to me, accords with the reason of the thing. In common parlance, to issue a county warrant means to take or send it out of the issuing office for use as a county warrant. Surely the lawmakers would not have so far departed from common usage as to use the word "issue," in the sense of "actually delivered into the hands of a person authorized to receive it," without saying so in express terms.

But it is said that the question was expressly decided in accordance with the ruling of the majority in the case of *State v. Pierce*, 52 Kan. 521, 35 Pac. 19. I do not so understand that case. There the defendants, who were members of the board of county commissioners of Barber county, state of Kansas, were informed against for doing certain acts as members of such board. The information contained eleven counts. The first count charged that the defendants unlawfully and fraudulently committed a fraud in their official capacity, and under color of their offices as members of the board of county commissioners, in unlawfully allowing greater sums on accounts against the county than were actually due thereon. The second, third, fourth, and fifth counts charged the defendants with allowing certain accounts in favor of certain named persons without such accounts being made out in separate items, or being verified according to the statute. The sixth, seventh, eighth, ninth, tenth, and eleventh counts charged the unlawful issuance of county warrants to the above named persons, in violation of the terms of the statute. Of the warrants ordered, only one—the subject of the sixth count—was in fact delivered, the others being, at the time of the trial, "in the office of the county clerk, and had not been delivered to any one." One of the defendants was convicted on all of the counts of the information, and the other on the first five. Both appealed. One of the contentions was that the defendant Pierce was wrongfully convicted on the sixth, seventh, eighth, ninth, tenth, and eleventh counts, because the warrants described had not been issued. Speaking to this question the court said (see, 52 Kans. 528, 35 Pac. 22):

"To issue county warrants or orders means 'to send out; to deliver; to put forth; to put into circulation; to emit— as, to issue bank notes, bonds, scrip,' etc. A county warrant or order is 'issued' when made out and placed in the hands of a person authorized to receive it, or is actually delivered or taken away. So long as a county warrant or order is not delivered or put into circulation, it is not 'issued,' within the terms of Sec. 1888. If a warrant or order, unlawfully directed to be issued by a board of county commissioners, remains in the hands of the county clerk, and is not delivered or sent out or put into circulation by the county clerk, or anyone else, the wrong attempted by the unlawful act does not succeed, because there is no actual issuance of the warrant or order. The trial court, therefore, should have given the instructions prayed for concerning the nondelivery and noncompletion of the county warrants or orders; but the refusal of those instructions was not prejudicial to D. L. Pierce, under the sixth count of the information, because the evidence is undisputed that the warrant or order to R. Lake was actually delivered. . . . As the only warrant or order for the purchase of the Lake City bridge ever delivered or put in circulation was the warrant or order for R. Lake, the only count in the information concerning the unlawful issuance of a county warrant or order supported by the evidence is the sixth count thereof."

This is all that is said in the opinion that is pertinent to the question here. It will be noticed that, while the court does say that a county warrant is issued when it is made out and placed "in the hands of a person authorized to receive it," it adds, in the same connection and as a part of the same sentence, the phrase "or is actually delivered or taken away;" showing to my mind, that a wrongful delivery would be, in the opinion of the court, an "issuance" of the warrant. This conclusion follows, also, from the tenor of the case. The court permitted the conviction to stand on the sixth count, because the warrant mentioned in that count had been delivered and put in circulation. But that warrant was never delivered to a "person authorized to receive it." It could not be so delivered. It was wrongfully and fraudulently ordered drawn and issued, and its taking from the clerk's office by the person in whose favor it was drawn was as much an unlawful taking, both in law and morals, as would be its taking by a stranger to the record.

The case cited from this state seems to me also to be equally far from the question. The quotation made in the majority opinion from that case covers everything said that is at all pertinent, but even that shows clearly that the court did not then have this question in mind.

There is a case from this court, however, not cited in the main opinion, which seems to me to be very much in point. I refer to the case of *State v. Raby,* 31 Wash. 111, 71 Pac. 771, where a judgment convicting the county auditor for embezzling the very warrant in question here was affirmed by this court. In that case we said:

"By virtue of his office, defendant became the legal custodian and bailee of the warrant by operation of law. He therefore had the warrant rightfully in his custody, and also, by operation of the law, held it as the agent of the owner. When he assumed the duties of the office, he assumed to act as agent for the owner, under provisions of the law, and he is estopped from denying such agency. If he is agent to receive the money for the owner, he is agent to deliver it to him. It would certainly be a puerile law that would constitute a public officer an agent to receive money for one with whom the municipality is dealing, and allow him to deny the agency for the purpose of escaping punishment for embezzling such property. The objection that there was no value to the warrant until it was delivered, and that the ownership was not properly alleged, is equally untenable. The warrant was duly authorized, legally drawn and issued by the proper officer for an approved claim against the county, by order of the proper authorities. Its proper place was in the auditor's files, and, when it was removed from those files by the officer and cashed, it was so removed and cashed because it was of value, notwithstanding the fact that it had not yet been delivered to the proper owners."

Unless this be dictum, and I am convinced it is not, it is a direct holding by this court that this very warrant was actually issued by the county auditor. It seems to me, therefore, both on reason and authority, that this warrant should be held, on the facts recited, to have been issued, within the meaning of that term as used in the statute.

Passing then to the second question: This action is waged as a special proceeding against the county officers to compel them to perform a supposed duty which it is alleged they have neglected and refused to perform. Its real purpose, however, is not thereby disguised. The simple facts are that the county auditor has embezzled a county warrant, which was drawn in favor of, and which ought to have been delivered to, a county creditor, and that creditor is now undertaking to hold the county responsible for the auditor's unlawful act. Whether the creditor should be permitted to do this is the real question involved in this proceeding, and the question which should have been met by the court. But I shall not enter upon an extended discussion of it. It is sufficient to call attention to the familiar rule that a county is not liable for the malfeasance or misfeasance of its officers unless expressly made so by statute. In this state there is no such statute, and in my opinion the judgment of the trial court should be affirmed.

[No. 5087.   Decided April 21, 1904.]

THE STATE OF WASHINGTON, *on the Relation of Daniel Fisher et al., Plaintiff,* v. H. L. KENNAN, *Judge of the Superior Court of Spokane County, Defendant.*[1]

PROHIBITION — AGAINST ENFORCEMENT OF INJUNCTION — EQUITY JURISDICTION. Prohibition will not lie against the threatened enforcement of a temporary injunction issued in a suit brought against a corporation, enjoining the relators from acting as stockholders in a corporation, during the pendency of the action, where the relators intervened in that suit, moved to dissolve the injunction, and appealed from the decision; since a court of equity manifestly has jurisdiction of the subject-matter of the action, and the court acquired jurisdiction of the persons of the relators, and prohibition will not lie to prevent an erroneous exercise of conceded jurisdiction.

Application filed in the supreme court March 21, 1904, for a writ of prohibition to prevent the threatened enforcement of an injunction by the superior court of Spokane county, Kennan, J. Writ denied.

A. H. Kenyon and *W. C. Jones,* for relators.

H. S. Stoolfire and *John C. Kleber,* for defendant.

1Reported in 76 Pac. 516.

PER CURIAM.—The Lucile Dreyfus Mining Company is a corporation organized under the laws of this state with a capital stock of fifty thousand dollars, divided into one million shares, of the par value of five cents each. It owns valuable mining property located in this state. For a considerable period preceding June 5, 1903, one Howard J. Kressly was the duly elected secretary of the corporation, and by virtue of his office had possession of its records. Kressly, while acting as such secretary, issued, over the seal of the company, something over one million shares of spurious and fraudulent stock, which he placed upon the market and sold to various persons. Differences afterwards arose among the holders of the stock as to who were actual stockholders of the corporation, when, to have the matter determined, an action was begun in the superior court of Spokane county, in which the mining company was plaintiff, and all of the holders of its stock, whether genuine or bogus, were made defendants.

While this action was pending, a stockholders' meeting was called by certain persons claiming to hold genuine stock, whereupon one Willard, who had been excluded from participating in the meeting, brought an action against such persons, seeking an injunction preventing them from acting as stockholders of the company, or doing any business as such, until the rights of the several parties claiming to be stockholders could be determined. This action was nominally against the corporation alone, but in it the court issued a temporary injunction against the several persons purporting to act as stockholders, as prayed for in the complaint. Afterwards the enjoined stockholders intervened in that suit, by leave of court, and moved to dissolve the injunction. This motion was denied, and they appealed to this court. Pending that appeal, the same persons apply here for a writ of prohibition, setting out the fact that the court intends to enforce its writ of injunction pending the appeal, and will punish them for contempt, if they violate its order; setting out, further, the fact that there is no board of trustees or persons authorized to take charge of the business of the company; that its property is being wasted and destroyed; that numerous suits are being brought against it; and that no persons are authorized to represent the company in defense of such suits; and they pray that this court will issue a writ of prohibition against the court, preventing him from enforcing the injunctive order.

Counsel for the applicants argue that the order was made without jurisdiction, either of the subject-matter of the action, or of the parties who are enjoined thereby, and, for that reason, is of no effect and void, and is a proper subject for the issuance of the writ. But, without entering into an extended discussion of the question, we are of the opinion that counsel's position is untenable. Manifestly, the court had jurisdiction of the subject-matter of the action; to enjoin certain of the stockholders of a corporation from proceeding illegally and wrongfully, at the suit of other stockholders injured thereby, is among the acknowledged powers of a court of equity. Nor do we think the question of lack of proper parties a material one now. It will be remembered that, since the writ issued, the stockholders enjoined intervened in the action, and thereby became parties to the same; even to the extent of appealing to this court from the order. Clearly, it is now too late for them to claim that the order was made without jurisdiction of their persons. But if the fact were otherwise, the result would be the same. As the court had jurisdiction of the subject-matter, prohibition will not lie to prevent an erroneous exercise of that jurisdiction. *State ex rel. Foster v. Superior Court*, 30 Wash. 156, 70 Pac. 230, 73 Pac. 690.

The application is denied.

[No. 4887.   Decided April 21, 1904.]

JOHN McCONKEY, *Appellant*, v. OREGON RAILROAD & NAVIGATION COMPANY, *Respondent*.[1]

RAILROADS—LICENSEE ON TRACK—BRIDGE MADE DANGEROUS BY REPAIRS—DUTY OF RAILROAD COMPANY. Although a railroad company has permitted its bridge to be used as a thoroughfare by pedestrians, it is not liable to a person using the same for his own convenience, for injuries sustained by reason of a hole thirty inches wide left by the company while repairing the bridge, since such defect does not create a concealed danger, and the company's liability to mere licensees is limited to avoiding wilful wrong and wanton carelessness.

SAME—WALKING ON RAILROAD BRIDGE AT NIGHT—CONTRIBUTORY NEGLIGENCE. A licensee upon a railroad bridge who was injured by falling through a hole, was guilty of contributory negligence as a matter of law in undertaking to walk thereon in the night, where the ties were some inches apart and it was so dark that he could not see the ties or the hole.

Appeal from a judgment of the superior court for Spokane county, Belt, J., entered July 3, 1903, upon sustaining a demurrer to the complaint, dismissing an action for personal injuries sustained by a pedestrian in falling through a railroad bridge. Affirmed.

Barnes & Latimer (Alfred M. Craven, of counsel), for appellant.

Cotton, Teal & Minor, Lester S. Wilson, and *Samuel R. Stern*, for respondent.

HADLEY, J.—This is an action whereby the plaintiff seeks to recover damages for injuries received from falling through a bridge on the line of defendant's railroad. The substantial allegations of the complaint are, that on the 16th day of November, 1902, between the hours of

[1]Reported in 76 Pac. 526.

seven and eight o'clock, p. m., the plaintiff was traveling
over and upon the defendant's right of way and track from
the town of Wardner, Idaho, to the town of Cataldo, Idaho;
that said railway between said places is constructed and
maintained through a deep and narrow canyon, with high
mountains on either side, and the defendant uses and occupies very nearly all, if not all, the space in said canyon, with
its railway line; that there was no road or passageway on
either side of the railway track for the plaintiff or the
public to use in going from one of said places to the other;
that the most direct and usual route for pedestrians,
when traveling between said places, was over said railway
track; that said railway track had been used by the public generally as a thoroughfare for people on foot, ever
since the construction of the railway, without objection on
the part of the defendant, and with its full knowledge and
consent; that, on said line of railway and near to the town
of Cataldo, the defendant maintains a bridge and trestle
over a stream of water in said canyon; that said trestle is
covered with ties, laid a few inches apart at right angles
with the rails upon said track; that the general topography,
and rugged condition of the country, on either side of said
bridge, is the same as heretofore described, and the only
means of crossing said stream by foot travelers, in going
from Wardner to Cataldo, was over said trestle and bridge;
that all of the above stated facts were known at the time by
the defendant, and it had permitted the public to so use
its track and bridge for a long period of time prior to the
date of plaintiff's injuries; that when plaintiff had partially crossed over said bridge, he fell into a hole between
the rails which had been previously left open and unguarded by the defendant; that ties at said place had been removed by defendant, leaving an open space about thirty

inches in width, all without notice to the plaintiff, and of
which he ·had no knowledge; that plaintiff was wholly
without fault on his part, and without any means of knowing of said defect or danger; that he could not, by the
exercise of ordinary diligence and care, have avoided or
discovered the danger, the night being dark and the danger
undiscoverable; that in consequence of the removal of said
ties, and the negligence of the defendant in not immediately
replacing same, the plaintiff fell through said opening, and
down a distance of twenty feet upon the rocks below, whereby he was injured. It is further alleged that the defendant
was negligent in not replacing said ties, in not warning
plaintiff of the danger, in leaving the hole unguarded, and
in not providing for proper inspection of the bridge at said
place.   The defendant demurred generally to the complaint, and the same was sustained by the court. Plaintiff
elected to stand upon his complaint, refusing to plead further, and thereupon judgment was entered dismissing the
action. The plaintiff has appealed.

It is assigned that the court erred in sustaining the demurrer to the complaint, and in entering judgment of dismissal.   It is appellant's theory that his complaint does
not show that he was a trespasser, but that, by reason of
the averment that respondent had for a long time permitted the use of its track and bridge by pedestrians and
had consented thereto, he became a licensee. Upon the
theory that his averments, as against demurrer, established the fact that he was a licensee, he urges that respondent owed him the duty of ordinary diligence and care
to avoid injury. Appellant cites a number of cases, which
he insists sustain the theory of respondent's liability here.
Among the cases cited by him are the following: *Cahill
v. Chicago etc. R. Co.,* 74 Fed. 285; *Hooker v. Chicago
etc. R. Co.,* 76 Wis. 542, 44 N. W. 1085; *Hansen v.*

Southern Pac. Co., 105 Cal. 379, 38 Pac. 957; *Thomas v. Chicago etc. R. Co.,* 103 Iowa 649, 72 N. W. 783, 39 L. R. A. 399; *Young v. Clark,* 16 Utah 42, 50 Pac. 832; *Barry v. New York etc. R. Co.,* 92 N. Y. 289, 44 Am. Rep. 377; *Cassida v. Oregon R. & Nav. Co.,* 14 Or. 551, 13 Pac. 438; *Roth v. Union Depot Co.,* 13 Wash. 525, 43 Pac. 641, 44 Pac. 253, 31 L. R. A. 855.

Each of the above cases involved the liability of a railroad company for injuries resulting from the movement of a train which ran over a person upon the railway track. In each case the location of the injured person with reference to the train, together with the topography and environment, were such as involved the question of recklessness and wantonness on the part of the engineer or train operators. Whether one be a trespasser or a licensee, a railroad company cannot escape liability, if it shall wantonly injure him when upon its track, and when his presence is discovered in time to avoid the injury by the exercise of reasonable care.

The distinction between the relations of a trespasser and a licensee to the railroad company seems to be as follows: In the case of the former, the company when moving trains is under no obligation to keep a special lookout for him, but if he is discovered upon the track in time to avoid injury by the exercise of reasonable care after such discovery, common humanity demands that such care shall be used. In the case of the licensee, the company when moving trains is charged with the additional duty of being in a state of expectancy as to the probable presence of persons upon the track at places where travel thereon is known to be customary and frequent. The care required in the case of the licensee, therefore, calls for both reasonable lookout in advance and a reasonable effort to avoid injury after presence is discovered. Thus, in either case, the duty is the same after actual presence upon the track is discovered. In the above cited cases, discovery was made in each instance before the injury, and, without regard to whether the injured person was a trespasser or a licensee, wanton negligence was the controlling question in the case. We therefore believe the cases are not decisive of the one at bar. Here appellant was not run down by a train, and his presence upon the track was neither known nor discovered. It is true, it is alleged that respondent consented to the use which was being made of the track and bridge, but the allegations, taken together, show that it was such consent as may have been merely implied because no asserted objection, or actual effort to prevent such use, had been made.

Assuming, however, that appellant was a licensee by reason of the fact that respondent had never actually prohibited him and others from traveling there, what new obligation did that fact create on the part of respondent, under the peculiar facts of this case? If he was a licensee, then, it is true, respondent, as we have already seen, was under obligation to be on the lookout, and not negligently run him down with a train. But was it required to have regard to his convenience, rather than its own, in the repair of its track and bridge? Respondent had never assumed to keep in repair a highway for footmen. Appellant was certainly not a licensee in the sense of being invited to cross the bridge. For his own benefit only, he assumed to cross because the privilege had not been denied. Under such circumstances, we think he must be held to have taken the situation as he found it. *Cusick v. Adams*, 115 N. Y. 55, 21 N. E. 673, 12 Am. St. 772; *Schreiner v. Great Northern R. Co.*, 86 Minn. 245, 90 N. W. 400, 58 L. R. A. 75; *Reardon v. Thompson,*

149 Mass. 267, 21 N. E. 369; *Morgan v. Pennsylvania R. Co.,* 7 Fed. 78; *Sterger v. Van Sicklen* 132 N. Y. 499, 30 N. E. 987. In *Reardon v. Thompson, supra,* Justice Holmes observes as follows:

"But the general rule is that a licensee goes upon land at his own risk and must take the premises as he finds them. An open hole, which is not concealed otherwise than by the darkness of night, is a danger which a licensee must avoid at his peril;"

citing many cases. The exception to the rule, as above stated, is noted in the following quoted extract from Pollock on Torts, at pages 503, 504 (6th ed.):

"Persons who by the mere gratuitous permission of owners or occupiers take a short cut across a waste piece of land, or pass over private bridges or have the run of a building, cannot expect to find the land free from holes or ditches, or the bridges to be in safe repair, or the passages and stairs to be commodious and free from dangerous places. If the occupier, while the permission continues, does something that creates a concealed danger to people availing themselves of it, he may well be liable. And he would of course be liable, not for failure in a special duty, but for wilful wrong, if he purposely made his property dangerous to persons using ordinary care, and then held out his permission as an inducement to come on it. Apart from this improbable case, the licensee's rights are measured, at best, by the actual state of the property at the time of the license."

This case cannot, in any reasonable view, be said to come within the exception. To leave an open space thirty inches wide between the ties of a railroad bridge does not create a concealed danger. Any person with the sense of sight can easily see such space, under ordinary and usual conditions, and can also easily step across it. It is not charged that the hole was left with any wilful purpose to make the property dangerous. We therefore think

the complaint, at most, shows that appellant was no more
than a bare licensee, and in such case respondent owed
him no duty, except to avoid wilful wrong and wanton
carelessness and neglect. In our view, the complaint
shows no such neglect of duty, and we believe it would be
so viewed in the minds of all reasonable jurors.

Other cases cited by appellant, not hereinbefore mentioned, we believe do not assist in the determination of
this case. We will briefly review those cases. In *Davis
v. Chicago etc. R. Co.*, 58 Wis. 646, 17 N. W. 406, 46
Am. Rep. 667, it was held, in the case of a licensee upon
a railway track, that it was for the jury to determine
whether it was negligence to leave a steam boiler and
engine upon its track unattended, and whether the ex-
plosion which caused the plaintiff's injury was the result
of such lack of attention. The act of leaving such a
dangerous agency as an unattended and heated boiler and
engine may well have been for the jury, on the principle
that it may have been wanton neglect. The same was
true in *Harriman v. Pittsburg etc. R. Co.*, 45 Ohio St. 11,
12 N. E. 451, 4 Am. St. 507, where a torpedo had been
left in an exposed condition near the track and was picked
up by a child of tender years, who was injured. In *Lillstrom v. Northern Pac. R. Co.*, 53 Minn. 464, 55 N. W.
624, 20 L. R. A. 587, the defendant had, for a long time,
itself maintained for the public a crossing of its track
at the place of injury. Planks were torn away from the
crossing, and it was claimed that the injured one's sleigh
caught in the defective crossing. The case was properly
for the jury on the theory that, as the company had assumed to maintain the crossing for the public, it was its
duty to keep it in repair. In *Tobin v. Portland etc. R. Co.*,
59 Me. 183, 8 Am. Rep. 415, the railroad company left

its depot platform in defective condition, and it was held
liable, although the place was within the limits of a
highway. This was also upon the theory that it had assumed to maintain the platform for the public, and thereby invited the presence of persons there. In *Campbell v.
Boyd,* 88 N. C. 129, 43 Am. Rep. 740, the defendant
permitted the public habitually to use his private bridge.
He knew it was unsafe. He was liable on the theory that
the injured party was, by his own conduct, induced to
pass over the bridge for a lawful purpose. The bridge
was used to reach defendant's mill. In *Graves v. Thomas,*
95 Ind. 361, 48 Am. Rep. 727, the public had by permission traveled on foot for years over an open city lot.
It was held that, upon making a cellar excavation in the
pathway, with a view to erecting a building, it was the
owner's duty to put up some guard or warning for public
protection. The court based its decision upon the ground
that for a long period, the public, using a near-by sidewalk, had been permitted to use the path where the plaintiff fell, as a part of the sidewalk. Knowing that it had
been for so long a time traveled as a sidewalk in a popu-
lous city, the defendant's conduct may well have been
classified as wanton neglect. We have thus noted appellant's cited cases, and do not find that they apply to the
facts of the case at bar.

We believe that the demurrer was properly sustained,
not alone upon the ground of want of negligence on the
part of respondent, but also upon the ground of contributory negligence. We think the complaint discloses, upon
its face, such facts as must be held, as matter of law, to
amount to contributory negligence. The conditions were
certainly unusual. Under the darkness of night appellant
was walking upon a mountain railroad. The place was in a

deep and narrow canyon. On either side the mountainous walls of the canyon rose precipitously. In this canyon was the trestle bridge over which appellant knew he must walk if he made the journey. He knew he must walk upon the ties of the bridge, placed some inches apart, and which, from the averments of his complaint, he could not see in the darkness. By the exercise of common judgment he should have known that, at best, the walk at such a time and place would be attended with great hazard. He knew that he was not upon a highway designed for pedestrians, but that it was built and maintained for railway purposes only. While he may have believed it was in such condition as would enable him to walk over it in safety, yet the environment, the time, and his relation to respondent, were such as gave him no right to act upon such belief, relying upon any duty of respondent to maintain for him a safe way. We believe any jury of reasonable men would be impelled to the conclusion that he took his chances, and that his injuries resulted from his own negligence. In such case it is the duty of the court to so decide, as a matter of law.

The judgment is affirmed.

FULLERTON, C. J., and DUNBAR, MOUNT, and ANDERS, JJ., concur.

[No. 5097½. Decided April 21, 1904.]

THE STATE OF WASHINGTON, *on the Relation of George S. Payson et al., Plaintiff*, v. W. O. CHAPMAN, *Judge of the Superior Court of Pierce County, Defendant.*[1]

TRIAL—NEW TRIAL—PRACTICE IN EQUITY. The practice upon entering judgment and the right to move for a new trial is the same in equity as in cases tried before a jury.

APPEAL—TIME FOR TAKING AND PROPOSING STATEMENT OF FACTS —JUDGMENT—WHEN FINAL—SUSPENDED BY MOTION FOR NEW TRIAL. The time for taking an appeal, and for proposing a statement of facts, begins to run from the time a motion for a new trial, seasonably made, is overruled, in an equity case as well as in law actions, since the judgment is not final until that time.

Application filed in the supreme court April 4, 1904, for a writ of mandate to the superior court for Pierce county, Chapman, J. Writ granted.

Wm. H. Pratt and *Walter Loveday*, for relators.

G. W. H. Davis, F. R. Baker, and *B. F. Jacobs*, for defendant, argued that compliance with the statute requiring the statement of facts to be filed within thirty days is jurisdictional. *Enos v. Wilcox*, 3 Wash. 44, 28 Pac. 364; *Snyder v. Kelso*, 3 Wash. 181, 28 Pac. 335; *State v. Hoyt*, 4 Wash. 818, 30 Pac. 1060; *Loos v. Rondema*, 10 Wash. 164, 38 Pac. 1012. The time for filing a statement of facts begins to run when the judgment is entered. *McQuestin v. Morrill*, 12 Wash. 335, 41 Pac. 56; *Wollin v. Smith*, 27 Wash. 349, 67 Pac. 561; *State ex rel. Dutch Miller etc. Co. v. Superior Court*, 30 Wash. 43, 70 Pac. 102; *National Christian Ass'n*, 21 Wash. 16, 56 Pac. 844; *Lamona v. Cowley*, 31 Wash. 297, 71 Pac. 1040.

[1]Reported in 76 Pac. 525.

MOUNT, J.—Original application for a writ of mandate requiring the judge of the superior court of Pierce county to settle and certify a statement of facts in the case of *Payson et al. v. Jacobs et al.,* now on appeal to this court.

It appears from the record herein that the cause of *Payson v. Jacobs* was an equity case, tried by the court without a jury. On January 4, 1904, the court made findings of fact and conclusions of law, and at the same time signed and entered a decree in said cause in favor of the defendant therein. Within two days thereafter, the plaintiffs served and filed a motion for a new trial in the said cause, which motion was heard by the court, and denied on February 3, 1904. The court thereafter refused to grant an extension of time within which to file a proposed statement of facts. Relators on March 3, 1904, within thirty days after the order denying the motion for a new trial, filed and served a proposed statement of facts in the case, to which statement no amendments were offered. The judge now refuses to settle and certify the proposed statement of facts, on the ground that the proposed statement was not served and filed within thirty days from the date of the entry of the judgment.

It will be readily seen that the proposed statement was filed within thirty days from the date of the order denying the motion for a new trial, but was not filed until sixty days after the date when the judgment was entered. Section 5062, Bal. Code, provides:

"A proposed bill of exceptions or statement of facts must be filed and served either before or within thirty days after the time begins to run within which an appeal may be taken from the final judgment in the cause, . . ."

The question presented here is, does the time for taking an appeal commence to run from the entry of the judg-

ment, in an equity case, or from the date of the order
denying the motion for a new trial? Section 5029, Bal.
Code, provides:

"Upon the trial of an issue of fact by the court, its
decisions shall be given in writing and filed with the
clerk. In giving the decision, the facts found and the
conclusions of law shall be separately stated. Judgment
upon the decision shall be entered accordingly."

Section 5030, Bal. Code, is as follows:

"The order of proceedings on a trial by the court shall
be the same as provided in trials by jury. The finding
of the court upon the facts shall be deemed a verdict, and
may be set aside in the same manner and for the same
reason, as far as applicable, and a new trial granted."

Section 5115, Bal. Code, as amended by Laws 1903, p.
285, is as follows:

"When a trial by jury has been had, judgment shall be
entered by the clerk immediately in conformity to the
verdict and a transcript of said judgment may be immediately filed in the office of the clerk of the superior court
of any other county in the state in the manner provided
by law: *Provided, however,* That if a motion for a
new trial shall be filed, execution shall not be issued upon
said judgment until said motion shall be determined:
And provided, further, That the granting of a motion
for a new trial shall immediately operate as the vacation
and setting aside of said judgment."

It clearly appears from these sections that the practice
in equity, and other cases tried by the court without a
jury, is governed by the rules applicable to jury trials.
It follows that a judgment or decree in an equity case
may be entered immediately upon the findings of the
trial court. The statute also provides, at § 5070, Bal.
Code:

"A new trial is a re-examination of an issue of fact
in the same court, after a trial and decision by a jury,
court or referees."

Section 5071 provides that the former verdict or *other decision* may be vacated or a new trial granted for causes therein named. And § 5075 provides that a party moving for a new trial must, within two days after the verdict of a jury, or two days after notice of a decision of the court, file and serve upon the adverse party his motion for a new trial, designating the grounds upon which the motion is made. These sections clearly give to a litigant the right to file a motion for a new trial within the time named—two days. No distinction is made between cases tried by a jury, and cases tried by the court without a jury. The result must be the same, viz., to suspend execution upon the judgment until the motion for a new trial is determined. The judgment, therefore, where a motion for a new trial is filed within time, is not *final* until such motion is disposed of. Elliott, Appellate Procedure, § 119; *New York etc. R. Co. v. Doane,* 105 Ind. 92, 4 N. E. 419; *Adrian Furniture Mfg. Co. v. Lane,* 92 Mich. 295, 52 N· W. 615.

It is true that § 6502, Bal. Code, provides that:

"In civil actions and proceedings an appeal from any final judgment must be taken within ninety days after the date of the entry of such final judgment."

This language must be construed in harmony with its evident intention, and, therefore, be held to mean within ninety days after the date when the judgment becomes *final,* which, of course, is the date when the order is entered denying the motion for a new trial. This court has held that a motion for a new trial is not necessary in order that questions once decided by the lower court may be reviewed here on appeal, but is necessary for a review of questions not presented to the trial court during the progress of the trial. *Dubcich v. Grand Lodge,* 33 Wash. 651, 74 Pac. 832. But the motion for a new trial is a *right* granted by statute, and questions already passed upon by the lower court, as well as those not passed upon, may be considered upon such motion, when seasonably made. We are therefore of the opinion that the time for taking an appeal begins to run from the date of the order denying a motion for a new trial, when such motion is seasonably filed.

The cases from this court, cited by respondent, to the effect that the time for filing the proposed statement of facts begins to run from the entry of the judgment, are all cases where a motion for a new trial was not filed at all, or, if filed, was not filed within the two days' time allowed therefor. In such cases the time begins to run from the date of the entry of the judgment. But motions or proceedings filed after the two days' time mentioned, seeking to vacate or set aside judgments, do not suspend the judgment regularly entered, or affect its finality, and for that reason do not suspend the time for taking an appeal.

For the reasons hereinbefore mentioned, the proposed statement of facts was filed within time, and should be certified by the trial court. The writ will therefore issue as prayed for.

FULLERTON, C. J., and HADLEY, ANDERS, and DUNBAR, JJ., concur.

[No. 5076.   Decided April 21, 1904.]

JACOB SWOPE *et al.*, *Plaintiffs*, v. CITY OF SEATTLE *et al.*,
Defendants.[1]

CERTIORARI—HEARING—AFFIDAVITS NOT PRESENTED BELOW. Upon
a hearing in the supreme court upon a writ of certiorari to review
an order of the superior court, affidavits not presented below cannot be considered, as the supreme court is restricted to the record
actually made in the lower court.

MUNICIPAL CORPORATIONS—STREETS—GRADING—DAMAGE TO ABUT-
TING PROPERTY—INJUNCTION AGAINST GRADING. Where a city has
let a contract and is about to change the grade of a street so as
to damage abutting property in excess of the benefits, injunction
is the proper remedy of the owner, and the city may be restrained
until just compensation has been paid, as required by Const.,
art. 1, § 16.

SAME—INJUNCTION—BOND—REQUIRING NEW BOND—DISCRETION
OF LOWER COURT. Before an injunction can issue against the
grading of a street by a city, the plaintiff must be required to give
a bond as required by Bal. Code, § 5438, and if insufficient, a new
bond may be required, in the discretion of the court, to be exercised legally and not arbitrarily.

SAME—REQUIRING NEW BOND—SUFFICIENCY OF SHOWING—ABUSE
OF DISCRETION. Where abutting property was about to be materially damaged by the grading of a street, and plaintiffs' right to
an injunction seemed clear, and an injunction was granted against
such grading until compensation should be made for such damage
upon the plaintiffs' giving a bond for $100, it is an abuse of dis-
cretion to require a further bond in the sum of $3,000, which is
more than the value of the property, upon the application of the
contractor, who did not deny any of the allegations of the plaintiffs, but merely made a showing that he would be greatly damaged by the delay, neither the city nor its officers applying for any
further bond.

Certiorari to review an order of the superior court for
King county, Bell, J., entered March 7, 1904, vacating
an injunction issued February 28, 1904, and requiring
an additional bond on the part of plaintiffs. Reversed.

[1]Reported in 76 Pac. 517.

C. L. Parker, for plaintiffs.

Mitchell Gilliam and *Hugh A. Tait,* for defendants.

ANDERS, J.—On February 26, 1904, Jacob Swope and wife filed a complaint in the superior court in and for King county, alleging in substance that they now are, and at all times therein mentioned, have been, the owners and in possession of lots 13 and 14, in block 20, in Brooklyn Addition to the city of Seattle, which said lots are situated at the northeast corner of Tenth avenue, N. E., and Fortieth avenue, E., in said city of Seattle, King county, state of Washington; that the surface of said lots is practically level and at a suitable and proper grade with said streets as they have heretofore existed for the past five or six years, and as said streets have heretofore been graded and used, and as the said plat was accepted by the city of Seattle; that, on or about the year 1900, the plaintiffs constructed a dwelling house upon their said lots at great expense, which they have ever since occupied as their home; that said Tenth avenue, N. E., has heretofore been graded and "sidewalked," and said grade is a suitable one, and the grade of said streets at their said intersection is already about five feet below the surface of plaintiffs' said premises, and said dwelling house was located and built on said premises with reference to the grade of said streets as they then existed; that there is no necessity, in order to improve said streets and make them suitable for public use, to make any cut or fill at their said intersection; that the city of Seattle, through its board of public works, has let a contract to the defendant William Stanley for regrading said Tenth avenue, N. E., in front of said premises, and for grading said Fortieth avenue, E., at the south side of said premises, in such a manner as to cut down said streets at their

said intersection to a depth of approximately ten feet
lower than the grade of said streets has heretofore been;
that, in pursuance of said contract, the said William Stanley has partially cut said Fortieth avenue, E., to a depth
lower than it heretofore was, and has partially removed,
and is removing, and is about still further to remove, the
earth from plaintiffs' said property so as to make a slope
from the surface thereof down to the grade established by
the city of Seattle, and to a depth of nine or ten feet below the present surface of said premises; that the said
contractor has removed earth from the plaintiffs' said premises to a distance of several feet back from the front and
west marginal lines of said premises, and is proceeding
to remove earth and soil from the said premises and intends to cut said premises, and the street in front of the
same, down to a depth of nine or ten feet below the present level of the street in front of said premises, and is
about to remove a strip of earth from the west part of said
premises to make them conform to the new grade as re-
cently established by the city of Seattle, for a distance
of eighteen or nineteen feet east and west, by a distance
of about eighty-three feet north and south, and for a depth
of from thirteen to fifteen feet; that the said city, through
its board of public works, and by its said contractor, is
about to lower the present grade of said streets about nine
or ten feet in front of plaintiffs' said premises; that, unless the defendants be restrained from so doing, they will
immediately change the street grade in front of plaintiffs'
lots as aforesaid and remove approximately twenty per
cent of the surface of plaintiffs' premises where they join
said streets, and leave the balance of said premises standing from thirteen to fifteen feet above the proposed new
grade of said streets, and that, by reason thereof, the said
premises will be greatly damaged and injured, and it

will be necessary for plaintiffs to spend a large sum of
money to build bulkheads around said lots to retain the
earth therein, and it will be impossible for plaintiffs to
drive onto said premises with fuel, and will hereafter
cause an increased annual expense for getting fuel and
other material from the streets to the surface of said lots,
and to the plaintiffs' said dwelling house; that the grade
of said streets as heretofore established is an easy and
suitable grade, and such that loaded wagons can be driven
therefrom onto plaintiffs' premises, and the change of
grade as proposed and now being carried out by defendants will not benefit the plaintiffs' property, but, on the
contrary, will damage it in the sum of $2,000; that none
of the defendants has made or paid into court for the
plaintiffs any compensation whatever for damaging their
premises as aforesaid, but, on the contrary, they claim
and assume the right to grade said streets and to remove
plaintiffs' soil from said premises without first making
compensation to plaintiffs, as provided by law and the
constitution of this state; and that the plaintiffs have no
remedy at law to enforce the payment of said damages
before such damages are committed.

In their complaint the plaintiffs prayed that a restraining order be issued, enjoining the defendants from
further proceeding in the grading of said streets, and
from removing any earth from plaintiffs' said premises,
until just compensation be made for taking and damaging
said premises, and that a time be set by the court in
said restraining order within which compensation shall
be made, and that it be further ordered that, upon failure to make such compensation within the time limited
by the court, the restraining order be made permanent,
and the defendants, and each of them, and their agents
and employees, be ordered and directed forthwith to cease

all work and all further proceedings in grading said
streets, until the further order of the court and for their
costs and disbursements.

At the time of filing their complaint, the plaintiffs
filed an affidavit of Jacob Swope, which is practically
a repetition of the allegations of the complaint, and, upon
the complaint and accompanying affidavit, they moved
the court for a restraining order directing the defendants
to refrain from doing any of the acts complained of in
the complaint until the further order of the court, and to
show cause why such temporary restraining order should
not be made permanent. An order was thereupon issued
directing the defendants, and each of them, to appear before Hon. W. R. Bell, one of the judges of said court, on
the 4th day of March, 1904, at 9:30 o'clock, A. M., of said
day, or as soon thereafter as counsel could be heard, to
show cause why such restraining order should not issue.
An emergency order was also entered, restraining the defendants and their agents and servants from suffering or
committing any of the acts complained of until the further order of the court. The amount of the bond to be
given by plaintiffs was fixed at $100, and such bond was
duly executed, approved, and filed according to law.

On March 3, 1904, the defendants William Stanley
& Co. appeared in the action and moved the court to require the plaintiffs to make, execute, and file in the cause
an additional bond, conditioned as required by law, in
the penal sum of $5,000. This motion was based upon
all the records and files in the cause, and upon the affidavit of Samuel Stanley, which was served and filed
therewith. The affidavit of Samuel Stanley, in support
of the motion for an additional or a larger bond, states
that the defendant William Stanley is a member of the
copartnership of William Stanley & Co., which company

was, at the time of the commencement of this action, engaged in grading the streets in front of the property described in plaintiffs' complaint, under and pursuant to a
contract theretofore entered into between the city of Seattle
and William Stanley & Co.; that said William Stanley
& Co. have a large number of men and teams employed
on said work, and, by reason of such fact, said William
Stanley & Co. are being damaged in the sum of not less
than $150 per day for each day they are prevented from
continuing said work; that said William Stanley & Co.
are limited by their contract with the city to a certain
time in which to complete said work, and are bound by
said contract to pay a large sum per day as penalty and
liquidated damages for each day the completion of said
work is delayed beyond the time agreed upon. And affiant further says that he has fully stated the facts regarding the action to one of his attorneys, and is advised by him, and therefore alleges the fact to be, that
said William Stanley & Co. have a good and valid defense
to said action.

Upon the showing thus made by the contractors, William
Stanley & Co., it was ordered by the court, on March 4,
1904, that the plaintiffs execute and file a good and sufficient bond, conditioned as required by law, in the sum
of $3,000, the same to be filed on or before March 7,
1904, and that, in the meantime, the temporary restraining order heretofore issued herein be suspended, and that
on failure of plaintiffs to file said bond on the morning
of said March 7, the temporary order heretofore issued be
vacated and set aside. The plaintiffs having failed to
comply with the order last above mentioned, within the
time therein designated, the court, on the 7th day of March,
1904, "vacated, set aside, and annulled" the temporary
restraining order issued on the 26th day of February,

1904. On the following day the plaintiffs, by their counsel, applied to this court for a writ of certiorari to review the said rulings and orders of the superior court. On March 11, 1904, the writ was accordingly issued, commanding the superior court in and for King county, and W. R. Bell, one of the judges thereof, to certify and transmit to this court, at the court room thereof in the city of Olympia, on the 25th day of March, 1904, at 10 o'clock in the forenoon of said day, a transcript of the record and proceedings in that certain action then pending in said superior court wherein Jacob Swope and Elizabeth Swope are plaintiffs and the city of Seattle *et al.* are defendants. And the said court and judge were further ordered and directed to show cause before this court, on said 25th day of March, 1904, why the order of said superior court made and entered on March 7, 1904, setting aside the temporary restraining order issued out of the said superior court on February 26, 1904, should not be vacated and annulled, and why the said temporary restraining order should not be reinstated without additional security from the said plaintiffs, upon the records, files, and proceedings before the said superior court at the hearing of the motion of the said William Stanley & Co., for additional security from said plaintiffs. The said court and the said defendants were also required and directed to desist from any further proceedings until the further order of this court.

In response to this writ the superior court certified and sent up to this court the records, files, and proceedings designated in said writ, and which we have hereinbefore set out. At the hearing the defendants appeared by counsel and produced affidavits going to show a defense to the action on the merits, but it seems plain to us that, in this proceeding, we are restricted to the consideration of the record as actually made in the court below. Matters which were not presented to the lower court cannot be received here to vary or contradict the record.

Our constitution, art. 1, § 16, provides that, "no private property shall be taken or damaged for public or private use without just compensation having been first made, or paid into court for the owner." And the plaintiffs, claiming that their property was being taken and damaged for public use, filed their complaint for an injunction, setting out the acts of the defendants, which they deemed violative of their constitutional rights. Upon the showing made by the plaintiffs—and which was certainly sufficient—the judge to whom the application was made issued the temporary restraining order above mentioned, and fixed the bond to be given by plaintiffs at a sum deemed by him proper and reasonable under the circumstances.

That injunction is a proper remedy in cases of this character has uniformly been held by this court. See, *Brown v. Seattle,* 5 Wash. 35, 31 Pac. 313, 32 Pac. 214, 18 L. R. A. 161; *Olson v. Seattle,* 30 Wash. 687, 71 Pac. 201, and cases cited. In *Brown v. Seattle, supra,* this court, after a careful consideration of the constitutional provision above quoted, and the decisions of other courts based upon similar provisions, announced the doctrine that damages are recoverable from a city, by the owner of land abutting upon a street, for any permanent injury inflicted upon such land by any material change of grade or obstruction to the abutter's access to the street, when the damages thus inflicted exceed the benefits derived from the grading or other improvement; and that when the proposed grading of a street will seriously depreciate the value of abutting property, the grading may be enjoined until the damages be ascertained and compensation made or paid into court for the owner. And the rule there laid down, as was said in *Olson v. Seattle, supra,* "has been followed in practice ever since." See, also, *State ex rel. Smith v. Superior Court,* 26 Wash. 278, 66 Pac. 385, wherein the question now under consideration was elaborately discussed.

But, while it is clear that an owner of property abutting upon a street may, by injunction, prevent a municipality from damaging the same, without first making compensation therefor, by materially changing the grade of the street in front thereof, it is equally clear that one who invokes the remedy of injunction and asks for an injunction or restraining order, *pendente lite,* must comply with the statute requiring the execution of a bond to the adverse party. Bal. Code, § 5438. When a statute requires the giving of a bond as a condition precedent to the granting of an injunction or restraining order, the court has not the power to disregard such statute and dispense with the bond. 2 High, Injunctions (3d ed.), § 1620; 1 Spelling, Injunctions (2d ed.), § 935. See, also, *Keeler v. White,* 10 Wash. 420, 38 Pac. 1134; *Cherry v. Western Wash. etc. Co.,* 11 Wash. 586, 40 Pac. 136. But where the bond given for obtaining a preliminary injunction is shown to be insufficient, a new bond may be required in a proper case, as a condition precedent to continuing such injunction to trial. 2 High, Injunctions (3d ed.), § 1626; 1 Spelling, Injunctions (2d ed.), § 941. No new bond, however, should be ordered in such cases, unless good reason be shown why the bond already given is insufficient. In injunctions and restraining orders, the legislature has confided the duty of fixing the amount of the bond to the court or judge granting the order (Bal. Code, § 5438), but this is a legal and not an arbitrary discretion, and, in the language of the supreme court of

Louisiana, "in case of abuse and denial of justice by unreasonable and oppressive requirements, we should not hesitate to extend relief." *Bell v. Riggs,* 37 La. Ann. 813.

The only question, therefore, for determination in the case at bar, is whether the superior court, upon the showing made by the defendants Stanley & Co., was justified, in the exercise of the discretion vested in it by law, in ordering the plaintiffs to execute a new bond, and in annulling and setting aside the bond originally required by the court, and given by the plaintiffs. Assuming that the allegations of the complaint are true, it clearly appears that the city, by its agents and servants, was inflicting great injury and damage upon the plaintiffs' premises, in direct contravention of one of the plain and mandatory provisions of the constitution. And, it thus appearing that the plaintiffs' rights were clear and that such rights were being illegally invaded by the defendants, the court, in the absence of a statute requiring the giving of a bond, would have been fully warranted in issuing the restraining order without any security whatever from the plaintiffs.

It must be borne in mind that neither the city nor its board of public works moved the court to require the plaintiffs to give additional security. That motion, as we have already said, was made by William Stanley & Co. alone, and was based upon the records and files in the cause, and the affidavit of Samuel Stanley. And it will be observed that that affidavit controverted none of the facts stated in the verified complaint, or the additional affidavit of Jacob Swope, one of the plaintiffs. It did not show that the city, its officers and contractors, or either or any of them, were rightfully interfering with the property of the plaintiffs, or even that the defendants were doing the things complained of in the exercise of a power conferred upon them

by statute, or by an ordinance of the city. It simply set
out facts showing that William Stanley & Co., who, as
we have said, were merely the agents and servants of the
city, will be greatly damaged if prevented from grading
the streets adjacent to plaintiffs' premises in accordance
with the terms of their contract. But the fact that the contractors may be bound to pay the penalty exacted by the
city for delay in the completion of their work certainly
constitutes no sufficient reason why the plaintiffs should
be deprived of their constitutional rights, or why the plaintiffs should be required to give a bond in an amount
equal to the full value of their property in order to secure
those rights. No brief has been filed or authorities cited
by either party to this proceeding, and we have based our
decision solely upon our view of the law, and the just
and equitable rights of the parties, as they are disclosed
by the record before us. Upon the showing made before
him, we are constrained to conclude that the learned judge
of the court below was not warranted, either in requiring the plaintiffs to execute the new bond designated in ·
his order, or in setting aside the bond theretofore given by
the plaintiffs in compliance with the previous order of
the court.

The judgment is therefore reversed, and the cause remanded, with instructions to reinstate the bond given by
plaintiffs on February 26, 1904.

FULLERTON, C. J., and HADLEY and MOUNT, JJ., concur.

[No. 4828.   Decided April 22, 1904.]

J. F. Adams, *Respondent*, v. Christopher C. Dempsey
et al., Appellants.[1]

Fraudulent Conveyances — Chattel Mortgage in Fraud of Creditors—Good Faith—Evidence—Sufficiency. Upon an issue as to whether a chattel mortgage given by a debtor was fraudulent and void as to attaching creditors, there is sufficient evidence to require the good faith of the transaction to be submitted to the jury, where it appears that the mortgage was given by the debtor to his brother when insolvent and on the brink of financial ruin, that the mortgage covered all his property, valued at from $3,000 to $4,000, while the debt secured was only $1,650, and that the debtor had repeatedly said that he owed his brother nothing.

Same—Fraud in Law—Instruction as to Facts Constituting Fraud. Upon an issue as to whether a conveyance was fraudulent as to creditors, it is proper to instruct that a debtor in failing circumstances, who transfers all his property to one creditor with a secret understanding to receive part of the proceeds or secure a benefit at the expense of other creditors, is guilty of a fraud upon his creditors; since such facts constitute fraud in law, and are more than mere evidence of fraud.

Appeal from a judgment of the superior court for Spokane county, Kennan, J., entered March 6, 1903, in favor of plaintiff, upon setting aside the verdict of a jury rendered in favor of the defendants, after a trial on the merits. Reversed.

Danson & Huneke, for appellants.

W. J. Thayer, for respondent.

Fullerton, C. J.—This action was begun in June, 1898, by the respondent, J. F. Adams, to recover from the appellant C. C. Dempsey, who was the sheriff of Spokane county, and his co-appellants, who were sureties on his official bond, the value of a stock of groceries and of

[1]Reported in 76 Pac. 538.

certain store fixtures, which, it was alleged, the respondent Dempsey, as sheriff of Spokane county, had wrongfully seized and sold. The record discloses that, some time prior to the date above mentioned, the respondent had been engaged in the grocery business, in the city of Spokane, and had sold such business to his brother, one Harry C. Adams; that Harry C. Adams thereafter conducted the business in his own name, and, while so doing, became indebted to sundry wholesale dealers, who began pressing him for payment; that he thereupon executed a chattel mortgage on all his stock and fixtures to his brother, J. F. Adams, to secure a purported indebtedness of $1,650, and immediately placed his brother in possession of the property. Certain of the creditors of Harry C. thereupon commenced actions on their accounts, and sued out writs of attachment, under which the sheriff seized the mortgaged property, which he afterwards sold on executions issued on judgments obtained in the attachment actions. The present action was thereupon begun, against which the sheriff and his co-defendants defended on the ground that the chattel mortgage was in fraud of the creditors of Harry C. Adams, and consequently void.

The case was tried before the court and a jury. At the conclusion of the appellants' evidence, the respondent challenged the legal sufficiency of such evidence to sustain the charge of fraud, and moved the court to discharge the jury, and enter a judgment in his favor, pursuant to the provisions of section 4994 of the Code (Ballinger's). This motion the court denied, and afterwards submitted the question of the good faith of the mortgage to the consideration of the jury, who returned a verdict in favor of the appellants. The respondent thereafter moved the court to set aside the verdict and grant a new trial, and, on the hearing of this motion, urged anew the question of the sufficiency of the evidence to justify the jury in finding the mortgage fraudulent. The trial judge reconsidered his former ruling, held the evidence insufficient, set aside the verdict of the jury, and entered a judgment in favor of the respondent for $2,083 and costs of the action. This appeal is from that judgment.

Counsel for the respective parties have discussed at length the interesting question, whether or not the trial court had power, after the return of the verdict of the jury, to review and reverse its former ruling on the sufficiency of the evidence, but we have found it unnecessary to determine the question. This was the fifth time this case had been tried, each trial being had before a jury. On two of these trials the jury disagreed, and on three of them they found for the defendants—the present appellants. The two former verdicts in favor of the defendants were set aside by this court, on the appeal of the present respondent, because of error in the instructions of the court; 22 Wash. 284, 60 Pac. 649, 79 Am. St. 933; 29 Wash. 155, 69 Pac. 738. It is not disputed that the evidence touching the validity of the chattel mortgage was, in all of these trials, substantially the same, and that in all of them, prior to the last one, it was assumed, if not conceded, that the evidence, if believed by the jury, was sufficient to sustain a judgment in favor of the defendants. While these facts may not require a reversal of the present judgment, if it be true that the evidence is insufficient to sustain such a judgment, still it would seem that it furnished some reason for doubting the soundness of the contention that it was insufficient to sustain the verdict.

But a perusal of the evidence itself does not, to our minds, leave the question in doubt. The transaction was between brothers. The mortgage was given to secure a purported debt to a person to whom the mortgagor had repeatedly declared he owed nothing. It was given when the mortgagor was insolvent, when he was on the brink of financial ruin, and its effect was, if valid, to defeat creditors who had sold the mortgagor on credit some of the very goods included in the mortgage. The stock of goods and fixtures were estimated by the mortgagor at $4,000, by the mortgagee at $3,000, and the debt was but $1,650; yet the parties included in the mortgage everything the mortgagor owned—not only the grocery and its fixtures, but a cow and her calf, four horses, two delivery wagons, one buggy, one set double harness, and one set single harness, a part of which only could be said to have any connection with the grocery. There was evidence of acts, participated in by the mortgagee, occurring subsequently to the execution, that were hardly consistent with the idea that the mortgage was given solely to secure a debt, but it is unnecessary to pursue the inquiry further. The evidence made the question of fraud one for the jury, and the court erred in holding otherwise.

This conclusion requires a reversal of the judgment, and it becomes material to inquire what form the order remanding the cause to the lower court should take. The respondent insists that he is entitled to a new trial in any event, on the ground of the erroneous instructions given the jury. The instructions complained of are as follows:

"16th. A debtor who is insolvent, or in failing circumstances, has no right to execute a chattel mortgage upon all of his property and surrender possession thereof to one creditor, and have a secret understanding with the mortgagee that said debtor shall secretly receive any part of said property or the proceeds thereof, so as to wrongfully deprive any other creditor thereof. And where such is the fact, such chattel mortgage is fraudulent and void.

"17th. If a debtor in failing circumstances makes a transfer of all his property, purporting upon its face to be absolute and without reservation, and at the same time there is a concealed agreement between the parties to it, inconsistent with its terms, intending to secretly secure a benefit or an advantage to the debtor at the expense of those whom he owes, such a trust thus secretly created is a fraud upon creditors."

It is claimed that these instructions are erroneous because the trial court has no right to say "that this or that circumstance showed fraud, as a matter of law, but that all the circumstances should be submitted to the jury as evidence only." But the respondent mistakes the rule. While it is error to say that particular acts, if proven, constitute fraud, when in fact they are only evidence of fraud, yet, if the circumstances proven do constitute fraud, it is not error for the court to so tell the jury. In other words, there are certain conditions that constitute fraud in law, whether it be the result of one or of a series of acts, and it is never error for the court to instruct the jury what these conditions are, if pertinent to the particular case. The instructions complained of here do not violate the rule. The court should have entered judgment on the verdict. The judgment is therefore reversed, and the cause remanded, with instructions to enter a judgment in accordance with the verdict of the jury.

MOUNT, DUNBAR, HADLEY, and ANDERS, JJ., concur.

[No. 4852.   Decided April 23, 1904.]

GUY WARING, *Appellant*, v. J. A. LOOMIS *et al.*, *Respondents.*[1]

CONTRACTS—CONSTRUCTION—AGREEMENT BETWEEN TENANTS IN
COMMON. Where L and W were in joint possession of government land, and enter into an agreement defining their interests
as owners of undivided halves, and whereby L agrees to hold
possession as trustee in the interest of both, paying certain rent,
and agrees to pay W $214 "as his part of the expense of erecting
the dwelling" thereon, the natural import of the language is that
L was paying the sum mentioned as L's part of the cost, and not
that he was buying W's half interest therein.

PUBLIC LANDS—POSSESSORY RIGHT OF SETTLERS AS CONSIDERA-
TION FOR CONTRACT—SUFFICIENCY. Parties who have entered upon
government land in good faith with the intent to lawfully acquire
title to the property at some future time, are not trespassers, and
may contract with reference to their right of possession, which is
a sufficient consideration for mutual agreements respecting the
same.

SAME—CONTRACTS RESPECTING POSSESSION OF—DESCRIPTION OF
UNSURVEYED LANDS—SUFFICIENCY. A contract between parties in
possession of unsurveyed public land sufficiently describes the
premises, as between the parties, by referring to it as upon a
certain creek and in their possession, where it was bounded by
fences and the contour of certain bluffs, which formed a natural
fence for a portion of the property.

PUBLIC LANDS—CONTRACT TO ACQUIRE TITLE FOR ANOTHER—
VALIDITY—FRAUD ON GOVERNMENT—COMPLAINT SHOWING NO IN-
TENT TO VIOLATE LAWS OF UNITED STATES, A contract between
parties in the possession of government land, referred to as a
"ranch," whereby one was to obtain a patent, if possible, and
hold a half interest in trust, is not necessarily void as a fraud
upon the United States, since there are various ways in which
title can be secured to government land, even if agricultural in
character, not inconsistent with a contract of that kind, and the
presumption is that a lawful way was contemplated, especially
where the complaint on such contract alleges that there was no
intent to acquire the land in violation of the laws of the United
States.

[1] Reported in 76 Pac. 510.

Appeal from a judgment of the superior court for Spokane county, Belt, J., entered January 13, 1903, upon sustaining a demurrer to the complaint, dismissing an action to recover an interest in real estate. Reversed.

Graves & Graves, for appellant.

Merritt & Merritt, for respondents, to the point that the parties were trespassers and there was no consideration for the contract, cited *Buxton v. Traver,* 130 U. S. 232, 9 Sup. Ct. 509, 32 L. Ed. 920; *Northern Pac. R. Co. v. McCormick,* 89 Fed. 659; 11 Rose's Notes, U. S. Rep. 735.

FULLERTON, C. J.—The appellant brought this action against the respondents to recover an undivided one-half interest in a certain tract of land situated on Sinlahekin creek, in Okanogan county. A demurrer was interposed and sustained to his second amended complaint, whereupon he refused to plead further, and appeals from the judgment of dismissal, entered after his refusal to so plead.

In the complaint it is alleged, in substance, that about the 26th of May, 1885, the appellant settled upon the land in question, which was then unoccupied and unsurveyed government land, and continued in the sole possession and occupancy of the same until about the 6th day of October, 1886, when he sold an undivided one-half interest therein and the improvements thereon to one J. A. Loomis, and formed a copartnership with him to carry on a general merchandise store on the property; that appellant and Loomis occupied the premises jointly from that time until the 28th day of May, 1888; that the appellant on the last mentioned date became desirous of leaving the property; whereupon, to settle and fix their mutual rights in the property, he and Loomis entered into the following written agreement, viz.:

"Be it known by these presents, That we, J. A. Loomis
of Sinlahekin ranch, near Sinlahekin creek, in the county
of Okanogan, and territory of Washington, party of the
first part, and Guy Waring, late of the same place, the
party of the second part, being the undivided one-half
owners of one hundred and sixty acres of land (subject
to the paramount title of the United States), located upon
Sinlahekin creek in said county of Okanogan, together
with the improvements thereon, and having heretofore been
in the joint occupancy thereof, and the said Waring being
about to remove therefrom and to leave said Loomis in
the sole use, occupation and possession of the same, have
agreed and concluded concerning said land and ranch
and improvements thereon as follows, viz.: (1) Loomis
is to pay Waring in cash money upon the signing of this
agreement the sum of two hundred and fourteen ($214.00)
dollars as his part of the expense of erecting the dwelling
house lately occupied by said Waring and his family on
said ranch. (2) Loomis is to have the sole use, occupation and possession of said land, ranch and improvements thereon, upon the following terms, viz.: (a) He
shall keep all boundary posts in position and in every
lawful manner protect the exclusive possession thereof,
and prevent said land from being jumped as unoccupied
lands of the United States, and when the same are in
the market, will apply for and obtain patent thereto if he
can. (b) Loomis is to pay to Waring one-fifth in quantity and quality of hay raised on the ranch each year,
delivered on said ranch, and shall have the privilege of
buying the same from Waring for cash at any time before
the end of the year in which the same was grown at the
current price for hay of similar class and quality, on
December 1st, of such year, and in any event, said Loomis
shall take one-fifth of the hay at the end of the year in
which it is grown, and pay Waring therefor in cash
money the current price of hay of similar class and
quality in that vicinity at the end of such year in which
the same is grown. (c) Loomis is hereby authorized at
any time to make a *bona fide* sale of said ranch, or any
part thereof, for the mutual and equal benefit of both
parties hereto, and to execute in Waring's name any

and all necessary conveyances thereof, and pay the proceeds of such sale one-half to himself and one-half, less 5 per cent commission, to Waring forthwith, provided that if Waring furnishes a purchaser for said ranch, Loomis shall not be entitled to retain any percentage as commission, but in all other respects this paragraph remains the same. (*d*) Loomis shall have no right to sublet or lease said land or any part thereof to any third person. (*e*) Loomis hereby acknowledges a trust in favor of said Waring for an undivided one-half interest in the whole of said land, and in the event of his obtaining the paramount title of the United States to said land in his own name, he hereby acknowledges an express trust to the extent of one undivided one-half thereof in favor of said Guy Waring for the faithful administration of which said express trust he hereby binds his heirs, executors and administrators to the same extent as himself. (*f*) Waring hereby warrants Loomis in the quiet and peaceable possession of said premises against his own acts and against any and all persons claiming by, through or under him. Witness our hands," etc.

It was further alleged that, although the tract was described as containing 160 acres of land, the exact quantity was not known, and was found afterwards to contain approximately 235 acres, but that it was, at the time the contract was entered into, marked and bounded by fences, buildings, and the contour of certain bluffs which formed a natural fence for a portion of the property, and that the property was generally known as the "Sinlahekin Ranch." It was further alleged, that, upon the execution of the contract above set out, the appellant moved from the property, leaving the said Loomis in the sole possession thereof, and that he continued in such sole possession until his insanity and death, which occurred since the commencement of this action; that said Loomis, at all times preceding his death, held the property under the contract mentioned, and, in express recognition thereof, paid the rent reserved therein; that between the 18th and 25th days

of September, 1891, Loomis located the land as quartz
claims, under the mineral land laws of the United States,
under various names and surveys, and filed the same
for record, and that the government of the United States,
on the 9th day of June, 1896, regularly issued patents
for the same in the name of the respondent Bogart, but
for the use and benefit of Loomis and the appellant; that
it was not the intention of the parties to the contract, at
any time, to procure, or attempt to procure, a patent to
the lands mentioned, under the homestead or preemption
laws of the United States, or in any unlawful way, but
that the method adopted by Loomis was followed with
the approval and consent of plaintiff, in order that a
lawful title to the property might be obtained.

The complaint concludes with the official description of
the property, as contained in the patents for the several
mining claims, and with appropriate allegations showing
the interests of the several defendants, averring that such
interests were acquired subsequent to, and with knowledge
of, the rights of the appellant.

The trial court sustained the demurrer, on the ground
that the contract sued upon was void, and the respondents
contend that the ruling was correct for three reasons: (1)
that the contract was without consideration; (2) that the
description of the property is ambiguous and uncertain:
and (3) that the contract contemplated a fraud upon the
government of the United States and is void as against
public policy.

In support of the first contention, it is argued that the
parties were mere trespassers on the land at the time of
the execution of the contract, and consequently the appellant had no interest therein which he could sell to Loomis;
that Loomis paid him in cash for all his interest in the
improvements on the property at the time of the execution
of the contract; and hence there was no consideration for

the contract, and the same was void as a *nudum pactum.*
But this contention is clearly untenable. In the first
place, the contract does not warrant the assertion that the
appellant was paid for all his interest in the improvements at the time of the execution of the contract. The
natural import of the language used is that Loomis was
to pay Waring the sum mentioned as Loomis' part of the
cost of the dwelling house lately occupied by Waring,
not Waring's part of the cost, and this natural construction
coincides with the other conditions of the lease, which the
construction put upon it by the respondents does not. In
the second place, the parties were not trespassers on the
land. While the United States statutes declare it unlawful, in certain instances, to inclose parts of the public
domain, such statutes have no application when the inclosure is made in good faith, with the intent lawfully to
acquire title to the property at some future time, under
the general laws of the government. While such occupation gives no right as against the government, the occupants are not technically trespassers. No individual can
interfere with their possession or compel them to leave—
both the laws of the United States and of this state contain
provisions for the prevention of that—and such possessory
rights have always been recognized, not only among individuals, but by the courts, as of value and subjects of
barter and sale. *Lamb v. Davenport,* 18 Wall. 307, 21
L. Ed. 759; *Tarpey v. Madsen,* 178 U. S. 215, 20 Sup.
Ct. 849, 44 L. Ed. 1042. There was, under any view
of the contract, a consideration sufficient to support it,
as between the parties and their privies.

The second objection is equally without merit. How
effective the description might be against an innocent
purchaser for value, having only constructive notice, it
is not necessary here to determine. But as between the
parties, the description is clearly sufficient.

The third objection can be sustained only on the assumption that the parties to the contract intended, at the time they entered into it, to obtain title to the land therein described in fraud of the United States. The contract, however, is far from declaring that such was their purpose. While it does refer to the land as a "ranch," and make provision concerning the payment of rent in hay, and provide that the vendee shall apply for and obtain patent thereto if he can," when the same are in the market," yet these provisions are not necessarily inconsistent with an honest intent on the part of the parties. There are various ways by which title can be acquired to the public land of the United States, even though it be agricultural in character, only some of which are inconsistent with a contract of this kind. This being the case, it will not be presumed that the parties intended to violate the law. On the contrary, it is a rule of interpretation that, when a contract is open to two constructions, by one of which it would be lawful and the other unlawful, the former must be adopted.

Moreover, it is alleged in the complaint that the parties had no intent to acquire title to the land in a manner inconsistent with the terms of the contract, or in violation of the laws of the United States, and it is further alleged that they did not so acquire it. It would seem that this alone would be sufficient, as against the naked presumption that the parties might have had some other thought in mind, when they entered into the contract.

We conclude, therefore, that the contract is not void on its face and that the complaint states a cause of action. The judgment will be reversed, and the cause remanded, with instructions to reinstate the case, and to require the defendant to answer to the merits.

DUNBAR, ANDERS, and HADLEY, JJ., concur.

[No. 4774.   Decided April 23, 1904.]

.E. E. INGERSOLL *et al., Respondents*, v. E. ROUSSEAU,
Appellant.[1]

NUISANCE—ADJOINING PROPERTY—RIGHTS RUNNING WITH LAND
—CONTINUING OFFENSE.   In an action to enjoin a continuing
nuisance upon adjoining premises, rendering plaintiffs' prop⁀ ty
unfit for residence purposes, it is immaterial that plaintiff pur·
chased his property after the commencement of the nuisance, as
the right of action existing in favor of plaintiffs' grantors runs
with the land, and, also, is a continuing offense, and lapse of time
bars recovery only for a completed offense.

NUISANCE—ABATEMENT—DISORDERLY HOUSES — TOLERATION BY
CITY NO DEFENSE.   The fact that city officials tolerate the maintenance of bawdy houses is no defense to an action to abate the
same as a nuisance specially injurious to adjoining property.

SAME—ABATEMENT AT SUIT OF PRIVATE CITIZEN — SPECIAL IN-
JURY.   The owner of adjoining premises may sue to abate the
maintenance of bawdy houses as a public nuisance specially injurious to his premises used for residence purposes, where the
occupants are compelled to witness indecent conduct and listen
to unseemly noises, the injury being special and different in kind
from that suffered by the general public.

SAME—INJUNCTION TO ABATE DISORDERLY HOUSE—REMEDIES AT
LAW—INADEQUACY.   Injunction lies to abate the maintenance of a
bawdy house as a public nuisance specially injurious to plaintiffs'
adjoining property used for residence purposes, the common law
remedies of indictment and action on the case being inadequate,
and this rule has not been changed by statute in this state.

Appeal from a judgment of the superior court for Snohomish county, Denney, J., entered April 3, 1903, upon
findings in favor of the plaintiff, after a trial before the
court without a jury, perpetually enjoining a nuisance.
Affirmed.

Brownell & Coleman, for appellant.

[1]Reported in 76 Pac. 513.

FULLERTON, C. J.—This action was brought by the respondents, who were plaintiffs below, to enjoin the appellant from maintaining, or permitting to be maintained, houses of ill fame on certain real property owned by him, situated in the city of Everett. The trial was had before the court without a jury, and resulted in a permanent injunction against the appellant.

The trial court found, in substance, that the respondents and appellant owned lots in the city of Everett lying adjacent to each other; that the respondents used their lots as places of residence for themselves and their families, while the appellant had erected on his property certain buildings or structures which he had divided into rooms or compartments known as "cribs," and which he leased to dissolute and abandoned women to be used as places of prostitution. The court further found that these women employ other dissolute and abandoned women as prostitutes, who exhibit themselves in the windows and at the doors of the houses, and on the verandas and sidewalks in front of the same, dressed in an indecent and immodest manner, and solicit men passing along the street to enter the houses for immoral purposes; that these women draw around them drunken and dissolute men, who engage with them in drunken orgies, and in loud and indecent talk and noisy and boisterous conduct. The court found that the effect of these acts was to render the respondents' properties unfit for residence puropses, and undesirable for any lawful business, greatly depreciating them in value; that the injury was irreparable, and incapable of being compensated for in damages, and would continue as long as the appellant permitted his premises to be used for such unlawful purposes.

The court further found, however, that the respondents purchased their property after the appellant had constructed his cribs and had begun to use his property for the above mentioned purposes. The evidence, also, perhaps justified findings to the effect that the appellant's property is in that part of the city of Everett where the city authorities compel, as far as they can, abandoned and dissolute women, who ply their noxious trade, to reside; and also, that the appellant, after the commencement of this action, but before the trial, remodeled his cribs, making them less conspicuous from the streets and surrounding property than they were before; but it appeared that they were still used, and intended to be used, as bawdy houses, and it did not appear that this change would materially affect the injury done to the surrounding property by the uses to which they were being put.

The appellant excepted to certain of the court's findings on the ground that they were not supported by the evidence, and has included his exceptions in his assignments of error. While he has not seriously pressed this point in his argument, we have, nevertheless, examined the evidence with that thought in view, and have no hesitancy in saying that the evidence abundantly sustains the findings. And we may state here, also, that the finding to the effect that the appellant began making this particular use of his property before the respondents purchased their properties, and the additional findings suggested, do not, in our opinion, affect the controversy, although the appellant seems to regard them as of some importance. The right of the respondents to maintain an injunction, if that right exists at all, is a property right; it runs with the land, so to speak, and existed in favor of the grantors of the respondents, and passed to them by the purchase of the properties. Moreover, the injury is a continuing one, constantly giving rise to a new cause of action, and lapse of time bars a recovery only for a completed offense.

As to the other matters suggested, if it be true that the city authorities tolerated bawdy houses on the appellant's property, that fact would not legalize their maintenance there, much less would it authorize their maintenance, if such maintenance injuriously affected the respondents' properties; and the change in the cribs could not be a defense unless it was shown—which it was not—that the change did away entirely with the injury.

The principal contention on the part of the appellant is that injunction is not the proper remedy. It is argued, (1) that it was not made to appear that the acts complained of were specially injurious to the respondents, or that they suffered a special injury differing in kind from that suffered by the general public; and (2) that the respondents had a plain, speedy, and adequate remedy at law for the nuisance, if it be one.

The first of these objections requires no serious consideration. The respondents suffer, not only all the inconveniences the general public suffers because of the maintenance of the nuisance, but in addition thereto, they are compelled to become witnesses to the boisterous and indecent conduct of the inmates of the houses, and listeners to the loud and unseemly noises made by them and their dissolute companions. The injury caused the respondents by these conditions is clearly special, and different in kind from that suffered by the general public, who are not compelled to be either such witnesses or listeners.

The second contention of the appellant, while not entirely free from difficulty, we think is also without merit. It will be remembered that courts of equity have, from the earliest times, exercised jurisdiction to prevent and abate public nuisances, notwithstanding there has concurrently existed the common law remedies of indictment and action on the case. The jurisdiction was grounded on the inadequacy of the legal remedies; it being within the power of courts of equity, not only to abate an existing nuisance, but to do what the courts of law could not do—interpose and prevent threatened nuisances, and, by a perpetual injunction, make their remedies effectual throughout all future time.

It may be true, as has been suggested, that no case can be found in the earlier English reports where a court of equity has interfered by injunction at the suit of a private person to enjoin the maintenance of a bawdy house, but it is equally true that there is no precedent the other way. Doubtless it is some evidence that jurisdiction does not exist, in a given case, to show that it has never been exercised in like cases, but the persuasive force of such evidence is weak or strong owing to the presence or absence of cases announcing the same or similar principles. Here such cases are plentiful. Precedents are abundant where equity has interfered by injunction to prevent and abate public nuisances against which there existed the same common law remedies of indictment and action on the case that existed against the maintenance of a bawdy house. 2 Story's Eq. Jurisp. §§ 921-924; *Attorney General v. Forbes,* 2 Mylne & Craig, 129, 130. It would seem, therefore, that, if equity refused to exercise such jurisdiction in the case of bawdy houses, it was for some reason other than for lack of jurisdiction.

The next question is, has the rule been changed by statute. The statutory legal remedies against public nuisances are much the same as those of the common law. They consist of an information or indictment, and a civil action for damages, with the added element of a warrant of abatement in case of a conviction or of a recovery. The first of these is notoriously inadequate to protect the rights of a person specially injured, for the

very sufficient reason that he has neither the right to institute such an action, nor to control it after it has been
instituted; these rights belong, properly enough, to the
public officers, who may or may not see fit to exercise them
in the particular case. The remedy afforded by an action
of damages is more efficient, but it is nevertheless inadequate because the judgment cannot be made continuing
in its operation. When the damages recovered are paid,
and the warrant of abatement is executed and returned,
the judgment is satisfied. The guilty party may, on the
next day, create a new nuisance of the same kind at the
same place, and the only legal remedy therefor is a new
action, a new recovery, and another warrant of abatement;
whereas a court can, by the equitable relief of injunction,
not only abate the existing nuisance, but it can forbid
the creation of other or similar nuisances in the future,
entering a judgment that will support an execution whenever its terms are violated. The jurisdiction of the courts
to interfere by injunction against public nuisances can rest
under the statute, therefore, on the same ground upon
which it rested while the common law remedies were in
force—on the ground of the inadequacy of the legal
remedies.

For precedents where the modern courts have interfered
to prevent and abate public nuisances, other than those
of the character in question here, we need not look beyond
our own decisions. In *Carl v. West Aberdeen Land etc.
Co.,* 13 Wash. 616, 43 Pac. 890, we affirmed a judgment
enjoining a boom company from obstructing a navigable
stream; and in *Smith v. Mitchell,* 21 Wash. 536, 58 Pac.
667, 75 Am. St. 858, we affirmed a judgment enjoining
the defendant from obstructing a public highway; each
of such acts being subject to the legal remedies of information or indictment, and an action for damages. It

is true this is the first instance in this state where the remedy has been sought against a bawdy house, but there is nothing in the character of this particular form of nuisance that prevents the exercise against it of the equitable remedy of injunction. If it can be exercised to abate such public nuisances as obstructions to highways, and the like, when they become specially injurious to particular individuals, it would be strange indeed if the courts were without jurisdiction to exercise it against this most baneful of all public nuisances, which not only destroys, for lawful use, all property surrounding it, but corrupts and degrades the morals of the community as well.

But we are not without precedent for the precise case. While the precedents are not many, the majority of those that do exist, and we think the better reasoned cases, hold that courts of equity have such jurisdiction. The earliest case called to our attention is that of *Hamilton v. Whitridge,* 11 Md. 128, 69 Am. Dec. 184. There the court noticed the absence of precedent, but rested its decision on analogous cases, the reason and spirit of which supported the rule; saying that there was jurisdiction in equity to enjoin whenever the nature of the injury is such that it cannot be adequately compensated by damages, or from its continuance or permanent mischief will occasion a constantly recurring grievance. In *Anderson v. Doty,* 33 Hun 160, the jurisdiction was denied; the court saying that a bawdy house is a nuisance because it is a crime, and that the proper tribunal in which to abate it is the criminal court. The appellate court of the same state, however, in *Crawford v. Tyrrell,* 128 N. Y. 341, 28 N. E. 514, without noticing the previous case, held that an injunction would lie; the court saying:

"One who uses his property lawfully and reasonably, in a general legal sense, can do injury to nobody. In the

full enjoyment of his legal rights in and to his property,
the law will not suffer a man to be restrained; but his
use of the property must be always such as in no manner
to invade the legal rights of his neighbor. The rights of
each to the enjoyment and use of their several properties
should, in legal contemplation, always be equal. If the
balance is destroyed by the act of one, the law gives a
remedy in damages, or equity will restrain. If the use
of a property is one which renders a neighbor's occupation and enjoyment physically uncomfortable, or which
may be hurtful to the health, as where trades are conducted
which are offensive by reason of odors, noises, or other
injurious or annoying features, a private nuisance is
deemed to be established, against which the protection of
a court of equity power may be invoked.

"In the present case the indecent conduct of the occupants of the defendant's house and the noise therefrom,
inasmuch as they rendered the plaintiff's house unfit for
comfortable or respectable occupation, and unfit for the
purposes it was intended for, were facts which constituted
a nuisance, and were sufficient grounds for the maintenance of the action. If it was a nuisance which affected
the general neighborhood and was the subject of an indictment for its unlawful and immoral features, the plaintiffs
were none the less entitled to their action for an injury
sustained and to their equitable right to have its continuance restrained."

In *Neaf v. Palmer,* 103 Ky. 496, 45 S. W. 506, the
jurisdiction was denied, or perhaps more accurately, the
court refused to exercise it in this class of cases. The
court noticed the cases of *Anderson v. Doty* and *Hamilton
r. Whitridge,* saying that it could not follow the latter
"without doing violence to the long established practice
in this state of relegating the enforcement of any laws
against crime to the criminal courts." Later cases are
Blagen v. Smith, 34 Or. 394, 56 Pac. 292, 44 L. R. A.
522, decided March 13, 1899, and *Weakley v. Page,* 102
Tenn. 178, 53 S. W. 551, 46 L. R. A. 552, decided March

16, 1899, each affirming the jurisdiction. These cases are ably argued by the judges rendering the opinions, and show, beyond question, that courts of equity have power to enjoin this particular character of nuisance, and that it is their duty to do so in all proper instances. Another case is *Marsan v. French,* 61 Tex. 173, 48 Am. Rep. 272. There it was held that one leasing his property to be used as a house of ill fame was responsible in damages to a proprietor residing with his family on adjacent property; and that he might be enjoined from continuing to permit such use of his property.

There is nothing in the case of *Coffer v. Territory,* 1 Wash. 325, 25 Pac. 632, 11 L. R. A. 296, which denies the power of a court, exercising equitable jurisdiction, to interfere by injunction at the suit of a private person specially injured to enjoin the maintenance of a bawdy house. That case is too long to be even epitomized here, but, if it is pertinent at all, it shows the inadequacy of the legal remedies in cases of the character of the one before us, and the necessity for a more effective remedy.

We are of the opinion, therefore, that the trial court had jurisdiction to enjoin the appellant from leasing his property to be used as houses of ill fame, and that the facts of the case warranted the exercise of the power. The judgment will stand affirmed.

DUNBAR, MOUNT, ANDERS, and HADLEY, JJ., concur.

[No. 4914.   Decided April 25, 1904.]

EDWIN J. ROWE *et al., Respondents, v.* NORTHPORT
SMELTING AND REFINING COMPANY, *Appellant.*[1]

APPEAL — REVIEW — MOTION FOR NEW TRIAL — NECESSITY OF.
Errors relating to rulings of the trial court during the progress
of the trial can be reviewed upon appeal without a motion for a
new trial.

NUISANCE — DAMAGES — FUMES FROM SMELTER — EVIDENCE OF
CONDITIONS AT ANOTHER PLACE.   In an action for damages to an
orchard and vegetation caused by fumes from a smelter, evidence
of the damage done in another place under different conditions,
while subject to criticism, is not prejudicial error, when the witness states that the damage was similar to that done to the
plaintiffs' property.

SAME.   In such a case, where there was evidence that the
smelter released sulphur on plaintiffs' farm two miles distant,
it is competent to prove the release of sulphur in the immediate
vicinity of the smelter, in corroboration.

SAME—EXPERT EVIDENCE OF EFFECT OF SULPHUR FUMES—EX-
PERIMENTS BEFORE JURY—COMPETENCY.   It is error, in examining
expert witness as to the effect of sulphuric acid, to permit experiments to be made before the jury with some substance when
there is no proof as to what the substance is, and none that the
elements which combined to produce the experimental results
were the same as combined to produce the injury to plaintiffs'
farm, or that there was any similarity of conditions.

SAME—DAMAGES SINCE COMMENCEMENT OF ACTION—INSTRUC-
TIONS WITHOUT EVIDENCE ON POINT.   In an action for damages to
plaintiffs' premises by fumes from a smelter, commenced by the
service of a summons in August, in which the complaint was not
filed until December, and in which there was no evidence as to
the damage sustained from August to December, it is error to
instruct the jury to assess damages sustained during the two
years next preceding December as the date of the commencement
of the action, since the action was commenced when the summons
was served.

SAME—INSTRUCTIONS—WAIVER OF ERROR—SUFFICIENCY OF EX-
CEPTION.   The objection to such an instruction is not waived by

[1]Reported in 76 Pac. 529.

failing to object to a preliminary statement of tho court that the date of filing the complaint would be considered as the date of commencing the action, where timely exception was taken to the instruction after retirement of the jury.

Appeal from a judgment of the superior court for Stevens county, Richardson, J., entered April 13, 1903, upon the verdict of a jury rendered in favor of the plaintiffs, after a trial on the merits, for $2,000 damages to premises, caused by fumes from a smelter. Reversed.

Voorhees & Voorhees and *D. H. Carey,* for appellant.

Robertson, Miller & Rosenhaupt, J. A. Kellogg, and *Jere Rochford,* for respondents.

Hadley, J.—Respondents are the owners of certain lands situate near Northport, in Stevens county, Washington, and appellant is the owner and operator of a smelter located at Northport. Respondents brought this suit against appellant and alleged, that, at all times continuously within two years last past, the appellant corporation has maintained and operated its said smelter plant; that, in connection therewith, it has caused sulphide ores to be roasted in heaps, and has smelted about one thousand tons of ore daily during said period; that the ore so smelted contained about ten per cent of sulphur, and that appellant, by causing it to be burned in the manner aforesaid, has daily caused to be released in the atmosphere of Northport about one hundred tons of sulphur; that the sulphur so released is in the form of sulphurous acid or gas; that the prevailing winds carry the fumes over and upon the lands of respondents, and that, by reason thereof, the orchard has been destroyed and the land rendered barren and unproductive. The prayer of the complaint asks damages in the sum of $10,000. A trial was had before the court and a jury, and a verdict was returned in favor of respondents in the sum of $2,000. Appellant moved for a new trial, which was denied. Judgment was entered for the amount of the verdict, and this appeal was taken from the judgment.

The first designated assignment of error is in the following words, "The court erred in denying appellant's motion for a new trial." Respondents urge at some length that the assignment is indefinite and cannot be considered, under rule 12 of this court, which provides that no alleged error will be considered unless the same be clearly pointed out in appellant's brief. Numerous claims of error are, however, distinctly pointed out in the brief, all of which relate to rulings of the court during the progress of the trial. Such rulings may be reviewed in this court even without a motion for new trial. *Dubcich v. Grand Lodge A. O. U. W.*, 33 Wash. 651, 74 Pac. 832. For a discussion of this point we refer to the above cited case, without repeating here.

We understand respondents to contend that, as no specific ground is mentioned in the criticized statement, quoted above, as a reason why the court erred in denying the motion for a new trial, there is therefore really nothing here to review. Under the rule already announced by this court, all the other claims of error assigned in this case could have been reviewed on appeal, if no motion for new trial had been made. While appellant nominally classified the statement made in its brief, concerning the ruling upon the motion for new trial, as an assignment of error, yet the statement in effect simply calls attention to the fact that the motion gave the court an opporunity to review its own rulings, and that, in denying the motion, the court erred for the reasons definitely set forth in the assignments which follow in the brief.

It is assigned that the court erred in permitting respondents, over objection, to ask one Gantenbein, a witness,
the following question: "What proportion of the trees
generally in the immediate vicinity of the smelter are
dead?" There was evidence to the effect that the lands
of respondents are distant from the smelter, on a direct
line and over the hills, about one and three-fourths miles,
and that, following the meanderings of the Columbia river,
the distance is about two and one-fourth miles. The purpose of noting the two measurements is by reason of the
contention of appellant that the fumes and smoke from
the smelter follow the meanderings of the river, and do not
cross in a direct course to respondents' lands. It will be
noted that the distance by way of the river is nearly one
mile greater than it is by the direct course, and that fact
is urged to emphasize appellant's claim that, after traveling
the greater distance, the sulphur fumes have become so
affected by the atmosphere that they are rendered harmless
to vegetation. The criticized question called for the condition of trees in the "immediate vicinity" of the smelter.
Appellant urges—and testimony was afterwards introduced
to that effect—that, as the distance of the point to be
affected from the place where the gas is generated increases,
the deleterious effect decreases. It is, therefore, contended
that the question called for the effect of the gases upon
vegetation at a point where conditions were materially
different from those which obtained at the location of
respondents' land. The limitation in the question, "immediate vicinity" was, indeed, indefinite. For some purposes the location of respondents' lands, considered from
the standpoint of either measurement above mentioned,
would be regarded as in the immediate vicinity of the
smelter. It is evident, however, from the examination of
the witness which preceded the question now under con-

sideration, that the inquiry was intended to relate to points nearer the smelter than respondents' land. The question standing alone would, therefore, seem to call for the effect of conditions different from those prevailing at respondents' land. The witness had, however, been previously interrogated, and had answered as follows:

"Q. You don't understand, Mr. Gantenbein. I mean that this dead timber, now, nearer the smelter, that was killed there, if it was killed by the fumes, when it first began to be affected by those fumes, how did it compare with the timber on the Rowe place at that time, in appearance? A. I should think very much similar."

The answer of the witness substantially stated as a fact that the effect upon timber nearer the smelter was the same as at respondents' farm, and the question criticized called for a more specific statement as to the extent of the effects upon the timber nearer the smelter. While the real question to be determined was the effect at respondents' farm, yet, from the witness' view as expressed, it followed logically that the same proportion of trees were dead in each locality, and the answer would, therefore, in effect, apply to each. The accuracy of the witness' view was to be tested by cross-examination, or by other testimony. While it would indeed have been more proper to inquire directly as to effects at respondents' farm, yet, in view of what the witness had already said, we believe that result was reached indirectly by the question.

Appellant cites and discusses a number of authorities under this assignment. Of the authorities cited, the following Massachusetts cases are particularly discussed by counsel: *Emerson v. Lowell Gas Light Co.*, 3 Allen, 410; *Lincoln v. Taunton Copper Mfg. Co.*, 91 Mass. 181; *Kelliher v. Miller*, 97 Mass. 71; *Hawks v. Charlemont*, 110 Mass. 110; *Campbell v. Russell*, 139 Mass. 278, 1 N. E.

345. Without reviewing all the cases cited, we will observe that, in each of the above cases, the offered evidence was rejected, and it was held that it was not error. Under the authorities cited by appellant, if the objection to this evidence had been sustained in the case at bar, we should probably have held that it was not error; but, inasmuch as it was allowed to go to the jury, we are disposed to the view that, when the whole testimony of the witness is considered together, the criticized portion thereof did not have such prejudicial effect as requires the reversal of the case upon this ground.

Several assignments of error, involving somewhat the same principle as above discussed, relate to questions asked the witness Sterrett, concerning the effect of the smelter fumes at his farm. The record shows that his farm is about one mile from the smelter, while that of respondents is near twice that distance by the direct course. The first objection to the questions asked this witness was when he was asked to tell the jury to what extent his strawberry crop was affected by the smelter fumes. The objection was made on the ground that the witness' farm is nearer the smelter than that of respondents, and that the condition of the gases at the two places was not the same. Objection was also made to other questions upon the same ground. This witness, in the course of his testimony, showed much familiarity with respondents' farm. He also testified that the trees at respondents' place were not quite as dead as those immediately around Northport and the smelter, but that they showed all indications of being killed. In practical effect the answer was that results were the same in the two localities, as was true of the answer of the other witness heretofore discussed. The location of this witness' place was between the two points and, if his statement—that the extreme points were simi-

larly affected—was true, then it would seem to follow that
his own place, occupying a position between the two, must
have been affected in like manner. The force of the witness' testimony was to the effect that what was true of
conditions at his own place was also true at respondents'
place. As we intimated in the case of the other witness,
while this indirect method of inquiring about effects at
respondents' farm may not have been the most acceptable
one, yet, in view of his whole testimony, we do not believe
appellant's case was prejudiced thereby, so as to call for
a reversal upon that ground alone.

Another assignment of error relates to the following,
which appears in the record:

"Q. Now, have you ever noticed the sidewalks in Northport after a rain, when they were smelting ores there? A.
I have. Q. I will ask you to state what, if anything, you
have seen on the sidewalks. Mr. Voorhees: I object.
These sidewalks are not on Rowe's place and Rowe's place
is virtually two miles away from Northport. Objection
overruled. Exception. A. I have noticed it on the sidewalks, the buildings, and in my yard and garden, and have
noticed it in the water barrels by the house, and have seen
considerable of it at various times. Q. What is that? A.
I don't know, but suppose it is sulphur. It is a yellow
substance."

Standing alone there would appear to be no pertinence
in merely showing the presence of sulphur upon the sidewalks and buildings in Northport, but one of the respondents had testified, that a precipitate lodged upon the roof
of the house at respondents' farm; that the same also
formed a scum on the water during the process of irrigation; that it was sulphur, and that it stopped the growth
of vegetation. In view of that testimony, and the claim
that the sulphur at the farm came from the smelter, we
think the testimony criticized under this assignment of
error was competent to show that the smelter did release

sulphur, and tended to corroborate the said testimony of Mr. Rowe, one of the respondents.

A number of other distinctly assigned errors may be grouped and discussed together as involving one general principle. While the witness Terwilliger, called by appellant as an expert, was upon the stand, counsel for respondents indulged in certain experiments before the jury with what was said by counsel to be sulphuric acid. One of the counsel handed the witness a bottle containing some substance, and asked him if he could detect sulphuric acid by smell. The witness replied, "It does not look like sulphuric acid to me," giving as a reason that it was not a proper color, and he afterwards stated that it was not sulphuric acid—at least, not chemically pure. Counsel dipped a wooden stick into the substance and said, "I will show you this stick. Explain to the jury, as that stick turns black in their presence, just the chemical action that goes on on that wood." The record then shows the following:

"Mr. Voorhees: We object. We do not know what this is in this bottle. Mr. Robertson: I will prove it. Objection overruled. Exception. We except on the ground that there has been no proof whatever as to what this is; just a mere statement of counsel."

Afterwards, over objection, the blackened stick was admitted in evidence. No proof was made as to what was the substance contained in the bottle. Appellant's counsel objected as follows:

"Mr. Voorhees: I object. I make the point that this witness has testified that sulphuric acid in this form—if this is sulphuric acid—is not the same, and will not have the same effect, which is made by the combination of SO_2 with the air and the water. There is affirmative evidence to that effect. Consequently the conditions are not the same. Consequently this piece of wood is not evidence.

This offer is incompetent, irrelevant and immaterial. Objection is overruled. Exception."
Thereafter counsel asked the witness what effect sulphuric acid has on leaves, and at the same time handed him a pine branch, after having poured thereon something from a bottle. Objection was again made that there was no proof that the substance in the bottle was the same as that thrown off from the roasting heaps of ore at the smelter. Again, counsel asked the witness the effect of sulphuric acid on cloth, and at the same time poured some substance from a bottle upon a piece of cloth. Objection was again made, but it was overruled.

We think the court erred in permitting the experimentation in the manner in which it was conducted. In the first place, it was not established that the substance in the bottle was sulphuric acid; and, in the next place, assuming that it was, the effect of the ocular demonstration before the jury may have been to so impress them that they were led to conclude that the acid thrown off from the roasting heaps, after traveling about two miles and becoming dilute by its contact with air, was as powerful and deadly in its effect as the substance before them appeared to be, when poured immediately from the hitherto closed bottle upon the stick, branch, and napkin. The court permitted the continuation of the experiments before the jury, notwithstanding the witness declared, concerning the contents of the bottle, "We have nothing like that at the smelter." There being no proof to show that the elements which combined to produce the experimental results before the jury were the same as those combined at respondents' farm, we think the court erred, and that appellant's rights were thereby prejudiced before the jury.

There must, at least, be identity of conditions before an experiment, or evidence of an experiment, can be sub-

mitted to a jury, as tending to prove the issue before them.
Klanowski v. Grand Trunk R. Co., 64 Mich. 279, 31
N. W. 275; *Newbold v. Mead,* 57 Pa. St. 487. It has
been held that the practical difficulty of bringing about
experimental conditions, in all respects identical with those
immediately before the jury, has the effect to render such
testimony more or less unreliable; that such experiments,
their results, and the inferences drawn from them by witnesses, are matters collateral to the issue before the jury,
and that many collateral issues are liable to arise when
an attempt is made to prove identity of conditions. *Libby
v. Scherman,* 146 Ill. 540, 34 N. E. 801, 37 Am. St.
191; *Chicago etc. R. Co. v. Champion,* 9 Ind. App. 510,
36 N. E. 221, 53 Am. St. 357; *Wise v. Ackerman,* 76
Md. 375, 25 Atl. 424. However, when substantial or
reasonable similarity of conditions has been made to appear, it has been frequently held that evidence of experiments is admissible. 12 Am. & Eng. Enc. Law (2d. ed.),
408, and cases cited. We therefore desire that we shall
not be understood as holding that evidence of experiments
may never be valuable or proper; but, rather, that in any
event such a similarity of conditions must be made to appear as will insure a reasonably just and accurate comparison.

Other errors are assigned upon the court's instructions,
and upon the refusal to instruct as requested by appellant. We believe no prejudicial error is shown under the
several assignments concerning the instructions, except in
one particular. The court instructed that respondents
could recover for such damages as had been caused by appellant within the period of two years next before the
commencement of the action, and then specifically limited
the time to two years next before December 22, 1902.
Counsel for both parties, during the entire examination

of witnesses, treated the action as having been commenced in August, 1902. All the testimony was confined to a period prior to that time, and no evidence was introduced relating to the period between August and December, 1902. The complaint was not filed until December 22, 1902, but it is conceded all through the case, that the summons was served in August of that year. Under § 4869, Bal. Code, the action was commenced when the summons was served, and it is, therefore, manifest that the time limit stated by the court in its instructions was incorrect, and included a period of about four months after the commencement of the action, covering which there was no evidence before the jury. Respondents, however, contend that appellant should not now be permitted to raise this question, because of what appears in the record. Just before the instructions to the jury the following appears:

"The evidence being concluded and the respective counsel for the plaintiffs and defendant having concluded their arguments to the jury, and the court being about to instruct the jury and to define the issues in the case to the jury, stated that, in instructing the jury he would treat the 22d day of December, 1902, the date of filing of the complaint, as the date of the commencement of the action; and that no objection was at that time interposed by counsel on either side."

Respondents urge that, as appellant did not at that time object, it should not be heard to do so now. From anything which appears in the record, the court unqualifiedly announced that it would instruct the jury that the action was commenced on the date the complaint was filed. An exception to an erroneous instruction could not have been taken until it had been given to the jury. Moreover, appellant timely excepted to the instruction, after the retirement of the jury and before a verdict was returned, but the error was not corrected by the court. Appellant, hav-

ing thus given an opportunity for the correction of the
instruction, did not waive the point, and, since the error
was not corrected, it remained before the jury. What
effect the instruction may have had upon the amount of
the verdict it is, of course, impossible to determine.

The foregoing reviews the principal points urged, and
we believe it is unnecessary to further extend the discussion. For the reasons assigned, the judgment is reversed
and the cause remanded with instructions to the trial court
to grant a new trial.

FULLERTON, C. J., and MOUNT and ANDERS, JJ., concur.

DUNBAR, J. (concurring).—I concur in the majority
opinion on the ground stated—that it was not established
that the substance in the bottle was sulphuric acid. Of
course, it would be error to permit the introduction of
evidence showing the effect of acid different from that
which was thrown off from the roasting heaps at the
smelter. But I do not agree with the statement that, assuming that the acid tested was the same as that which
was thrown from the roasting heaps, error was committed
by introducing evidence of its effect upon vegetation, for
the reason that the conditions were not the same. Of
necessity the conditions would be different after the transmission of the acid through the air for two miles to the
farm of the respondents, and it seems to me that, if the
rule announced were adopted, it would prevent the respondents from proving that the effects on the vegetation
at their place were brought about through the agency of
the acid emanating from the smelter works. If plaintiffs
had proved the condition of the vegetation and the finding thereon of a deposit, and it was shown by the defense that the acid which was found upon the vegetation

was harmless, and such proof, if true, would have been admissible by experiments offered by the defendant showing that the acid, before it was diluted by the air, would not have a deleterious effect upon vegetation, plaintiffs' case would fail. So that, it seems to me, it was competent to show primarily the effect of sulphuric acid on vegetation; and the diluting effect of the air, in the transmission of the acid for two miles or more, would be a subject for explanation on cross-examination or otherwise, and a deduction which must necessarily be made by the jury in consideration of all the facts proven, viz., the difference in the conditions, the distance traveled, the effect of the air on the acid, and any other circumstance which was pertinent and explanatory.

[No. 4934.   Decided April 26, 1904.]

ALMA K. LAMONA et al., Respondents, v. ODESSA STATE BANK et al., Appellants.[1]

APPEAL—DISMISSAL—COSTS. An appeal involving only a question of costs will be dismissed on motion.

Appeal from a judgment of the superior court for Lincoln county, Neal, J., entered October 3, 1903, in favor of defendants for costs, upon plaintiffs' voluntary dismissal of the action. Appeal dismissed.

Myers & Warren, for appellants.

Merritt & Merritt, for respondents.

PER CURIAM.—Respondents brought this action in the superior court of Lincoln county, against appellants and others, to recover $725, alleged to be due upon a promis-

[1]Reported in 76 Pac. 534.

sory note. Appellants filed a demurrer to the complaint, which demurrer was sustained by the court. Respondents thereupon voluntarily dismissed the action. Appellants filed a cost bill, claiming $10 as the statutory attorney's fee to be taxed as costs. Respondents filed a motion to retax this item of costs. The trial court sustained the motion, and retaxed this item of costs at $5. This appeal is prosecuted from that order.

Respondents move to dismiss the appeal. We think the motion should be granted. We have several times held that the mere question of costs in a cause cannot be litigated here. *State ex rel. Scottish-Am. etc. Co. v. Meacham,* 17 Wash. 429, 50 Pac. 52; *State ex rel. Land v. Christopher,* 32 Wash. 59, 72 Pac. 709. It is true that, in *Bringgold v. Spokane,* 19 Wash. 333, 53 Pac. 368, the question of costs was the only question considered, but there appears to have been no motion to dismiss that case.

The cause will be dismissed.

[No. 4991.   Decided April 26, 1904.]

HIRAM L. POST, *Appellant,* v. CITY OF SPOKANE, *Respondent.*[1]

APPEAL — FINAL ORDERS — VACATION OF JUDGMENT FOR FRAUD. An order vacating a judgment and granting a new trial, for fraud, made upon petition under Bal. Code, § 5153, must be treated as a proceeding in the original cause, and is not appealable, since it is not a final order and is reviewable on appeal from the final judgment in the case.

Appeal from an order of the superior court for Spokane county, Kennan, J., entered June 6, 1903, vacating a judgment recovered by the plaintiff, after a hearing on

[1]Reported in 76 Pac. 510.

the merits of defendant's petition to vacate the judgment for fraud in procuring it. Appeal dismissed.

Norman Buck, Alfred M. Craven, Sullivan, Nuzum & Nuzum, and *Barnes & Latimer,* for appellant.

John P. Judson and *A. H. Kenyon,* for respondent.

PER CURIAM.—In November, 1901, Hiram L. Post recovered a judgment in the superior court of Spokane county against the city of Spokane. The city appealed from that judgment to this court. The appeal was dismissed and the judgment affirmed. Thereafter the said city applied to this court for permission to file a petition in the lower court to vacate the judgment, on the ground that the same was obtained through fraud. Permission to file this petition was granted by this court as prayed for. *Post v. Spokane,* 28 Wash. 701, 69 Pac. 371, 1104. Thereupon a petition was filed in the superior court of Spokane county, setting up the facts in relation to the fraud, and praying that said judgment be set aside and a new trial granted, under the provisions of § 5153, *et seq.,* Bal. Code. The petition came on regularly for hearing, evidence was taken on behalf of both parties to the litigation, and the court sustained the petition, vacated the judgment, and ordered a new trial of the original case. Mr. Post has appealed from the order vacating the judgment. The city of Spokane now moves to dismiss the appeal, upon the ground that the order appealed from is not an appealable order.

This same question was presented in *State ex rel. Post v. Superior Court,* 31 Wash. 53, 71 Pac. 740, which was an application by the appellant for a writ of prohibition in this case, and we there held, in substance, that these proceedings must be treated as within the original cause, and that appellant's remedy for errors is by appeal from the final judgment which may be rendered in the original cause. We there said:

"The reason for the holding of this court that an appeal does not lie from an order vacating a judgment is that such order may be reviewed on appeal from the final judgment, and thus avoid the probable necessity of more than one appeal in the same action. The rule is based upon the theory that all the proceedings are in the same action."

Under the rule there announced the motion must be granted and the appeal dismissed.

[No. 5121.   Decided April 26, 1904.]

THE STATE OF WASHINGTON, *on the Relation of M. G. Royal, as Guardian etc., Plaintiff,* v. O. V. LINN, *Judge of the Superior Court of Thurston County, Defendant.*

APPEAL—STATEMENT OF FACTS—CERTIFYING AS PROPOSED—WITHDRAWAL FOR PURPOSE OF AMENDMENT. After a proposed statement of facts has been filed, and no amendments proposed, the same should be certified as proposed, and the superior court has no power to permit the same to be withdrawn, on motion of the party proposing the same, for the purpose of amending, refiling, and serving the same, although the time for filing and proposing a statement has not expired.

Application filed in the supreme court April 18, 1904, for a writ of prohibition to prevent the superior court of Thurston county, Linn, J., from permitting the withdrawal and amendment of a proposed statement of facts. Writ granted.

Troy & Falknor, for relator.
Israel & Mackay, for defendant.

[1] Reported in 76 Pac. 513.

PER CURIAM.—This is an original application in this court for a writ of prohibition, directed to the superior court of Thurston county, and to the Hon. O. V. Linn, judge thereof. The conceded facts are substantially as follows: In a certain cause pending in said court, the relator herein procured a judgment against the Northern Pacific Railway Company. The latter filed and served a proposed statement of facts. Ten days expired, and no amendments were offered by the relator, and thereupon the court certified the proposed statement; but there was included in it as certified a page of purported exceptions concerning the court's instructions, which was not included in the proposed statement as originally filed and served. Thereafter this relator moved the court to strike said page from the statement of facts, for the reason that the contents thereof were never made part of the record, and no copy was ever served upon the relator as a part of the proposed statement. The motion also asked the court to correct its certificate to the statement of facts, so as to show the truth with regard to said page, and that it was incorporated in the statement without notice to the relator. The facts stated in relator's said motion, and in affidavits supporting the same, were not controverted, but the aforesaid defendant in that action thereupon moved the court for permission to withdraw, and strike from the files, the said statement, for the purpose of amending, refiling, and serving the same, with a view to its settlement as amended. The defendant was about to grant the latter motion, when the application herein was made for a writ from this court to prevent such threatened action. An alternative writ was issued and, upon the return thereto, a hearing was had.

Defendant urges that, by reason of the order extending the time for filing a statement of facts in said cause, the time has not yet expired; that the statement now on file may be withdrawn, and a new proposed statement filed within the time limit. We think not, within the statute and the former rulings of this court. Section 5058, Bal. Code, provides that, when a proposed statement of facts has been filed and served, if no proposed amendments thereto shall be served within ten days, the statement as proposed "shall be deemed agreed to," and shall be certified by the judge. In *State ex rel. Hersner v. Arthur*, 7 Wash. 358, 35 Pac. 120, this court held that in such case the trial judge has no duty of investigation imposed upon him, and shall certify the statement as proposed. The above case was followed, and the same rule adhered to, in *State ex rel. Fetterley v. Griffin*, 32 Wash. 67, 72 Pac. 1030. By the filing and service of a proposed statement, the proposing party thereby waives any further time included within the statutory or extended limit. In the absence of some fraud in the premises, he must be presumed in law to know what the proposed statement contains, and to intend that its contents shall be what they are. When, therefore, he has proposed a statement which is unobjectionable to his adversary, the law provides that, after ten days, the court shall certify it as if it were an agreed statement in the case. We therefore think the respondent should deny the motion for leave to withdraw and refile the proposed statement in amended form, and also that the original statement as proposed should be certified.

The writ should issue accordingly.

[No. 4990.   Decided April 30, 1904.]

R. M. HESTER, *Appellant,* v. R. H. THOMSON *et al.,*
Respondents.[1]

MANDAMUS—WHEN LIES—ISSUANCE OF BUILDING PERMIT—DIS-
CRETIONARY POWERS OF BUILDING INSPECTOR—APPEAL TO BOARD OF
PUBLIC WORKS—DECISION BY QUASI JUDICIAL BODY—NO WRIT TO
COMPEL CHANGE OF JUDGMENT. Where a building inspector must
hear protests against the issuance of building permits, and refer
reasonable objections to the board of public works, and his decisions are binding until reversed, and an appeal may be taken
therefrom to said board, which hears the matter upon evidence
taken, mandamus will not lie to compel such officers to issue a
building permit for a livery stable, after objections and a hearing
duly had before said board, upon which the board refused the
permit, since the inspector and board exercise discretion, and
have determined the matter in a judicial capacity, and mandamus
does not lie to compel a change of judgment.

SAME — ACTION BY BOARD — CONSTRUCTION OF ORDINANCE. In
such a case it cannot be claimed that the board has not acted,
under an ordinance suspending proceedings until the matter is
"adjusted" by the board, since that signifies simply a determination by the board.

SAME—MOTION TO QUASH WRIT—DEMURRER—CONCLUSIONS NOT
ADMITTED. A motion to quash a writ of mandamus for want of
sufficient facts performs the office of a demurrer, and only admits
the facts stated, and not the conclusions drawn therefrom; and
a conclusion that defendants acted capriciously and arbitrarily is
unavailing in the absence of facts in the petition showing such
action.

Appeal from a judgment of the superior court for King
county, Albertson, J., entered September 8, 1903, dismissing the action, upon sustaining a demurrer to the
petition. Affirmed.

Wakefield & Petrovitsky and *Ballinger, Ronald & Battle,* for appellant, contended, *inter alia,* that the mere

[1]Reported in 76 Pac. 734.

declaration of a local municipal board cannot preclude a judicial investigation or restrict the absolute dominion of an owner over his property. 1 Dillon, Mun. Corp. §§308-374; *Bostock v. Sams,* 95 Md. 400, 52 Atl. 665, 1130, 59 L. R. A. 282; *Yates v. Milwaukee,* 10 Wall. 505; *State v. Mott,* 61 Md. 297, 48 Am. Rep. 105; *Yick Wo v. Hopkins,* 118 U. S. 356, 6 Sup. Ct. 1064, 30 L. Ed. 220; *Baltimore v. Radecke,* 49 Md. 217, 33 Am. Rep. 239; *State v. Tenant,* 110 N. C. 609, 14 S. E. 387, 28 Am. St. 715, 15 L. R. A. 423; *Newton v. Belger,* 143 Mass. 598, 10 N. E. 464; *Richmond v. Dudley,* 129 Ind. 112, 28 N. E. 312, 28 Am. St. 180, 13 L. R. A. 587; *May v. People,* 1 Colo. App. 157, 27 Pac. 1010; *Anderson v. Wellington,* 40 Kan. 173, 19 Pac. 719; *Sioux Falls v. Kirby,* 6 S. Dak. 62, 60 N. W. 156, 25 L. R. A. 621. The ordinance is void since it restricts the owner's right of dominion, not according to any general or uniform rule, but subject to the arbitrary will of the authorities. *State v. Hunter,* 106 N. C. 796, 11 S. E. 366, 8 L. R. A. 529; *Bills v. Goshen,* 117 Ind. 221, 20 N. E. 115, 3 L. R. A. 261; *State v. Wcbber,* 107 N. C. 962, 12 S. E. 598; 22 Am. St. 920; *Tugman v. Chicago,* 78 Ill. 405; Horr & B., Mun. Ord., §13; and cases *supra.* A livery stable is not a nuisance *per se,* and a court of equity cannot restrain the building or use of one. *Kirkman v. Handy,* 11 Humph. (Tenn.) 406, 54 Am. Dec. 45; *Shiras v. Olinger,* 50 Iowa 571, 32 Am. Rep. 138. That a trade is disagreeable and lessens the value of adjacent property is not sufficient ground to prohibit it, when it is not a nuisance. Addison, Torts (Wood's ed.), §219; *Huckenstine's Appeal,* 70 Pa. St. 102, 10 Am. Rep. 669; *St. Helen's Co. v. Tipping,* 11 H. L. C. 642, 11 Eng. Rep. Reprint 1483; *Ross v. Butler,* 19 N. J. Eq. 294, 97 Am. Dec. 654. Mandamus lies

if there has been in fact no actual and bona fide exercise
of judgment and discretion. 19 Am. & Eng. Enc. Law
(2d ed.), 739; .Wood v. Strother, 76 Cal. 545, 18 Pac.
766, 9 Am. St. 249; State v. Barnes, 25 Fla. 298, 23
Am. St. 516; Hull v. Supervisors, 19 Johnson 259, 10
Am. Dec. 223. Also if the discretion is exercised in
an arbitrary or capricious manner. 19 Am. & Eng.
Enc. Law (2d ed.), 737; 13 Enc. Plead. & Prac., 527;
Moody v. Fleming, 4 Ga. 115, 48 Am. Dec. 210.

M. Gilliam and John B. Hartman, for respondents.

HADLEY, J.—Appellant brought this action against respondents, and seeks a writ of mandate to compel respondents to adjust the matter of appellant's application
for a permit to erect a livery and feed stable, and to
issue a permit to erect such building upon certain property described as follows: Lots 1 and 4, in block 36,
of C. D. Boren's addition to the city of Seattle.   An
alternative writ of mandate was issued, and the respondents thereupon moved to quash the writ, for the reason that the petition does not state facts sufficient to
constitute a cause of action.   The motion was granted,
and, the appellant having elected to stand upon his petition, declining to plead further, judgment was entered
dismissing the action.   This appeal is from that judgment of the superior court.

By the petition for the writ of mandate the following
facts are made to appear: Section 478 of the Revised
Ordinances of the city of Seattle is as follows:

"No building, any part of which is within the limits
or within forty feet of the property of any adjoining
owner, shall be erected for or converted to use as a
stable, unless such use is authorized by the board of
public health, after public hearing is had, after written
notice to the adjoining owners, and after public notice,

published at least three times, and at least ten days before the hearing, in the city official paper."

The petition alleges a compliance with the above ordinance provision, and that, after a regular public hearing before the board of public health, that body granted the petitioner authority to erect the stable on the premises described. Section 446 of the Revised Ordinances of the city is as follows:

"When any person or corporation desires to erect, alter, repair, raise, lower or remove any structure within the corporate limits of the city of Seattle, before beginning any work on same, such person or corporation shall make formal application to the inspector of buildings for a permit to do the work, restoration of plastering or painting excepted. Such application must be filed at least two full days before a permit is issued, for first or second class buildings or other buildings in the fire limits, if required by the inspector."

It is alleged that, in pursuance of the above section, the petitioner filed his application with the inspector of buildings, together with the evidence of authority granted by the board of public health, as aforesaid, and also blue print copies of the drawings, and typewritten specifications of the proposed building, as by ordinance required; but that said officer refused to grant the permit. Section 451 of the Revised Ordinances is as follows:

"In case objections are filed against any structure to be erected, the same shall be referred to the board of public works, and the permit for doing the work shall not be issued, or if the same has been theretofore issued, shall be considered as of no effect until the matter is adjusted by said board."

The petition further shows that the inspector of buildings refused to grant the permit for the reason that objections thereto had been filed, and that he referred the matter to the board of public works, under the terms of the last quoted section. It is alleged that thereafter a hearing was had before the board of public works, and that, at said hearing, no objections were made that the plans and specifications of the proposed building do not comply with the building ordinances of the city; but that certain objections were filed and urged against the erection of a livery stable upon the premises described. It is further averred that the board of public works failed and refused to adjust the matter of said permit, as required by §451, *supra,* and that they have wrongfully, capriciously, and arbitrarily refused to grant the permit. The foregoing is a substantial statement of the essential facts appearing from the petition for the writ of mandate.

It is assigned that the court erred in holding that the petition does not state facts sufficient to constitute a cause of action, and also in holding that the acts of respondents, of which complaint is made, were discretionary. Appellant argues that, when an owner's absolute dominion over his property is restricted by ordinance, it should not be left to the arbitrary will of the governing authorities; that whether a certain use of property is a nuisance or not is a question which the owner has a right to have determined by judicial authority, and that the mere declaration of a local municipal board cannot preclude a judicial investigation as to the alleged nuisance. Many authorities are cited as supporting the above argument, but we do not deem it necessary to enlarge upon the points suggested therein, in view of the facts shown by the petition in this case, considered with reference to the ordinance provisions of the city of Seattle.

If it appeared that the city had attempted to leave the determination of the matters involved here to the arbitrary will of the governing authorities, then we should probably be called upon to determine the constitutionality of such a course. We, however, do not find that the city has so attempted. We have seen that, by § 446, *supra,* applications of this character must be made to the inspector of buildings, and §449 of the Revised Ordinances provides, among other things relating to the duties of the inspector, that, ". . . if there is no reasonable objection to the work from the owner of adjoining property, a permit shall be granted, . . ." It is thus apparent that discretion is lodged with the inspector of buildings, and he shall determine whether the protest of adjoining property holders amounts to a "reasonable objection." If he shall decide that it is such, then, under § 451, *supra,* he shall refer the matter to the board of public works.

Section 452 also provides for an appeal from any decision or order of the inspector of buildings to the board of public works, and the latter shall hear the matter, receiving testimony for that purpose. It is also provided that the decision of the inspector shall be valid and binding until reversed by the board. Manifestly, therefore, the inspector must act with discretion, and in a quasi judicial capacity. Otherwise he would not be left to determine what may be reasonable objections, and there would be no appeal from his decisions. It is also clear that the board of public works must exercise like discretion, and act in .a similar capacity, basing their action upon evidence which they shall receive and hear. The duties of these officers in the premises are not, therefore, purely ministerial, since they involve discretion and are judicial in their nature. In such a case mandamus does not lie for the purpose of reviewing a decision, and compelling a change of judgment. If such an officer

or board should refuse to act at all, then mandamus would
lie to compel action.

"Where the duty to be performed is judicial or involves
the exercise of discretion upon the part of the tribunal
or officer, mandamus will lie to compel such tribunal to
take some action in the premises and exercise its judgment or discretion. But the function of the writ is merely
to set in motion. It will not direct how the duty shall
be performed or the discretion exercised. To do so would
be to substitute the judgment and discretion of the court
issuing the mandamus for that of the court or officer
to whom it was committed by law. No particular act
can be commanded, and if the discretion is to act or
not to act at all, mandamus will not lie. After the tribunal or officer has exercised the judgment or discretion
vested in him, and has acted, mandamus will not lie for
the purpose of reviewing the decision and compelling
a change of judgment or any further action in the premises. The writ cannot be used for the correction of errors."
19 Am. & Eng. Enc. Law, p. 732, *et seq.*

The citation of authorities in support of the above quoted
text covers pages of said volume, and we believe it is
unnecessary to refer to authority with more particularity.
The respondents in this proceeding have *acted*. They
heard and considered the application for the permit, and
denied it. Appellant urges that the petition shows that
respondents have not *acted* within the scope of § 451,
supra, which provides that,' in case of objection, the action
of the inspector shall be considered as of no effect until
the matter is "adjusted by said board." It is urged
that the board had not "adjusted" the matter. The context, we think, signifies simply that proceedings under
the inspector's decision shall be suspended until the board
shall *determine* the matter. The board has determined
this matter, and, having acted within their discretionary
duties, mandamus does not lie.

It has been held that, when discretion has been exercised in an arbitrary or capricious manner, mandamus will lie to compel a proper exercise thereof. Appellant, in his petition for the writ of mandate, avers the conclusion that respondents have acted capriciously and arbitrarily, and that, in denying the application for a permit, they "acted under personal prejudice and caprice, as is clearly shown by the aforementioned ordinances of the city of Seattle," etc., further referring, also, to exhibits attached to the petition, including the findings of the board, as facts to sustain the conclusion so averred. We do not think any facts are made to appear by the petition which show that respondents acted in such a manner. Mandamus therefore will not lie upon that ground.

We need not discuss the question of appellant's further remedy, if he has any. It would be ineffective, if we should undertake to pass upon that subject here, since it is not involved in this case. The city ordinances do not appear to provide for any appeal from the decision of the board of public works. But whether, under § 5741, Bal. Code, resort may be had to the writ of review for the purpose of reviewing discretionary or quasi judicial acts of said board, we in no sense now intimate or decide. The only question that can be effectively decided here is, whether the remedy by mandamus is the proper one in the premises, and, for the reasons heretofore stated, we think it is not.

It is assigned as error that the court sustained the motion to quash the alternative writ of mandate, and entered judgment of dismissal. It is stated in the brief that the motion to quash performs the office of a general demurrer, and that the demurrer admits the truth of all allegations in the pleading to which it is directed. We have, in our foregoing discussion, treated the motion as effecting the same purpose as a general demurrer. With that view, it admits the facts alleged, but not the conclusions drawn therefrom. We think the facts stated are insufficient to warrant the writ of mandamus. The record shows that, after the motion to quash the writ was sustained, the appellant elected to stand upon his amended petition, and declined to plead further. The court then entered judgment of dismissal. Such judgment followed in logical order.

We find no error, and the judgment is affirmed.

FULLERTON, C. J., and ANDERS, MOUNT, and DUNBAR, JJ., concur.

[No. 4993.   Decided May 2, 1904.]

THE STATE OF WASHINGTON, *Respondent*, v. FRANK FAIR, *et al., Appellants.*[1]

STATUTES — ENACTMENT — LEGISLATURE — EXTRA SESSION — RESTRICTING LEGISLATIVE ACTION—CRIMINAL LAW—VALIDITY OF SAVING CLAUSE FOR PENDING PROSECUTIONS. Const., art. 3, § 7, authorizing the governor to call an extra session of the legislature for a particular purpose, which shall be stated in the call, does not restrict legislative action at such session to that purpose, nor has the governor power to do so, hence the legislature had power to enact Laws Ex. Sess. 1901, p. 13, saving pending criminal prosecutions in cases of repeal, at the extra session called for the purpose of amending the law relating to capital punishment.

CRIMINAL LAW — ROBBERY — INFORMATION — VARIANCE — OWNERSHIP OF PROPERTY TAKEN. Under an information for robbery charging that the money taken was the property of M, there is no variance by proof that it belonged to a partnership of which M was a member, and that it was in his immediate and exclusive control, since Bal. Code, § 6944, so providing as to property stolen or fraudulently received, is applicable to robbery although robbery is not specifically mentioned.

[1]Reported in 76 Pac. 731.

CRIMINAL LAW—EVIDENCE OF ALIBI—SUFFICIENCY. There is sufficient evidence to justify a conviction of robbery, where the defendant's evidence as to an alibi was contradicted by two witnesses who identified the defendant.

TRIAL—VERDICT—CONFLICTING EVIDENCE. The verdict of the jury will not be disturbed upon conflicting evidence where there is testimony which, if true, is sufficient to justify it, and the trial court passed upon its sufficiency in refusing a new trial.

APPEAL—PARTIES—WITNESSES NOT ENTITLED TO APPEAL—DISALLOWANCE OF COSTS. Witnesses for the defendant in a criminal case, whose fees were disallowed by the lower court, are not parties to the action, and cannot appeal from the order of the court disallowing their fees.

Appeal from a judgment of the superior court for Spokane county, Kennan, J., entered August 29, 1903, upon a trial and conviction of the crime of robbery. Affirmed.

Robertson, Miller & Rosenhaupt, for appellants.

Horace Kimball and *R. M. Barnhart,* for respondent.

ANDERS, J.—On and prior to the night of Saturday, April 4, 1903, Robert G. Miller and his brother, under the firm name of Miller Bros., were conducting a meat market on East Sprague avenue, in the city of Spokane. About nine o'clock on the evening of that date, and while Robert G. Miller and Charles Johnson, the driver of the market wagon, were preparing to close the market for the night, three masked men, with pistols in their hands, suddenly entered the room, "held up" Miller and Johnson, and took from the cash register—which was on the corner of the counter—and carried away, $70 belonging to said Robert G. Miller and his brother. At the time of the robbery, the market and its contents, including the cash register and the money therein, were in the care and possession of said Robert G. Miller.

Some time in June following, Frank Fair and Sam Eder were arrested and identified as being two of the persons who committed the offense. The third and unknown man, the one who rifled the cash register, has never been apprehended or discovered. Subsequently to the arrest of Fair and Eder, the prosecuting attorney filed an information against them in the superior court for Spokane county, the charging part of which is as follows:

"That the said defendants, Frank Fair and Sam Eder, on the 4th day of April, 1903, in the county of Spokane, and state of Washington, then and there being, did then and there wilfully, unlawfully, feloniously, and forcibly take from the immediate presence of Robert G. Miller, and against his will, a certain article of value, to wit, seventy dollars in money of the value of seventy dollars, the property of and belonging to Robert G. Miller, by then and there wilfully, unlawfully, and feloniously pointing at said Robert G. Miller a loaded revolver thereby putting said Robert G. Miller in fear."

At his own request the defendant Fair was tried separately, and at the trial he set up an alibi, viz., that at the time of the robbery he was at the town of Prosser, Washington, which, according to the evidence, is about 186 miles distant from the city of Spokane. To establish this defense the defendant testified, and produced several witnesses who also testified, that he was at Prosser at the time the robbery with which he was charged was committed. The jury, however, found the defendant guilty as charged, and the court, after denying a motion in arrest of judgment, and also a motion for a new trial, sentenced the defendant to imprisonment in the penitentiary for the term of fifteen years. To reverse this judgment and sentence, the defendant has appealed.

Section 829 of the Code of Washington, commonly known as the Code of 1881 (§ 7103, Bal. Code), defined the crime of robbery, and provided that every person convicted of that offense should be punished by imprison-

ment in the penitentiary not less than one nor more than
twenty years. This section of the statute was amended
by an act of the legislature, approved February 5, 1903,
which changed the minimum imprisonment for the offense
from one to five years. Laws 1903, p. 5. This amenda-
tory statute, not carrying an emergency clause, did not
take effect until after the commission of the crime with
which appellant is charged. Neither did it contain a saving clause as to pending prosecutions, or as to offenses
committed under the old statute. In 1901, however, the
legslature, at an extraordinary session, passed a general
act saving prosecutions in cases of the repeal or amendment of criminal statutes. Laws, Ex. Sess. 1901, p. 13.

The trial of the appellant occurred on July 17, 1903,
which was after the amending statute of the 5th of
February became effective. And it is contended by the
learned counsel for appellant that, at the time of the trial,
there was no law in existence defining the crime of robbery, or prescribing the punishment therefor, and that
the trial court erred in holding the contrary. This contention is based upon the notion that the general act above
mentioned, of June 13, 1901, is invalid for the reason
that the legislature had not the power to pass it at that
extraordinary session. Section 7 of art. 3 of the state
constitution, relating to the powers of the governor, provides as follows:

"He may, on extraordinary occasions, convene the legislature by proclamation, in which shall be stated the purposes for which the legislature is convened."

By virtue of the power thus vested in him by the constitution, Governor Rogers convened the legislature in extraordinary session on June 11, 1901, and the purpose for
which it was so convened was stated in his proclamation
as follows:

"The purpose for which the legislature is called together is that it may pass upon, confirm or amend the law relating to capital punishment."

It was the exclusive province of the governor, under the constitution, to determine whether an occasion existed of sufficient gravity to require an extra session of the legislature, and his conclusion in that regard is not subject to review by the courts. *Farrelly v. Cole,* 60 Kan. 356, 56 Pac. 492, 44 L. R. A. 464. That such is the law is not disputed by counsel for appellant, but they do earnestly insist that the legislature, at its extra session, had no right to legislate upon any subject not mentioned in the governor's proclamation. And, if this position is well taken, it necessarily follows that the general saving statute above mentioned is void, and constituted no authority whatever for the prosecution and punishment of appellant. The solution of this question depends upon the effect of the constitution on the power of the legislature at its extra session.

It seems to be assumed, on behalf of the appellant, that the provision of the constitution above quoted restricted legislative action to matters specifically designated by the governor in his proclamation, and the following authorities are cited in support of this proposition: Sutherland, Stat. Constr., § 26; *Davidson v. Moorman,* 2 Heisk. 575; *Jones v. Theall,* 3 Nev. 233; *Wells v. Missouri Pac. R. Co.,* 110 Mo. 286, 19 S. W. 530; *In re Governor's Proclamation,* 19 Colo. 333, 35 Pac. 530. It is true, it was held in each of those cases that the particular statute or act in question was void because the legislature was inhibited by the express terms of the constitution from passing it. For instance, the constitutional provision involved in the Nevada case was the following:

"The governor may, on extraordinary occasions, convene the legislature by proclamation, and shall state to both houses, when organized, the purpose for which they have been convened, and the legislature shall transact no legislative business except that for which they were specially convened, or such other legislative business as the governor may call to the attention of the legislature while in session."

The decisions in the other cases cited were based upon constitutional provisions substantially like that of Nevada, and their soundness can hardly be doubted. The rule announced by them, as to the power of the legislature when assembled in extraordinary session, is tersely and correctly stated by Sutherland in his work on Statutory Construction at § 26 (cited by appellant), as follows:

"When convened in extra session and limited by the constitution to business for which the session was specially called, all acts passed relating to other subjects will be void."

But, inasmuch as our constitution does not restrict the legislature, at its extra sessions, to the consideration of the particular business for which it was convened, or to such other matters as may be called to its attention, while in session, by the governor, it would seem that the authorities relied on by appellant are not applicable to the case at bar. All legislative power is declared by the state constitution to be vested in a senate and house of representatives, or, in other words, in "the legislature of the state of Washington." Const., art. 2, § 1. But such powers are not specially defined by the constitution, nor are they, strictly speaking, granted by that instrument.

"The people in framing the constitution committed to the legislature the whole law-making power of the state, which they did not expressly or impliedly withhold. Plenary power in the legislature, for all purposes of civil government, is the rule. A prohibition to exercise a particular power is an exception. In inquiring, therefore, whether a given statute is constitutional, it is for those who question its validity to show that it is forbidden." *People v. Draper,* 15 N. Y. 532, 543.

It is stated in a recent legal publication that "the legislature of a state has power to enact any laws that are not expressly, or by necessary implication, prohibited, either by the federal constitution or by the constitution of the state enacting the law, the constitutionality of which is called in question." 8 Cyc. p. 806. Many cases are cited which hold the doctrine thus announced, and none has been cited by counsel, or discovered by us, announcing a different rule. The question of the extent of legislative power is fully and intelligently discussed in *Kimball v. Grantsville City,* 19 Utah 368, 57 Pac. 1, 45 L. R. A. 628; *State ex rel. Nichols v. Cherry,* 22 Utah 1, 60 Pac. 1103; and *People v. Richmond,* 16 Colo. 274, 26 Pac. 929. See, also, Cooley, Const. Lim. (6th ed.), p. 197.

The legislature was lawfully convened by the governor and, not being limited by the constitution to the consideration of the legislative business for which it was called together, we think it had ample power and authority to enact the general saving statute of June 13, 1901, and it, therefore, follows that that act is constitutional and valid. While the constitution empowers the governor to call extra sessions of the legislature, and defines his duty respecting the same, it does not authorize him to restrict or prohibit legislative action by proclamation or otherwise. *Morford v. Unger,* 8 Iowa 82; *Farrelly v. Cole,* 60 Kan. 356, 56 Pac. 492, 44 L. R. A. 464; Cooley, Const. Lim., *supra.*

It is insisted, on the part of the appellant, that there was a variance between the pleading and the proof in regard to the ownership of the property designated in the information. It will be observed that the information alleged that the money taken was the property of Robert G. Miller. The evidence showed, however, that it really belonged to a copartnership of which said Robert G. Miller was a member, but that at the time of the robbery it was in his presence, and under his immediate and exclusive control. Was this proof sufficient to sustain the allegation of the ownership of the property described in the information? We have no doubt that it was. Our statute (Bal. Code, § 6944, Pierce's Code, § 2016) provides:

"In the prosecution of any offense committed upon, or in relation to, or in any way affecting any real estate, or any offense committed in stealing, embezzling, destroying, injuring, or fraudulently receiving or concealing any money, goods, or other personal estate, it shall be sufficient, and shall not be deemed a variance, if it be proved on the trial that, at the time when such offense was committed, either the actual or constructive possession, or the general or special property, in the whole or any part of such real or personal estate, was in the person or community alleged in the indictment or other accusation to be the owner thereof."

Robbery is a compound or aggravated larceny, and larceny is only another name for stealing or theft. And, says Mr. Bishop:

"The indictment for robbery charges a larceny, together with the aggravating matter which makes it, in the particular instance, robbery. For example, the property is described the same as in larceny; the ownership is in the same way set out, and so of the rest." 2 Bish., New Cr. L., §1159.

Although robbery is not specifically mentioned in the statute last quoted, we think it is clearly within its spirit, and that that section of the code is therefore applicable to the case at bar. Under this statute this court has held that, if the actual or constructive possession of a building is in the person alleged in an information for arson to be the owner, it is no variance if it be proved on the trial that he was in such possession at the time of the commission of the offense, although the actual ownership be shown to be in another. *State v. Biles,* 6 Wash. 186, 33 Pac. 347. And we see no reason why the same rule should not be applied in this case.

In *People v. Clark,* 106 Cal. 32, 39 Pac. 53, the information charged the defendant with having robbed the Wing Hing Company of $210. The evidence showed that sum was taken, but that only $175 belonged to the company. And upon the question whether there was a variance between the allegation and proof of ownership, the supreme court of the state said:

"The court properly refused to instruct the jury that such variance entitled the defendant to an acquittal; nor did the court err in charging the jury that it was not necessary that the property alleged to have been taken was, in its entirety, the property of that company."

That case would seem to be directly in point here. See, also, *State v. Adams,* 58 Kan. 365, 49 Pac. 81; and *Brooks v. People,* 49 N. Y. 436, 10 Am. Rep. 398.

It is claimed by appellant that the court erred in refusing to grant a new trial on the ground that the evidence is not sufficient to justify the verdict of the jury. We have carefully examined and considered all the evidence in the record, and we are not convinced that it was not sufficient to warrant the jury in returning a verdict of guilty. That a robbery was committed at the time and place designated in the information, there can be no reasonable doubt. The prosecuting witness, Miller, and Charles Johnson testified that the appellant was one of the

persons who committed the offense; and Detective Mc-
Dermott, who had known the appellant for several years,
testified that he saw him in Spokane at 8 o'clock in the
evening of the robbery. This evidence on the part of
the state was contradicted by appellant, who, as a witness
in his own behalf, testified that he was not in the butcher
shop of Miller Brothers, or in Spokane, at the time of
the robbery, but was then in Prosser, nearly 200 miles
from the scene of the robbery. Four other witnesses were
introduced by the defense, each of whom testified to the
same effect. But it was the exclusive province of the
jury to weigh the evidence, and, in so doing, to determine
the credibility of the various witnesses. And it is evident that the jury concluded that the witnesses for the
defense were not entitled to credit, and that those for the
prosecution spoke the truth. Moreover, the trial judge
must have been of the same opinion, for he passed upon
the sufficiency of the evidence in determining the motion
for a new trial. And, under such circumstances, this
court will not disturb the verdict of the jury, where there
is testimony which, if true, is sufficient to justify it.
State v. Kroenert, 13 Wash. 644, 43 Pac. 876; *State v.
Maldonado,* 21 Wash. 653, 59 Pac. 489; *State v. Mitchell,*
32 Wash. 64, 72 Pac. 707; *State v. Ripley,* 32 Wash. 182,
72 Pac. 1036.

We perceive no error in the record, and the judgment
as to appellant Frank Fair is therefore affirmed.

The witnesses for the defendant and appellant Fair,
viz., Frank Rutledge, O. Johnson, G. L. Eichenhauer,
and J. H. Bailey, have appealed from the order of the
trial court disallowing their fees for attendance on the
trial, and for mileage, as certified by the clerk. The
respondent moves to dismiss this pretended appeal for
the reasons, among others, that none of said persons was

a party to this action in the trial court; that said persons
are not proper parties appellant herein, and that this court
has no jurisdiction of the subject matter of the attempted
and pretended appeal of said persons. This motion must
be granted. Our statutes provide that, "any *party* aggrieved may appeal to the supreme court in the mode
prescribed in this title, . . ." (Laws 1901, p. 28);
that "any *party* aggrieved by the taxation of costs by the
clerk of the court may, upon application, have the same
retaxed by the court in which the action or proceeding is
had" (Bal. Code, § 5185, Pierce's Code, § 1122); and
that "the party commencing the action shall be known
as the plaintiff and the opposite party the defendant"
(Bal. Code, § 4794, Pierce's Code, § 251). As these so-
called appellants were not parties to the action at any
stage of the proceeding, it seems clear to our minds that
they were not authorized by law to prosecute an appeal
from any order or judgment made or rendered by the
court therein. They were simply witnesses at the trial
of the cause, and were therefore in no sense parties to the
action, or to the ruling of the court rejecting their claim
for witness fees. *Fiedelday v. Diserens,* 26 Ohio St. 312;
Perkins v. Delta etc. Co., 66 Miss. 378, 6 South. 210,
See, also, *Nicol v. Skagit Boom Co.,* 12 Wash. 230, 40
Pac. 984, and *Montgomery v. Leavenworth,* 2 Cal. 57.

For the foregoing reasons the appeal of Rutledge, Johnson, Eichenhauer, and Bailey is dismissed.

FULLERTON, C. J., and MOUNT, DUNBAR, and HADLEY,
JJ., concur.

[No. 4451. Decided May 8, 1904.]

M. M. Teater, *Respondent,* v. Terry King, *Appellant.*[1]

Trial—Appearance—Waiver of Special Appearance—Motion to Dismiss Action of Unlawful Detainer. Where a special appearance is made to quash a summons in unlawful detainer and the writ of restitution, for want of jurisdiction, and a motion is subsequently made to dismiss the action for the reason that no summons has been issued or served, the motion to dismiss invokes the jurisdiction of the court on the merits, and waives the special appearance.

Unlawful Detainer—Notice to Quit—Sufficiency of Time Allowed—Monthly Rental. Where rent was paid November 23d for one month in advance under a tenancy from month to month, a notice to quit on December 23d, served on December 2d, was in time.

Landlord and Tenant—Unlawful Detainer—Validity of Sublease—Evidence—Sufficiency—Question for Jury. In an action of unlawful detainer brought by a tenant of the whole premises against a subtenant of a part, there is sufficient evidence to require the submission to the jury of an issue as to whether defendant was rightfully in possession under a sublease prior to plaintiff's lease, where it appears that the owners originally leased to D for an indefinite period, and D subleased for two years, subject to the continuance of her own term, and the owners in writing recognized the sublease, and for a valuable consideration agreed to approve the same, and the evidence tended to show that plaintiff, who bought out D before the expiration of said two years, had knowledge at the time, of the sublease, and of the owner's recognition thereof.

Same—Owner's Recognition Conclusive. In such case, the plaintiff cannot raise the question of the validity of the original lease, nor of the owner's recognition of the sublease, when those questions are not raised by the owner.

Same—Defenses. In an action of unlawful detainer against a subtenant, where the evidence tended to show that he was not guilty of the wrongful detention, it cannot be claimed that his rights in the premises can only be enforced in an equitable action.

[1]Reported in 76 Pac. 688.

Appeal from a judgment of the superior court for King county, Emory, J., entered May 20, 1902, upon granting plaintiff's motion for a directed verdict, after a trial on the merits before the court and a jury. Reversed.

Allen, Allen & Stratton, for appellant.

Shank & Smith, for respondent.

PER CURIAM.—Action for unlawful detainer, brought by M. M. Teater, plaintiff and respondent, against Terry King, defendant and appellant, in the superior court of King county. The plaintiff recovered judgment, and defendant appeals.

The complaint was filed in the clerk's office of the lower court on December 26, 1901. It alleged that respondent was, and had been since May 15, 1901, in possession of lot 1, and the north half of lot 4, excepting the dwelling house situated upon the easterly end thereof, in block 32 of C. D. Boren's Plat of an addition to Seattle, under verbal lease thereof from month to month; that on November 23, 1901, the respondent sublet to the appellant, from month to month, at a rental of $100 per month, payable in advance, the storeroom comprising the main floor of the building, erected upon the westerly portion of said lot 1. The complaint further alleged the payment by appellant of $100, one month's rental, on November 23, 1901; that, at the city of Seattle, on the 2nd day of December, 1901, the respondent served upon appellant personally a written notice to quit and surrender possession of said premises to respondent on or before Dec. 23, 1901, with which notice appellant refused to comply. Respondent demanded judgment for restitution of the premises, and damages.

On the day of the filing of this complaint, summons and writ of restitution were issued. On the 31st day of

December, 1901, pursuant to such writ, appellant was ousted
by the sheriff from the possession of the premises. On
the same day the appellant made a special appearance by
written motion to quash the summons and service thereof.
On January 4, 1902, appellant made and filed an amended
motion in form of a special appearance, wherein he moved,
(1) to quash the summons, and set aside the service thereof; (2) to set aside and quash the writ of restitution,
for the reason that the same was prematurely issued,
and that the court had no jurisdiction to issue the same;
and (3) to dismiss the said action, for the reason that no
summons had been issued and served in said cause as required by law. This amended motion came on for hearing on January 11, 1902. The trial court sustained the
motion to quash the summons and set aside the service
thereof, but refused to quash the writ of restitution or
dismiss the action, to which ruling appellant excepted.

The appellant, by his amended answer, filed Jan. 24,
1902, denies the material allegations of the complaint,
except the payment of the month's rent, and the refusal
to vacate the premises in question, as required by the
above notice to quit. He specially denies that he unlawfully and wrongfully detained the possession of said
premises to respondent's damage. And for an affirmative
defense the answer alleges, that on or about the 23d day
of September, 1900, one Mrs. R. J. Dodds, who was
rightfully in possession of the property described in the
complaint, did, in writing, lease and demise to one C. M.
Spores and one Joseph Gavin, the whole lower or main
floor of said building (the storeroom described in the
complaint), for the period of two years after that date;
that said property was a part of the estate of Mary N.
Welch, deceased; that on October 1, 1900, in consideration of the payment of $500 by said Dodds, this lease

was recognized and ratified by the executor of said estate, who reported the same to the superior court of King county, which lease was approved by said court; that respondent acquired, by contract from Mrs. Dodds, her interest in said property, on or about May 15, 1901, and thereby went into possession of said property, save the storeroom theretofore leased to Spores and Gavin; that respondent agreed to, and did, take said property subject to said lease, recognized the same, and received rental for such storeroom from Spores and Gavin and their successors in interest; that appellant became, and was, after the 14th day of November, 1901, in the rightful possession of said storeroom, as the successor in interest of said Spores and Gavin, by purchase; that the said Spores and Gavin, their successors in interest therein, and this appellant, complied in all respects with the terms of said lease; and that, on the 31st day of December, 1901, respondent wrongfully and illegally ejected appellant from said storeroom in pursuance of the writ of restitution issued herein. Appellant asked judgment restoring to him the possession thereof, and for costs. The reply puts in issue the material allegations contained in the affirmative defense, and specially alleges, that respondent went into possession of the premises on May 15, 1901, under a new and independent tenancy from month to month, and, until December 23, 1901, he sublet said storeroom and collected rent therefor.

(1) The first two assignments of error allege that the trial court erred in overruling appellant's motions to quash and set aside the writ of restitution and dismiss the action. The record shows that a second summons issued herein, on January 13, 1902, pursuant to the order of the court below of that date, above noted, quashing the original summons and setting aside the service thereof.

We are of the opinion, that a writ of restitution, when
issued at the commencement or during the pendency of
an action, is governed, in the main, by the same principles of law as a writ of attachment, or other ancillary
process in the main cause. The appellant's position is
that the action abated, when the original summons and
service thereof were quashed and set aside, and therefore carried the proceedings for the writ of restitution
with it, as an incident, and that the trial court erred in
not quashing the writ and dismissing the case. There
would be much force in appellant's contention, if he had
not asked the court below to dismiss the action. The
appearance of appellant was in form special, for the purpose of objecting to the court's jurisdiction over his person, but in the body of his motion he invoked the jurisdiction of the court below on the merits, when he asked
for a dismissal. A party desiring to successfully challenge
jurisdiction over his person should not call into action the
powers of the court over the subject-matter of the controversy. By so doing, he waives his special appearance,
and will be held to have appeared generally. *Fitzgerald
Const. Co., v. Fitzgerald*, 137 U. S. 98, 11 Sup. Ct. 36,
34 L. Ed. 608; *Sayward v. Carlson*, 1 Wash. 29, 23 Pac.
830; 2 Enc. Plead. & Prac. 625; *Bucklin v. Strickler*,
32 Neb. 602; 49 N. W. 371. Some courts hold that in
a proceeding, as contradistinguished from an ordinary
civil action, a party may move to dismiss such proceeding
for defective notice or service thereof, but that jurisdiction over the person is waived by going further and asking the court or tribunal to grant relief relative to the
merits of the controversy. See, *Perkins v. Hayward*, 132
Ind. 95, 31 N. E. 670; 2 Elliott's Gen. Pract., §§ 474-476,
and authorities cited. In the light of the rules of law
enunciated in the foregoing citations, we reach the conclu-

sion that the trial court committed no error in denying appellant's motion to dismiss the cause.

(2) The next contention of appellant presents the proposition regarding the sufficiency of the notice to quit possession of the premises in question. The notice was served on appellant on December 2, 1901, requiring him to surrender possession and vacate the premises "on or before December 23, 1901, being the expiration of the current monthly period." Appellant urges that this notice was not given and served a sufficient length of time prior to the expiration of the tenancy to have terminated it under the statute. We think his position untenable, under the decision of this court in *Yesler Estate v. Orth,* 24 Wash. 483, 64 Pac. 723. See, further, *Steffens v. Earl,* 11 Vroom 128, 29 Am. Rep. 214, 218. Moreover, it is questionable whether appellant is in a position to question the sufficiency of this notice or its service, when the complaint squarely tendered an issue in that behalf, and appellant not only failed to meet such issue, but alleged right of possession in himself under his affirmative defense. The notice to quit is for the protection of the tenant and may be waived. *Dale v. Doddridge,* 9 Neb. 138, 1 N. W. 999.

(3) The alleged errors respecting the rulings of the court, in denying appellant's motion for a nonsuit, and in granting respondent's application to take the case from the jury, direct a verdict, and enter judgment in his favor, may be considered together. There was no error in denying the motion for a nonsuit. The respondent was the only witness examined in his own behalf. His testimony tends to support the allegations of his complaint. The chief issue tendered by this pleading was the unlawful detention of the premises in question by appellant. It appeared from this evidence, that on May 15, 1901, one Mrs. R. J.

Dodds sold her furniture in the Russell hotel or lodging house to Teater; that, shortly prior to that date, Teater made arrangements with M. M. Carraher, executor of the Welch estate, to rent this lodging house from month to month; that Teater sublet the lower floor of the above house to King, appellant, on November 23, 1901, received $100, one month's rental in advance therefor, notified King to vacate and surrender possession as above stated, and that he refused to comply with the requirements of such notice. Respondent, Teater, denied that there was any privity between Mrs. Dodds, the former lessee of the lodging house, and himself, concerning her relations with Spores and Gavin, assignors of King, or that he (Teater) recognized King's interests in such property in any manner, other than as tenant of respondent for an indefinite term.

The evidence introduced in appellant's behalf at the trial tended to show, that on the 21st of September, 1900, Mrs. R. J. Dodds was lessee of this hotel property, for an indefinite term, from M. M. Carraher, executor of the Welch estate; that at that date Mrs. Dodds leased, by written indenture, this lower floor (the property in dispute) to C. M. Spores and Joseph Gavin for the term of two years. This lease contained the following provision: "Provided, however, that said party of the first part continues to have the lease or possession of the said property during said term of two years." Appellant then introduced in evidence the following paper writings:

"Seattle, Washington. September 21st, 1900. In consideration of C. M. Spores and Joseph Gavin entering into a written lease with Mrs. R. J. Dodds for two years for the Russell House in the city of Seattle, it is hereby agreed that in case Mrs. R. J. Dodds should for any reason lose or not have the right to rent said premises so leased to said Spores and Gavin for two years that we, as executors of the estate owning the land described in

said lease, will recognize the lease of said Spores and
Gavin for said two years provided that said Gavin and
said Spores shall perform all their conditions of said lease.
(Signed) C. M. Spores. Joseph Gavin. M. M. Carraher,
as executor of the estate of Mary A. Welch, deceased.
Pierre P. Ferry, attorney for said executor."

"Seattle, Washington, October 1, 1900. In consideration of the sum of five hundred dollars ($500) to me
in hand paid by C. M. Spores and Joseph Gavin, the
receipt of which is hereby acknowledged, I hereby release
said C. M. Spores and Joseph Gavin from the certain
provision in the lease hereinafter referred to requiring
said C. M. Spores and Joseph Gavin to lower the floor
of the certain building heretofore leased by me to said
C. M. Spores and Joseph Gavin, said lease bearing date
September 21, 1900, it being mutually understood and
agreed that said payment of said money in no way affects
any covenant or conditions in said lease, excepting as
hereinbefore provided. Mrs. R. J. Dodds."

"Received from Mrs. R. G. Dodds the above sum of
five hundred dollars ($500.00) in consideration of our
recognition of the said lease hereinbefore referred to. Dated
at Seattle, Washington, this 1st day of October, 1900.
M. M. Carraher, as executor of the estate of Mary M.
Welch, deceased. Pierre P. Ferry, as attorney for said
executors."

It further appeared that Spores and Gavin, on October
17, 1900, assigned, in writing, their interest in the above
lease to the Seattle Brewing and Malting Company, as
collateral security for money loaned; that this lease was
recorded June 1, 1901; that Spores and Gavin were running a bath house on this lower floor, at the time respondent entered into possession of the Russell House property, of which respondent had notice; that thereafter
Teater collected rents from such parties and their successors in interest; that, through certain mesne transfers,
appellant, on or about November 14, 1901, became the

owner, by purchase, of the rights and interests of Spores
and Gavin in and to the above lease. Mrs. Larimer (formerly Mrs. Dodds) testified in part as follows:

"At the time I sold out the house to M. M. Teater,
these parties [Spores and Gavin] were still running the
bath house, and at the time I sold to Mr. Teater I told
him about this lease I had made to Spores and Gavin,
and showed Mr. Teater a copy of the lease, and I told
Mr. Teater at that time I did not want to have any trouble
about it, and that he must protect me on that lease, and
he said he would; and at the time I closed up the deal
with Mr. M. M. Teater I turned the lease over to him,
that I had made to Spores and Gavin."

M. M. Carraher, the executor, swore that respondent
"got into possession by buying Mrs. Dodd out." Witness
Jensen, in behalf of appellant, swore that, when the $100
rental was paid by King to Teater, the former said to the
latter: "I have come up here to pay you the rent, $100,
subject to that lease." There was further evidence tending to show that Teater took the property designated as
the Russell House with knowledge of Spores and Gavin's
lease of the lower floor, subject to the above condition,
and that King was the successor in interest of those lessees.
True, much of this evidence is vague and inexplicit on the
question whether Teater, at the time he bought Mrs.
Dodds out, obligated himself to assume the burden of this
lease to Spores and Gavin. After a careful reading of the
testimony adduced in appellant's behalf, we think that
it tends to sustain the allegations of his answer, and that
the learned trial court erred in taking the case from the
jury, directing a verdict, and entering judgment for respondent.

The learned counsel for respondent argue that the
so-called recognition of the executor could have, at most,
only a future contingent operation. This argument, as

it appears to us, assumes one of the very points in issue. This court cannot so hold as a matter of law, in the light of the evidence. Whether the tenancy of Spores and Gavin, as between themselves and the executor, was created with all the formalities required by the statute, is not pertinent to this appeal, as we view the record. The executor is not attempting to dispute the validity of the original lease between Mrs. Dodds and Spores and Gavin, or of the alleged rights of appellant as their assignee under such instrument. Can the respondent properly raise that question in the present controversy? We think not. We are of the opinion that the respondent is not in a position to affirm that part of the above transaction which he deemed beneficial to his interests, and repudiate that part which he may consider otherwise, to the prejudice of appellant. *Ansonia v. Cooper,* 64 Conn. 536, 30 Atl. 760; *Weaver v. Coumbe,* 15 Neb. 167, 17 N. W. 357.

We cannot agree with respondent's contention, that whatever rights appellant may have in the premises can only be enforced in an equitable action. The gravamen of this controversy is the alleged unlawful detention on the part of the appellant. The question of respondent's recognition of the lease from Mrs. Dodds to Spores and Gavin was one of fact for the consideration of the jury. The evidence in behalf of appellant tended to show that he was not guilty of the unlawful and wrongful detention of this property, as charged in the complaint. The proposition regarding the sufficiency of this evidence, as opposed to the testimony of respondent, was a matter that should have been submitted to the jury. The trial court was not justified in deciding, as a matter of law, that respondent was entitled to recover in the action at bar.

The judgment of the superior court is reversed, and the case is remanded for a new trial.

[No. 4881. Decided May 3, 1904]

CRASSUS STEWART, *Appellant,* v. E. K. HANNA *et al.,*
Respondents.[1]

APPEAL—WHEN LIES—AMOUNT IN CONTROVERSY—TENDER BY
DEFENDANTS REDUCING AMOUNT. In an action to recover $300,
in which the defendants tendered and brought into court the
sum of $270, no appeal lies to the supreme court, since the
amount in controversy is less than $200.

Appeal from a judgment of the superior court for Whitman county, Chadwick, J., entered July 1, 1903, upon
the verdict of a jury in favor of the defendants, after a
trial on the merits. Appeal dismissed.

J. W. Brooks and *Guy Bartlett,* for appellant.

Thomas Neill and *H. W. Canfield,* for respondents.

MOUNT, J.—Plaintiff brought this action to recover
$300 from the defendants. The complaint alleges that
defendants collected that amount of money for the use
and benefit of plaintiff, and wrongfully refuse to pay
the same to plaintiff. The answer admitted possession
of the sum of $300, but alleged that $30 thereof belonged
to defendants as fees for collecting the said $300. De-
fendants also pleaded a tender to plaintiff of the sum of
$270 before the action was begun, and deposited that
amount in court for plaintiff's use. Plaintiff, for reply,
admitted the tender, but denied that there was any greater
sum than $10 due defendants for collecting the said sum
of $300. On a trial of the issues thus made, a verdict
was returned in favor of defendants, and from a judgment thereon plaintiff appeals.

Respondents move to dismiss the appeal, upon the

[1]Reported in 76 Pac. 688.

ground that this court has no jurisdiction because the original amount in controversy is less than $200. This motion must be sustained. There is not now, and never has been, any controversy over plaintiff's right to the $270. The only controversy is over the $30 claimed by defendants. The verdict and judgment is in favor of defendants, but plaintiff is entitled to $270 deposited in court for his use, because there is and has been no controversy over that sum. It is true, plaintiff prayed for judgment against defendants for $300, but the answer of defendants showed that the only amount in controversy was the sum of $30, and this allegation was admitted in plaintiff's reply. *Puyallup Light etc. Co. v. Stevenson,* 21 Wash. 604, 59 Pac. 504. Appellant relies upon the case of *Taylor v. Spokane Falls & N. R. Co.,* 32 Wash. 450, 73 Pac. 499, but that case is not in point here, because, under the admitted facts in this case, the original amount in controversy is less than $200, and neither party therefore can appeal to this court.

The appeal is dismissed.

FULLERTON, C. J., and DUNBAR, ANDERS, and HADLEY, JJ., concur.

[No. 4833. Decided May 2, 1904.]

THE STATE OF WASHINGTON, *Respondent,* v. FRANK OLESON, *Appellant.*[1]

CRIMINAL LAW—RECEIVING DEPOSIT AFTER INSOLVENCY OF BANK—DEFENSES—INDIVIDUAL LIABILITY OF OFFICER. Const., art. 12, § 12, making officers of a bank individually responsible for receiving a deposit after knowledge that the bank was insolvent, does not preclude the legislature from passing a law making them criminally liable therefor.

[1]Reported in 76 Pac. 686.

SAME—INFORMATION—VARIANCE—NAME OF DEPOSITOR—CORPORA-
TION SUCCEEDING PARTNERSHIP—IDEM SONANS. Under an information against a bank officer for receiving, after the insolvency
of the bank, a deposit from the B. G. Co., a corporation, it is
a fatal variance to prove a deposit by B. & S., a copartnership,
consisting of the incorporators of the B. G. Co., which was not
in existence at the time alleged, and the fact that the corporation was the successor of the copartnership does not bring the
two names within the principle of *idem sonans*.

SAME—NAME OF DEPOSITOR NECESSARY TO IDENTIFY DEPOSIT.
The fact that the bank was insolvent at a particular time, and
that a deposit of $113 was made at that time, does not identify
the act of such deposit with certainty, without the name of the
depositor, within the provision of Bal. Code, § 6846, respecting
material variances.

Appeal from a judgment of the superior court for Whatcom county, Neterer, J., entered December 19, 1902, upon
a trial and conviction of the crime of receiving a deposit
in an insolvent bank. Reversed.

Harry Fairchild, Will H. Morris, and *Morris & Southard,* for appellant.

Parker Ellis, A. E. Mead, and *John B. Hart,* for respondent.

MOUNT, J.—Appellant was convicted by a jury in the
court below, under an information charging him with
receiving a certain deposit in an insolvent bank of which
he was cashier, knowing the bank to be insolvent. Appellant insists, first, that the statute under which the
information was filed is unconstitutional, because the
constitution in terms provides that an officer receiving
such deposit shall be individually responsible therefor
and, therefore, by implication, prevents the legislature
from making the act criminal. The statute is as follows:

"Any president, director, manager, cashier or other
officer of any banking institution who shall receive or
assent to the reception of deposits after he shall have

knowledge of the fact that such banking institution is
insolvent or in failing circumstances, shall be guilty of
felony and punished as hereinafter provided." § 7121,
Bal. Code.

The constitution provides as follows:

"Any president, director, manager, cashier, or other
officer of any banking institution, who shall receive or
assent to the reception of deposits after he shall have
knowledge of the fact that such banking institution is
insolvent or in failing circumstances, shall be individually
responsible for such deposits so received." § 12, art. 12,
of the constitution.

This court, in *State ex rel. Murphy v. McBride*, 29 Wash.
335, 70 Pac. 25, said:

"The constitution of this state is a limitation upon
the powers of the legislature, and not a grant of power.
Hence, before an act of the legislature may be declared
unconstitutional, it must appear that the act is in conflict
with some express provision of the constitution which
prohibits the act or parts of the act complained of."

See, also, Cooley, Const. Lim. (7th ed.), pp. 126, 236, 242.
There is no contention that the provision of the constitution quoted expressly prohibits the legislature from making the reception of such deposits by an officer of the
bank criminal; but it is argued that, because the constitution provides that the officer shall be "individually responsible for such deposits so received," there is an implication that he shall not be made criminally liable. If
the constitution, by the term "individually responsible,"
means that such officer shall be liable civilly, we think
it does not follow, as a *necessary implication,* that he shall
be only liable civilly; and therefore the legislature may
make him liable both civilly and criminally. The demurrer was therefore properly denied.

Appellant next insists that there was a fatal variance between the essential allegations of the information and the proof. The information is as follows, omitting the caption:

"In the name and by the authority of the State of Washington, I, A. E. Mead, prosecuting attorney of Whatcom county, state of Washington, come now here and give the court to understand and be informed, and on oath do accuse Frank Oleson of the crime of larceny, committed as follows: That for more than six months immediately preceding the 27th day of February, A. D. 1901, the Scandinavian-American Bank was a banking corporation organized and existing as such and doing business in the city of New Whatcom, Whatcom county, Washington, and on the 27th day of February, A. D. 1901, and for more than six months immediately preceding said date did during said time conduct a general banking business therein by receiving money for deposit and otherwise in the said city of Whatcom, Whatcom county, Washington; that on the 27th day of February, A. D. 1901, during all of the times aforesaid, the said Scandinavian-American Bank, a banking corporation as aforesaid, was insolvent and in failing circumstances; that on, to wit, the said 27th day of February, A. D. 1901, and for the six months immediately prior thereto, one Frank Oleson was the cashier of said banking institution and as such cashier of such banking institution did, on the 27th day of February, A. D. 1901, receive and assent to the reception of a certain sum of money, to wit, the sum of one hundred and thirteen dollars ($113), as a deposit in said bank, from the Byron Grocery Company, a corporation, and said Frank Oleson then and there at all times well knowing that the said Scandinavian-American Bank, said banking institution, was then insolvent, and in failing circumstances, contrary to the form of the statute in such cases made and provided and against the peace and dignity of the state of Washington."

The undisputed evidence introduced on the part of the state shows, that the deposit alleged in the information

was made for a partnership composed of H. C. Byron,
Will Shumway and X. S. Byron, known as Byron &
Shumway, by their bookkeeper, John H. Lloyd; that the
Byron Grocery Company, a corporation, was not in existence at that time and never did any business with the
said bank. The evidence also shows that all the partners
in the firm of Byron & Shumway were the incorporators
of the Byron Grocery Company, a corporation, which was
organized some two or three weeks after the alleged deposit. The deposit slip, which was introduced in evidence,
is as follows:

"Deposited by Byron & Shumway with the Scandinavian-American Bank, New Whatcom, Washington, February 27, 1901:

"Gold 70
"Silver 13
"Currency 10
"Checks 20
                          ———
                          "113"

When the state had introduced this proof and rested,
the appellant moved the court for an instructed verdict,
upon the ground of a material variance. This motion
was denied. There can be no doubt that this proof is a
variance from the allegation, which charged the deposit
to have been made by the Byron Grocery Company, a
corporation, for the corporation is an entirely different
and distinct person from Byron & Shumway, a copartnership. The rule is well settled that an information charging larceny from a particular person is not sustained by
proof of larceny of the same property from another person,
or from a person by another name, unless the names are
idem sonans. Larceny and Kindred Offenses, by Rapalje,
§§ 241, 242, and cases cited; *State v. Van Cleve,* 5 Wash.

642, 32 Pac. 461. The fact that the Byron Grocery Company, a corporation, is the successor of Byron & Shumway, does not bring the two names within the rule of *idem sonans,* because they are, in fact and in law, two distinct and different persons, notwithstanding that the stockholders of the corporation may in fact be identical with the partners in a partnership which was the predecessor in interest of the property of the corporation. Respondent contends, however, that the variance is immaterial, by reason of the following provision of the code:

"When the crime involves the commission of or an attempt to commit a private injury, and is described with sufficient certainty in other respects to identify the act, an erroneous allegation as to the person injured or intended to be injured is not material." §6846, Bal. Code.

And it is argued that, because the date and amount of the deposit are described with certainty, these facts are sufficient to identify the act. The fact that the bank was insolvent or in failing circumstances at the time of the deposit is, no doubt, material, but the precise date of the deposit, so long as it was within the time when the bank was in failing circumstances, is not a material ingredient in the crime. § 6845, Bal. Code.

The question then is, do the facts that the bank was insolvent at a particular time, and that a deposit of $113 was made at that time, identify the act of such deposit with certainty. It seems clear that it does not do so. The first and most important inquiry to identify such an act would naturally be, who made the deposit? Without this fact, a person charged might find upon his books different deposits for the same amount upon the same day. It would then be impossible to identify the act charged. Banks, as a rule, receive many deposits on the same day, and frequently, no doubt, in the same amount.

The date and amount of a deposit are material to identify
it, but these items alone could not be relied upon to
identify it with certainty. The name of the depositor
is equally as important as either the date or the amount,
if not more so. All three of the items, particularly the
amount and name of the depositor, are necessary to identify the deposit with certainty. The statute, therefore,
does not apply to the facts in this case.

Furthermore, the facts in this case illustrate, as clearly
as any that could be supposed, the danger of permitting
misleading allegations intended to identify the act charged.
The information alleges that the defendant, on February
27, 1901, knowing the bank to be insolvent, received and
assented to the reception of "$113 as a deposit in said
bank from the Byron Grocery Company, a corporation."
The pleader evidently supposed that the name of the depositor was necessary to an identification of the deposit
and, therefore, alleged that the deposit was made by the
Byron Grocery Company, a corporation. The defendant,
from his personal knowledge or from an examination of
the books of the bank, knew that no such person had made
a deposit in said bank, and had a right to rely upon this
fact as a complete defense. He was certainly not required
to prepare to meet some other accusation. This allegation, even if immaterial, would have the effect to mislead
the accused, because he had a right to suppose that the
state would attempt to prove the charge as made. If the
prosecution may be permitted to allege that the deposit
was made by one person, and then, at the trial, prove that
it was made by another and entirely different person, there
is no virtue in the constitutional provision that an accused
person shall have a right to know the nature and *cause* of
the accusation against him. § 22, art. 1, of the constitution. And the state might, in prosecutions of this kind,

entirely mislead accused persons by alleging that such deposits were made by one person, when they were in fact made by another. In the language of *State v. Gifford,* 19 Wash. 464, 53 Pac. 709, "we do not think it was the intention of the legislature, in the passage of this law, to set a trap for the feet of defendants."

The appellant's motion for a directed verdict should have been granted. The judgment is therefore reversed.

FULLERTON, C. J., and DUNBAR, ANDERS, and HADLEY, JJ., concur.

[No. 4889. Decided May 7, 1904.]

ELIZA J. LEWIS, *Appellant,* v. JOSEPH MAUERMAN *et al.,*

Respondents.[1]

HOMESTEADS—EXEMPTIONS—OCCUPATION NOT ESSENTIAL AFTER SELECTION. Where a homestead has been duly selected by recording the declaration under Laws 1895, p. 109, actual occupancy of the same is not necessary to maintain the right to the homestead exemption.

SAME—EXECUTION SALE—FAILURE TO COMPLY WITH LAW RESPECTING EXEMPTION—INCREASE OF EXEMPTION BY SUBSEQUENT LAW. Where the law respecting the sale of homesteads was not complied with and no exemption at all allowed, an execution sale of premises that have been duly selected as a homestead, cannot be sustained on the theory that since the judgment was obtained the exemption for a homestead was increased from $1,000 to $2,000, and the premises were worth more than $1,000.

SAME—CONFIRMATION OF EXECUTION SALE—COLLATERAL ATTACK—HOMESTEAD CLAIM NOT CONCLUDED BY CONFIRMATION. An action to recover possession of a homestead, sold under execution without complying with the law regulating such sales, is not a collateral attack upon the confirmation of the sale, since the only matter that can be determined on the confirmation is

[1]Reported in 76 Pac. 737.

the regularity of the procedings concerning the sale, and the same does not constitute an adjudication upon the question of the homestead claim.

Appeal from a judgment of the superior court for Chehalis county, Irwin, J., entered May 9, 1903, upon findings in favor of the defendants, after a trial on the merits before the court without a jury, dismissing an action to quiet title. Reversed.

B. G. Cheney, for appellant.

W. H. Abel, for respondents, argued, *inter alia,* that an execution sale cannot be collaterally attacked by an action to quiet title. Van Fleet, Collateral Attack, § 3; *Christofferson v. Pfennig,* 16 Wash. 491, 48 Pac. 264; *Kalb v. German Savings Bank,* 25 Wash. 349, 65 Pac. 559; *Morrill v. Morrill,* 20 Ore. 96, 25 Pac. 362, 11 L. R. A. 155; *Vorhees v. Jackson,* 10 Peters 450; *Sumner v. Moore,* 2 McLean 59, Fed. Cas. No. 13,610.

DUNBAR, J.—This is an action brought by the appellant to quiet title to certain lands in controversy. The complaint alleges, plaintiff's ownership in, and possession of, the lands; that the defendants claim some right, title, or interest in and to said lands adverse to plaintiff, and that the said claim is without any right whatever; and asks, that the defendants be required to set forth the nature of their claim; that, by decree, it be declared and adjudged that the defendants have no estate, right, title, or interest whatever in or to said land; that the title of the plaintiff thereto be declared and adjudged to be valid; that the title thereof be quieted as against any and all claims of any kind whatever; and that defendants be perpetually enjoined from asserting or setting up any estate, right, title, or interest whatever in or to said land; and prays for costs and general relief.

The answer, after denying the allegations of ownership
and possession, alleges, that on July 13, 1891, J. M.
Lewis, for the benefit of the community consisting of
himself and plaintiff, together with one W. H. Lewis,
made, executed, and delivered to defendant Joseph Mauerman two certain promissory notes, aggregating $300; that
thereafter an action was duly commenced by defendant
Joseph Mauerman, as plaintiff, against the said J. M.
Lewis and the plaintiff in this action, and against W. H.
Lewis, and that the result of said action was a judgment
for $80, with interest thereon at twelve per cent per
annum from the date of said note until paid, and for
$40 attorney's fees, and $9.40 court costs; that thereafter
and on July 27, 1901, execution was duly issued out of
said court upon said judgment, and the sheriff of Chehalis
county, Washington, duly levied the same upon the land
described in the complaint; that said lands, at all times
since July 13, 1891, up to the time of said levy, had been,
and were then, used by the said J. M. Lewis and Eliza
J. Lewis as community property; that thereafter the said
lands were sold upon said levy and execution in due
form of law, and regularly purchased at sheriff's sale by
defendant Joseph Mauerman, for the sum of $465.80;
that a certificate of such sale was duly executed and delivered to said Joseph Mauerman, by the sheriff of Chehalis county, on the 7th day of September, 1901; that the
sale was, on February 21, 1902, regularly confirmed by
order of the court duly entered in said cause; and the
defendants assert an interest in said lands as owners in
fee, and allege that they were such owners at the time
of the commencement of this action, under and by virtue
of such sale.

The reply admits the commencement of the action set
forth in the answer, the obtaining of the judgment, issu-

ance of execution, levy and sale of the lands and premises described in the complaint, and the order of court confirming said sale; but alleges, that, prior to the sale, the
plaintiff with her husband resided upon said lands and
premises with their minor children, and claimed the same
as their homestead; that said lands and premises did not
exceed in value the sum of $2,000; that on the 28th day
of January, 1901, said J. M. Lewis, husband of plaintiff
and head of his family, made and executed his declaration
of homestead covering the lands and premises described
in the complaint, and thereafter, to wit, on the 30th of
January, 1901, filed the same in the office of the auditor
of Chehalis county; that the same was duly acknowledged
so as to entitle it to be recorded, and the same was duly
recorded; and alleges, in substance, that the sale to Mauerman was void by reason of not being in compliance with
the statute in regard to sales under such circumstances.

The court found the issues, in relation to the maintaining of the homestead right by the plaintiff, against her;
and judgment was entered dismissing the action, with
costs to defendant. From that judgment this appeal is
taken.

The cause was tried on the theory that it was the duty
of the appellant to maintain her right to the selected
homestead by actual occupancy of the same, and the judgment was rendered against her for the reason that, in the
opinion of the court, such occupancy had not been proven,
and for the further reason that the debt contracted was
antecedent to the passage of the homestead law of 1895,
wherein the value of the homestead exempt was raised
from $1,000 to $2,000. But the question of occupancy
is not a material one in the case, for § 7 of chap. 64, p.
109, of the Sessions Laws of 1895, an act defining a homestead and providing for the manner of selecting the same,

provides that a homestead can be abandoned only by a declaration of abandonment, or a grant thereof, executed and acknowledged, (1) by the husband and wife, if the claimant is married; (2) by the claimant, if unmarried. Section 8 provides that a declaration of abandonment is effectual only from the time it is filed in the office in which the homestead was recorded.

Nor could the judgment of the court be sustained on the theory that the appellant was entitled to an exemption of only $1,000, instead of $2,000; for, in this instance, the property was not sold in the manner provided by law for the sale of homesteads, and no exemption at all was allowed. The law points out definitely the manner in which such sales shall be conducted, and the homestead cannot be legally disposed of in any other way.

It is insisted by the respondents that, in any event, this judgment must be affirmed, for the reason that this is a collateral attack upon the judgment of sale and confirmation of the lands in dispute, and that the judgment cannot be avoided by reason of any irregularities or illegality in obtaining it, even though it be void, if, upon the face of the judgment, it is legal. This is true as a general proposition, but, under the provisions of our statute, as they have been construed by this court, the only question that can be determined upon the confirmation of the sale of lands is the regularity of the sale. In *Krutz v. Batts,* 18 Wash. 460, 51 Pac. 1054, after quoting the statute governing confirmations, it was said:

"It will thus be seen that the only question which the court has a right to investigate is a question of irregularity in the proceedings concerning the sale. The law is plain and imperative on that proposition, and the matters objected to by the respondents here were not matters concerning the irregularity of the sale, but concerning the jurisdiction of the court which rendered the judgment in the first instance."

It was also decided, in *Harding v. Atlantic Trust Co.,* 26 Wash. 536, 67 Pac. 222, that the confirmation by the court of an execution sale of realty, after it had been claimed as exempt as the homestead of the judgment debtors, would not constitute an adjudication upon the question of the homestead claim, since the only question the court could properly investigate upon application for confirmation was that of irregularity in the proceedings concerning the sale.

The judgment is reversed, and the cause remanded, with instructions to proceed in accordance with this opinion.

FULLERTON, C. J., and HADLEY, ANDERS, and MOUNT, JJ., concur.

[No. 4983. Decided May 23, 1904.]

JENSEN-KING-BYRD COMPANY, *Respondent,* v. C. H. WILLIAMS, *Appellant.*[1]

INSOLVENCY—FEDERAL BANKRUPTCY ACT—STATE LAWS NOT SUSPENDED. The federal bankruptcy law, approved July 1, 1898, did not supersede or suspend the state insolvency law, in existence at that time, where no proceedings in bankruptcy were instituted.

ASSIGNMENT FOR CREDITORS—JUDGMENT OUTSIDE INSOLVENCY PROCEEDINGS—ENFORCEMENT—SUPPLEMENTAL PROCEEDINGS. An assignment for the benefit of creditors, not objected to, discharges the debtor, and may be set up to defeat supplemental proceedings upon a judgment obtained by a creditor pending the insolvency proceedings.

SAME—STATUTES—TITLE. Section 15 of the insolvency act [Laws 1890, p. 88] entitled "An act to secure creditors a just

[1]Reported in 76 Pac. 934.

division of the estate of debtors who conveyed to assignee for
the benefit of creditors," is not unconstitutional as embracing
more than one subject: since it embraces but one subject, which
is sufficiently expressed in the title.

Appeal from an order of the superior court for Spokane
county, Richardson, J., entered September 4, 1903, upon
overruling a motion to quash supplemental proceedings,
ordering defendant to pay a judgment. Reversed.

O. C. Moore, for appellant.

P. F. Quinn, for respondent, argued that the state insolvency law was superseded by the national bankruptcy
act of 1898. *In re Sievers*, 91 Fed. 368; *Boese v. King*,
78 N. Y. 471, *s. c.* 108 U. S. 379, 27 L. Ed. 760; *Par-
menter Mfg. Co. v. Hamilton*, 172 Mass. 178, 51 N. E.
529; *In re Etheridge Furniture Co.*, 92 Fed. 332; *In re
Bruss-Ritter Co.*, 90 Fed. 651; *Boedefield v. Reed*, 55 Cal.
299. The provision of § 15 for the discharge of insolvent
debtors is not embraced within the title of the act. *Boese
v. King, supra.*

DUNBAR, J.—This is an appeal from a final order in a
proceeding supplemental to execution. On July 30, 1903,
respondent filed its motion for the issuance of a citation
against appellant, requiring him to appear and give testimony respecting the amount and location of his property,
in order that the same might be reduced to the satisfaction
of a judgment, held by respondent against him in the above
entitled cause. In support of this motion, respondent filed
an affidavit, setting forth that on October 7, 1898, it obtained a judgment against the appellant for the sum of
$501, and $16 costs, and interest; that the sum of $458.85
still remains due and unpaid on said judgment, and that
execution had been issued thereon, and returned with the
report that no property could be found; that appellant

Williams possessed money and personal property which he
failed and neglected to produce and apply to the satisfaction of said judgment, and that an order of court was
necessary in order that said Williams might be required to
submit his property to the satisfaction of said judgment.

Appellant appeared in response to the citation, and made
a motion to quash the service and return thereof, on the
ground that the issuance of said citation was inadvertent,
wrongful, and without the jurisdiction of the court, said
motion being based upon all the records in said action and
upon the affidavit of appellant. The affidavit set forth
that, during the years 1897 and 1898, prior to the 6th day
of August, 1898, appellant was engaged in the mercantile
business in the state of Washington, under the name and
style of Columbia Hardware Company; that on the 6th
day of August, 1898, he made a general assignment of all
his assets, of every kind and character, for the benefit of
all his creditors; that, in his said deed of assignment,
appellant gave a list of all of his creditors and the creditors
of said Columbia Hardware Company and the amount of
their claims; that thereafter, on the 25th day of August,
1898, Morton Doty, as assignee of said estate, filed his
bond as required by law, took possession of all the assets
and property belonging to the said assigned estate, and
filed in the office of the clerk of the superior court of the
state of Washington in and for Stevens county, where said
assignment was made, his inventory of the assets of said
estate, showing the same to be of the value of $2,071.11;
that the assignee thereafter gave notice of said assignment,
as required by law, to all the creditors of affiant, and the
said Columbia Hardware Company, including respondent;
that the judgment in this action, and upon which said supplemental proceeding is based, is for an indebtedness of
this affiant and of the Columbia Hardware Company, on

account of goods purchased by said Columbia Hardware
Company prior to the 6th day of August, 1898, and that
the judgment creditor herein, Jensen-King-Byrd Company,
was duly and regularly notified of the making of said assignment by said assignee, as required by law, and that
neither the Jensen-King-Byrd Company, nor any other
creditor of the appellant, nor of the Columbia Hardware
Company, at any time instituted bankruptcy proceedings
against affiant or the said Columbia Hardware Company,
under the federal bankruptcy law, notwithstanding the fact
that respondent, and all other creditors of affiant, had full
knowledge and information, by notice to them by said assignee, of the fact that said assignment had been made;
and that affiant was led to believe, by respondent's silence
and inaction, that respondent acquiesced in and ratified
appellant's assignment for the benefit of his creditors, and
would be satisfied with its proportionate share of the assets
of said estate.

Controverting affidavits denied that the respondent had
acquiesced in, or would be satisfied with, its proportionate
share of the assets of said estate. The court overruled the
motion to quash, and, the appellant having admitted his
ability to pay said judgment, the court made and entered
an order requiring appellant to pay to the clerk of the said
superior court the sum demanded.

It is assigned that the court erred in denying appellant's
motion to quash, and in entering the order appealed from
requiring appellant to pay the clerk of the superior court
the sum of $458.85, with interest and costs, in satisfaction
of respondent's judgment. So that it will be seen that the
vital question to be determined in this case is whether or
not the bankruptcy law, which was passed by the United
States Congress and approved on July 1, 1898 [30 Stat.
544; U. S. Comp. St. 1901, p. 3418], supersedes or sus-

pends the state insolvency law which was in existence at
the time of the passage of said bankruptcy act.

There is some conflict in judicial decisions on this question, but it was decided by this court, in *State ex rel. Strohl
v. Superior Court*, 20 Wash. 545, 56 Pac. 35, 45 L. R. A.
177, that the enactment of the federal bankruptcy law of
July 1, 1898, did not suspend the jurisdiction of state
courts in insolvency cases, where there had been no proceedings in bankruptcy instituted respecting the matter in
controversy. This doctrine was reaffirmed in *State ex rel.
Heckman v. Superior Court*, 28 Wash. 35, 68 Pac. 170,
92 Am. St. 826, where the doctrine was unequivocally announced that an adjudication of bankruptcy, made in the
federal court under the United States bankruptcy law, will
not deprive a state court of jurisdiction in a pending suit,
in which such bankrupts are involved as parties; citing
Eyster v. Gaff, 91 U. S. 521, 23 L. Ed. 403, where the following language was used:

"It is a mistake to suppose that the bankrupt law avoids
of its own force all judicial proceedings in the state or other
courts the instant one of the parties is adjudged a bankrupt.
There is nothing in the act which sanctions such a proposition. . . . The same courts remain open to him in
such contests, and the statute has not divested those courts
of jurisdiction in such actions. If it has for certain classes
of actions conferred a jurisdiction for the benefit of the
assignee in the circuit and district courts of the United
States, it is concurrent with and does not divest that of the
state courts."

This case falls within the rule announced in the cases just
cited, and the motion of the appellant should have been sustained.

The contention of the respondent, that § 15 of the act
entitled, "An act to secure creditors a just division of the
estate of debtors who conveyed to assignee for the benefit

of creditors" [Laws 1890, p. 88], is not constitutional, being in conflict with § 19, art. 2 of the constitution of the state of Washington—which is to the effect that no bill shall embrace more than one subject and that shall be expressed in the title—is without merit and cannot be sustained under the uniform holdings of this court. The cause will be reversed, and remanded with instructions to dismiss the proceeding.

FULLERTON, C. J., and HADLEY, MOUNT, and ANDERS, JJ., concur.

[No. 4915.   Decided May 23, 1904.]

W. M. WINDHAM et al., Respondents, v. INDEPENDENT TELEPHONE COMPANY et al., Appellants.[1]

MECHANICS' LIENS — FORECLOSURE — EVIDENCE — SUFFICIENCY—SUBSTANTIAL COMPLETION OF BUILDING—ACCEPTANCE BY OWNER—ARCHITECT'S CERTIFICATE. An action to foreclose a mechanics' lien should not be dismissed, because it appears that it would take the trifling sum of $57 to complete a $3,850 building, where the record shows a substantial compliance with the contract, together with an offer on the part of contractors to complete any work, and where the building was received and occupied, and the refusal of the architect to furnish the required certificate was whimsical.

Appeal from a judgment of the superior court for King county, Morris, J., entered June 1, 1903, upon findings in favor of the plaintiffs, after a trial on the merits before the court without a jury, foreclosing a mechanics' lien. Affirmed.

Piles, Donworth & Howe, for appellants.

Smith & Cole, for respondents Windham et al.

Hastings & Stedman, for respondents Baker et al.

[1]Reported in 76 Pac. 936.

DUNBAR, J.—This is an appeal from a judgment establishing a lien in favor of each of the respondents upon lot 3, block 15, C. D. Boren's addition to the city of Seattle, and decreeing a sale of the premises to satisfy said liens. The liens grew out of a building contract entered into between the appellant owners of the property and respondents Windham & Combs, building contractors. The other respondents furnished materials for the building. The respondents Windham & Combs sued for a balance on the original contract of $3,850, and for an amount due by reason of deviations from the original contract, in the sum of $1,723. The defendants prayed for the dismissal of the complaint, and for damages for violation of the contract in the sum of $2,000.

This case rests entirely upon the evidence, and, from a careful examination of the statement of facts, we are satisfied that the facts found by the court were justified by the evidence, and that the findings of fact justified the conclusions of law and the judgment. This case does not fall within the principles announced in *Schmidt v. North Yakima,* 12 Wash. 121, 40 Pac. 790, which is cited by appellants to sustain the contention that the action should have been dismissed for the reason that it appears that it would take $57.25 to complete the building, and for the further reason that no certificate had been furnished by the architect. In the first place, the item is trifling, compared with the amount which was due on the contract; in the second place, the record shows not only a substantial compliance with the contract, but an offer on the part of the contractors, seasonably made, to complete any work that might be found to be incomplete, and to make such slight repairs or corrections as might be required; and, in the third place, the building was re-

ceived by the appellants, who moved into and occupied
it with the understanding, upon the announcement made
by the architect and by the contractors, that the occupancy of the building at that time would constitute an
acceptance of it. So that any question of the refusal of
the architect to furnish a certificate becomes immaterial.
In addition to this, the record shows a practical compliance
with the contract, and the refusal of the architect to furnish a certificate was whimsical, and such refusal cannot
prevent a recovery.

We are unable to discover any objection to the lien
notices, and are not inclined to disturb the judgment of
the court in relation to attorney's fees; and, without entering into a detailed analysis of the evidence, we are satisfied that substantial justice was done by the lower court,
and the judgment is therefore affirmed.

FULLERTON, C. J., and HADLEY, MOUNT, and ANDERS,
JJ., concur.

[No. 5056. Decided May 22, 1904.]

THE STATE OF WASHINGTON, *on the Relation of W. B.*
Stratton, Respondent, v. C. W. MAYNARD, *as*
State Treasurer, Appellant.[1]

STATE OFFICERS — ATTORNEY GENERAL — SALARY — TERRITORIAL
LAW ALLOWING FEES—REPEAL. Territorial Laws, 1887-8, providing that the attorney general shall receive an annual salary of
$1,800, and the further sum of ten per cent on all money collected
upon legal process instituted to enforce claims due the territory,
is repugnant to Const., art. 3, § 21. providing that he shall receive
an annual salary of $2,000, which may be increased by the
legislature, but shall never exceed $3,500, since it is clearly the

[1]Reported in 76 Pac. 937.

intent of the constitution that the whole compensation of the
executive officers should be fixed by salary, as distinguished
from the fee system.

Appeal from a judgment of the superior court for Thurston county, Linn, J., entered January 11, 1904, upon
overruling a demurrer to the complaint, granting a writ
of mandate, as prayed for. Reversed.

Frank C. Owings, for appellant.

E. W. Ross and *C. C. Dalton,* for respondent. The
terms "compensation" and "salary" are used in the constitution with distinct meanings. Const. art. 3, §§ 21,
25; art. 2, § 25; art. 4, § 13; art. 11, §§ 5, 8. There is
a clear distinction between compensation and salary; the
former includes the latter, but not *vice versa. Kilgore
v. People,* 76 Ill. 548; *State ex rel. Murphy v. Barnes,*
24 Fla. 29; *Dane v. Smith,* 54 Ala. 47; *Benedict v.
United States,* 176 U. S. 357, 20 Sup. Ct. 458; *Thompson v. Phillips,* 12 Ohio St. 617; *Cox v. Holmes,* 14
Wash. 255, 44 Pac. 262. Other state constitutions expressly provide that the compensation by fees shall be paid
to the state. *State ex rel. Att'y Gen. v. Leidtke,* 12 Neb.
171; New York Const. art. 5, § 1; Ark. Const. art. 6,
§ 11; Cal. Const. art. 5, § 19; Colo. Const. art. 4, § 19.
The territorial provision for compensation by fees is still
in force because not expressly repealed or repugnant to
the constitution. Laws 1887, p. 7, § 8; Const. art. 27,
§ 2; *Hamilton v. St. Louis County Court,* 15 Mo. 5;
Bandel v. Isaac, 13 Md. 202; *People v. Gies,* 25 Mich.
82; *Stewart v. Sup'rs of Polk County,* 30 Iowa 9, 1 Am.
Rep. 238; *Lafayette etc. R. Co. v. Geiger,* 34 Ind. 185.
To repeal it by implication it must appear to be in conflict with an express constitutional provision. *State ex
rel. Murphy v. McBride,* 29 Wash. 341, 70 Pac. 25;

State v. Clark, 30 Wash. 439, 71 Pac. 20; *State v. Vance,*
29 Wash. 459, 70 Pac. 34; *Smith v. Seattle,* 25 Wash.
308, 65 Pac. 312. And this must be clear and unquestioned. *Nelson v. Troy,* 11 Wash. 438, 39 Pac. 974;
Reeves v. Anderson, 13 Wash. 20, 42 Pac. 625; *Ah Lim
v. Territory,* 1 Wash. 156, 24 Pac. 588, 9 L. R. A. 395;
State v. Stoll, 17 Wall. 425; *United States v. Claflin,*
97 U. S. 546; *Tacoma Land Co. v. Pierce County,* 1 Wash.
482, 25 Pac. 904; *Coler v. Rhoda Tp.,* 6 S. D. 640, 63
N. W. 158. None but inconsistent laws were repealed
by the constitution. *Cass v. Dillon,* 2 Ohio St. 607;
State ex rel. Evans v. Dudley, 1 Ohio St. 437. The
constitution is to be construed with reference to existing
laws. *Board of Directors v. Peterson,* 4 Wash. 147, 29
Pac. 995; *Peterson v. Dillon,* 27 Wash. 83, 67 Pac. 397;
Winsor v. Bridges, 24 Wash. 544, 64 Pac. 780; *State ex
rel. Atty. Gen. v. Seattle Gas Co.,* 28 Wash. 496, 68
Pac. 946, 70 Pac. 114; *State ex rel. Clark v. Neterer,* 33
Wash. 535, 74 Pac. 668; *Collins v. Tracy,* 36 Tex. 546;
Cass v. Dillon, 2 Ohio St. 607; *Rich v. Flanders,* 39 N.
H. 304; *Snyder v. Compton,* 87 Tex. 374, 28 S. W. 1061;
Bandel v. Isaac, 13 Md. 202; *Mayor v. State,* 15 Md.
376, 74 Am. Dec. 572; *Servis v. Beatty,* 32 Miss. 52.
The fact that the attorney general was receiving compensation by fees, and the constitution did not prohibit
it, indicates an intention to continue it. *O'Gorman v.
Mayor,* 67 N. Y. 486; *Cox v. Holmes, supra.* The terms
salary and compensation must be given the same meaning
in the constitution as in the former laws. *Duramus v.
Harrison,* 26 Ala. 326. The former laws and the constitution should be read and construed together as parts of
one act. *Billingsley v. State,* 14 Md. 369, 74 Am. Dec.
544; *Fowler v. Poor,* Dallam (Tex.) 401; *Austin v.*

Gulf etc. R. Co., 45 Tex. 236.   The following cases are
squarely in point upon the law and the merits of this
case: *Pillsbury v. Brown*, 45 Cal. 46; *O'Gorman v.
Mayor*, 67 N. Y. 486; *Thon v. Commonwealth*, 77 Va.
289; *Smith v. City*, 54 Conn. 174, 7 Atl. 17; *Chatfield
v. Washington County*, 3 Ore. 318; *Commonwealth ex
rel. Wolfe v. Butler*, 99 Pa. St. 535.

PER CURIAM.—This is an application for a writ of
màndate, made by respondent, who is attorney general,
to compel the state treasurer of the state of Washington
to receive the amount recovered in a judgment, which the
state of Washington obtained against the city of Seattle,
less ten per cent of the amount of said judgment, which
has been retained by the attorney general, and which he
claims he is entitled to under the provisions of the law.
This money was recovered in an action brought by the
attorney general, claiming the same to be due the state
on account of liquor licenses, collected by said city of
Seattle. To a complaint setting up substantially these
facts, the appellant demurred generally in the lower court,
which demurrer was overruled. Whereupon appellant refused to plead further, and the court entered judgment
against him. From that judgment this appeal is taken.

Section 8, chapter 7, of the acts of the territorial legislature of 1887-8, reads as follows:

"The attorney general shall receive an annual salary of
$1,800, payable out of the territorial treasury. He shall
also receive the further sum of ten per centum on all
money collected and paid into the territorial treasury,
upon legal process instituted to enforce the payment of
any claim due the territory for money, property, or damages which per centum, in addition to the other legal costs
incident to the procedure, shall, unless otherwise directed

by the court, be paid by the party defendant, and allowed
as costs in the action."

Section 21 art. 3, of the state constitution, is as follows:

"The attorney general shall be the legal adviser of the
state officers, and shall perform such other duties as may
be prescribed by law. He shall receive an annual salary
of two thousand dollars, which may be increased by the
legislature, but shall never exceed thirty-five hundred
dollars per annum."

There has been no compensation for the attorney general fixed by legislative enactment, since the admission
of the state into the Union and the adoption of its constitution, and it is the contention of the respondent that
the territorial provision, in relation to the per centum
to which the attorney general is entitled, is now in force,
and that the constitutional provision affected only that
portion of the territorial law which related to the salary;
while the appellant contends that, upon the admission of
the state into the Union, the territorial statute became
inoperative, because of its repugnance to § 21, art. 3,
of the state constitution, quoted above, and that the word
"salary," as used in the constitution, should be construed
to be synonymous with the word "compensation."

Conceding the contention of the respondent that existing laws are not to be changed by the adoption of the
constitution, except as far as they may be inconsistent
with its provisions, we are of the opinion that the provisions of the territorial act are in conflict with the provisions of the constitution, in relation to the compensation
of the attorney general, and that the constitution sought,
in § 21, supra, to prescribe the compensation for such
officer. The language of the constitution appears to us
so plain that it seems scarcely susceptible of construction,
but, if construction be resorted to, there are two rules

of construction which must be applied and which, it
seems to us, are controlling: (1) If the intention of
the lawmaking power is plainly discernible from the language employed, the law must be construed in accordance with such manifest intention, without the aid of
other rules of construction; for the object of all canons
of construction is to aid in properly arriving at the intention of the framers of the law in question; (2) a constitution being adopted by the votes of the common people,
its language must be particularly construed in accordance
with the common understanding of the words and language employed; although, if there were no difference
in the rule of construction employed in interpreting constitutional and legislative enactments, it would be equally
clear to us that the contention of the respondent could not
be maintained. For we think it is plain, not only from
the language used, but from the connection of the language with other provisions of the constitution, that it
was the intention of the framers of the constitution that
the attorney general should be fully compensated by the
salary prescribed.

Article 3 undertakes to define the duties and fix the
salaries of all the executive officers of the state. Section
14 provides that the governor shall receive an annual
salary of $4,000, which may be increased by law, but
shall never exceed $6,000. Section 16 prescribes the
qualifications of the lieutenant governor, and provides
that he shall receive an annual salary of $1,000, which
may be increased by the legislature, but shall never exceed
$3,000 per annum. Section 17, after prescribing the
qualifications of the secretary of state, provides that he
shall receive an annual salary of $2,500, which may be
increased by the legislature, but shall never exceed $3,000

per annum. Section 19 provides that the treasurer shall receive an annual salary of $2,000, which may be increased by the legislature, but shall never exceed $4,000 per annum. Section 20 specifies the qualifications of the auditor, and provides that he shall receive an annual salary of $2,000, which may be increased by the legislature, but shall never exceed $3,000 per annum. Section 21 prescribes the qualifications and duties of the attorney general, and provides that he shall receive an annual salary of $2,000, which may be increased by the legislature, but shall never exceed $3,500 per annum; and section 22 makes similar provisions for the salary of the superintendent of public instruction, with a limitation of $4,000 per annum.

Upon reading this chapter, disconnected from any other law, the first and only thought would be that the compensation, and the whole compensation, of the executive officers, regardless of what word was used to express it, was fixed by this article of the constitution; and, while it is true that the laws which were in existence at the time of the adoption of the constitution, and not in conflict with its provisions, remained in force and effect, it is plain to us that the territorial law relied upon by the respondent is in conflict with the plainly expressed intention of the framers of the constitution in relation to the salary of the attorney general, and that there was no thought of adding the old compensation to the new one prescribed in connection with the salary of the other executive officers, but that the act was complete within itself, governing all the compensation of all the officers mentioned therein. The fact must not be lost sight of that the main office of a state constitution is to limit legislative power, and it is too evident for discussion

that a limitation on the compensation to be allowed the
attorney general was sought to be imposed in § 21, when
it said, "He shall receive an annual salary of $2,000,
which may be increased by the legislature, but shall
never exceed $3,500 per annum." We must not impute
to the framers of the constitution the commission of so
foolish and vain an act as that of prescribing a limitation which, in effect, is no limitation at all; for while,
under the construction contended for, the legislature was
limited to prescribing a salary not exceeding $3,500, it
could indirectly, through the medium of fees allowed,
increase indefinitely the amount of pay allowed the officer.
It was the compensation of the officer which was the
material thing with which the constitution was dealing;
in plain phrase, the amount of money which the state
would have to pay out of its treasury for his services.
Whether that amount should be paid out under the term
"compensation," "salary," or "fees" was unimportant.

It is said that the constitution nowhere provides that
the compensation of the attorney general shall be fixed
by salary; that it provides what his salary shall be, but
does not fix his compensation. This contention is answered
by what we have said above, viz., that it was the compensation to which the constitution was prescribing a
limit. It is argued that the same rule will not obtain
in construing this law, as in construing the law in relation to the salaries of county officers, because § 8, art.
11, prescribes that the legislature shall fix the compensation, by salaries, of all county officers; and that there is
no such provision in the constitution in relation to the
attorney general, but there is simply a provision that the
legislature shall fix his salary with certain limitations,
and that, therefore, it follows that the framers of the

constitution did not use the word "salary" in the large sense in which the word compensation is used in § 8, referred to above. We are not able to gather from the language of the constitution itself, or from any of its provisions in any other respect, that there was any intention to make a distinction in this respect. There was no necessity to use the expression "fix the compensation by salary," with relation to the state officers, for the constitution itself fixed the salaries of state officers, leaving discretion in the legislature as to the county officers, and providing only for a limitation on the power of the legislature in raising the salaries of state officers, which had already been fixed by the constitution.

We see nothing in the opinion of this court in *Cox v. Holmes,* 14 Wash. 255, 44 Pac. 262, to sustain respondent's contention. That was a case where the provisions of art. 11, § 8, of the constitution, providing that the legislature shall fix the compensation, by salaries, of all county officers (except certain enumerated ones), were construed with relation to the provision contained in the laws of 1890, p. 361, § 17, providing that county superintendents shall receive compensation at the rate of three dollars for each school visited, such law being held invalid, as being opposed to the constitutional provision. The court, in discussing the case, said:

"We think that the system which the framers of the constitution intended to provide by § 8, *supra,* was that of 'fixed' and established 'compensation by time,' as distinguished from the system of specific fees for specific services which had theretofore prevailed; and, although the word 'salary' is sometimes used to denote compensation paid for a particular service, it was used in the constitution to mean 'a payment dependent on the time and not on the amount of the service rendered' by the officer."

So, we think here that the whole idea of the constitution was of compensation by salary, as distinguished from the fee system, which had theretofore prevailed, and that the word 'salary' was used in the constitution to mean a payment dependent on the time, and not upon the amount of the services rendered; or, in other words, when the salary for a year was prescribed, it was meant that the prescribed salary should be the compensation for a year. The respondent has filed a very learned and elaborate brief, citing many cases on many propositions, a review of which we do not think it advisable to undertake; for, under the plain provisions of the constitution itself, we are forced to the conclusion that the compensation of the attorney general is limited to the salary prescribed by the constitution, there having been no other or different salary prescribed by the legislature since.

The judgment will be reversed, and the cause remanded, with instructions to sustain the demurrer to the complaint.

[No. 4795. Decided May 31, 1904.]

Azoa Foster, *Appellant*, v. Seattle Electric Company, *Respondent*.

Carriers—Negligence—Instructions—Duty Owed to Passengers—Highest Degree of Care Consistent with Practical Conduct of Business. In an action against a street railway company to recover damages for personal injuries, an instruction to the effect that the company is not liable if it exercises towards its passengers the highest degree of care consistent with the practical conduct of its business, is a correct statement of defendant's legal duty.

Same. While it is incorrect in giving such an instruction, to further state that the conductor of the car should exercise the

[1]Reported in 76 Pac. 995.

highest degree of care "consistent with the proper discharge of
all the other duties of such employes," yet it is not prejudicial
error where there was no evidence to the effect that the injury
was caused by the fact that he was engaged in the performance
of any other duty.

SAME—DUTY OF CARRIER TO ONE DESIRING TO BECOME A PASSEN-
GER. Street railway employes are not required to exercise the
highest degree of care in ascertaining whether a person desires
to become a passenger, hence it is not error to instruct that
the company is not liable to one injured in attempting to
board a car, if the conductor, by the exercise of ordinary care,
could not have seen him before starting the car.

SAME—RELATION OF PASSENGER AND CARRIER. To give rise to
the relation of passenger and carrier, there must be the intent
of the former to become a passenger, and an implied or express
acceptance of the latter, and one who attempts to board a
starting car from a position where he could not be seen by the
company's employes, by the exercise of ordinary care on their
part, is not a passenger.

APPEAL—REVIEW—HARMLESS ERROR—INSTRUCTION NOT PERTI-
NENT. An instruction is not necessarily prejudicially erroneous
because it includes an abstract error which is not pertinent to
the balance of the instructions nor to any of the evidence, when
it does not take any question of fact from the jury.

Appeal from a judgment of the superior court for King
county, Morris, J., entered February 11, 1903, upon the
verdict of a jury in favor of the defendant, after a trial
on the merits. Affirmed.

Benson & Hall, for appellant.

Struve, Hughes & McMicken, for respondent.

FULLERTON, C. J.—The appellant was injured while
attempting to board one of the respondent's street cars
in the city of Seattle, and brought this action to recover
for her injuries, averring that they were caused by the
negligence of the agents and servants of the respondent.
The trial resulted in a verdict and judgment for the respondent.

The car which the appellant was attempting to board was a large vestibuled car, having but one place open, at the time of the accident, where passengers could board the same, which was at the right hand side of the rear platform. As the car proceeded along its route, it passed westerly along Pike street to the intersection of Second avenue, where it turned south, stopping at a few feet south of Pike street. The evidence of both sides agrees that, while the car was standing where it had stopped, two passengers entered it, and that the conductor thereupon signalled the motorman to proceed, and that the car started just as the appellant was in the act of boarding the same. The appellant's evidence tended to show that she was following immediately after the two passengers who did enter the car in safety, so close, in fact, that she was compelled to wait an instant for the last one, and that she was in such a position, when the conductor signalled the car to start, that he could have seen her, had he looked in that direction. The defendant's evidence tended to show that the conductor was in a position where he could plainly see the entrance, when the car came to a stop on Second avenue. He testified that, when the car stopped, he ceased the work he was engaged in, and looked back to the car entrance, and saw the two passengers enter; that, when the second one got on, he looked to ascertain if any one else was entering, or desirous of entering, and, seeing no one, gave the signal to go ahead, and began again his regular duties. There was evidence tending to corroborate the conductor; and evidence, also, to the effect that the appellant approached the car from the rear, out of the sight of the conductor, reaching it after the signal to go ahead had been given, and just as the car started; that others, standing by, saw and appreciated her danger, and sought to warn her by hallooing; that the place where the accident occurred was a busy thoroughfare, and that more than the ordinary number of people were there at that time, owing to the fact that some social gathering had been held during the evening at the Masonic Temple, which stood near this place, and people were then leaving that place.

The court in charging the jury gave, among others, the following instructions:

"(2) I instruct you, second, that if you believe from the evidence in this case that the plaintiff, in her efforts to get upon the defendant's car at the time and place and manner alleged in her complaint, acted as an ordinarily prudent woman generally acts under circumstances entirely similar to all those which then surrounded the plaintiff; and if you believe, from a preponderance of the evidence, that the plaintiff attempted to get upon the defendant's car while the same was standing still and immediately after the other passengers had boarded the train, and that the defendant's servants started said car without having exercised the highest degree of care reasonably practicable under the circumstances and conditions existing at the time and place in question, to see that all persons who were in the act of boarding the said car were in places of safety, and that the negligent starting of the said car threw the plaintiff to the pavement and injured her as alleged in the complaint, then and in that event, your verdict will be for the plaintiff.

"(3) If you find for the plaintiff, you will by your verdict award her one such gross sum, not exceeding the demand of her amended complaint, which is fifteen thousand dollars, as will in your opinion from the evidence justly, fairly, and fully compensate the plaintiff for all suffering, if any, which she has necessarily endured, as well as all that she will necessarily endure in the future, if any; for all time which the plaintiff has necessarily lost, if any, and all which she will necessarily lose, if any; for all permanent impairment of health, if any, which she has sustained; for all medical treatment, if any, for which she has become obligated; provided, however, that you will not permit the plaintiff to recover for anything which was not the proximate, natural, and necessary result of the negligent acts complained of in the plaintiff's complaint.

"(4) Contributory negligence is pleaded as a defense in this case, and the burden of proving the same is upon the defendant. To sustain this defense it must appear to you, by a fair preponderance of the evidence, that the plaintiff contributed to her own injury by failing to act as ordinarily prudent women generally act under circumstances entirely similar to all those which surrounded the plaintiff at and just prior to her injury. Every person who rightfully attempts to board a street car as a passenger, at a place where such car usually receives passengers, has a right to assume that the men in charge of such car will exercise the highest degree of care reasonably practicable under the circumstances for the safety of all persons upon the said car or who may be lawfully attempting to get upon the same; and no passenger should be held guilty of contributory negligence because he or she failed to anticipate negligence, if such there was, upon the part of the men in charge of the car which he or she was attempting to board.

"(6) With respect to the degree of care owed by the defendant to its passengers, you are instructed that the duty enjoined by the law upon its conductor and motorman does not require the exercise of the highest degree of care possible to avoid an accident, but only the highest degree of care reasonably practicable under the circumstances and conditions existing at the time and place in question and consistent with the proper discharge of all the other duties of such employes. By the term 'highest degree of care' used in these instructions is meant that degree of care which would be exercised under like circumstances by careful, prudent, and experienced conductors and motormen generally.

"(7) The plaintiff in this case would not be a passenger within the meaning of the law, unless you find from the evidence that plaintiff in the exercise of reasonable care and prudence on her part was actually attempting to board the said car, or so near thereto and in such a position as to indicate her intention so to do, in such manner as reasonably careful and prudent persons ordinarily board cars under like circumstances, and that the conductor either saw, or in the exercise of reasonable care should have seen, her intention so to do, before giving the signal for said car to start.

"(8) If you believe from the evidence that the plaintiff came up to the said car from the rear, and was in a position where the conductor in the exercise of ordinary care in looking for intending passengers at the rear entrance of his car would not ordinarily see plaintiff, and if you further find that the said conductor, in the exercise of such care, did look and did not in fact see the plaintiff, and at once gave the signal to go ahead, and the car thereupon started, then there can be no recovery in this case and your verdict will be for the defendant.

"(9) You are further instructed that if you find from the evidence that the conductor of said car, at the time of arriving at the corner of Pike street and Second avenue, was engaged in collecting fare or making change for a passenger, and after said car had stopped and before starting the same again, he was in a position where he could plainly see the rear entrance of said car through which passenegrs are permitted to board the same; and if you further find from the evidence that before giving the signal to his motorman to start said car he did, in fact, look to see whether there were any other persons about to board said car, and if in so doing he exercised the degree of care and prudence that would be employed by reasonably careful conductors under like circumstances, and did not see that plaintiff was approaching said car or was about to attempt to board the same, before giving his signal, then you should not find him guilty of negligence.

"(10) If you find from the evidence that the car in question stopped on Second avenue on the south side of Pike street for the purpose of receiving passengers in the usual way, and if you further believe from the evidence that the plaintiff came running towards said car from the rear thereof across the intersection of Pike street, and grabbed the handle-bar and attempted to board said car after the signal had been givèn and the said car was starting forward in the usual manner, then plaintiff assumed all the natural risks incident to such attempt to board the car, and under such circumstances she cannot hold defendant responsible therefor.

"(11) You are further instructed that if you find from the evidence that while said car was standing still, waiting to receive passengers on the south side of Second avenue, the plaintiff ran diagonally across Pike street towards the rear of said car, and if you believe that after the signal had been given to start said car the plaintiff caught hold of the handle-bar of said car and attempted to board the same after it was in motion, and that in so doing she did not exercise the degree of care and prudence that would be exercised by ordinary persons under like circumstances, then it will be your duty to return a verdict for the defendant."

The assignments of error are all based on the instructions. It is urged that the sixth instruction is erroneous, because it reduces the degree of care required of the appellant's servants, while looking after the safety of its passengers, to that of ordinary care, and because, "by it the conductor was practically excused from looking after the plaintiff at all during such times as he was engaged in performing any duty for the defendant." It seems to us these criticisms are not well founded. It is evident that the court was endeavoring, by this instruction, to define the phrase, "highest degree of care," used in the second instruction above quoted, and to explain to the jury its applicability to the case before them. Leaving out the clause with reference to the other duties of the

employes, the rule there laid down is not inconsistent
with the rule as we have heretofore announced it in,
Sears v. Seattle Consol. etc., Co., 6 Wash. 227, 33 Pac.
389, 1081, and *Payne v. Spokane Street R. Co.*, 15 Wash.
522, 46 Pac. 1054. It is not the rule that a street
car company is an insurer of the safety of its passengers.
There are dangers attending on their transportation which
it seems no human prudence can foresee, while there are
others which can be foreseen, but which cannot be effectually guarded against, because to do so would make the
conduct of the business so burdensome as to prohibit it
altogether. Hence, when a street car company exercises
towards its passengers the highest degree of care consistent with the practical conduct of its business, it performs towards them its full legal duty, and is not liable,
even for injuries which might have been foreseen and
prevented, if the means required to prevent them would
involve a burden amounting to a practical prohibition of
the business. The instruction is consistent with these
principles, and therefore is not erroneous.

With reference to the remaining part of the objection,
it is, doubtless, incorrect to say, without further qualification, that the duty of the conductor and motorman of an
electric street car towards the passengers thereon, is to exercise the highest degree of care consistent with the proper
discharge of all the other duties of such employes, yet
we do not think it reversible error in this case. There
was no evidence to the effect that the injury to the appellant was caused by the fact that the conductor or motorman was engaged in the performance of another duty,
and therefore could not look out for the appellant. As
to the motorman, no blame at all can be attached to him.
He obeyed the signals given him by the conductor, and it

is not in evidence that he saw or knew that to obey such signals would result, or was likely to result, in an injury to the appellant. The negligence, if any, was on the part of the conductor, and, as to negligence on his part, there was a sharp conflict in the evidence. If the appellant's evidence was to be believed, then he was guilty of negligence in starting the car at the time he did start it, no matter what other duty he was performing at the time, and the court practically so told the jury. On the other hand, if the evidence on behalf of the respondent was to be believed, the conductor performed towards her his full duty, and the injury was the result of the conduct of the appellant herself, rather than the result of negligence on the part of the conductor. Under these circumstances, the error could not have been prejudicial, and, as we have repeatedly held, error without prejudice is not cause for reversal.

Instruction numbered seven is objected to, because it is said that it reduces the degree of care required of the appellant's servants to that of ordinary care, while the true rule is that the highest degree of care reasonably practicable under the circumstances should be exercised. But the rule contended for by appellant is applicable only after one has become a passenger. The company is not required to exercise the highest degree of care to ascertain whether or not a particular person walking or standing on a public street desires to become a passenger on its car. Ordinary care is all that is necessary in such a case. The instruction here complained of was intended to define the degree of care required of the respondent's servants in ascertaining whether or not a particular person desired to become a passenger, and is a correct statement of the rule in that regard.

The eighth instruction is objected to for the same reason, but we think the instruction without error. "To give rise to the relation of passenger and carrier there must be not only an intent on the part of the former to avail himself of the facilities of the latter for transportation, but also an express or implied acceptance by the latter of the former as a passenger." 6 Cyc. 538. Under the conditions described in the instruction, the appellant had not yet become a passenger, and, as we said in answer to the last objection, the servants of the company owed her only the duty of ordinary care. *Gaffney v. St. Paul City R. Co.*, 81 Minn. 459, 84 N. W. 304.

It is objected to the ninth instruction that it took from the jury one of the material issues of fact, in that it did not leave to them the question what is, and what is not, a proper time to take up fares, but we think the appellant misinterprets it. The matter relating to the making of change for a passenger could well have been omitted, as it was neither pertinent to the balance of the instruction, nor to any of the evidence in the case, but it takes no question of fact from the jury. Nor does it require a reversal of the judgment because it is not pertinent. Mere abstract error is never sufficient for that purpose; it must be prejudicial.

The tenth and eleventh instructions are so clearly free from error as not to require comment.

The judgment is affirmed.

DUNBAR, ANDERS, MOUNT, and HADLEY, JJ., concur.

[No. 5009.   Decided May 31, 1904.]

A. A. PHILLIPS *et al., as Executors of the Estate of
Abbie H. H. Stuart, Deceased, Appellants,* v. THURS-
TON COUNTY *et al., Respondents.*[1]

TAXATION — ASSESSMENT — OMITTED PROPERTY — DUTY OF AS-
SESSOR—UNAUTHORIZED ORDER OF COMMISSIONERS. The county
assessor may, on his own motion, enter for assessment on the
list of the current year, any property omitted from the list of
any preceding year, and the fact that the county commissioners
made an unauthorized order that he do so, does not affect the
validity of such an assessment, or show that the assessor did
not exercise his own discretion in the matter.

SAME — EXCESSIVE ASSESSMENT — VALIDITY — JURISDICTION OF
COURTS TO RESTRAIN COLLECTION. Where the assessor adds to
the current assessment, personal property omitted in the preceding year, in a grossly excessive amount, or makes an assessment based upon property not owned by the party or not subject to taxation, the same is void, and the courts have jurisdiction to inquire into the propriety thereof, and to set aside the
excess, or restrain its collection.

SAME—TENDER OF TAX JUSTLY DUE—BRINGING TENDER INTO
COURT—ESTATE ALREADY IN COURT. In such a case a tender of
the amount of the tax due, made before suit and renewed in
the complaint, need not be brought into court, where the property assessed belonged to an estate in the process of administration then under the control of the same court, at least, not
without a specific objection on that ground.

Appeal from a judgment of the superior court for
Thurston county, Linn, J., entered November 17, 1903,
upon sustaining a demurrer to the complaint, dismissing
an action to restrain the collection of a tax. Reversed.

T. N. Allen, for appellants.

F. C. Owings, for respondents.

FULLERTON, C. J.—The appellants, as executors of the
estate of Abbie H. H. Stuart, deceased, brought this action

[1]Reported in 76 Pac. 993.

to enjoin the respondent and its officers from attempting to collect a tax levied against personal property formerly belonging to their testatrix. The trial court sustained a general demurrer to the complaint, and, upon the refusal of the appellants to plead further, entered a judgment of dismissal, and for costs, in favor of the respondents. The ultimate question therefore is, does the complaint state facts sufficient to constitute a cause of action.

In the complaint it is alleged, in substance, that on April 17, 1901, Mrs. Stuart made out a detail list of her personal property subject to taxation in Thurston county, subscribed and made oath to the same as required by law and delivered it to the county assessor, who assessed the property thereon listed at $2,075. Later, Mrs. Stuart died without having paid the taxes. In her will she named the appellants as her executors. They accepted the trust, and, in the performance of their duties as such, paid the taxes assessed upon her property for the year named. Afterwards, and in 1902, the board of county commissioners of Thurston county, conceiving apparently that Mrs. Stuart had omitted from her detail list a large amount of personal property, then owned by her and subject to taxation, directed that the assessor assess the same for the year 1901, as property omitted from the assessment roll for that year, at a valuation of $35,746. Later they directed that the amount of tax paid by the executors on the personal property of the estate for that year be deducted from the amount of the levy. The assessor thereupon assessed the personal property mentioned, for the year 1901, at the amount named in the commissioner's order, as property "inadvertently omitted in that year," notice of which was duly given the executors. On this valuation, a tax was levied of $1,284.45. In making the assessment, however, the assessor did not undertake to list the property omitted. He valued it in one lump sum under the general head of "personal property." On receipt of the notice above mentioned, the executors undertook to ascertain what personal property Mrs. Stuart owned subject to taxation in Thurston county in the year 1901. As a result of their investigation, they found property which might possibly have been subject to taxation for that year, of the value of $10,849.80, which, after deducting the amount given in by Mrs. Stuart, would leave $8,814.80 that had not been assessed. On this sum they offered to pay taxes for the year 1901, as in full for all of the taxes legally due for that year on testatrix' personal property, but this offer was rejected by the county officers. The complaint concludes with allegations to the effect that the attempted assessment was made without any reference to the property actually owned by Mrs. Stuart, and subject to taxation for the year named, and was wholly arbitrary and void. They offer, however, in satisfaction of the claim of the county, to pay taxes on the property to a valuation equal to $8,814.80, which they concede might possibly have been subject to taxation for the year 1901.

The appellants have proceeded on the theory, and their counsel contend in this court, that there is no authority or warrant in law for the board of county commissioners, sitting as a board of equalization or otherwise, to order the assessor to make an assessment of property omitted from the assessment roll of a previous year, and no warrant in law for the assessor to make any such assessment. The appellants are mistaken, however, as regards the assessor. The statute provides that the assessor, upon his own motion, or upon the application of any taxpayer, shall enter in the detail and assessment list of the current year, any property shown to be omitted from the list of any preceding year. Pierce's Code, § 8640. This is ample authority to warrant the assessor in placing on the list for the current year any property omitted for the previous year, and warranted the assessor in making the assessment he made in this case, if it be true that personal property of Mrs. Stuart, to the value mentioned, had not been assessed for the year 1901. The fact that the board of county commissioners, sitting as a board of equalization, may have directed the assessment to be made, does not alter the case. The assessor, notwithstanding the direction may come to him in the form of an order from that board, has the right to exercise his discretion in the matter, and there is nothing in the complaint to show that it was not so exercised in this instance. The assessment is valid, therefore, to the extent of the value of the property assessed.

But, notwithstanding this, we think there is enough in the complaint to show that the valuation of the property omitted was either grossly excessive, or that the assessment was based on property not owned by Mrs. Stuart, or not subject to taxation in Thurston county in the year 1901. For these excesses, the levy was clearly void, and the complaint, we think, was sufficient to require the court to inquire into them, and, if he found either such a disparity in the valuations as the complaint discloses, or that a part of the levy was made on property not subject to taxation, to set aside the excess of tax. In this state the courts have jurisdiction to inquire into the validity of a tax levy on personal property, and to restrain the collection thereof, if found void, at the suit of the injured party, if the tax be due and payable and a levy on the

part of collecting officers is threatened. *Phelan v. Smith,*
22 Wash. 397, 61 Pac. 31; *Northwestern Lumber Co.
v. Chehalis County,* 24 Wash. 626, 64 Pac. 787.

The respondents contend, however, that the demurrer
was properly sustained because the complainants do not
bring into court the amount of tax they concede to be
due. The appellants prosecute this action in a fiduciary
capacity. The trust fund which they represent is now
under the control of the court. For these reasons, we
think it may be doubtful whether the rule requiring a
tender of the tax admitted to be due applies with all of
its strictness. A tender in fact, however, was made, and
the appellants have in their complaint renewed their offer
to pay. Their action will not be dismissed for a mere
failure to bring the money into court, unless a specific
objection is made on that ground, and they have been
placed in default for not so doing.

The judgment appealed from is reversed, and the cause
remanded for further proceedings.

ANDERS, MOUNT, and HADLEY, JJ., concur.

DUNBAR, J., concurs in the result.

[No. 4975. Decided June 9, 1904.]

J. S. INGRAM, *Respondent,* v. WISHKAH BOOM COMPANY,
Appellant.[1]

PLEADINGS — DEFINITENESS — BILL OF PARTICULARS—UNNECES-
SARY TO PLEAD EVIDENCE—DISCOVERY OF FACTS. It is not error
to refuse to require the complaint to be made more definite
and certain or to refuse to require a bill of particulars, where
the complaint pleads the ultimate facts, and the object was
to require the plaintiff to plead his evidence, or to obtain a

[1]Reported in 77 Pac. 34.

discovery of facts in possession of the plaintiff, since the remedy
is by interrogatories served and answered before the trial.

WATERS—RIPARIAN RIGHTS—OVERFLOW IN FLOATING LOGS IN
UNUSUAL MANNER—NEGLIGENCE NOT ESSENTIAL—COMPLAINT—
SUFFICIENCY. A complaint by a riparian owner against a logging
company using the stream for floating and driving logs need
not allege negligence on the part of the defendant, where it is
alleged that the defendant created log jams and by dams and
artificial freshets floated the logs and overflowed plaintiff's
premises, since these acts are wrongful and an abuse of the
right of navigation.

TRIAL—VERDICT—WHEN NOT DISTURBED. A verdict will not
be disturbed where there is substantial evidence in support of
all the issues, and there is nothing to indicate that it was
the result of passion or prejudice.

DAMAGES—EVIDENCE—TESTIFYING TO AMOUNT IN MONEY—
WHEN PERMISSIBLE. In an action by a riparian owner for
damages caused by a boom company in floating logs down a
stream, it is not prejudicial error to allow the plaintiff to testify
to his damage in money, where the injury consisted in the
depreciation of the value of the land and the destruction of
personal property, and he testified as to the values and afterwards stated the sum total, which could have been arrived at
by a mathematical calculation.

EVIDENCE—ADMISSION OF ANSWER WITHOUT THE COMPLAINT—
HARMLESS ERROR. The admission in evidence of an answer to
contradict the statement of the party verifying it, without
introducing the complaint, is harmless where the only part
of the answer read could not have been explained by anything
in the complaint.

Appeal from a judgment of the superior court for Chehalis county, Irwin, J., entered July 25, 1903, upon the
verdict of a jury rendered in favor of the plaintiff, after
a trial on the merits. Affirmed.

Greene & Griffiths (*Sidney Moor Heath*, of counsel),
for appellant.

J. C. Cross, for respondent.

FULLERTON, C. J.—In this action the respondent sued
to recover damages for injuries to his real property, al-

leged to have been caused by the appellant in the operation of its sluice dams on the Wishkah river. After issue
had been joined, a trial was had, resulting in a verdict
and judgment for respondent, from which this appeal
is taken.

The appellant first complains that the trial court erred
in overruling its motion to make the complaint more definite and certain, and in refusing to require the respondent to furnish it with a bill of particulars. The complaint
alleged, in substance, that the appellant was a boom company, organized under the laws of this state, owning and
operating certain sluice dams on the Wishkah river, a
stream navigable for the purpose of floating sawlogs; that
the respondent owned lands through which the Wishkah
river ran, lying below the sluice dams of the appellant;
that he used his lands for a home, and had improvements
thereon consisting of cleared and cultivated lands, buildings, fencing, and certain other structures; and that the
appellant "has never procured from the respondent, by
condemnation or otherwise, any right to the use of his
land whatsoever, as it might do by virtue of the statutes
authorizing its incorporation." The paragraphs of the
complaint containing the allegation of damage are as
follows:

"That during all the times herein mentioned and at
the present time the defendant, the Wishkah Boom Company, has been and is engaged in the sluicing, driving,
booming, and rafting of sawlogs in said river, and through
the lands of this plaintiff, hereinabove described; that, in
the driving of the said sawlogs down the said river, the
said defendant has employed and is employing dams,
whereby and by virtue of which, great and large artificial
freshets are made in said river through the lands of this
plaintiff, and that by reason of such dams and such arti-

13-35 WASH.   .

ficial freshets, through the lands of the plaintiff aforesaid,
and by reason of the driving of large bodies or quantities
of sawlogs by virtue of such artificial freshets through
the lands of this plaintiff, and by reason of the creation
of large jams of sawlogs in said river and within the
boundaries of plaintiff's lands by the said defendant, in
its endeavor to drive the said sawlogs by means of artificial freshets aforesaid through the lands of this plaintiff aforesaid, and on account of each of the said reasons
and uses the said defendant has greatly injured and damni-
fied or damaged the lands of this plaintiff, such damages
being, primarily, as follows, to wit: (1) By creating and
producing great and lasting erosions of the banks of plaintiff's said lands. (2) By causing great quantities of
water, logs, and debris and sediment to flow in, and upon
and over the plaintiff's said lands, thereby destroying the
crops upon the said lands. (3) By causing great quantities
of water, logs, and debris to flow in and upon plaintiff's
said lands, thereby destroying the improvements upon said
lands.

"That by reason of the facts hereinbefore alleged, this
plaintiff has been and is damaged as follows: (1) On
account of erosions, since March 1, 1900, as hereinbefore
set forth in the full and just sum of $200. (2) On ac-
count of injury to the improvements, since March 1, 1900,
as hereinbefore alleged in the full and just sum of $100.
(3) On account of injury and damage to crops, since
March 1, 1900, as hereinbefore alleged in the full and
just sum of $200."

The motion of the appellant, which is too long to set
out here in detail, practically called for the evidence on
which the respondent relied to maintain his cause of
action. But plainly these were not matters which the
plaintiff was required to set out in his complaint. Only
ultimate facts need be pleaded in order to state a cause
of action. There is no requirement that evidence relied
upon to support the facts need be set out. Nor was the
matter demanded the subject for a bill of particulars.

While a bill of particulars may be demanded in certain
kinds of actions as a matter of right (Bal. Code, §4930),
this was not such an action. A bill of particulars may be
ordered when the demand is for particulars of the general items set out in the complaint, but it is not the remedy where discovery is sought of facts in possession of the
plaintiff material to the defense of an action. For discovery of facts in the possession of the other party, the
code provides a remedy by interrogatories served and to
be answered before trial, or by an examination of the
party as a witness at the trial, not by demanding a bill
of particulars.

The appellant next contends that the court erred in
overruling its demurrer to the complaint. It argues that,
inasmuch as the stream was a navigable one, the appellant, along with the public generally, had the right to
use it for the purpose of floating or driving logs, and
that the rights of riparian owners are subordinate to this
use, when reasonably exercised; hence, the complaint, in
order to state a cause of action, must contain an allegation
to the effect that the damage was caused by the negligent
use of the stream. Whether it be the rule that, had the
appellant been using the stream for the purpose of floating and driving logs in the usual and ordinary manner,
and, in spite thereof, had injured the respondent's property, no action would lie against it for such injury, it is
not necessary here to determine. The complaint does not
make that kind of a case. The appellant was not using
the stream in the usual and ordinary manner. It not
only suffered and permitted the logs it was driving to
jam and accumulate in the stream on the respondent's
property, but it sought to remove them by artificial freshets, thereby causing the water to back up and overflow

the respondent's land, washing away the banks of the
stream and the fences protecting the land, destroying the
crops growing thereon, and covering the land with logs
and other debris that would have passed on without damage but for the acts of the appellant.

· As we said in *Watkinson v. McCoy*, 23 Wash. 372,
63 Pac. 245, "The right to float logs down a stream
does not carry with it the right to boom logs in said
stream, or to obstruct it in any way so that it will either
interfere with the rights of other navigators, or cause
damage to riparian proprietors." And we conclude here,
as we concluded in that case, that it is not necessary, where
the injury is caused by a misuse of the stream, or an
abuse of the rights of navigation, to allege in the complaint that the acts were done negligently in order to state
a cause of action for damages arising from such misuse
or abuse. It is sufficient to set out the acts showing the
misuse or abuse of the right navigation, as it is these
acts that give rise to the cause of action. The acts themselves are wrongful; it is not a case of a rightful act
negligently performed.

The appellant challenges the sufficiency of the evidence
to justify the verdict, but we find no cause to interfere
with the verdict on this ground. There was substantial
evidence in support of all of the issues necessary to be
maintained by the respondent, and, unless the verdict
was the result of passion and prejudice, rather than a due
consideration of the evidence, this is sufficient to sustain
it in this court. Of passion and prejudice on the part of
the jury, we find nothing in the record.

The court permitted the respondent to testify to the
amount of his damages in money, and this is assigned as
error by the appellant. We are of the opinion, however,

that the evidence, if not strictly within the rule, was harmless. The damages consisted of a depreciation in value of the real property, and a total destruction of certain personal property. The respondent could properly testify to the value of the real property, both before and after the injury, and to the value of the personalty at the time it was destroyed. This the respondent did do, and for him afterwards to state the sum total of his different losses could not be error, as the ascertainment of the total was a mere solution of an arithmetical problem, the terms of which were stated when he testified to the different values.

But it is said this court has announced a contrary view in *De Wald v. Ingle,* 31 Wash. 616, 72 Pac. 469. In that case we did hold that it was error to permit the plaintiff, in an action for personal injuries, to testify to the amount of his damages in money. The cases rest, however, on widely different principles. In a personal injury case the damages are not capable of anything like exact admeasurement, and cannot be made any more certain by the mere opinion of witnesses. In other words, the question is treated as one not capable of ascertainment by expert or peculiar knowledge, but one resting within the knowledge of the generality of mankind, which the jury alone are qualified to determine, after being made acquainted with the nature and effect of the injury and the circumstances under which it was inflicted. But value, when applied to property, is capable of at least approximate admeasurement, and is a subject on which a person can acquire a knowledge not possessed by the generality of mankind, and is held everywhere to be a proper subject for opinion or expert evidence. Indeed, values could hardly be proved in any other way, and it would practically be a denial of the right to recover for injuries to property, if witnesses were not permitted to give their opinion as to the amount a particular piece of property has depreciated from a given cause.

Many errors are assigned going to the admission and exclusion of evidence, but as the appellant passes all of these with one exception, without comment, we shall treat them in the same manner, saying merely that we have examined each of them, but find nothing that requires a reversal of the case. The exception mentioned is to the admission of an answer, filed by the appellant in an action brought by one Hayes, against the appellant and others, for services performed in driving the logs the respondent contends caused the injury to his property. The answer was verified by a Mr. Emerson, and was introduced to contradict certain statements Mr. Emerson made while testifying for the appellant in this case. The appellant contends that the answer should not have been admitted without introducing, in connection with it, the complaint in the action it purported to answer, and assigns error on that ground. But the only part of the answer read to the jury as material was an allegation describing the corporate powers of the appellant, and the complaint could hardly have explained or aided in an understanding of that paragraph. It is somewhat difficult to discover from the record the materiality of the evidence, but its admission, if error at all, was harmless error.

Lastly the appellant assigns that the court erred in giving, and in refusing to give, certain instructions to the jury. The exception taken to the instructions given was in the following words: "The defendant excepts to that part of the charge given by the court saying in effect that if the jury find that the defendant, or its officers, agents, or employes assisted in breaking the jam, the company would be liable." A careful perusal of the charge as reported in the record fails to disclose any instruction to this effect, unless it is found in the following:

"If you find that there was any such use of this stream by any person in driving these logs or in the use of these dams, as has caused the injury to the plaintiff for which he would be entitled to recover, then you should inquire whether it was done by these defendants, or this defendant company—when we speak of the defendant company we mean its acts through its employes or agents; and that fact must be established by a fair preponderance of the evidence also; if you cannot find that from the preponderance of the evidence or if the evidence is such as to leave you in a condition of uncertainty as to who among the drivers of these logs did cause this damage, or in the operation of the dams, if it was caused in that way, and you cannot say from a fair preponderance of the evidence who did it, then you cannot find the defendant liable. If you can say from a fair preponderance of the evidence that it was done or caused by this defendant company, or its employes, then the plaintiff would be entitled to recover from the company; if you cannot find from a preponderance of the evidence that the employes of the company were operating this dam, nor were driving these logs nor were breaking this jam at the time this alleged injury was sustained, then they are not liable."

There is nothing in this, when read as a whole, that can be said to be prejudicial to the appellant.

The instructions requested and refused merely suggest the appellant's theory of the case, which we have discussed in passing upon its objection to the sufficiency of the complaint, and require no further discussion.

As we find no reversible error in the record, the judgment appealed from will stand affirmed.

DUNBAR, HADLEY, ANDERS, and MOUNT, JJ., concur.

[No. 5105. Decided June 9, 1904.]

THE STATE OF WASHINGTON, *on the Relation of Patrick J. Flaherty et al., Plaintiff,* v. THE SUPERIOR COURT OF KING COUNTY, *Defendant.*[1]

APPEAL — SUPERSEDEAS — INJUNCTION AGAINST OBSTRUCTION OF HIGHWAY. An injunction against the obstruction of a public highway by the locking of gates and the erection of fences cannot be superseded on appeal, since a supersedeas operates only upon orders or judgments commanding some act to be done, and does not reach a case of a forbidden act.

Application filed in the supreme court April 11, 1904, for a writ of mandate to compel the superior court for King county, Tallman, J., to fix the amount of a supersedeas bond on appeal. Writ denied.

George McKay, for relators.

PER CURIAM.—One Edward Van de Vanter brought an action in the superior court of King county, against the relators, to enjoin them from fencing up or otherwise interfering with a certain road leading from his premises, across the premises of the relators, to a recognized public highway. In his complaint he alleged, that the road in question was the only way leading from his premises to the public highway, and that the same had been used by him and his predecessors in interest, without hindrance or interruption, for more than seventeen years last past; that the appellant had attempted to obstruct the way by means of fences, locking of gates, and other acts, and would close the same entirely unless restrained by the court. He prayed a temporary restraining order, which was granted and continued in force until the final trial of the case, when a perpetual

[1]Reported in 77 Pac. 33.

injunction was granted. The relator, desiring to appeal to
this court, applied to the superior court to fix the amount
of a supersedeas bond to be given in order to stay the judgment pending the appeal. That court declined to fix the
amount of the bond, holding that the injunction granted
was not such an injunction as could be superseded, and the
relators apply here for a writ of mandate compelling it to
fix the amount of such bond.

In *State ex rel. Commercial Electric Light & Power Co.
v. Stallcup*, 15 Wash. 263, 46 Pac. 251, we held, construing the statute now in force, that a supersedeas, from its
nature, operated only upon orders or judgments commanding some act to be done, and does not reach a case where
the relief granted merely forbids the doing of some act; in
other words, mandatory injunctions could be superseded,
while those merely preventive could not. The injunction
in the present case is of the latter kind. It is preventive
merely, and cannot be rendered inoperative by a supersedeas.

The application is denied.

[No. 5215. Decided June 9, 1904.]

THE STATE OF WASHINGTON, on *the Relation of Austin
Corbin, 2nd, et al., Plaintiff*, v. THE SUPERIOR
COURT OF LINCOLN COUNTY *et al.,
Defendants.*[1]

CERTIORARI—WHEN LIES—AMOUNT IN CONTROVERSY LESS THAN
$200. A writ of review will not lie to review a judgment from
which no appeal lies because the amount in controversy is
less than $200, and the fact that the judgment is not merely
erroneous, but is void for want of jurisdiction, is immaterial.

[1]Reported in 77 Pac. 33.

Application for a writ of review to review a judgment of the superior court for Lincoln county, Neal, J., entered May 3, 1904. Writ denied.

Hamblen, Lund & Gilbert, for relators.

Myers & Warren, for defendants.

PER CURIAM.—This is an application for a writ of review. Briefly, the relators allege that the defendant, the superior court, at the instance of its co-defendant, entered a judgment against the relators, and in favor of such co-defendant, for the sum of $112, without authority, right, or jurisdiction; that the judgment is by reason thereof void, but that the relators have no right of appeal because the amount of the judgment is not sufficiently large to bring the cause within the appellate jurisdiction of this court, and have no other speedy or adequate remedy at law; wherefore they pray that this court cause the record to be brought before it by a writ of review, and, on the hearing thereof, declare void and set aside the judgment.

The relators concede that this court has held that it will not issue a writ of review in a cause not within its appellate jurisdiction, but argue that this case does not fall within the rule, because here the judgment is void, while in the cases determined by this court the review was sought to correct mere error in the record of the superior court. But, in our judgment, the distinction sought to be made is not sound. As we have construed the constitution, it makes the superior court the court of last resort in all civil actions at law, when the original amount in controversy does not exceed the sum of two hundred dollars. In other words, it matters not whether that court decides that it has jurisdiction when it has not, or whether it erroneously decides some other matter of law, its judgment is final in all causes not within the appellate jurisdiction of this court.

The application is denied.

[No. 4862. Decided June 20, 1904.]

WESLEY DAVIS *et al., Respondents*, v. TACOMA RAILWAY
AND POWER COMPANY *et al., Appellants.*[1]

APPEAL—NOTICE—SERVICE ON CO-PARTIES—DISMISSAL. An appeal by one of two joint wrongdoers from a judgment against
both of them must be dismissed where no notice of appeal
was served upon the co-party, and no joinder was made in the
subsequent appeal of such co-party.

TORTS — PERSONAL INDIGNITIES — DEFAMATION OF CHARACTER—
PUBLIC RESORTS—RIGHT TO REMAIN AT—DAMAGES FOR EXCLUDING
FROM—WORDS NOT ACTIONABLE PER SE. Any person not belonging to a proscribed class who goes to a public pleasure resort
or park, and is not guilty of improper conduct, may recover for
personal indignities inflicted by an employe of the parties owning and in charge of the place, in being publicly ordered out
in an insulting manner as an unfit and improper person, without showing that the language used was actionable *per se*, if
any special damages were suffered.

SAME—MALICE OR WILFUL CONDUCT. In such a case, it is not
necessary for the plaintiff to show malice or a wanton or wilful
wrong in order to recover actual damages, the same being
material only to enhance the damages.

SAME—MEASURE OF DAMAGES—MENTAL SUFFERING IRRESPECTIVE
OF BODILY INJURY. A wrong having been committed by the
defendant in ordering the plaintiff out of a public park where
she had a right to be, it is proper to instruct that the jury,
in estimating the damages, may consider the plaintiff's mental
suffering, even though no bodily injury was inflicted.

SAME — DAMAGES — EXCESSIVE VERDICT DUE TO PASSION OR
PREJUDICE. In an action for personal indignities inflicted upon
the plaintiff in being ordered from a public resort as a disreputable woman, in which it appears that it was due to a
mistake of the defendant's employe, who immediately apologized therefor, and the defendant also openly apologized for the
mistake, and the evidence showing actual damages is very
meager, a verdict for the sum of $750 is not warranted, and is
clearly the result of passion and prejudice, requiring a reversal.

[1]Reported in 77 Pac. 209.

Appeal from a judgment of the superior court for Pierce
county, Chapman, J., entered February 21, 1903, upon the
verdict of a jury rendered in favor of the plaintiff, after a
trial on the merits, for $750 damages by reason of personal
indignities inflicted in ordering plaintiff from a public
resort. Reversed.

B. S. Grosscup and *A. G. Avery,* for appellant Tacoma
Railway and Power Co.

Frank S. Carroll, for appellants Shreeder et al.

John C. Stallcup, J. W. A. Nichols, and *Albert E. Joab,*
for respondents.

FULLERTON, C. J.—This is an action for damages. The
respondents, who were plaintiffs below, alleged in their
complaint, that the appellant railway company was, in the
year 1902, operating a line of street railway from the city
of Tacoma to Spanaway Lake; that, for the purpose of increasing its passenger business, it had acquired certain
lands at the lake named, which it had made into an attract-
ive park, or place of resort, and had placed the appellants
Shreeder & Green in charge thereof; that, on June 8th of
the year named, the respondents, attracted by the announce-
ments for that particular day, visited the park, where the
wrong occurred of which they complain. This wrong is
thus described in the complaint:

"That these plaintiffs, seeing said advertisement, procured tickets and took their seats in one of the cars of said
defendant railway company and were thereby conveyed to
said park on said day, arriving there a few minutes after
nine o'clock in the evening; that the cars and the park were
covered with people, and music and other attractions were
there, for the entertainment of the visitors; that, a very
few minutes after alighting from the car, upon said
grounds, and while plaintiffs were quietly viewing the at-

tractions then upon the said park grounds of said defendants, one Charles W. Cromwell, an employe of said defendants in charge of said grounds, approached the plaintiff Lenora Davis, and, after staring her in the face in a rude and insolent manner, seized her by the arm in a rough, brutal, and insulting manner, and, in a loud tone of voice, in the presence and hearing of a large group of people, said to this plaintiff Lenora Davis: 'You must leave these grounds. You can take the next car, coming in, or going out. You are not allowed on these grounds,' at the same time exhibiting a metallic star or badge, and claiming to be an officer and a deputy, attracting the attention of a large number of people to said plaintiff, meaning and imputing, by his words and action, that said plaintiff Lenora Davis was a lewd and base woman, unfit to be or remain upon said grounds; that she, the said plaintiff, is of the age of twenty-seven years, has always conducted herself as a lady of refinement and respectability, and has never at any other time been charged with anything derogatory to her good name, character, and reputation, always having enjoyed a good and spotless name and the high esteem of all her acquaintances; that she was then and there so dazed, shocked, humiliated, insulted, and wounded in her feelings, by said words and actions of said Cromwell, that she became faint and sick and could scarcely remain standing, and has not yet recovered in physical health, nor from the great mental anguish and wounded feelings, resulting from such treatment; that the defendant Green was upon the said grounds, at the time, and directed the said Cromwell to order the said plaintiff off the said grounds, and aided and participated in said violent and unjust treatment of said plaintiff."

Damages were demanded in the sum of $5,000. Issue was joined on the complaint, the defendant railway company and the defendants Shreeder & Green appearing separately, and by different counsel. On the issues made a trial was had before a jury, resulting in a verdict and judgment against all of the defendants for the sum of $750.

The evidence introduced at the trial did not support the complaint in all of its particulars. It appears that the managers of the park, desiring to keep the place suitable as a place of resort for respectable people, had employed one Cromwell to warn off of the grounds all persons whose conduct, demeanor, or dress marked them as belonging to, or being associated with, the criminal or vicious classes; that Cromwell had been informed that such a person had entered the ground and had taken a certain direction, whereupon he went in the direction indicated, and finding no other woman there, mistook Mrs. Davis for the person meant, and addressed her, asking her to leave the grounds; that he discovered his mistake almost immediately, and apologized to her and her husband for so accosting her. He also called the attention of the railway company's manager to his mistake, who likewise openly apologized to them therefor. The evidence discloses clearly that there was nothing wilful or malicious in the action of the employe. It was a mistake simply, and one that was atoned for by the employe and the manager of the railway company, who was present, in the only manner then possible.

Notice of appeal was first given by Shreeder & Green, and afterwards by the railway company. The respondents move to dismiss the appeal of Shreeder & Green for the reason that they did not serve their notice of appeal on their co-defendant, the railway company, nor join in the appeal of the railway company, when appeal was taken by it. This motion must be granted. Under the statute a notice of appeal, to be effectual, must be served on all of the parties who have appeared in the action, and who do not join in the notice of appeal. This was not done in this case. The appeal of the defendants Shreeder & Green is therefore dismissed.

The appellant railway company insists that, if any actionable wrong is stated in the complaint at all, it is an action for defamation of character, and that the proofs are insufficient to support a recovery for that wrong, because there was no publication of the defamatory matter, and because, further, the words alleged and proved to have been spoken are not actionable *per se,* and no special damages were proved to have been suffered because of them. But whether this may be called an action for defamation of character, for insult, or for personal indignities, or by some other name, we are clear that an actionable wrong was both alleged and proven. Every person not belonging to a proscribed class has a right to go to any public place, or visit a resort where the public generally are invited, and to remain there, during all proper hours, free from molestation by any one, so long as he conducts himself in a decorous and orderly manner. This right to freedom from molestation extends not only to freedom from actual violence, but to freedom from insult, personal indignities, or acts which subject him to humiliation and disgrace, and any one guilty of violating any of these rights is liable in all cases for the actual damages suffered therefrom by the injured person. It matters not whether the wrong be one of pure negligence, or a wanton and wilful wrong, an action will lie for the actual damages suffered. Actual malice, or wanton and wilful conduct, on the part of the wrongdoer, is material only on the question of punitive or exemplary damages, and must be shown in order to recover such damages, but the injured person may recover actual or compensatory damages regardless of whether there was any actual malice or intent to commit a wrong on the part of the other. When the employe of the appellant ordered Mrs. Davis from the grounds in question, he committed a wrong for which she is entitled to recover for any actual damages suffered. If it were true that the company had the right to exclude from these grounds persons whose conduct, dress, or demeanor generally proclaimed them to be, or whom it knew to be, members of a class with whom decent people do not associate, this fact would not exempt it from liability for a mistake it made in the effort to exercise that right. An actual voluntary injury must be compensated for by the person who commits the injury, no matter how innocent he may be of intentional wrong.

It is unnecessary, therefore, to inquire whether the words spoken at the time were of themselves defamatory, or whether they were published, in the legal sense of the term, as the words spoken were not of themselves the basic wrong. The wrong consisted of the act itself, of the violation of a right of the plaintiff, and the manner in which the act was done and the words spoken are material only on the question of the amount of damages. If the conduct of the employe was rude and insolent, if his tone was loud and boisterous, if the words spoken were indecent or profane, or if a number of people were witnesses to the transaction, the insult, indignity, humiliation, and disgrace felt by the injured person would be much greater than it would be if the conduct of the party and the situation were the opposite of these. While the act partakes of the nature of defamation of character, it has in it, in addition, some of the elements of an assault, although strictly speaking it is neither. It must not be understood, however, that we hold mere words of common abuse actionable *per se*. They are not so unless a special injury be shown. But, if an actionable wrong is otherwise committed, it can be shown that it was accompanied with words of common abuse, to enhance the damages.

The court instructed the jury that they were not limited to the actual physical injuries suffered by the person injured, but might take into consideration her sense of wrong, feeling of humiliation, disgrace, and mental suffering, in estimating her damages. The appellant assigns error on this instruction, contending that mental suffering, apart from a physical injury, is not an element of damages. The rule, however, is not so broad as this. It is probably true that no court has allowed a recovery for mental suffering, even though it resulted in a bodily injury, where the defendant has been guilty of no wrongful act as against the person seeking the recovery. If, for example, a person passing along a public street should be forced to witness an injury inflicted upon the person of another by the negligence of a third person, there could be no recovery by the first against the third, even though the shock, caused by the horror of the sight, produced such mental suffering as to materially affect the health of the first person. But, when the mental suffering is the result of some wrongful act against the sufferer, even though there may be no actual physical injury, this court has held, and the courts generally hold, that such mental suffering may be taken into consideration in assessing the damages for the wrong. *Wilson r. Northern Pac. R. Co.,* 5 Wash. 621, 32 Pac. 468, 34 Pac. 146; *Gray v. Washington Water Power Co.,* 30 Wash. 665, 71 Pac. 206. See, also, Voorhies, Measure of Damages, §§ 97, 98, and cases cited. Furthermore, mental suffering on the part of the person wronged has always been held a proper subject for consideration in estimating damages in an action for slander or libel, and the principle which allows such damages in cases of that character applies with all its force to a case of this kind. We do not think the court erred in giving the instruction complained of.

What we have said covers the exceptions to the purely
legal phases of the case, but the appellant complains, and
we think justly, that the verdict is so grossly disproportion-
ate to the injury proven as to show that it was the result of
passion and prejudice on the part of the jury, and not the
result of a consideration of the evidence. The evidence going
to show actual damages was meager indeed. As we view it,
it showed but little more than a bare violation of a technical
legal right, which caused a momentary annoyance to the respondents. But giving them the benefit of all doubts, and
making a liberal allowance for the mental suffering the
injured respondent testified that she had been subjected to
because of the wrongful act of the respondent, we can find
no warrant for the verdict of the jury. It seems clearly to
have been the result of passion and prejudice. The judgment will be reversed as to the respondent the Tacoma Railway and Power Company, and a new trial awarded as to it.

MOUNT, HADLEY, DUNBAR, and ANDERS, JJ., concur.

[No. 4661. Decided June 20, 1904.]

RIVERSIDE LAND COMPANY, *Appellant,* v. FRANZ PIETSCH
et al., Respondents.[1]

EJECTMENT—DEFENSES—ESTOPPEL—ENTRY AND IMPROVEMENTS
UNDER ORAL REPRESENTATIONS OF OWNER—MATERIAL AVERMENTS
RESPECTING THE ESTOPPEL—ORAL AGREEMENT TO TAKE CASE OUT
OF STATUTE OF FRAUDS—PLEADING AND PROOF. In an action of
ejectment, in which the defendants pleaded affirmatively an
equitable estoppel, in that the land in question, being a hillside
and valueless, the plaintiff induced the defendants to enter
thereon and inclose, irrigate, and improve the same at great
expense, under the oral representation that after ten years'
possession the defendants would have title thereto, which improvement enhanced the value of plaintiff's other lands in the

[1]Reported in 77 Pac. 195.

vicinity, the defendants can recover only on the theory of the
equitable estoppel as alleged, and the allegations that the land
was valueless when the defendants entered, and that its improvement enhanced the value of plaintiff's adjoining property,
are material allegations, necessary to be shown as part of the
oral contract for the sale of the property, by clear and satisfactory evidence, in order to take the case out of the statute
of frauds.

SAME—INSTRUCTIONS. Accordingly, in such a case, it is error
to instruct that the only question for the jury is whether the
plaintiff put the defendants in possession with the understanding
aforesaid, thereby eliminating the said allegations as to non-
value and enhancing the value of other lands, and requires a
reversal and a new trial.

APPEAL—REVIEW. A case is to be determined upon appeal on
the same theory on which it was tried in the court below.

Appeal from a judgment of the superior court for Spokane county, Prather, J., entered November 1, 1902, upon
the verdict of a jury rendered in favor of the defendants.
Reversed.

James Dawson and *F. E. Langford,* for appellant.

W. S. Lewis, for respondents.

PER CURIAM.—This action was brought in the superior
court of Spokane county by plaintiff, Riverside Land Company, against defendants, Franz Pietsch and Augusta
Pietsch (husband and wife), to recover possession of certain lots situated in the Second Addition to West Riverside
Addition to the city of Spokane. The cause came on for
trial before the court and a jury, resulting in a verdict and
judgment for defendants. Plaintiff appeals.

The complaint alleges, appellant's incorporation under
the laws of this state; that it is, and has been for eleven
years last past, the owner in fee simple of the above described real estate; that the respondents are in possession
of said premises; that they wrongfully and unjustly with-

hold the same from appellant; that on March 20, 1902, appellant served notice in writing upon respondents to vacate and surrender possession of said property, and to remove the fence erected around the same. Appellant asks judgment for restitution and possession, together with its costs and disbursements. Respondents by their answer deny the incorporation of appellant, and also the material allegations of the complaint. The allegations of their first affirmative defense are as follows:

"(1) That for more than twelve years last past the defendants have been, and they now are, in the actual, open, and peaceful possession of the premises described in the plaintiff's complaint, to wit: lots 12, 13, 14, 15, 20, 21, 22, and 23, in block 8, of the Second Addition to West Riverside Addition to Spokane Falls (now Spokane), in the city and county of Spokane, Washington, with color of title thereto, and have cultivated and improved the same and planted thereon and grown and cultivated a large and fruitful orchard which is of great value. (2) That at the time the defendants entered upon said premises it was wild, hilly and rugged waste and in its natural state, a steep hillside covered with rock and undergrowth and small pine timber, and regarded as of no value whatsoever, and destitute of any water rights for irrigation and cultivation. (3) That by and with the knowledge and consent of the plaintiff, defendants entered upon the said land and cleared and improved the same, and reduced it to a high state of cultivation, and purchased and obtained water rights therefor and conducted water thereon, and in and about so doing expended large sums of money, labor, skill, and care, and during the time that defendants were so doing plaintiff very well knew of such facts and directed the defendants so to do, and positively assured the defendants that, by so doing and with ten years' peaceable possession, they should become the absolute owners thereof, free from any claim or alleged claim of the plaintiff thereto, because of the fact that the improvements being made thereon by these defendants was of great value to other real estate claimed by the plaintiff in the immediate vicinity, and because the said premises in the natural state were totally valueless, without which assurance the defendants would not have so acted nor made such improvements, nor purchased such water rights, nor so rested upon their said rights thereto, and the defendants further allege that the improvements and cultivation and fruit trees and other improvements are of such a character and so attached to the soil that they cannot be removed, but would be an utter loss to the defendants, at a great profit to the plaintiff, should these defendants be ejected therefrom, and that plaintiff is, and ought to be, estopped from questioning the defendants' right or possession thereof or title thereto, or from in any manner interfering with the peaceable and quiet enjoyment of the premises and improvements."

The second affirmative defense alleges ten years' adverse possession of the premises, prior to the commencement of the action. This defense seems to have been abandoned at the trial. The reply denies the material allegations of the first affirmative defense, except that respondents entered upon these premises with the knowledge and consent of appellant.

Under the issues, as formulated and tendered by the pleadings, the burden of proof was cast upon respondents regarding their plea of estoppel, as alleged in their first affirmative defense above noted. Respondents' evidence at the trial tended to show, that in the month of February, 1892, they were the owners, by purchase from appellant company, of lots 16, 17, 18, and 19, in said block 8, which are contiguous to the lots in question; that at such time respondents inclosed these lots, with the lots in question, and also four other lots in said block 8, then being the property of appellant, by building a fence around all such real estate, except portions of lots 12 and 27 abutting upon the east line of this block 8. Respondent Pietsch testified

that in April and May, 1891, he cleared and grubbed the
lots in controversy; using the following language:

"Well, those are side hills, you know, steep hills; they
were overgrown with large pine timber, and with dense
growth of underbrush, and those trees were overshadow-
ing it; one side is on the east, and the other side is on the
south, so when the sun came around, it would shade it, I
could not raise anything; so I was to establish a nursery
there, so I had to make me sunshine and air. . . .
Q. State whether or not it was in its natural state, . . .
when you went upon it. A. What it was, in the natural
state? Q. Yes. A. A wilderness, that is all; rocks, that
is all it was, and trees."

Mr. Pietsch further testified, that he bought another lot
of appellant, on which property there was located a spring,
in order to irrigate the lots in controversy, and expended
considerable labor and money in order to get water thereon
from that spring; that, without water upon these lots, they
were utterly worthless to witness; that witness in these
transactions dealt with one C. F. Clough, as the agent of
the appellant; that witness, during his occupancy of such
lots, put the same in a high state of cultivation, planted
thereon two hundred bearing fruit trees, which cannot be
moved without great injury being done them; that the improvements and labor placed and expended on such lots
by these respondents were over $1,500 in value, and are
of a permanent nature; that Clough, president Perkins,
and secretary Stevens, of appellant company, were cog-
nizant of respondents' acts regarding the improvement and
cultivation of this real estate, and encouraged his acts in
that regard. It seems that Mr. Clough, who was the resident agent of appellant company, testified that he had authority to sell this real estate and receive payments therefor.
Mr. Pietsch swore that, in the spring of 1892, Mr. Clough
came there, looked everything over, and smiled and said.

"Mr. Pietsch, when you have this garden ten years in peaceful possession, it will be yours." His testimony continues:

"And he came occasionally and told me the same story over and over again, more than five times to me, and I believed it in him, too; I took his word for it. . . Q. Do you remember Mr. Clough being down there at any time with the president of the company? A. Yes sir. . . Q. What did they say, Mr. Perkins and Mr. Stevens and Mr. Clough, on the occasion of that visit; state what they said and did, with reference to this particular land now in controversy? . . . A. They tapped me on the shoulder and they said, 'We wish we had half a dozen more men on our place here like you are yourself.' Q. Well, what did they say about your work there on the garden, this disputed land, now? A. Well, they said, 'You have done just right, nobody can make—the hillsides are no good, anyhow; nobody can make use of those hillsides but you, and you done just right,' they said, 'and we only wish we had half a dozen more such men on the land as you are.' "

This witness also testified that he induced appellant to sell four of the lots inclosed with those now in controversy, one of which was sold to one Murphy in 1895, and the other three to one Pritchard. Respondent Franz Pietsch was corroborated by members of his own family testifying regarding the knowledge of Clough of these improvements, which testimony is not seriously disputed. Augusta Pietsch, wife of Franz Pietsch, and one of the respondents herein, testified that, four years after they went into possession of this property, the following conversation occurred between Mr. Clough and her husband:

"Mr. Clough he said—he was outside of the fence, and I was inside of the fence, and Mr. Pietsch was there, too; he said, 'Mr. Pietsch, if you have these ten years in possession,' or how you call it, 'then it is yours,' he say; and we lived over it for awhile. . . . He said last year [1901] . . . 'Mr. Pietsch, do you want to buy those lots?' Mr. Pietsch said, 'I don't have any money.' Then he said, 'If

you have that one year more, it must be about the time
when you have that ten years, then it is yours; must be
about around the time.'"

Louis Pietsch, a son of respondents, testified that the
value of the labor and improvements expended and placed
on these lots by his father was from $1,000 to $1,200.
Respondents offered no testimony tending to show that the
alleged improvements on these lots in controversy enhanced the valuation of other property in that vicinity
belonging to appellant. The record shows that counsel
for appellant made frequent objections, and took numerous exceptions, to the rulings of the trial court as to the
introduction of testimony in behalf of respondents, concerning the alleged statements of agent Clough and the
president and secretary of appellant company, pertaining
to the acts of respondents in improving the property in
question. Clough testified in part as follows: "At some
time in the summer or fall of 1891, Mr. Pietsch asked
if there would be any objection to his cultivating a portion of the hillside, and I told him I did not think there
would, providing when the property was wanted by the
company he would vacate it; he says, 'Certainly'." Witness denies telling Mr. Pietsch that, if he went on these
hillside lots, cultivated, and improved them for ten years,
he (Pietsch) would get title to the same.

It further appeared, from the evidence, that this realty
was valuable property when respondents took possession
thereof; that the appellant had kept the taxes paid up on
the same; that respondent Franz Pietsch offered to pay
Clough, for appellant, the money which the company had
already paid for the taxes of 1901 and 1902 on these lots,
and the company refused to receive the same. The verdict and judgment above noted in effect established an

estoppel against appellant's "claiming any estate or right of possession in said property." The judgment decreed, among other things, that respondents' "title to said land be and the same is hereby confirmed."

The assignments of error practically present but one question for the consideration of this court on the hearing of this appeal: Whether the evidence adduced by respondents was sufficient, under their first affirmative defense, to warrant the verdict and judgment rendered in the trial court. After a careful consideration of all the evidence found in the record, in connection with the able arguments of counsel on both sides of the present controversy, we are impelled to the conclusion that it was incumbent upon respondents to establish, by a preponderance of testimony, that appellant is estopped from asserting its title to the premises in question, by reason of an alleged parol contract between appellant and respondents, when the latter entered into the possession of and inclosed these lots with the other realty, or shortly thereafter. In other words, respondents took the burden of proving that they were in possession of this property under a parol agreement, complete and definite in its terms, for a valuable consideration moving from them to appellant; and that they (respondents) had fully complied, or were ready and willing to comply, with the terms of such contract on their part, entitling them to a specific performance thereof as against appellant. We are unable to conceive of any other theory, under the issues as formulated by the pleadings and the evidence adduced on the trial, by which respondents were legally or equitably entitled to have judgment entered in their behalf confirming their title in and to the lots described in the above complaint, as against the appellant company.

It is true that, in many instances, while a defense including matters pleaded as an equitable estoppel may
not entitle a defendant to affirmative relief in a given case,
still, such defense performs the office of a negative resist-
ance to, and defeats, plaintiff's cause of action. Pomeroy,
Code Remedies (3d ed.), § 91. A defendant seeking
affirmative relief in his answer becomes, *quoad hoc*, plaintiff, and must state the requisite facts constituting his
right of action as if he were stating them in a complaint,
except that he may refer to and adopt matters stated in
the complaint. Phillips, Code Plead., § 260.

There is no question but that, at the time of the commencement of the present action, the legal title to this
property was in the appellant. If the respondents are
entitled to recover, they must do so under the allegations
of their answer, and the proofs in support thereof submitted at the trial. They failed to show that, at the time
they entered into possession, "the said premises in their natural state were totally valueless," and, "because of the fact
that the improvements being made thereon by these defendants [respondents], was of great value to other real
estate claimed by the plaintiff [appellant] in the immediate vicinity," as alleged in their answer. As we read the
record, the testimony, though somewhat obscure, tends to
show that the market value of this real estate was at that
time greater than the alleged improvements. It seems
too plain for argument, even granting, without deciding,
the sufficiency of this first affirmative defense as a matter
of pleading, that the respondents could not ignore such
important matters of proof at the trial, in support of their
alleged estoppel. Under their pleading in that behalf,
the respondents became actors in this controversy. They
were not entitled to the relief awarded them by the court

below, confirming and quieting their title in and to these
lots, unless they showed, by clear and satisfactory testimony, an oral contract for the sale thereof, made between
appellant company and themselves, in conformity to the
issues tendered, sufficient to take the transaction out of
the operation of the statute of frauds. 2 Warvelle, Vend-
ors, p. 783, quoted with approval in *O'Connor v. Jackson,*
23 Wash. 229, 62 Pac. 761. Courts of equity in the
matter of defenses of this nature, will look to the substance
rather than to the form thereof. The calling this defense
an equitable estoppel does not lessen the responsibility of
the parties invoking this doctrine, or warrant us in ig-
noring fundamental principles as the proper basis for the
granting of equitable relief. As we view it, there is nothing disclosed by this record which would divest the legal
owner of its title and interest in the property and vest
it in the respondents. *Chicago etc. R. Co. v. Reno,* 113
Ill. 39.

It is further assigned that the trial judge erred in giving the following instruction to the jury:

"I will relieve the jury of some of the issues in the
case, by holding and finding that the evidence on the
part of the plaintiff shows that it is a corporation, competent to sue in this court, and that the evidence on the
part of plaintiff shows a fee simple title in the plaintiff,
except that the allegations of the defense should be true—
that is, that the plaintiff had placed the defendant in
possession of the property with the understanding as I
have mentioned. So that the only question of fact which
the court will submit to you, to find from the evidence
in the case, is whether or not the claim of the defendants
that the plaintiff put them in possession, with the understanding that I have mentioned, was true, is the only
issue which the court will submit to you."

This instruction, and the understanding therein referred to, eliminate from the jury's consideration the above allegations in the answer pertaining to the non-value of this real estate, when respondents took possession thereof, and the improvements, placed by respondents thereon, enhancing the valuation of other real estate in the immediate vicinity, claimed by appellant. These were questions of fact under the issues, which the trial court had no right to ignore. This instruction was, therefore, misleading and prejudicial to appellant. Matters alleged as an estoppel must be proven as charged. "Estoppels never arise from ambiguous facts; they must be established by those which are unequivocal, and not susceptible of two constructions." *Fredenburg v. Lyon Lake M. E. Church*, 37 Mich. 476. 8 Ency. Plead. & Prac., 9-11.

Whether the respondents are entitled to relief, or to recover compensation for their improvements, under issues properly tendered with that end in view, is a proposition not pertinent to this inquiry. This court on appeal will only consider those matters presented to the court below for decision. Within the scope of the issues, the case is considered and determined on the same theory in the appellate as in the trial court. *Sanders v. Stimson Mill Co.*, 34 Wash. 357, 75 Pac. 975, and authorities cited. Having reached the conclusion that the judgment of the court below must be reversed, it becomes unnecessary to consider the remaining assignments of error.

Judgment reversed, and cause remanded for further proceedings not inconsistent with this opinion.

[No. 4770. Decided June 21, 1904.]

W. J. Allen, *Appellant*, v. Northern Pacific Railway Company, *Respondent*.[1]

CARRIERS—RAILROADS—NEGLIGENCE—PRESUMPTION FROM ACCIDENT TO PASSENGER. The fact of an injury to a passenger on a railroad train does not alone raise a presumption of negligence in all cases regardless of the circumstances and nature of the accident.

SAME—SUDDEN LURCH OR JERK AS EVIDENCE OF NEGLIGENCE. That an injury to a passenger was due to a sudden lurch or jerk imparted to a train is not prima facie proof of negligence, where it appears that the same was necessary to effect the movement of the train up an incline from a ferry boat.

SAME—OBSTRUCTION NEAR TRACKS—NECESSARY SUPPORT FOR RAILROAD FERRY. That a passenger on a railroad train slowly moving from a ferry boat was injured while attempting to board the train by coming in contact with a post twenty-six inches from the car, is not prima facie proof of negligence when it appears that the post was a necessary support or appliance for the operation of the ferry as constructed.

SAME — INJURY TO PASSENGER WHILE MOVING TRAIN FROM FERRY BOAT—EVIDENCE OF NEGLIGENCE—SUFFICIENCY. In an action against a railroad company brought by a passenger for personal injuries, there is no evidence of negligence upon the part of defendant warranting a submission of the case to the jury, where it appears that the plaintiff alighted from the train for the purpose of getting breakfast while it was being ferried across the Columbia river, as he was told that he could do, and upon learning that the train was being moved off the boat, he attempted to board the train while it was moving slowly, no warning being given to him that it was dangerous so to do, and while in such act, lost his balance by reason of a sudden lurch necessarily imparted to the train in moving it off the boat, bringing plaintiff in contact with an upright twenty-six inches from the platform of the car, which was a necessary support for the operation of the boat; since there was no duty to warn and there is no presumption of negligence from an injury to a passenger under such circumstances (HADLEY and DUNBAR, JJ., dissenting).

[1]Reported in 77 Pac. 204.

Appeal from an order of the superior court for King county, Albertson, J., entered April 14, 1903, after a trial on the merits, setting aside the verdict of a jury rendered in favor of the plaintiff, and granting a new trial. Affirmed.

Walter S. Fulton and *Vince H. Faben*, for appellant. The court erred in setting aside the verdict upon the ground that there was no proof of defendant's negligence, after the jury had found that there was such negligence. *Tibbals v. Mt. Olympus Water Co.*, 10 Wash. 329, 38 Pac. 1120; *Brookman v. State Ins. Co.*, 18 Wash. 308, 51 Pac. 395; *Morris v. Frye-Bruhn Co.*, 20 Wash. 257, 55 Pac. 50; *Lane v. Spokane etc. R. Co.*, 21 Wash. 119, 57 Pac. 367, 75 Am. St. 821, 46 L. R. A. 153; *Traver v. Spokane etc. R. Co.*, 25 Wash. 225, 65 Pac. 284; *Latimer v. Baker*, 25 Wash. 192, 64 Pac. 899; *Jordan v. Seattle*, 26 Wash. 61, 66 Pac. 114; *Richmond R. Co. v. Powers*, 149 U. S. 43, 13 Sup. Ct. 748; *Northern Pac. R. Co. v. Adams*, 116 Fed. 324. An injury to a passenger raises a presumption of the carrier's negligence. *Gleeson v. Virginia Midland R. Co.*, 140 U. S. 435, 11 Sup. Ct. 859; *McCurrie v. Southern Pac. R. Co.*, 122 Cal. 558, 55 Pac. 324; Sherm. & Redf., Negligence, § 59; 3 Thompson, Comm. Law of Neg., § 2830. A sudden lurch or jerk is prima facie evidence of negligence. 5 Am. & Eng. Enc. Law, 573; *Consolidated Traction Co. v. Thalheimer*, 59 N. J. L. 474, 37 Atl. 132; *Osgood v. Los Angeles Traction Co.*, 137 Cal. 280, 70 Pac. 169, 92 Am. St. 171; *Dixie v. Philadelphia Traction Co.*, 180 Pa. St. 401, 36 Atl. 924; *Doolittle v. Southern R. Co.*, 62 S. C. 130, 40 S. E. 133; *Parlier v. Southern R. Co.*, 129 N. C. 262, 39 S. E. 961; *Scott v. Bergen etc. Co.*, 63 N. J. L. 407, 43 Atl. 1060; *Kulman v. Erie R. Co.*, 65 N. J. L. 241, 47 Atl. 497;

McCurrie v. Southern Pac. R. Co., supra; Choate v. San Antonio etc. R. Co., 90 Tex. 82, 36 S. W. 247, 37 S. W. 319; *Houston etc. R. Co. v. Rowell* (Tex.), 45 S. W. 763; *Baltimore & O. R. Co. v. Kane,* 69 Md. 11, 13 Atl. 387, 9 Am. St. 387; *Distler v. Long Island R. Co.,* 151 N. Y. 424, 45 N. E. 937, 56 Am. St. 630, 35 L. R. A. 762. It was for the jury to say whether defendant was negligent in maintaining an obstruction within 26 inches of the platform of the car. *North Chicago St. R. Co. v. Williams,* 140 Ill. 275, 29 N. E. 672; *Anderson v. City etc. R. Co.,* 42 Ore. 505, 71 Pac. 659. Defendant was negligent in failing to warn plaintiff of the danger. 5 Am. & Eng. Enc. Law (2d ed.), 581; *Kulman v. Erie R. Co.,* 65 N. J. L. 241, 47 Atl. 497; *Houston etc. R. Co., v. Pereira* (Tex.), 45 S. W. 766.

James F. McElroy and *B. S. Grosscup,* for respondent. Under the testimony the sudden acceleration of speed was not negligent. *Blakney v. Seattle Electric Co.,* 28 Wash. 608, 68 Pac. 1037; *Etson v. Ft. Wayne etc. R. Co.,* 110 Mich. 494, 68 N. W. 298; *Bradley v. Ft. Wayne etc. R. Co.,* 94 Mich. 35, 53 N. W. 915; *Black v. Third Ave. R. Co.,* 37 N. Y. Supp. 830; *Hoffman v. Third Avenue R. Co.,* 61 N. Y. Supp. 590; *Armstrong v. Metropolitan St. R. Co.,* 48 N. Y. Supp. 597; *Schmidt v. North Jersey St. R. Co.,* 66 N. J. L. 424, 49 Atl. 439; *Pitcher v. Peoples St. R. Co.,* 174 Pa. St. 402, 34 Atl. 567; *Hite v. Metropolitan St. R. Co.,* 130 Mo. 132, 32 S. W. 33, 51 Am. St. 555; *Picard v. Ridge Ave. etc. R. Co.,* 147 Pa. St. 195, 23 Atl. 566; *Byron v. Lynn etc. R. Co.,* 177 Mass. 303, 58 N. E. 1015; *Jones v. New York etc. R. Co.,* 156 N. Y. 187, 50 N. E. 856, 41 L. R. A. 490. Under the circumstances, no inference of negligence can be drawn from the maintenance or position of the upright. *Georgia etc.*

R. Co. v. Cartledge, 116 Ga. 164, 42 S. E. 405, 59
L. R. A. 118; *Moore v. Edison etc. Co.,* 43 La. Ann. 792,
9 So. 433; *Craighead v. Brooklyn City R. Co.,* 123 N. Y.
391, 25 N. E. 387; *Favre v. Louisville & N. R. Co.,* 13
Ky. 116, 16 S. W. 370. An accident to a passenger
while in the carrier's charge does not necessarily raise a
presumption of negligence. *Hawkins v. Front St. Cable
R. Co.,* 3 Wash. 592, 28 Pac. 1021, 28 Am. St. 72, 16
L. R. A. 808; *Rothchild v. Central etc. R. Co.,* 163 Pa.
St. 49, 29 Atl. 702; *Baltimore etc. Road v. Cason,* 72
Md. 377, 20 Atl. 113; *Saunders v. Chicago etc. R. Co.,*
6 S. D. 40, 60 N. W. 148; *Byron v. Lynn etc. R. Co.,*
supra; Cincinnati etc. R. Co. v. Jackson, 22 Ky. L. 630,
58 S. W. 526; *Picard v. Ridge Ave. etc. R. Co., supra.*

PER CURIAM.—This action was brought in the superior
court of King county, by W. J. Allen, plaintiff, against
Northern Pacific Railway Company, a corporation, defendant, to recover compensation for personal injuries.
The cause was tried before the court and a jury. A verdict was returned for plaintiff, which, upon the motion
of defendant, was set aside and a new trial granted by the
lower court, upon the sole ground, as stated in the record,
"that the evidence introduced at the trial herein failed
to show any act or acts of negligence on the part of the
defendant." The plaintiff excepted, and appealed from
the order granting the new trial. The only error assigned
is that the trial court erred in making said order. The
court having stated the ground of its decision in the
order granting the new trial, the sole proposition presented for our consideration upon this appeal is whether
any act or acts of negligence on the part of respondent
appeared in the evidence which became a question for the

consideration of the jury at the trial. *Gray v. Washington Water Power Co.,* 27 Wash. 713, 68 Pac. 360.

On January 13, 1902, appellant, W. J. Allen, was a passenger on one of respondent's trains, bound from Portland, Oregon, to Seattle, Washington. When this train reached the Columbia river, an employe thereon informed appellant that he would have sufficient time in which to get breakfast on the ferry. Thereupon, the appellant left the train, went into the restaurant on the ferry, and ordered his breakfast. Ordinarily the time occupied in crossing this river on the ferry was about 20 minutes. Soon after commencing his meal, he heard the train give what he believed to be a signal for its departure from the ferry. The man in charge of this eating house said to appellant, "You better hurry up; the train will pull out and leave you." Mr. Allen testified in this connection, on his direct examination, as follows:

"So I just quit eating right there and paid him for my meal, and walked out, and as I went out the train was moving off. Q. Let me ask you right there, where was the train when you went out, with reference to where you were, that is, on the ferry? A. Well, it was towards the other end of the boat. Q. That is, it was towards this side, the Washington side? A. Towards the Washington side, yes sir. Q. And you saw it moving, did you, as you come out? A. Yes sir. Q. And believed that to be your train, did you? A. Yes sir. Mr. McElroy: I object, now, to the leading of the witness, if the court please. The Court: I think the questions are leading. Q. What did you do, then, upon coming out and seeing your train? A. Well, I saw the train moving out, and started to catch the train, and I started with a little run to catch it, and it was close to the other end of the ferry, and as I jumped on the step of the platform—on to the platform of the last car, why I got one foot on and stepped up to the second step, and as

I did so the train gave a very sudden lurch or jerk and overbalanced me and threwed me off the car, and I struck some timber or piling or something—I don't know what. Q. How fast was the train moving when you came out of the eating house there? A. Well, it was not going fast at all. I did not have no trouble to catch it. I have often caught trains . . . It was not going over a mile an hour, I don't think. . . . Q. Now, where was this obstruction, with reference to the right of way or the passage way leading from the ferry up on to the main land? . . . A. Well, it could not have been only just—it was right close to the car, because I remember when I overbalanced on the step with the jerk—with the forcible jerk that the engine or the car gave—it overbalanced me, and I just tipped backwards and it struck me some way; I don't know how."

Appellant suffered severe injuries and was picked up in an unconscious condition, in which state he remained for several days. Appellant testified that he received no warning that he should not board the train. Timothy Mahoney, a witness for respondent, testified in part, that in January, 1902, he was a deckhand on this ferry boat; that witness had his regular work to perform; that it was witness' duty, if he saw anybody about to board the train who he thought was liable to get hurt, to stop him. "The train was in motion; Mr. Allen made a move to get on the train, and I told him not to get on; and that is all there is to it." E. E. Weymouth, one of respondent's witnesses, testified that he was the supervisor of bridges and buildings on the Pacific division of the respondent company; that the clearance between the platform of the coach and the lever or upright, with which appellant came in contact when injured, was about 26 inches; that this appliance was absolutely necessary for the operation of the pontoon and the receiving of the ferry boat. It also appeared by the testimony that the engine, while attached

to the cars, first moved slowly, and then, as the incline
from the ferry to the station at Kalama was approached,
it was necessary to increase the speed in order to make
the ascent. It would seem from the evidence that the
cars must have been in motion for at least 200 feet, when
appellant boarded this particular car. The following statement, explanatory of appellant's contentions, appears in
the brief of his counsel:

"The acts of negligence which were alleged, and found
by the jury, to have caused appellant's injuries were, the
failure of respondent to provide facilities which would have
enabled the appellant to safely board the train; starting
the train suddenly after appellant had boarded the same;
and placing and maintaining in the passage and right of
way leading from the ferry a pile, or obstruction of like
nature, which rendered the right of way dangerous to
passengers situated as was appellant on trains leaving the
ferry."

The jury, by its verdict, affirmed that appellant was
free from contributory negligence in boarding the train,
and that he was not warned against so doing by any employe of respondent. All conflict in the testimony was
settled by the jury. Therefore the sole question raised
on this record is, whether the evidence adduced at the trial
shows, or tends to establish, that appellant was injured
by the negligence of respondent company, as alleged. Appellant, under the issues as formulated by the pleadings,
assumed the burden of proof in that behalf.

The question of negligence is one of law for the court
only where the facts are such that all reasonable men
must draw the same inference from them, and when the
conclusion follows, as a matter of law, that no recovery
can be had upon any view which can properly be taken of
the facts the evidence tends to establish. *Towle v. Stimson Mill Co.*, 33 Wash. 305, 74 Pac. 471.

It is urged by appellant that, whenever a passenger is injured by something which is under the control of the carrier, the fact of the injury is itself prima facie evidence of negligence on the part of the carrier. In *Hawkins v. Front Street Cable R. Co.*, 3 Wash. 592, 28 Pac. 1021, 16 L. R. A. 808, 28 Am. St. 72, which was an action to recover compensation for injuries sustained by Marie Hawkins, one of the respondents, while she was a passenger riding upon one of appellant's street cars, the trial court, among other things, instructed the jury that, "It is the law that where a passenger being carried on a train is injured without fault of his own, there is legal presumption of negligence, casting upon the carrier the burden of disproving it." This court held that, "Such is not the law as laid down by very numerous authorities." At page 597, in the opinion delivered by Stiles, J., the following language from *Meier v. Pennsylvania R. Co.*, 64 Pa. St. 225, 3 Am. Rep. 581, is quoted with approval:

"Prima facie, where a passenger, being carried on a train, is injured without fault of his own, there is a legal presumption of negligence, casting upon the carrier the onus of disproving it. This is the rule when the injury is caused by a defect in the road, cars or machinery, or by a want of diligence or care by those employed, or by any other thing which the company can and ought to control as a part of its duty, to carry passengers safely; but this rule of evidence is not conclusive."

Again, in the opinion of the court in *Klepsch v. Donald*, 8 Wash. 164, 35 Pac. 622, this language is used: "A passenger on a railroad train is injured, and the fact of injury alone does not sustain a charge of negligence; but if the train was derailed by reason of a broken wheel, the presumption arises that the carrier was negligent in not providing a sound one." In *Gleeson v. Virginia Mid-*

land R. Co., 140 U. S. 435, 11 Sup. Ct. 859, 35 L. Ed. 458, the court held that an accident, happening to a passenger riding on the railway of the carrier, caused by the train coming in contact with a land slide, raises, when shown, a presumption of negligence on the part of the carrier, and throws upon it the burden of showing that the slide was in fact the result of causes beyond its control. The general language employed in the court's opinion, quoted by the appellant, should be considered with reference to the facts of the particular case decided.

"It is, therefore, too broad a statement of the rule to say that, in all cases, a presumption of negligence on the part of the carrier arises from the mere happening of the accident or an injury to a passenger regardless of the circumstances and nature of the accident. The true rule would seem to be that when the injury and circumstances attending it are so unusual and of such a nature that it could not well have happened without the company being negligent, or when it is caused by something connected with the equipment or operation of the road, over which the company has entire control, without contributory negligence on the part of the passenger, a presumption of negligence on the part of the company usually arises from proof of such facts, in the absence of anything to the contrary, and the burden is then cast upon the company to show that its negligence did not cause the injury." 4 Elliott, Railroads, § 1644, and authorities cited.

In *Fearn v. West Jersey Ferry Co.,* 143 Pa. St. 122, 22 Atl. 708, 13 L. R. A. 366, the court said:

"The cause of the accident was known as well to the appellant as to the company. In such case the presumption of negligence arising from the mere fact that a passenger was injured while on the appellant's boat has no application. . . . As the appellant failed to show any omission or violation of duty by the company, in connection with the cause of the accident, we think the nonsuit was properly ordered."

The presumption "arises not from the naked fact that an injury has been inflicted, but from the cause of the injury, or from other circumstances attending it." *Pennsylvania R. Co. v. MacKinney,* 124 Pa. St. 462, 17 Atl. 14, 2 L. R. A. 820, 10 Am. St. 601. In a case where the fact of no negligence is fixed by the proofs, a mere presumption cannot overcome it. *Bernhardt v. West Penn. R. Co.* 159 Pa. St. 363, 28 Atl. 140. See, also, exhaustive note, *Barnowski v. Helson,* 15 L. R. A. 33. *Etson v. Ft. Wayne etc. R. Co.* 110 Mich. 494, 68 N. W. 298, was an action to recover damages for alleged negligence on the part of the carrier. The point decided is succinctly presented in the syllabus: "In an action against an electric street railway, by a passenger for personal injuries, evidence merely that plaintiff, who was upon the platform to alight as soon as the car, which was slowing up, stopped at the far side of the street, its usual stopping place, was thrown from the car, by a sudden jerk, when the car was only halfway across the street, is insufficient, in the absence of evidence as to the cause of the sudden jerk, to warrant a recovery by plaintiff." If this proposition be correct, it follows logically, that, if it had appeared that such lurch was necessary to effect a legitimate purpose, there would have been no negligence on the part of the railroad company. See, further, *Schmidt v. North Jersey St. R. Co.,* 66 N. J. L. 424, 49 Atl. 438.

The able counsel for appellant argue that the case of *Anderson v. City & Sub. R. Co.,* 42 Or. 505, 71 Pac. 659, is an authority directly in point in support of their contentions in the present controversy. It appeared that a street railway company constructed its tracks so near the superstructure of a bridge as to leave only eighteen inches between the frame thereof and the outer edge of the foot-

board of its open cars; that a passenger, while riding on
the footboard, with the knowledge and consent of the carrier—the seats inside of the car all being occupied—was
injured by coming in contact with a strut of the bridge;
and there was evidence tending to show that the car was
going at an unlawful rate of speed, and that no warning
was given. It was held—and we think correctly—that the
company's negligence was a question for the jury.

In the case at bar it is not pretended that appellant,
when injured, was on this particular step or platform of
respondent's car with the knowledge or consent of any of
respondent's servants or trainmen. The engine and cars
thereto attached had proceeded a considerable distance
from their starting point on the ferry, when appellant
boarded the car without invitation, express or implied,
on the part of respondent. In so doing, could he impose
upon respondent company the duty of warning him of
possible danger? Was the respondent bound, at its peril,
to know that a passenger was liable to board one of its
cars while in motion, at an unusual place, just as the
engine was about to make the ascent of this incline? We
think that these questions must be answered in the negative.

The lurch or jerk of the car on which appellant was
riding, and of which he complains, was occasioned by the
increase of power necessary to ascend such incline. We
fail to see how the appellant can justly charge negligence
on respondent or its servants, by reason of such sudden
movement of the engine and cars, under the evidence and
circumstances as disclosed by this record. True, this
lurch caused appellant's body to swing out about twenty-
six inches from the car, which brought him in contact with
the upright; but it appeared in evidence that this appli-

ance was necessary to operate the pontoon, and there was no testimony tending to show that it was in a dangerous position.

The verdict of the jury settled the question in appellant's favor that he received no warning at or about the time he boarded the car in question. Still, we think that respondent was not bound to warn passengers against boarding its cars, under the circumstances shown by this record. A carrier, acting as a prudent and careful person with a proper regard for human safety, cannot be held as an insurer against all possible accidents happening to its passengers, in consequence of boarding its trains at unusual places, while in motion, and coming in contact with objects near the railway track rightfully placed there for the purpose of operating its line of railroad. We are unable, after a careful research, to find any authority which goes to the extent for which appellant contends.

Appellant quotes from *North Chicago St. R. Co. v. Williams,* 140 Ill. 275, 29 N. E. 672, the following paragraph: "Where a railroad company places its tracks so near an obstruction, which it is necessary for its cars to pass, that its passengers, in getting on and off the cars and while upon them, are in danger of being injured by contact with such obstruction, it is a fair question for the jury whether the company is or is not guilty of negligence." But that case is plainly distinguishable in principle from the action at bar. The court then adds: "The negligence charged against the company is, that it placed the temporary track too near the curb line of the street and the telegraph poles on the east side thereof." Plaintiff Williams boarded one of defendant's cars propelled by horse power, while the car was in motion, came in contact with the telegraph pole, and was injured. An important feature in the case is mentioned in the opinion: "When an open car was passing, there were from nine to twelve inches between the telegraph pole and the east ends of the seats; and if a man stood on the rail or platform running along the east side of an open car passing that point, the distance between his shoulders and the pole would vary from two to five inches in different cars." The evidence tended strongly to show that the street railroad company was negligent in laying its temporary track so near the telegraph pole which was an obstruction. This pole was in no sense an appliance necessary to operate its business pertaining to the conveyance of its passengers along its line of road. In that case the proof also showed that the conductor saw the plaintiff before he stepped upon the car, and shouted to him to "look out," just before he was struck by the pole. In the present controversy, it is not claimed that the conductor or any of the train crew saw appellant board the car, or had any reason to believe that he had placed himself in a position to receive injuries, when the engine and car made this sudden movement which became necessary, under the evidence, as we have heretofore stated. While it has been held that boarding a slowly moving train of cars is not *per se* negligence on the part of the passenger, in case of accident resulting therefrom, still, it would seem to follow, as a corollary of this proposition and as a logical sequence, that the carrier ought not to be held liable for actionable negligence in such cases, unless the passenger is able to show affirmatively that the carrier was in some manner at fault in causing the injuries for which damages are sought to be recovered. Elliott, Railroads, *supra,* and citations.

Applying the foregoing propositions of law to the facts in this controversy, we think that the evidence fails to make out a case of actionable negligence against respondent, that the trial court committed no error in granting the motion for a new trial, and that the order appealed from should be affirmed.

HADLEY, J. (dissenting).—I dissent from the conclusion reached by the majority of the court in this case.

Briefly stated, testimony as to the following facts appears in the record. The appellant was a passenger upon one of respondent's trains, making the trip from Portland, Oregon, to Seattle, Washington. The trains of respondent between Portland and Seattle are transferred across the Columbia river upon a large ferry boat. Coming from Portland this boat starts at Goble, on the Oregon side of the river, and lands at Kalama, on the Washington side. Three sets of tracks are arranged upon the boat and, by means of pontoon approaches, the engines and cars of the trains are run upon these tracks and drawn from the boat to the shore in the same manner. The trains are usually separated into sections, which are placed upon the tracks aforesaid. At one end of the boat is a lunch room, which, upon the occasion in question, was toward the Oregon shore. Appellant inquired of some employe upon the train if he would have time to get breakfast in the lunch room. He was informed that he would have sufficient time. The usual time consumed in crossing the river is about twenty minutes. Appellant thereupon left his car, went to the lunch room and ordered some breakfast. He testified that, before he had finished eating, the bell rang, and that the man in charge of the lunch room said: "You better hurry up. The train will pull out and leave you." That he thereupon quit eating immediately, paid for his meal, and walked out; that as he went out the train was moving away, and he

started to catch it; that he jumped on to the step of the
last car; that, while holding to the railing, he got one
foot on, and stepped up to, the second step, and as he
did so the train gave a sudden lurch or jerk, by which
he was overbalanced and thrown against a piling, or some
timber placed in the boat.

After he was struck he says he does not remember what
occurred. Other testimony shows that he was thrown off
the boat, and fell upon some timbers resting upon the
water below. He was taken up and left at Kalama in
charge of a physician. The accident happened on the
13th of January, and he says he did not recover conscious-
ness until the 1st of February following. He testified,
that he believed it was his train which he saw moving out;
that the person in charge of the restaurant told him it
was, and that he had to catch it to go through; that he
had no trouble in getting on, but, by the sudden lurch of
the train, he was thrown against the timber aforesaid.

It appeared in evidence that the car in which appellant
had been riding was not in the section of cars which he
saw moving, but it was still standing upon another track
on the boat. He testified, however, that he saw no one
to give him warning, and that no one did so except the
man at the restaurant, who told him his train was leaving and he would have to catch it. Another witness testified that he was an employe of respondent, and that he
was at the time stationed upon the boat; that it was his
duty to warn passengers against danger, and that he did
warn the appellant. From his testimony the warning
which he says he gave must have been given as appellant
was about in the act of getting upon the steps. He says
that after he gave the warning he turned away and did
not look further after appellant. It was testified that the

lurch of the train was necessary in its operation at that
place, by reason of ascending the incline leading from the
boat to the shore. It was also testified that the timber, against
which appellant was thrown, was about twenty-six inches
from the steps of the car, and that it was a necessary
timber for the operation of the boat as constructed. The
foregoing is a substantial statement of the material testimony that may be said to relate to the question of negligence on the part of respondent. The court denied the
challenge to appellant's evidence, and afterwards submitted the case to the jury, evidently believing at the
time that sufficient evidence of negligence had appeared
to require its submission. Upon motion for new trial the
court, however, concluded that negligence had not been
shown.

It may well be said that the conditions surrounding appellant at the time of the accident were not ordinary.
It is not usual to transfer trains of cars across streams
in the manner described. The method used is doubtless
reasonably safe, and no criticism is to be lodged against
respondent for adopting such method. But the method
required the separation of the cars of the train into sections. These were placed upon different tracks, and were
necessarily moved at different times. It was also necessary to pull them up the incline from the boat to the
shore, thus involving the application, suddenly or otherwise, of the required power to effect the ascent. It is
manifest that, under such circumstances, a high degree
of care was required of respondent, both in the construction and operation of its boat, in the movement of its
cars, and in guarding its passengers against confusion and
danger. If passengers were permitted to leave the cars
at all, the duty rested upon respondent to see that they

were warned against danger, and so informed as to train
movements that they need not become confused thereby.

No restrictions seem to have been placed upon passengers leaving the cars. The porter of the rear car, called
the observation car, testified that the rear platform thereof was surrounded by an inclosed railing, with a gateway
opening through it; that he opened the gateway when
upon the boat, and that a number of passengers went out
upon the boat, and returned to the cars by the same way.
He says when the train started he closed this gateway, so
that no one could have entered the car from that way
afterward. This was the car which appellant attempted
to enter, and by way of this platform. Appellant testified that, when he jumped upon the steps, the way to
the platform was open so that he could have entered.
This fact is in dispute between the porter and appellant.
But, be that as it may, it appears in any event that a
number of passengers, including appellant, were out of
the cars and moving about the boat. Passengers thus permitted upon the boat were under the special care of respondent, and were entitled to reasonable warning of lia-
bilty of danger, and against the probability of confusion
by train movements. Appellant says that he received no
warning, and saw no one there to give it. This testimony, if true, I think under all the circumstances showed
at least some negligence upon respondent's part. It is
true, as stated, that a witness for respondent testified that
he gave appellant warning, but that made the matter of
warning merely a disputed fact, which it was the jury's
province to determine.

Again, while it was testified that the upright timber
which appellant struck was necessary for the operation
of the boat as constructed, yet it became a question whether

its location so near the side of the cars was necessary and proper, in view of the apparently necessary lurching of the train as it passed that point. It has been often held that it is not necessarily negligence *per se* for one to get aboard a slowly moving train, the fact of negligence depending upon the circumstances of each particular case. Respondent was therefore bound to take notice that, in the absence of proper care or warning, passengers might attempt to get aboard slowly moving cars at or about the point in question, and might possibly, by the necessary lurch of the train, be thrown in contact with the timber only twenty-six inches in the clear from the cars. I think all these circumstances, bearing upon the question of respondent's negligence, were at least sufficient to call for their submission to the jury.

It is said in the briefs that the court was mainly influenced in its ruling on the motion for a new trial, by the decision of this court in *Blakney v. Seattle Electric Co.,* 28 Wash. 607, 68 Pac. 1037. The negligence alleged in that case was the sudden lurch of a street car, by which the respondent claimed she was thrown to the ground while in the act of getting off the car. The evidence, uncontradicted in the record, showed that the respondent did not fall at a street crossing, but at a point near the middle of a block, while she was attempting to step off the car. She did not notify the conductor, who was busy collecting fares, that she desired to leave the car, but she went to the rear platform for the purpose of getting off. She admitted that she was preparing to alight when she fell, and claimed that a sudden lurch of the car caused her to fall. She was in the act of getting off while the car was in motion, and at a place where it did not usually stop, without any notice to the operators of the car that

she desired, or was attempting, to do so. Witnesses called
by the respondent herself testified that there was no jerk
of the car; but that the car, already in motion, simply increased its speed while the respondent was in the act of
stepping off about the middle of a block. The court held
that it was not negligence *per se* to increase the speed of
the car, and that it was not negligence to do so when a
passenger was in the act of alighting unless the car company knew, or by the exercise of reasonable diligence could
have known, of that circumstance.

I do not think that the circumstances of that case are
similar to those in the one at bar. The accident occurred
at a place where the car company could not reasonably
have expected that a passenger would attempt to alight
without notice to that effect. It was at a place where
the car was properly proceeding on its course, and the
company had a right to increase the speed under those
circumstances. In the case at bar, however, the passenger was attempting to board a train at a place where it
was just starting. Other passengers had gone outside of
the cars and returned. The testimony of the porter showed
that this was a common occurrence. Respondent must
have known that those who had been permitted to leave the
cars would expect to return when the train was ready to
move. It must have known that, if it permitted its passengers to go out upon the boat, the necessary and reasonable information, warning, and facilities for their safe
and timely return should be provided, and those in accordance with the peculiar nature of the surroundings
and possibility of attendant danger. Respondent was also
chargeable with knowledge of all the conditions, appliances, and surroundings attending the movement of the
train at that time and place, and the possibility of acci-

dents happening to passengers returning to the cars. It
was therefore for the jury to say whether due care was
exercised at that time and place, whether there was lack
· of proper care in placing the timber so near the cars, particularly when the lurch of the train was necessary as it
passed that point, and whether these, conspiring together,
were the proximate cause of appellant's injury.

"It is well settled that where there is uncertainty as
to the existence of either negligence or contributory negligence, the question is not one of law but of fact and to
be settled by a jury; and this whether the uncertainty
arises from a conflict in the testimony or because the facts
being undisputed fair-minded men will honestly draw
different conclusions from them." *Richmond etc. Co. v.
Powers,* 149 U. S. 43, 45, 13 Sup. Ct. 748, 37 L. Ed.
642.

See, also, *Lane v. Spokane Falls etc. R. Co.,* 21 Wash.
119, 57 Pac. 367, 46 L. R. A. 153, 75 Am. St. 821. As
based particularly upon facts somewhat similar to those
here involved, and where the question of negligence was
held to be for the jury, see *North Chicago etc. Co. v.
Williams,* 140 Ill. 275, 29 N. E. 672; *Anderson v. Railway Co.,* 42 Ore. 505, 71 Pac. 659; *Kulman v. Erie R.
Co.,* 65 N. J. L. 241, 47 Atl. 497; 5 Am. & Eng. Enc. Law
(2d ed.), 581.

I believe the court's first impression of the evidence
in this case was the correct one, within the rules governing the facts which are for the jury. I therefore think
the verdict should not have been set aside on the ground
that there was no evidence of negligence on respondent's
part.

DUNBAR, J., concurs with HADLEY, J.

[No. 4414. Filed June 23, 1904.]

ALVIN LEWIS CULLY, *Appellant*, v. NORTHERN PACIFIC
RAILWAY COMPANY *et al., Respondents.*[1]

DISCOVERY—INTERROGATORIES—ACCIDENT REPORT—CONFIDENTIAL
COMMUNICATIONS. In an action against a railroad company
for personal injuries to an employe, it is proper to strike out
from interrogatories for a discovery, propounded to the defendant under Bal. Code, § 6009, one that compels the defendant
to produce the accident report and confidential correspondence
touching the case, since such communications are privileged.

SAME—INSPECTION OF PAPERS. Doubted whether the production of documentary evidence can be enforced by interrogatories
under Bal. Code, § 6009, in view of § 6047, making provision for
their inspection.

MASTER AND SERVANT—NEGLIGENCE—SAFE PLACE—INJURY TO
SERVANT BY SLIDE IN GRAVEL PIT. An employe working in and
about a gravel pit cannot recover for injuries received by reason
of a slide, where there was no evidence of negligence on the
part of the master in failing to discover the danger or to give
warning thereof, since the rule that he must furnish a safe
place in which to work has no application to that class of cases.

Appeal from a judgment of the superior court for
Skagit county, Joiner, J., entered June 11, 1902, upon
granting a nonsuit, after a trial on the merits before the
court and a jury, in an action for personal injuries sustained through a slide in a gravel pit.

Gable & Seabury and *Million & Houser,* for appellant,
cited the following cases as sustaining the liability under
similar facts, viz: *Chicago etc. Brick Co., v. Sobkowiak,*
148 Ill. 573, 36 N. E. 572; *Haas v. Balch,* 56 Fed. 984;
Holden v. Fitchburg R. Co., 129 Mass. 268, 37 Am. Rep.
343; *Rogers v. Leyden,* 127 Ind. 50, 26 N. E. 210;
Lynch v. Allyn, 160 Mass. 248, 35 N. E. 550; *Hennessy*

[1]Reported in 77 Pac. 202.

v. Boston, 161 Mass. 502, 37 N. E. 668; *Daly v. Kiel,*
106 La. 170, 30 So. 254; *Cook v. St. Paul etc. R. Co.,* 34
Minn. 45, 24 N. W. 311; *Fitzsimmons v. Taunton,* 160
Mass. 223, 35 N. E. 549; *Bartolomeo v. McKnight,* 178
Mass. 242, 59 N. E. 804; *Breen v. Field,* 157 Mass. 277,
31 N. E. 1075; *Connolly v. Waltham,* 156 Mass. 368,
31 N. E. 302; *McMillan Marble Co. v. Black,* 89 Tenn.
118, 14 S. W. 479; *Kranz v. Long Is. R. Co.,* 123 N. Y.
1, 25 N. E. 206, 20 Am. St. 716; *City of LaSalle v.
Kostka,* 190 Ill. 130, 60 N. E. 72; *Coan v. City of Marl-
borough,* 164 Mass. 206, 41 N. E. 238; *Carlson v. Northwestern Tel. Co.,* 63 Minn. 428, 65 N. W. 914; *Soyer v.
Great Falls Water Co.,* 15 Mont. 1, 37 Pac. 838; *Christianson v. Pacific Bridge Co.,* 27 Wash. 582, 68 Pac. 191.

Jas. F. McElroy, B. S. Grosscup, and *Wilbra Coleman,*
for respondents, cited the following cases as denying the
liability under similar facts, viz: *Walsh v. St. Paul
etc. R. Co.,* 27 Minn. 367, 8 N. W. 145; *Olson v. Mc-
Mullen* 34 Minn. 94, 24 N. W. 318; *Pederson v. Rush-
ford,* 41 Minn. 289, 42 N. W. 1063; *Quick v. Minnesota
Iron Co.,* 47 Minn. 361, 50 N. W. 244; *Welch v. Brainerd,*
108 Mich. 38, 65 N. W. 667; *Showalter v. Fairbanks,
Morse & Co.,* 88 Wis. 376, 60 N. W. 257; *Swanson v.
Great Northern R. Co.,* 68 Minn. 184, 70 N. W. 978;
Naylor v. Chicago & N. W. R. Co., 53 Wis. 661, 11
N. W. 24; *Johnson v. Ashland Water Co.,* 77 Wis. 51,
45 N. W. 807; *Consolidated Coal etc. Co. v. Clay's
Admr.,* 51 Ohio St. 542, 38 N. E. 610; *Galveston R. Co.
v. Lempe,* 59 Tex. 19, 11 Am. & Eng. R. Cas. 201; *Paule
v. Florence Min. Co.,* 80 Wis. 350, 50 N. W. 189; *Fin-
layson v. Utica Min. Co.,* 67 Fed. 507; *Anderson v. Winston,* 31 Fed. 528; *What Cheer Coal Co. v. Johnson,* 56
Fed. 810; *Minneapolis v. Lundin,* 58 Fed. 525; *Balch
v. Haas,* 73 Fed. 974.

PER CURIAM.—This is an action brought in the superior court of Skagit county, by Alvin Lewis Cully, by Charles Cully, his guardian *ad litem,* plaintiff, against Northern Pacific Railway Company and T. B. McDermott, defendants, to recover compensation for personal injuries sustained by said plaintiff. From a judgment of nonsuit and dismissal entered against him in the lower court, plaintiff appeals.

Appellant alleges in his complaint that, on or about August 5, 1901, he sustained serious injuries through the negligence of respondents in failing to provide him a safe place in which to work. The following facts are amply borne out by the record: On or about the 29th day of July, 1901, respondent Northern Pacific Railway Company was engaged in taking gravel from a gravel bank, near the town of Sedro-Woolley, in Skagit county. The crew of men engaged in the work of excavating the gravel and loading it on the cars was under the direction and control of respondent T. B. McDermott, as foreman of the crew. On or about the day last mentioned, appellant, being at that time between seventeen and eighteen years of age, although doing a man's work and drawing a man's pay, was employed by said McDermott to assist the crew in the work in hand, the particular duties assigned him being to assist those of the crew whose duty it was to attend the jackscrews on the steam shovel, and take up and relay the track, upon which the steam shovel was operated, as the necessity of the work from time to time required its position to be changed.

In the process of removing gravel from the bank and loading it on the cars, a steam shovel was used. Respondents had been engaged for some time in taking gravel from the bank in question, prior to the employment of appel-

lant, and, in the process of so doing, had cut into the
face of the bank to a considerable extent, necessitating
the building of the track, on which the steam shovel was
being operated, and the side track used for the gravel
cars, within the cut. The excavation had advanced into
the bank to such an extent that the height of the embank-
ment, caused by the excavation, was between thirty and
forty feet, on the day of the accident. Either early on
the same day or the day before, a stratum of blue clay
had been struck, which undoubtedly added to the danger
of a slide taking place.

On the afternoon of the 5th day of August, 1901, appellant was assisting another workman by the name of
Hale Rhodes in laying and spiking down track in the
rear of the steam shovel, preparatory to moving the shovel
to another position. Rhodes was engaged in spiking, and
appellant was holding or "pinching" the rails in position
to be spiked, by the use of a "claw" or "pinch" bar, respondent McDermott standing by. The bar which appellant was using was not working satisfactorily, and some
one—it does not clearly appear who—suggested, "Get a
line bar;" whereupon McDermott, by pointing, directed
attention to a bar lying a short distance away, between
the steam shovel and a car standing opposite on a parallel
track. Appellant immediately proceeded down between
the steam shovel and the standing car to get the bar pointed
to, and was in the act of picking it up, when a large mass
of the bank broke away from the top, and, before appellant had time to change his position, came down with
great violence, striking the steam shovel with such force
as to carry it off the track, carrying it over against the
opposite car, and pinning appellant between the steam
box of the steam shovel and the deck of the car, resulting in the injury.

The separate answers of respondents put in issue the material allegations of the complaint, and further alleged, as separate defenses to the action, assumed risk, contributory negligence, and negligence of fellow-servants. The affirmative matter in each answer was denied in the reply.

Prior to the trial, appellant, pursuant to § 6009, Bal. Code, propounded to respondent company certain written interrogatories, to all of which the respondent made answer, except interrogatories numbered 19 and 20, which are as follows:

"No. 19. If such report was ever made, who made it, and to whom was it made, and what action, if any, was ever taken by the company with reference thereto ?

"No. 20. Attach to your answers herein all reports regarding the accident, and all correspondence with the person or persons reporting said accident with reference thereto."

On motion of counsel for the railway company, these two interrogatories were stricken out by the lower court, on the ground that the same were incompetent, irrelevant, and immaterial, to which ruling appellant excepted. It appears from the transcript that the respondent company answered in the affirmative interrogatory No. 18, that a report of appellant's said injury was made to the company.

We are clearly of the opinion that these interrogatories were properly stricken. It seems to us that it would be a very dangerous and unjust practice to require the defendant, in this character of cases, to produce all of the correspondence, reports, and documents which he may have touching a case at issue, all of which must necessarily be of a strictly confidential character. Assuming that this correspondence disclosed admissions of the confidential agents of the defendants against the interests of the defendants, they are not such admissions as would be admissible in evidence. We can conceive of no reason why a different rule should apply in this case than prevails in the case of privileged communications generally. The statute which authorizes the filing of "interrogatories for the discovery of facts and documents material to the support, etc., of the action," does not contemplate that the plaintiff shall be permitted to have free access to the defendant's private correspondence and papers, in order that he may not only discover whether facts and documents, material to the issue, existed therein, but learn the defendant's line of defense as well. It is highly probable that §§ 6009 and 6047, Bal. Code, were intended to supersede the old practice which authorized a bill of discovery, but Mr. Pomeroy, in his work on Equity Jurisprudence, at § 201, in referring to the old practice, says:

"The fundamental rule on this subject is, that the plaintiff's right to a discovery does not extend to all facts which may be material to the issue, but is confined to facts which are material to his own title or cause of action; *it does not enable him to pry into the defendant's case,* or find out the evidence by which that case will be supported," etc.

The record fails to disclose the particular evidence sought to be obtained. Mr. Hageman, in his work on Privileged Communications, at page 32, says:

"So where a plaintiff at the instance of the solicitors sent out a gentleman to India for the express purpose of acting as the solicitors' agent in the collection of evidence respecting a pending suit, letters written by the agent either to the plaintiff or his solicitors on the subject of the evidence have been regarded by the court 'as confidential communications."

At page 750, Vol. 6, Enc. Plead. & Prac., the rule is laid down that,

"Communications to any person whose intervention is
necessary to secure and facilitàte the communication between attorney and client are privileged."

It seems to us that the communications sought to be obtained in his suit come squarely within the rule above
laid down as privileged. It may well be doubted whether,
under § 6009, *supra,* the production of any documentary
evidence could be demanded, in view of the provisions of
§ 6047, Bal. Code, which makes ample provision for the
inspection of books and papers in the hands of the opposite party material to the issue, and for permission to
make copies thereof.

Granting a nonsuit is the next error assigned. The
appellant seeks to invoke the rule in this case that it is
the duty of the master to furnish the servant with a safe
place in which to work. This rule, however, has no application to this class of employment. As was said in *Kath
v. Wisconsin Cent. R. Co.,* (Wis.), 99 N. W., at page 221:

"The place to work is being changed constantly, and is
necessarily incomplete and dangerous; and the employe
knows it, and accepts such risks as are ordinarily present
in such operations;"

citing *Porter v. Silver Creek etc. Co.,* 84 Wis. 418, 54
N. W. 1019; *Gulf etc. R. Co. v. Jackson,* 65 Fed. 48;
Moon Anchor etc. Mines v. Hopkins, 111 Fed. 298; *Ar-
mour v. Hahn,* 111 U. S. 313, 4 Sup. Ct. 433, 28 L. Ed.
440. To the same effect also is *Swanson v. Great Northern R. Co.,* 68 Minn. 184, 70 N. W. 978, and the statement of facts in that case is almost identical with that in
the case at bar. In a concurring opinion by one of the
justices, it is said:

"In this case the inferior servant injured knew, or
should have known, as much about the dangers which he

was encountering as the foreman knew, or could have been expected to know. They 'stood upon an equal footing. . . . In this respect the case is different from *Carlson v. Exchange Co.,* 63 Minn. 428, [65 N. W. 914], where a large crack had formed in the soil above the excavation, which the foreman knew, but which the inferior servant injured did not know, and was not in a position to observe. He was injured by reason of the foreman's neglect in failing to warn him.''

The evidence shows that the foreman repeatedly informed the workmen of the danger incident to the employment, that the workmen frequently talked over the liability of a slide occurring, and were constantly on the lookout for a slide; and, although the plaintiff went upon the stand, he failed to give any evidence to the effect that he was not warned, or that he did not hear the talk between the workmen to the effect that a slide was likely to occur at any time. The appellant uses this language in his brief: "Nor is there a scintilla of proof to show that appellant ever joined in these discussions or ever heard them." From this statement we are led to believe that the appellant must have been laboring under the impression that the law imposed the duty upon the defendant to prove want of negligence. This, however, is not the law. The burden was upon the appellant to prove negligence upon the part of the respondents. The labor being performed was of a hazardous character, and the appellant's own witnesses, upon cross-examination, testified that the respondents constantly kept men upon the top of the bank to watch for indications of a slide, to keep the bank clear of logs, etc., and shoot down the bank when it became undermined. And there is no evidence that these men were not carefully selected with reference to the duty which they had to perform.

In our judgment the respondents were clearly entitled to a nonsuit. The judgment is affirmed.

[No. 5190. Decided June 23, 1904.]

THE STATE OF WASHINGTON, *Respondent*, v. FRANK
ZENNER, *Appellant*.[1]

CRIMINAL LAW—LIVING OFF EARNINGS OF PROSTITUTE—SCIEN-
TER. Laws 1903, p. 320, § 2, making it a felony for any male
person to accept or live off the earnings of a prostitute is not
unconstitutional because it fails to require that the same be
knowingly done.

SAME—INFORMATION—ACT WILFULLY COMMITTED—KNOWLEDGE.
An information charging the crime of accepting the earnings
of a prostitute is not insufficient for failure to allege that it
was knowingly done, where it is alleged that the defendant
wilfully committed the act.

Appeal from a judgment of the superior court for Chehalis county, Irwin, J., entered October 9, 1903, upon
a trial and conviction of the crime of accepting the earnings of a prostitute. Affirmed.

W. H. Abel and *T. H. McKay*, for appellant.

Sidney Moor Heath and *J. A. Hutcheson*, for respondent.

DUNBAR, J.—Frank Zenner, the defendant and appellant, was charged by information as follows:

"The said Frank Zenner, on the 4th day of September,
A. D. 1903, in the county of Chehalis, in the state aforesaid, then and there being, did wilfully, feloniously and
unlawfully, then and there being a male person, lived with
and for a long time previous thereto, had been living
with, and lived off of, and accepted the earnings of one
Queen Adams, so called, she being then and there a prostitute."

A verdict of guilty was rendered, motion for new trial
and motion in arrest of judgment denied, and judgment

[1]Reported in 77 Pac. 191.

of conviction rendered. From such judgment this appeal was taken.

The following errors are assigned: (1) The information fails to state a crime; (2) the evidence was insufficient to support a verdict of guilty. It is argued by the appellant that the information is insufficient, first, because the act on which it was based is unconstitutional; second, because, in any event, an offense is not charged under the act. Section 2 of chapter 123, p. 230, Laws of 1903, provides:

"Any male person who lives with, or who lives off of, in whole or in part, or accepts any of the earnings of a prostitute, or connives in or solicits or attempts to solicit any male person or persons to have sexual intercourse, or cohabit with a prostitute, or who shall invite, direct or solicit any person to go to a house of ill-fame for any immoral purpose; or any person who shall entice, decoy, place, take or receive any female child or person under the age of eighteen years, into any house of ill-fame or disorderly house, or any house, for the purpose of prostitution; or any person who, having in his or her custody or control such child, shall dispose of it to be so received, or to be received in or for any obscene, indecent or immoral purpose, exhibition or practice, shall be deemed guilty of a felony and upon conviction thereof shall be imprisoned in the penitentiary not less than one year nor more than five years, and fined in any sum not less than one thousand dollars nor more than five thousand dollars."

And it is contended, that under the act the acceptance of the earnings of a prostitute renders the acceptor guilty, irrespective of whether such acceptor knew that the person from whom he accepted such earnings was a prostitute; that the law does not say that "knowingly accepting," etc., renders the person guilty, and that it is an acceptance, however innocent, that is made unlawful by the act; and that, therefore, the law is unconstitutional.

This contention is not supported by authority. The rule
is thus laid down in 16 Am. & Eng. Enc. Law, p. 138:

"Where the statutes are silent as to any *scienter*, as
where they do not use the words 'knowingly,' 'wilfully,'
and the like in describing the offense, it will not be necessary to allege and prove affirmatively that the defendant
knew the relationship existing between him and the parti-
ceps;"

citing many cases in support of this proposition, and laying down the doctrine that the defendant's ignorance of
such fact would constitute a valid defense.

This identical question, embracing the construction of
a statute of Washington territory, was passed upon by the
federal court in, *In Re Nelson,* 69 Fed. 712, in the following language:

"It has been further argued in behalf of the petitioner
that the statute of Washington territory is invalid because of the omission of the word 'knowingly,' or any
equivalent word or phrase to make knowledge of the relationship an element of the crime. I find by comparison,
however, that the statute of Washington territory is in
this respect not unlike other statutes which have been
upheld in numerous prosecutions, and there is really no
merit in the argument. Bish. Stat. Crimes, §§ 727, 729."

The same question was discussed by this court in *State
v. Glindemann,* 34 Wash. 222, 75 Pac. 800, and the constitutionality of a similar statute sustained.

On the second proposition, if it were held to be necessary to allege knowledge, the information in this respect
is sufficient, for it alleges that the defendant wilfully
committed this act, and it would be a strange construction
of language to hold that one could wilfully do a thing
without knowingly doing it. In our opinion the law is
a valid law, and the information is sufficient under the

provisions of the law.   We are not inclined to disturb
the verdict of the jury on the question of the insufficiency
of the evidence.

The judgment will therefore be affirmed.

FULLERTON, C. J., and HADLEY, ANDERS, and MOUNT,
JJ., concur.

[No. 4976. Decided June 22, 1904.]

THE HENRY H. SCHOTT COMPANY, *Appellant*, v. STONE,
FISHER & LANE, *Respondent*.[1]

SALES — REFUSAL OF PURCHASER TO COMPLETE SALE — AGREE-
MENT TO RETIRE FROM BUSINESS AND FOR SACRIFICE SALE OF
STOCK—PURCHASER'S COVENANT TO KEEP UP STOCK DURING SALE—
BREACH—MEASURE OF DAMAGES. Upon the breach by defendant
of a contract to purchase a stock of goods from the plaintiff,
in which the defendant agreed to pay eighty-five per cent of the
inventoried cost of the remaining stock after a sacrifice sale
conducted under directions of the defendant, reducing the value
thereof to $25,000, the defendant to keep up the stock during the
sale, the measure of plaintiff's damages upon the defendant's
refusal to take the remnant of the goods after the completion
of the sacrifice sale, is the difference between the contract price
and the value of the goods; hence it was proper to strike from
the complaint claims for damage for loss of goods sold at the
sacrifice sale, loss of customers by reason of failing to keep
up the stock during the sale, and by reason of being unable to
procure goods for the following trade, and loss to business reputation and financial credit.

SAME. In such a case, it is error to strike from the complaint a claim for damages by reason of the unsalable condition
of the remaining stock, because not kept up during the sacrifice sale; since the same is based on the difference between the
actual value of the remnant of the stock and the price agreed
to be paid, and the court was not justified in striking it, although
it may have been pleaded on a different theory from the above.

SAME—LEASE—REFUSAL OF TENANT TO ACCEPT—MEASURE OF
DAMAGES. In such a case, the fact that the purchaser had also

[1]Reported in 77 Pac. 192.

agreed to rent the premises for a term at a certain rental,
does not change the rules ordinarily applicable to a breach
of contract for the sale of goods, or render the damages uncertain, since the measure of damages as to the lease is the
difference between the rental value and the amount agreed to
be paid.

Appeal from a judgment of the superior court for Pierce
county, Chapman, J., entered July 10, 1903, dismissing
the action, upon striking the complaint. Reversed.

Graves & Englehart, for appellant.

Hudson & Holt and *Kerr & McCord,* for respondent.

FULLERTON, C. J.—The appellant brought this action
against the respondent to recover damages for a breach
of contract. The lower court, on the motion of the respondent, struck out, as immaterial and irrelevant, the
several allegations of the complaint relating to the damages alleged to have been suffered because of the breach,
and dismissed the action on the refusal of the appellant
to plead further. The case is here on the sufficiency of
these allegations.

The contract, the breach of which is complained of,
is set out in the complaint in the following language:

"That the plaintiff on or about the 10th day of October, 1902, and while engaged in carrying on its general
merchandise business in said city of North Yakima, which
said business was fully established, and had been carried
on by it since about July, 1900, in said city, duly made
and entered into a certain contract and agreement with
the defendant above named wherein and whereby it was
agreed by and between said plaintiff and said defendant
that said plaintiff would sell its entire business, which
it was then conducting in said city, together with the
good will thereof, and would retire from said business
in said city, and would sell its stock of merchandise and
store fixtures then owned by it and used by it in conduct-

ing its said business in North Yakima, except its shoe,
clothing, hat, crockery, tinware, and grocery business
and stock, and such articles used in conducting the same.
That said defendant at said time agreed to purchase the
same, for the purpose of acquiring all the business, good
will, stock, fixtures, etc., of said plaintiff in said business,
and for the purpose of establishing said defendant in the
said business of said plaintiff in said North Yakima, and
for the purpose of getting said plaintiff to retire from its
said business in North Yakima, and allowing said defendant to engage in said business in said North Yakima
in its place and stead. The terms and conditions of which
said agreement were as follows, to wit: That said plaintiff would immediately surrender the sale of its entire
stock of goods, then held by it in its said stores, in said
city of North Yakima, to said defendant, which would
remark all of said stock of goods of the said plaintiff and
sell the same for such prices as said defendant thought
best and desired, and apply the proceeds of the sale, first,
to pay current expenses and advertising expenses; second,
accounts payable; third, bills payable. Said stock to be
sold under the direction of said defendant as aforesaid
until the same was reduced to the value of about twenty
five thousand dollars, exclusive of shoes, clothing, hats,
crockery, tinware and groceries; that said defendant should
receive 1% commission on all sales made under its direction; that said defendant would supply all necessary new
merchandise to keep up the said stock in a fair condition
while said sales were being made, and receive as compensation for said stock so furnished the invoice price of the
same with 10% added, the same to be payable monthly,
and also receive the expenses of Mr. George Stone, the
duly acting agent and president of said defendant, while
engaged in working on said sales. In consideration of
which said defendant agreed that when said stock had been
so sold as to be reduced to the value of about $25,000,
not including shoes, clothing, hats, crockery, tinware and
groceries, that said defendant would receive and purchase the said remaining stock of said plaintiff and pay
therefor the sum of eighty five cents on the dollar of the

inventoried cost of said remaining stock; said inventoried
cost to be fixed between January 1st and January 15th,
1903, the said stock to be received and paid for in cash,
at said time by said defendant. That said plaintiff then
and there also agreed to transfer and convey all its said
business, good will of the business, store fixtures, etc.,
except said crockery, hat, shoe, tinware, clothing and
grocery stock and business, to said defendant at the agreed
price of twenty seven hundred (2,700) dollars in addition
to the sale of the above stock of about twenty five thousand
dollars of merchandise, said defendant to have a lease of
the premises then occupied by said plaintiff with its said
business, exclusive of the departments used for shoe and
groceries, for five years, at a monthly rental of two hundred (200) dollars. That said defendant should also have
the refusal of the space then used by said plaintiff for
its grocery department, at a monthly rental of twenty-
five (25) dollars, for the term of five years, in so far as
the influence of E. B. Moore and Henry H. Schott, stockholders in said plaintiff corporation, could be used to obtain the same. That said plaintiff and defendant then
and there agreed, as a part of the consideration for the
purchase of said business, store fixtures, good will of the
business and merchandise by said defendant, that said
plaintiff would retire from its said business in said North
Yakima, and that said defendant would succeed to the
same."

It is then alleged that the appellant, pursuant to such
agreement, took control of the stock of goods mentioned
about October 12, 1902, and placed the same on the
market as a sacrifice sale at an average reduction of about
twenty-five per centum of what the same were reasonably
worth where they then were, and between that date and
January 1, 1903, made sales amounting in all to $61,-
539.70, reducing the stock to a cost value of between
$25,000 and $26,000; that on the latter date the appellant, following instructions received from the respondent,
proceeded to make an inventory of the goods remaining

on hand, which it shortly thereafter completed, and so informed the respondent, requesting the respondent at the same time to carry out the agreement; that the respondent, in reply thereto, notified the appellant that it would not further comply with the agreement, saying that the appellant could either retain the business or dispose of it elsewhere as it saw fit—that the transaction, in so far as the respondent was concerned, was closed and at an end, and that it would proceed no further towards a compliance therewith. The appellant further alleged that, up to the time the respondent repudiated the contract, it had faithfully and fully complied with all of its terms and conditions on its part to be performed, and stood ready to comply with all of its remaining conditions, had the respondent consented to carry out its part of the contract.

The items of damage claimed in the complaint because of the breach of the contract, and which were struck out by the trial court, were in substance these: (1) For loss on the goods sold at the sacrifice sale while the stock was being reduced to $25,000, being the difference between the amount received and their actual value, the sum of $20,-513.24. (2) For losses between October 15, 1902, and January 15, 1903, caused by the fact that its stock of goods was sold out and run down so low that it was unable to supply many of its customers, thereby losing its customers and profits on sales, etc., the whole aggregating $7,500. (3) For losses between January 15, 1903, and October 15, 1903, caused by the fact that the appellant was unable to procure suitable goods for the spring, summer, and fall trade, after the respondent gave notice that it would not perform its part of the contract, thereby losing many of its customers, and profits on goods it would otherwise have made, aggregating the sum of $15,000. (4) For damages to its business reputation and financial credit with the wholesale houses and commercial agencies of the United States, aggregating $10,000.   (5) The allegation concerning the fifth item of loss was as follows:

"That when said defendant refused to purchase said business of said plaintiff and refused to receive and pay for said stock of merchandise, it left said plaintiff with a stock of merchandise on hand of the apparent value of about twenty five thousand (25,000) dollars; that said stock of merchandise consisted of remnants of a large stock of merchandise, which said plaintiff had on hand in the month of October, 1902, when said agreement was made with said plaintiff; that said stock so left was unsalable by reason of the fact that many of the articles necessary to be on hand and a part of said stock were missing; that said stock was, by reason of its having been so sold down and sold out by said defendant under said agreement, unsalable, and of a market value of not more than ten thousand (10,000) dollars; that the action of said defendant in selling said stock as aforesaid and reducing the same, depreciated the market value thereof to the injury of this plaintiff in the sum of ten thousand (10,000) dollars."

The complaint concluded with a demand for judgment for the several items above mentioned, which aggregate the sum of $63,013.24.

The argument, by which the appellant seeks to justify the several items of damage set out in its complaint, can hardly be better stated than counsel on its behalf have stated it in their brief.   They say:

"This was no mere sale of personal property; it was a contract containing several covenants to be kept and performed by The Henry H. Schott Company.   In order to carry out this contract, The Henry H. Schott Company was compelled to and did notify the wholesale houses with whom they dealt that they would go out of business, thereby severing their business connection with the wholesale firms, from whom they purchased certain goods which could not be purchased elsewhere. They were compelled to and did notify the people who were in the habit of buying goods from them that they were going out of business.

"To reduce the stock they were compelled to, and did make a sacrifice sale, thereby losing several thousand dollars.

"When Stone, Fisher & Lane refused to comply with their part of the contract, The Henry H. Schott Company were compelled to re-establish their business relations with the wholesale houses at a loss. They were also without enough goods to continue their business, and they had lost heavily by making the sacrifice sale. They were losers by having a remnant stock of goods left on their hands, which could only be sold at a loss.

"The complaint in this action pleads a contract with several covenants and conditions to be kept and performed by The Henry H. Schott Company. It then pleads a breach on the part of Stone, Fisher & Lane, and then pleads actual losses by The Henry H. Schott Company by reason of said breach of Stone, Fisher & Lane.

"All the damages pleaded are the direct result of the breach by Stone, Fisher & Lane. Stone, Fisher & Lane had all the acts performed by The Henry H. Schott Company in contemplation. At the time the contract was entered into it was fully understood by Stone, Fisher & Lane that The Henry H. Schott Company would perform the acts alleged in the complaint to have been performed by it. Each party was fully informed as to all that was to be done by each party to carry out the contract."

Plausible as this reasoning may appear, when first presented to the mind, we cannot think it sound. It is not disputed that the contract had been performed, by both the parties thereto, down to the time the transfer was ready to be made. The respondent, to relieve itself from

any liability on account of the terms of the contract at
that time, was only required to do three things, viz: (1)
purchase the stock of goods then on hand at the rate of
eighty five cents on the dollar of the inventoried cost of
the same; (2) purchase the "business, good will of the
business, store fixtures, etc," at the agreed price of $2,700;
and (3) enter into a lease of the store building for a
term of five years at a rental of $200 per month. These
being the only things the respondent was required to do
in order to comply with the contract, it is plain that the
damages suffered and recoverable by the appellant are
such as were caused by the failure of the respondent to
comply therewith; that is to say, the appellant is entitled to recover for any loss it sustained because of the
failure of the respondent to purchase the remaining stock
and business, good will of the business, store fixtures,
etc., at the prices agreed upon, and to enter into a lease
of the store building at the rent reserved for the time
named.

As the utmost measure of the respondent's liability, had
it taken the property, was the contract price, so the measure of its liability, after its refusal to take it and the
appellant had elected to keep it, was the difference between the contract price and the actual value of the property, if the actual value was less than the contract price.
On the failure of the respondent to comply with the contract the appellant, of course, had a choice of remedies;
(1) it could store and hold the personal property subject
to the respondent's order, tender a lease of the store room,
and sue for the contract price; (2) it could sell the property, including the lease, after notice to the respondent,
and recover the difference between the price received
and the contract price; or (3) it could retain the property

as its own, and recover the difference between the market
value of the same, at the time and place of delivery, and
the contract price, if the market value was less than the
contract price. But, as it elected to keep the property,
it is clear that its measure of damages is found in the
last of the three remedies mentioned.

The contract, as we view it, was nothing more than
a contract relating to the purchase and sale of personal
property, and the remedies for a breach of the contract
are such as ordinarily apply in such cases. It is suggested, however, that, while this remedy is definite and
certain in so far as the goods themselves and the good will
of the business and store fixtures are concerned, it is
uncertain when applied to the lease, and hence the rules
ordinarily applicable to a breach of contract for the sale
of personal property do not apply. But we think dif-
ferently. The respondent agreed to take the lease at a
fixed rate per month for five years. The damage sustained by its failure to take it, if any, is the difference
between the actual rental value of the property and the
amount the respondent agreed to pay as such rent, and
is as capable of just admeasurement as is the loss on the
personal property.

For these reasons, therefore, we are of the opinion
that the court committed no error in striking from the
complaint the allegations concerning items one to four
inclusive, as we have numbered them above. With reference to the item numbered five, being paragraph eleven
of the complaint, we think the court erred in striking it
out. It was based upon the difference between the actual
value of the remnant of the stock of goods, and the price
the respondent agreed to pay for the same. As such, it
was a legitimate item of damage, and one for which re-

covery could be had. It may be, as the respondent suggests, that the appellant based its right of recovery even for this item on a different theory from that upon which we hold the item a legitimate one, but this would hardly justify the court in denying it the right to recover altogether. Moreover, the respondent's motion was not directed to this paragraph of the complaint with the idea of having it made to conform to correct pleading, but on the theory that it stated a non-recoverable item of damage, and it was stricken out on that theory. As we hold it states a recoverable item, clearly it was error for the court to strike it out. The view we have taken of the pleading, however, may have rendered an amendment of the complaint desirable, and the remittitur will go with leave to amend, if the appellant so elects.

The judgment is reversed, and the cause remanded, with instructions to reinstate the case.

HADLEY, ANDERS, MOUNT, and DUNBAR, JJ., concur.

[No. 4328. Decided June 23, 1904.]

THE STATE OF WASHINGTON, *Respondent,* v. W. A. LEWIS *et al., Appellants.*[1]

APPEAL—BRIEFS—TITLE OF CASE—SUFFICIENCY. The appellants' brief will not be struck out on motion of the respondent on account of error in the title of the case, where the notice of appeal and appeal bond were correctly entitled and gave the supreme court jurisdiction, and the respondent entitled its brief in the same style and was not misled or prejudiced.

APPEAL—DISMISSAL—WITHDRAWAL OF CO-PARTY. An appeal will not be dismissed because one of the co-appellants withdrew his appeal.

CRIMINAL LAW—INFORMATION—TIME FOR FILING—DISMISSAL OF PROSECUTION AFTER THIRTY DAYS. Where the accused, after

[1]Reported in 77 Pac. 198.

being held to answer to the superior court by a justice of the
peace, gives a bail bond for his appearance, and no information
is filed against him for thirty days, as required by Bal. Code,
§ 6910, the prosecution must be dismissed unless good cause for
the delay is shown, and the burden of showing such cause is
upon the state.

SAME — BAIL — RELEASE OF SURETIES — FAILURE TO PROSECUTE
WITHIN TIME PRESCRIBED—DISMISSAL OF PROSECUTION WITHOUT
PRESENCE OF DEFENDANT. Where the accused on being held to
answer by a justice of the peace, gave a bail bond conditioned
for his presence in the superior court when required, and no
information was filed against him within thirty days and he
was not brought to trial within sixty days, pursuant to Bal.
Code, §§ 6910, 6911, and no cause for such delay is shown by
the state, the sureties are released; and it is error to enter
judgment on the bail bond and to deny the sureties' motion to
dismiss the prosecution because they fail to produce the defendant in court at the time the motion is made, especially
when the prosecution is subsequently dismissed upon a motion
confessed by the state, showing that the state had no case against
the defendant.

Appeal from a judgment of the superior court for Spokane county, Richardson, J., entered October 14, 1901,
against sureties upon a bail bond, upon the motion of the
state, after the failure of the accused to appear. Reversed.

William O. Lewis and *George M. Nethercutt* (*W. M.
Murray* and *T. C. Griffitts,* of counsel), for appellants.

Horace Kimball and *Miles Poindexter,* for respondent.

PER CURIAM.—On May 24, 1901, W. A. Lewis, waiving preliminary examination before a justice of the peace,
was held to answer to the superior court of Spokane
county, on the charge of embezzlement. On May 25,
1901, W. A. Lewis, as principal, and E. F. Boyles, Otto
Bringgold, M. L. Lewis, H. G. Brown, and Harry Green,
as sureties, entered into a bail bond or recognizance to the

state of Washington, in the penal sum of $3,000, for the appearance of said Lewis before the superior court. This instrument contained the following conditions: "Now, therefore, if the said W. A. Lewis shall be and appear in said superior court aforesaid at the city of Spokane, to answer the said charge whenever it shall be prosecuted, and, at all times required until discharged according to law, render himself amenable to the orders and process of the said superior court, then, this obligation to be void and of no effect, otherwise to be and remain in full force, virtue and effect." This bail bond was approved by the justice May 31, 1901. The certified transcript of the justice of the peace and the bond were filed in the clerk's office of the superior court on June 13, 1901.

On the 25th day of June, 1901, the defendant, W. A. Lewis, appeared in person, and made and filed his motion in said court to dismiss such prosecution. Such motion, omitting title, is as follows:

"Comes now the defendant in the above entitled action and appearing in his own proper person, and in open court makes this motion, and files the same with the clerk and moves the court: That the above entitled action and the prosecution thereof, be by the court dismissed, upon the following grounds, to wit: That on the twenty-fourth day of May, A. D. 1901, the defendant was, by H. L. Kennan, a justice of the peace in and for Spokane county and precinct, held to answer the charge of larceny by embezzlement, theretofore preferred against him in the said justice court, and the proceedings therein were, by the said justice, duly certified and returned to the clerk of the above entitled court wherein the above entitled and said action ever since has been and now is pending, and more than thirty days have elapsed since the defendant was held to answer as aforesaid, and no indictment has been found, and no information has been filed, against him within thirty days or at all. Wherefore the defendant demands that this

action, and the prosecution thereof, be dismissed and he
go hence without day, and that his bond be exonerated and
his bondsmen discharged of and from any, all and further
liability thereon. This motion is made upon the record,
pleadings, files, and papers in this action, and upon the
annexed affidavit."

This motion was accompanied by an affidavit on the part
of Lewis purporting to substantiate the grounds thereof,
and which alleges:

"That this defendant has called the attention of Horace
Kimball [prosecuting attorney] to this matter at divers
times, the last time being Saturday, June 22, 1901, at
which time this affiant informed the said Horace Kimball
that he had been waiting here at Spokane for over four
weeks to answer any information that might be filed against
him in the premises, and that this affiant had business interests elsewhere, which demanded his attention, and that
it would be very inconvenient for this affiant to wait longer
than Monday, the 24th day of June, A. D. 1901, for the
said Kimball to take action in the premises."

On the 27th day of June, 1901, defendant Lewis filed
his affidavit in the above prosecution, that on the 25th day
of June, 1901, he personally served upon Horace Kimball,
at the city of Spokane, true copies of such motion and
affidavit. The record further shows that defendant Lewis,
on the 26th day of June, 1901, served upon the prosecuting attorney a written notice, stating "that the defendant
has called your attention thereto at divers times during the
last month, the last time being Saturday, June 22, 1901,
and at all times told and informed you he was ready to
plead and dispose of the said action at the earliest possible
time."

On September 23, 1901, no indictment having been
found nor information filed against defendant, W. A.
Lewis, this cause came on for hearing in the court below

on motion of defendant to dismiss the prosecution. The order thereon recites that the court was of the opinion that the presence of defendant was necessary at such hearing, and thereupon "ordered that bench warrant issue forthwith for the arrest of the defendant W. A. Lewis, and that he be brought before the court at 9:30 A. M. tomorrow, to wit, Tuesday, September 24, 1901, to which time the hearing of this motion is adjourned." On September 26, 1901, this motion was again called up in the superior court, when the sheriff of Spokane county reported in open court that he had made diligent search for defendant, Lewis, and could not find him. The hearing of this motion for dismissal was continued from time to time, on account of the absence of such defendant, until October 10, 1901, when the motion again came on for hearing in the lower court, the defendant appearing by his counsel, Messrs. W. S. Lewis and Frank H. Graves. The court below at that time ordered that the hearing of this motion be continued till the defendant should be personally present in court. The defendant, by his counsel, excepted to this order.

On October 9, 1901, the prosecution, without making any showing, filed in the court below an information, charging defendant, Lewis, with the crime for which he was held by the justice of the peace on May 24, 1901, and October 14, 1901, was the time set for the arraignment of defendant on such charge. On October 10, 1901, the prosecution was granted leave to withdraw its motion to forfeit the above bail bond. On October 14, 1901, the defendant, by W. S. Lewis, insisted on the hearing of the motion to dismiss the prosecution, and also moved a discharge of the bail bond as against the principal and sureties thereon, on substantially the same grounds as stated in the defendant's motion to dismiss.

On the day last named, on motion of plaintiff (the state of Washington), the court below, on default of defendant W. A. Lewis to appear personally and answer such charge, rendered judgment against defendant for $3,000, and against the sureties in the amounts following: M. L. Lewis, for $1,000; E. F. Boyles, $500; Otto Bringgold, $500; Harry Green, $500, and H. G. Brown, in the sum of $500. The defendant and appealing sureties excepted to the entry of this judgment. On the 2d day of December, 1901, the motion to dismiss the prosecution came on for hearing in the superior court, and the prosecution confessed this motion, which was granted, the action was dismissed, and the defendant was discharged from custody. He did not appear personally at this hearing, but was represented by counsel. The sureties, E. F. Boyles, M. L. Lewis, H. G. Brown, and Otto Bringgold, appeal from this judgment, which was entered herein on October 14, 1901. H. G. Brown afterwards withdrew from such appeal.

The respondent moves to strike from the files herein appellants' opening brief, for the reason that neither such brief, the appeal bond, "nor any of the papers in the said appeal, after the notice of appeal had been given and served, are entitled as required by statute and by rule of this court." Respondent also moves the dismissal of the appeal of H. G. Brown, on account of his withdrawal of the same as above noted.

No question is raised by respondent as to the correctness of the title of the cause in the notice of appeal, which is as follows: "In the superior court of the state of Washington in and for the county of Spokane. The State of Washington vs. W. A. Lewis, Harry Green, E. F. Boyles, M. L. Lewis, H. G. Brown, and Otto Bringgold, sureties, on bail bond." On the appeal bond the title of the cause is iden-

tical down to and including the name of "W. A. Lewis;"
then follows the words and names, "defendant, Harry
Green, E. F. Boyles, M. L. Lewis, H. G. Brown, and Otto
Bringgold, sureties on bond or recognizance of defendant."
We think, unquestionably, that the notice of appeal and
bond are sufficient to give this court jurisdiction. Respondent's counsel do not claim to have been misled or prejudiced
by the action of appellants in the premises. The state has
entitled its brief in the same manner and style as that of
appellants. Sec. 6535, Bal Code, provides: "The supreme court shall hear and determine all causes removed
thereto in the manner hereinbefore provided, upon the
merits thereof, disregarding all technicalities, and shall
upon the hearing consider all amendments which could
have been made as made." The withdrawal of H. G.
Brown, as one of the appealing parties, cannot work to the
prejudice of the other appellants in the present controversy.
The motions to strike and to dismiss the appeal are therefore denied.

The assignments of error present the single proposition
of law for our consideration: Were the proceedings, had
in the court below, regular and valid with regard to the
forfeiture of the above bail bond, and in rendering judgment in the case at bar against the appellants now before
the court? Section 6910, Bal. Code, provides:

"When a person has been held to answer, if an indictment be not found or information filed against him within
thirty days, the court must order the prosecution to be dismissed, unless good cause to the contrary be shown."

The next section, 6911, further provides:

"If a defendant indicted or informed against for an
offense, whose trial has not been postponed upon his application, be not brought to trial within sixty days after the
indictment is found or the information filed, the court must

order it to be dismissed, unless good cause to the contrary
be shown."

This court, in *State v. Brodie,* 7 Wash. 442, 35 Pac. 137,
while having the latter section under consideration, used
the following language:

"As the record stands, we are of the opinion that no
sufficient cause appears for not having brought the defendants to trial, and in the absence of such cause they were
entitled to their discharge under said section. The failure
to call a jury, without any good reason being made apparent why one was not called, was not sufficient to warrant
holding them in custody beyond the time specified in said
section."

The same line of reasoning when applied to the above section, 6910, clearly implies that the provisions of this section are mandatory; that, "if an indictment be not found
or information filed against him [the defendant] within
thirty days, the court must order the prosecution to be dismissed, unless good cause to the contrary be shown;" that
such cause should appear, or be shown by, the record, unless
waived in some manner by the defendant or accused. In
other words, when the indictment shall not have been
found, nor information filed, within the thirty days after
the defendant has been held to answer a criminal charge,
the prosecution must assume the burden of showing a reasonable excuse or justification for its omission so to do.
Otherwise, the defendant is entitled to his discharge, and
a dismissal of the prosecution, as a matter of right.

When it shall have been determined that such right to discharge and dimissal exists in defendant's behalf, it would
seem to logically follow that this right inures to the advantage of the sureties on the defendant's bail bond. The
above sections contained in Ballinger's Code are substantially identical with § 1382 of the California Penal

Code. In *People v. Wickham*, 113 Cal. 283, 48 Pac. 123,
defendant was convicted in the trial court of embezzlement,
and appealed. In the opinion the following language is
used: "The only point made for a reversal is that the
court erred in denying defendant's motion to dismiss the
prosecution upon the ground that the information against
him was not filed within thirty days after he was held to
answer." The court held in this case that, "if there was
any good cause for not filing the information sooner, the
burden was on the prosecution to show it." The judgment
of conviction was reversed for want of such showing in the
record. There are authorities holding that, where a bail
bond has been executed by a defendant and sureties, conditioned that the principal shall appear at the next term of
the court named in the instrument, to answer a criminal
charge, and continuances are had from term to term without the finding of any indictment or the presentment of
any information against the principal, such delays are sufficient in law to release the sureties from liability on the
recognizance. *Rogers v. State,* 79 Ala. 59; *Jones v. State,*
11 Tex. App. 412; *Lane v. State,* 6 Kan. App. 106, 50
Pac. 905.

Bail bonds should be construed with reference to the
laws of the sovereign jurisdiction where given. While the
liability of the principal and sureties is to be measured by
the terms of the bond, the obligors, especially the sureties,
have the right to expect and insist that the prosecution
observe the mandates of the statute. While the defendant
Lewis in the case at bar may not have had sufficient excuse
or justification to absent himself from the jurisdiction of
the trial court, still such conduct did not excuse the prosecution in neglecting to perform a positive duty, enjoined

by the provisions of § 6910, Bal. Code, to either file an information within the thirty days as therein provided, or show good cause for the delay in that particular. The record fails to show any good cause for the neglect, on the part of the state, to file the information until October 9, 1901, more than three months after the expiration of the time limited. If the state can omit the performance of so important a duty for three months, why may it not do so for six months, or for an indefinite period, and in the meantime insist upon the forfeiture of defendant's recognizance? We cannot conceive this to be the law. True, the sureties may seize the person of their principal and surrender him into the custody of the law, and thus exempt themselves from future liability. Still, we think that they should not be mulcted, simply because they omitted so to do, having acted on the presumption that the prosecution would discharge its duties as required by the statute, or that otherwise it had elected to abandon such prosecution.

The following language is found in the brief of the learned counsel for respondent:

"The dismissal of the prosecution does not necessarily follow the failure to file an information within thirty days, and is not an absolute right, but 'good cause to the contrary may be shown,' . . . Defendant's sureties had no right to suppose either that they were exonerated or that the prosecution would be dismissed because an information was not filed within 30 days. This was a matter which could only be determined upon a hearing, when the prosecution might have shown 'good cause to the contrary.'"

But, as we view the record of the judgment entered on December 2, 1901, wherein the prosecution confessed defendant Lewis' motion of June 24, 1901, in open court, which was granted, judgment of dismissal was thereupon entered, and the defendant ordered discharged from custody. In our opinion, this entry is a very significant feature in the present controversy. It shows on the face of the record, in the absence of any explanation, that, at the time the above motion was made, June 24, 1901, the prosecution had no case against the principal, Lewis, and had no right to hold him further in these proceedings; that he (Lewis) was then entitled to his discharge. In view of these facts, we think that it would be illegal and inequitable to uphold the judgment of the court below against these sureties who are now before this court insisting upon their legal rights; that such judgment should be reversed, and the proceedings ordered dismissed as against these appellants.

[No. 5093. Decided June 28, 1904.]

F. F. WILLIAMS, *Respondent*, v. H. L. PITTOCK *et al.*, *Appellants.*[1]

TAXATION—FORECLOSURE OF LIEN—NOTICE—SUMMONS BY PUBLICATION—NAME OF OWNER—DUE PROCESS OF LAW. A summons by publication in a tax certificate foreclosure against nonresident owners need not name or be addressed to the real owner of the property, in order to constitute due process of law, and is sufficient under the statute if directed to the person in whose name the property was assessed, and to all persons, unknown, if any, having an interest in the property; since the proceeding is *in rem*, and the owner is bound to take notice of the tax and all steps towards its collection.

SAME—REQUISITES OF SUMMONS. The general statutes as to summons by publication are applicable to tax foreclosure proceedings under Laws, 1901, p. 383, § 1.

PROCESS—SUMMONS—DATE OF FIRST PUBLICATION. The requirement of the general statute that a summons for publication shall contain the date of the first publication is sufficiently com-

[1]Reported in 77 Pac. 385.

plied with where immediately below the attorney's signature the
"Date of the first publication" is stated.

JUDGMENT—VACATION WITHIN ONE YEAR—GOOD CAUSE TO BE
SHOWN. Under Bal. Code, § 4880, a nonresident defendant, served
by publication in a tax lien foreclosure, is not entitled to the
vacation of the judgment, upon a tender of the tax and interest
and application made within one year, but good cause therefor
must be shown, and mere neglect to pay the taxes is not sufficient cause.

Appeal from a judgment of the superior court for Chehalis county, Joiner, J., entered February 1, 1904, dismissing the action, upon sustaining a demurrer to a petition to
vacate a judgment. Affirmed.

B. G. Cheney and *Coovert & Stapleton,* for appellants,
to the point that a tender of the tax, being a complete defense, entitled the parties to a vacation of the decree within
one year, cited, *Woodham v. Anderson,* 32 Wash. 500, 73
Pac. 536; *Hauswirth Admn'x v. Sullivan,* 6 Mont. 203,
9 Pac. 798.

John C. Hogan, for respondent.

HADLEY, J.—Respondent, as the holder of a delinquency
tax certificate, brought suit to foreclose the same. Judgment by default was entered. The sale of the premises
was ordered, and respondent became the purchaser at treasurer's sale. Within a year from the date of its entry, appellants, by petition, asked for the vacation of the judgment. Respondent demurred to the petition on the ground
that it does not state facts sufficient to support the relief
asked, and also that the court has not jurisdiction to entertain the petition. The demurrer was sustained. Appellants elected to stand upon their petition, and judgment
was entered dismissing the same. This appeal is from the
judgment.

It is assigned that the court erred in sustaining the demurrer, for the alleged reason that the allegations of the petition show that the foreclosure proceedings amounted to an attempt to deprive appellants of their property without due process of law. The petition avers that appellants are, and ever since 1871 have been, the owners of the land, and that, in the foreclosure proceedings, they were neither served with process nor made parties. It is alleged, however, that service upon them was attempted to be made by publication, directed to W. L. Pittock and Mrs. W. L. Pittock, his wife, and to R. L. Pittock and Mrs. R. L. Pittock, his wife; but that the court did not acquire jurisdiction of the subject matter of the action, for the reason that neither the actual owners nor the reputed owners were made defendants, and that neither were served with process. It is also alleged that neither of the appellants had actual notice or knowledge of the pendency of the action, the publication of the summons, the entry of the judgment, or the sale of the property, until some months thereafter.

Reference to the application for judgment in the foreclosure proceeding, which is attached to the petition as an exhibit, discloses that the property was assessed for these taxes in the name of R. L. Pittock, who was made a party together with the other persons named above, "and all persons unknown, if any, having or claiming to have an interest in and to the real property hereinafter described." The publication summons was directed to the same persons. Appellants do not contend that they were residents of this state, but allege in their petition that they have, at all times mentioned, been and now are residents of the state of Oregon. It is manifest, therefore, that, as far as appellants were concerned, publication summons became the proper process in the case under our statutes. Such being true, are they bound by the notice that was given, although they were not named therein? That the summons was specifically directed to the person in whose name the property was assessed, must be taken as true, since the exhibit attached to appellants' petition so states, and it is not denied by other averments. It appears, therefore, that good faith was exercised by naming in the summons the persons whose names appeared upon the tax records as the owners. We think no more was required. Tax proceedings under our statutes are purely *in rem*. *Coolidge v. Pierce County*, 28 Wash. 95, 68 Pac. 391. The same is true of tax foreclosure proceedings. *Washington Timber & Loan Co. v. Smith*, 34 Wash. 625, 76 Pac. 267. Our statutes permit property to be assessed to an unknown owner, when the owner's name is unknown. § 1699, Bal. Code. Also, Sess. Laws 1899, p. 287, § 3. It is also provided that the notice in the foreclosure proceedings shall contain the name of the owner, if known. § 1751, subd. 1, Bal. Code. Also, Sess. Laws 1901, p. 383, § 1, subd. 1. The fair inference to be drawn from these statutes is that, if the property has been assessed to an unknown owner, and the certificate of delinquency has been so issued, the foreclosure may be had in form against an unknown owner. It would appear that the actual name of the real owner is made no more essential in the proceedings to foreclose, than it is in the assessment. The whole procedure, including the assessment, foreclosure, and sale, is for the purpose of establishing and enforcing a lien for public revenue, which, under the policy of the state, is chargeable to the property only, and not personally to the owner. It is the land itself with which the state is concerned, and its dominion over the land for revenue purposes exists without regard to who may be the owner. All owners know that such is the fact, and that the power of taxation will be exercised each year. In the very nature of our revenue procedure, the statutory provisions with regard to owners must have been intended to be directory, rather than mandatory—of the form, and not of the essence, of the proceedings.

"Proceedings of this nature are not usually proceedings against parties, nor, in the case of lands or interests in lands belonging to persons unknown, can they be. They are proceedings which have regard to the land itself rather than to the owners of the land, and if the owners are named in the proceedings, and personal notice is provided for, it is rather from tenderness to their interests, and in order to make sure that the opportunity for a hearing shall not be lost to them, than from any necessity that the case shall assume that form. As in all other cases of proceedings *in rem*, if the law makes provision for publication of notice in a form and manner reasonably calculated to bring the proceedings to the knowledge of the parties who exercise ordinary diligence in looking after their interests in the lands, it is all that can be required." Cooley, Taxation (2d ed.), p. 527.

If the property is assessed to an unknown owner, or to one not the real owner, the holder of a certificate should not be required to determine in advance who may be the real owner. That may be a difficult matter, and may often be the subject of serious dispute. The supreme court of Minnesota, in *McQuade v. Jaffray*, 47 Minn. 326, 50 N. W. 233, aptly observed as follows:

"In several cases, as in *Association v. McComber*, 41 Minn. 20, 42 N. W. 543, it appeared that the ownership of the land was erroneously stated in the published list; but no suggestion was ever made that this invalidated the judgment. Any such rule would subvert the whole policy of our tax law. The statute nowhere makes it the duty of assessors or county auditors to search the records with a view of ascertaining the names of the real owners. Such a search would impose upon them an impossible labor, and, even if it were possible to perform it, it would often still remain a doubtful question of law who was the real owner; for, as is said in the McComber case, the ownership of land is often a matter of grave doubt and uncertainty."

The above reasoning is clearly as applicable to the holder of a delinquency certificate as to assessors and county auditors. If the duty to determine in all cases who is the real owner rests upon individual certificate holders, then, in the event of foreclosure by a county, the officers must determine the real ownership of the long lists of property usually included in such cases. Such a requirement would be impracticable, and, as said by the Minnesota court above quoted, "would subvert the whole policy of our tax law." This summons contained a proper description of the land, and the name of the person shown by the tax records to be the owner. Commenting upon what the notice in such proceedings shall contain, the opinion in *McQuade v. Jaffray, supra,* further observes:

"It is elementary that no reference to the name of the owner is necessary in proceedings *in rem.* It is, however, a common practice in such proceedings to give the name of the owner, if known, 'for frankness' sake,' to increase the chances of his attention being called to the notice. The provisions of our statute on the subject are but declaratory of this established practice, and are to be construed as merely directory. The essential thing in such proceedings is the description of the *res* (the land), and this is complete without the name of the owner. We think it has been the uniform understanding, ever since our present statute was adopted, that no error or omission in stating the name of the owner affected the jurisdiction of the court over the land."

The principle decided in the above case seems to be directly in point here against appellants' contention. In *Leigh v. Green,* 193 U. S. 79, 24 Sup. Ct. 390, a recent de-

cision of the supreme court of the United States, the subject
of due process of law under the tax procedure of the state
of Nebraska is fully discussed. The notice in that case, as
in the one at bar, was directed to all persons interested in
the property. The federal question presented was, did the
failure of the Nebraska statute to make provision for service of notice of the pendency of the proceedings upon a
lien holder amount to a deprivation of property without
due process of law, within the protection of the fourteenth
amendment? It was held that it was not such deprivation
and that the notice given by publication to all persons interested in the property was sufficient process, inasmuch as
the proceeding was *in rem,* and was in aid of the collection
of public taxes. Following an extended discussion of authorities, the opinion concludes as folows:

"The principles applicable which may be deduced from
the authorities we think lead to this result: Where the
state seeks directly or by authorization to others to sell land
for taxes upon procedings to enforce a lien for the payment
thereof, it may proceed directly against the land within the
jurisdiction of the court, and a notice which permits all
interested, who are 'so minded,' to ascertain that it is to be
subjected to sale to answer for taxes, and to appear and be
heard, whether to be found within the jurisdiction or not,
is due process of law within the fourteenth amendment to
the Constitution. In the case under consideration the
notice was sufficiently clear as to the lands to be sold; the
lien holders investigating the title could readily have seen
in the public records that the taxes were unpaid and a lien
outstanding, which, after two years, might be foreclosed
and the lands sold and, by the laws of the state, an inde-
feasible title given to the purchaser. Such lien holder had
the right for two years to redeem, or, had he appeared in
the foreclosure case, to set up his rights in the land. These
proceedings arise in aid of the right and power of the state
to collect the public revenue, and did not, in our opinion,
abridge the right of the lien holder to the protection guar-

anteed by the Constitution against the taking of property without due process of law."

If, as held in the above case, a lien holder is chargeable with knowledge that taxes are unpaid, by so much more should an owner be so chargeable. The primary duty rests upon him to see that the taxes are paid, if he would prevent his land from being sold therefor. He is chargeable with knowledge of every step in the tax procedure, including the listing by the assessor, the sitting of the board of equalization to hear complaints, the completion of the rolls, their delivery to the treasurer, and the issuance of the certificate of delinquency. He must also know that, after the lapse of the statutory period, the right of redemption will be foreclosed. With such knowledge, and after his neglect to pay the taxes within the long period which the state has graciously given him, he cannot complain when he is given the same notice of foreclosure proceedings which may be given to others interested in the property. Within the authority of our statutes already cited and discussed, together with the liberal curative provisions of § 18, p. 299, Sess. Laws 1899, and subd. 6, § 1767, Bal. Code, the notice issued in this case was sufficient, and the above cited decision of the federal supreme court is authority that a judgment, founded upon such notice, does not amount to a taking of property without due process of law.

The petition further alleges that the summons was insufficient to confer jurisdiction, for the reason that it did not set out therein the date of the first publication, and was therefore too indefinite to inform the defendants therein named, or the appellants, when they were required to appear and defend the action. Respondent argues that a tax foreclosure is a special proceeding, governed by the special revenue statutes only, and that, inasmuch as those statutes do not specifically require that the date of the first publication of the summons shall be stated, it is therefore unnecessary. Subd. 2 of § 1, pp. 383, 384, Session Laws 1901, relates to the special tax procedure, and declares that service by publication of summons may be had. There is no requirement in such summons different from those described by the general statute. We therefore think the law of 1901 requires a reference to the general statute, for a description of what the summons shall contain. That statute, as found in § 4878, Bal. Code, requires that the date of the first publication shall be named. It follows that a tax foreclosure publication summons shall state such date. Such, in effect, was said by this court in *Thompson v. Robbins,* 32 Wash. 149, 72 Pac. 1043, and afterwards approved in *Smith v. White,* 32 Wash. 414, 73 Pac. 480. If it be true, therefore, that the summons in question did not disclose the date of its first publication, it was insufficient to confer jurisdiction.

Immediately following the attorney's signature to the summons is the following: "Date of first publication, October 9th, 1902." Appellants contend that the above words, not being in the body of the summons, are not contained therein, within the meaning of the statute. They also argue that, since the words follow the signature of counsel, it does not appear that they were authorized by the plaintiff in the case; that they may have been placed there by the printer, or by some one else not representing the plaintiff, and by whose acts the plaintiff was not bound. The words were, however, in a conspicuous place, and where they must have been seen, if the summons was read. It was the duty of the defendants in the action to presume that the correct date was stated, and to act accordingly. If it afterwards developed that the date was incorrect, the diligence of the defendants would have saved them from any prejudicial consequences. The fact that the words followed the signature of counsel we think is immaterial. They conveyed as much information as if they had preceded the signature, and their location is analogous to that of the postoffice address of counsel, which usually follows the signature upon the summons. In *Wagnitz v. Ritter*, 31 Wash. 343, 71 Pac. 1035, it was held that § 4870, Bal. Code, which contemplates that the postoffice address of the attorney shall be contained in the summons, was sufficiently complied with when such address followed the signature. It is true that § 4872 sets forth a form of summons which places the postoffice address after the signature, but the section descriptive of the summons contemplates that the statement as to the postoffice address shall be a part of the summons itself. The form section is a mere legislative construction of the meaning of the prior one, to the effect that, when the address follows the signature, it is sufficiently a part of the summons, and the case cited is a judicial approval of that construction. We think the essence of that construction is applicable to the subject matter here. The recital, stating the date of the first publication, was attached immediately at the conclusion of the summons. One could not, with ordinary care, have read the entire summons without seeing this recital, and we think it should be held to have been a part of the summons. Nothing short of a substantial departure from the statutory requirements for a summons should be held to be fatal to a proceeding under it, and unless it is clear that a defendant has been prejudiced, the variation in form is not such substantial departure. *Shinn v. Cummins*, 65 Cal. 97, 3 Pac. 133. To the same effect is *Ralph v. Lomer*, 3 Wash. 401, 28 Pac. 760. We are unable to see that the defendants in the action were prejudiced by the form of this summons. We therefore conclude that, in both particulars discussed by appellants, the summons was sufficient to confer jurisdiction.

Appellants further urge that, even if the court acquired jurisdiction, they are in any event entitled to have the judgment vacated under the provisions of § 4880, Bal. Code, inasmuch as their application was made within one year from the rendition of the judgment, accompanied with a tender of the taxes and interest. That section, however, provides that for "sufficient cause shown" one shall be entitled to such relief. In *Whitney v. Knowlton*, 33 Wash. 319, 74 Pac. 469, which involved a tax foreclosure, we held that one is not entitled, as a mere matter of right, to the vacation of the judgment, and that, in the absence of a showing of sufficient cause, the petition will not be granted. There is no such showing here. The petition does not allege that the taxes had been paid, or that by mistake, fraud, or other sufficient cause, appellants have been misled to their prejudice. The petition presents a case of mere neglect to pay the taxes, which is not a showing of sufficient cause. Respondent contends that, under the provisions of subdivision 6, §1767, Bal. Code, the appellants are in any event estopped to raise objections to the judgment. It is urged that said section is a special provision of the revenue law, and that tax foreclosure judgments are thereby excepted from the general provisions of § 4880, *supra,* relating to ordinary judgments. It is not necessary that we shall decide that question now, inasmuch as sufficient cause has not been shown in this case, even under the terms of § 4880. When a case arises where meritorious cause is made to appear, it will then be our duty to ascertain if there is any conflict between the statutory provisions, and to construe them if such conflict is found to exist.

The judgment is affirmed.

FULLERTON, C. J., and DUNBAR, MOUNT, and ANDERS, JJ., concur.

[No. 5214. Decided June 29, 1904.]

Charles Graves, *Appellant,* v. H. L. Thompson, *Respondent.*[1]

Appeal — Jurisdiction — Amount in Controversy—Value of Personal Property Found by Jury. In an action for the recovery of the possession of personal property, the value of the property in controversy, determining the jurisdiction of the supreme court on appeal, is the amount found by the court or jury, and not the amount claimed in the complaint.

Same—Value of Personal Property—Damages For Detention. Upon an appeal from a judgment in favor of defendant in an action for the recovery of the possession of personal property, and for damages for its detention, alleged in the sum of $475, the value of the property as found by the court or jury, and not the damages alleged, is the amount in controversy, and where the value fixed is $200, the appeal will be dismissed.

Appeal from a judgment of the superior court for Lincoln county, Neal, J., entered March 24, 1904, upon the verdict of a jury rendered in favor of the defendant. Appeal dismissed.

W. E. Southard, for appellant.

Myers & Warren, for respondent.

Dunbar, J.—Plaintiff brought an action to recover the possession of two certain horses and a set of harness, all described in the complaint; also alleging damages for the detention, in the sum of $475. The jury found a verdict in favor of the defendant, and also found that the value of the property was $200. Judgment was entered in favor of the defendant for costs, and from such judgment this appeal is taken.

The respondent moves to dismiss the appeal, for the reason that this court has no jurisdiction, because this is

1Reported in 77 Pac. 384.

an action for the recovery of personal property and the value thereof does not exceed $200. The decisions of this court seem to be somewhat conflicting on this proposition. In *Freeburger v. Caldwell*, 5 Wash. 769, 32 Pac. 732, which was an action for the recovery of personal property, in the course of the discussion the following announcement was made: "The amount in controversy was $200, value of the goods, and $500 damages for their detention. This court, therefore, has jurisdiction of the case." This was all the discussion of the question that was indulged in in that case. The question was discussed at some length, however, in *Herrin v. Pugh*, 9 Wash. 637, 38 Pac. 213, where it was held that the allegation of the pleader that the value of the property in controversy was a sum in excess of $200, was not sufficient to give the supreme court jurisdiction on appeal; but that, before the appellate court will assume jurisdiction, there must be a finding as to the value by the lower court. After quoting the constitutional provision that the jurisdiction of this court shall not extend to civil actions at law for the recovery of money or personal property when the original amount in controversy, or the value of the property, does not exceed the sum of $200, it was said:

"Under this provision it has been held that the amount claimed by the plaintiff in his complaint is the original amount in controversy, but so far as we are advised it has never been held that the bare allegation that property sought to be recovered is of a certain value establishes such value for the purpose of giving jurisdiction on appeal. An examination of the language of the constitution will lead to the contrary holding. 'The original amount in controversy' is the language of one clause, and must refer to the amount claimed and not to the amount which may ultimately be established upon trial. But the lan-

guage of the other clause, 'the value of the property,' is
not qualified by the amount in controversy or by the word
'original,' and must be construed as referring to such
value as found by the court or jury. To hold otherwise
would be to enable every case for the recovery of personal
property to be brought within the jurisdiction of this
court on appeal. The statement of the value of the property is purely a matter of opinion on the part of the
pleader. and such opinion cannot give this court jurisdiction."

So that, yielding our allegiance to the doctrine announced in the last case—which we are constrained to
do—the only remaining question is, whether the jurisdiction is affected by the amount claimed for damages. This
proposition has also been squarely decided by this court
in favor of respondent's contention, in the case of *Doty
v. Krutz,* 13 Wash. 169, 43 Pac. 17, where it was said
in the course of the discussion:

"   .   .   .   but appellant insists that the amount alleged in the *ad damnum* clause in the complaint, and for
which judgment was prayed, was the amount involved,
so far as the constitutional inhibition on appeals where
the amount is less than $200 is concerned. We do not
think the constitution can be so construed. If so, any
claim for a judgment, which could not possibly be obtained under the pleadings, would permit an appeal and
destroy the object of the constitutional enactment."

And this, we think, is the construction placed upon statutes of this kind by the great weight of authority. See
1 Enc. Plead. & Prac., 728, where it is said:

"In suits to test the title to or for the recovery of
specific personal property the damages claimed or recovered are generally merely an incidental matter. It is
the value of the property which is the determinative factor
upon the question of jurisdiction *vel non.*"

The same rule is announced in *Astell v. Phillippi*, 55 Cal.
265; *Peyton v. Robertson*, 9 Wheat. 527, 6 L. Ed. 151;
Higgins v. Deloach, 54 Miss. 498.

The motion will be sustained, and the appeal dismissed.

MOUNT, HADLEY, and ANDERS, JJ., concur.

FULLERTON, C. J., did not sit in this case.

[No. 4942. Decided June 30, 1904.]

ROBERT TISCHNER, *Respondent,* v. WILLIAM RUTLEDGE
et al., Appellants.[1]

APPEAL — NOTICE — PROOF OF SERVICE — SIGNATURE OF PARTY
WITHOUT PROOF OF GENUINENESS. An appeal will not be dismissed because the only proof of service upon one .of the co-
parties not joining therein, and who had appeared in the action,
was an admission of service over his own signature, without
any proof of its genuiness, since the lower and appellate court
must judicially notice the signature of any party that has appeared in the action.

LANDLORD AND TENANT — LEASE — CONSTRUCTION — PERPETUAL
RENEWALS. An intention to create a perpetual lease by a clause
for perpetual renewals must be clear and unequivocal, and is
not shown by reserving a monthly rental terminating at a certain time "with the privilege at the same rate and terms each
year thereafter from year to year," where the lease contains
only covenants applicable to a short fixed period without employing any terms of perpetuity.

Appeal from a judgment of the superior court for Lincoln county, Neal, J., entered July 23, 1903, upon findings in favor of the plaintiff, after a trial on the merits
before the court without a jury. Affirmed.

Thayer & Belt, for appellants.

Martin & Grant, for respondent.

[1]Reported in 77 Pac. 388.

PER CURIAM.—This is an action of unlawful detainer. The facts are not in dispute and are substantially these: On April 9, 1900, the respondent, being the owner of a store building and the lands on which the same was situate in the city of Davenport, in this state, leased the same to the defendant, Anderson, at a rental of $33.33 per month, payable monthly, for a term terminating on the 8th day of April, 1901, "with the privilege at the same rate and terms each year thereafter from year to year." Anderson held under the lease until September 30, 1902, when he transferred his interests in the premises to the appellant William Rutledge, who in turn sublet a portion thereof to the appellant G. K. Birge. On February 23, 1903, the respondent caused notice to be served on the appellants and the defendant, Anderson, notifying them that the lease would be terminated on April 8, 1903, and that they were required to quit the possession of the premises and surrender the same to the respondent on that day. In the month following, the appellant William Rutledge notified the respondent that he elected to continue to hold possession of the premises, under the clause of the lease above quoted, and that he would refuse to surrender possession on the date named by the respondent. Demand for possession was again made on April 8, which being refused, this action was brought under the statutes of forcible entry and detainer to recover such possession. The case was tried before the court without a jury, and resulted in findings of fact substantially as above outlined, from which the trial court concluded, as a matter of law, that the respondent was entitled to recover, and entered a judgment accordingly.

This appeal is taken by Rutledge and Birge, the defendant Anderson not joining therein. Anderson appeared separately, and by separate counsel in the court below, and the respondent moves to dismiss the appeal, because, as he contends, the notice of appeal was not served on Anderson as required by statute. The record shows an acceptance of service of the notice, over the signature of Anderson, but unaccompanied by any proofs of its genuineness. It is said that this is insufficient, because the court will not take judicial notice of the signatures of persons other than public officers or officers of the court, and that the signatures of persons other than such officers must be accompanied by proofs of their genuineness.

It is undoubtedly true that a court will not notice, judicially, the signature of a defendant unaccompanied by proofs of its genuineness, when it is sought to show thereby the service of an original process by which the defendant is brought into court (*Downs v. Board of Directors,* 4 Wash. 309, 30 Pac. 147); but this is as far as the rule extends. After a party has once appeared in an action, he may be served with all notices and motions pertaining to that proceeding, and his signature to an acceptance of service thereof is entitled to recognition by the court, without other proof of its genuineness than the court requires of any fact it knows judicially. If this were not so, a party would be without power to conduct his own case. The taking of an appeal is not the commencement of a new action, nor is a notice of appeal in any sense an original process by which parties are brought into court. *Philadelphia Mtge. & Trust Co. v. Palmer,* 32 Wash. 455, 73 Pac. 501, and cases cited. This being so, it must necessarily follow that the signature of a party to the notice of appeal must receive the same consideration it would receive if to any other notice or paper served in the cause, not an original process. In other words, it must be noticed judicially.

It is suggested, however, that, while the trial court might notice judicially the signature of a party who has appeared before it, the rule is different in the appellate court. But we think not. The rule is that an appellate court will notice judicially whatever the court of original jurisdiction is bound to notice judicially, and hence, as the superior court before whom this cause was pending was bound to take notice of the signature of Anderson, when signed to papers in the cause before it, so must this court take notice of it in the same cause. The motion to dismiss is denied.

On the merits of the controversy, the appellants contend that the lease confers upon the lessee and his assigns the right of perpetual renewal; while the respondent argues (1) that the writing does not bear that construction, and (2) that, if it does, then it is void because it creates a perpetuity.

Whether or not a lease providing for perpetual renewals is valid, is a question upon which the authorities are not agreed, though perhaps the weight is with the holding that such leases are valid. On principle, it would seem that where a person has the right to convey, in fee absolute, his whole estate, he could convey in the same manner a part of it less than the whole. But, be this as it may, the authorities are uniform on the proposition that the law does not favor perpetual leases of the character claimed for this one, and that the intention to create such lease must be expressed in clear and unequivocal language, and not be left to mere inference. Courts will, also, whenever it is possible without doing violence to the plain meaning of words, so construe the language used as to avoid a perpetuity by renewal.

We think it clearly appears from the instrument in question here, when examined as a whole, that the parties did not intend to provide for perpetual renewals. With the exception of the clause above quoted, the lease contains only covenants applicable to a short fixed term. It makes no provision for waste, for repairs to, or for rebuilding in case of the destruction of the buildings on the property by fire or accidents of any kind. It provides that, upon the "expiration of the time mentioned in this lease, peaceable possession of said premises shall be given to said" lessor, "in as good condition as they now are, the usual wear, inevitable accidents, and loss by fire excepted." It does not employ the terms, "in perpetuity," "forever," or words of similar import, such as one would expect to find in instruments granting perpetual rights. Moreover, the phrase used, which is thought to create the perpetual right, is of itself likely to conceal its real meaning. When we speak of a thing as continuing from year to year, it is only on second thought that we conclude it means forever. This, we think, is not the direct and unequivocal language necessary to create a lease of the character contended for. We are of the opinion, therefore, that the lessee and his assigns became tenants from month to month, after the expiration of the year mentioned in the lease, and that their tenancy was terminated by the notice to that effect, given by the lessor.

The judgment appealed from is affirmed.

[No. 4911. Decided June 30, 1904.]

PAUL SMITS, *Appellant,* v. JOHN C. HOGAN, *Respondent.*[1]

CHAMPERTY—ATTORNEY AND CLIENT—AGREEMENT TO PAY COSTS
AND PROSECUTE FOR CONTINGENT FEE. It is doubtful if the doctrine of champerty was ever in force in this state, and if it
was, it was repealed by Bal. Code, § 5165, declaring that the
compensation of attorneys shall be left to the parties, and hence
an agreement whereby the attorney agrees to pay the costs and
to prosecute a case for a percentage of the recovery is legal.

SAME—DAMAGES TO DEFENDANT BY REASON OF CHAMPERTOUS
AGREEMENT — MALICE — MALICIOUS PROSECUTION. In an action
brought against an attorney for damages for maliciously inciting an insolvent person to prosecute an unfounded action against
the plaintiff, and which was prosecuted under a champertous
agreement, it is proper to instruct that the plaintiff must show
malice and want of probable cause, as in an action for malicious
prosecution, and the action is not maintainable as a claim for
damages for champerty irrespective of malice, since the doctrine of champerty does not prevail in this state.

Appeal from a judgment of the superior court for Chehalis county, Irwin, J., entered July 21, 1903, upon the
verdict of a jury rendered in favor of the defendant. Affirmed.

J. C. Cross and *C. B. Rawson,* for appellant.

W. H. Abel and *John C. Hogan,* for respondent.

HADLEY, J.—Appellant brought this suit against respondent to recover alleged damages. The complaint, in
substance, avers, that respondent is an attorney at law;
that he maliciously, and without reasonable or proper
cause, stirred up one Erickson, the latter being insolvent
and in indigent circumstances, to prosecute an action
against appellant for alleged malpractice as a physician

[1]Reported in 77 Pac. 390.

and surgeon; that the following written agreement was
executed between said Erickson and respondent, to wit:

"It is hereby agreed by and between John C. Hogan and
John Erickson as follows: That the said Hogan is to
act as attorney for said Erickson in the matter of bringing suit against Paul Smits, to recover for negligent and
unskillful setting of fractured finger, and to prosecute
said case to final judgment in the superior court of Chehalis county, and pay the necessary court disbursements
in prosecuting said case.

"And for said services the said Erickson agrees to give
him one-third of the amount recovered in said action as
full compensation. And neither of the parties hereto
shall settle said case without the consent of the other."

It is alleged, that the suit for malpractice was prosecuted by respondent, as attorney for said Erickson, in
pursuance of the above agreement; that the same resulted
in a judgment against Erickson for costs, and that he
should take nothing by his action. Appellant avers damages to himself, for necessary attorney's fees and expenses
incurred in the former suit, and demands recovery from
respondent. Issue was joined upon the complaint. A
trial was had before the court, and a verdict was returned
for respondent. Appellant moved for a new trial, which
was denied. Judgment was entered in accordance with
the verdict, and this appeal was taken.

The alleged errors assigned as stated in the brief are,
(1) "in the giving of certain instructions," and (2) "in
refusing to give certain instructions." The second ground
of error, as stated above, is waived in the brief, the first
only being discussed. The general and indefinite assignment as to the instructions given is of no practical assistance to the court, and we are compelled to resort to the
general discussion in the brief to discover what objections
are intended to be urged. From the general discussion,

we understand that the instructions are criticised on the
theory that it was error for the court to instruct that
appellant must show that respondent maliciously stirred
up or incited the bringing of the former suit. We think
this was not error, for the reason that the complaint alleges, with much emphasis, that respondent did act maliciously, and it seems to have been drawn upon the theory
that the action is one for malicious prosecution.

We understand from appellant's argument, however,
that he contends now that, by reason of the written agreement above set forth, the action is based upon a claim of
damages for champerty or maintenance. It is insisted
that the agreement was champertous, and that appellant
is entitled to recover, even though malice in fact is not
shown. It is doubtful if the doctrine of champerty was
ever in force in this state, as a part of the common law,
under the authority of decision by American courts.

"Nor is the contract void as being contrary to the policy
of any law of this state in regard to maintenance. That
offense was created by statute in England in early times,
in order to prevent great and powerful persons from en-
listing in behalf of one party in a lawsuit, by which the
opposite and feeble party would be oppressed and prevented from obtaining justice. It has been said by English judges that under the enlightened and impartial administration of justice in later times the object of the
law had ceased and the law itself had become nearly ob-
solete. It has been said in America that the law against
maintenance was peculiar to early English society, and
inapplicable to American society, and, therefore, that it
would not exist here unless by statute enacted here. At
an early day in the history of the State of New York
a statute was enacted against maintenance. At the revision of the laws of that State in 1830, the revisors, in
a report to the Legislature, say: 'It is proposed to abolish the law of maintenance and to qualify that of champerty, by permitting mortgages of lands in dispute to

raise money, under guards and restrictions which will prevent abuse,' and the mode adopted to 'abolish the law of maintenance' was simply to omit enacting any statute upon the subject and repealing the old statute by which it was created or adopted. There was no special repeal of this old statute, but it was included in the general repealing act, nor was there any law directly abolishing the offense of maintenance. Under these circumstances Judge Paige, in the case of *Hoyt v. Thompson,* 1 Selden, 347, said: 'Since the adoption of the revised statutes, maintenance has not, under our laws, been recognized as an offense, and champerty only remains an offense in a qualified form.' Chancellor Walworth, in the case of *Mott v. Small,* 22 Wend. 405, said: 'I am prepared to say that all the absurd doctrines of maintenance that grew out of the statutes which might have been necessary in a semi-barbarous age were swept away by the recent revision of the laws, and many of them had been virtually abrogated long before that time.' Chancellor Sanford, in the case of *Thalheimer v. Brinkerhoff,* 3 Cowen, 647 [15 Am. Dec. 308], said: 'In many States of this Union these laws are not in force, and the want of them is said to be no inconvenience.' These remarks show that, in the opinion of these judges, in the absence of a statute creating it, the offense of maintenance does not exist in America as a part of the common law." *Mathewson v. Fitch,* 22 Cal. 86, 94, 95.

In *Courtright v. Burnes,* 13 Fed. 317, 320, the court observed:

"The tendency in the courts of this country is stronger in the direction of relaxing the common-law doctrine concerning champerty and maintenance, so as to permit greater liberty of contracting between attorney and client than was formerly allowed, and this for the reason that the peculiar condition of society which gave rise to the doctrine has in a great measure passed away. In some of the states the common-law rule is altogether repudiated, and it is held that no such contract is now invalid unless it contravenes some existing statute of the state."

See, also *Sedgwick v. Stanton,* 14 N. Y. 289; *Richardson v. Rowland,* 40 Conn. 565; *Lytle v. State,* 17 Ark. 608.

If, however, the doctrine of champerty ever was in force
in this state, then, as far as it relates to the mode of compensation between attorney and client, it must have been
repealed by our statute as found in § 5165, Bal. Code,
which is as follows:

"The measure and mode of compensation of attorneys
and counselors shall be left to the agreement, express or
implied, of the parties. . . ."

There is nothing in the above statute which prevents the
making of the contract set out above, but the parties were
left to make such contract as to the compensation of the
attorney, if they saw fit to do so. In Utah it has been held
that a statute of practically the same words as our own,
quoted above, has modified the common law rule as to
champertous contracts, so as to leave client and attorney
free to contract as they choose with reference to the attorney's compensation. *Croco v. Oregon etc. R. Co.,* 18 Utah
311, 54 Pac. 985, 44 L. R. A. 285. The same has been
held in Michigan. *Wildey v. Crane,* 63 Mich. 720, 30
N. W. 327.

Under either view of the case at bar, therefore, the contract mentioned was not an illegal one, for, if the rule as
to champerty ever prevailed here, it has been modified by
our statute. If it should be said that the statute of 1903,
page 68, Session Laws of that year, upon the subject of
barratry, bears upon the subject matter of this contract, it
is sufficient to say that said statute was not in force when
the contract was made. The contract not being illegal in
itself, it was proper for the court, under the issues, to instruct the jury that appellant should show malice and want
of reasonable or probable cause before he could recover, for

the reason that, with the illegality of the contract eliminated, the only remaining issue was that of malicious prosecution.

Respondent insists that, even if this contract came within the rule as to champerty, still appellant could not recover of respondent, and counsel assert in respondent's brief that they have been unable to find, in the whole range of American cases, a single case where an attorney has been held to respond in damages to the opposite party because of having made a champertous agreement with his client. It is true appellant has not cited such cases, but that question we do not now decide, for the reason, as we have seen, that no champertous contract is involved.

The judgment is affirmed.

FULLERTON, C. J., and ANDERS, MOUNT, and DUNBAR, JJ., concur.

[No. 5125. Decided July 2, 1904.]

MARTIN BAILEY, *Respondent*, v. CASCADE TIMBER COMPANY, *Appellant*.[1]

MASTER AND SERVANT — NEGLIGENCE — SAFE APPLIANCES — INSTRUCTIONS—SUFFICIENCY. In an action for personal injuries sustained by an employe upon the breaking of a swamp hook, instructions sufficiently submit to the jury the question whether defendant furnished proper appliances, where the jury are told that the burden of proof as to whether defendant furnished a reasonably safe swamp hook was upon the plaintiff, and that the plaintiff could not recover unless that was shown to be the proximate cause of the injury.

SAME—SELECTION OF APPLIANCES—APPEAL—DECISION—LAW OF THE CASE. The supreme court having decided upon a former appeal that the removal of a heavy tank was not a mere ordinary detail of the work of a logging crew that could be delegated

[1]Reported in 77 Pac. 377.

to fellow-servants of the plaintiff, the same becomes the law of the case and is conclusive.

SAME—FELLOW-SERVANTS—DELEGATED DUTIES—IMMATERIAL BY WHOM DISCHARGED. The supreme court having decided upon a former appeal that a hook tender charged with the duty of selecting a proper swamp hook to be used in moving a heavy tank is not a fellow-servant, but a vice-principal with respect to such duties, it is immaterial whether that duty was discharged by him or by some other employe, as in either case it is a duty owed by the master.

DAMAGES — EXCESSIVE VERDICT — POWER OF TRIAL COURT TO REMIT EXCESS—NEW TRIAL. Where the trial court was of the opinion that the damages for personal injuries awarded by the jury were excessive, it has power to require the plaintiff to remit the excessive amount or submit to a new trial.

DAMAGES—WHEN EXCESSIVE. Where $6,000 was awarded for personal injuries sustained in the fracture of the ulna and a dislocation of the head of the radius, resulting in limiting the turning motion of the forearm, but which did not destroy the usefulness of the arm or greatly lessen plaintiff's earning ability, a finding of the trial court that the verdict was excessive and should be reduced to $4,000 will be sustained.

Appeal from a judgment of the superior court for Pierce county, Snell, J., entered December 14, 1903, upon the verdict of a jury rendered in favor of the plaintiff for $6,000 damages for personal injuries sustained by the breaking of a swamp hook. Affirmed on condition of remitting $2,000.

John A. Shackleford and *E. M. Hayden,* for appellant.

Govnor Teats, for respondent.

HADLEY, J.—This case was once before in this court, and the opinion upon the former appeal will be found reported in 32 Wash. 319, 73 Pac. 385. For a statement of the issues and facts, we refer to that opinion without repetition here. At the first trial, when the evidence of both parties had all been introduced, the defendant moved

that the court discharge the jury and render judgment for
the defendant, which motion was granted.   This court reversed the judgment on the ground that there was evidence
which should have been submitted to the jury, and the
cause was remanded for a retrial.   At the second trial the
jury returned a verdict for the plaintiff.   Thereupon the
defendant moved for a new trial, which was denied, and
judgment was entered in accordance with the verdict.   The
defendant has appealed.

Many alleged errors are assigned relating to the instructions given by the court and to the refusal to give certain
requested instructions.   In argument appellant groups what
it claims to be the principles involved in its assignments of
error under the following general statement:

"Appellant contends that whether proper appliances for
moving the tank had been furnished by the master was a
question for the jury; whether the work of moving the tank
was an ordinary detail of the work of the crew was a question for the jury; and that it was for the jury to say
whether it was the duty of the hook tender to select, from
those on hand, the appliance to be used in attaching the
line to the tank, or whether such selection was a part of the
duty of the rigging slinger, as an incident to his duty to
use and attach the appliance.   By the instructions, all of
these questions were taken from the jury."

The different assignments relate to segregated parts of the
instructions.   It is our duty to examine the instructions as
a whole and determine whether, when construed together,
they fairly state the law applicable to the case.   Referring
to the first proposition included in the above statement of
counsel—that is to say, that it was a question for the jury
whether proper appliances had been furnished by the master—the court did specifically state to the jury, that one
of respondent's allegations was that appellant had neglected

to furnish a reasonably safe and suitable swamp hook or appliance for the work to be performed in the removal of the tank; that the burden of proof as to the respondent's allegations was upon him; and that, even if the jury should find the defendant negligent in not having furnished suitable appliances, still respondent was not entitled to recover for the wrong alleged, unless it was shown by the evidence to be the proximate cause of the injury. We think the instructions sufficiently left it with the jury to say whether suitable appliances had been furnished or not.

The next criticism as to the instructions, suggested by counsel's statement, is that it was a question for the jury whether the work of moving the tank was an ordinary detail of the work of the crew, it being contended that, if it was such, then the duty of the master did not extend to the supervision of details such as the selection of appliances, and that injuries arising from such circumstances should be held to be due to the neglect of a fellow-servant, and not of the master. We said of the circumstances of this case, when it was here before, as follows:

"We think the circumstances were such that it ought not to be said that the selection of appliances could properly be left to the judgment of a fellow-servant, but that such duty properly rested with the master, acting through a directing mind supposed to be skilled from experience in such matters."

It will be remembered that the station of respondent, at the location of the donkey engine, was such that his safety depended upon the security of the appliances used to connect with the heavy tank. He was at a distance from the tank, and his duty called him to remain at his post ready to control his engine, in accordance with signals given him. He had not the opportunity to inspect the appliances used unless he left his post for that purpose, and such was not his duty.   His situation was such that, if the appliance broke, the large cable would recoil toward him, involving him in much danger, as the result proved.   It was because of such peculiar surroundings that we before held it to be the duty of the master to select the appliances, acting through a directing mind skilled from experience in such matters.   Under that view of the case, which we reiterate here, the removal of this heavy tank cannot be classified as a mere ordinary detail of the work of the crew to be left entirely with fellow-servants, and calling for no immediate duty from the master.   This view had become the law of the case at the last trial, and the question whether the removal of the tank was a mere ordinary detail of the work of the crew was therefore not one for the jury.

Counsel's next suggestion of error is that the court should have left it to the jury to say whether it was the duty of the hook tender to select, from appliances on hand, the one to be used, or whether such selection was a part of the duty of the rigging slinger, as an incident to his duty to attach the appliance.   This contention also seeks to classify the rigging slinger as a fellow-servant in charge of the detail of selection, with the master relieved from any share in the duty. The facts in evidence were in all material respects the same as were before this court on the former appeal.   We then declared the relations of the hook tender to the crew of men, and the duties he admittedly discharged to be such as made him a vice-principal, for the reason that it was his duty to direct the men to determine what appliances should be used, and the method of adjusting them.   Such being the case then, as we held before, the duties discharged by the rigging slinger pertaining to the selection and adjustment of appliances were delegated duties, and passed to him from the hook tender, the master's primary representative.

The environment called for the exercise of skill and a high
degree of care in order to preserve the safety of life and
limb, and which should have been exercised by the master
or his representative.   It therefore became immaterial
whether the immediate act of selection was done by the hook
tender or by the rigging slinger, since, in either case, it was
a duty of the master which was being discharged.   We
think the instructions as a whole fully and fairly stated the
law of the case, and we find no error.

Appellant next urges that the verdict was excessive.   The
amount returned was $6,000.   Respondent's injury con-
sisted of a fracture of the ulna of the forearm and a dis-
location of the head of the radius.   The turning motion of
the forearm was somewhat limited by the injury, although
not destroyed, and respondent is also unable to bend the
arm at the elbow to the full extent.   The injury was severe,
and the condition resulting therefrom undoubtedly entails
much inconvenience to the respondent, but the arm is still
useful for many purposes.   Respondent himself testified
that, during the time intervening between the two trials of
this case, he was a part of the time engaged in cutting wood.
He also said he was able to earn about $700 per year before
the accident, and that, for about five weeks prior to the last
trial, he had been earning more than $2 per day—$2 net
after paying car fare.   It would thus appear from his testimony that his present earning capacity is not greatly less
than it was before the accident.   He has, however, a crippled arm, which he must carry through life, and, at best,
either his earning power is in some degree impaired, or he
must undergo great inconvenience, with the possibility of
increased impairment with advancing years.   Under such
circumstances, the jury having determined other questions
in his favor, he is entitled to recover a substantial amount,

based, however, upon the nature of his injury, and its bearing upon his usefulness. The trial court was of the opinion that the verdict is excessive, and so found. The following appears in the order denying the motion for new trial:

"The court finds: That the verdict of the jury was excessive, unreasonable, and exceeded in amount the damages sustained by the plaintiff, and that the amount of said verdict should not in any event exceed the sum of four thousand dollars ($4,000); but that this court has no power to reduce said verdict without granting a new trial; and that with the findings heretofore made in this order, the supreme court can pass upon the question of the excessiveness of said verdict without prejudice to the rights of the defendant, by reason of the refusal of this court to grant a new trial."

We think it was within the power of the trial court to have required respondent to remit the excessive amount or submit to a new trial. But the court declined to do so, seemingly under the belief that it had not such power. It is therefore for this court to determine whether it will confirm the court's finding, as made in its said order concerning the excessive amount of the verdict, or whether it is excessive in any amount. Taking into consideration the evidence as above discussed, together with the fact that the trial court heard the witnesses testify, and more particularly observed the nature of respondent's injury, we shall adopt the views of that court as to the excessive amount.

The judgment is approved in all particulars except as to amount. But, as entered, it is reversed, and the cause remanded with instructions to the lower court that, within thirty days from the time the remittitur is filed in that court, it shall, in the alternative, require respondent to file a remittance of $2,000 from the amount of the verdict, or submit to a new trial. In the event such remittance shall be filed within the specified time, judgment shall then be entered for $4,000, and if respondent shall refuse to file such remittance, the motion for new trial shall be granted. Appellant shall recover the costs of this appeal.

FULLERTON, C. J., and ANDERS and MOUNT, JJ., concur.

[No. 4962.   Decided July 2, 1904.]

JAMES A. TEMPLEMAN, *Appellant*, v. FRED T. EVANS, JR., *Respondent*.[1]

APPEAL—STATEMENT OF FACTS—AFFIDAVITS IDENTIFIED IN CERTIFICATE—HOW BROUGHT UP. Upon an appeal from an order made after a hearing upon affidavits, a statement of facts will not be struck out for the reason that it failed to incorporate therein the affidavits, where, after amendments were proposed to the statement, the court certified, upon notice, that the matter was heard upon the affidavits, which were specifically referred to and attached to the record, and that they constituted all the evidence before the court.

Appeal from an order of the superior court for King county, Tallman, J., entered August 1, 1903, discharging an attachment, after a hearing upon affidavits. Affirmed.

C. L. Parker, for appellant.

Jerold Landon Finch, for respondent.

MOUNT, J.—This appeal is from an order of the lower court discharging an attachment upon real estate. Respondent moves to strike the statement of facts and dismiss the appeal, for the reason that the evidence consists of affidavits which were not incorporated in any statement of facts or bill of exceptions. A bill of exceptions, however, was filed and served upon respondent's attorney, who thereupon filed certain amendments thereto. Thereafter, upon

[1]Reported in 77 Pac. 381.

notice, the court certified that the motion to discharge the attachment was heard upon affidavits, which affidavits were specifically referred to and attached to the record; and also certified that the said affidavits constituted all the evidence before the court upon the hearing of the said motion, on the part of both plaintiff and defendant. We think this was sufficient under the statute, and the motion to strike and dismiss is therefore denied.

On the merits of the case the question is one entirely of fact. It is sufficient to say that the affidavits are somewhat conflicting, but, upon a careful reading thereof, we think the appellant has failed to show, by a preponderance of the evidence, that the defendant was attempting to dispose of his property in order to defraud his creditors, as alleged in the application for the writ.

The judgment appealed from is therefore affirmed.

FULLERTON, C. J., and HADLEY, DUNBAR, and ANDERS, JJ., concur.

[No. 5226. Decided July 2, 1904.]

THE STATE OF WASHINGTON, *on the Relation of Kent Lumber Company, Plaintiff,* v. THE SUPERIOR COURT OF KING COUNTY, *Defendant.*[1]

EMINENT DOMAIN—MUNICIPAL CORPORATIONS—PUBLIC PURPOSE—ELECTRIC LIGHT PLANT. The city of Seattle is authorized to exercise the right of eminent domain for the purposes of an electric light plant, under Bal. Code, § 739, subd. 6, authorizing cities of the first class to appropriate property for corporate purposes, and subd. 15, authorizing it to erect and maintain plants for furnishing lights to the city or its inhabitants.

SAME—CONDEMNATION OF LANDS OUTSIDE CITY LIMITS. Such power may be exercised to appropriate lands outside of the city limits.

[1]Reported in 77 Pac. 382.

SAME—ORDINANCE AUTHORIZING CONDEMNATION. An ordinance condemning the land, providing for a proceeding in the superior court to appropriate it, and authorizing the corporation counsel to conduct the proceedings, is sufficient to confer authority upon the city to maintain the action.

Certiorari to review an order of the superior court for King county, Griffin, J., entered June 13, 1904, declaring a public use upon a condemnation of certain lands for the purposes of a lighting plant, after a hearing on the merits, before the court without a jury. Affirmed.

John G. Barnes, for relator.

M. Gilliam, for defendant.

MOUNT, J.—The city of Seattle, a city of the first class, brought an action in the superior court of King county for the purpose of condemning a right of way over certain lands to be used for pole and transmission lines for an electric lighting plant, which the city is now constructing for its use. The whole of the lands sought to be condemned are without the city of Seattle. The Kent Lumber Company, a corporation, is the owner of certain of the lands sought to be condemned. This company appeared in the action and filed a demurrer to the petition of the city upon the grounds, (1) that it appears upon the face of the petition that the superior court has no jurisdiction of the subject matter of the action; (2) that the petitioner has no capacity to prosecute said proceedings; and (3) that said petition does not state facts sufficient to constitute a cause of action, or to entitle the city to the relief demanded. This demurrer came on for hearing, and was denied by the court. The relator duly excepted to the order denying the demurrer, and then filed its answer. Thereupon a hearing was had, and, upon evidence taken, the lower court made findings and entered an order declaring the use of the lands sought to be condemned to be a public use, and also ordered a jury to assess the damages. Relator thereupon filed his petition in this court, praying for a writ of review. The writ was issued, and the case is now here for review upon the questions presented by the demurrer.

(1) Relator insists, first, that the power of eminent domain does not exist in the city of Seattle because such power has never been expressly conferred upon it, and therefore the court has no jurisdiction to maintain the action. Section 739, Bal. Code, in defining the powers of cities of the first class, provides, at subd. 6, that such city shall have power, "to purchase or appropriate private property within or without its corporate limits, for its corporate uses, upon making just compensation to the owners thereof, and to institute and maintain such proceedings as may be authorized by the general laws of the state for the appropriation of private property for public use." This same section also confers power upon the city, "to provide for lighting the streets and all public places, and for furnishing the inhabitants thereof with gas or other lights, and to erect, or otherwise acquire, and to maintain the same, or to authorize the erection and maintenance of such works as may be necessary and convenient therefor, and to regulate and control the use thereof." § 739, subd. 15, Bal. Code.

This latter provision clearly authorizes the city to erect and maintain works for *furnishing gas or other lights* to the city and its inhabitants. Lights so furnished are for corporate uses. The former provision clearly authorizes the city to condemn private lands, either within or without the city, for such uses. By enacting these provisions, we think the legislature of the state has authorized the city of

Seattle to exercise the right of eminent domain, and to maintain the action. Since the decision in *Tacoma v. State*, 4 Wash. 64, the legislature has passed an act authorizing, regulating, and prescribing the procedure by which municipal corporations of the first class may condemn land for any public use within the authority of such city. § 775 *et seq.*, Bal. Code. This procedure was followed in the case at bar. Holding as we do upon the provisions above considered, it is unnecessary to consider other provisions of the statute claimed by respondent to authorize the condemnation.

(2) It is next contended that the city is without legal capacity to maintain the proceedings, because the lands sought to be condemned lie wholly without the corporate limits of the city. As we have seen above, subd. 15 of § 739, Bal. Code, gives the city power to provide for lighting the streets and all public places, and for furnishing the inhabitants with gas or other lights, and to erect or otherwise acquire and maintain the same. This power is one of the corporate functions which may be exercised by the city, and property used for such purposes is for a corporate use. It is true that subd. 14 of the same section, referring to water works, provides that such works may be erected, purchased, or acquired within or without the corporate limits, while subd. 15, relating to works for lighting purposes, makes no reference to the same being within or without the city limits. This omission makes room for argument, but is not conclusive, that the legislature thereby intended to limit works for lighting purposes within the corporate boundaries, especially when it had provided that the city might appropriate property within or without its corporate limits for corporate purposes. We are therefore of the

opinion that the city is authorized to erect works for lighting purposes without its corporate boundary.

(3)   It is next contended by the relator that no ordinance has been passed by the city authorizing the lands to be condemned and paid for, but we find attached to the return as a part of the petition, Ordinance No. 10,723, which condemns the land in question, and provides for a proceeding in the superior court to appropriate the lands in question, and to assess to the owner his damages, and which authorizes and directs the corporation counsel to conduct the necessary proceedings therefor. This ordinance is not mentioned by the relator in his brief. As it appears regular upon its face in all respects, we think it is sufficient, under the statute, to confer authority upon the city by the proper officer to maintain the action.

No question is made here as to the finding of the lower court that the contemplated use is a public use. The other questions presented go to the question of damages, which are not properly before us upon this review, and will therefore not be considered. We find no error of the lower court in overruling the demurrer, or in adjudging the contemplated use to be a public use. The order made thereon is therefore affirmed.

FULLERTON, C. J., and HADLEY, DUNBAR, and ANDERS, JJ., concur.

[No. 5145.   Decided July 2, 1904.]

GEORGE D. FARWELL, *Appellant,* v. CLARISSA D. COLMAN, *Respondent.*[1]

ATTORNEY AND CLIENT — CONTRACT FOR SERVICES — ABANDON-
MENT — FAILURE TO PROSECUTE ACTION — TERMINATION OF EMPLOY-
MENT.   In an action to recover for services performed by an
attorney under a special agreement to receive seven per cent
of the amount recovered for the defendant upon the final judgment in a condemnation proceeding instituted by a railroad
company, in which it appears that a judgment for the defendant
for $9,500 was reversed by the supreme court for error, and a
new trial ordered, and that the defendant repeatedly requested
the attorney to proceed with the case, but he failed to do so for
over ten years, giving as a reason that owing to the hard times
the company would abandon the suit if pressed, and that he
would thereby lose his fee, such refusal was a termination of the
employment, justifying the defendant in making any settlement
with the railroad company, and warranting a finding that nothing was due the attorney under the terms of his special contract
of employment.

Appeal from a judgment of the superior court for King
county, Albertson, J., entered January 19, 1904, upon
findings in favor of the defendant, after a trial before
the court without a jury, in an action to recover for legal
services.   Affirmed.

George D. Farwell, and *Bauer & Buchanan,* for appellant.

Jacobs & Jacobs, for respondent.

DUNBAR, J.—The complaint in this case alleges that
the plaintiff was an attorney and counsellor at law, duly
qualified, and the defendant was indebted to him in the
reasonable sum of $750, balance due for legal services

[1]Reported in 77 Pac. 379.

and other valuable services rendered, furnished, and performed for defendant by plaintiff, at her special instance
and request, between the dates of October 1, 1890, and
June 20, 1903, which amount was unpaid, and prays
judgment against the defendant in said sum. The answer
denies the rendition of the services alleged, and alleges
that the cause of action mentioned in plaintiff's complaint did not accrue within three years from the commencement of said. action, that the contract of liability
set forth in plaintiff's complaint is not in writing, and
did not arise out of any written agreement. The second
affirmative defense, by way of new matter, alleges that
the cause of action set forth in plaintiff's complaint did
not accrue within six years from the commencement of
plaintiff's said action. For a third affirmative answer
she alleges, that in A. D. 1890, the Northern Pacific &
Puget Sound Shore Railroad Company filed in the superior court of King county a petition for the condemnation of a right of way over and across certain described
lands of defendant; that plaintiff solicited employment
in said proceeding, and represented to the defendant that
he had requisite knowledge, experience, and ability to
secure to defendant her rights in such proceedings; alleges
want of knowledge, experience, and skill on the part of
plaintiff to her damage, in that he filed an answer to said
petition of condemnation in which he confined the damages to be recovered by the defendants therein, to the value
of the land actually taken, and excluding all right to
recover damages done to abutting lands belonging to
defendants; and because evidence was introduced of damages to such abutting lands and such evidence was considered by the jury, the judgment was reversed by the
supreme court, to the great damage of the defendant;

alleges that, by a verbal contract of employment, plaintiff
was to have and recover, as full compensation for said
services, seven per cent of the final judgment recovered,
and alleges that no final judgment was ever recovered in
said action; that a verdict and judgment for $9,500 and
costs was rendered in the superior court of the State of
Washington, in favor of the defendants therein; that before
appeal was taken the railroad petitioner in said proceedings tendered the amount of said judgment, less the interest on the same, which tender was refused by the plaintiff, to her damage in the sum of five thousand dollars;
alleges that it was the duty of plaintiff to have submitted
all propositions of compromise or settlement to her; and
asks that she may go hence with her costs. The reply
denies substantially the affirmative allegations of the
answer. The case was tried by the court, and the following findings of facts and conclusions of law were made by
the court:

"(1) The court finds that this is a cause of action
for compensation for legal services performed by the
plaintiff for defendant in the matter of the condemnation
of the right-of-way of the Northern Pacific & Puget Sound
Shore Railroad Company against this defendant and
others, being cause No. 9269, in this court, and a further
action of this defendant and others against said Northern
Pacific & Puget Sound Shore Railroad Company, being
cause No. 9338, in this court, restraining them from going
across the lands of plaintiff.

"(2) The court finds that the services were performed
between 1890 and 1893, inclusive; said services consisted
in contesting the petition of said railroad companies for
a condemnation of a right-of-way over and across the
premises belonging to said defendant and others and the
subsequent issuance of an injunction prohibiting work
on the said premises by said companies during the continuance of the litigation.

"(3) The court finds that there was a special contract
entered into between plaintiff and defendant as to the

compensation plaintiff was to receive for his legal services; by the terms of said special contract plaintiff was to receive seven per cent of all monies which should be collected from said companies or either of them in such proceedings, as his full compensation.

"(4) The court finds that no final judgment was ever recovered against said companies, or either of them, and that no money was ever collected from said companies, or either of them.

"(5) The court finds that the petition for condemnation was tried in the fall of 1890, and a judgment was rendered for defendant; an appeal was taken to the supreme court and the judgment was reversed and a new trial granted; a remittitur was sent down in the summer of 1892, and plaintiff in said year obtained permission to, and did, file an amended answer, and that this was the last court service he ever performed for the defendant in the case.

"(6) In the summer of 1892 I find defendant went to plaintiff's office in the city of Seattle and personally requested and urged him to proceed in the retrial of the condemnation case, telling him she had placed ample funds for costs and expenses in the hands of Judge Orange Jacobs, subject to his order; that he would act for her, as she would be out of the city for some time; I further find that a few days after said personal interview defendant wrote a letter to plaintiff and duly and properly addressed, paid the postage thereon and placed the same in the postoffice, in which letter she requested and directed plaintiff to proceed in said action, again assuring him that she had placed ample funds in the hands of Judge Jacobs for cost and all other expenses; I find that he neglected and refused to proceed with said litigation; I further find that the reason he gave for his neglect and refusal, as stated by himself, was that it was an inopportune time; that the railroads had stopped construction, and if he attempted to proceed, the railroad companies would withdraw their petition, and he would lose his fee; I further find that after the filing of the amended answer, in the fall of 1892, the plaintiff performed no service for defendant; that he kept the ordinary office files, remained and still remains attorney of record; that he lives in the city of Seattle, and has continuously maintained an office and practice in said city, where service of papers could be had upon him; I further find that said cause of action No. 9,269 and cause of action No. 9,338 are each still pending, at issue and undisposed of. That said condemnation suit renders a cloud on the defendant's title to said land.

"(7) I find that for over ten (10) years plaintiff did not, notwithstanding defendant's said requests and direction to proceed in the action, do anything except to retain the ordinary office files and to remain attorney of record and maintain an office in the city of Seattle, as aforesaid; and I find that in the meantime the Northern Pacific & Puget Sound Shore Railroad Company had become owned and absorbed by the Northern Pacific Railway Company as successor in interest to its rights and privileges; I further find that the injunction proceeding, being cause No. 9,338, restraining the defendant company and its successors named therein from going across the lands of the defendant in this action, is still pending.

"(8) This court further finds that in June, 1903, the defendant, Clarissa D. Colman, without the knowledge or consent of the plaintiff, George D. Farwell, sold the identical land and right-of-way theretofore involved in litigation in the condemnation proceedings and injunction proceedings between the Northern Pacific & Puget Sound Shore Railroad Company and the defendant, Clarissa D. Colman, and others, to the Northern Pacific Railway Company, a corporation that is the successor in interest to the Northern Pacific & Puget Sound Shore Railway Company, for four thousand two hundred and ninety-five dollars ($4,295). Done in open court this 4th day of January, 1904.   (Signed) R. B. ALBERTSON, Judge.

"CONCLUSIONS OF LAW.

"The court finds, as conclusions of law from the above findings of fact, that plaintiff is not entitled to recover and that the defendant is entitled to judgment for her costs and disbursements herein. Done in open court this 4th day of January, 1904. (Signed) R. B. Albertson, Judge."

Judgment was entered in accordance with the findings, and from such judgment this appeal was taken.

The plaintiff excepted to the material findings of fact made by the court. The testimony in this case was exceedingly brief, and from its examination we are not able to say that the facts found by the lower court are not justified. It is true that some services were rendered by the appellant to the respondent in this action, but we think, with the lower court, that the testimony shows that this work was done under an agreement that the appellant should have, for his legal services, seven per cent of the amount of the judgment recovered by the defendant, and that, for more than ten years after the reversal of the case by this court, nothing was done in the case by the appellant, although its prosecution was urged by the respondent, and that the respondent was justified in concluding, under the circumstances, that the appellant had failed and refused to proceed with the work under the agreement which had been entered into. Upon rebuttal the appellant testified, among other things, as follows:

"Q. Was it a fact that Mrs. Colman requested you to press the trial of this action after the case was reversed by the supreme court? A. She asked me if the case could not be brought up a long time after this. She insisted upon making the railroad company pay, but I realized, and knew very well, and told her at the time, that I was in no position to press the matter. That if I attempted to make a move and brought the case on for trial, that the times were hard, that we were in the midst of a panic, that the land wasn't worth a quarter what it was worth in 1890, and that the company had abandoned construction, and if we pressed for trial then, that they would dismiss their action and I would be unable to get anything.

The Court: Was that the ground of your refusal? A. That was the reason. The Court: But was that the ground of your refusal? A. That was the ground of my refusal, because in such case I lost any chance to recover." This is the last testimony offered in the case; the attorney for the plaintiff then announcing that he did not desire to argue the case. Upon this statement alone, we think the appellant should not recover—certainly not, if the respondent's construction of the testimony is correct, namely: that the appellant refused to proceed with the case lest it should result in the loss of a fee to him. And such a construction we think would not do violence to the language used, and was evidently the construction placed upon the testimony by the trial judge, as shown by the questions so pointedly asked.

The principal and ultimate object of a lawsuit is for the benefit of the client, and it is the client's interests that must be considered by the attorney throughout the trial of the case, and he must not place himself in a position where his personal interests will interfere with a full performance of his duty to his client. It is, however, insisted by the appellant that the use of the personal pronoun "I" was not intended to refer to the personal interests of the attorney, but referred to the interests of the client. But even conceding that this construction of the testimony is reasonable, it would still not justify the attorney in refusing to proceed with the trial of the case when requested so to do by the client, and when the necessary funds for prosecuting the suit were placed at his disposal; for the object of a defense to an application for a condemnation, in a case of this kind, ought simply to be to obtain legitimate damages, and not to encourage the railroad company to proceed with the suit for the purpose of obtaining a judgment that would more than compensate for the loss sustained, and this must have been appellant's idea, or there would have been no objection to the withdrawal of the suit by the railroad company.

We think, under all the circumstances of the case, that the respondent was justified in concluding that the appellant had failed to carry out the conditions of the contract entered into, and that the relation of attorney and client had been severed by the refusal of the appellant to perform the duty for which he had been employed, and that she was justified in moving in the matter on her own account to settle with the railroad company in any manner which she considered advantageous to her interests.

In consideration of the whole record, the judgment is affirmed.

FULLERTON, C. J., and HADLEY, MOUNT and ANDERS, JJ., concur.

[No. 5157. Decided July 5, 1904.]

J. J. MULHOLLAND, *Respondent,* v. WASHINGTON MATCH COMPANY, *Appellant.*[1]

PROCESS—SUMMONS—WAIVER OF DEFECT BY APPEARANCE. A motion to quash the service of a summons for insufficiency in form is properly overruled, where defendant had already entered a full appearance in the action, and filed an answer to the complaint.

FRAUD—BY CORPORATION—RESCISSION OF SALE OF STOCK—DUTY OF PURCHASER TO INVESTIGATE REPRESENTATIONS—TRUTH NOT AT HAND. The purchaser of treasury stock from a corporation may rescind the sale for fraud where he relied upon false representations of the officers and promoters with regard to the ownership by the corporation of a device for manufacturing matches and the patents therefor, and a prospectus containing false representations as to the capacity of such machine, since the facts with reference to the existence of the machine and the patents therefor were not at hand, and the representations involved a special skilled knowledge, concerning which the plaintiff was not under obligations to investigate for himself.

RESCISSION—FRAUD—LACHES—DILIGENCE IN BRINGING SUIT. A delay of eighteen months in bringing an action for rescission of a sale of stock in a corporation on the ground of fraud will not estop the plaintiff, where the complaint alleged that the action was commenced within a reasonable time after the discovery of the fraud, and the plaintiff testified that he believed the representations to be true until one month before the commencement of the action.

RESCISSION—SALE INDUCED BY FRAUD—ESTOPPEL—COLLATERAL SECURITY NOT AFFECTING FRAUD IN ORIGINAL CONTRACT. Where a purchase of treasury stock in a corporation was induced by fraud, the purchaser is not estopped to rescind the contract by the fact that afterwards certain other shares of stock were pledged as a guaranty, and other stock was put up as collateral, and that plaintiff had availed himself of the guaranty and collateral, since such guaranty and collateral do not affect the fraud in the original contract, or carry with it any estoppel.

Appeal from a judgment of the superior court for Pierce county, Snell, J., entered October 19, 1903, upon findings in favor of the plaintiff, after a trial on the merits before the court without a jury, decreeing the rescission of a sale for fraud. Affirmed.

H. E. Foster, for appellant.

Jas. J. Anderson, for respondent.

HADLEY, J.—The respondent, as the holder of stock in the appellant corporation, brought this suit to rescind the contract of purchase and sale by which he obtained the stock, and also to obtain judgment for the amount originally paid therefor. The material allegations of the complaint are, that the capital stock of the corporation, as stated in its articles of incorporation, is the sum of $1,200,000, divided into 240,000 shares, of the par value

of $5 per share; that one Lucius T. Holes subscribed for
239,996 shares of the stock upon the organization of the
company, and that four other persons, named as co-defendants with appellant herein, each taking one share, subscribed for the remaining four shares; that said persons
became the incorporators, trustees, and officers of the corporation; that thereafter said Holes transferred to said
corporation 108,000 shares of said capital stock, which
was known as treasury stock, the same to be sold by the
company, and the proceeds thereof to be placed in the treasury; that afterwards the said company and its officers
issued and published a certain circular or prospectus, for
the purpose of advertising the company and its stock, in
which circular the names of said original stock subscribers
were set forth as the promoters, incorporators, trustees and
officers of the company, for the purpose of inducing persons who should read said prospectus to believe that the
several matters and things therein set forth and represented were true; that in said circular said persons, for
the purpose aforesaid, represented, that said Holes had
invented a certain match machine, called the "Holes Match
Machine," and that said invention or machine was then
the property of said company; that said machine was
capable of producing, and was producing, five times as
much finished product in any given length of time as any
other match machine, and at one-fifth the cost for labor;
that the machine was capable of making, and was making,
a complete match; that it would put the matches into the
boxes, and would wrap the boxes into packages containing
from one dozen to one gross of the boxes; that it would
turn the packages out of the machine ready to ship, and,
if desired, would print advertising matter on each and
every match; that the machine had a capacity of 86,400,-

000 matches, or 4,000 gross of 150 matches in each box, for every ten hours operated; that said Holes was a practical match manufacturer, as well as the inventor of said machine; that said company had letters from "the trade" (meaning the dealers in matches), containing more orders for matches than the factory proposed to be constructed by the company could produce. A copy of the alleged circular is made a part of the complaint, and contains, among other things, substantially what is stated above as alleged by respondent.

It is further averred that the said officers and agents of said company caused to be exhibited to respondent a copy of a certain writing, purporting to be an assignment or bill of sale from said Holes to said company of a certain machine, therein represented to have been invented and perfected by said Holes for the purpose of manufacturing and boxing matches, and in which it was stated and represented that said Holes was the owner of the machine; that one of the machines described in the assignment was represented to be then in the city of Philadelphia, Pa., but that certain parts thereof were then in Seattle, Wash.; that said writing also contained certain other of the representations hereinbefore set forth, and was exhibited to respondent for the purpose, and with the intent, of inducing him to believe that said Holes had invented and perfected such a machine, and that said company was then the owner thereof; that it was also exhibited to him for the further purpose of inducing him to purchase shares of the capital stock of the said company; that at various times one Lanning, also a co-defendant, who is alleged to have been assistant manager of said company and its duly authorized agent, and also the said Holes, acting for themselves and for their co-defendants, including the appellant company, repeated the representations hereinbefore recited, together with others of similar import; that said Lanning represented to respondent that he had actually seen the machine making matches; that all of said representations were made to respondent prior to the time that he purchased any stock in said company; that respondent, believing said statements and representations to be true, and relying upon them, did purchase from said corporation 250 shares of the so-called treasury stock, and paid therefor to the said company the sum of $250, and afterwards, further believing and relying upon said statements, he purchased an additional 150 shares of said stock, for which he paid to said company the further sum of $150; that said sums, aggregating $400, were received by said company and turned into the treasury of the company for its benefit; that the same is retained by the company, and no part thereof has been repaid to respondent.

It is further alleged that each and all of the said statements are, and were at the time they were made, wholly false; that said Holes never did invent or perfect any machine for the manufacture of matches; that there has at no time been any perfected machine known as the "Holes Match Machine;" and that the said corporation did not own such a machine. The truth of practically every representation hereinbefore set forth is negatived, and it is averred that their falsity was known to the company and its said officers and agents, at the time they were made. It is further alleged that, prior to the commencement of this action, and within a reasonable time after respondent ascertained that said representations were false, he tendered to said company the said 400 shares of stock, purchased as aforesaid, and demanded the repayment of said $400 paid for the stock; that the company refused, and still refuses, to accept the return of the stock or to repay the money; and that respondent now brings the shares of stock, and deposits them with the clerk of the court, to await the orders of the court in the premises. The complaint prays judgment for $400, and that the contract of purchase of the said 400 shares of stock be rescinded.

The appellant was the only defendant that joined issue upon the complaint, the other defendants not having been served with summons. Appellant demurred to the complaint, which was overruled, and after answer a trial was had before the court without a jury, resulting in a judgment according to the prayer of the complaint. The company has appealed from the judgment.

Appellant's first assignment of error is that the motion to quash the summons and service was overruled. It is asserted that the summons was insufficient in form, but we are unable to appreciate the criticism, since every essential statutory requirement seems to be contained in the summons. It is unnecessary for us to examine the record as to the service of the summons, since appellant entered a full appearance in the action, as shown by respondent's supplemental transcript. In such case no service of summons was necessary. On September 12, 1903, a full appearance for appellant was entered by demurrer to the complaint, through J. W. A. Nichols, its attorney. The same counsel also, on the 22d day of September, 1903, served upon respondent's counsel an answer in the cause, which was filed October 13, 1903. It is true that the record brought here by appellant shows that counsel who appears for appellant in this court did, on October 12, 1903, file a motion to quash the summons and service, and stated therein that the appearance was limited to the

purposes of the motion only; but the motion was then of
no effect, for the reason that appellant had, a month prior
to that time, entered a full appearance through accredited
counsel. The court did not err in denying the motion to
quash.

It is next assigned that the complaint is wholly insufficient, upon its face, to authorize the court to make and
enter any judgment, or to grant any relief. By reason
of this assignment, we have set forth above at some length
the more material averments of the complaint. It seems
to be appellant's theory that respondent was dealing with
it at arm's length. It is argued that, since no fiduciary relation existed, and since it is not alleged that respondent
was overcome by cunning or artifice, by reason of being
frail of body, or of weak and imbecile mind, caused by
advanced age or disease, he does not show a ground for
relief.

It cannot be the law that a person of ordinary faculties
may never rely upon representations made to him, even
though no fiduciary relation may exist. Each case must
depend upon its own circumstances. Where the subject
matter is at hand, and the truth easily ascertainable, this
court has held that one must use his senses, and cannot
afterwards be heard to say that he has been defrauded,
if he neglects to avail himself of a present and reasonable opportunity to learn the truth. The above rule was
applied in *Washington Central Imp. Co. v. Newlands,*
11 Wash. 212, 39 Pac. 366; *West Seattle Land & Imp.
Co. v. Herren,* 16 Wash. 665, 48 Pac. 341; *Griffith v.
Strand,* 19 Wash. 686, 54 Pac. 613; *Walsh v. Bushell,*
26 Wash. 576, 67 Pac. 216.

Under the circumstances detailed by the complaint, as
hereinbefore set out, we think the rule of the above cases

does not apply here. The representations with regard to
the ingenious device for manufacturing matches upon the
proposed new plan, and upon such an extensive scale,
involved a special, skilled knowledge of the mechanism
itself. Even if respondent had been sufficiently skilled
to analyze and pass upon the merits of the mechanism,
or even if it had been his duty to cause it to be done by
some one known to be skilled, yet, under the allegations
of the complaint, the machine was not at hand, and did
not in fact exist. The facts with reference to the existence of such a machine and the patent therefor, together
with the ownership thereof by appellant, were peculiarly
within the knowledge of appellant's officers and agents
who made the representations. It even appears by the
complaint that a paper purporting to be a transfer of
such ownership was shown to respondent, for the fraudulent purpose of misleading him. It is manifest, from
the nature of the subject matter, that the value placed
upon the stock in respondent's mind was due to the belief
that this so-called match machine of extraordinary capacity actually existed, and was also the actual property
of appellant company. The statements made in the prospectus which was placed in respondent's hands are alleged to have been false. This circular is alleged to have
been issued by authority of the trustees and officers of the
corporation for the purpose of inducing the purchase of
treasury stock.

"A prospectus issued by the authority of the directors
or the stockholders of a corporation may be relied upon
by a person in subscribing for stock, and if the prospectus
contains a false representation, and the subscription is
made by reason thereof, such representation is binding
upon the corporation. . . . Nevertheless a subscriber
may have rescission where the prospectus is not an honest,

candid, straightforward document, but suggests that which
is untrue, and is in a high degree misleading." Cook,
Stock & Stockholders (3d ed.), § 143.

The same rule is stated in Thompson's Commentaries on
the Law of Corporations, vol. 1, § 452, as follows:

"Where the promoter of a company, together with the
directors, puts forth a fraudulent prospectus, on the faith
of which a person is induced to purchase shares of the
company, he may bring a bill in equity against the company, the directors and the promoter, and under it he
will be entitled to a rescission of his contract."

The foregoing statements of the principle involved here
made by eminent authors seem to be founded in natural
justice, and the minds of reasonable men instinctively
accept them as correct statements of the rule that should
govern the conduct of men under the circumstances named.
The authors do not, however, state the rule upon their
own authority alone, but they cite the decisions of able
courts in support thereof. Concerning the general principle governing fraud in obtaining subscriptions to the
capital stock of a corporation, the above cited volume of
Cook on Stock & Stockholders, at § 140, further states the
rule as follows:

"The modern doctrine, however, both in this country
and in England, has completely exploded the theory that
corporations are not chargeable with the frauds of their
agents in taking subscriptions. The well-established rule
now is that a corporation cannot claim or retain the benefit of a subscription which has been obtained through the
fraud of its agents. The misrepresentations are not regarded as having actually been made by the corporation,
but the corporation is not allowed to retain the benefit of
the contract growing out of them, being liable to the
extent that it has profited by such misrepresentations.
The question of the authority of the agent taking the
subscription is immaterial herein. It matters not whether

he had any authority, or exceeded his authority, or concealed its limitations. The corporation cannot claim the benefits of his fraud without assuming also the representations which procured those benefits."

The above stated rule pertaining to subscribers for stock applies with equal force here. It is true, respondent was not an original subscriber for stock, but he was a purchaser of shares which belonged to the company, theretofore set apart as treasury stock. The contract of purchase was with the company, and the money paid was as much for the benefit of the company as if paid on an original subscription. For all the foregoing reasons, we think the complaint states a cause of action for the relief asked.

Errors are assigned upon the introduction of evidence, but the cause is triable *de novo* here, and, as we have often held, if there is sufficient competent evidence to sustain the judgment, it will be affirmed, even though some incompetent evidence may have been erroneously admitted.

Errors are assigned upon the findings of facts and conclusions of law. The evidence is sufficient to support the material allegations of the complaint, which have already been recited. The findings are in substantial accord therewith, and we think were not erroneously made. The conclusions of law follow from the findings, within the law as hereinbefore discussed.

It is argued that respondent should be estopped to wage this action, for the reason that he waited about eighteen months before seeking a rescission. The complaint alleges that, within a reasonable time after respondent ascertained that the statements and representations were false, he tendered back the stock and demanded a rescission. The allegation was sufficient, as against de-

murrer, and in the absence of a motion for more definite
statement of the time. Respondent himself testified that,
until within six months of the time of the trial, he had
always believed that such a match machine existed, and
that it belonged to the company. The discovery of the
falsity of the representations, as shown by the evidence,
must have been made about the month of May, 1903.
The complaint was verified June 24th of that year, and
the demand for rescission alleged therein must have been
made within the period of one month after discovery.
Respondent therefore acted with sufficient diligence.

It appears that, some time after respondent became
the holder of the aforesaid stock, the said Holes, the
alleged inventor of the match machine, and a large holder
of stock, caused to be pledged to respondent 1,000 shares
of stock in appellant company, as a guaranty that respondent's stock would, within ninety days from the
date of the pledge, become worth $1.50 per share. The
guaranty contract not being fulfilled, respondent proceeded
to dispose of the collateral stock by exchanging it for
other stock in another corporation. Whether the stock
received in exchange was of any actual value does not
appear. We refer to this circumstance for the reason
that appellant argues that it shows respondent to have
been trafficking in appellant's stock, and that such fact
should estop him to rescind his contract of purchase of
his original stock. We do not see that the disposition of
the stock held as collateral bears any relation to the original contract of purchase. If that contract was induced
by fraud, respondent is entitled to have it rescinded.
The transaction as to the collateral stock concerns only
the pledgor, the respondent, and the latter's transferee.
It does not affect the questions before us in this appeal.

The same is also true of 600 other shares taken by respondent as collateral security for a loan of $450, made by him to a Mr. Lanning, hereinbefore mentioned as assistant manager of appellant company. This circumstance is also urged by appellant as in some way carrying with it the element of estoppel. We are unable to see that the fact of respondent's accepting said stock as security for an actual loan, even though afterwards absolutely transferred to him, in any way estops him to assert his rights under his original stock purchase contract, fraudulently procured.

The judgment is affirmed.

ANDERS, DUNBAR, and MOUNT, JJ., concur.

FULLERTON, C. J., did not sit in this case.

[No. 5207. Decided July 8, 1904.]

THE STATE OF WASHINGTON, *Respondent*, v. DUKE DEATHERAGE, *Appellant*.[1]

CRIMINAL LAW—BURGLARY — EVIDENCE—COMPETENCY. Where, in a prosecution for burglary, a witness testified that he saw the defendant enter a stable and take away two saddles, and that he notified the police by phone, it is not reversible error to sustain an objection, on cross-examination, to the question why witness did not notify the owners of the stable.

SAME—FLIGHT. Upon a witness' testifying that he saw defendant twenty-five miles from the place where the burglary was committed, and only eight hours thereafter, it is not error to permit the witness to answer the question, "Was defendant under arrest?" it not appearing that the witness was not qualified, and the primary purpose of the testimony being to show the fact of flight.

SAME. Where there is evidence that defendant committed a burglary at 2 o'clock A. M., and upon being discovered, dis-

[1]Reported in 77 Pac. 504.

appeared, and admits that he walked twenty-five miles by 10 o'clock of the same morning, without giving any reason therefor, there was sufficient evidence of the flight of defendant to submit the fact to the jury.

CRIMINAL LAW—TRIAL—FAILURE OF DEFENDANT TO TESTIFY—INSTRUCTIONS. An instruction that no inference of guilt shall arise against the accused because of his failure to testify in his own behalf is not objectionable because the court states that the statute makes it the duty of the judge to so instruct the jury.

CRIMINAL LAW—TRIAL—INSTRUCTIONS AS TO FACT OF FLIGHT. An instruction that evidence of flight of the accused may be considered in determining his guilt, is not objectionable as a comment on the evidence.

SAME. Neither is such an instruction objectionable because it fails to explain that circumstances explaining the fact of flight may be considered, where there were no facts or circumstances to explain or excuse the flight.

BURGLARY—EVIDENCE—SUFFICIENCY—CONFESSION BY ANOTHER—CONFLICTING EVIDENCE—NEW TRIAL. A conviction of burglary will not be set aside as unwarranted by the evidence, because another states positively that he and not the defendant committed the crime, where, upon cross-examination, the witness was unable to state any of the surrounding circumstances, and admitted to having been convicted of a felony and to have occupied the same cell with defendant, and his evidence was squarely contradicted, since a new trial should not be awarded on conflicting evidence where there was evidence clearly sufficient to warrant the verdict.

Appeal from a judgment of the superior court for Spokane county, Kennan, J., entered January 2, 1904, upon a trial and conviction of the crime of burglary. Affirmed.

Alex. M. Winston, for appellant.

Horace Kimball, for respondent.

ANDERS, J.—The defendant was convicted of burglary upon the trial of an information of which the following, omitting formal parts, is a copy:

"That the said defendant, Duke Deatherage, on the 4th day of November, 1903, in the county of Spokane

and state of Washington, then and there being, did then
and there wilfully, unlawfully, feloniously and burglari-
ously enter in the night time a certain stable there situate, the property of, and belonging to, C. O. Wilson and
W. M. Moore, copartners doing business as the Klondike
Stables, and then and there used by them as such, in
which certain goods and valuable property of the said
C. O. Wilson and W. M. Moore, copartners as aforesaid,
was then and there kept for use, with intent then and
there unlawfully, wilfully, and feloniously, to steal, take
and carry away the said goods and valuable property of the
said C. O. Wilson and W. M. Moore, copartners as aforesaid, then and there kept for use as aforesaid."

A motion for a new trial was denied, and the defendant
has appealed from the judgment.

The errors assigned and relied on by the appellant
for a reversal of the judgment call in question the ruling
of the court in sustaining objections to certain questions
propounded to witnesses, in refusing to strike from the
records the testimony of the witness McPhee, in giving
certain instructions to the jury, and in denying appellant's motion for a new trial. At the trial the state called
one Fisher, who testified, in substance, that he lived in
Spokane and was employed in a stable adjoining the
Klondike stables; that he was acquainted with the appellant; that on the night of November 3, 1903, he was in
the stable adjoining the Klondike stables on First avenue; that about 1:30 or 2 o'clock on that night his attention was attracted by the barking of a dog in the Klondike stables; that he went to the rear of the stable and
hid behind an open swinging door; that he saw the appellant coming out of the Klondike stable with a saddle under each arm (which saddles were produced in court and
identified by the witness); that the appellant then walked
up the alley and disappeared from sight; that in about

five minutes he returned and went into the stable where
the witness was secreted, and in a few moments came
out leading a horse belonging to the proprietor of the stable; that when appellant came out, he, the witness, asked
him, "What are you going to do with that horse?" whereupon he dropped the horse and ran away.

This witness further testified, that he then telephoned
the police station and reported the matter to the police,
and two policemen came up to the barn; that he and the
policemen looked for the saddles, and that he found them
and the bridle, about one hundred and fifty feet from
the barn, in a wagon which was in the alley. On cross-
examination the witness stated that he did not enter the
Klondike stables, after the saddles were taken, until the
next day, and that he reported the taking of the saddles
that night to the police by "phone." Counsel for the defendant then asked the witness the following questions: "Q.
Did you report to Mr. Wilson or Mr. Moore the taking
of the saddles, that night? Ans. I did not. Q. Why
did you not report to Wilson or Moore the taking of the
saddles that night?" This question was objected to by
counsel for the state on the ground that it was immaterial. The objection was sustained by the court, and the
defendant, by his counsel, excepted.

It is claimed that this ruling of the court was erroneous and prejudicial to the appellant, and it is insisted
that the appellant had the right to know why the witness did not inform the proprietors of the Klondike stables that a burglary had been committed; and it is, in
effect, argued in support of this contention that, if the
witness had no good reason for not promptly reporting
the burglary to the proprietors of the stables, counsel for
the appellant could have argued to the jury that, as a

matter of fact, no burglary was committed, or, if that
offense was committed, that the witness himself or some
person other than the appellant committed it. Although
this interrogatory, as propounded to the witness, may
not be deemed to have been wholly irrelevant or immaterial, yet we are convinced that the sustaining of the
objection thereto constitutes no sufficient ground for the
reversal of the judgment. The witness had already testified that he reported the burglary to the police, but did
not report to Wilson or Moore that night that the saddles
had been taken from the stable; and it would seem that
the reason why he did not report to them was, at most,
a circumstance only remotely, if at all, material to appellant's defense. Whether the answer to the question would
have been beneficial or not to the appellant is merely a
matter of pure speculation. If any inference favorable
to appellant could be drawn from the fact that the witness did not report the taking of the saddles to Wilson
or Moore, the appellant was certainly entitled to the benefit of it, and his counsel could have so argued to the
jury.

It is next insisted that the trial court erred in permitting the witness McPhee, over appellant's objection,
to answer the question, "Was defendant under arrest?"
and in refusing to strike from the record the statement
of the witness that the defendant was under arrest, when
he saw him at Reardon, Washington, at about 10 o'clock
in the forenoon of November 4, 1903. These two assignments of error are based upon the proposition that
an arrest may be proved in two ways only; first, by
a person who made the arrest or who saw it made; and,
second, by a certified copy of a public record showing
the arrest. But conceding, without deciding, that this

proposition is correct, still we find nothing in the record showing that the witness was not qualified to testify that the appellant was under arrest at the time he saw him and conversed with him at Reardon. The fact that the appellant was not handcuffed does not show that he was not under arrest. On the contrary, as stated by counsel for the state, this shows, if it shows anything, that appellant was in no way resisting arrest. Nor does the fact that the sheriff was not in the store when McPhee was there throw any light, either one way or the other, on the subject of the arrest of appellant. McPhee was a police officer of the city of Spokane, and he testified that, while he was on the railroad going from Davenport to Spokane, he was informed that appellant was at Reardon, in custody, and that he found him there sitting in a store at the time above mentioned. In fact, it appears that the question of appellant's arrest was not deemed of any special importance by the prosecuting attorney, as there was no attempt to ascertain from the witness the details of the original arrest of appellant, if he was arrested by some person other than the witness himself. If the appellant, as seems to have been the fact, was in the actual custody, or within the power, of McPhee, he was, in contemplation of law, under arrest. *Gold v. Bissell*, 1 Wend. 210, 19 Am. Dec. 480. We think the court did not err either in overruling appellant's objection to the question as to appellant's arrest, or in denying the motion to strike the answer thereto from the record.

Nor do we think the court erred in refusing to strike from the record the entire testimony of the witness McPhee. It is admitted that the primary purpose of the testimony of this witness was to show that appellant had precipitously fled from the scene of the crime with which he was charged. But the learned counsel for the appellant earnestly insists that such testimony was wholly insufficient to prove flight, and therefore should have been excluded from the consideration of the jury. It is true that the testimony in question was not alone sufficient to establish the fact that the appellant was fleeing from justice, but it was nevertheless competent and material evidence upon that question. It constituted at least one link in the chain of circumstances from which flight might be inferred, and was therefore properly submitted to the jury. That McPhee saw appellant at Reardon, a town twenty-five miles from Spokane, at 10 o'clock in the morning of November 4, 1903, and that appellant told him he had walked all the way from Spokane the night before, is not disputed. And the materiality of this testimony becomes at once apparent, when viewed in connection with the positive testimony of the witness Fisher to the effect that he saw the appellant at or about 2 o'clock in the morning of the same day, carrying saddles from the Klondike stable, in the city of Spokane, and trying to steal a horse from the adjoining stable. Why the appellant walked on that particular night from Spokane to Reardon is not disclosed by the record, and, that being true, it cannot be said there was no evidence of flight on the part of appellant. It is not necessary, in order to prove the flight of one charged with crime, to show that he escaped from jail or from an officer having him in custody, for it often happens that persons conscious of guilt seek safety by flight, even before they are suspected of crime. "The wicked flee when no man pursueth."

The fifth assignment of error is that the court erred in instructing the jury as follows:

"While the statute of this state provides that a person charged with crime may testify in his own behalf, he is under no obligation to do so, and the statute expressly makes it the duty of the court to instruct the jury that no inference of guilt shall arise against the accused if the accused shall fail or refuse to testify as a witness in his own behalf, and the court so instructs the jury in this case."

It is conceded that this charge of the court complies with the letter of the statute, but it is contended on behalf of appellant that it is not within the spirit of the law; and it is urged that the appellant was entitled to an unqualified instruction, without reference to any statute whatever; or, in other words, that the appellant was prejudiced by the statement to the jury that "the statute expressly makes it the duty of the court to instruct the jury that no inference of guilt shall arise against the accused if the accused shall fail or refuse to testify as a witness in his own behalf." It is stated, in effect, by counsel for appellant, that the judge, by this instruction, virtually told the jury that "the law requires me to so instruct you, and for that reason only I do it." This instruction is clearly in accordance with the law, and the statement of the court that it was made its duty, by the statute, to so instruct the jury, did not, in our judgment, abridge or injuriously affect any right of the appellant. Where the jury is properly directed as to the law upon a particular question, the language used by the court is a matter of no special importance. In *State v. Mitchell*, 32 Wash. 64, 72 Pac. 707, this court ruled that an instruction which substantially complies with the provisions of the statute is sufficient, and we think such is the general rule. The instruction now under consideration is not only substantially but literally in the language of the statute (Bal. Code, § 6941), and is therefore not subject to legitimate criticism.

Upon the question of flight the court charged the jury as follows:

"If you find that burglary was committed as charged in the information, evidence of flight of the accused may be considered in determining the question as to whether he was the one who committed the act."

It is contended by appellant that this instruction is erroneous for the reasons, (1) that there is no evidence of the flight. of the appellant, and no evidence of any attempt to escape from the officers; (2) that it comments upon the facts in the case; and (3) that this is not a proper case for such an instruction, and that the instruction fails to state the law correctly. What we have said in discussing appellant's fourth assignment of error disposes of the proposition that there was no evidence of flight of appellant, and therefore a further consideration of the question of flight is unnecessary. Nor do we think that this instruction is violative of section 16 of art. 4 of the constitution, which provides that judges shall not charge juries with respect to matters of fact, or comment thereon. The learned judge made no statement to the jury as to the evidence which had been introduced upon the question of flight. Neither did he make any remarks indicating his own opinion upon that question or suggesting the conclusion which should be arrived at by the jury. In short, he did not "comment thereon."

The contention that this instruction does not state the law is based upon the proposition, if we understand appellant's argument, that the court should have gone further and informed the jury that the circumstances explaining or excusing flight should be taken into consideration, and

no doubt the jury should be so instructed in cases where
the evidence warrants such instruction. Wharton's Crim.
Ev. (9th ed.), § 750. But, in this case, there were no
facts or circumstances explaining, or tending to explain
or excuse, the flight of appellant, and, consequently, no
countervailing conditions for the consideration of the jury.
Although the court might properly have charged the jury
that the flight of the accused would not, by itself, warrant
a conviction, yet the omission to do so did not, in our
opinion, vitiate the instruction as given. Indeed, this
instruction plainly implies that a conviction might not
be based solely on the fact of flight. In *State v. Gee,*
85 Mo. 647, the supreme court of Missouri approved an
instruction couched in the following language:

"The court instructs the jury that flight raises the presumption of guilt, and if you believe from the evidence
that the defendant, after having shot and killed Minnick,
as charged in the indictment, fled the country and tried
to avoid arrest and trial, you may take that fact into consideration in determining his guilt or innocence."

The instruction given in this case does not state that guilt
may be inferred from flight, or even, as was said in the
Missouri case, that flight raises the presumption of guilt.
It simply says to the jury that evidence of flight may be
considered in determining whether the accused was the
one who committed the offense, and the court committed
no error in so charging the jury.

Lastly, it is contended by appellant that the court erred
in refusing to grant a new trial on the ground that the
verdict was contrary to the evidence. This contention is
absolutely untenable. We have read and carefully considered all the evidence contained in the record, and are
thoroughly satisfied that it justifies the verdict of the jury.

It is true, one Ingalls, a witness on behalf of the defendant, testified at the trial substantially as follows:

"On the evening of November 3d, about nine or ten o'clock, I called at the Klondike stables and defendant and I went to town and had several drinks together, among other places, at the Judge saloon. About 12 o'clock or thereafter, the defendant left me, stating he was going back to the barn to sleep. After that time I went to the barn, walked into the door, took these saddles from the barn and carried them away. Deatherage was not with me. After I had taken the saddles out, I went upstairs to the place where Deatherage was asleep, and told him what I had done. He remonstrated with me, and said he did not want to have anything to do with it, and if the saddles were taken he would be accused of it."

Of course, if this testimony was true, appellant was entitled to a new trial. But evidently the jury and the judge, having observed the demeanor of this witness and heard his testimony, disbelieved the statements above set forth. And an examination of his testimony as a whole, even as it appears in the record, is sufficient to convince any unbiased mind that it is wholly unworthy of belief. Although he testified positively and without hesitation, in his examination in chief, that he took the saddles from the barn and afterwards went upstairs where appellant was sleeping and told him what he had done, and that appellant remonstrated with him, he was utterly unable to recount the surrounding circumstances, or to give a more detailed account of the transaction. For instance, the following are questions asked this witness on cross-examination, and his answers thereto:

"Q. How many saddles did you take? A. Two. Q. Did you take anything else besides the saddles? A. No. Q. Are you sure about that? A. Yes. Q. From where did you take the saddles? A. I got them in the

stable. Q. Did you take the saddles from the same
identical place in the stable; were they hanging together
at the time you took them? A. Yes. Q. Where was
Deatherage at this time? A. Upstairs. Q. Did you
go upstairs thereafter? A. Yes. Q. How did you get
upstairs—by stairs or by ladder? A. I don't know. Q.
Where was Deatherage sleeping—on a bed or on the
floor? A. I can't tell you. Q. Why can't you tell? A.
I don't know. Q. Who else, or was there any one else
in the room with Deatherage at that time? A. I don't
know. Q. How could you see him—was there a light
in the room? A. I don't know. Q. Describe the room
in which Deatherage slept. A. I cannot. Where did
you put the saddles after taking them? A. I don't remember. Q. Which way did you go with the saddles
after leaving the stable—north, south, east or west? A.
I don't remember. Q. Where have you been during the
last two or three weeks? A. I have been confined in
the county jail. Q. In what cell were you confined in
the county jail with reference to the defendant Deatherage? A. I was confined in the same cell. Q. For how
long a time were you confined in the same cell with Deatherage? A. For several weeks. Q. Have you not been
heretofore convicted of felony in the county of Whitman,
State of Washington, and served sentence by reason thereof? A. Yes sir."

It seems plain to us that the testimony of this witness,
Ingalls, taken all together, bears upon its face the brand
of untruthfulness, and that the jury was fully justified
in regarding it as a mere fabrication. But even if Ingalls' testimony were considered as worthy of serious
consideration, it was squarely contradicted by other evidence, which the jury had the right to believe, and did
believe, and which was clearly sufficient to sustain their
verdict. Under such circumstances this court has uniformly declined to award a new trial on the ground of in-

sufficiency of the evidence. See, *State v. Ripley*, 32 Wash. 182, 72 Pac. 1036, and cases therein cited.

We have discovered no error in the record, and the judgment is, therefore, affirmed.

FULLERTON, C. J., and HADLEY, MOUNT, and DUNBAR, JJ., concur.

[No. 4996. Decided July 12, 1904.]

THE STATE OF WASHINGTON, *Appellant*, v. THE FRA-
TERNAL KNIGHTS AND LADIES, *Respondent*.[1]

STATUTES — TITLE — BENEFICIAL ASSOCIATIONS — REGULATION —
PRESCRIBING MINIMUM RATE. Laws 1901, p. 356, entitled "An act regulating fraternal beneficiary societies," does not violate the constitutional prohibition against a bill's embracing more than one subject, by reason of the inclusion of § 12, p. 362, which fixes a minimum rate for insurance by all such associations thereafter authorized to transact business in this state, since "regulation" is broad enough to include said section.

BENEFICIAL   ASSOCIATIONS — STATUTES — CONSTRUCTION — CER-
TAINTY—REFERENCE TO MORTALITY TABLE—MINIMUM RATE. The act of 1901, p. 356, regulating beneficial societies by fixing a rate for assessments not lower than as indicated by the table designated "Fraternal Congress Mortality Table," is not objectionable as vague and uncertain, nor because the same belongs to the domain of evidence and ought to be subject to impeachment, since it is competent for the legislature to determine the rate by adopting such tables and incorporating them into the law.

SAME—CONSTITUTIONAL LAW—CLASS LEGISLATION—EQUAL PRO-
TECTION—REGULATIONS APPLYING TO NEW CORPORATIONS. Laws 1901, p. 356, regulating new corporations to be thereafter authorized to do business in this state, and making them a class unto themselves, does not violate the constitution, art. 1, § 12, forbidding the granting of special privileges to any citizen or class; nor does it violate art. 12, § 7, providing that no corporation outside the limits of the state shall be allowed to transact business on more favorable conditions than those prescribed for

[1]Reported in 77 Pac. 500.

domestic corporations, where the law applies equally to all foreign and domestic corporations thereafter to be authorized to
transact business, since it is only necessary that the laws operate
alike upon all similarly situated.

Appeal from a judgment of the superior court for King
county, Tallman, J., entered October 8, 1903, dismissing
the action, upon sustaining a demurrer to the complaint.
Reversed.

The Attorney General and *E. W. Ross, C. C. Dalton,*
and *Root, Palmer & Brown,* for appellant.

J. W. Langley, W. H. Merritt, and *Robert D. Hamlin,*
for respondent.

HADLEY, J.—The state of Washington, the appellant
in this appeal, instituted this proceeding against the respondent to enjoin and prohibit it from continuing or
carrying on the business of fraternal insurance, until
certain alleged violations of law have been corrected.
The complaint avers, that the respondent is a fraternal
beneficiary corporation, organized and existing under and
by virtue of chapter 174, of the session laws of 1901; that
the corporation was organized on the 16th day of April,
1903, and ever since said date has been, and now is, transacting a fraternal beneficiary business, and issuing to
its beneficiary members certificates entitling their beneficiaries to payment in the event of death of the member,
or in case of sickness or accident, of the sums set forth
in a table or schedule, such payments being in consideration of the monthly payment of installments or assessments in sums set forth in the same table; that the mortuary assessment rates, heretofore charged and collected,
and now being charged and collected, by said corporation,
have been, at all times since the organization of the com-

pany, and are now, less than the mortuary assessment
rates indicated as necessary by the fraternal congress
mortality table set forth in said chapter 174 of the laws
of Washington, 1901, and less than the mortuary rates
required by law; that said corporation ever since its
organization has been, and now is, transacting and carrying on business in violation of § 12 of said chapter 174;
that the commissioner of insurance of the state of Washington has repeatedly demanded of said corporation, its
officers and agents, that the mortuary assessment rates
charged and collected by it be increased and made to
correspond with the rates indicated as necessary by said
fraternal congress mortality table, and as required by
law, but that it has refused, and still refuses, to increase
said rates, or to comply with the requirements of law;
that the said commissioner of insurance has served upon
the attorney general notice in writing that said corporation has been, and is, exceeding its powers, is conducting
its business fraudulently, has failed and refused to comply with the law, and that this proceeding is prosecuted
at the request of said commissioner of insurance.   The
complaint prays that the corporation be enjoined from
continuing its business until the said violation shall have
been corrected, and the costs of this action paid.   The
corporation demurred to the complaint, on the ground
that it does not state facts sufficient to constitute a cause
of action.   The demurrer was sustained.   The state elected
to stand upon its complaint, and judgment was entered
that the injunction be denied and the action dismissed.
The state has appealed.

Respondent concedes that chapter 174, Laws 1901, is
a complete act for all the purposes expressed in its title,
without § 12 of the act, but contends that said section is

repugnant to § 19, art. 2, of the state constitution, which
is as follows: "No bill shall embrace more than one
subject, and that shall be embraced in the title." The
title of the act of 1901 is as follows: "An act regulating
fraternal beneficiary societies, orders, or associations."
Section 12 of the act, which it is claimed is not within
the above title is as follows:

"No association not admitted to transact business within
this state prior to the passage of this act shall be incorporated or given a permit or certificate of authority to transact business within this state, as provided for by this
act, unless it shall first show that the mortuary assessment rates, provided for in whatever plan of business
it has adopted, are not lower than is indicated as necessary by the following mortality table:" (Here follows
a table designated as "Fraternal Congress Mortality Table."

Respondent's argument is that this objection would be
less forcible, if the minimum rate and the manner of
determining it, provided by § 12, applied alike to all
associations doing business in this state; but that, inasmuch as the section attempts to apply the rate to a
class not yet in existence, and exempts from its operation all associations already doing business in the state,
the matter of fixing a minimum rate for the only members the act can affect becomes a material part, if not
the sole purpose, of the act itself, and is not sufficiently
indicated by its title. If it is competent for the legislature to make the classification required by § 12, then we
think the title of the act is broad enough to include it,
for the reason that the words "regulating fraternal beneficiary societies," etc., seem broad enough to require the
reader to examine the body of the act for every feature
that may properly come within the scope of regulation.

The adoption of minimum mortuary assessment rates, and their application under stated conditions, are matters of regulation, and come within the title of the act. Whether it is competent for the legislature to regulate by classification we shall hereinafter discuss.

Respondent's next contention is that § 12 aforesaid is vague and uncertain, in that it is alleged no minimum mortuary assessment rate is in fact written in the law itself as the legislative judgment and will. It is true it is designated as, "Fraternal Congress Mortality Table," but the section so refers to the table that its terms become a part of the act itself, and it is wholly immaterial by whom it was prepared or by what, if any, name it is designated. It may be true, as respondent argues, that the table was originally prepared by some body of men bearing no official relation to the legislative body, but that does not prevent the legislature from adopting the table, and incorporating it into law as a regulative feature. It is further argued that such tables belong to the domain of evidence, and that, like other evidentiary matters, they should receive the scrutiny of the courts, and be held subject to impeachment. We think, in the light of modern experience, that it is entirely competent for the legislature to incorporate such tables into law, and require that they shall be applied. It may be a matter of difference of opinion as to whether the table includes the rates most approved by experience, but that is a question which the legislature may determine, and it is not necessarily one of evidence to be weighed by the courts.

Respondent's principal contention, however, is that § 12 attempts to make an arbitrary and unreasonable classification of corporations, with reference to the application of assessment rates, and grants unequal privileges and immunities in violation of § 12, art. 1, of the state constitution, which is as follows:

"No law shall be passed granting to any citizen, class of citizens, or corporation other than municipal, privileges or immunities which upon the same terms shall not equally belong to all citizens or corporations."

It is insisted that, inasmuch as the law of 1901 exempts corporations then existing and doing business from the operation of the rates named in the act, but applies them to corporations thereafter created or admitted to do business, there is for that reason an attempted discrimination which is violative of the above constitutional requirement. It will be observed, however, that all corporations thereafter created or admitted to do business are placed in a class to themselves, and no discrimination is made between any of the class, but the law is operative alike upon all corporations similarly situated. It is further suggested that, inasmuch as foreign corporations which had been admitted to transact business within this state prior to the passage of the act are exempt from the application of the statutory assessment rates, the fact that the rates are made to apply to respondent, a domestic corporation, is violative of § 7, art. 12, of the state constitution, which is as follows:

"No corporation organized outside the limits of this state shall be allowed to transact business within the state on more favorable conditions than are prescribed by law to similar corporations organized under the laws of this state."

It will also be observed, in this connection, that all foreign corporations, thereafter admitted to do business in this state, are classified with such as respondent, and no more favorable conditions are extended to the one than to the other. Thus all corporations, whether domestic or foreign, which are admitted to do business in the state after the passage of this law, are placed upon equal footing. What may have been the legislative reasoning may be surmised. Doubtless it was believed that experience had shown that assessment rates lower than those incorporated in the act were insufficient to secure payment of benefits and insurance to beneficiaries. It may have also been the view that certain contractual relations as to assessment rates then obtained between certificate holders and existing corporations, which prevented the application of the new rates to old members. It may have been believed to be impracticable for existing corporations to carry two sets of rates, one for old and another for new certificate holders. It may be supposed that the legislature, actuated by such reasoning, decided to arrange the associations in two classes as aforesaid, and that, by so doing, it would the more effectively correct what it must have believed to be a prevailing evil, viz., the charging and acceptance of mortuary assessment rates too low to secure payments to the beneficiaries of trusting, but uninformed and inexperienced, certificate holders. It must be assumed that it was the object of the legislature to establish such regulative conditions as will best serve and protect the rights of the citizen. Based upon such grounds as above indicated, the classification seems to be neither unreasonable nor arbitrary, and such reasonable classifications are held to be not violative of the constitutional principles invoked here, where all persons who come within the operation of the law are affected alike, even though they may constitute a class. Equal protection of the laws, given by the constitution, requires that the law shall have equality of operation, but that does not mean equality of operation on persons merely as such, but on persons according to their relations, *State v. Carey,* 4 Wash. 424, 30 Pac. 729; *Redford v. Spokane St. R. Co.,* 15 Wash. 419, 46 Pac. 650; *Fitch v. Applegate,* 24 Wash. 25, 64 Pac. 147; *State v. Nichols,* 28 Wash. 628, 69 Pac.

372; *State v. Clark*, 30 Wash. 439, 71 Pac. 20; *McDaniels v. Connelly Shoe Co.*, 30 Wash. 549, 71 Pac. 37, 60 L. R. A. 947, 94 Am. St. 889; *People v. Phippin*, 70 Mich. 6, 37 N. W. 888; *Magoun v. Illinois Trust & Sav. Bank*, 170 U. S. 283, 18 Sup. Ct. 594, 42 L. Ed. 1037; *Ames v. Union Pac. R. Co.*, 64 Fed. 165; *Chicago etc. R. Co. v. Iowa*, 94 U. S. 155, 24 L. Ed. 94; *Missouri Pac. R. Co. v. Mackey*, 127 U. S. 205, 8 Sup. Ct. 1161, 32 L. Ed. 107; *Indianapolis v. Navin*, 151 Ind. 139, 47 N. E. 525, 51 N. E. 80, 41 L. R. A. 337; *Central Iowa R. Co. v. Board of Supervisors*, 67 Iowa 199, 25 N. W. 128; *In re Oberg*, 21 Ore. 406, 28 Pac. 130, 14 L. R. A. 577; *Ex parte Koser*, 60 Cal. 177; *Hayes v. Missouri*, 120 U. S. 68, 7 Sup. Ct. 350, 30 L. Ed. 578; *American Sugar Ref. Co. v. Louisiana*, 179 U. S. 89, 21 Sup. Ct. 43, 45 L. Ed. 102; *New York etc. R. Co. v. New York*, 165 U. S. 628, 17 Sup. Ct. 418, 41 L. Ed. 853; *Fidelity Mut. Life Ass'n v. Mettler*, 185 U. S. 308, 22 Sup. Ct. 662, 46 L. Ed. 922.

The principle under discussion here has been so frequently held, not only in the above cited cases, but in many others, that we deem it unnecessary to further pursue the subject. The act of 1901 operates alike upon respondent, and upon all other corporations similarly situated. Such legislative classification is not in conflict with the constitution. No acquired rights or privileges have been taken from respondent. Its existence followed that of the law, and its incorporators were bound to know its limitations, in the light of existing law. We think the complaint states a cause of action.

The judgment is reversed, and the cause remanded, with instructions to the lower court to overrule the demurrer to the complaint.

FULLERTON, C. J., and ANDERS, MOUNT, and DUNBAR, JJ., concur.

[No. 5152. Decided July 12, 1904.]

A. E. BRAYMER, *Appellant*, v. SEATTLE, RENTON AND
SOUTHERN RAILWAY COMPANY, *Respondent*.[1]

CARRIERS—EJECTION OF PASSENGER—STREET CAR NOT RUNNING
TO END OF LINE—PAYMENT OF ADDITIONAL FARE—NONSUIT. In an
action by a passenger for damages by reason of being ejected
from a street car, a nonsuit is properly ordered where it appears
that the plaintiff boarded a car that did not run to his destination, paid a five-cent fare, without stating his destination, and,
upon reaching the end of the run of that car, was told by the
superintendent, who was acting as motorman, to take the next
car, and that the conductor thereof would be told to pick him
up and carry him to his destination, since the minds of the
parties did not meet in a contract to carry him to such point for
one fare.

SAME—CONTRACT OF CARRIAGE—TRANSFER CONTRARY TO CUSTOM.
The statement of the superintendent that he would tell the conductor of the next car to pick him up and carry him on was not
sufficient to create a contract to carry him without the payment
of another fare, there being no custom to transfer passengers
without an additional fare under such circumstances.

SAME—PROMISE OF EMPLOYE. The fact that the superintendent testifies that he intended to so notify the next conductor,
but forgot to do so, does not create any obligation on the part
of the company to carry the passenger further without pay.

SAME—EVIDENCE—DISPOSITION OF CONDUCTOR EJECTING PASSEN-
GER. In an action for forcibly ejecting a passenger from a street
car, based entirely on the contract of carriage, evidence of the
general character and disposition of the conductor who ejected
the plaintiff is inadmissible, in the absence of allegations of incompetence.

SAME—EVIDENCE AS TO CAR SCHEDULES. In an action against
a street car company for failing to carry a passenger to his
destination, where there is no question as to the destination of
a certain car boarded by plaintiff, and he made no inquiry as to
the same, it is not error to strike out evidence relating to the
car schedules of the defendant.

[1]Reported in 77 Pac. 495.

Appeal from a judgment of the superior court for King
county, Albertson, J., entered November 9, 1903, upon
granting a nonsuit at the close of plaintiff's case, in an
action for damages by reason of ejection from a street car
for nonpayment of fare. Affirmed.

Tucker & Hyland, for appellant, to the point that the
superintendent's promise, under the circumstances, constituted a complete contract of carriage through to Fairview, cited: *Sloane v. Southern Cal. R. Co.,* 111 Cal. 668,
44 Pac. 320, 32 L. R. A. 193; *O'Rourke v. Citizens' St. R.
Co.,* 103 Tenn. 124, 52 S. W. 872, 46 L. R. A. 614, 76
Am. St. 639; *Gulf etc. R. Co. v. Rather,* 3 Tex. Civ. App.
72, 21 S. W. 951; *Gulf etc. R. Co. v. Copeland,* 17 Tex.
Civ. App. 55, 42 S. W. 239.

Peters & Powell, for respondent.

HADLEY, J.—Appellant sued respondent to recover alleged damages. The complaint avers, that appellant for hire
became a passenger upon respondent's road, paid the fare
demanded of him, and rode in one of respondent's cars to a
point near Brighton Beach, his destination being Fairview,
upon said line of road; that at said point near Brighton
Beach the respondent, through its officers and agents, with
force and without any cause whatsoever, ejected appellant
from respondent's car. He avers that he was thereby greatly
humiliated, and was damaged in the sum of $2,500, for
which amount he demands judgment. The answer of respondent denies the material allegations of the complaint,
and affirmatively alleges, that appellant boarded one of
respondent's cars at or near Brighton Beach; that he refused to pay the fare demanded of him by the conductor,
as necessary to entitle him to ride as a passenger in said
car, and upon such refusal he was, by said conductor, with-

out unnecessary force or violence, ejected from the car. The cause was tried before the court and a jury. At the conclusion of the plaintiff's testimony the defendant moved for a nonsuit, which was granted, judgment was thereupon entered dismissing the action, and the plaintiff has appealed.

The evidence shows that on Sunday, February 1, 1903, appellant boarded one of respondent's cars at the corner of Second avenue south and Washington street, in Seattle. It appears that he desired to go to his home at Fairview, a station on the line of said road outside of the city of Seattle. The conductor demanded his fare, and he paid five cents, the customary amount. He did not inform the conductor that he desired to go to Fairview, and he made no inquiry as to how far that car would go. It also appears by the evidence that the company intended that the car upon which appellant was riding should go no further than Hillman City, which is a station nearer Seattle than Fairview, where appellant desired to go. It appears that appellant did not know that the car would stop at Hillman City, and inasmuch as a car by schedule should have left at 4:30 P. M., bound for a point on the line beyond Fairview, he supposed that this car, which left about that time, would go beyond his station.

Before the car reached Hillman City, a Mr. Brown, the superintendent of respondent company, boarded it and directed the motorman of this car to take another to the barn while he (Brown) acted as motorman of the car which carried appellant until it reached Hillman City. Upon reaching the latter place, Brown concluded that he had time to carry a few passengers as far as Brighton Beach, a station beyond Hillman City, while waiting for the next car to come. He seems to have made this run as a matter of mere accommodation to certain Brighton Beach passengers, it being no part of the regular run of the car. Appellant remained upon the car until it reached Brighton Beach. At the latter point he was requested by Brown to retire from this car and take the next one coming from the city. Appellant testified as follows:

"I says, 'All right,' and after he got on his car and I got off he says, 'I will tell the conductor on the other car to pick you up and take you on.' I says, 'All right,' and he went back and went into the switch, and just then the other car came along."

After appellant boarded the other car, the conductor demanded fare, which he refused to pay, stating as a reason that he had paid his fare once and was entitled to ride through. He also testified that he attempted to explain, and ask if Brown had not spoken to the conductor, but the latter would hear no explanation, and informed him that he must pay fare or get off. Appellant then said: " 'Well,' I says, 'not quite so fast. I have paid my fare once. If you want me off this car, you will have to put me off.' " Thereupon the conductor called the motorman, and, without violence, they removed appellant from the car. No injury was done to his person or clothing.

Appellant's complaint in effect alleges, a contract on the part of respondent to carry him to Fairview station for the price of a fare, which he then paid; that respondent afterwards refused to carry him beyond an intermediate station, demanded further fare from him, and, upon his failure to pay, ejected him. If there was a contract to carry appellant as far as Fairview, then the minds of appellant and respondent's agents must have met upon that subject. Nothing, however, was said to the conductor upon the subject of appellant's destination. The conductor knew that

his car was bound to Hillman City and not beyond. Under
such circumstances it was impossible for their minds to
have met in an agreement to carry appellant to Fairview
for the fare he then paid. The evidence shows that it was
a common thing for cars to go no further than Hillman
City, and there is no evidence that there was any system of
issuing transfer tickets to passengers upon those cars, which
were good for passage upon others going beyond there.
Even if such system obtained, there is no evidence that
appellant asked for such transfer ticket. He contends,
however, that if his contract was not, in the first instance,
sufficient to carry him beyond Hillman City, it became
sufficient when the superintendent said to him: "I will
tell the conductor on the other car to pick you up and take
you on." It will be observed that Brown did not say that
appellant would be carried upon the other car for the fare
already paid. Doubtless appellant so inferred, but the language used was not sufficient to make a contract to that
effect, at least when unaided by any custom of the company to transfer passengers from one car to another to be
carried further without additional fare. We therefore think
appellant had no contract except one for carriage as far as
the car he first boarded was intended to go, viz.; to Hillman
City. When he was carried to the latter place, the contract
was at an end. His carriage beyond that point, as we have
seen, was a mere gratuity, a license to him, revocable at
pleasure, until he should pay fare and thus effect a contract
for further carriage upon another car.

Appellant sought to show by a witness that Brown, the
superintendent, said to him the next day after the incident
that it was more his (Brown's) fault than that of the conductor, as he intended to tell the conductor to pick appellant up and take him out, but that he forgot to do so. The

witness did so testify, and it is not clear from the sweeping motion to strike testimony in connection with the motion for nonsuit, whether the court intended to strike this part of the testimony or not. But, for the purposes of this discussion, we shall treat that evidence as before the jury. If one may infer from what Brown said the next day, that he intended to have appellant carried further without additional fare, still it does not appear that such a course of transferring fare-paying passengers was authorized by any custom or regulation of the company. What Brown said to appellant, or what he may have said the next day of his intentions, was no part of the original contract, and amounted to no more than an intention to authorize gratuitous carriage of appellant from Brighton Beach out. Such intention was, however, not carried out, the conductor was not so authorized, appellant presented no evidence of right ta free passage, and, in any event, such passage would have been without consideration from appellant to support a contract, and, in the absence of injury from excessive force used to expel him from the car, or from other inexcusable negligence, would furnish no ground for recovery.

We regard this case as wholly unlike that of *Lawshe v. Tacoma Railway & Power Co.,* 29 Wash. 681, 70 Pac. 118, 59 L. R. A. 350, cited by appellant. In that case the system of transferring from one car to another, under payment of a single fare, prevailed, and an actual contract for such a transfer and passage was made; but the conductor of the first car, having made the transfer check read over the wrong line, the second conductor ejected the passenger. It was held that the passenger had, in consideration of the fare paid, and of his application for a proper transfer check, an actual contract for continuous passage, and was therefore wrongfully ejected. We have seen, however, that in the case at bar there was no contract for continuous passage, and it was therefore limited to the extent of the run of the car upon which the fare was paid. We believe the court did not err in granting the nonsuit.

Error is assigned upon the court's refusal to admit evidence touching the general character and disposition of the conductor who ejected appellant. We think this was properly rejected, since his conduct and disposition, as manifested upon the particular occasion, were the only proper subjects for inquiry. Moreover, appellant's complaint does not allege, as a ground of recovery, the employment of an incompetent conductor, but it is based merely upon an alleged breach of contract for carriage.

It is assigned that the court erred in striking certain evidence relating to car schedules. Even if we consider all of that evidence, we are unable to see that it affects the actual contract hereinbefore discussed, and which the court must have considered in granting the nonsuit. While it may be true that the car appellant boarded left Seattle about the time a car ordinarily left for points beyond Hillman City, still there is, we think, no room for argument under the evidence that this particular car was started for points beyond Hillman City, and appellant made no inquiry as to the destination of the car.

The judgment is affirmed.

FULLERTON, C. J., and ANDERS, MOUNT, and DUNBAR, JJ., concur.

[No. 5030. Decided July 13, 1904.]

FRED A. COOKE, *Appellant*, v. JOHN CAIN *et al., Respondents.*[1]

PLEADINGS—AMENDMENT—MISTAKE IN ANSWER—NECESSITY OF AFFIDAVITS AND NOTICE—SURPRISE. Where, after sustaining demurrers to defendants' affirmative defenses, an action based upon a written contract went to trial upon issues raised by general denials, it was not error to permit the defendants to file a trial amendment setting up affirmatively an oral rescission of the contract and the substitution of an oral agreement providing a different consideration which was paid in full, without requiring an affidavit and notice to the plaintiff under Bal. Code, §4953, where it appeared by sworn statements of the defendants as witnesses that a mistake was made in the first attempt to draw the answer, and the plaintiff had early notice at the trial of the defendants' claim and defense, and no continuance was asked and no claim made that the plaintiff was surprised.

APPEAL—REVIEW—EVIDENCE ON TRIAL DE NOVO. The erroneous admission of testimony is not ground for a reversal where on appeal there is a trial *de novo*.

EVIDENCE—WRITTEN CONTRACT—ORAL RESCISSION—UNCORROBORATED TESTIMONY OF A PARTY—FINDINGS ON CONFLICTING EVIDENCE. It seems that the uncorroborated testimony of a party may establish that a written contract was orally rescinded, the only requirement being that the testimony be "clear, cogent and convincing," and a finding of a rescission based wholly on oral evidence will not be disturbed upon conflicting testimony, where a corroborating circumstance supports the finding and the trial court had the demeanor of the witnesses for a guide.

Appeal from a judgment of the superior court for Clallam county, Hatch, J., entered July 27, 1903, upon findings in favor of the defendants, after a trial on the merits before the court without a jury, dismissing an action for an accounting and a balance due for commissions. Affirmed.

[1]Reported in 77 Pac. 682.

Trumbull & Trumbull, for appellant.

William Ritchie and *G. M. Emory*, for respondents.

HADLEY, J.—Appellant brought this action against respondents and alleged, that, at the times mentioned, the latter composed a copartnership, doing business as dealers in real estate, under the firm name of Cain Investment Company, with their principal place of business in the city of Port Angeles, Washington; that on the 23d day of January, 1900, and for many years prior thereto, appellant was a resident of the city of Boston, Massachusetts; that on said date respondent Cain was in said city of Boston, representing said firm in the business of selling real estate situate in the city of Port Angeles and vicinity, and was endeavoring to effect sales in Boston; that on said date appellant entered into a written agreement with said firm, the essential part of the memorandum of which is as follows:

"Port Angeles, Wash., January 23rd, 1900.

"Memorandum of Agreement by and between John Cain of Port Angeles, Washington, and Dr. Fred A. Cooke, of Boston, Mass. It is agreed between the parties hereto that John Cain will pay to Dr. Fred A. Cooke fifty per cent of all profits and commissions of such sales of Port Angeles real estate as said Dr. Cooke is instrumental in bringing about or assists said Cain in consummating.
                                                "John Cain."

The complaint then enumerates numerous sales alleged to have been effected through the assistance of appellant, stating the amounts for which the respective lots and parcels were sold. It is also alleged that the respondents represented certain amounts as the cost prices at Port Angeles and vicinity of the various lots and tracts, which amounts are set forth in the complaint, and that appellant has been paid one-half the difference between the said several amounts and the selling prices of the, respective tracts. It is further averred that respondents falsely represented to appellant the actual cost of said real estate; that in each instance such actual cost was less than the represented amount, and that such false representations were made for the purpose of defrauding appellant out of his just share of the profits arising from the sales under said contract. It is averred that, prior to the making of said sales, appellant had never been in Port Angeles or the state of Washington, and knew nothing of real estate values in said city and vicinity, except as stated to him by respondents; that all of said sales were made prior to the 1st day of February, 1901, and that appellant did not discover the false representations as to the cost of said property until after he came to Port Angeles in October, 1901; that about July 1, 1902, he demanded of respondents an accounting of the profits and commissions actually arising from said sales, but that they have refused and neglected to so account. The complaint concludes with a prayer for an accounting to determine the amount due appellant under said contract, and that he be given judgment against respondents for the amount so found to be due.

The respondents first answered the complaint separately, each denying all allegations of the complaint, and respondent Cain further answered affirmatively that, on or about said 23d day of January, 1900, at Boston, he entered into an agreement with appellant, whereby he agreed to pay him fifty per cent of all net profits upon sales of real estate situate within the city of Port Angeles which appellant might assist in consummating. A list of lands and lots sold, located within the city of Port Angeles, is then set out, together with the alleged cost

thereof to said Cain, the selling price, and the amount
of the difference, one-half of which it is alleged has been
paid to appellant, and accepted by him in full satisfaction
of all demands.   A further affirmative defense of said
Cain's first answer is to the effect that the sales of lands
outside of the city of Port Angeles were not included in
said contract, and that appellant has been fully paid on
account of all sales of outside lands.

Appellant demurred to the said affirmative defenses of
respondent Cain's first answer, and the demurrer was
sustained.   The purpose of mentioning these pleadings
will more fully appear hereinafter.   Respondents did
not further plead affirmatively at that time, and the cause
then went to trial before the court without a jury, upon
the issues formed by the complaint and the general denials of the separate answers.   At the conclusion of the
plaintiff's testimony, the court denied a motion for nonsuit, and stated that, as the evidence then stood, the plaintiff was entitled to recover.   This occurred on the 16th
day of May, 1903, and, by reason of an approaching
jury session, the court at this juncture postponed the further trial of the cause until June 5, 1903, at which
time the trial was resumed.   Before proceeding with the
trial, however, respondents on the said day asked and obtained leave to file an amended answer.   The permission
was granted over the urgent protest of appellant.

The amended answer was jointly made by the respondents, and admitted that respondent Cain did, on or about
January 23, 1900, subscribe and deliver the writing set
forth in the complaint, but averred, that said memorandum of agreement was never acted upon by any of the
parties, and that no sales were made thereunder; that said
agreement was, in the month of October, 1900, by the

parties thereto, mutually abandoned; that, subsequent to
said abandonment, the respondents entered into an oral
agreement with appellant, whereby he agreed to assist
them in selling various parcels of real estate in Clallam
county, Washington; that it was agreed that the specific
parcels of property should be furnished to appellant at
certain and definite prices, from which fixed prices appellant's commissions should be ascertained; that it was
agreed that appellant should receive as commissions one-
half of the difference between the selling prices and the
prices specifically agreed upon, at which the parcels of
land should be furnished; that the prices agreed upon
were, in each instance, the same as those alleged in the
complaint to have been represented as the cost prices;
that the prices for which the lands sold were the same
as the amounts alleged in the complaint as the prices for
which they were sold; and that appellant has been fully
paid all his share of commissions, under the terms of said
agreement. The trial thereafter proceeded under the issues formed by the complaint and amended answer. Respondents introduced evidence to support the new answer,
and appellant introduced rebuttal testimony. The court
made findings of facts substantially in accord with the
amended answer, and concluded that the agreement under the written memorandum was abandoned and rescinded by the alleged subsequent oral agreement, and
that all commissions under the new oral agreement had
been paid. Judgment was entered dismissing the action,
and the plaintiff has appealed.

Appellant assigns as error that the court permitted the
amended answer to be filed after the plaintiff had rested
his case. This point is urged at great length in the
briefs, and counsel manifest much earnestness in the

argument. It is urged that the court had no authority to
allow an amendment of this character, without notice to
appellant and without a showing by affidavit, and we are
referred to § 4953, Bal. Code, in support of this position. Counsel maintain that the proposed amendment
could not come within the first part of the section relating to the correction of mistakes, and that an affidavit
showing good cause, after notice to the adverse party,
became necessary to establish any right to the amendment
under the latter part of the section. This section has
ordinarily received a very liberal construction. The first
part relates not only to amendments with reference to
correcting names, but also to "mistake in any other respect," when it may be "in furtherance of justice." During the introduction of testimony on behalf of appellant,
both respondents were placed upon the witness stand by
appellant, and Mr. Cain testified at that time that the
real estate was sold under another and oral agreement,
made about nine months after the written memorandum
was made. It thus became manifest, at that early stage
of the trial, from an examination conducted by appellant's
own counsel, that respondents' position was that the written agreement had been rescinded and superseded by another and oral one.

It will be remembered that, in respondent Cain's first
affirmative defense, an agreement was pleaded to the effect that the commissions were to be based upon an equal
division of "net profits." The court sustained a demurrer to that defense, apparently, from what the record discloses, upon the theory that the agreement named
in it was the same as that set out in the complaint, inasmuch as the date laid for it was the same as that alleged
in the complaint. It seems to us, however, that the legal

effect of the two is not necessarily the same. That alleged in the complaint is based merely upon "profits," which is susceptible of the construction placed upon it by appellant, viz., that the profits meant should include the difference between the actual cost and selling prices; whereas, the contract alleged in the answer is based upon "net profits," which may be construed to mean what is left, after deducting from the selling price the actual cost price together with all expenses incidental to the procurement of the property in the first instance and to its sale thereafter. It is contended by respondents that their expenses were large, including the expenses of an almost continuous sojourn of Mr. Cain in Boston, for the purpose of effecting sales. They claim that appellant's assistance was rendered chiefly by way of introducing persons to Mr. Cain, but that the conclusive work of making the sales was done by the latter, and such in effect is admitted by appellant. It therefore appears to us that the court may have overlooked the above mentioned difference between the two alleged contracts, in ruling upon the demurrer to the first affirmative answer of Mr. Cain, and may have been misled to the conclusion that the two contracts were the same, by the fact that the same date was laid for both.

We make these observations by way of trying to make it clear that the first verified answer is not, in its legal effect, necessarily inconsistent with the last answer, wherein it is specifically averred that the agreement evidenced by the written memorandum was rescinded by a subsequent oral agreement. That being true, and it having already appeared in the testimony that respondents claimed that such rescission had been made about nine months after the date of the written memorandum, whereas, the date alleged for it in the pleading was the same as that of the former, it is evident that some mistake existed with reference to the pleading, and we think the court did not err in permitting it to be corrected by amendment. Evidence was afterwards introduced with reference to the inception of the mistake. It is true, this was not before the court at the time of the ruling upon the application for leave to amend, but it serves to emphasize the view that a mistake existed, and that the court did not err in allowing its correction from what already appeared in the record, without affidavit and without notice to appellant. The latter was already advised of respondents' position by what had appeared in the testimony, brought out by his own examination of Mr. Cain.

The testimony concerning the mistake, in its inception, to which we refer, was given by the two respondents, and by two of their counsel, Judge McClinton and Mr. Ritchie, who represented respondents at the beginning of the litigation. Each of these witnesses testified that the respondents, at all times, including their first interview with counsel, stated the facts about the subsequent oral agreement and their claim that all the property was sold under it. Just how the error in date, and the failure to more specifically state the terms of the new contract, occurred, counsel were unable to say, but all agreed that counsel had drawn the answer under some misapprehension, and that a mistake had manifestly been made. Mr. Cain stated that he did not observe the error in the date, and, not knowing the legal effect of the answer, relied upon counsel therefor, and verified the pleading.

In view of the existence of all these circumstances, we think good cause appeared in the record by way of sworn

testimony, which was as forcible as a formal affidavit
could have been, and that, under the latter part of § 4953,
supra, the amendment was authorized, even if we should
not take into account the authority to correct a mistake
given by the first part of the section. Appellant cites
cases to the effect that, at so late a stage in the progress
of a cause, amendments will not be permitted which radi-
cally change the theory of the former pleadings. From
what we have already said, we think the legal effect of the
amended pleading was not fundamentally different from
the first, in its bearing upon the written contract, and
that this case does not come within the rule invoked, particularly since respondents themselves asserted to their
counsel, from the beginning, the position stated in the
amended answer, and relied upon them for its maintenance by the necessary pleading in the premises. Appellant at no time, not even after all the testimony concerning the mistake was introduced, asked for a continuance
on the ground of surprise, and it is not contended that he
would, under any circumstances, have been able to produce other testimony than that which was introduced by
him. Hard and fast rules concerning amendments in
furtherance of justice during the progress of a trial cannot
well be established. The trial court must be vested with
much discretion, and exercise of that discretion will not
be disturbed, unless it appears that the adverse party has
been prejudiced and surprised, and makes timely objection for relief on such grounds. The above rule has not
only been sustained by this court in repeated decisions,
but, among many others which might be cited, we refer
to the following in support of the rule: *Aultman & Taylor Co. v. Shelton,* 90 Iowa 288, 57 N. W. 857; *Burns
v. Fox,* 113 Ind. 205, 14 N. E. 541; *Osborne & Co.*

v. Williams, 37 Minn. 507, 35 N. W. 371; *Hedges v. Roach,* 16 Neb. 673, 21 N. W. 404; *McPherson v. Weston,* 85 Cal. 90, 24 Pac. 733; *Excelsior Mfg. Co. v. Boyle,* 46 Kan. 202, 26 Pac. 408. We have given much space to the discussion of the subject of the amendment for the reason that the attendant circumstances, urged by appellant as the basis of error, could not well be made clear without it, and for the further reason that counsel have so earnestly and extensively pursued that subject, both in the opening and reply briefs.

Errors are assigned upon the rejection and introduction of certain testimony. We do not believe the rejection of testimony became prejudicial, in view of evidence that was admitted, and we think no good purpose will be served by a detailed discussion of it. Referring to testimony which it is claimed was erroneously admitted, it is sufficient to say that this court has often held that, in a trial *de novo,* it will not disturb findings of the trial court merely because immaterial or incompetent testimony may have been admitted, when, in its opinion, there is sufficient competent testimony to support the findings.

It is next vigorously urged that certain of the material findings are not supported by the evidence. Both respondents testified, in support of the facts alleged in the amended answer, to the effect that an oral agreement to rescind the written one was made in October, 1900, that a new oral one was then made, and that the sales were all made under the new agreement. Appellant denied that such new agreement was made. If the testimony of respondents is to be accepted as the truth, then appellant's commissions have been fully paid by the $7,000, and more, already received by him. If, however, appellant's testimony is correct, then he is entitled to recover about $6,000 more. There seems to be no way of harmonizing the testimony. It is that of two parties upon one side, against one upon the other, and all are vitally interested in the result of the litigation.

Appellant urges that the uncorroborated oral evidence of a party should not be held to be sufficient proof that a written contract has been orally rescinded. We find that a few of the cases practically go so far as to announce such a rule, but the language of most of the opinions is restricted to the statement, in effect, that the oral evidence necessary must be "clear, cogent, and convincing," as against the party who denies it, and who seeks to sustain the writing. In *Quinn v. Parke & Lacy Mach. Co.*, 9 Wash. 136, 37 Pac. 288, this court, in a majority opinion, used somewhat strong language declaratory of the rule contended for by appellant. The application of the rule so broadly stated seems not to have been required in that case, since the opinion states that there was no evidence to sustain the allegations concerning a rescission except the mere assertion of one that the machinery was not delivered under the written agreement, there being actually no testimony, by even a party, that an *agreement* to rescind was made. Appellant also cites the opinion of this court in *Western Loan & Sav. Co. v. Waisman*, 32 Wash. 644, 73 Pac. 703, where we refused to hold that a certificate of acknowledgment had been impeached by the uncorroborated testimony of two mortgagors. We, however, based the decision upon the view that a certificate of acknowledgment is a record of an official act of such dignity and importance that it ought not, for reasons of public security, to be held that it may be overcome by the mere uncorroborated testimony of an interested party.

Were we now confronted with a case with no corroboration whatever to support the testimony of parties, we

should hesitate to say that rescission is not established for
the mere reason alone that such corroboration may be
lacking.   It seems to us that the application of an inflexi-
ble rule of that kind might, in some cases, preclude the
doing of what the courts may be firmly convinced should
be done, and that the deciding mind should, in each case,
be free to accept that which is "clear, cogent, and convincing," even though it be the testimony of a party only.
It is none the less true, however, that such testimony
should be scrutinized with great care and caution, and
its convincing force must depend upon the character of
the witnesses and the circumstances of each case.   Indeed, in most of the cases there are probably attending
circumstances which may, of themselves, be either cor-
roborative of the testimony of the party, or may weigh
against it.   In the case at bar there is one circumstance
which, to our minds, tends to corroborate respondents.
It is this: Both respondents testify that in October,
1900, about nine months after the date of the written
memorandum, they met the appellant in the Adams hotel
in Boston; that respondent Hartt and appellant had never
met before, and, during the first conversation between
the two in the hotel office, appellant disclosed to Mr. Hartt
that he understood his commissions were to be based upon
an equal division of the difference between actual original
cost prices at Port Angeles and the selling prices in Boston; that Mr. Hartt had not before known of the written
contract or its terms, it having been made by Mr. Cain;
that Hartt at once, in vigorous language and in a boisterous manner, declared he would not abide by such an
arrangement; that Cain, hearing the two, and wishing to
avoid a further scene in the hotel office, got them in the
elevator and took them to his room; that there Cain took

up the conversation, and said to appellant that they could
not work under the agreement he had made with him
in the previous January, for the reason that their expenses were so heavy in procuring property at Port Angeles, and his own traveling and hotel expenses in Boston,
together with expenses of entertaining customers in order
to effect sales, were so great that they would have to add
a sum to the original cost price in each instance, at least
sufficient to cover these expenses, and put the property
to appellant at definite and agreed prices which he should
accept, and that he should receive one-half the difference
between the prices thus fixed and the selling prices; that
appellant, after some further conversation, agreed to accept the new proposition, and all three then agreed upon
said terms. Now, appellant admits the above details of
the first interview between himself and Hartt, and that
Cain, after he got the two to his room, took up the conversation; but he says that Cain was endeavoring to convince Hartt that the written agreement was all right. He
does not say, however, that Hartt ever acquiesced in such
view, and, from the admitted temper of his mind at
that time, it seems extremely improbable that he did so. In
view of the fact that the commissions were earned after
that time, and inasmuch as appellant admits that this
vigorous and seemingly unyielding protest was made by
Hartt before the sales were made, it seems the more
reasonable to us that respondents' version of the result
of that interview is the true one. We shall therefore not
disturb the findings of the trial court, who had these parties before him, and, in addition to the spoken testimony
and circumstances we have mentioned, had, also, the demeanor of the parties for a guide to such impressions
as may be instinctively gathered from the manner of
a witness, and which an appellate court cannot observe.

The conclusions of law and judgment follow from the findings. We believe no prejudicial error appears, and the judgment is affirmed.

FULLERTON, C. J., and ANDERS, MOUNT, and DUNBAR, JJ., concur.

[No. 4980. Decided July 14, 1904.]

LUCIEN H. ALEXANDER, *Appellant*, v. CITY OF TACOMA et al., *Respondents.*[1]

MUNICIPAL CORPORATIONS — LOCAL IMPROVEMENTS — ASSESS-MENTS—HEARING ON OBJECTIONS—PROMISE OF CITY TO GIVE NOTICE OF ADJOURNMENT. Where proceedings are instituted before a city council to reassess property for local improvements and, pending a hearing thereon, adjournments are taken, and the city officials promise an objector to give notice of the time to be thereafter set for the hearing, the promise relates only to the pending proceeding, and not to a subsequent proceeding begun after the abandonment of the first.

SAME—INDEFINITE ADJOURNMENT—RIGHT TO RELY ON PROMISE OF NOTICE. A property owner objecting to proceedings to reassess property has no right to rely upon an oral promise made by city officials that he would be given notice of the time to be thereafter set for hearing his objections, after the hearing had been adjourned to an indefinite date.

SAME—OBJECTIONS TO BE MADE BEFORE CITY COUNCIL. Objections to assessment proceedings not going to the jurisdiction must be made before the city council on the hearing pending the confirmation of the proceedings.

SAME—OBJECTIONS NOT GOING TO JURISDICTION—WAIVER. Objections to a local improvement assessment, that it was made without regard to benefits, that it exceeded the actual cost, that it included the cost of future repairs, and exceeded the benefits, do not go to the jurisdiction of the council to make a reassessment under the act of 1893, and are waived if not made before the city council.

[1]Reported in 77 Pac. 686.

SAME—CONSTITUTIONAL LAW—DUE PROCESS—PROMISE OF NOTICE OF HEARING OBJECTIONS. The fact that a property owner was lulled into security by a promise of city officials to give him notice of the time to be fixed for a hearing upon his objections to an assessment for local improvements does not deprive him of his property without due process of law, where he had no right to rely upon the promise.

Ellis & Fletcher and *Arthur Remington,* for appellant.

Emmett N. Parker, Harvey L. Johnson, and *E. R. York,* for respondents.

Appeal from a judgment of the superior court for Pierce county, Chapman, J., entered June 20, 1903, upon findings in favor of the defendants, after a trial on the merits before the court without a jury, dismissing an action to cancel an assessment for local improvements. Affirmed.

FULLERTON, C. J.—On May 14, 1892, the city council of the city of Tacoma passed a resolution declaring it to be its intention to improve that part of Tacoma Avenue between the center of North Fourth street and the center of North Fifth street, by "paving the roadway fifty-four (54) feet wide with bituminous rock, upon six (6) inch concrete foundations." Thereupon the city engineer made a survey of the contemplated improvement, prepared a diagram of, and specifications for, the same, and made an estimate of the cost thereof, including within his survey, diagram, specifications, and estimate of cost, 640 lineal feet of eight foot walk, and 677 lineal feet of concrete curb, not mentioned in the resolution of the city council. Bids for the work according to the diagrams and specifications of the city engineer were advertised for, and a contract let to the lowest bidder thereon, being for the sum of $5,795. Included in this contract was a clause by which the contractor guaranteed to keep the pavement in repair for a period of five years. The contractor entered immediately upon the performance of the work, and completed the same about the middle of September, 1892. Thereupon the city council levied an assessment upon the property benefited, to pay the cost of the work, in the sum of $5,800, or five dollars in excess of the contract price.

On January 28, 1893, and after the city officers had commenced proceedings to enforce collection of the assessment, one J. D. McAllister brought an action against the city to restrain collection of the assessment, and to cancel the same. Issue was taken on the allegations of the complaint, a trial had, and a judgment entered dismissing the action. This judgment was reversed on appeal to this court (9 Wash. 272, 37 Pac. 447), and the cause remanded, with instructions to enter a judgment cancelling the assessment.

On February 15, 1896, the city council attempted a reassessment of the property, under the act of 1893, by passing an ordinance authorizing such a reassessment. Under this ordinance a reassessment was made by the assessing officers, according to benefits, the officers finding that the several lots were benefited equally, and to an amount equal to the original assessment. After the assessment roll had been returned, notice was given of the filing of the same and a time fixed when objections thereto would be heard. The appellant, within the time required, filed objection to the assessment, and at the time fixed appeared to contest the same, when the hearing was postponed by the committee of the council having the matter in charge, to a day certain, and on the latter day to no fixed date, but with the understanding that it might be called up after notice to the parties interested. Nothing further

was done in the matter until July 11, 1896, when the city
council, without notice to the appellant, dismissed the
proceedings by repealing the ordinance authorizing the
assessment. At this same date a new ordinance was
introduced, providing for a reassessment of the property,
which passed the council on July 18, 1896. This last
ordinance was in turn repealed on July 15, 1897, and
on July 18, 1897, the council passed ordinance No. 1214,
being the fourth ordinance providing for an assessment
of the property benefited, and the ordinance under which
the assessment now in question was made.

This last ordinance recited, among other things, the
making of the original improvement and the original
assessment to pay the cost of the same; the fact that the
original assessment was approved and confirmed by the
city council, but was thereafter declared void by the
courts; and that it was intended, by the ordinance in
question, to reassess the property to pay the cost of the
original improvements, reciting further that the cost of
the improvement was $5,800. The ordinance directed
that an assessment be made by the commissioner of public
works on the lots benefited by the improvement, in an
equitable manner according to benefits, to an amount
equal to the cost of improvement, as recited in the ordinance, and interest thereon from November 30, 1892, at
the legal rate.

The officer named in the ordinance made a new assessment in accordance therewith, valuing the benefits to
the several lots equally, and at sums the aggregate of
which equaled the amount of the original costs and interest, as directed in the ordinance. On the filing of the
assessment roll with the city clerk, that officer caused
to be published the required notice of the time and place

when and where objections thereto could be heard. On
the day fixed for the hearing, no objection having been
filed, the city council examined the roll, and by ordinance
approved and confirmed the assessment, as made by the
commissioner, and directed that the city treasurer proceed to collect the same. No notice, other than that required by statute, was given the appellant of any of these
subsequent proceedings, and he had no actual notice
thereof until after the actual proceedings had been confirmed by the city council, and his right of appeal therefrom to the superior court had expired.

The appellant owns a lot abutting upon the improved
street, which is among the lots assessed to pay for the
improvement, and he brings this action asking the court
to direct that the city council reopen the assessment proceedings, and, after permitting the appellant to file his
objections thereto, reconsider and rehear the matter in the
light of such objections, the same as if they had been
presented in due time at an original hearing; and, in the
meantime, enjoin a sale of the property. He contends
that, because he once appeared before the city council
in opposition to the reassessment, and was promised by
the city officers that his counsel should be personally
notified of the subsequent proceedings taken in the matters
then pending, he was entitled to be personally notified of
the last attempt at reassessment, and that the failure
of the city officers to so notify him or his counsel of such
attempt was so far arbitrary and in fraud of his rights
as to require a vacation of the order confirming the assessment, notwithstanding the city proceeded with reference
to giving notice in accordance with the statute, and
actually gave such notice as is therein required. The
appellant also contends that the superior court is the

proper forum in which to urge this objection, and that that court, as a court possessing powers of an equitable nature, has the right to grant the relief demanded.

Whether or not the proposition last mentioned is sound in law we shall not now stop to inquire, as it is manifest that such a power will not be exercised until the applicant has made a reasonably clear case calling for its exercise, and it seems plain to us that the record here does not present such a case. The appellant's claim that he was prevented from having a hearing on his objections to the reassessment, before the city council, by the arbitrary action of the city authorities, is rested solely on the oral promise that his counsel should be notified personally of any subsequent proceedings, made by certain of the city officers at the time the hearing on the first attempt to reassess was continued indefinitely. It seems to us, from an examination of the evidence, that the promise related only to the proceedings then pending, and meant that notice would be given the appellant before any action looking to the completion of those proceedings should be taken. It could hardly have meant that notice would be given of an abandonment of the proceedings. To defeat the proceedings, was the purpose of the objections made by the appellant, and when the city confessed the soundness of the objections, by dismissing and abandoning its attempt to perfect the proceedings, notice of such abandonment could have been of no benefit to the appellant; the thing he desired was accomplished. Hence, it would seem that, if the promise was one which bound the city, there was no breach thereof.

But there is another and broader ground on which the contention must be denied. The promise was not one on which the appellant had a right to rely. The conduct

of public officers is governed by fixed rules, prescribed
by public statutes, beyond which the officers cannot go
and bind the public interests, and their promises outside
of their prescribed duties are no more binding on the
public than are the promises of strangers, and one relying
thereon does so at his peril. He may possibly have a
remedy against the individual making the promise, but
he cannot successfully claim the right to arrest the performance of a public duty, which is being performed in
the statutory way, because the officers have promised him
that some other or additional conditions, not required by
the statute, will be complied with, before such performance will be attempted. Public policy forbids such a rule,
and requires that statutory duties be performed in the
statutory way.

The appellant stands, therefore, as one making a collateral attack upon the assessment proceedings, and his
rights are governed by the rules applicable to that form
of attack. The statute governing reassessment proceedings gives to the order of the city council confirming
such proceedings the conclusiveness of a judgment of a
court, and we have repeatedly held the statute valid in
that regard. In *Lewis v. Seattle*, 28 Wash. 639, 69 Pac.
293, we said:

"This court has repeatedly held that all questions affecting the assessment proceedings, not going to the jurisdiction of the municipality to make the assessment, must
be taken before the city council on the hearing pending
the confirmation of the assessment proceedings by that
body, and appealed therefrom to the courts, before the
courts have authority to inquire as to mere error therein."

And see, *New Whatcom v. Bellingham Bay Imp. Co.*, 16
Wash. 131, 47 Pac. 236; *New Whatcom v. Bellingham Bay
Imp. Co.*, 18 Wash. 181, 51 Pac. 360; *Heath v. McCrea*,

20 Wash. 342, 55 Pac. 432; *Annie Wright Seminary v. Tacoma*, 23 Wash. 109, 62 Pac. 444; *McNamee v. Tacoma*, 24 Wash. 591, 64 Pac. 791; *Potter v. Whatcom*, 25 Wash. 207, 65 Pac. 197; *Tacoma, etc. Paving Co. v. Sternberg*, 26 Wash. 84, 66 Pac. 121.

It remains, then, to inquire whether the matters complained of as affecting the assessment are such as go to the jurisdiction of the city council, or whether such matters are, if errors at all, errors committed in the exercise of acknowledged jurisdiction. The objections made in the brief against the validity of the assessment are these: (1) that it was made without regard to benefits; (2) that it was for more than the actual cost of the improvements; (3) that it includes the cost of future repairs for five years; (4) that the amount imposed upon the appellant's lot exceeds the benefits conferred on that lot; and (5) that the appellant is about to be deprived of his property without due process of law because the notice given of the assessment was not such as is contemplated by law, and insufficient under the peculiar circumstances of this particular case.

With regard to the first objection, it is not disputed that the assessment is purported to have been made according to benefits, and that the city council found that it was so made, but it is said that this finding is merely colorable and perfunctory, because it appears that all of the lots were assessed alike, and for the precise amount they were assessed for when the apportionment was made according to the front foot plan, and concededly without reference to benefits. It seems to us, however, that these facts argue nothing. Surely it cannot be denied that a possible condition could exist where an improvement of a street would benefit all of the lots thereon precisely alike, yet it must be so denied in order to overturn this

assessment in this proceeding. The assessment to be
overturned in this proceeding must be void on its face,
and it could only be void for the reason here given on
the theory that under no conceivable conditions could
lots abutting upon an improvement be equally benefited
thereby. But so far from this being impossible, it would
seem that it would be found to actually exist in many
instances. To pave and curb a street which has already
been brought to grade, and the abutting property built
upon with reference thereto, would seem rather to benefit
each part of it alike than otherwise, especially where, as
in this case, no unusual or special conditions are shown
to exist.

It appears by the terms of the contract that the actual
cost of the improvement was $5,795, while the reassess-
ment was for $5,800, or $5 more than the original cost.
On this discrepancy the second objection is founded. In
tax sales, where the proceedings were wholly ex parte,
courts have set aside titles acquired thereunder apparently
for some not very substantial reasons, and cases can be
found where differences even less than are shown here
have been held to avoid the proceedings. The reasoning
on which such judgments are justified, however, has no
application to proceedings such as our statutes prescribe.
They were rendered in cases where the proceedings were
such that no opportunity was given to make the objection
until after the sale. Such is not the fact here. The
appellant had the right to appear before the city council
and make this objection. Had he done so doubtless it
would have been corrected. But having failed to appear
and make the objection he must be deemed to have waived
it. *Tumwater v. Pix*, 18 Wash. 153, 51 Pac. 353.

The third objection is that the reassessment included
the cost of keeping the street in repair for a period of

five years from the time the work was completed. It was
held in *McAllister v. Tacoma*, 9 Wash. 272, 37 Pac. 447,
658, that the city could not contract for such a result
originally, and create a lien for such cost, because its
charter did not authorize it to do so. But it was pointed
out in that case (see opinion on petition for rehearing),
that the statute under which this reassessment was made
was passed to cure defects of this very character. And
we have since held that the act of 1893 was passed for the
purpose of permitting a reassessment of property benefited by a street improvement, the original assessment
for which might be invalid under the existing laws, no
matter what might have been the defect in the law which
caused the invalidity of the original assessment. *Frederick v. Seattle*, 13 Wash. 428, 43 Pac. 364; *Lewis v.
Seattle*, 28 Wash. 639, 69 Pac. 393. To include in the
assessment items not proper to be included therein does
not render the assessment void, or subject it to collateral
attack. As the city had power to make the reassessment,
the objection that it was made for too much, must, to
be available, be taken before the city council when it
sits to hear objections to the assessment. *Young v. Tacoma*, 31 Wash. 153, 71 Pac. 742.

The fourth objection is without merit for the reason
last stated. If it be true that the assessment exceeded the
benefits conferred on the appellant's property by the improvement, the objection should have been urged before
the city council. It is not a matter for a collateral attack
on the assessment proceedings.

The last objection, namely, that the appellant is being
deprived of his property without due process of law, we
think is also without merit. It is not contended that the
notice provided by the statute is not sufficient in itself

to constitute due process of law, nor is it contended that such notice was not given. It is argued that the notice was insufficient, in this particular case, because the appellant was lulled into security by the promise of the city officers and was not, for that reason, as diligent as he might otherwise have been. We have heretofore in this opinion attempted to show that this promise was one on which the appellant had no right to rely, and, if it be true that he had no right to rely on the promise, no question of due process of law is involved in the failure of the city officers to give it.

We conclude, therefore, that however pertinent the objections urged might be were we permitted to review the proceedings for mere error, they are insufficient to render them void; and, as they are not void, they cannot be overturned in this form of attack. The judgment appealed from is affirmed.

HADLEY, ANDERS, MOUNT and DUNBAR, JJ., concur.

[No. 4943. Decided July 14, 1904.]

RICHARD O'CONNELL et al., Respondents, v. CHARLES BAKER et al., as the Board of County Commissioners, etc., Appellants.[1]

COUNTIES AND COUNTY OFFICERS—DRAINAGE DISTRICTS—ESTABLISHMENT—PETITION SIGNED BY COUNTY—CONFLICTING DUTIES OF COUNTY COMMISSIONERS—DISQUALIFICATION. A board of county commissioners cannot be permanently enjoined from entertaining a petition for the establishment of a drainage district, because the county and the chairman of the board, on behalf of the county, signed the petition praying for the establishment of the district, since a subsequent board could not be thereby disqualified; neither is the present board disqualified because the

[1]Reported in 77 Pac. 678.

statute may have imposed conflicting duties upon the board, since
the power to act is expressly conferred by the statute, and the
members of the board, as individuals, are not interested in the
result.

Appeal from a judgment of the superior court for King
county, Hon. William H. Brinker, Judge *pro tempore,*
entered May 13, 1903, upon overruling a demurrer to the
complaint, enjoining the county commissioners from entertaining a petition to establish a drainage district; and,
also, from an order entered July 6, 1903, adjudging that
the defendants had violated said judgment. Reversed.

Ballinger, Ronald & Battle, for appellants.

George McKay and *Preston, Carr & Gilman,* for respondents.

FULLERTON, C. J.—On April 30, 1903, after due notice
given as required by statute, Allen Clark and others presented a petition to the board of county commissioners of
King county, praying for the organization into a drainage
district of certain territory particularly described in the
petition. Among the signatures to the petition was the
following: "Charles Baker, chairman of board of commissioners, owner of 4½ acres in proposed district." The
petition, however, was signed by persons owning a majority of the acreage of the proposed district without including the four and one-half acres here mentioned. On
the day fixed for the presentation of the petition to the
board, the respondents appeared before that body and
moved a dismissal of the petition, on the grounds, as
stated in the motion, that the board had no jurisdiction
to hear the petition, and was interested in the result, and
therefore disqualified to hear the same. This motion was
overruled by the board, whereupon the respondents brought

this action to enjoin the board from proceeding further with the matter.

The complaint sets out the proceedings had up to that time, copying the petition for the establishment of the drainage district in full, showing the signature of Charles Baker thereto, and avers: "That the said board is a party petitioner in the said petition, and is a party interested in the granting of the said petition, and has, as such board, requested and petitioned itself to grant the prayer of such petition, and the said Charles H. Baker, as chairman of said board, and by direction of said board, and on behalf of said board, signed the said petition." The complaint concluded with pertinent allegations showing the interest of the complainants in the subject-matter of the petition. A general demurrer to the complaint was interposed by the appellants, and overruled by the court, a judge *pro tempore* presiding. The appellants then refused to plead further, whereupon the court entered a judgment forever restraining and enjoining them from proceeding further with the organization of the drainage district, or from taking any further steps or proceedings therein.

Immediately after the entry of the judgment, another petition for the establishment of a drainage district was prepared and presented to the board of county commissioners. This petition was precisely like the first one, with the exception that it was not signed by Charles Baker. The board was proceeding to take action thereon, when the respondents instituted proceedings against them to restrain them from so doing, before the attorney, sitting as judge of the court, who presided as judge *pro tempore* in the original action. Objection was made to the attorney hearing the cause as judge, this motion was overruled, and afterwards an order was entered holding the members of the board to be acting in violation of the original injunction. This appeal is from both the original judgment, and the order adjudging the commissioners to have violated the same.

From the foregoing statement, it will be observed that the complaint does not make it clear just what matter it was thought disqualified the board of county commissioners from entertaining the petition for the establishment of the drainage district, but the parties in their briefs have interpreted it to mean that the county of King owned the four and one-half acres of land, mentioned in connection with the signature of Charles Baker, and that Baker, as chairman of the board, was petitioning on behalf of the county, and it is in this manner we shall interpret the complaint. The question presented, then, is this: Is a board of county commissioners forever disqualified from entertaining a petition for the establishment of a drainage district, because the county of which they are commissioners owns land in the proposed drainage district, and the chairman of such board, on behalf of such county, has signed a petition praying for the establishment of the district? It would seem that to state the proposition was to refute it. The only possible ground upon which the disqualification could be urged against the existing board is that they, by the signature of their chairman, became parties to the proceedings, and to subsequently sit in judgment on the petition would be to become judges in their own cause. But if it were conceded that this fact disqualified the present board, it could hardly be successfully contended that this taint would follow the office, and forever disqualify any subsequent board from entertaining such a petition. The judgment appealed from would therefore have to be reversed because too sweeping in its terms, if for no other reason.

But we think it wrong as applied to the present board and the present petition. The allegations of the complaint, when given their broadest signification, simply present a case where the board of county commissioners as officers may be said to be charged with conflicting duties. As county commissioners they are charged with the conduct of the business of the county, and are the conservators of its property, and it is their duty to act in reference thereto so as to best subserve and protect the interests confided to their charge. As county commissioners the law has vested in them certain powers, and put upon them certain duties, with reference to the establishment of drainage districts, among which is the power and duty to determine whether the proposed drainage system "will be conducive to the public health, welfare and convenience, increase the public revenue, and be of special benefit to the majority of the lands included within the boundaries of said proposed district," and it is their duty to act in that behalf, also, so as to best subserve the interests intrusted to them. In a case, therefore, where the county owns real estate in a proposed drainage district, it might be to the best interests of the county, considered with reference to such property, to establish the district, while its establishment might not be conducive to the public health, welfare or convenience, or subserve any public interest whatsoever; and, in the sense that the commissioners have the power to pass upon both of the questions, their duties are conflicting. But this is not a sufficient reason for denying them the right to act. The power to act in each instance is conferred upon them by express legislative enactment, and to deny them the right is to deny to the legislature the power to confer on them the right. We think the power of the legislature in this respect is not to be questioned, and this being so, it is not within the province of the court to interfere with their exercise of it.

The case of *State ex rel. Barnard v. Board of Education*, 19 Wash. 8, 52 Pac. 317, 40 L. R. A. 317, 67 Am. St. 706, cited and relied upon by the respondent, is not in conflict with these principles. In that case a certain member of the board, who proposed to sit as judge of the cause, had a personal interest in its result, and had publicly announced, in advance of the trial, what his judgment was going to be. In the case before us there is no allegation that the members of the board as individuals have a personal interest in the result, and they cannot, in any sense, be said to be judges of their own cause. It is not their own cause they are adjudicating, but the cause of the public, and the maxim that no one can be a judge in his own cause does not apply.

It was strenuously argued that the judge *pro tempore* in the original case had no right to sit in judgment of the subsequent proceedings, but as the conclusion reached in the main case must dispose of the subsequent proceedings, even if a valid order, we expressly refrain from deciding the point.

The judgment and order appealed from are reversed, and the cause remanded, with instructions to sustain the demurrer to the complaint.

HADLEY, ANDERS, MOUNT, and DUNBAR, JJ., concur.

[No. 4890. Decided July 14, 1904.]

C. G. JOHNSON *et al., Respondents*, v. SEATTLE ELECTRIC
COMPANY, *Appellant*.[1]

CARRIERS—NEGLIGENCE—INJURY TO PASSENGER ON STREET CAR—
DEGREE OF CARE REQUIRED OF COMPANY—INSTRUCTIONS. In an
action for personal injuries sustained by a passenger while
alighting from a street car, it is error to instruct that while the
company is not an insurer, the law calls upon it to do whatever
can be done to insure the protection of passengers, since the
company is only bound to exercise the highest degree of care
consistent with the practical conduct of its business, and such an
instruction is reversible error where it is the only one defining
the measure of defendant's duty to passengers.

Appeal from a judgment of the superior court for King
county, Albertson, J., entered May 25, 1903, upon the
verdict of a jury rendered in favor of the plaintiff, in an
action for injuries sustained in alighting from a street
car. Reversed.

Struve, Hughes & McMicken, for appellant.
Root, Palmer & Brown, for respondent.

PER CURIAM.—The appellant is a street car company,
operating a line of street cars in the city of Seattle. The
respondent Betse Johnson was a passenger on one of the
appellant's cars, and was injured while alighting therefrom. The injury is alleged to have been caused by the
negligence of the appellant's servants in suddenly starting
the car while the respondent was in the act of alighting,
and one of the principal issues in the case was whether
or not the appellant's servants were guilty in the manner
so alleged. On the question of the degree of care necessary to be exercised by a carrier of passengers, the court
gave to the jury the following instructions:

[1]Reported in 77 Pac. 677.

"Now, in arriving at a solution of the question whether the plaintiff was injured through the negligence of the defendant corporation, you must consider what was the duty of the corporation in that regard at the time, under the circumstances. A corporation engaged in the transportation of passengers is held by the law to the exercise of the highest degree of care in the equipment of its road and the manner of operation of its road. A transportation company is not an insurer of the lives or limbs of its passengers, but the law calls upon it to do whatever can be done to insure their protection while they are being transported."

This instruction is complained of, we think justly. While the jury are told that a common carrier is not an insurer of the lives and limbs of its passengers, yet they are told that it is liable if it has not done everything that could have been done to insure their safety. The rule is not so onerous as this. There are many things that a carrier could do which would conduce to the safety of its passengers, but which it is not required to do, simply because the practical prosecution of the business will not permit of it. The carrier could, for example, by simply increasing its force of attendants, reduce to a minimum the happening of accidents like the one complained of here, but this, simple as the remedy may seem, might so increase the cost of operation as to compel the abandonment of the business. Hence the carrier cannot be held bound to do everything that can be done to insure the safety of its passengers, but only to the highest degree of care consistent with the practical conduct of its business. The measure of duty, as laid down by the trial court, was more than the law requires of the carrier, and for that reason erroneous.

It is said by the respondent that this instruction even though it may be erroneous, when considered by itself, is not so when taken with the other instruction given. But a careful perusal of the entire charge shows that this is the only place where the court undertook to define the measure of the appellant's duty to its passengers, and the jury could not have understood, from expressions made use of elsewhere, that they were intended as modifications of the language used here. Nor do we think the instruction is supported by the cases of *Northern Pac. R. Co. v. Hess,* 2 Wash. 383, 26 Pac. 866, and *Clukey v. Seattle Electric Co.,* 27 Wash. 70, 67 Pac. 379. While the first states the rule of liability in strong language, and the second upholds an instruction that goes to the utmost extent of the rule, in neither of them was it said that the carrier, to escape liability for negligence, must do everything that can be done to prevent accidents.

Other objections are urged against the regularity of the trial, but, as these will not recur on a retrial, it would be unprofitable to discuss them now.

The judgment is reversed, and a new trial awarded.

[No. 5024. Decided July 15, 1904.]

N. McINNES, *Respondent,* v. H. SUTTON, *Appellant.*[1]

APPEAL—WAIVER OF ERROR—MOTION FOR NEW TRIAL A WAIVER OF MOTION FOR JUDGMENT. Where a defendant against whom a verdict is rendered moves for judgment in his favor upon a special verdict, and also moves for a new trial, and the motion for judgment is denied, and that for a new trial is granted, the granting of the new trial determines any rights of the defendant on his motion for judgment, since he did not stand thereon.

ATTORNEY AND CLIENT—REMOVAL OF ATTORNEY—VOLUNTARY WITHDRAWAL—NOTICE—CONTINUANCE. Bal. Code, § 4771, providing for twenty days' notice of further proceedings upon the death or removal of a party's attorney, does not apply to a voluntary

[1] Reported in 77 Pac. 736.

withdrawal by the attorney, since a twenty days' delay could thereby be secured by collusion.

SAME—WITHDRAWAL AS GROUND FOR CONTINUANCE. When a case is regularly set for trial, the voluntary withdrawal of defendant's attorney is not ground for a continuance, and a judgment entered after hearing plaintiff's evidence is not irregularly entered, where no leave of court was obtained for such withdrawal, since the relation of attorney and client cannot be so severed as to affect the rights of others or to secure a delay of the trial.

APPEAL—REVIEW—JUDGMENT—VACATION—ERROR OF LAW. Error of law cannot be corrected upon a petition to vacate a judgment, but only by an appeal from the judgment.

Appeal from a judgment of the superior court for King county, Morris, J., entered June 16, 1903, upon findings in favor of the plaintiff, after a hearing before the court without a jury, dismissing a petition to vacate a judgment. Affirmed.

H. E. Foster, for appellant.

Humes, Miller & Lysons and *Ralph Simon,* for respondent.

HADLEY, J.—Respondent brought suit for damages against appellant, and charged wanton injury and destruction of property of the respondent. Issue was formed, a trial was had, and a verdict returned against appellant. With the general verdict, a special one was returned by way of answer to submitted interrogatories. The defendant moved for a new trial, and also moved for judgment in his favor on the special findings of the jury. The latter motion was denied, but the motion for new trial was granted. The cause came on for trial a second time in pursuance of regular assignment, the plaintiff with his witnesses being present in court and ready for trial. At that time counsel who then represented the defendant applied to the court for a continuance, but made no showing by way of affidavit or otherwise. The request was denied, and said counsel then sought to withdraw from the case, by announcing his withdrawal, and by serving upon the plaintiff, and filing with the clerk of the court, a notice thereof, and by refusing to proceed with, or participate in, the trial. The court, however, proceeded with the trial. A jury was impaneled, and the plaintiff's evidence submitted. A verdict was returned in favor of the plaintiff.

Before judgment was entered upon the verdict, the defendant appeared by other counsel, being the same who now represents him in this court. Said counsel filed in the cause what he designated as a "protest against the signing or entering of judgment," in which he recited the facts about the attempted withdrawal of former counsel, and stated that the defendant had no knowledge that the cause was to be called for trial at the time it was called, and did not know that his said attorney intended to withdraw from the case. The paper filed also states that the defendant was neither present nor represented by counsel at the trial. The court heard counsel upon the matters suggested by the paper filed in the record, and, after duly considering the same, denied the protest against entering judgment. Judgment was thereupon signed in accordance with the verdict, on the 22d day of May, 1903, and the same was filed June 16, 1903. Afterwards, on the 3d day of July, 1903, the defendant filed a petition to vacate the judgment, claiming that it had been irregularly entered, because of the facts concerning the attempted withdrawal of counsel, which are again recited in the petition. The petition also avers that the defendant has a good defense, as shown by his answer, that the plaintiff has no right of action, and that the complaint is insufficient to sustain a judgment. It is also alleged that the defendant is entitled to a judgment in his favor on the special find-

ings of the jury heretofore mentioned. The court denied
the petition to vacate, and the defendant has appealed.

We think the claim that the judgment was irregularly
entered is not well taken. . The complaint undoubtedly
states a cause of action, and is sufficient to sustain the
judgment. It recites a plain, wanton, and malicious removal, injury, and destruction of respondent's property.
Referring to the point that the appellant was entitled to
judgment upon the special findings of the jury, it will be
remembered that those findings were returned at the first
trial. Appellant both moved for judgment upon the findings, and for a new trial, evidently intending the motions
filed under the same cover to be in the alternative. With
the granting of the motion for a new trial, the other motion
was of course denied, and any rights of appellant under
the motion for judgment were effectively determined by
the granting of the other motion. Having asked for a
new trial, he was not in position to complain, since he did
not stand upon his motion for judgment. The final judgment entered is therefore not irregular by reason of the
denial of judgment upon the special findings.

If any element of irregularity attended the entry of
the judgment, it must, therefore, have been through the
attempted withdrawal of counsel. The statutory method
for effecting withdrawal of counsel is found in § 4771,
Bal. Code, as follows:

"When an attorney dies, or is removed or suspended, or
ceases to act as such, a party to an action for whom he
was acting as attorney must, at least twenty days before
any further proceedings against him, be required by the
adverse party, by written notice, to appoint another attorney, or to appear in person."

It seems to be appellant's view that the withdrawal was
complete when his counsel announced in open court, after

the case was called for trial, and when a mere request for
continuance was denied, that he would withdraw from the
case, and followed this by then serving upon respondent
a written notice to that effect. We do not think the terms
of the above quoted section relate to a mere voluntary
refusal to proceed with a case when it is regularly called
for trial, and the adversary is prepared with his witnesses
to proceed. If such were the meaning of the statute, it
could, by collusion between attorney and client, easily
be used as a means for effecting at least a twenty days'
delay, which, in some instances, might amount to a practical denial of justice. The relation of attorney and client,
when once established in a case, is not to be so easily
severed, when the rights of others depend thereon. The
interdependent relation is such that what is the client's
duty is often the attorney's duty, and the client cannot
escape his obligation to the court and to his adversary
to proceed with a trial, for the mere reason that his duly
appointed confidential agent—his attorney—may have
declined to act.

In *Coon v. Plymouth Plank Road Co.*, 32 Mich. 248,
250, the supreme court of Michigan, speaking of a statute
in all essential respects like our own, said:

"We do not understand this to apply to a case where
a practicing attorney for any reason declines to go on
with a particular case while still continuing in practice.
It might be made the means of serious mischief, if it
could have such a construction. The plain meaning of
the statute is to provide for cases in which the attorney or
solicitor, by reason of death, disability, or other cause, has
ceased to practice in the court. His refusal to proceed
in a particular case is not ceasing to 'act as such' attorney
or solicitor; it does not even disconnect him with the case;
for that can only be accomplished by consent of the parties,
or of the court, or by regular proceedings for the substitution of another."

Again, the supreme court of Maryland, in *Henck v. Todhunter,* 7 Har. & J. (Md.) 275, 16 Am. Dec. 300, when speaking of striking the name of an attorney of record, said:

"When, therefore, an attorney on the record applies for permission to cause his name to be stricken out, it is presumed to be done at the instance and by the authority of the party for whom his appearance has been entered. But it will never be permitted to a party, or his attorney, to obtain a continuance of a cause beyond the time allowed him by law, by striking out the attorney's appearance at the term at which the cause stands for trial; otherwise, by collusion between client and attorney, the trial of a cause might be delayed without limit. Hence, though the court will, on application, permit the attorney's name to be stricken out, considering him as acting on that very application as the attorney, and at the instance of the party, yet it will not be done to the prejudice of the other party, and the cause will be made to progress as if the appearance had not been stricken out."

In *Rio Grande Irrigation Co. v. Gildersleeve,* 174 U. S. 603, 19 Sup. Ct. 761, 43 L. Ed. 1103, it was held that, when a defendant, who has been served with process, causes an appearance to be entered by an attorney, and the latter subsequently withdraws his appearance but without obtaining leave of court, the record is left in a condition in which a judgment by default may be entered. To the effect that a voluntary withdrawal is not effective without leave of court, see, 3 Am. & Eng. Ency. Law (2 ed.), 410. The following case, cited in support of the above mentioned text, we especially note as being in point: *United States v. Curry,* 6 How. 106, 12 L. Ed. 363.

No leave of court was given in the case at bar, and, under the above authorities, appellant could not delay the trial by reason of the then attempted withdrawal of his counsel. The trial, theerfore, proceeded regularly. The

protest against the judgment on the verdict was in effect
an application for a new trial, and the ruling thereon
amounted to a denial of the new trial.

The judgment having been regularly entered, it was
not error to deny the petition to vacate. All matters of
substance contained in the petition had already been passed
upon by the court adversely to the petitioner, and it was
therefore proper to dismiss the petition. *Friedman v.
Manley,* 21 Wash. 675, 59 Pac. 490; *Greene v. Williams,*
13 Wash. 674, 43 Pac. 938. Mere errors of law cannot
be corrected by a petition to vacate a judgment, but the
remedy is by appeal from the judgment. *Kuhn v. Mason,*
24 Wash. 94, 64 Pac. 182.

The judgment is affirmed.

FULLERTON, C. J., and MOUNT, ANDERS, and DUNBAR,
JJ., concur.

[No. 5098. Decided July 15, 1904.]

DANIEL McKENZIE *et al., Appellants,* v. ROYAL DAIRY *et
al., Respondents.*[1]

APPEAL—BRIEFS—ASSIGNMENT OF ERRORS—SUFFICIENCY. A brief
will not be struck out because it contains no formal assignment
of errors, where it is clear that the only error alleged is the
sustaining of a demurrer to the complaint, and all the argument
is directed to that point.

MALICIOUS PROSECUTION—CONVICTION OF PLAINTIFF ADMITTED.
An action for a malicious prosecution cannot be maintained
where the plaintiffs were admittedly convicted of the offense
charged against them.

TORTIOUS INJURY—DAMAGES—SALE OF POISONOUS MILK—CON-
NIVANCE OF STATE DAIRY COMMISSIONER—INJURY BY PROSECUTION
AND DAMAGE TO BUSINESS AND REPUTATION. In an action for
damages by reason of the sale of poisonous milk to the plain-

[1]Reported in 77 Pac. 680.

tiffs, resulting in their arrest and prosecution for innocently reselling the same, thereby injuring their reputation and business,
the complaint states a cause of action against the state dairy
commissioner, as one of the defendants, where it alleges that he
was a stockholder in the defendant corporation making the sale,
and engaged in selling supplies to it, and to further his own
interests connived at the poisoning of the milk, and afterwards
caused the arrest and prosecution of the plaintiffs for using and
reselling the same, since he would be a joint tort feasor.

APPEAL—DECISION—ASSIGNMENT OF ERRORS—DISMISSAL—COSTS.
Where, in appellant's brief, no error is assigned as to one of two
joint tort feasors, as to whom the action was dismissed upon
its separate appearance, and no claim is made that the court erred in entering judgment in its favor, the appeal will be dismissed as to such defendant, with costs where a separate brief
was filed.

APPEAL—COSTS.   Upon dismissing a joint appeal, as to one of
the respondents, and reversing the case as to the other, the appellant is allowed only one-half of his costs of the appeal.

Appeal from a judgment of the superior court for King
county, Morris, J., entered November 9, 1903, upon sustaining a demurrer to the complaint, dismissing an action
for damages for the sale to plaintiffs of poisonous milk,
resulting in their arrest and prosecution. Reversed.

P. C. Dormitzer, for appellants, contended, among other
things, that a ministerial officer may exercise discretion
without possessing the immunity of a judicial officer. *Mc-
Cord v. High,* 24 Iowa 336; *Hicks v. Dorn,* 42 N. Y. 47,
affirming, s. c., 54 Barb. 172; *Owen v. Hill,* 67 Mich. 43.
A ministerial officer is liable in a civil action for nonfea-
sance, misfeasance, or malfeasance. *Boyden v. Burke,* 14
How. 575; *Dow v. Humbert,* 91 U. S. 294; *Eslava v.
Jones,* 83 Ala. 139, 3 Am. St. 699; *Harris v. Carson,* 40
Ill. App. 147; *Haverly v. McClelland,* 57 Iowa 182; *Rob-
inson v. Chamberlain,* 34 N. Y. 389, 90 Am. Dec. 713;
Adsit v. Brady, 4 Hill 630, 40 Am. Dec. 305.

Shank & Smith, for respondent E. A. McDonald. The complaint does not sustain an action for malicious prosecution. *Swepson v. Davis,* 109 Tenn. 99, 59 L. R. A. 501; *Stewart v. Sonneborn,* 98 U. S. 187; *Crescent etc. Co. v. Butchers' etc. Co.,* 120 U. S. 141, 7 Sup. Ct. 472; *Holliday v. Holliday,* 123 Cal. 26, 55 Pac. 703; *Woodworth v. Mills,* 61 Wis. 44, 20 N. W. 728, 50 Am. Rep. 135. The duties called for the exercise of discretion, and vested the commissioner with judicial power. 23 Am. & Eng. Encyc. Law, 376. And he was, therefore, not liable. *Porter v. Haight,* 45 Cal. 631; *Williams v. Weaver,* 100 U. S. 547; *Anderson v. Park,* 57 Ia. 69, 10 N. W. 310.

D. B. Trefethen, for respondent Royal Dairy.

Hadley, J.—Appellants, as copartners under the firm name and style of "Fashion Cafe," brought this suit against respondents to recover damages. It is alleged, that the respondent Royal Dairy is a corporation under the laws of Washington, and that respondent McDonald has been the duly and regularly appointed dairy commissioner of the state of Washington; that, while assuming to discharge the duties of said office, said McDonald has, in connivance and collusion with his co-respondent, aided, abetted and protected said corporation in the sale of milk to appellants, which contained a poisonous ingredient known as formaldehyde, well knowing that the milk so sold contained said poisonous ingredient; that appellants purchased said milk from said Royal Dairy for the purpose of mixing the same as a cooking ingredient, and that they also served the milk in its raw state as an accommodation to their patrons; that all milk, so served by appellants, was served to their patrons in the exact state that it was when purchased from the Royal Dairy, and that respondent McDonald had knowledge thereof. It is averred that said McDonald was a stockholder in said Royal Dairy, and was also engaged in the business of selling dairy supplies to dairy firms, and particularly to said Royal Dairy, which corporation was the largest consumer and purchaser of said McDonald's merchandise; that he shielded said corporation to further his own interests in the sale of dairy equipment, and that he at all times had full knowledge that said corporation was placing said ingredient in its product for the purpose of selling it, and with the intent to defraud and deceive the consumers, particularly the appellants. It is also alleged that appellants at no time had actual knowledge of the presence of said ingredient in the milk, and that they rested in the assurance of said corporation that the milk sold to them was pure, of standard quality, and free from all poisonous ingredients; that the placing of said ingredient in the milk was a fraud and deception upon appellants, of which fraud said McDonald, as dairy commissioner, at all times had knowledge, and that, with knowledge of all the foregoing facts, he did, while in the pretended exercise of his duties as dairy commissioner, by virtue of a sworn complaint, filed by him, cause the arrest of both appellants on the charge of selling milk containing said poisonous ingredients; that each of said appellants was found by the court to be technically, though not intentionally, guilty, and each was fined $25, the minimum fine required by law; that, in so doing, said McDonald was in connivance and collusion with said corporation, and acted maliciously and without probable cause; that the acts and conduct on the part of respondents advertised and branded appellants' place of business as being a place which supplied its patrons with poisonous, unwholesome, and impure food and milk; that appellants and their said business were thereby brought

into contempt and disrepute. The damages are laid in
the aggregate at $10,000. Respondent McDonald sepa-
rately demurred to the complaint, on the general ground
that it does not state facts sufficient to constitute a cause
of action against him. The demurrer was sustained. The
record before us does not disclose any appearance or pleading on the part of respondent Royal Dairy, except as shown
in the final order of the court. In that order, after reciting that the demurrer of McDonald is sustained, the following appears:

"And it further appearing that defendant corporation,
Royal Dairy, have herein also interposed a motion for
themselves and in their own behalf to strike certain parts
of plaintiff's amended complaint herein, and argument
having been heretofore had upon defendant E. A. McDonald's demurrer and said demurrer having been sustained:—
It is hereby ordered and adjudged that further argument
be not had upon defendant Royal Dairy's motion, or that
further pleading on the part of defendant Royal Dairy,
be had upon said amended complaint. And it further
appearing by the statement of P. C. Dormitzer, Esq., as
attorney and counsel for plaintiffs herein, that he elects
to stand upon his amended complaint filed in this cause,
and that he refuses to plead further in this cause—it is.
hereby further ordered and adjudged that said action be,
and the same is, hereby dismissed, at plaintiff's costs, as to
both and each of the defendants herein."

The plaintiffs have appealed from the judgment. Respondent McDonald moves, for several reasons, to strike
appellants' brief. We think it unnecessary to refer to more
than one of the grounds urged, viz., that the brief does not
point out the errors relied upon, as provided by the rules of
this court. It is true no so-called and formal assignment of
error appears in the brief, but, at the conclusion of appellants' statement of the case, is the following: "From the
order sustaining defendant E. A. McDonald's demurrer,

plaintiffs appeal." To the above subject, the argument is
wholly directed, and it seems to be sufficiently clear that
the only error urged is as to the ruling sustaining the demurrer of McDonald. The motion to strike the brief is
therefore denied.

We shall now consider the ruling upon the demurrer to
the complaint. If the complaint be treated as one for
malicious prosecution, the ruling of the court upon the
demurrer was manifestly right, for no recovery of damages
can be predicated upon the action of McDonald in causing
the arrest of appellants on a charge under which they were
admittedly convicted. If he knew they were conducting a
restaurant and, as the proprietors thereof, were selling milk
to their customers which contained the poisonous substance,
there was not only probable cause, but it was his duty as
dairy commissioner to cause their arrest, under the provisions of chapter 94 of the session laws of 1901. In such
case sufficient probable cause existed to excuse McDonald
from liability.

The remaining question is whether there are sufficient
allegations, as against demurrer, to render McDonald liable
on any other theory than that of malicious prosecution. On
motion, doubtless, appellants would have been required to
elect upon what theory they would proceed; but upon general demurrer, the only question is whether sufficient facts
are stated to constitute a cause of action upon any theory.
We are inclined to think that the broad allegations of this
complaint do state a cause of action against McDonald.
While it is not alleged—except by way of mere information and belief, and this we do not regard of any force,
since it is not actually alleged—that he directly contributed
to bring about the condition of the milk, yet it is repeatedly
averred that he, for some time, had knowledge thereof, and

that, for purposes of personal benefit, he declined to interfere in an official way and prevent the dairy company from selling appellants the poisoned milk. We think such a state of facts would make him a joint tort feasor with the dairy company. IIis counsel argue that in his official capacity he acts quasi judicially, and is not therefore liable in damages. The acts, as charged in this complaint, cannot well be classified as being of a judicial nature, since they cannot be other than basely wrong and tortious toward appellants. We think such a cause of action appears that respondent McDonald cannot be relieved upon mere demurrer, and that the persons making such serious charges as to the conduct of a public official should be required to prove them, or go out of court by failure to establish them.

The respondent Royal Dairy moves to dismiss the appeal as to it, for the reason that appellants have not assigned as error the action of the lower court in entering a judgment in favor of it and against appellants; also, for the further reason that they, in their opening brief, have made no argument to the effect that the lower court was in error in rendering a judgment in favor of the Royal Dairy and against appellants. It is also true that, in appellants' reply brief, no claim whatever is made that the court erred in its judgment in favor of the dairy company. The only error in any way pointed out, or argued in the briefs, is that of the ruling upon the separate demurrer of McDonald hereinbefore discussed. The motion of the dairy company must therefore be granted. We must assume from the briefs that appellants do not wish to disturb the judgment as to said company. There being no other questions before us for decision at this time, the appeal as to respondent Royal Dairy is dismissed, and the judgment as to it is affirmed, and it shall also recover its costs on appeal, it having filed a separate brief. As to respondent McDonald, the judgment is reversed, and the cause remanded, with instructions to overrule the demurrer to the complaint interposed by said respondent, and, inasmuch as the appeal is joint as to both respondents, and whereas, appellants have prevailed as to one only, they shall recover of respondent McDonald but one-half of their costs on appeal.

FULLERTON, C. J., and MOUNT, ANDERS, and DUNBAR, JJ., concur.

[No. 4939. Decided July 19, 1904.]

PETER HARVEY *et al.*, *Appellants*, v. DENA IVORY, *Respondent.*[1]

REPLEVIN—PLEADINGS—ANSWER—DEFENDANT'S TITLE UNDER A GENERAL DENIAL. In an action of replevin the defendant may, under a general denial of plaintiff's title and right of possession, show title to the property in himself.

REPLEVIN—JUDGMENT FOR RETURN OF PROPERTY—RELIEF TO DEFENDANT WITHOUT PROOF OF TITLE. Where plaintiff replevins and obtains possession of property, and fails at the trial to establish his title or right thereto, upon dismissal of the action the defendant is entitled to judgment for the return of the property, or its value if return cannot be had, without allegation or proof in support of such relief.

NEW TRIAL—NEWLY DISCOVERED EVIDENCE—CREDIBILITY OF WITNESS. A new trial should not be granted for newly discovered evidence which merely goes to the credibility of the opposite party as a witness, rather than to the right of recovery.

Appeal from a judgment of the superior court for King county, Albertson, J., entered May 28, 1903, upon the verdict of a jury rendered in favor of the defendant, in an

[1]Reported in 77 Pac. 725.

action of replevin, directing a return of the property, etc.
Affirmed.

James Kiefer, for appellants. The defendant in replevin
must plead his title. *Dennott v. Wallach,* 1 Black 96;
Richardson v. Smith, 29 Cal. 530; *Woodworth v. Knowl-
ton,* 22 Cal. 164; *Swasey v. Adair,* 88 Cal. 179, 25 Pac.
1119; *Banning v. Marleau,* 101 Cal. 238, 35 Pac. 772;
Hill v. Fellows, 25 Ark. 11; *McIlvaine v. Holland,* 5 Harr.
(Del.) 226; *Lamping v. Payne,* 83 Ill. 463; *Kern v.
Potter,* 71 Ill. 19; *Darter v. Brown,* 48 Ind. 395; *Mc-
Intire v. Eastman,* 76 Iowa 455; *Pope v. Jackson,* 65
Me. 162; *Mathias v. Sellers,* 86 Pa. St. 486, 27 Am. St.
723. The answer must demand a return of the property.
Liebmann v. McGraw, 3 Wash. 520, 28 Pac. 1107; *Gould
v. Scannel,* 13 Cal. 430; *Pico v. Pico,* 56 Cal. 453; *Acock
v. Halsey,* 90 Cal. 215, 27 Pac. 193; *Chandler v. Lincoln,*
52 Ill. 74; *Hinchman v. Doak,* 48 Mich. 168; *Capital
Lumbering Co. v. Hall,* 10 Ore. 202; *Gallagher v. Bishop,*
15 Wis. 276.

Bennett & Whitham, for respondent. A general denial
is all that is necessary under the code system. Pomeroy,
Rem. & Rem. Rights, § 642; Work, Prac. & Plead. (3d
ed.), §§ 414, 579, 1491; Cobbey, Replevin (2d ed.),
§§ 746, 751; *Ross v. Banta,* 140 Ind. 120; *Matlock v.
Straughn,* 21 Ind. 128.

FULLERTON, C. J.—The appellants brought this action
against the respondent to recover the possession of certain
personal property, consisting of a piano and certain household furniture. In their complaint they alleged ownership
and right of possession of the property, its unlawful seizure
and detention by respondent, that it was of the value of
$390, and that the respondent had refused to surrender pos-

session thereof to the appellants, on demand made therefor. At the time of filing the complaint they executed and delivered to the sheriff the statutory affidavit and bond, claiming an immediate delivery of the property. On receipt of the affidavit and bond, the sheriff took possession of the property, held it for the statutory time, when, no redelivery bond being filed, he delivered the property to the appellants, who had possession of it at the time of the trial. The respondent thereafter answered the complaint, admitting that she had possession of the property, that demand had been made upon her for it by the appellants, and that it was of the value of $390; and denied generally all of the other allegations of the complaint. The prayer was that the appellants' action be dismissed, and that the respondent recover costs. On the issues thus found, a trial was had before a jury, which returned a verdict in favor of the respondent. On this verdict a judgment was entered adjudging that the respondent was the owner and entitled to the possession of the property, and directing its immediate return to her by the appellants, and, in case its return could not be had, that she have judgment against the appellants for its value, viz., the sum of $390.

At the trial the court permitted the respondent to prove ownership and right of possession to the property in herself. This is assigned as error, on the ground that she had not pleaded title or right of possession in herself to the property; her answer, as we have said, being merely a general denial of the allegations of ownership and right of possession made in the complaint on behalf of the appellant. But, whatever may be the rule elsewhere, it is not the rule in this state that a defendant in an action of replevin may not, under a general denial, show title in himself to the property in controversy. On the contrary, the rule and the practice have been the other way ever since the case of *Chamberlain v. Winn*, 1 Wash. 501, 20 Pac. 780, decided by the territorial supreme court. It was there held that, in an action brought to recover possession of specific personal property, the defendant could, under a general denial, prove ownership or right of possession in a third person, and, of course, if it be permissible to prove title in a third person under such an answer, it is permissible to show title in one's self.

It is next urged that the court erred in entering a judgment for the return of the property, or its value in case return could not be had, because the respondent had not asked for such return in her answer. There are cases which maintain this position, but we do not feel inclined to follow them. They proceed on the theory that judgment for the return of the property is affirmative relief, and that a defendant, to be entitled to it, must allege and prove himself entitled to it. But plainly this is not sound. The plaintiff obtains possession of the property under the delivery bond by virtue of the statute, not by making good his title thereto. The remedy is allowed him in furtherance of justice, that he may not lose the fruits of his victory, if he succeeds in proving his right to the property, when the question of right is tried out. But his right to possession is not thus absolute; it is conditional only, dependent on his ability to make good his title and right of possession, when these rights are called in question by the defendant. If he fails to make good his title or right of possession, the right of the defendant to have the property returned to him, or to have its value in case it cannot be returned, follows as a matter of course. The plaintiff is the actor, and it is his duty to prove his right to take the property from the defendant, not the defendant's duty to prove the taking

ing wrongful. When, therefore, the plaintiff fails to prove his title or right of possession, the defendant's right to have it returned to him, or have its value in case return cannot be had, is absolute, and needs no allegations or proofs to support it, and judgment in his favor requiring such return or payment of the value of the property is a matter of right. The statute (§ 5020, Ballinger) does not prescribe a different rule.

The last assignment is that the court erred in denying the appellants' motion for a new trial. The ground of the motion is that of newly discovered evidence, but we are clearly of the opinion that there was no error here. The newly discovered evidence goes to the credibility of the respondent as a witness, rather than to her right to recover, and for this reason, were the matter unexplained, it would seem that the motion was properly overruled by the trial court. 14 Enc. Plead. & Prac. 807. But the respondent offers an explanation of the transaction seemingly satisfactory to the trial court. And so satisfactory, indeed, does it seem to us, that we think it more likely that the impeaching witness is mistaken, as to the matter to which he avers, than is the respondent.

As we find no error in the record, the judgment will stand affirmed.

MOUNT, ANDERS, HADLEY, and DUNBAR, JJ., concur.

[No. 5023. Decided July 19, 1904.]

ELIZA DODDS et al., Respondents, v. THOMAS GRAVES GREGSON, Appellant.[1]

APPEAL—STATEMENT OF FACTS—TIME FOR FILING—EXTENSION. The time for filing a statement of facts may be extended by stipulation of the parties without any order of court, under Bal. Code, § 5062.

SAME—TIME FOR CERTIFYING STATEMENT OF FACTS. Bal. Code, § 5058, providing that there shall be no extension of time for filing a statement of facts beyond ninety days, limits the time for filing only, and not the time for its settlement by the court, for which no limit is prescribed.

SAME—NOTICE OF SETTLEMENT—SUFFICIENCY—APPEARANCE. A statement of facts will not be struck out for failure to give notice of the time of settlement of proposed amendments, where notice was once duly given, continuances taken, and later when both parties were in court the time was set for two days thereafter without objection on account of want of notice, and respondents' counsel appeared at the hearing, and many of his amendments were adopted.

APPEAL — DISMISSAL — RECOGNIZING VALIDITY OF JUDGMENT — PAYMENT WHEN NOT VOLUNTARY. An appeal will not be dismissed on the ground that the appellant recognized the validity of the judgment by making a partial payment, where it appears that, there being no supersedeas, the respondents issued garnishment proceedings under the judgment, and the payment was made thereunder, after a contest, since the same was not voluntary.

PLEADINGS—DEPARTURE—CONSISTENCY OF COMPLAINT AND REPLY. Where a complaint alleges that a note for $400 belonging to the plaintiff came into the defendant's possession through his employment as the plaintiff's attorney, and alleges its conversion, and the answer sets up the defense that it was given to him in payment for his services, a reply admitting the allegations of the answer but averring that afterwards the defendant received other pay for his services and agreed to return the note, which he failed to do, is not inconsistent with the complaint, and a motion for judgment on the pleadings and an objection to any evidence on that account are properly overruled.

[1]Reported in 77 Pac. 791.

APPEAL—TRIAL—INSTRUCTIONS—EXCEPTIONS. Error cannot be predicated upon instructions where no exceptions thereto were taken.

APPEAL—REVIEW—VERDICT ON CONFLICTING EVIDENCE. The verdict of a jury upon conflicting testimony will not be disturbed on appeal.

ATTORNEY AND CLIENT—ACTION FOR SERVICES—EVIDENCE—RELEVANCY OF IMPROPER CONDUCT IN SECURING ADMISSION TO PRACTICE. In an action against an attorney for the alleged conversion of money and notes belonging to his client, in which it is alleged and admitted that he is duly admitted to practice in this state, it is prejudicial error to permit cross-examination suggesting that he had resorted to bribery in order to obtain his admission, since it is immaterial and irrelevant and would have the effect of arousing the passions of the jury.

SAME—EVIDENCE—OBJECTION—SUFFICIENCY. Where such cross-examination is objected to in the beginning and the court rules the same pertinent, further objection might increase the prejudice of the jury, and is not essential to secure a review of the ruling on appeal.

Appeal from a judgment of the superior court for King county, Bell, J., entered June 16, 1903, upon the verdict of a jury rendered in favor of the plaintiff, in an action for conversion. Reversed.

Ballinger, Ronald & Battle, for appellant.

James A. Snoddy, for respondents.

HADLEY, J.—Respondents, being husband and wife, brought this suit as plaintiffs against appellant as defendant. They allege, that the defendant is an attorney at law and a member of the bar of Washington; that the wife plaintiff employed defendant, as such attorney, to collect for her a sum of $165, due to her upon a note and mortgage from one Meyer; that he collected thereon $175 principal and interest, and $15 as attorney's fees, but has refused to pay the same to said plaintiff, and has converted it to his own use. It is further alleged that, while defendant was employed by the wife plaintiff as the latter's attorney in an

action to procure a divorce for her from her said husband,
a certain note and mortgage for $400, belonging to said
wife, came into the possession of the defendant by and
through his said employment, and which he promised to
return to said wife; that he sold said note for the sum of
$200, and converted the proceeds to his own use. Judg-
ment is demanded for $375.

The answer first denies the material allegations of the
complaint, and then affirmatively avers, that said wife employed defendant to institute for her an action for divorce
from her said husband, and for the recovery of alimony,
which suit was brought by him; that said wife agreed to
pay defendant, as a fee for his services, one-third of the
amount of money and property which should be allowed by
the court as alimony, or, in the event of a settlement in
any manner, such sum was to be paid as attorney's fees;
that, pending the action, the settlement of the claim for
alimony was effected through defendant's efforts, the settlement being in the sum of $2,000, to be paid by the husband
to the wife; that, under the agreement as to attorney's fees,
defendant was entitled to $665 of said sum; that in part
payment thereof said wife transferred to him the $165
note and mortgage mentioned in the complaint, and that in
further payment she also transferred to him the other note
and mortgage, named in the complaint, in the sum of $400,
which note had been given by the husband to the wife as a
part of the $2,000 settlement; that the said notes and mort-
gages thereby became the absolute property of defendant;
that thereafter said wife delivered back to the husband a
$1,600 note received by her in said settlement, and that
she—claiming that the husband had perpetrated a fraud
upon her by procuring the surrender of said note—again
employed defendant to take the necessary steps to protect
her rights, and to effect a settlement with the husband;

that, for the services to be so rendered, she agreed to pay defendant one-fourth of the amount of the property and money that should be thereafter realized from any settlement, which one-fourth should be in addition to the sums hereinbefore alleged as paid for services up to and including the first settlement; that an adjustment of the alleged fraud was afterwards effected through the efforts of defendant, by which the husband executed and delivered to the wife a note for the sum of $2,250, and agreed to execute to her an additional note for $750; but that, by direction of the wife, the latter note was made directly to defendant in payment of his fees, the new settlement being for $3,000 and the last named note representing one-fourth thereof, the alleged agreed amount of the attorney's fees for the later services.

The reply denies that defendant was entitled to receive $665 as fees under the first settlement, but avers that he agreed to accept, and did accept, said $400 note and mortgage in full for all services rendered. It is denied that the Meyer note of $165 was transferred to the defendant as a part payment on attorney's fees. It is further averred, in reply, that the agreement as to fees the second time was not for one-fourth of what should be thereafter recovered, in addition to what had been theretofore paid, but that said $750 note should be in full for all services rendered from the beginning of the entire employment, and that defendant then agreed to surrender and return the said $400 note. Upon issues in effect as above stated, the cause was tried before the court and a jury, and a verdict was returned for the plaintiffs in the action in the sum of $375 and interest. Motion for new trial having been denied, judgment was entered for the amount of the verdict, and the defendant has appealed.

Respondents move to strike the statement of facts and
to dismiss the appeal. The motion to strike the statement
is based upon several grounds. The first ground stated is
that the proposed statement was not filed within the time
allowed by law after judgment, and that no order granting
an extension of time was ever made by the court. It is true
the proposed statement was not filed within thirty days
after judgment, but there is in the record a written stipulation, signed by counsel representing the respective parties,
whereby it was agreed that the time should be extended "for
an additional thirty days after the expiration of the first
thirty days after the time begins to run within which an
appeal may be taken from the judgment rendered in this
cause; that is, until the 16th day of August, 1903." The
proposed statement was filed August 15, 1903, which was
clearly within the extended time under the stipulation.

Respondents' counsel, however, argues that an order of
court was absolutely necessary to effect an extension of
time, and cites the following decisions of this court: *Zindorf Construction Co. v. Western Amer. Co.*, 27 Wash. 31,
67 Pac. 374; *Wollin v. Smith*, 27 Wash. 349, 67 Pac. 561;
Crowley v. McDonough, 30 Wash. 57, 70 Pac. 261; *Lamona v. Cowley*, 31 Wash. 297, 71 Pac. 1040. It is true
expressions are used in those opinions to the effect that an
order of court is necessary, but there was no stipulation
involved in any of those cases, and the remarks of the court
were intended to apply to such conditions as were then under consideration. The extension by the stipulation is authorized by § 5062, Bal. Code, wherein it is provided that
the time may be enlarged either before or after the expiration of thirty days "by stipulation of the parties, or for
good cause shown and on such terms as may be just, by an
order of the court or judge," etc. Thus the extension may

be made either by stipulation or by order of court, and when by stipulation, no order is necessary.

The second ground urged for striking the statement is that it was not presented and settled by the court within the time required by law.   It is counsel's position that it must, in any event, be settled within ninety days, the period within which it may be filed under extension. Counsel cites *Loos v. Rondema,* 10 Wash. 164, 38 Pac. 1012, and *McQuesten v. Morrill,* 12 Wash. 335, 41 Pac. 56.   Again, expressions are used in those opinions which, at first glance, seem to treat both the filing and settlement of a statement of facts as being governed by the fixed time.   It is manifest, however, that the real subject under discussion was the time for filing.   That time is fixed by statute, but no such limit is fixed for the settlement under the terms of § 5058, Bal. Code.

The third point alleged on the motion to strike the statement is that the settlement was made without notice, the respondents having filed proposed amendments.   The record shows that notice was once regularly given, and several continuances were thereafter noted on the journal for definite times, and it was then continued indefinitely. Later, counsel for both parties were in court when appellant's counsel asked the court to set a time for settlement. Respondents' counsel simply objected, but stated no reason to the court other than that he wished to raise the point that the settlement could not be made after ninety days.   The court set the hearing for two days thereafter. The point was not made that the objection was for want of sufficient notice, and the record shows that, at the time of the settlement, respondents' counsel appeared, and that many of the proposed amendments were allowed.   Under such circumstances the court was authorized to settle the statement, and the motion to strike it is denied.

The motion to dismiss the appeal is based upon the contention that, since the appeal was taken, appellant has made a payment upon the judgment, and thereby acknowledged its validity. The facts as shown by the record are as follows: No supersedeas bond was filed by appellant, and respondents proceeded, by authority of the judgment, to garnish a debtor of appellant. The answer of the garnishee was controverted by appellant in part, and he also claimed that $19.88 in the garnishee's hands was exempt. A hearing was had, and judgment entered to the effect that the $19.88 was all that the garnishee held as the property of appellant, that the same was not exempt, and should be paid to respondents. This was not a voluntary payment upon the judgment which amounted to an acknowledgment of its validity. Some effort is made by way of affidavits to show that appellant voluntarily consented to the garnishment judgment, but the record of the garnishment proceedings shows a contest and a judgment thereon, with no consent of appellant appearing. The motion to dismiss the appeal is denied.

Appellant assigns that the court erred in not granting his motion for judgment on the pleadings, for the reason, as alleged, that the reply admits the correctness of the affirmative defense, and that the complaint and reply, taken together, show that respondents had no cause of action. Objection was also made to the introduction of any evidence for the same reason. It will be remembered that the complaint avers that the $400 note and mortgage came into appellant's possession by and through his employment as attorney for this wife respondent. The answer avers that it was turned over to him in payment of attorney's fees. The reply admits that it was first so turned over to him, but alleges that, by subsequent agree-

ment, appellant accepted another $750 note in payment
of all fees, and then agreed to turn back the $400 note
to the wife respondent. We do not think the reply is
inconsistent with the complaint. The reply still makes it
clear, on respondents' theory, that the note did not belong
to appellant when he sold it, but did belong to the wife respondent. It still remains true, even under the reply,
that the note belonging to said respondent came into appellant's possession in the course of the latter's employment as her attorney. The court did not err in denying
the motion for judgment upon the pleadings, and in overruling the objection to the introduction of any evidence.

Errors are assigned upon the court's instructions. One
instruction with reference to the burden of proof is criticised, but no exception to it is disclosed by the record, and
we shall therefore not discuss it. We think the other instructions discussed by counsel were not erroneous under
the issues and testimony, and we believe it is unnecessary
to extend this opinion as would be required for their discussion.

There was conflict in the testimony, and it is argued
that neither the general nor special verdict returned was
supported by the evidence. We have read all the evidence. It is much in conflict, but it was for the jury to
pass upon the conflicting testimony, and upon that ground
we find no reason to disturb the verdict. There is, however, another assignment of error which we regard as
serious. The record discloses the following in the cross-
examination of appellant:

"Q. How long have you been a member of the bar?
Mr. Battle: Don't make any difference. They have alleged he is, and it is admitted. The Court: Objection
overruled. A. I have been a member of the bar for four
years, this and the Oregon bar. Q. You were admitted

to the bar of this state upon examination, or upon certificate from some other state? A. I was admitted to the bar of this state on a certificate from the supreme court of Oregon. Q. Did you bring in those certificates? A. I have got them. Q. Will you produce them? A. Certainly. Q. What is the date of the original certificate? A. 25th of September, in the year of our Lord, 1899. Q. What is the date of the Washington certificate? A. 27th day of March, A. D. 1901. Q. Were you admitted to the supreme court of the state of Oregon on examination? A. Yes. Q. In open court? A. In open court, by the full bench. Q. By the full bench? A. Yes, sir; as my certificate states. Q. Were you there? A. Oh, yes. Q. Are you acquainted with the firm of Joseph, Slager & Watson of Portland? A. I am. Q. Did you make them a note of $750 payable on condition that you get admitted to the supreme court of the state of Oregon? A. No. Q. Hasn't one been in Seattle for collection in the last year for collection? A. No. Do you mean to tell me that I could bribe the supreme court of Oregon? You have no more respect for American courts? Q. I am talking about Joseph, Slager & Company. Did you give Joseph, Slager & Company a note? A. No, sir. Q. Endorsed on the back in your own handwriting that it should be payable when you got admission to the supreme court of Oregon? A. I never gave a note for any such purpose, nor yet have I ever had a note presented to me. Q. There was no such a note as that presented to you for payment in the last year? A. At no time. Q. Did Joseph, Slager & Watson procure your admission to the bar? A. No sir. Q. You didn't give any note in connection with your admission? A. Oh, no sir; not at all."

It is urged that appellant was highly prejudiced by the foregoing examination. We think it must be so held. That he was a member of the bar of this state was a fact alleged by respondents in their complaint, and admitted by the answer. It was therefore wholly immaterial how long he had been such a member, or what circumstances had attended his admission to the bar. If any irregularity attended his admission to the bar, corrupt or otherwise, that was not a matter for investigation in this case, and it was not for the jury to try. The whole of the above cross-examination was immaterial and irrelevant, and its natural effect must have been to arouse the passions of the jury against appellant. His acts as an attorney were under examination, and this sensational and purely collateral matter must have been highly inflammatory and prejudicial. It is suggested that the examination proceeded without objection. Appellant did, however, object in the beginning to any examination touching his membership of the bar, for the reason that it was an admitted fact. The objection was overruled and the examination proceeded. Appellant was placed in a peculiar position. The court having once ruled that the examination was pertinent, further objection to it might have had the effect to increase the jury's prejudice by lodging in their minds the belief that he was endeavoring to prevent a disclosure of the truth. We think the examination was erroneously permitted.

The judgment is reversed, and the cause remanded with instructions to the lower court to grant a new trial.

FULLERTON, C. J., and MOUNT, ANDERS, and DUNBAR, JJ., concur.

[No. 5037. Decided July 19, 1904.]

In the Matter of the Estate of PAUL DRASDO, *Deceased.*[1]

APPEAL — DISMISSAL — BOND — SUPERSEDEAS — ORDER FIXING AMOUNT—NECESSITY. Upon an appeal from an order other than a judgment for the recovery of money, the amount of a bond to effect a stay of proceedings must be fixed by the court, and a bond given both as an appeal and supersedeas bond in the sum of $500, without any order of court fixing the amount, is insufficient to give jurisdiction of the appeal, and the appeal must be dismissed.

Appeal from an order of the superior court for King county, Bell, J., entered September 4, 1903, requiring the payment of the fees of a special administrator, and other sums, upon the allowance of his account, against the objection of the executors. Appeal dismissed.

William Martin and *W. A. Keene,* for appellants.

Wm. Hickman Moore, pro se.

PER CURIAM.—This is an appeal from an order of the superior court allowing to William Hickman Moore, as special administrator of the estate of Paul Drasdo, deceased, the sum of $1,000 as fees for his services as such special administrator, together with certain other minor sums, allowed in the order to be paid to other persons than the special administrator, and which he is directed to pay. The executors of the will of the deceased are prosecuting the appeal. The respondent moves to dismiss the appeal on the ground, among others, that the appellants did not furnish an appeal bond as required by law. A bond was given in the sum of $500, which purports to stay proceedings. Respondent contends that the appeal is from an order which is a judgment for the recovery

[1]Reported in 77 Pac 735.

of money, and that the bond, in order to effect a stay of
proceedings, should be in double the amount of the judgment, which would require a bond for more than $2,000.
Whether the order appealed from is a judgment for the
recovery of money, within the meaning of § 6506, Bal.
Code, is a question that admits of controversy. If it be
such a judgment, then manifestly the bond is insufficient,
but without deciding that point, and conceding, for the
purposes of this motion, that an order fixing and allowing
the compensation of an administrator should not be classified as a judgment for the recovery of money, still, under
the section of the statute cited, the amount of the bond
must in any event be fixed by the court, in order to stay
proceedings. The record is silent upon that subject. No
order or entry of any kind appears by which we can determine that the court fixed the amount of the supersedeas
bond at $500, or at any other sum. Respondent in his
brief asserts that the court did not fix the amount. Appellants' counsel, in the reply brief, does not dispute the
assertion, but in a mere inferential manner, following
argumentative matter, says: "We take it that this was
the reason that the lower court fixed the amount of the
bond in the sum of $500." He, however, points out noth-
ing in the record to verify the statement, and, after diligent search, we are unable to find any order in the record
fixing an amount for the supersedeas bond. The appeal
must therefore be dismissed.

[No. 4376. Decided July 19, 1904.]

WILLIAM DICKERSON, *Appellant*, v. CITY OF SPOKANE, *Respondent*.[1]

CONTRACTS—CONSTRUCTION—CITY ORDER—PAYABLE FROM CERTAIN FUND. An order, drawn upon a city by a contractor constructing water works, requesting payment of a certain sum "out of any moneys belonging to me, or that may hereafter be due me . . . on the water works contract, either in the twenty per cent reserve, or on account of money to be due me on account of final estimate," is payable only out of said reserve or final estimate, and not out of semimonthly payments falling due as the work progressed.

MUNICIPAL CORPORATIONS — ORDER PAYABLE ACCORDING TO ITS TERMS — CITY COMPTROLLER'S ADMISSION. A city comptroller, upon filing an order on the city, drawn by a contractor, has no power to bind the city or create a liability beyond the terms of the order, by stating that it is all right and would be paid.

SAME—PLEADING AND PROOF—ORIGINAL CONSIDERATION FOR ORDER WHEN INADMISSIBLE. In an action upon an order, drawn by a contractor upon a city, seeking to recover thereon and not on the original consideration, evidence showing that such consideration was labor or material furnished the contractor, making it a preferred claim, is inadmissible, although such consideration is alleged in the complaint, as plaintiff cannot assert that the order is payable otherwise than according to its terms.

Appeal from a judgment of the superior court for Spokane county, Bell, J., entered January 11, 1902, upon the verdict of a jury rendered in favor of the defendant. Affirmed.

James Dawson, for appellant.

John P. Judson, A. H. Kenyon, and *E. O. Connor*, for respondent.

PER CURIAM.—This is an action brought by appellant, William Dickerson, against the city of Spokane, defend-

[1]Reported in 77 Pac. 730.

ant and respondent, in the superior court of Spokane
county, on a certain written order for the payment of
money, issued by one R. A. Jones to appellant, as follows:

"Spokane, Washington, January 27th. 1895.
"To the City Comptroller of the City of Spokane. Dear
Sir: Please pay to William Dickerson the sum of $294
out of any moneys belonging to me, or that may hereafter
be due me from the city of Spokane, on the water works
contract, either in the twenty per cent reserve, or on account of money to be due me on account of final estimate
on said water works contract.   Said sum of $294 to bear
interest at the rate of one and one half per cent per month
until paid, which principal sum and interest please pay
in the manner as aforesaid. R. A. Jones."

This cause was here on a former appeal taken by appellant from a judgment of dismissal, rendered by the
lower court at the first trial on the ground that the complaint did not state facts sufficient to constitute a cause
of action.   The judgment of the superior court was reversed and the case remanded.   26 Wash. 292, 66 Pac.
381.   The allegations upon which the present cause of action is founded sufficiently appear from the opinion of this
court delivered on the former appeal, which renders it
unnecessary to restate such averments in this connection.
The amended answer of the city of Spokane denies the
material allegations of the complaint charging it with any
liability whatever to appellant by reason of the drawing
and presentation of the above written order to respondent, admits that it has neglected and refused to pay the
same, and avers that, under the contract between R. A.
Jones and the respondent city, "it was expressly provided
that defendant should not be obliged to accept or pay
orders like the one described in the complaint."   It is
alleged in the first affirmative defense, "That at no time,
since the filing of said order, has the defendant had any

money or funds of said R. A. Jones subject thereto, nor
has said Jones, at any time since said order was filed,
had any credit or account with said defendant, on account
of said contract or otherwise, from which said order, or
any part thereof, could be paid." The reply denies the
allegations of new matter contained in the above answer.
The cause came on for trial before the lower court and
a jury. Verdict was rendered and judgment entered in
favor of respondent city, and plaintiff, William Dickerson, appeals.

On January 5, 1894, R. A. Jones and the city of Spokane entered into a written contract for the construction
of a water works system for such city, for the consideration of $339,880, to be paid Jones, the contractor, by the
respondent city in the manner and amounts, and at the
times, therein provided. This contract contains the following provision with reference to the times and manner of
payments:

"And the said city of Spokane, hereby agrees to make
payment of the said sum for said work in manner and
at the times following, to wit: Said payments to be made
semimonthly, on or about the first and fifteenth day of
every month, upon estimates of the value of the materials
delivered at the site, and the labor performed upon the
said work, during the preceding half month, . . . less
20 per centum of the amount of each estimate, which 20
per centum shall be retained by the city of Spokane until
all and every part of said work shall be entirely complete,
and accepted by the said board of public works."

On September 21, 1895, Jones assigned all of his interest in this contract to Philip Buehner, one of his sureties.
At that time he also gave Buehner a general power of
attorney authorizing and empowering Buehner to act in
his place and stead and complete this contract. The city
council of Spokane consented to the change. The 20 per

cent, reserved by the terms of the original contract, was
reduced to 10 per cent. At the trial in the court below
before a jury, on December 20, 1901, appellant's evidence
tended to show that, when the order was issued, he filed
the same with the comptroller of the city of Spokane.
Over the objection of respondent's counsel, appellant testified that Mr. Liebes, the comptroller, told him this order
was all right and would be paid. Appellant offered in evidence a certain affidavit purporting to have been made
by him October 19, 1895, in which it is stated: "That
the indebtedness which formed the basis of said order was
incurred by said Jones for work and labor performed
on said water works by J. L. Martin and Thos. Olsen,
and said claim has been heretofore assigned to this affiant."
His counsel contended that, if this document were not
proper testimony to show the true consideration of this
order, still, it was sufficient to put the city upon inquiry
as to the nature of the claim. The trial court rejected the
offer, and appellant excepted. The court also ruled out
appellant's offers of estimates Nos. 16, 17, and 18 as
tending to show the amounts due from the city to Jones
under the contract on January 27, 1895, when the order
was filed. Witness R. A. Jones testified that the order
was given to William Dickerson at the request of Thomas
Olsen, as payment for labor performed on, and piling furnished for, the water works by Thomas Olsen. Appellant
took the order for a debt which Olsen owed him. The trial
court, in explanation of its position, remarked that, if it
were shown that this order was given on account of work
and labor performed, or material furnished, in the construction of the water works, and ought to have gone into one
of their estimates, and by some mistake of the city it was
omitted, the respondent would be liable primarily. The

appellant, however, failed to show any state of facts leading to such conclusion.

On behalf of the defense, Mr. E. F. Gill, city commissioner, and a member of the board of Public Works of
Spokane in 1895 and 1896, testified, that, when the water
works contract was turned over by Jones to Buehner on
the 21st of September, 1895, $260,000 had been expended
under the contract; that the final estimate, which included
all other estimates, was 388,000 and some hundred dollars; and that there was not money enough left of the
contract price remaining unexpended, when Philip Buehner took charge of the work, to pay the claims for labor
and material then due, or thereafter incurred in completing the works. This witness further testified that more
than one thousand dollars was expended over and above
the contract price, and that there were a great number
of bills not allowed. The evidence of Messrs. Jones and
Buehner, as well as the documentary evidence adduced
in behalf of the defense, tended to show that there was
no money due the contractor, unless, on the final settlement, there was a balance in the reserve fund; that, upon
the completion of the contract, there was no money to
turn over to the contractor. The transcript shows that
the appellant's counsel objected to nearly every item of
evidence, oral and documentary, offered by the city at
the trial.

The trial court, among other things, instructed the
jury as follows:

"The defendant admits the contract, as alleged; admits
that the order, as alleged, was delivered to the comptroller
of the city; denies that the comptroller endorsed it or
promised to pay anything upon it; admits that the water
works plant was completed and accepted by the city.   It

denies, however, that anything was due to Jones on the contract upon the final settlement, so that the issue raised for you to determine, gentlemen, is whether or not, upon the final settlement between Jones and the city, there was anything due from the city to Jones upon that contract. . . . Now gentlemen, this order is that the city pay to the plaintiff out of the reserve that is kept back by the city upon the contract with Jones, or out of anything that may become due him on the final estimate or final settlement. . . . The comptroller had no authority to bind the city by any statement that he may have made to Dickerson, or any one else, with regard to the payment of this order outside of the terms of the contract, and outside of the legal liability of the city, as I have explained to you."

Appellant excepted to the giving of each of these instructions.

In our opinion these instructions, in connection with the evidence above noted, present the two material questions for our consideration under the assignments of error: (1) the proper interpretation of the terms of the written order described in the complaint, and upon which the present action is founded; (2) the liability of the city of Spokane, respondent, to appellant on such written instrument. The main contention arises as to the proper significance and meaning of the terms contained in this written order: "Out of any moneys belonging to me, or that may hereafter be due me from the city of Spokane, on the water works contract, either in the twenty per cent reserve, or on account of money to be due me on account of final estimate on said water works contract." The lower court decided that it was payable from the 20 per cent reserve or the amount found due on final estimate.

The learned counsel for appellant forcibly urges that, "instead of designating two funds, as the trial judge held, it designated really three funds: (1) his [Jones'] semi-

monthly earnings, earned when the order was given and
presented; (2) the 20 per cent reserve; and (3) the
amount due on final estimate." In support of this position he directs our attention to the following language,
found in the former opinion: "Certainly the written order from Jones, when filed by appellant with the proper
accounting officer of the city, was an equitable assignment
of any of the funds belonging to Jones in the possession of
respondent." *Dickerson v. Spokane,* 26 Wash. 292, 294,
66 Pac. 381. This language should be considered in connection with the written order declared upon in the complaint. This court did not undertake to decide out of
just what funds this order was made payable, but the
language employed referred only to the funds designated
in the order. There was nothing in the record at that
time outside of the complaint to enlighten us regarding
the condition of the funds designated in the order, or in
the water works contract; neither were we called upon to
consider that matter.

After a careful consideration of the record in this case,
in connection with the arguments of able counsel, we are
of the opinion that the trial court committed no error
prejudicial to the rights of appellant in its rulings respecting the admission and rejection of evidence, or in any
of the instructions given to the jury at the trial, and that
there is ample evidence to sustain the verdict. It seems
plain to us that this order was drawn upon the 20 per
cent reserve fund, or the balance due the contractor upon
completion of the water works. This fund was reserved
for the protection of the city against any liability which
might arise under, or in connection with, the contract between the city and Jones. When the water works system

was completed, it was found that there were no funds available with which to pay the order in question, and therefore the appellant cannot recover thereon as against the respondent. The comptroller had no authority to bind the respondent by any admission or statement he may have made pertaining to the payment of, or the liability of the city of Spokane on, this order.

We think the trial court committed no error in refusing to admit in evidence plaintiff's exhibit No. 1 as to the alleged consideration of this order being for labor or material furnished by Thomas Olsen at the instance of contractor Jones, and that this order was, therefore, a preferred claim against the city under the water works contract, operating as an assignment of Olsen's claim. The appellant is seeking to recover against respondent on this written order, and not on the original consideration. True, he alleges such consideration in his complaint, but it is plain that his right of action is measured by the terms of the written instrument upon which this action is founded. It does not lie with appellant to assert that it is payable otherwise than in the manner designated by the instrument itself.

The judgment of the superior court is clearly right, and should be affirmed.

[No. 4447. Decided July 19, 1904.]

CARRIE B. FRIEND, *Respondent,* v. F. H. RALSTON *et al.,*
Respondents, and THE UNITED STATES FIDELITY
AND GUARANTY COMPANY, *Appellant.*[1]

INDEMNITY—BUILDING CONTRACT—AGREEMENT TO FURNISH ALL
MATERIAL—BREACH—FILING OF MECHANICS' LIEN—SUIT ON BOND
BEFORE DISCHARGE OF LIEN. Where an indemnity bond guarantees the faithful performance of a building contract in which the
contractors agree to furnish all the material for the building,
the failure of the contractors to pay for the materials furnished,
resulting in the filing of a mechanics' lien, is a breach of the contract and the bond, entitling the owner to maintain a suit on the
bond before the payment and discharge of the lien claim for
materials.

SAME—DEFENSES—FAILURE TO PAY CONTRACTORS—CREDITS FOR
BALANCE DUE ALLOWED ON CLAIM AGAINST CONTRACTORS. In an
action upon a bond guaranteeing a building contract, in which the
owner seeks to recover the amount of a judgment establishing a
mechanics' lien for material furnished to the contractors, it is no
defense that the plaintiff had refused to pay the contractors two
small items for a balance due and for extras, where due credits
were received therefor by the contractors and inured to the benefit of the surety on the bond, having been deducted from the
amount of the plaintiff's claim.

SAME—JUDGMENT AGAINST PRINCIPAL—NOTICE TO THE SURETY
TO DEFEND—ESTOPPEL. Where a surety company guaranteed, by
its bond, the faithful performance of a building contract in which
the contractors agreed to furnish all the material, and is given
due notice to defend an action commenced by materialmen to
foreclose a lien for material furnished to the contractors, a judgment obtained in good faith against the contractors, the principals in the bond, establishing the claim and foreclosing the lien,
is binding upon the surety, to the same extent that it binds the
contractors, and in an action on the bond estops the surety company from claiming that there was no breach of the contract.

Appeal from a judgment of the superior court for King
county, Griffin, J., entered April 29, 1902, upon the ver-

[1]Reported in 77 Pac. 794.

dict of a jury rendered in favor of the plaintiff by direction of the court, after a trial on the merits, in an action on an indemnity bond guaranteeing a building contract.

James B. Murphy, for appellant.

Ralph. Simon, for respondent.

PER CURIAM.—This action was begun in the superior court of King county by Carrie B. Friend, plaintiff, against H. F. Ralston and D. A. Royea, copartners doing business under the firm name and style of Ralston & Royea, and the United States Fidelity and Guaranty Company, defendants. On the trial of the issues between the plaintiff and the defendant United States Fidelity and Guaranty Company, before the court below and a jury, a verdict was rendered in favor of plaintiff for $1,206.41, under direction of the trial court, April 10, 1902. Judgment was entered on this verdict April 29, 1902, from which the United States Fidelity and Guaranty Company appeals.

On the 21st day of January, 1901, at the city of Seattle, respondent Carrie B. Friend entered into a written contract with the respondents Ralston & Royea for the construction, in said city, on the real estate of Mrs. Friend, of a certain two story frame building, for the consideration of $7,753. On the 25th day of January, 1902, Ralston & Royea, as principals, with appellant company as surety, executed a bond to Carrie B. Friend in the penal sum of $3,000. Such bond by recitals referred to this building contract, and contained the following conditions: "Now, therefore, the condition of the foregoing obligation is such that, if the said principals shall well, truly, and faithfully comply with all the terms, covenants, and conditions of said contract on their part to be kept and performed, according to its tenor, then this obligation to be null and void, otherwise to be and remain in full force and virtue in law." The above contract, among other things, provided that the contractors, at their own expense, should provide and supply all manner of materials and labor for the construction of this building, and complete the same on or before May 1, 1901. The provisions of the third and fifth paragraphs of the contract are as follows:

"Third: Should the owner at any time during the progress of said building require any alterations, deviations, additions to, or omissions from the said contract, specifications or plans, she shall be at liberty to have such changes made, and the same shall in no way affect or avoid the contract, but the additional costs (if any) of such changes will be added to the amount of such contract price, and deductions shall be made from said contract price for all omissions of work specified, at a fair and reasonable valuation."

"Fifth: Should any dispute arise respecting the true construction or meaning of the drawings or specifications, the same shall be decided by McManus & Walker, architects, and their decision shall be final and conclusive, and should any dispute arise respecting the true value of any extra work, or omitted work, the same shall be valued by two competent persons, one employed by the owner and the other by the contractors, who, in case they cannot agree as to the value of such extra work or omitted work, shall name an umpire, whose decision shall be binding on all parties."

These contractors, Ralston & Royea, purchased from the Kerry Mill Company lumber and material which was used in the construction of this building. The balance remaining due therefor was $1,179.49. On June 15, 1901, the architects, McManus & Walker, issued their final certificate with regard to the completion of the building under the contract. The Kerry Mill Company, on August

21, 1901, filed a lien upon said property, and brought
action in the court below to foreclose the same, making
Carrie B. Friend and Ralston & Royea defendants therein.
Ralston & Royea also filed a lien on said premises for
$152, the balance due on the contract, and, also, for
$1,410.25, on account of extra work and materials, and
brought suit to foreclose such lien. Mrs. Friend answered
the complaint of the contractors, denying the material allegations thereof, except an item of $8. She further alleged
in her answer a demand for $599.90 for work and materi-
als omitted; also, a claim for demurrage in delaying the
completion of the building till June 16, 1901, and the
filing of the lien of the Kerry Mill Company, and the
action instituted for the foreclosure thereof. The reply
of the contractors admitted that the building was not completed till June 16, 1901, and denied allegations regarding the omission of any work or materials.

The contractor's bond provides, "that any suits at law
or proceedings in equity brought against this bond . . .
must be instituted within six months after the first breach
of said contract;" that a registered letter, mailed to the
president of appellant company, at its principal office in
Baltimore City, Md., shall be deemed sufficient notice.
On September 18, 1901, Mrs. Friend, by her attorney,
notified appellant by registered letter of the bringing of
the Kerry Mill Company's lien suit, and tendered the
defense thereof to appellant. It appears, from the recitals in such notice, that Mrs. Friend was served with
the summons and complaint in such action on September
17, 1901. The appellant disregarded such notice, and
failed to take any part in such defense.

These two lien cases were consolidated, and tried together. The lower court found in favor of the Kerry

Mill Company in the sum of $1,280.04, and also decreed that its lien therefor, together with an attorney's fee and costs, be foreclosed against said premises. The court further found that Mrs. Friend was indebted to the contractors in the sums of $28 for extra work, and $152 for balance due on the contract price, and on February 13, 1902, rendered judgment in her favor against Ralston & Royea for $1,100.04 and costs.

This action was instituted by Carrie B. Friend to recover damages on the bond, for the failure on the part of Ralston & Royea to perform their part of said contract, and by reason of the foregoing facts and judicial proceedings. On the 3rd day of March, 1902, respondent Carrie B. Friend, by order of the trial court, based on the stipulation of the parties, filed her amended and supplemental complaint in the action, wherein, among other things, she alleged notice to appellant to defend as above stated, the rendition of said judgment against the contractors, Ralston & Royea, and appellant company's knowledge of the matters litigated, limiting her demand for judgment to the amount of the judgment recovered by her against Ralston & Royea.

Appellant answered the complaint, in which answer it denied certain allegations thereof, admitted the execution of the contract and bond, and set forth several affirmative defenses. The first affirmative defense in substance alleges, that certain changes, deviations, and alterations were made by the mutual consent of the contractors and Mrs. Friend, as outlined in the plans and specifications; that the reasonable value of such extra work and material was greater than the amount sought to be recovered in this action, and the penalty of the contractors' bond; that no allowance was made to the contractors for such material

and labor, and that Mrs. Friend was still indebted to them
for the same. The second affirmative defense alleges
matters with regard to extra work and material furnished
pursuant to oral agreements, made between the contractors and owner contrary to the plans and specifications
which were a part of the building contract. The provision claimed to have been violated is as follows: "No bills
or accounts for extra work will be allowed or paid unless
authority for contracting same can be shown by a certificate from the owner, countersigned by the architect."
It is further charged in this defense that such charges
were made without the knowledge or consent of appellant. The third separate defense, after alleging that there
was extra work and material furnished in the construction
of this building, charges that the contractors and owner
were unable to agree upon the allowance therefor, that the
contractors, pursuant to the provisions of the above paragraph five of the building contract, offered to submit the
value of such extras to arbitration, and that Carrie B.
Friend refused to select an arbitrator or submit such dispute to arbitration. The fourth and last of these affirmative defenses charges that respondent Mrs. Friend failed
and refused to make payments to the contractors, as provided in the building contract, and withholds the same.

After respondent had submitted her evidence at the
trial, including the notice to defend and judgment roll
above mentioned, appellant insisted that the complaint
did not state facts sufficient to constitute a cause of action,
and further that the evidence in behalf of respondent
Friend was insufficient to entitle her to any relief. The
trial, including the notice to defend and judgment roll
which rulings it duly excepted. The trial court excluded
all evidence in support of the affirmative defenses, respectively, and appellant excepted. Thereafter the following

written stipulation between the parties to this action was filed in the trial court:

"Whereas, upon the trial of this cause, no opportunity was given to the United States Fidelity & Guaranty Company, one of the defendants herein, to introduce testimony in support of its denials, and in answer to the evidence introduced on behalf of the plaintiff after the motion to exclude testimony under the affirmative defenses set out in its answer were passed upon by the court:

"It is now stipulated that under the order offered in evidence by the plaintiff, given by Ralston & Royea to Calhoun, Denny & Ewing, dated ————, the said plaintiff paid the sums represented by the receipts from said agents, and did not pay nor offer to pay to them any other, or further sum, and that she, the said plaintiff, did withhold from the said Ralston & Royea and the said agents, the sum of $152.00 on the original contract price as named in the building contract which is an exhibit herein, and the $28.00 for extra work, these being the same amounts found by the court to be due Ralston & Royea according to the findings of fact offered in evidence and marked (Plaintiff's Exhibit ——).

"And it is further stipulated that the defendant aside from testimony to the above effect, had no testimony to offer in support of its denials or in answer to the testimony offered on behalf of the said plaintiff, except in support of the matters set out in its separate affirmative defenses; and the said defendant hereby waives any claim or error which it might have predicated upon the action of the court above referred to and that if said cause be appealed to the supreme court no error will be claimed or assigned by reason thereof.

"Dated at Seattle, Washington, this 24th day of April, A. D., 1902."

Under direction of the lower court, the jury returned a verdict in behalf of respondent Carrie B. Friend, on which the judgment appealed from was entered.

After the perfection of the present appeal, Carrie B. Friend died. On suggestion of her death, by order of this court, her executor, Ralph Simon, was substituted herein as respondent in her stead. The propositions of law arising upon this record, under the assignments of error, are: (1) That the original and supplemental complaints fail to state a cause of action; (2) that the court below erred in denying appellant's motion for a nonsuit, and (3) error in excluding the evidence in support of appellant's four affirmative defenses respectively.

In support of the first assignment, it is urged that, in order to entitle respondent Friend to recover in the present controversy, she must have paid the judgment of the Kerry Mill Company against Ralston & Royea, which, as we understand by appellant's contention, includes the original demand constituting the consideration of such judgment, as the action at bar was originally begun prior to the rendition of that judgment; that, therefore, both the original and supplemental complaints, failing to allege such payment prior to the commencement of this action, do not state facts sufficient to constitute a cause of action against this appellant company.

The building contract was made a part of the bond in question. The contractors, among other things, undertook, by the express terms of their contract, to provide and supply, at their own cost and expense, all the materials necessary for the completion of said building and the fulfillment of such contract. The appellant company, for a consideration, guaranteed that these contractors should well, truly, and faithfully comply with all the terms, covenants, and conditions of such agreement on their part to be performed. These complaints respectively allege, that Ralston & Royea purchased materials for this building of the Kerry Mill Company, in furtherance of their said contract with Mrs. Friend, the owner of the premises; that, by their (the contractors') failure to pay for the same, Mrs. Friend's property became subject to a lien at the instance of the Kerry Mill Company. "Where the contractor for the erection of a building gave a bond with sureties to 'faithfully perform all the covenants and agreements contained in the building contract,' etc., and the building contract provided that he was 'to furnish all the material, such as lumber, hardware, brick, lime, sand, paints, oils, etc., as per specifications,' held, that a failure to pay for such materials, whereby a mechanics' lien was filed on the building and lot, was a breach of the condition of the bond, and rendered the builder and his sureties liable thereon." *Kiewit v. Carter,* 25 Neb. 460, 41 N. W. 286.

The learned counsel for appellant cites numerous authorities with reference to the nonliability of sureties on bonds or covenants of indemnity "to save and keep harmless the obligee from certain outstanding debts, or that the party indemnified shall not sustain damage incurred through the omissions or acts of the principal, etc., until the obligee shall have paid or discharged such debts, or may have otherwise sustained financial loss. *Miller v. Fries,* 66 N. J. L. 377, 49 Atl. 674. But there is a marked distinction between covenants of that description and agreements that the obligors shall perform specific acts. *Litchfield v. Cowley,* 34 Wash. 566, 76 Pac. 81; *Wright v. Whiting,* 40 Barb. 235. The covenant in the building contract on the part of the contractors with Mrs. Friend is, as between them, equivalent to a direct promise to pay for materials used in the construction of the building, and a breach of the contract occurred when the contractor suffered the obligation to become a charge on her property; at least, she was entitled to treat it as

a breach. It may be true that she was not obligated to
do so; that she could have waited until the lien had become fixed and determined by judgment against her property, and treated that as the breach of the bond, thus
escaping the onus of establishing, at the trial, the validity
of such lien and the amount of the indebtedness, but she
was not obliged to delay action in that behalf. She could
treat the failure of the contractors to keep her property
free from such incumbrance as a breach of the contract.
Therefore, the position of appellant's counsel that this
action was prematurely brought is untenable. In the
light of the above authorities relative to primary and
affirmative covenants to perform some particular act, we
conclude that the original and supplemental complaints
state sufficient facts to constitute a cause of action.

The assignments of error pertaining to the refusal of
the lower court to grant appellant's motion for a nonsuit,
and in excluding its evidence in support of the several
affirmative defenses, may properly be treated and consid
ered under one head, and in the same connection. The
appellant contends that the testimony in respondent's behalf disclosed that she had not fulfilled her agreement with
her contractors, in that she had refused to pay them the
above items $152, balance on contract price, and $48 for
extra work, and that therefore the lower court erred in
denying the nonsuit.

The case of *Cowles v. United States Fidelity and Guaranty Co.*, 32 Wash. 120, 72 Pac. 1032, was similar in
many of its salient features to the action at bar. In that
case this court held (quoting from the syllabus, which
tersely presents the points decided):

"A guaranty company which, for a compensation, becomes surety upon the bond given by a building contractor
for the faithful performance of his contract cannot escape

liability by reason of deviations from the exact terms of
the contract, where such provisions were waived by the
contractor and no damage is shown as resulting to the
surety by reason thereof."

In the consolidated actions above noted, it fully appeared
that the contractors, Ralston & Royea, received due credits
for the two items of $152, balance of contract price, and
$48 for extra work, which inured to the benefit of this
appellant. The stipulation as to these credits in terms
related to the action of the lower court regarding its decision denying the · nonsuit; still, it contained admissions
which were properly in the case for all purposes, and it
is questionable whether appellant could, in any event, be
permitted to controvert such admissions as to these several
amounts withheld from the contractors by Mrs. Friend,
when it thereafter undertook to sustain any of the averments of these affirmative defenses at variance with such
stipulation. *Sherman v. Sweeny,* 29 Wash. 331, 69 Pac.
1117.

However, we consider that the vital question with regard to the sufficiency of such defenses is, whether the
judgment in the consolidated lien cases above noted, which
is described in the supplemental complaint, estops the
appellant. It had due notice of the pendency of the Kerry
Mill lien suit, one of the cases consolidated, and it was
offered the defense thereof on the part of this respondent
Mrs. Friend. Such action was instituted to recover on
a demand for materials purchased by the contractors in
furtherance of their said building contract, the faithful
performance of which, on the part of Ralston & Royea,
was guaranteed by the appellant company. The judgment
in favor of Mrs. Friend against her contractors was obtained in good faith without fraud or collusion. This
judgment related exclusively to matters connected with the

contract and bond, in which appellant was closely identified and directly interested. The following language is
quoted from the opinion of the court in *Cowles v. United
States Fidelity and Guaranty Co., supra:*—

"It is the contract instead of the bond which is primarily to be construed, and the construction of the contract cannot be affected by the fact that a bond is given
for its performance. It must be construed with reference
to the gathered intention of the parties to the contract, and
whatever is binding upon them is binding upon the surety,
who becomes a party to the contract, identified with the
contractor."

We are of the opinion that, under the facts appearing in
this record, the appellant company is bound by the judg-
ment recovered against the contractors in favor of the
owner, Mrs. Friend; that this case in that regard falls
within the principles of law enunciated in *Douthitt v.
MacCulsky,* 11 Wash. 601, 40 Pac. 186, and *Doremus v.
Root,* 23 Wash. 710, 63 Pac. 572, 54 L. R. A. 649. See,
Lovejoy v. Murray, 3 Wall. 1, 18, 18 L. Ed. 129; 6 Rose's
Notes on U. S. Rep., p. 458; *Prichard v. Farrar,* 116
Mass. 221.

Appellant's counsel has directed our attention to many
authorities in support of his position, that a judgment
rendered against the principal on a bond does not estop
the surety from relitigating the merits of the controversy,
where such judgment was obtained in an action on the
original contract, as distinct from the bond for its faithful
performance, without making the surety a party defendant. The case of *McConnell v. Poor,* 113 Iowa 133, 84
N. W. 968, 52 L. R. A. 312, is an authority upon which
appellant places its principal reliance, but we fail to discover wherein it is in conflict with the conclusions heretofore declared respecting this feature of the present contro-

versy. Notwithstanding the statement in the syllabus, the case fails to show that the surety had notice of the prior suit against his principal, or was given any opportunity to appear and defend such action, and it further appeared that the plaintiff had elected to treat the bond and contract as separate instruments for the purposes of the litigation. The able court properly held that a judgment, rendered in favor of the obligee for breach of the contract against the principal, did not estop the surety when sued on the contractor's bond. Again, in this Iowa case, the record fails to show that the surety had any further interest in the contract of his principal other than that of a mere surety without compensation. The facts in the case before us, as we have shown, are entirely dissimilar, and render the rule of the Iowa case inapplicable.

No reversible error appearing in the record, it follows that the judgment of the lower court must be affirmed, with costs, and it is so ordered.

[No. 4848. Decided July 19, 1904.]

FRANK A. JONES *et al.*, *Appellants*, v. JOSEPHINE C. HERRICK *et al.*, *Respondents.*[1]

APPEAL—REVIEW—HARMLESS ERROR. Where a judgment for defendants is based upon certain defenses, error in refusing to sustain a demurrer to certain other separate defenses of the defendants is not prejudicial.

MORTGAGES—FORECLOSURE SALE—PURCHASER WITHOUT NOTICE OF UNRECORDED INTERESTS—QUIETING TITLE—PLEADING. An answer in an action to quiet title, pleading title in the defendants through a foreclosure sale, need not allege that the plaintiffs were parties to the foreclosure proceeding, where it is alleged that plaintiffs had no interest of record at the time, and that the purchaser had no notice of any such interest or claim, since he holds as an innocent

[1]Reported in 77 Pac. 798.

purchaser for value as to outstanding unrecorded liens of which
he has no notice.

ADVERSE POSSESSION—COLOR OF TITLE—PLEADING. An answer
pleading title by adverse possession is not demurrable for failure
to allege "color of title," where it is averred that defendants held
under a warranty deed from the owner.

QUIETING TITLE—RIGHT TO REDEEM FROM MORTGAGE—PROFFER OF
REDEMPTION—BARRED BY LAPSE OF TIME. An action to quiet title,
brought by one who only had the right to redeem from a mortgage, must fail where, after foreclosure and sale to an innocent
purchaser, the plaintiff made no proffer of redemption, and where
the right to redeem was barred by lapse of time prior to the commencement of the action.

Appeal from a judgment of the superior court for King
county, Tallman, J., entered March 24, 1903, upon findings in favor of the defendant, after a trial on the merits
before the court without a jury. Affirmed.

S. S. Langland, for appellants.

Mitchell Gilliam, for respondents.

FULLERTON, C. J.—The appellants brought this action
against the respondents to quiet title in themselves to some
eighty acres of vacant and unoccupied land, situated in
King county, in this state. They alleged title by virtue
of a judgment of the circuit court of the United States
for the district of Washington against one W. P. Sayward, an execution sale of the property as the property of
Sayward, its purchase at such sale by one A. A. Johnson,
and the subsequent conveyance of the property to themselves by Johnson. The answer of the respondents consisted of a general denial of the allegations of the complaint, and some five separate defenses. In three of these
the respondents claimed title in themselves, first, by a
warranty deed from the common owner, antedating the
inception of the proceedings through which the appellants
claimed title; second, through a foreclosure proceeding

in which the rights of the appellants, if any they had, were foreclosed and sold; and third, by virtue of the statute of limitations. The fourth was a partial defense only, being a claim for taxes paid, which they prayed to have adjudged to be a lien on the land, in case it should be found that the appellants had a superior title. The fifth defense was in the nature of a cross-complaint, asking that the respondents' instruments of title be adjudged to be liens upon the land for the amounts advanced by them and their predecessor in interest in acquiring the same, if such instruments of title should not be adjudged to convey title in fee, and that such liens be foreclosed as against the appellants, and the property sold in satisfaction of the amount found due. To these separate answers, with the exception of the first, general demurrers were interposed, which were overruled by the trial court, whereupon a reply was filed, denying generally the affirmative matter pleaded therein, and pleading new matter by way of defense and estoppel thereto. Subsequently a motion was made to require the respondents to elect between their first and second defenses, on the ground that they were inconsistent. This motion, also, was overruled, and thereafter a trial had on the merits of the contrversy, resulting in findings of fact, conclusions of law, and a judgment in favor of the respondents.

The statement of facts certified to this court was stricken prior to the hearing; the cause, however, was retained on the suggestion that there were questions presented by the record not dependent upon the statement of facts. The appellants now insist that the court erred in overruling the demurrers to the separate defenses, but we think those of them necessary to uphold the judgment were clearly sufficient. The court found that the respondents were the

owners in fee of the premises, hence it makes no difference
whether or not the matters alleged in the fourth or fifth
of the separate defenses were sufficient to entitle the respondents to relief.   The fourth, as we have stated, only
purported to be a partial defense, and could only be material in case the court should hold the respondents to be
without title.   The fifth was material only under a like
condition.   The failure, therefore, of the court to rule
correctly on the demurrer to these defenses would not require a reversal of the case, as the judgment was not
founded on the allegations of either of them.

As to the other defenses demurred to, we think they
were clearly sufficient.   The second separate defense was
a deraignment of title through foreclosure proceedings,
based on an instrument antedating any right the appellants
may have obtained by virtue of the execution sale under
which they claim.   The precise objection to the pleading
is that it does not appear that the appellants or their
grantor was made a party to the foreclosure proceedings,
and that they were not, for that reason, bound by them;
but the answer avers that there was nothing of record at
the time of the foreclosure proceedings showing that either
the appellants or their grantor had any claim to, or interest in, the property, and that the purchasers under that
proceeding had no notice, actual or constructive, of such
claims or interests.   If this be true, the interests of the
appellants were as effectually cut off by the foreclosure
proceedings as they would have been had their claims been
of record, and they had been made parties to the proceedings.   A purchaser at a sale, had under foreclosure of a
mortgage or other lien, holds as an innocent purchaser for
value, and is bound by only such outstanding unrecorded
liens or claims to the property as he has actual notice of.

The defense, therefore, as a pleading, could not be objectionable for the reason stated.

The third defense was a plea of the statute of limitations under section 5504 of the Code (Ballinger's). The objection to it is that it is not alleged that the respondents had "color of title" to the property during the time they paid taxes thereon. But the allegation is that they held under a warranty deed from the owner, which we think is equivalent to alleging they held under "color of title," and this being true the pleading was sufficient as against a general demurrer. Moreover, this was such a defect as could be cured by amendment, and, if the findings of fact justified holding that the respondents had title to the property by virtue of having paid taxes thereon for seven consecutive years, having color of title thereto made in good faith, this court would treat the pleading as amended to correspond therewith.

The appellants contend further, however, that the findings made by the trial court are not as broad as the pleadings, and argue that, if the pleadings do support the judgment, the findings of fact do not. But here again we think the appellants are mistaken. The facts, as found, show that Sayward, at the time of the execution sale, under which the appellants purchased, had in the property only a right of redemption, the legal title having passed from him by the deed under which the respondents claim. This being true, the appellants could have acquired by the execution sale no greater rights than Sayward had; namely, the right to redeem, and could not, under any circumstances, have the title conveyed to them and quieted in themselves without first redeeming from the respondents. This they did not do, nor proffer to do, and there could be no recovery by them in this action in any event. And

·we think the court did not err in quieting the title in the respondents. Lapse of time alone has now barred any right the appellants may have had to redeem the property, and they have never possessed any other remedy. The respondents' right, therefore, to have the litigation ended and their title put at rest is absolute.

The judgment appealed from is affirmed.

MOUNT, ANDERS, HADLEY, and DUNBAR, JJ., concur.

[No. 5149. Decided July 21, 1904.]

JOHN BJORKLUND, *Respondent,* v. THE SEATTLE ELECTRIC COMPANY, *Appellant.*[1]

COMPROMISE—RELEASE OF DAMAGES SECURED BY FRAUD—PARTIES NOT ON EQUAL FOOTING—QUESTION FOR JURY. In an action to recover for personal injuries sustained by an employe, whether the plaintiff was fraudulently misled and induced to sign a release of his damages is a question for the jury, where it appears that the company's physician told the plaintiff that his injury was slight and he would be well in a short time, but wrote a letter showing a serious injury, and when it appears that the plaintiff understood English imperfectly, and supposed he was signing a receipt for wages for the time he had lost, then paid to him, under a promise for future employment, and under the representations of the company's claim agent that it was such receipt, and that from long service he placed reliance in the defendant's agents and physician; since the jury could reasonably find that the parties did not stand upon an equal footing, and that the plaintiff was justified in placing confidence in the representations because of his long established relations with the company.

SAME—EXPRESSIONS OF OPINION. In such a case it is for the jury to say whether the physician's statements concerning the extent of the plaintiff's injuries were mere expressions of opinion or statements of fact upon which the plaintiff had a right to rely.

SAME—SURRENDER OF AMOUNT PAID ON SETTLEMENT. It is not necessary to return a sum received in a settlement induced by

[1]Reported in 77 Pac. 727.

fraud, before bringing action on the demand, but the same may
be credited thereon.

MASTER AND SERVANT—RELEASE SECURED BY FRAUD—SERVANT'S
CONTINUANCE OF EMPLOYMENT—ESTOPPEL. Where a servant was
induced, by an agreement for future employment and false representations respecting the extent of his injuries, to sign a release for personal injuries sustained through the negligence of
the master, the fact that he shortly afterwards went back to
work under representations of the master's claim agent and
physician that his injuries were slight, and worked and received
wages for about a year and a half, does not militate against his
recovery for the injuries received.

Appeal from a judgment of the superior court for King
county, Hatch, J., entered November 16, 1903, upon the
verdict of a jury rendered in favor of the plaintiff for
$2,500 for personal injuries. Affirmed.

Hughes, McMicken, Dovell & Ramsey, for appellant.

George F. Aust and *G. Meade Emory*, for respondent.

HADLEY, J.—This is an action for damages for personal
injuries received by respondent while traveling as a passenger upon one of appellant's cars. Respondent was at
the time, and for several years prior thereto had been, an
employe of appellant, engaged in rendering services about
the car barn of the railway company, but when he received
his injuries he was a passenger on his way to his home,
after completing a day's work, and he says he had paid
his fare as the other passengers had done.

The question of want of original liability is not urged
upon this appeal, but it is contended that respondent had,
prior to bringing the action, for a consideration, fully
released appellant from all claims for damages. In reply
to the answer setting up the release, respondent alleged,
that, by reason of his long employment by appellant, he
had great confidence in the company's agents, physician,

and representatives; that he understands, very imperfectly,
the English language, and can, with great difficulty, only
read the simplest English words and phrases; that at the
time of signing the alleged release he did not obtain legal
advice, and was entirely ignorant of his legal rights, and
of the extent of his injury; that appellant, well knowing
the above facts, did, by its agents, to wit, its superintendent, claim agent, and physician, with intent and purpose of intensifying respondent's ignorance as to his legal
rights and physical condition, falsely and fraudulently
represent to him that it was inadvisable for him to consult a lawyer; that his injuries were such that, without
doubt, he would be entirely well within six weeks' time at
most, and that he was even then able to return to work;
that appellant was willing to pay him his wages until he
was able to return to work, and was also anxious to have
him continue in its service; that it would give him a good
easy job, soon raise his wages, and give him ample opportunity for promotion; that appellant's claim agent and
superintendent then informed him that, in order to carry
out said arrangement for him to draw his wages and get
an easy job, it was necessary for him to sign a writing,
which was then for the first time produced; that respondent could not read it, and that said claim agent then pretended to read it to him, but that he could not understand
its meaning, and the claim agent knew he could not understand it; that he then told the claim agent that he could not
understand it; that the claim agent thereupon told him
that the only purpose of the paper was to have respondent
go to work again for appellant, to give him a good easy
job, with promise of promotion and raise of wages, and
to enable him to draw his wages for the time he had been
off duty; that appellant, its agents, servants, and physi-

cian, well knew of respondent's ignorance of his rights,
and of the extent of his injuries; that he was relying upon
their representations, and that but for such false representations he would not have signed any paper, a release
or otherwise; that he was ignorant of the fact that he was
signing any purported release for injuries of any extent
or duration contrary to said representations, or any purported representations whatever, and that he never intended to release appellant; that the aforesaid promises,
made by appellant's agents, have not been carried out;
that respondent did not recover from his injuries within
six weeks, has not yet recovered, is now unable to work
by reason thereof, and is informed and believes that his
injuries are of a permanent nature, and that he will always
remain crippled and deformed. A trial was had before the
court and a jury, and a verdict was returned for respondent in the sum of $2,500. Motion for new trial having
been denied, judgment was entered upon the verdict, and
the defendant has appealed.

It is assigned that the court erred in overruling appellant's challenge to the legal sufficiency of the evidence.
Respondent was injured in a "head on" collision between
two of appellant's cars, and his hand was severely cut, and
his thigh was struck in such a manner as to cause a bad
bruise to the muscles and to the bone, accompanied with
sub-acute inflamation of the periosteum. Such was
shown to be his condition by a letter in the record, written
by the company's surgeon. This letter was written January 23, 1903, a short time before this suit was begun. The
injury occurred April 23, 1901, nearly two years prior to
the writing of this letter. In the course of the testimony
of the doctor upon the witness stand, he said that he, as
the company's surgeon, examined respondent's injuries
soon after they were received, and that he then told re-

spondent that he thought he would be well in a short
time. It is easy for us to believe, from a personal standpoint, that the doctor was originally simply mistaken in
his judgment, but in view of the fact that his letter stated
that "there was a bad bruise to the muscles and to the
bone," and in view of his entire testimony upon the stand,
we think it became a question for the jury whether the
doctor, as surgeon of the company, knew at the time that
respondent was seriously injured. He admits that he did
not so inform respondent. If he knew the fact, and if his
failure to so inform respondent misled the latter to his
injury, it amounted to a legal fraud upon his rights. Appellant suggested that respondent had no right to rely upon
the physician's statement, and that it is not bound thereby.
We think the relation of employer and employe, having
long existed between appellant and respondent, the latter
had the right to place trust and confidence in the statements of the company's surgeon, who had examined the
injuries at the instance of the company. It therefore
became a question for the jury, even if they found that
respondent knowingly signed a release, whether he did
so as the result of being fraudulently misled by appellant's
agents as to the extent and character of his injuries.

The testimony of respondent as to what occurred at the
time of the signing of the alleged release is in substantial
accord with the allegations of the reply hereinbefore set
out. The chief negotiations leading up to the signing of
the paper, aside from the statements of the physician heretofore discussed, were between the claim agent and respondent. The sum of $70 was paid by the claim agent
to respondent at the time the paper was signed. That was
the amount of wages, at respondent's rate, for the time
he had been unable to work, and he says he was informed

by the claim agent, and that he understood, that he was simply signing a receipt for the wages, so that he could go to work again and get his easy job. The paper signed contained a release provision. It was prepared upon a printed blank and contained technical words, both in the printed and written matter, and bore evidence of careful and skillful preparation with a view to making it an effective release. In view of respondent's testimony as to his inability to read and understand English, and particularly such technical words and phrases as were contained in this paper, it became a question for the jury whether he did understand it, and whether the claim agent had intentionally and fraudulently misrepresented to him what it contained, and thereby purposely misled him into signing what he would not have signed, if its actual contents and legal effect had been fully made known to him. The jury could reasonably find, under the evidence, that appellant and respondent did not stand upon an equal footing, by reason of the latter's imperfect understanding of English and the legal effect of what he signed, or the nature and extent of his injuries, while the agents of the former were fully informed. They could also reasonably find that respondent was justified in placing confidence in what appellant's agents told him, because of his long established relations with the company.

That it is for the jury to say whether one has been fraudulently misled into signing a release of this character, under similar circumstances, is expressly held in the following cases: *Pioneer Cooperage Co. v. Romanowicz,* 186 Ill. 9, 57 N. E. 864; *Meyer v. Haas,* 126 Cal. 560, 58 Pac. 1042; *International etc. R. Co. v. Harris,* (Tex.) 65 S. W. 885; *Great Northern R. Co. v. Kasischke,* 104 Fed. 440; *Schus v. Powers-Simpson Co.,* 85 Minn. 447, 89 N. W. 68, 89 Am. St. 571, 57 L. R. A. 297; *Whitney & Star-*

rette Co. v. O'Rourke, 172 Ill. 177, 50 N. E. 242; *Indiana etc. R. Co. v. Fowler,* 201 Ill. 152, 66 N. E. 394, 94 Am. St. 158; *Burik v. Dundee Woolen Co.,* 66 N. J. L. 420, 49 Atl. 442; *St. Louis etc. R. Co. v. Phillips,* 66 Fed. 35. This court also discussed the general prinicples governing the procurement of a release by fraud in *Sanford v. Royal Ins. Co.,* 11 Wash. 653, 40 Pac. 609. There it was held that false statements as to the law, for the purpose of inducing one to sign a release of an insurance company, amounted to fraud, where the assured believed the insurer's agent to be his personal friend, and relied upon his statement that it would do no good to consult a lawyer, and also relied upon his superior knowledge and experience in such matters. In essential features that case contained elements not unlike those in the case at bar.

Appellant urges that the evidence is insufficient to establish fraud. It is true there is conflict, but the weight of the evidence must be determined by the jury. We think there is sufficient evidence bearing upon the question of fraud, if true, to support the verdict, and it is clearly established by the above authorities that when a purported release has been procured by fraud, it does not become a release, and is not a defense to an action of this kind. The cases cited by appellant are lacking in some elements found in the issues of this case. In *Pederson v. Seattle Consolidated St. R. Co.,* 6 Wash. 202, 33 Pac. 351, 34 Pac. 665, urged by appellant as decisive of this case, the respondent testified that he could understand and speak the English language, but could not write in that language; that the language used in the release was not read to him, and that if the words therein found had been read to him he would have understood them. It thus appeared that he was capable of understanding the paper upon merely hearing it read, and there was much testimony that it was read to him. In the case at bar the respondent testified that he did not, even at the time of the trial, understand the meaning of terms used, such as "release," "acquit," "discharge," etc. In the Pederson case there was no evidence that even any false statement was made to him. He merely claimed that the paper he signed was not read to him. He did not deny that a paper was read to him, but asserted that it was not the one he signed; thus leaving it to be inferred that, if he signed the paper, which was present at the reading, it was not correctly read. Moreover, in that case there was no evidence that any representations were made respecting the nature or duration of the injuries. In *Albrecht v. Milwaukee etc. R. Co.*, 87 Wis. 105, 58 N. W. 72, 41 Am. St. 30, the opinion expressly states that "there is no pretense that the plaintiff was induced to sign the release through fraud or misrepresentation or that any deception was practiced by misreading it to him." In *Wallace v. Chicago etc. R. Co.*, 67 Ia. 547, 25 N. W. 772, the party who signed the release stated in his testimony that there was nothing to hinder him from reading the papers before signing them, and that nothing was done to keep him from reading them. It is stated that he was a railroad conductor, had been a deputy sheriff, could read writing, make out papers and transact any kind of ordinary business. The court concluded from these facts that no fraud appeared, and that he was therefore bound by the writing which he signed. In *Fuller v. Madison Mut. Ins. Co.*, 36 Wis. 599, an insurance policy was involved. The applicant had been previously insured in the same company, and was held chargeable with notice of its bylaws and routine of business. The opinion states: "There is no pretense that he was overreached or deceived otherwise than in the fact that he could not and did not read the policy. That was his own negligence. His want of English is no excuse." *Hawkins v. Hawkins,* 50 Cal. 558, was determined upon demurrer, and it is said that no relation of special trust or confidence existing between the parties appeared, and that the terms and conditions of the writing were equally open to both. In *Chicago etc. R. Co. v. Belliwith,* 83 Fed. 437, the party who signed the contract testified that he did not ask any one to read it to him, and moreover his own attorney was present and assisted in the negotiations. In *Spitze v. Baltimore etc. Co.,* 75 Md. 162, 23 Atl. 307, 32 Am. St. 378, no representations of any kind were made when the release was signed, and no explanation was asked. The court found that the testimony did not prove fraud on the part of defendant, but carelessness on the part of plaintiff, and that such carelessness is not ground for the granting of any relief. In *Gulliher v. Chicago etc. R. Co.,* 59 Iowa 416, 13 N. W. 429, there was no evidence of any false representation when the release was signed. It neither appeared that the party was unable to read, nor that he was refused an examination and reading. The court say that they have searched the record in vain for any evidence of fraud in procuring the release. Having thus noted the cases cited by appellant upon this subject, we believe, for reasons above indicated, that they are all distinguishable from the case at bar, by reason of testimony in this case bearing upon fraudulent representations. The court therefore did not err in denying the challenge to the sufficiency of the evidence.

This disposes of appellant's chief contention in this case. Errors are assigned on the introduction of testimony. It is contended that evidence was improperly admitted as to statements made by the physician concerning the duration of respondent's injuries. Under the issues of the case, and within the authorities first above cited, the testimony was proper. It was for the jury to say whether the statements were intended to be, and were understood to be, mere expressions of opinion, upon which respondent had no right to rely; or whether it was intended that they should be received, and whether they were received, as the statements of facts, upon which he might and did rely, by reason of the relation of trust and confidence between himself and the agents of his long-time employer, and also by reason of the superior and peculiar professional knowledge of the physician. The same rule applies to statements said to have been made by the claim agent at the time the release was signed, and prior thereto. We think the instructions were clear and covered the law of the case.

The jury found the whole damage to be $2,570, and, following the court's instructions, they deducted $70 from said sum, which was the amount paid respondent when he signed the alleged release. Due credit was therefore given for the sum in respondent's hands, and, under the authorities, there was no necessity for its return before bringing this suit. It is true, respondent worked for and received wages from appellant for about a year and a half after his injuries, but he was presumably giving value received. A few weeks after the injury he began work again, as he says, under the statement of the physician, reinforced with that of the claim agent, that his injury was slight and that he would soon recover. But during the time he worked he seems to have suffered continually, and made no apparent progress toward recovery, which is not remarkable in view of the testimony of the physician that the bone was badly bruised. We do not see that his struggle to earn a living, even though as an employe of appellant, should militate against his recovery for the injuries previously received, if he never released appellant from liability. The verdict of the jury says that he did not release the company in fact.

We see no reason for disturbing the verdict, or for granting a new trial, and the judgment is affirmed.

FULLERTON, C. J., and MOUNT. ANDERS, and DUNBAR, JJ., concur.

[No. 5019. Decided July 25, 1904.]

MONA GERTRUDE LOUGH, BY HER GUARDIAN AD LITEM, FREDERICK LOUGH, *Respondent,* v. JOHN DAVIS & COMPANY, *Appellant.*[1]

DANGEROUS PREMISES—NEGLIGENCE—PRINCIPAL AND AGENT—DUTY TO REPAIR—LIABILITY OF AGENT IN CHARGE OF BUILDING—OWNER A NONRESIDENT. Agents in charge of a building, charged with the duty to make repairs, are liable for failure to keep the same in a safe condition, resulting in personal injuries to the child of a tenant, especially if the owner is a nonresident, or if service of process upon him is impossible.

SAME—EVIDENCE—AUTHORITY OF AGENT—IMPLIED FROM CONDUCT. In an action against an agent of a nonresident owner of a building, for damages sustained by the child of a tenant, through want of repairs, the fact that certain other repairs were authorized and paid for by the agent, who collected the rents and had funds that could be applied thereto, coupled with the fact that the owner was a nonresident or absent, is admissible to show that the agent had authority to make repairs, where the authority was not in writing, since it may be proved by parol and the agency implied from the conduct of the parties.

SAME—EVIDENCE OF AGENT'S AUTHORITY—SUFFICIENCY—QUESTION FOR JURY. In an action against agents alleged to be charged

[1]Reported in 77 Pac. 732.

with the duty to make repairs, brought on behalf of the child of a
tenant to recover for injuries sustained by the breaking of a rotten railing on the second floor, a nonsuit is properly refused,
where it appears that the agents, who collected the rents, ordered
and paid for similar repairs, and personally supervised the same,
apparently on their own authority, and the owner was a nonresident, or, at least, was never seen about the premises.

TRIAL—INSTRUCTIONS—COMMENT ON EVIDENCE.   It is not reversible error to state the issues raised by the pleadings, although there may have been no evidence offered as to some of
them, where the jury is properly instructed to base their findings entirely upon the evidence.

DANGEROUS PREMISES—NEGLIGENCE—AGENT CHARGED WITH DUTY
TO REPAIR — EVIDENCE OF AUTHORITY — SUFFICIENCY — DENIAL OF
AUTHORITY BY AGENT — DIRECTION OF VERDICT. The fact that
agents testify that they had no authority to make repairs to a
building except where it was specially given, and that none was
given to repair a railing and banister, which was necessary for
the safety of the occupants, does not warrant a directed verdict
for the defendants, where the agents made some repairs apparently on their own authority, and testified, as to their authority,
that the owner did not want to spend any more money than
absolutely necessary, and where the janitor, under their orders,
made and oversaw many small repairs such as securing the guard
rail in question.

Appeal from a judgment of the superior court for King
county, Griffin, J., entered July 28, 1903, upon the verdict
of a jury rendered in favor of the plaintiff for personal
injuries sustained by a child through the breaking of a
second-story railing or banister. Affirmed.

Chas. F. Munday, for appellant.

Frederick R. Burch and *Robert H. Lindsay*, for respondents.

HADLEY, J.—This cause was once before in this court.
See, *Lough v. John Davis & Co.*, 30 Wash. 204, 70 Pac.
491, 59 L. R. A. 802, 94 Am. St. 848. A demurrer to
the complaint had been sustained by the lower court, and

this court reversed the judgment, holding that the complaint stated a cause of action. The essential facts averred in the complaint will be found stated in the former opinion. The question involved is that of the liability of an agent in charge of a building, for injuries received by a child who fell from an upper porch, by reason of a rotten and unsafe railing, the father and guardian *ad litem* of the child being a tenant of the building. The complaint averred that the defendant, a corporation, as agent of the owner, had full power and authority from the principal to keep the property in repair, and in safe condition for tenants. Upon the return of the cause to the superior court, the defendant answered, admitting that it had authority to rent the property and collect the rents, but denying the said allegations as to authority to repair. A trial was had before the court and a jury, resulting in a verdict for the plaintiff. The defendant moved for a new trial, which was denied, and judgment was entered upon the verdict. The defendant has appealed.

It is first assigned that the court erred in overruling the demurrer to the complaint. That question was passed upon by this court in the former appeal. Appellant now asks us to overrule that decision. The question was exhaustively examined and discussed before, and the decision is supported by eminent authority. We shall therefore adhere to the former ruling.

The property was owned by one Webb, and both he and the appellant were made parties defendant. Webb, however, was not served with process, and the question of his liability in the premises is therefore not before us. Respondent's complaint alleges that Webb was a nonresident of this state. The allegation was disputed by appellant, and there was testimony to the effect that he was a resident of King county, and was available for the service of process. The record, however, shows an evident earnest effort on the part of respondent's counsel to find his location for the purpose of making service upon him, and this was supplemented by the sheriff's return that he could not find him in King county. There is also in the record a certified copy of a deed executed by Webb, bearing date December 18, 1901, in which he recites that he was "formerly of King county, state of Washington, but now of Staunton county, state of Virginia." The complaint was verified and filed a little more than one month before the date of said deed, to wit, on November 4, 1901. It also appears from the evidence that Webb was never seen by the tenants of the building. They knew no one as being in charge thereof except the appellant, and it does not appear that Webb was ever about the property, or gave it any personal attention. The circumstances, therefore, make the fact of his residence in this state at least a doubtful one, and also show that, even though he may in fact have been a resident, yet he practically eluded a personal service of the summons.

The building was a large four-story frame structure, occupied by numerous tenants. The rotten and insecure condition of the railing which gave way cannot be doubted, and this was, also, accompanied by other similar dilapidated conditions about the premises. The evidence also shows that it was bought for speculative purposes, and this is given as a reason for the limited repairs. The child fell from an upper porch by reason of the insecure railing, and received serious injuries, which must be lifelong in effect, thus entailing upon her permanent suffering and inconvenience, through the neglect of some one. We make these observations at this time, not because the owner of the property, under the theory of the complaint, was a necessary party, and not because it is material in this case whether the owner was in fact a resident or nonresident, but by way of argument, in order to show what we believe to be the wisdom of the rule declared by this court in its former decision—that any one under such circumstances as appear in this case, who is charged with a duty respecting the repair of property, shall not escape the consequences of his neglect, when serious harm to an innocent person has resulted therefrom. Particularly should this be so if the owner is a nonresident, or may so direct his whereabouts as to make the service of personal process upon him a difficult, if not an impossible, thing. It must always be remembered, however, that, in order to charge an agent, he must have authority to make repairs at the owner's expense, which places upon him the duty to do so. This was what was decided before, and its application to the facts of this case will be hereinafter examined.

It is assigned that the court erred in permitting testimony to be given as to certain repairs made by one Case and others, in the absence of a showing that the authority to make the repairs was vested in appellant by Webb, the owner. It is not disputed that Case and the others made the repairs by authority of appellant, and were paid therefor by appellant. It is also admitted that appellant was the owner's agent to the extent of renting the property and collecting the rents. The evidence was therefore proper as tending to show that appellant had, also, authority to repair, inasmuch as it had undertaken to make at least some repairs. It appeared that appellant collected and handled the rents, thus having in its possession funds of the owner which could have been applied upon repairs. The fact that repairs were made by authority of, and paid

for by, appellant was, therefore, proper to go before the
jury as a circumstance connected with the conduct of the
parties, coupled also with the fact that the owner at no
time appeared to be personally present and directing as to
repairs. Under the evidence complained of, there must
have been some authority to repair, and whether that authority was general, or special and limited, was a fact for
the jury to determine from the conduct of the parties and
attending circumstances. It is not claimed by appellant
that its authority as agent was created by writing. It was
therefore competent to prove it by parol. In such case,
the agency may be implied from the conduct of the parties,
and both the fact and scope of the agency are for the jury,
under proper instructions from the court. *London Sav.
Fund Soc. v. Hagerstown*, 36 Pa. St. 498, 78 Am. Dec.
390. In the above case the court said: "And in all
instances where the authority, whether general or special,
is to be implied from the conduct of the principal, or
where the medium of proof of agency is *per testes*, the jury
are to judge of the credibility of witnesses and of the im-
plications to be made from their testimony." See, also,
Nicoll v. Amer. Ins. Co., 3 Woodb. & M. (U. S.) 529,
Fed. Cas. No. 10,259; *Dickinson County v. Mississippi
Valley Ins. Co.*, 41 Ia. 286; *Nicholson v. Golden*, 27 Mo.
App. 132; *Golding v. Merchant & Co.*, 43 Ala. 705; *Jacobson v. Poindexter*, 42 Ark. 97.

It is next assigned that the court erred in overruling
the defendant's motion for nonsuit. It had already appeared that the aforesaid Case made, and caused to be
made, repairs, under the direction of appellant. It was
shown that Case himself connected the toilets to the sewer,
nailed up the railing which broke, put a brace against a
board in the alley, worked at tarring the roof, repaired the
rear steps, nailed a board across the north stairway, and

fixed the windows. Others, employed through and directed by Case, but paid by appellant, repaired the fence, built a bulkhead on the side of the house to prevent the earth in the alley, which was higher than the foundation of the house, from coming against the house, put boards in the walks around the house, put shores under the house, cleaned away the dirt which had fallen down from the house against the next property, and cleared away some evaporating works from the south side of the house. There was also testimony that John Davis, the president of appellant company, was about the premises and gave immediate and peremptory orders concerning certain repairs, the necessity for which appeared to have then first come to his notice. The directions were given in such a manner as to warrant the jury in concluding that he had authority to act upon his own judgment, and without consulting the owner as to such small details as the repairing and strengthening of a porch banister and railing. It having been admitted that appellant was the owner's agent for at least some purposes, and it having appeared that all the repairs were made and paid for under the direction of appellant, the owner never being seen in connection therewith, it was for the jury to say, under the circumstances, whether appellant derived its authority from the owner to make the repairs it did make, and, if so, whether its authority was extended to as simple a matter as the repair of this railing, which was, in grade and character, similar to a number of other repairs that were made. In *Wilcox v. Chicago etc. R. Co.*, 24 Minn. 269, the following instruction was requested and refused:

"In order to raise a presumption that a person is authorized to act for another, the acts and recognitions of acts relied upon as evidence of authority must be more than one act of the alleged agent, and one recognition of the

act by the principal. They must have been done often
enough to raise in the mind of a person of ordinary care
a presumption of authority given by the principal to the
alleged agent."

The supreme court, commenting upon the refused instruction, said:

"This request is bad; a single act of the agent and a
recognition of it by the principal may be so unequivocal
and of so positive and comprehensive a character, as to
place the authority of the agent to do similar acts for the
principal beyond any question. The value of such proof
does not depend so much on the number of acts as upon
their character."

Even if it be conceded that the rule as stated by the court
is too strong, we think it must, also, be conceded that the
requested instruction did comprehend the law, and the
frequent similar acts on the part of the agent in the case
at bar bring the case within the terms of said requested
instruction. The court did not err in denying the motion
for nonsuit.

It is urged that the court erred in its statement of the
issues to the jury, in that it referred to certain averments
of the complaint which, it is claimed, are not supported
by any evidence. It is appellant's position that the court
should either not have referred to such allegations of the
complaint, or should have told the jury that there was no
evidence upon the subject. Should the court have made
the latter statement to the jury, it might have subjected
itself to the criticism of commenting upon the evidence.
We see no error in stating the issues, as laid in the pleadings, when the jury are instructed that they must base
their findings entirely upon evidence. Such was made
sufficiently clear to the jury in this case. No other errors
are urged upon the instructions given, but assignments are
made upon the refusal to give several requested ones. We

think the instructions given fully and fairly cover the law of the case, and that no prejudicial error was committed in refusing the requested instructions.

The next claims of error, which are considered together, are that the court refused to instruct the jury to return a verdict for the defendant, and also that the motion for a new trial was overruled. This contention is based upon the claim that there was not sufficient evidence upon which to base the verdict. We have already referred to the evidence introduced prior to the motion for nonsuit, and which we have held sufficient for submission to the jury. The testimony in behalf of defendant was to the effect that it had no general authority to repair, and that the repairs which were made by it were made under special authority and direction. There was also testimony by officers of the defendant, and also by a Mr. Smith, an uncle of Webb, the owner, that no special instructions were given to repair the guard rail in question. Smith appears to have, in some manner, represented Webb in Seattle, and it is claimed that authority to repair came only through him. Webb, the owner, did not testify at the trial. As already stated, there were at least some repairs ordered by appellant, under circumstances which justified the jury in finding that they were ordered without waiting for special directions. The secretary of the company testified that appellant was authorized to keep the building clean and do the janitor work. Just what was comprehended in the janitor work was not stated, but the man Case, who made and oversaw so many of the small repairs, was the janitor, and these circumstances were such as we think justified the jury in concluding that such small repairs as the nailing and securing of this guard rail were included in the janitor's duties.

Mr. Davis, the president of appellant company, was asked the following question: "What power or authority or direction from Webb, or any one representing Webb, did John Davis & Company have as to repairs to the property?" to which he answered: "Well, they did not want to spend any more money than was absolutely necessary on it." From the above the jury could reasonably imply an authority to make no more repairs than were absolutely necessary, and it certainly appeals to any reasonable mind that the repair of this guard rail and banister was necessary for the safety of the occupants of the building, who paid rent with the expectation of enjoying reasonably safe premises. It is true, Mr. Davis afterwards testified, in answer to further questions, that his company had no authority to make repairs except such as were specifically directed, but the above was his answer to a plain and direct question, the first upon the subject, and was as much for the consideration of the jury as any of his other answers. The case was fairly submitted to the jury. They were not left to the realm of speculation for the verdict they returned, as suggested by appellant, but they had substantial evidence, as above outlined, and from said facts, the attending circumstances, and the conduct of the parties, they found that appellant had authority to make the repair in question. The evidence is such that we do not deem it our province to disturb that finding. Not only did the jury find the fact, but the trial court, who heard and saw the witnesses, also passed upon the sufficiency of the evidence by a denial of a new trial. With the fact of authority to repair established, the duty to do so arose within the former decision in this case. That duty having been neglected, it follows that the appellant is liable. The evidence upon other features necessary to establish liability is ample and unquestioned. The judgment is affirmed.

FULLERTON, C. J., and MOUNT, ANDERS, and DUNBAR, JJ., concur.

[No. 4737. Decided July 26, 1904.]

B. BERTELSON, *Respondent*, v. D. M. HOFFMAN, *Appellant.*[1]

BROKERS—ACTION TO RECOVER COMMISSION—DISCLOSING IDENTITY OF PURCHASER—COMPLAINT—SUFFICIENCY. A complaint in an action to recover a real estate broker's commission is not demurrable because of failure to allege that the agent disclosed to the defendant the identity of the purchaser, where it does not appear that he refused to do so, or that the defendant made demand therefor, or suffered any injury from the fact of concealment.

TRIAL—VERDICT—CONFLICTING EVIDENCE. The verdict of a jury will not be disturbed upon conflicting testimony, when supported by substantial evidence.

BROKERS—ACTION TO RECOVER COMMISSION—EVIDENCE—MATERIALITY OF OTHER DEALS. Where, in an action to recover commissions, plaintiff was asked on cross-examination what other property he had ever been asked to sell for defendant, besides that involved in the suit, an objection on the ground of immateriality was properly sustained.

SAME—VALUE OF LAND. Evidence that the actual value of property is $20,000, and its rental value $1,500, is not admissible as tending to show the improbability of an agreement to sell for $18,000, since the disparity is not sufficient to warrant this class of evidence.

SAME—CUSTOMARY COMMISSIONS—PLEADING AND PROOF—INSTRUCTIONS. It was proper to refuse to instruct that under the pleadings plaintiff could not recover unless the jury should find an express promise by defendant to pay the commission, where the allegations of the complaint are predicated upon both an express promise and an agreement to pay the usual and customary commission for like sales, and evidence was received in support thereof, it not appearing that defendant objected to the complaint on the ground that it alleged duplicate causes of action.

Appeal from a judgment of the superior court for Pierce county, Huston, J., entered December 5, 1902, upon the

[1]Reported in 77 Pac. 801.

verdict of a jury rendered in favor of the plaintiff. Affirmed.

B. F. Heuston, for appellant.

J. W. A. Nichols (*John C. Stallcup,* of counsel), for respondent.

PER CURIAM.—B. Bertelson, plaintiff, commenced an action in the superior court of Pierce county against D. M. Hoffman, defendant, to recover $500, alleged to have been earned by Bertelson as a broker's commission in procuring a purchaser for defendant Hoffman's real estate, situate in the city of Tacoma, known as the Board of Trade saloon. The complaint alleges, the listing of the property by the defendant with plaintiff for sale, upon terms fixed by Hoffman, being five thousand dollars in hand, or to be paid on consummation of sale, and the balance—thirteen thousand dollars—to be paid on or before five years from date of sale, with six per cent interest on such deferred payment; "that plaintiff did procure a purchaser for said property, at the said price and upon the said terms, fixed by defendant as aforesaid, who was ready, able, and willing to buy the same at the said price and terms, and who did accept from plaintiff his said offer of said property; that, on or about the 29th day of May, 1902, plaintiff notified defendant that the said property was sold according to defendant's directions, and upon the terms and at the price fixed by defendant as aforesaid, and the said sum of five thousand dollars was ready for payment." The complaint further alleges, that the defendant declined and refused to make said contract of sale, and still refuses so to do; that "plaintiff became entitled to receive his commission, at the usual and customary rate for like sales, and which defendant had agreed to pay plaintiff for procuring such purchaser, to wit; in the sum of five hundred dollars."

The answer was a general denial. There was a jury trial. A verdict was rendered in plaintiff's favor for $500, the amount claimed. The defendant made and filed his motion for a new trial, which was denied, and judgment was entered on the verdict. Defendant appeals.

(1) Appellant contends (quoting from the language used in the brief of his counsel) that "the complaint is defective in failing to allege that appellant knew or that knowledge of the identity of the proposed purchaser was communicated to him by respondent. Our contention in this respect is that it is not enough for a broker to find a purchaser ready and willing to buy, but that he must bring the parties together, that it may be fairly said that the principal has also found a buyer." This is undoubtedly the general rule, which has been frequently recognized and affirmed by text book writers and the decisions of the courts. *Carstens v. McReavy*, 1 Wash. 359, 25 Pac. 471; *Barnes v. German Sav. and Loan Soc.*, 21 Wash. 448, 58 Pac. 569; *Baars v. Hyland*, 65 Minn. 150, 67 N. W. 1148. The question to be decided is, how far this general rule applies to the facts presented in the action at bar. In *Veasey v. Carson*, 177 Mass. 117, 58 N. E. 177, 53 L. R. A. 241, the court decided that the concealment of the name of the actual purchaser of land, and the substitution of the name of a fictitious vendee, is not the concealment of such a material fact as will prevent the broker from recovering his commission, unless it appears that the owner was in some manner prejudiced by such concealment; that the court could not, in such case, declare, as a matter of law, that the broker had forfeited his right to recover his commission.

"Even if ordinarily a broker is required to furnish the name of the purchaser as a condition precedent to his right to claim commissions on the sale, as the defendants inter-

posed no objection on that ground and absolutely disavowed
the sale, they waived the right to insist upon any such condition.   The rule no doubt is that when a broker, employed
to effect a sale, has found a purchaser willing to take upon
the terms named and of sufficient responsibility, he has
performed his contract and is entitled to the commissions
agreed upon, and the rule claimed, that the minds of the
parties did· not meet, has no application." *Duclos v. Cunningham,* 102 N. Y. 678, 6 N. E. 790.

In the above complaint, it nowhere appears that the
appellant ever demanded of respondent that he furnish
the name of the would-be purchaser, or that respondent
ever refused to disclose the name of such purchaser, or that
appellant suffered any injury from the fact of such concealment.   Testing the complaint by the propositions of
law enunciated in the two cases last cited, we are of the
opinion that the complaint states a cause of action, and
that our position in this respect is not inconsistent with
the other authorities cited, and the general principles of
law applicable to real estate brokers.

(2)   It is next urged that the evidence was insufficient
to sustain the verdict of the jury.   The record shows that,
regarding the material issues in this controversy, the testimony was squarely in conflict.   It was the peculiar province of the jury to determine these issues arising on such
conflict.   The learned counsel for appellant does not dispute this proposition of law, but argues that the uncontradicted testimony fails to sustain such verdict.   We think
that the contentions of the counsel in this respect are untenable.   The principal argument of appellant under this
head has been answered in the preceding paragraph of this
opinion, wherein we considered the attack upon the complaint on the ground that it failed to state facts sufficient to
constitute a cause of action.   The other points made by appellant on this branch of the case relate chiefly to the good

faith of the respondent in the transaction, and the credibility that should be attached to the testimony adduced in his behalf at the trial. These are questions of fact, which were settled by the verdict. This record shows that there was substantial evidence tending to support the material averments of the complaint.

(3) It is further assigned and argued that the lower court committed reversible error in ruling out certain testimony offered by appellant at the trial. The respondent testified regarding the listing of the property with him for sale, and the refusal of appellant to sell on the terms fixed. The latter's counsel, after having asked respondent some preliminary questions on his cross-examination, proceeded as follows:

"Q. Did you ever do any other business for Mr. Hoffman in the real estate line? A. No, sir. Q. Did he ask you to sell any other property? A. Yes, sir. Q. What other property? Objected to as immaterial. The court: What is the object of this? Mr. Heuston: The object is to show the status of the parties with reference to one another, and to show that they have a bearing as to whether or not Mr. Hoffman entered into this contract. The court: I think you can do that, so far as this contract is concerned, with reference to this property. Mr. Heuston: We want to show that this plaintiff was the agent of the other party, instead of the agent of Mr. Hoffman. The court: . That is a matter of defense, and does not belong to this cross-examination. Objection sustained. Exception noted."

It is to be borne in mind that this cross-examination did not relate to any matter brought out on the direct examination. We fail to discover how this offer could have any bearing on the contract upon which suit was brought, or that such offer was, at that stage of the proceedings, pertinent to any matter connected with the subject of the action. We therefore conclude that the trial court committed no error in excluding such testimony.

The contention of appellant that the court below erred
in not permitting him to introduce testimony with regard
to the value and rentals of this property cannot be successfully maintained. Such offer tended to show that the
actual value of this property was $20,000, and the annual
rental thereof $1,500, at the time respondent claimed that
it was placed in his hands to sell. Therefore, according to
appellant's theory, this evidence, if admitted, would tend
to show the improbability of appellant having entered into
this agreement, fixing a definite compensation to be paid
respondent, as alleged in the complaint, on the basis of the
valuation contended for by respondent. In the case of
Wheeler v. Buck & Co., 23 Wash. 688, 63 Pac. 566, this
court held that, "In an action on a contract for work, when
the testimony is conflicting as to the price agreed upon for
the work, it is competent to show the value of such work
at the time the contract was made, as tending to show what
the agreed price was." In support of this proposition, the
case of *Allison v. Horning,* 22 Ohio St. 138, is cited in the
opinion, "in which the plaintiff claimed that the agreed
price for the work was $1.50 a perch, and the defendant
claimed that the contract price was $1.35 a perch, the
plaintiff was permitted to prove what it was worth to do
the work embraced in the contract." The ruling in this
Ohio case seems to have been based upon *Kidder v. Smith,*
34 Vt. 294, in which the court decided that, "When the
testimony is conflicting as to the price agreed upon in the
sale of personal property, it is competent to show the
value of the property at the time of sale, as tending to
show what the real contract was." The judge, delivering
the opinion of the court in this case, uses the following
language:

"Where the disparity between the value of the property,
and what is claimed to have been the contract price, is

small, and within the fair range of what different persons
might esteem to be a fair value, such evidence would be
very slight, perhaps too slight to be admissible, but when
the difference is very great, and beyond the range of fair
difference in judgment, it might be entitled to much weight,
and the wider the difference, proportionably stronger would
be the evidence furnished by it."

The significance of this language is very apparent when
applied to the appellant's position regarding this assignment of error. The difference between the contentions of
the respective parties to this litigation as to the valuation
of this property was not sufficient to justify the trial judge
in admitting this class of testimony, which we think was
properly excluded.

(4) Appellant urges that the trial court erred in refusing to give the following instruction to the jury: "Under
the pleadings in this case, plaintiff cannot recover unless
you find an express promise by defendant to pay the commission." The allegations of the complaint are predicated
upon both an express promise, and an agreement to pay the
usual and customary commission for like sales as above
noted. The record fails to show that the appellant ever
moved against the complaint on the ground that respondent
alleged therein duplicate causes of action, or in any other
manner. Moreover, it has been held in actions of this kind,
that it is not error to admit evidence as to the reasonable
value of services performed under allegations of an express
promise. *Sussdorff v. Schmidt*, 55 N. Y. 320; *Bûcking-
ham v. Harris*, 10 Colo. 455, 15 Pac. 817. Evidence having been introduced and received on behalf of respondent
in support of those allegations, no error was committed in
the refusal of the court below to grant appellant's request
restricting the jury's consideration to the alleged express
promise to pay respondent for services rendered.

No reversible error appearing in the record, the judgment of the superior court must be affirmed.

[No. 4845. Decided July 26, 1904.]

THE MINNESOTA SANDSTONE COMPANY, *Respondent*, v.
F. LEWIS CLARK, *Appellant*.[1]

EVIDENCE—VARYING WRITING BY PAROL—CONTRACTS—LEGALITY
—AGREEMENT AS TO REFUND ON FREIGHT SHIPPED. Where the purchaser of stone agreed in writing to pay the freight, and alleges
an oral agreement whereby the vendor guaranteed that the same
should not exceed thirty cents per cwt., agreeing to pay any excess, or to turn over to the purchaser any amount that the railroad company might refund, oral evidence will not be held admissible to vary the terms of the written agreement, as in the
case of an illegal contract, on account of the illegality of such
refund, where the illegality of the contract was not pleaded, and
the evidence touching such illegality was meager, and fails to
show any intent to violate the law, except by indulging in forced
construction or innuendo.

SAME—CONTRACTS—ILLEGAL PART SEPARABLE. If such an agreement were illegal, plaintiff could still recover on the balance of
the contract, since the consideration is legal and the illegal provision is separable from the rest of the contract.

SAME—CONSTRUCTION OF CONTRACT—ORAL AGREEMENT VARYING
TERMS OF WRITING. Where a written contract of sale provided
that the purchaser will pay the freight charges "as agreed upon
between you and I, the above price being f. o. b.," parol evidence
of an oral agreement that the seller would pay any freight
charges in excess of a certain rate is inadmissible, as contradicting the writing.

Appeal from a judgment of the superior court for Spokane county, Richardson, J., entered March 21, 1902, in
favor of the plaintiff, by direction of the court upon withdrawing the case from the jury at the close of the evidence,
in an action for a balance due for stone sold and delivered.
Affirmed.

Thayer & Belt, for appellant, to the point that the oral
agreement made in this case did not vary or contradict the

[1]Reported in 77 Pac. 803.

written contract, cited, Jones, Evidence, §§ 444, 445;
Browne, Parol Evidence, § 50; *Ruggles v. Swanwick*, 6
Minn. 526; *King v. Dahl*, 82 Minn. 240, 84 N. W. 737;
Gibbons v. Rush Co., 65 N. Y. Supp. 215; *Mt. Vernon Stone
Co. v. Sheely*, 114 Iowa 313, 86 N. W. 301; *John Hutchison
Mfg. Co. v. Pinch*, 107 Mich. 12, 64 N. W. 729, 66 N. W.
240; *Hines v. Willcox*, 96 Tenn. 148, 33 S. W. 914, 34
L. R. A. 824; *Anderson v. National Surety Co.*, 196 Pa.
St. 288, 46 Atl. 306.

Moore & Corbett, for respondents.

PER CURIAM.—The Minnesota Sandstone Company,
plaintiff, commenced this action against F. Lewis Clark,
defendant, in the superior court of Spokane county, to recover a balance due said company on a written contract.
Judgment was rendered herein in favor of plaintiff, and
defendant appeals.

Respondent company's cause of action is founded upon
a written contract, executed to it by appellant, which is as
follows:

"September 13, 1900.
"Mr. W. W. Butler, Agent Minnesota Sandstone Co., Spokane, Washington. Dear sir: We accept your proposal
for the sum of five thousand and two hundred and fifty
dollars for the cut stone for the Spokane Club Building, to
be erected at the corner of Washington St. and Riverside
Ave., Spokane, Washington. With the following conditions: The stone is to be the Kettle River Sandstone, from
the quarries of the Minnesota Sandstone Co., at Sandstone,
Minnesota; the stone to be cut, fitted and finished ready
for placing in the wall; the finish to be ten cut, patent ham-
mered face, all stone to be of the best quality and free from
flaws, seams or streaks, and as good as sample submitted
and now on file at this office. The work to be done in accordance with the plans, specifications, sections and details
prepared by John K. Dow, architect, and such further draw-

ings as may be necessary to illustrate the work to be done,
so far as they may be consistent with the original drawings, and to the satisfaction of the architect; the work to
be finished and delivered complete on or before the 5th day
of October, 1900.   We will pay the freight charges, as
agreed upon between you and I, the above price being f. o.
b. Sandstone, Minnesota.   Respectfully yours, John K.
Dow, architect.

"The above conditions accepted.   W. W. Butler, Agent."

The complaint alleges that respondent furnished and delivered to appellant the aforesaid stone at the agreed price
of $5,250, and that appellant has paid respondent, on ac-
count of this contract, $4,500, leaving a balance due of
$750, for which, with legal interest from January 1, 1901,
respondent asks judgment.   Appellant in his answer admitted the execution of the contract, but alleged that it
comprehended other stipulations pertaining to the payment of the freight on said stone from Sandstone, Minnesota, to Spokane, Washington; alleged that it was agreed,
as a part of said contract, that respondent would guarantee
that the freight rate, to be charged by the Great Northern
R. Co. for transporting said stone from the above point in
Minnesota to Spokane, Wash.; should not exceed thirty
cents per cwt.; that, "if said railway company should
charge, and defendant should pay, more than said rate,
then, that plaintiff would refund to defendant any excess
that defendant should be obliged to pay said railway company in excess of said rate, and that, if said railway company should refund or rebate any moneys paid by defendant to it in excess of said rate, then that such moneys, so
refunded, should belong to defendant and be delivered and
paid over by plaintiff to defendant."

The first affirmative defense reiterates this alleged agreement pertaining to the refunding of the excess of freight
charges, which were paid by appellant at the rate of eighty-

five cents per cwt., amounting to the sum total of $2,561.90. This defense further alleges that, "thereafter said railway company paid to plaintiff, through its said agent, W. W. Butler, as a rebate on said freight, so as to make the freight charges amount to thirty cents per cwt., the sum of $1,657.70, and said plaintiff received said sum of $1,657.70 from said railway company on or about the 1st day of January, 1901, and still retains and holds the same, but the plaintiff refuses to pay same to defendant, and wrongfully withholds same, although payment thereof has been demanded of it." It is further alleged that appellant was obliged to recut and refit a portion of the stone furnished, at an expense of $121.38. The second affirmative defense alleges that respondent company received from the Great Northern R. Co. the sum of $1,657.70 for the use and benefit of appellant, which it refused to pay over to appellant. Appellant demanded judgment in accordance with the allegations of his said answer. Respondent, by its reply, denies the new matter alleged in the answer, except as to the above credit of $121.38, which it admits.

There is very little dispute between the parties to this controversy with regard to its salient features. There was no showing made in the court below at the trial that respondent ever received from the railway company the rebates alleged on the part of appellant. It appears from the transcript that appellant offered evidence tending to show that respondent guaranteed that the above freight charges on this stone between the above points should not exceed thirty cents per cwt., and that respondent would repay appellant the excess over and above such rate, if he should be compelled to pay the carrier company a greater rate; that appellant was compelled to and did pay the railway company, as freight charges for transporting such stone, eighty-five cents per cwt. Respondent company objected to the introduction of this evidence on two grounds: (1) that such testimony tended to prove an oral agreement inconsistent, and at variance, with the above written contract; (2) that such oral agreement was in violation of the federal statute commonly known as the interstate commerce law. This evidence was admitted tentatively, but, after all of the evidence was submitted, the trial court discharged the jury, and entered judgment in favor of respondent for the amount claimed in its complaint less the above credit of $121.38. It would seem from the remarks of the trial judge, as noted in the statement of facts, that both of the foregoing objections on the part of respondent were sustained.

The material questions raised on this record, necessary to the proper disposition of this appeal from appellant's standpoint, are presented by the first assignment of error: "The court erred in discharging the jury and ordering judgment for plaintiff." The theory of appellant, as stated in his answer, on which he seeks to maintain his counterclaim, is that respondent had collected certain rebates from the railway company, for which it had refused to account to appellant, in violation of the alleged oral agreement referred to in the written contract with regard to the payment of freight charges. From the testimony adduced at the trial, it would seem that appellant shifted his ground, and undertook to prove an oral guaranty on the part of respondent company, whereby it agreed to refund to appellant the amount of freight charges paid by him for the transportation of this stone over and above the thirty cents per cwt.

The testimony appearing in this record, touching the question of the illegality of this alleged oral contract or guaranty with reference to these freight charges, is very meager. After giving careful consideration to all the testimony regarding this feature of the transaction, we entertain grave doubts whether it tends to show that there was any intent or sinister purpose, on the part of both, or either, of the parties, to violate the law. It would seem to possess less strength in that behalf than the allegations appearing in the answer of appellant, who denies that such alleged oral agreement was illegal, and contends that it is perfectly consistent with the written contract, and that, if this oral contract were unlawful, and if the appellant could not recover on his counterclaim, the respondent is precluded from maintaining the present action, because the taint of illegality effects the entire contract.

On the other hand, respondent argues, that this written contract is complete in all of its terms; that, therefore, no oral testimony is permissible to vary or add to its provisions, in the absence of allegations of accident, fraud, or mistake; that the law will not presume that parties have entered into the unlawful arrangement upon which appellant bases his claims respecting these freight charges; and that, in any event, the illegal portion of this written contract may be eliminated and disregarded, and the respondent permitted to recover on the remaining provisions of the agreement. There is no question about the correctness of the proposition of law that, notwithstanding the general rule that parol evidence is inadmissible to contradict, vary, or add to a written contract, such rule does not preclude the admissibility of such evidence to show the illegality of a contract or that it was the result of accident, fraud, or mistake. It is also true, as a general rule, that none of these matters can be proven in the absence of pleadings tendering appropriate issues, where the party claiming relief in that respect has had the opportunity of so pleading, and failed so to do. It is also true that, "Whenever the illegality appears, whether the evidence comes from one side or the other, the disclosure is fatal to the case. No consent of the defendant can neutralize its effect. A stipulation in the most solemn form to waive the objection, would be tainted with the vice of the original contract, and void for the same reasons." *Coppell v. Hall,* 7 Wall. 558, 19 L. Ed. 244. See, 6 Rose's Notes on U. S. Rep. p. 1033; *Ah Doon v. Smith,* 25 Or. 89, 34 Pac. 1093; *Sampson v. Shaw,* 101 Mass. 145, 3 Am. Rep. 327.

The allegations in appellant's answer, with reference to this alleged oral agrement respecting freight charges, being denied by respondent in its reply, we are not inclined to indulge in any forced construction of the facts, and hold, from mere innuendo, that there was testimony tending to show that either of these litigants intended to evade or violate the law in entering into the alleged arrangement concerning these freight charges. If, however, we were of the contrary opinion, we would not be warranted in holding the entire contract illegal. The illegality would affect only that portion of the transaction relating to the refunding of the excess of freight charges. That part relating to the sale and purchase of this stone is plainly separable from, and independent of, that part respecting the freight charges, which brings this feature of the case at bar within the rule that, where the consideration of an agreement is legal, a separable illegal provision, free from the imputation of *malum in se,* may be rejected. *Gelpcke v. City of Dubuque,* 1 Wall. 221, 17 L. Ed. 519; *Webb v. Allington & Anderson,* 27 Mo. App. 570.

The last proposition presented for our consideration is whether the court below erred in deciding that this written

contract is complete in itself, and whether the reception of
oral testimony was not permissible to explain the meaning
of this provision in the instrument: "We will pay the
freight charges, as agreed upon between you and I, the
above price being f. o. b. Sandstone, Minnesota." "The rule
as to the inadmissibility of parol evidence which tends to
vary, alter, or modify a written contract is not infringed by
proof of any collateral parol agreement which does not
interfere with the terms of the written contract, although
it may relate to the same subject-matter." This quotation
is taken from the syllabus formulated by the court in the
case of *King v. Dahl,* 82 Minn. 240, 84 N. W. 737, and is
one of the numerous authorities, to which our attention has
been directed by the learned counsel for appellant, bearing
on this feature of the transaction. All of appellant's citations in that behalf seem to be of the same general import.
If the written contract involved in this controversy were
silent on the matter of the payment of freight rates, counsel's contention would be entitled to great. weight. But
does this alleged oral contract, on which appellant bases his
counterclaim, come within the purview of this rule of law
enunciated in the Minnesota case? We think not. This
stipulation provides that the appellant was to pay the
freight charges for the transportation of this stone, uncon-
ditionally—not a portion thereof. The price of the stone
was definitely fixed by the terms of the written agreement,
"free on board" the cars of the carrier company, at Sandstone, Minnesota. We are of the opinion that, to allow appellant to prove the verbal agreement for which he contends
respecting the payment of these transportation charges, in
the absence of allegations of accident, fraud, or mistake,
would be inconsistent with the express provisions of the
written agreement, and in violation of well settled princi-

ples of law, recognized and applied by the courts from time
immemorial, relative to the interpretation of written agreements.   The words found in the written instrument, "as
agreed upon between you and I," do not add to, or take
from, such instrument, in any legal sense, and may be rejected as surplusage.   This language denotes on its face
that the payment of the freight charges had theretofore
been agreed upon between these parties, and that appellant
would pay the same, as agreed upon prior to the execution
of the original contract, on which respondent bases its cause
of action.   In other words, appellant employs his own language to advise respondent that he will pay the stipulated
price for the stone, and also the freight charges thereon
from Sandstone to Spokane.   "Of course, if the testimony
was for the purpose of contradicting the written instrument
or to defeat the operative effect of it, in the absence of
fraud, or mistake, it would not be admissible." *Wright v.
Stewart,* 19 Wash. 184, 52 Pac. 1020.   See, further,
Pacific Nat. Bank v. San Francisco Bridge Co., 23 Wash.
425, 63 Pac. 207, wherein this court quotes with approval
the following language from the opinion in the case of
Eighmie v. Taylor, 98 N. Y. 288: "If we may go outside
of the instrument to prove that there was a stipulation not
contained in it, and so that only part of the contract was
put in writing, and then, because of that fact, enforce the
oral stipulation, there will be little of value left in the rule
itself."   We think that the principle of law embraced in
this language applies with full force to the facts presented
in the case at bar, and that, if we should hold with appellant and decide that oral testimony should have been received in the trial court in support of his contention above
noted, we would, in effect, have to ignore and discredit this
salutary proposition of law many times enunciated by this
and other courts, and long recognized by jurists.

Testing the facts in the present controversy by the foregoing propositions of law, no reversible error appearing in the record, we are of the opinion that the judgment of the superior court is correct, and must be affirmed.

[No. 5003. Decided July 26, 1904.]

T. K. ROBE, *Appellant*, v. SNOHOMISH COUNTY, *Respondent*.[1]

BRIDGES—NEGLIGENCE—COLLAPSE THROUGH DECAY OF TIMBERS—NOTICE OF DEFECT—DUTY OF COUNTY—INSTRUCTIONS. In an action against a county for personal injuries caused by the collapse of a bridge through the decay of timbers, an instruction commencing with the statement that the county cannot be held liable unless the authorities had been notified of the defect, is not prejudicial error, where the instructions as a whole properly state the duty of the authorities to exercise care to detect and guard against such defects, and that it was not necessary to prove actual notice, and properly defining constructive notice.

APPEAL AND ERROR—REVIEW—SPECIAL VERDICT—HARMLESS ERROR ON ANOTHER BRANCH OF CASE. Where a special finding establishes that the county authorities had no notice of defects in a bridge, and there is a general verdict for the county, error committed on another branch of the case is harmless, as the county would not be liable in any event.

Appeal from a judgment of the superior court for Snohomish county, Denney, J., entered June 5, 1903, upon the verdict of a jury rendered in favor of the defendant. Affirmed.

Brady & Gay and *John Francis McLean*, for appellant.

H. D. Cooley, for respondent.

FULLERTON, C. J.—The appellant sought by this action to recover damages for personal injuries, and for injuries

[1]Reported in 77 Pac. 810.

to his personal property, caused by the collapse of a bridge
over which he was crossing. The bridge was on a public
road in the respondent county, and the action was based on
the alleged failure of the county to keep the bridge in repair. The defect was found to consist of decayed timbers
not visible from a casual inspection of the bridge. The
jury, along with a general verdict in favor of the county,
returned a special verdict in which they found that the
county officers, charged with the maintenance of the bridge,
had no knowledge of its defective condition prior to the
accident, although they had used due diligence in its care
and maintenance. Judgment was entered on the verdict in
favor of the county, and this appeal is taken therefrom.

Among other assignments of error, it is contended that
the court erred in its instruction to the jury on the question
of what constituted notice to the county of the defective
condition of the bridge, the contention being that the instructions were conflicting and misleading. On this branch
of the case the court gave the following:

"You are instructed that before you can return a verdict
in favor of plaintiff upon either of the causes of action set
forth in plaintiff's complaint, you must find from a preponderance of the evidence . . . that the authorities
of said defendant county had been notified of such condition for a reasonable time prior to the happening of said
accident, or that such bridge had been so notoriously unsafe
as to amount to constructive notice to the authorities of said
county; and by reasonable time is meant such length of
time as would have allowed the repair of said bridge, or
prevention of its use, by said county; . . . that it is
the duty of the county not only to construct its bridges in
such a manner as that they shall be safe, but to use ordinary
care in keeping them in a safe condition for travelers and
all persons passing over said bridge, by removing therefrom timbers which by use have become, or may have become, decayed and rotten, and thus rendering the bridge

unsafe and dangerous; that the law charges the county with
the knowledge of the natural tendency of timber to decay,
and places upon the county the duty of exercising ordinary
care to detect and guard against any decay or rottenness
that might exist; that a failure to exercise such care upon
the part of the county will render the county liable, although it may have no actual notice of the condition of the
bridge; that it is not necessary, in order to charge the
county with negligence in suffering the bridge in question
to remain out of repair, for the plaintiff to prove actual
notice of it, but that such notice may be inferred if the
defect in the bridge was of such a character, and had continued for such a length of time as that the officers of the
county charged with the supervision and repair of the
bridges of the county might and probably would have discovered it if they had used ordinary care in the discharge of
their duties; that the county is liable in damages if it negligently suffered rotten and decayed timbers to remain in
the bridge in question, thus rendering it unsafe and dangerous."

While it may be true that the first part of this charge could
have been more happily expressed, we do not think it wrong
when taken in connection with the latter portion, which
expresses clearly the measure of the county's duty. It is a
familiar rule that instructions must be read as a whole,
and, if the whole charge fairly states the law of the case,
it will not work a reversal, even though disconnected portions of the charge may state the law too broadly. Tested
by this rule, these instructions are not erroneous.

The conclusion reached on this branch of the case renders
it unnecessary to notice the assignments of error pertaining
to the other branches of the case. It being true that the
officials of the county, having in charge the care and maintenance of the bridge, had no notice of its defective condition, and had used due diligence in its care and maintenance, there can be no recovery against the county in any

event, and it is useless to inquire whether the court committed error on a branch of the case which could only be material had it been found that the county was chargeable with notice of such defect.

The judgment is affirmed.

MOUNT, HADLEY, and ANDERS, JJ., concur.

[No. 4998. Decided July 26, 1904.]

E. J. CASETY, *Respondent,* v. ARTHUR C. JAMISON, *Appellant.*[1]

JUDGMENT—TRANSCRIPT FROM FOREIGN STATE—CERTIFICATE—REFERENCE TO SUMMONS—SHERIFF'S RETURN OF SERVICE PART OF SUMMONS. A transcript of a foreign judgment, in which the certificate of the clerk specifically refers to each of the papers attached, including the summons, but without mention of the sheriff's return of service, is not insufficient as failing to show the service, since the sheriff's return is part of the summons and is sufficiently described by the reference thereto.

TRIAL—VERDICT—FAILURE TO ASSESS AMOUNT—No DISPUTED QUESTION OF FACT. Where a verdict is returned without assessment of the amount of the recovery, but there was no disputed question of fact and the amount is known, the irregularity does not require a reversal, since the court could either direct a verdict or discharge the jury and enter the judgment.

Appeal from a judgment of the superior court for Spokane county, Richardson, J., entered February 23, 1903, upon the verdict of a jury rendered in favor of the plaintiff. Affirmed.

Hamblen & Lund, for appellant.

Ellis G. Soule, for respondent.

FULLERTON, C. J.—The respondent brought this action upon a personal judgment recovered by him against the

[1]Reported in 77 Pac. 800.

appellant in the municipal court of the city of Duluth, in the state of Minnesota. The appellant filed an answer putting in issue the existence of the judgment, and a trial was had, resulting in a judgment for the respondent for the full amount demanded.

The only question raised at the trial by the appellant was the sufficiency of the certificate to the transcript of the record of the Minnesota court by which it was sought to establish the existence of the judgment. The transcript consisted of a copy of the complaint, the summons and sheriff's return thereon showing personal service on the defendant, a notice of the withdrawal of certain attorneys who had purported to appear for the respondent, and the entry of final judgment. The clerk's certificate thereto recited that he had "carefully compared the foregoing papers writing with the original complaint, summons, notice and judgment in the action therein entitled, now remaining of record in my office, and that the same is a true and correct copy and transcript of said original papers and the whole thereof." It is insisted that this certificate is insufficient to permit the introduction of the sheriff's return on the summons because it makes no mention of such return; the contention being that it was necessary, in order to show jurisdiction in the Minnesota court to enter a personal judgment against the appellant, to show personal service on him within the jurisdiction of that court. Inasmuch as the judgment, which is conceded to be properly certified, recites that personal service of summons was made upon the appellant, we think it may fairly be questioned whether the return of the sheriff on the summons is material. *Ritchie v. Carpenter,* 2 Wash. 512, 521, 28 Pac. 380, 26 Am. St. 877. But conceding the rule to be otherwise, we think the certificate sufficient. At common law, and under the statute of this state—and we must presume the law of Minnesota to be the same—an officer's return of a summons is a certificate of the officer, indorsed upon or attached to the summons, reciting what he has done by virtue of its commands. When so indorsed upon, or attached thereto, the return becomes a part of the summons, and a copy of the summons, in order to be a true copy, must contain a copy of such return. The return being a part of the summons, it is, of course, sufficiently described by the word "summons."

The trial was had before a jury, which returned a verdict in favor of the respondent, but did not assess the amount of the recovery therein. The verdict was insufficient under section 5023 of the code, and, were there a conflict in the evidence as to the amount the respondent was entitled to recover, this irregularity would require a reversal of the judgment. But there was no disputed question of fact in the case, and there was nothing to submit to the jury for their determination. Under our practice the court was authorized, at the conclusion of the evidence, to either direct a verdict for the full amount sued for, or discharge the jury and enter a judgment for such amount. Its rights in these respects were not changed because the jury returned an irregular and insufficient verdict. It still had the power to direct the entry of such a judgment as the justice and law of the case required, and, as it did no more than this, the judgment ought not to be disturbed by this court.

The judgment appealed from is affirmed.

MOUNT, HADLEY, ANDERS, and DUNBAR, JJ., concur.

[No. 4546. Decided July 26, 1904.]

DAVID O'SULLIVAN, *Respondent*, v. MARGARET O'SUL-
LIVAN, *Appellant.*[1]

DIVORCE — CRUELTY — ABUSIVE LANGUAGE — FINDINGS OF TRIAL
COURT. In an action for a divorce brought by the husband, where
there was evidence that the wife was in the habit of applying
vile and opprobrious epithets to her husband without reason, and
that she had been carried into the house while under the influence
of liquor, and when in such condition was quite abusive, findings
of the trial court, who heard and saw the witnesses, that the
husband was entitled to a divorce on the ground of cruel treatment, will not be disturbed on appeal.

SAME—DIVISION OF PROPERTY. Findings of the trial court, upon
granting a divorce, that all of the property was community property, and making an equal division thereof, will not be disturbed
on appeal, upon the claim of the wife that her separate earnings,
accumulated before marriage, constituted the sole consideration
for a certain part of the property, where the evidence showed
that the same was purchased about one year after the marriage,
that both parties were industrious and accumulated money, and
there was not sufficient evidence to overcome the presumption
that property acquired after marriage belonged to the community.

Appeal from a judgment of the superior court for King
county, Griffin, J., entered August 7, 1902, upon findings
in favor of the plaintiff, after a trial on the merits before
the court without a jury, decreeing a divorce on the ground
of cruelty. Affirmed.

James Hamilton Lewis, Thomas B. Hardin, and *John E.
Humphries* (*Leroy V. Newcomb,* of counsel), for appellant.

John Arthur, for respondent.

PER CURIAM.—This was an action for divorce, instituted
by David O'Sullivan, plaintiff, against Margaret O'Sulli-

[1]Reported in 77 Pac. 806.

van, defendant, in the superior court of King county. Defendant appeals from the following judgment, entered in the trial court in such action:

"This cause having been regularly tried on the 4th day of August, 1902, upon the issues framed by the complaint, the answer, and the reply of the respective parties, the plaintiff appearing in person and by his attorney of record, and the defendant appearing in person and by her attorneys of record, and the testimony of witnesses in behalf of the respective parties having been duly submitted to the court, and the court having heretofore made its findings of fact and conclusions of law herein, making and stating the same separately, and having filed the same herein, from which it appears that all the material allegations of the complaint are sustained by the testimony, that there is no issue of the marriage between the plaintiff David O'Sullivan and the defendant Margaret O'Sullivan, and that all the property held by them, with the exception of lots numbered one (1) and two (2) in block numbered thirty (30) in Burke's Second Addition to the city of Seattle, is community property, and all and singular the law and the premises being by the court understood and fully considered, it is hereby

"ORDERED, ADJUDGED and DECREED, And this court does order, adjudge and decree, that the marriage between the plaintiff David O'Sullivan and the defendant Margaret O'Sullivan be dissolved, and the same is hereby dissolved, and the said parties are, and each of them is, free and absolutely released from the bonds of matrimony and all the obligations thereof; and the said parties are, and each of them is, expressly prohibited from contracting any marriage with a third party within the period of six months from the date of the entry of this decree, or if an appeal is taken, not until after the said appeal is finally determined.

"It is further ordered, adjudged and decreed that the property held by them be divided and awarded as follows: The plaintiff shall have his personal clothing and personal effects; also lots numbered severally one (1) and two (2) in block numbered thirty (30) in Burke's Second Addition to the city of Seattle; also that portion of lot numbered

one (1) in block numbered four (4) in W. R. Brawley's
Addition to the city of Seattle, commencing at the northeast corner of said lot and running thence south sixty-eight
(68) feet, thence west fifty-three (53) feet, thence north
sixty-eight (68) feet to the north line of said lot, being the
place of beginning; also that portion of lot numbered two
(2) in block numbered four (4) of said W. R. Brawley's
Addition to the city of Seattle, described as follows, to wit:
beginning at the northwest corner of said lot and running
thence south one hundred and twenty (120) feet, thence
east thirty-four (34) feet, thence north one hundred and
twenty (120) feet to the north line of said lot, thence west
thirty-four (34) feet to the northwest corner of said lot,
being the place of beginning; also all the rights and interests in mining claims in the Yukon Territory, Dominion
of Canada, mentioned in said Findings of Fact.

"The defendant shall have all the personal property other
than the personal clothng and personal effects of the plaintiff; said personal property for her including all the household furniture and the pianoforte; also all the remaining
portion of said lots numbered severally one (1) and two
(2) in block numbered four (4) in W. R. Brawley's Addition to the city of Seattle; also the west thirty (30) feet of
the east sixty (60) feet of lot numbered five (5) in block
numbered seven (7) in Terry's Fifth Addition to the city
of Seattle.

"It is further ordered, adjudged and decreed that the
plaintiff shall pay to the defendant, within one year from
the date of this decree, the sum of seven hundred and fifty
dollars ($750), with interest thereon at the legal rate until
paid, which said sum of seven hundred and fifty dollars
($750) shall be, until paid, a lien upon all of said real prop-
erty awarded to the plaintiff. The costs of this suit and the
attorneys' fees shall be paid by the respective parties. It is
further ordered that each party to this action shall have
right of access over any alleys now existing to the several
parcels of real property above mentioned, which right may
be taken away, restricted or modified by order of the court
if the privilege granted be abused by either party to the
injury of the other."

The assignments of error practically present but two questions for our consideration on this appeal.

(1) It is contended that the court below erred in granting respondent a divorce from appellant on the grounds of cruelty as alleged in the complaint. The trial court found, on this branch of the present controversy, that,

"The defendant has for several years last past treated the plaintiff with great cruelty and inflicted upon him indignities which have rendered his life burdensome. She has habitually called him improper and degrading names and frequently scolded him in a loud and boisterous manner. The plaintiff and the defendant can no longer live together as husband and wife. The plaintiff has used improper language in the presence of the defendant and her family; but offenses in this regard have been principally committed by the defendant."

This court has held, in numerous decisions, that, where we deemed the evidence adduced in the trial court as evenly balanced, or not clearly in appellant's favor, we were inclined to sustain the finding of the judge, who saw and heard the witnesses. *Hamar v. Peterson,* 9 Wash. 152, 37 Pac. 309; *Skeel v. Christenson,* 17 Wash. 649, 50 Pac. 466; *Washington Dredging etc. Co. v. Partridge,* 19 Wash. 62, 52 Pac. 523; *Cullen v. Whitham,* 33 Wash. 366, 74 Pac. 581; *Cochran v. Yoho,* 34 Wash. 238, 75 Pac. 815. Applying this rule to the facts in the case at bar, we are not prepared to hold that the trial court erred in finding appellant guilty of acts of cruelty towards respondent, as charged in the complaint. The testimony abundantly shows that respondent and appellant were industrious and frugal individuals; that respondent was a person of even temper, possessed the faculty of getting along smoothly with his employers, and was generally considered a good neighbor. There was also testimony in respondent's behalf tending to show that appellant was in the habit of applying vile and opprobrious epithets to her husband, without cause or reason; that respondent did not retaliate, but remained passive. Witness Jonathan Gifford testified that about one year before the trial, he took appellant off the street one evening and carried her into the house, at a time when she was under the influence of liquor and somewhat disorderly; that when in such a condition she was quite abusive, and had a good command of rough language. Mrs. O'Sullivan, while on the witness stand, denied that she had ever called her husband vulgar names or had applied to him opprobrious epithets, and emphatically contradicted all the statements of Gifford as to having been drunk and disorderly, and that he had picked her up off the street and carried her into the house. There was, also, some evidence in appellant's behalf tending to show that respondent had used improper language in the presence and hearing of Mrs. O'Sullivan and her family. We feel, after a careful examination of the record, that we would not be justified in setting aside the above finding, or in reversing the decision of the lower court on the main issues of the present controversy.

(2) The more serious contentions respecting this litigation arise over the adjustment of the property rights between the parties. The able counsel for appellant contend, vigorously, that their client was treated very inequitably in this respect; that Mrs. O'Sullivan should have been awarded the premises designated in the record as No. 925 Washington street in the city of Seattle, in addition to other property given her. The valuation placed on this property, by competent witnesses who testified at the hearing, was $4,250, and it constituted a part of the property awarded respondent in the division made by the superior court. It appears from the evidence that, at the time re-

spondent and appellant intermarried in 1888, he was the
owner of lots 1 and 2 in block 30, Burke's Second Addition
to Seattle, which was of the value of $400.   These lots
were set over to respondent.   The trial court found, among
other things, that all the real estate and household furniture
described in the above decree, save these two lots in Burke's
Second Addition, were acquired by them since their marriage, and in its decree divided the same approximately
equally between the parties, giving to each property of
the value of about eight thousand dollars.

The appellant urges that the testimony showed that her
individual earnings, accumulated prior to her marriage
with respondent, constituted the sole and exclusive consideration for the purchase of the property described as the
west 30 feet of east 60 feet of Lot No. 5, Blk. 7, in Terry's
Fifth Addition to Seattle.   The value of this property,
as shown by the testimony, was $1,300.   It appears, how-
ever, that this property was purchased by appellant a little
over one year after her marriage with Mr. O'Sullivan, and
that both members of the community were frugal and industrious, and accumulated money.   All property accumulated by husband and wife, during the continuance of the
marriage relation, is presumed to be community property,
and we fail to find sufficient evidence to overcome such presumption with regard to the property in question.   Under
the showing made, we think we would not be warranted in
taking from respondent, and setting off to appellant, the
property known as 925 Washington street, Seattle, in addition to the property and interests which had already been
awarded to her.

As we find no reversible error in the record, the judgment of the court below must be affirmed, and it is so ordered.

[No. 4846. Decided July 26, 1904.]

MONROE MILL COMPANY, *Respondent, v.* GEORGE MENZEL,
Appellant.[1]

WATERS—STREAM NAVIGABLE FOR SHINGLE BOLTS—PLEADINGS—
COMPLAINT TO ENJOIN OBSTRUCTION—AVERMENTS NOT INCONSIST-
ENT. An averment in a complaint that a stream is navigable for
shingle bolts is not negatived by another averment that plaintiff
had constructed a dam for the purpose of furnishing a sufficient
supply of water to conveniently and rapidly float shingle bolts
and other timber products down said stream; and it was not
error to admit evidence supporting such a complaint.

SAME—RIPARIAN RIGHTS—ACQUIESCENCE IN UNLAWFUL USE OF
STREAM—ESTOPPEL—PLEADINGS—SUFFICIENCY OF COMPLAINT. Averments in a complaint that plaintiff cleared a stream of obstructions on defendant's land, in order to facilitate the floating of
shingle bolts, that defendant acquiesced therein, assisted in clean-
ing out such obstructions, and thereafter used the benefits therefrom and the flow of water as furnished by a dam constructed
by plaintiff for a period of two years, are not sufficient to plead
an estoppel against defendant's objecting to the interference by
plaintiff with the natural flow of the stream; but such failure to
show an estoppel does not defeat the plaintiff's action for an injunction, where by other averments it appears that the stream is
navigable and defendant threatens to obstruct the same.

SAME—NAVIGABILITY OF STREAM—FRESHETS—LOWER RIPARIAN
RIGHTS. A stream which in its natural state is capable of floating shingle bolts after heavy rains and during freshets which
occur with periodic regularity in the spring and fall of each year,
without the storage of water by a dam, is a navigable stream for
that purpose, and plaintiff is entitled to use it as such across the
lands of a lower riparian proprietor, and interference with such
right will be enjoined.

SAME — OBSTRUCTIONS — DETENTION AND RELEASE OF WATER —
OVERFLOW. The maintenance of a dam and the detention of the
water in a stream which is navigable for the purpose of floating
shingle bolts, and the release of the water at irregular intervals,

[1]Reported in 77 Pac. 813.

causing the stream to overflow and wash the lands of a lower riparian proprietor, and obstructing his navigation thereof, is such an interference with the natural flow of the water as will be enjoined.

SAME—RIGHT TO BANKS OF UNMEANDERED STREAM. One who makes use of an unmeandered stream for driving timber is not entitled to go upon the banks of a riparian owner unless the land owner consents, or until the right to their use has been acquired in a lawful way.

Appeal from a judgment of the superior court for Snohomish county, entered May 2, 1903, upon findings in favor of the plaintiff after a trial on the merits before the court without a jury, enjoining interference with plaintiff's use of a stream for the purpose of floating shingle bolts. Reversed.

Coleman & Fogarty, for appellants. Waters which can be made navigable only by artificial means are not public highways. 21 Am. & Eng. Enc. Law (2d ed.), 428; Gould, Waters (3d ed.), §§ 108, 109; *Morgan v. King,* 35 N. Y. 453, 91 Am. Dec. 58; *Thunder Bay etc. Co. v. Speechly,* 31 Mich. 336, 18 Am. Rep. 184; *Wadsworth v. Smith,* 11 Me. 278, 26 Am. Dec. 525; *Moore v. Sanborne,* 2 Mich. 519, 59 Am. Dec. 209; *Treat v. Lord,* 42 Me. 552, 66 Am. Dec. 298; *Pearson v. Rolfe,* 76 Me. 385; *Koopman v. Blodgett,* 70 Mich. 610, 38 N. W. 649; *East Hoquiam Boom etc. Co. v. Neeson,* 20 Wash. 142, 54 Pac. 1001; *Haines v. Hall,* 17 Ore. 165, 20 Pac. 831; *Nutter v. Gallagher,* 19 Ore. 375, 24 Pac. 250; *Murray v. Preston,* 106 Ky. 561, 50 S. W. 1095; *Banks v. Frazier,* 111 Ky. 909, 64 S. W. 983; *Witheral v. Muskegon Booming Co.,* 68 Mich. 48, 35 N. W. 758, 13 Am. St. 325; *Morgan v. King,* 35 N. Y. 453, 91 Am. Dec. 58. If the stream is navigable, the dam is an unlawful obstruction. Gould, Waters (3d ed.), § 134; *Carl v. West Aberdeen Land etc.*

Co., 13 Wash. 616, 43 Pac. 890; *United States v. Bellingham Bay Boom Co.,* 176 U. S. 211, 20 Sup. Ct. 343, 44 L. Ed. 437; *People v. Vanderbilt,* 26 N. Y. 287; *Blanchard v. Western U. Tel. Co.,* 60 N. Y. 510; *Wisconsin River Imp. Co. v. Lyons,* 30 Wis. 61; *People v. Gold Run etc. Co.,* 66 Cal. 138, 4 Pac. 1150; *Commonwealth v. Church,* 1 Pa. St. 105, 44 Am. Dec. 112; *Stevens Point Boom Co. v. Reilly,* 46 Wis. 237, 49 N. W. 978; *McPheters v. Moose River etc. Co.,* 78 Me. 329, 5 Atl. 270; *Gifford v. McArthur,* 55 Mich. 535, 22 N. W. 28; *Sultan Water & P. Co. v. Weyerhauser Timber Co.,* 31 Wash. 558, 72 Pac. 114. The riparian owner is entitled to the natural flow of the water. Gould, Waters (3d ed.), §§ 204, 218; Cooley, Torts (2d ed.), 694; *Crook v. Hewitt,* 4 Wash. 749, 31 Pac. 28; *Lux v. Haggin,* 69 Cal. 255, 10 Pac. 674; *Rigney v. Tacoma Light & W. Co.,* 9 Wash. 576, 38 Pac. 147, 26 L. R. A. 425; *Whatcom v. Fairhaven Land Co.,* 24 Wash. 493, 64 Pac. 735, 54 L. R. A. 190; *Brewster v. Rogers Co.,* 169 N. Y. 73, 62 N. E. 164; *Noonan v. Albany,* 79 N. Y. 470, 35 Am. Rep. 540; *McCormick v. Horan,* 81 N. Y. 86, 37 Am. Rep. 479; *Lone Tree Ditch Co. v. Rapid City L. Co.* (S. D.), 93 N. W. 650; *East Jersey Water Co. v. Bigelow,* 60 N. J. L. 201, 38 Atl. 631; *Watkinson v. McCoy,* 23 Wash. 372, 63 Pac. 245.

Cooley & Horan, for respondent. A stream is navigable if it will float logs during periodical freshets. *Falls Mfg. Co. v. Oconto River Imp. Co.,* 87 Wis. 134, 58 N. W. 257; *Morgan v. King,* 35 N. Y. 454. The test of navigability is whether the stream in its nature is capable of being used to float boats, rafts or logs. *Moore v. Sanborne,* 2 Mich. 520; *Brown v. Chadbourne,* 31 Me. 9; *Hickok v. Hine,* 23 Ohio St. 523. That it is customary to go upon the banks to assist in driving logs does not affect the question of

navigability. *Olson v. Merrill*, 42 Wis. 203. One may
enter upon the land of a riparian owner to reclaim logs
stranded without negligence. *Weise v. Smith*, 3 Ore. 445,
8 Am. Rep. 621; *Carter v. Thurston*, 58 N. H. 104, 42
Am. Rep. 584; *Brown v. Chadbourne, supra; Hooper v.
Hobson*, 57 Me. 273, 99 Am. Dec. 769. The riparian
owner may dam up the water for the purpose of floating
logs, so long as such dam does not constitute an obstruction
to navigation, even though it may interfere with the ordinary flow of water across the lands of a lower proprietor.
Buchanan v. Grand River etc. Co., 48 Mich. 364, 12 N. W.
490; *Beard v. Clarke*, 35 Minn. 324; *Merriman v. Bowen,*
33 Minn. 445; *Kroll v. Nester*, 52 Mich. 70, 17 N. W.
704; *Kretzschmar v. Meehan*, 74 Minn. 211, 77 N. W. 41;
Mabie v. Matteson, 17 Wis. 1; *Patten v. Marden*, 14 Wis.
513.

HADLEY, J.—The respondent brought this action
against appellant to procure an injunction against an alleged threatened interference with the use of a stream for
the floating of shingle bolts. The stream is known as the
West Fork of Woods creek. It commences at the foot of
Lake Roesiger, in Snohomish county, and flows therefrom
in a southwesterly direction, passing through the lands of
both appellant and respondent. Respondent owns an extensive body of timber lands adjacent to the lake and
stream, and owns the lands upon both sides of the stream
at its source. Appellant's lands lie below those of respondent. The respondent has constructed, and has heretofore
operated, a dam at the lower end of the lake, for the purpose of storing the waters within the lake to be used in
flooding the stream in order to accelerate the movement of
shingle bolts. The complaint charges that appellant threat-

ens, by obstruction, to prevent respondent from driving its
bolts through the stream where it crosses appellant's land.
It is alleged that the stream is navigable or floatable for
shingle bolts, and that respondent has now about three
thousand cords of bolts stored in the lake ready for movement, which it will be unable to move unless appellant is
restrained.

The answer denies that the stream is navigable, and
alleges that, by reason of the storing of the water in the
lake, the flow of the stream is at times entirely stopped,
and that at other times respondent suddenly and without
warning releases the stored water, and that it runs down
and overflows the lands of appellant adjacent to the stream,
washes away the soil, and destroys appellant's roads and
landings constructed for the movement of his own shingle
bolts; that appellant is engaged in removing the cedar timber from his own land, and that by reason of respondent's
obstruction of the natural flow of the water, it is impossible
for him to run his shingle bolts down said stream. The
answer prays for damages, and for an injunction perpetually restraining respondent from interfering with the
natural flow of the water in the creek, and from flooding
appellant's lands.

The cause was tried before the court without a jury.
Findings of facts and conclusions of law were entered, and
the decree provides that appellant shall be perpetually enjoined from in any manner obstructing or interfering with
the navigation of said stream, or the driving of respondent's
shingle bolts across the lands of appellant. It is further
provided that appellant shall be restrained from in any
manner interfering with or preventing respondent's employes from going upon the banks of said stream for the
purpose, only, of breaking jams of bolts which may occur,

so long as the going upon said banks does no injury to appellant or his land. This appeal is from that decree.

The first alleged error is that the court permitted any testimony to be introduced in support of the complaint. This contention is based upon the theory that the complaint shows that the stream in question is not navigable or floatable for shingle bolts, in its natural condition. It is expressly averred that the stream is navigable for said purpose, but it is argued that other allegations have the effect to negative such fact. The following averment is pointed out as destroying the force of the positive allegation as to navigability:

"That it (respondent) has at great expense constructed a dam across the foot of Lake Roesiger for the purpose of storing water, thereby furnishing a sufficient supply of water in the aforesaid stream to conveniently and rapidly float shingle bolts and other timber products down the same to the mill of this plaintiff."

We think the conclusion which appellant draws does not necessarily follow when the two averments are taken together. The quoted allegation amounts to no more than the statement that respondent's own convenience, in the moving of its shingle bolts, is better served by the storing of the water and the operation of the dam. But it does not say that the stream is not floatable in its natural state. The court did not err in overruling the objection to the introduction of any testimony upon the above mentioned ground.

A further point raised under the objection to the introduction of any testimony is that an attempt is made in the complaint to plead an estoppel against appellant, but that the allegations are insufficient to charge an estoppel. The complaint avers that respondent, at its own expense, cleared the said stream of obstructions across appellant's land, in order to facilitate the movement of shingle bolts; that ap-

pellant acquiesced therein, actually assisted in the clearing
out of such obstructions, thereafter used the benefits accruing therefrom, and also the flow of water as furnished by
the dam and improvements constructed by respondent at the
lake. We agree with appellant's contention that the facts
stated are not sufficient to estop him from claiming now
that respondent is interfering with the natural flow of the
water. The mere fact that he made no objection to clearing the bed of the stream from obstructions, or that he may
even have assisted therein, does not necessarily establish
that he consented that the floatage of the stream should be
conducted in any other manner than as provided by the
natural flow of the water. The further fact that he may
have used the water, as it was sent down the stream by the
occasional opening of the dam, during a period of about
two years, does not establish his acquiescence in the continued interruption of the natural flow of the water, and
amounts to no more than a mere license for a temporary
interruption, revocable at will. Such facts do not contain
the essential elements of estoppel. *Rigney v. Tacoma Light
& W. Co.,* 9 Wash. 576, 38 Pac. 147, 26 L. R. A. 425;
Hathaway v. Yakima Water etc. Co., 14 Wash. 469, 44
Pac. 896, 53 Am. St. 847. It is true, therefore, that appellant is not estopped to assert that the complaint shows
that respondent, through the operation of its dam, is interfering with the natural flow of the water. But in view of
the allegation that the stream is navigable, it is also true
that appellant has no right to interfere with its navigation
by respondent, as it is alleged he threatens to do, and it was
not error, under the averments of the complaint, to admit
evidence upon that subject.

The court found that, with the removal of the artificial
obstructions, the stream is capable of navigation by shingle
bolts after heavy rains and during freshets, which occur

with periodic regularity in the spring and fall of each year,
and that it is so navigable without the storage of the water
in the lake, and without the aid of said dam. It is assigned
that the court erred in so finding. We think not, under the
evidence. There was sufficient evidence to sustain the finding that the stream, in its natural state, can be practicably
used for the floatage of shingle bolts to market, at the times
and seasons specified in the court's findings. Such makes
it a navigable stream within the holding of this court in
Watkins v. Dorris, 24 Wash. 636, 64 Pac. 840, 54 L. R. A.
199. In that case the trial court found Elochoman creek
to be an unmeandered stream, and that it can, during annually recurring freshets, be used profitably for the floating
of sawlogs to market. This court held it to be navigable,
and a highway for that purpose. Woods creek is much
smaller than Elochoman creek, is also unmeandered, and is
doubtless non-navigable for sawlogs. But the evidence
shows that it has sufficient capacity, in its natural state,
during annually recurring periods, to float shingle bolts,
and while a single shingle bolt contains but a small amount
of timber, compared with a sawlog, yet, in the aggregate,
timber in that form in this locality is relatively of equal
commercial value with sawlogs, and its carriage to market
is, perhaps, as important to the timber industry of this state
as that of sawlogs. Elochoman creek was declared to be navigable, for the reason that it furnishes a natural highway
for the product of the great logging industry in this state,
and Woods creek should, also, be held to be navigable, because it furnishes a similar highway for the product of
another branch of the same industry. Elochoman creek
was held to be a navigable stream because it is navigable
in fact for the floatage of logs or timber to market. Its
navigable character is restricted to a certain commercial
and industrial purpose, and does not comprehend naviga-

bility in the broad sense, as applied in America to the great
rivers and water highways. The rule that navigability in
fact for commercial purposes makes a water course a navigable one was also declared in *Dawson v. McMillan,* 34
Wash. 269, 75 Pac. 807. The reasons leading to the holding in this state and others, where the timber industry is
important, that streams which are navigable in fact for the
floatage of timber to market shall be public highways for
that purpose, are founded upon commercial convenience
and necessity, because of the environment of the industry.
Much of the timber grows in the mountains, also upon the
foothills, and in other localities which are inaccessible by
means of transportation facilities, without great expense.
Nature has, however, provided numerous streams which
flow out from these timber centers, and which are available
highways for the carriage of the timber to market. In a
locality so situated, it seems reasonable that these highways should be used for such purposes. It is true, the
majority of these streams, being unmeandered, pass over
private property, and their beds are owned by the adjacent
land owner. But the lands are naturally burdened, if it be
a burden, by the streams themselves, with their defined
banks and flowing water, and it is not an additional burden
to the land owner for the timber product to float along with
the already running water, provided it is so done as not to
damage his land. His rights in the latter particular must,
however, be strictly and carefully guarded. Under the
former decisions of this court, and for the further reasons
herein assigned, the court did not err in holding that Woods
creek is a navigable stream for the floatage of shingle bolts.
The provision in the decree properly followed, whereby appellant is restrained from interfering with the running of
respondent's shingle bolts along said stream where it crosses
appellant's lands.

It being established that the stream is a navigable one,
and that appellant shall not interfere with respondent's
navigation of it, we must next inquire as to the methods
and limitations of that navigation. The court refused to
grant appellant an injunction preventing respondent from
continuing the storage of the water in Lake Roesiger, and
the periodic flushing of the stream. We think this was
error. Under well established principles, appellant is entitled to the natural flow of the water across his land. *Crook
v. Hewitt*, 4 Wash. 749, 31 Pac. 28; *Rigney v. Tacoma
Light & W. Co., supra; New Whatcom v. Fairhaven Land
Co.*, 24 Wash. 493, 64 Pac. 735, 54 L. R. A. 190. It is
said that, although language used in the above cases declares the general principle, yet there was an actual threatened diversion of a substantial portion of the water in each
case, while, in the case at bar, there is no diversion,
but simply a detention, followed by a restoration of all the
water before it reaches appellant's lands. This detention,
however, amounts practically to a total detention for irregular periods, and at times unknown to appellant, without
warning, it is released in such quantities as to greatly increase the natural flow and, according to testimony in the
record, actually causes an overflow of his lands. The general principle governing the fundamental rights of all
riparian proprietors is well stated as follows:

"Riparian proprietors upon both navigable and unnav-
igable streams are entitled, in the absence of grant, license,
or prescription limiting their rights, to have the stream
which washes their lands flow as it is wont by nature, without material diminution or alteration. Each proprietor
may, therefore, insist that the stream shall flow to his land
in the usual quantity, at its natural place and height, and
that it shall flow off his land to his neighbor below in its
accustomed place and at its usual level." Gould, Waters
(3d ed.), § 204.

That such a detention of water as is shown in this case is prejudicial to the appellant's rights appears from the following authority:

"It is an unreasonable detention of the water to gather it into reservoirs for future use in a dry season, or for the purpose of obtaining a greater supply than the stream affords by its natural flow in ordinary stages, or in order that, by letting it off occasionally, a flood may be obtained for the purpose of floating logs; . . ." Cooley, Torts (2d ed.), p. 694.

The maintenance and operation of the dam prevents appellant from navigating the stream himself at times when he may wish to do so, thereby obstructing navigation, and, unless he consents to its maintenance, the dam is to him a nuisance, which he is entitled to have enjoined. *Carl v. West Aberdeen etc. Co.*, 13 Wash. 616, 43 Pac. 890; *Sultan W. & P. Co. v. Weyerhauser Timber Co.*, 31 Wash. 558, 72 Pac. 114. We therefore think appellant was entitled to an injunction, preventing respondent from maintaining and operating the dam, and requiring it to permit the water to flow across appellant's lands in its natural and regular way, and respondent must conduct its own navigation of the stream over such natural flow.

Another provision of the decree, with reference to the methods attending respondent's navigation, also calls for examination. It will be remembered that, by its terms, the decree prohibits appellant from interfering with respondent's employes in the way of preventing them from going upon the banks of the stream upon appellant's lands, for the purpose of breaking jams of shingle bolts, so long as the going upon the banks does no injury to appellant or his lands. We think this provision of the decree is also erroneous. We believe we went as far as we should go in the interest of public convenience, when we held, in *Watkins*

32-35 WASH.

v. Dorris, supra, that private land owners hold the beds of unmeandered streams subject to the easement of driving timber products over the land. But we tried to make it clear in that case that the timber driver must confine himself and his operations to the highway itself—the bed of the stream, until the land owner consents to the use of the banks, or until the right to their use has been acquired in a lawful way. If more emphatic statement of that rule is necessary, we now wish to be understood as making it, with all needed emphasis. The fundamental principle of right in the land owner to control his own premises, outside of the bed of the stream, must not be violated. To leave parties under such terms as this decree provides would, in many instances, invite trouble and litigation. Each one would assume to be his own judge as to whether any injury is done to the land. What might appear to the land owner as injury might not so appear to the timber driver, and thus a controversy would at once arise, probably requiring repeated litigation to settle. The driver must know from the beginning that he must, in no event, go upon the banks of the stream in his operations without the owner's permission, and thus controversies about damages accruing in that way will be avoided. Enough controversies will arise about the manner of operating in the bed of the stream to the possible damage of the adjacent land, without adding thereto those arising from semi-legalized trespass upon private premises, which would be the case if it were judicially held that one may operate upon private lands against the owner's consent, and without compensation.

The court found that respondent's acts have produced no actual injury or damage to appellant or his lands. Appellant contends that it was error to so find. The evidence conflicts upon this subject, and we shall not disturb the finding. No judgment for damages will therefore be directed.

The decree should be modified in accordance with what has been herein said. The cause is remanded, with instructions to the trial court to enter a decree conformable to this opinion. The appellant shall recover the costs of the appeal, and neither party shall recover costs in the lower court.

FULLERTON, C. J., and MOUNT, ANDERS, and DUNBAR, JJ., concur.

[No. 4832. Decided July 26, 1904.]

REBECCA JONES, *Appellant,* v. P. B. M. MILLER *et al.,* *Respondents.*[1]

ABATEMENT—ACTIONS— INJURY TO PERSON — DEATH—SURVIVAL. Bal. Code, § 5695, read in connection with other parts of the act, was not intended to provide that "all other causes of action" survive to the personal representatives, but relates only to causes of action which the law had provided should survive; hence an action by a widow to recover damages for the mutilation of the body of her deceased husband, being an injury to the person, abates upon her death.

SAME — APPEAL — ABATEMENT BY DEATH—COSTS—DISMISSAL. Where the cause of action abates by the death of the party, the executor cannot be substituted and the cause retained on appeal for the purpose of determining the question of costs.

SAME—SUBSTITUTION OF PARTY ON APPEAL. Where a cause of action abates by the death of a party, an executor cannot be substituted for the purpose of continuing the action in his individual interest affected by the same wrong.

Motion to substitute party, and counter motion to dismiss an appeal from a judgment of the superior court for

[1]Reported in 77 Pac. 811.

King county, Albertson, J., entered July 21, 1903, upon granting a nonsuit. Action dismissed.

G. Ward Kemp, for appellant.

Fred H. Peterson and *Norwood W. Brockett,* for respondents.

FULLERTON, C. J.—Rebecca Jones, the appellant above named, brought this action to recover damages for the alleged unlawful mutilation and dishonor of the body of her deceased husband. The mutilation and dishonor complained of consisted of an incision made in the abdominal cavity, sufficient to explore the stomach and other digestive organs, by the respondents Miller and Ross, for the purpose of ascertaining the cause of death. The body was, at the time, in the custody and charge of the respondents Butterworth & Sons. As the grounds of her injury, the appellant alleged that, upon learning the facts and viewing the "body so cut, mutilated and dishonored" she "was most grievously distressed, mortified and humiliated, and received a severe nervous shock, and suffered great mental pain and distress, and has ever since grieved and suffered humiliation and mental pain and distress, and . . . has been damaged in the sum of five thousand dolars." On the trial the appellant was nonsuited on the motion of the respondents, on the ground that she had failed to prove a sufficient cause for the jury. From the judgment following the order of nonsuit, this appeal was taken.

After the appeal had been perfected, and the cause argued and submitted in this court, Mrs. Jones died, leaving a will in which she named her eldest son, William J. Jones, as her executor. The executor named duly qualified as such, and thereafter moved this court to be substituted as plaintiff and appellant, with leave to continue the prose-

cution of the action in his own name. The respondents
oppose the motion, and move to dismiss the appeal on the
ground that the action is not one that survives to heirs or
personal representatives. These motions present the questions to be determined.

At common law an action for an injury to the person,
such as the one in question here, abated on the death of the
person injured, and could not thereafter be revived by his
heirs or personal representatives. The executor does not
seriously question the correctness of this proposition, but
contends that the action survives by virtue of section 5695
of the Code (Ballinger's), which provides: "All other
causes of action [than those enumerated in section 4828
supra] by one person against another, whether arising on contract or otherwise, survive to the personal representatives of the former and against the personal representatives of the latter. . . ." When we read this section
as if it stood alone, and apart from its context, it doubtless
bears the construction put upon it, but we held in *Slauson
v. Schwabacher Bros. & Co.,* 4 Wash. 783, 31 Pac. 329, 31
Am. St. 948, that it had no such meaning. There we said
that the legislature, when it enacted this section, was legis-
lating with reference to causes of action which had already
survived, and was not attempting to announce what causes
of action should survive; and, further, that if the contrary
contention were correct, there was no limit whatever to
causes which would survive the death of the person injured; "for causes of action for assault, slander, and for
other purely personal causes, would survive; and this would
be so wide a departure from the established rule that the
legislature would hardly be deemed to have intended it
without plainly expressing such intention." That this is
the correct construction of the statute is made clear by reading it in connection with the act of which it formed a part

when originally enacted, and being so, it does not warrant
the holding that causes of action, such as the one at bar,
survive to heirs and personal representatives.

It is insisted, however, that the executor is entitled to be
substituted, and to a decision on the merits of the controversy, for the purpose of determining who is entitled to
costs; but such is not the rule.   Where there is no longer
a controversy between the parties, or the right of action has
ceased to exist, the action will be dismissed by the court,
even though it may leave the question of costs undeter-
mined.   *Hice v. Orr,* 16 Wash. 163, 47 Pac. 424; *State
ex rel. Coiner v. Wickersham,* 16 Wash. 161, 47 Pac. 421;
Lynde v. Dibble, 19 Wash. 328, 53 Pac. 370; *Watson v.
Merkle,* 21 Wash. 635, 59 Pac. 484; *State ex rel. Taylor
v. Cummings,* 27 Wash. 316, 67 Pac. 565.

The last contention, viz., that the executor has a right to
be substituted individually as the son of the person mutilated, and proceed in this action to recover damages for his
own sufferings caused by the mutilation, is without merit.
If he has any cause of action as an individual, his remedy
is to prosecute it first in the court of original jurisdiction;
he cannot commence such an action in this court.

The respondents are entitled to a dismissal of the action,
and the order will go to that effect.

MOUNT, J., HADLEY, ANDERS, and DUNBAR, JJ., concur.

[No. 5011. Decided July 26, 1904.]

SEATTLE & LAKE WASHINGTON WATERWAY COMPANY *et al., Respondents,* v. SEATTLE DOCK COMPANY, *Appellant.*[1]

STATUTES—TITLE—SUFFICIENCY—EXCAVATION OF WATERWAYS AND PROVISION FOR LIENS. The title to Laws 1893, p. 241 (Bal. Code, § 4080), the main purpose of which is to provide for the excavation of public waterways by private contract, which is specified in the title, is broad enough to include a provision for liens for the work performed, as that is merely incidental to the main subject and a means of accomplishing the main purpose, and the act is not objectionable as embracing more than one subject, although the title also embraces the subject of such liens and the granting of rights-of-way across the lands, and might have been included in three separate acts.

TIDE LANDS—STATUTES—CONSTRUCTION OF ACT FOR EXCAVATION OF WATERWAYS—LIENS—CONSTITUTIONAL LAW—VESTED RIGHTS. Bal Code, §§ 4080 *et seq.,* providing for the excavation of public waterways by private contract, does not confer power upon the land commissioner to encumber private property with liens for filling in such property against the owner's will, but the same intends to give such liens only where the state was the owner of the tide lands when the contract was entered into.

SAME—STATUTES—TITLE—SUFFICIENCY—POWERS OF LAND COMMISSIONER. If such act gave such power, it would not be necessary to refer thereto in the title, as the title need not be a complete index to the act.

SAME — CONSTITUTIONAL LAW — DUE PROCESS OF LAW — STATE CONTRACT FOR EXCAVATION OF TIDE LANDS—RIGHTS OF SUBSEQUENT PURCHASERS. The act of 1893, authorizing the excavation of public waterways by private contract, and providing for liens upon the filled in tide lands belonging to the state, and which the state afterwards sells, does not violate the state and federal constitutions, in that, by the foreclosure of such liens, it deprives the subsequent purchasers from the state of their property without due process of law, since the state could make any contract with reference to filling up its tide lands, and subsequent purchasers

[1]Reported in 77 Pac. 845.

take subject thereto, and are not entitled to notice or opportunity to be heard touching the improvements.

SAME—ABUTTERS ON TIDE LANDS—VESTED RIGHTS. Abutters, with only a preference right to purchase tide lands, have no vested rights therein, and are not entitled to notice or opportunity to be heard respecting the improvement thereof, contracted for by the state while the state is still the owner.

SAME—DECISION OF COMMISSIONER OF PUBLIC LANDS. In the absence of fraud, the decision of the commissioner of public lands upon the right of the contractor, excavating a public waterway under the act of 1893, to a certificate, is as conclusive upon subsequent purchasers as it would be upon the state, if the state were still the owner.

SAME—LOANING CREDIT OF STATE—STATE NOT LIABLE FOR IMPROVEMENTS. The act of 1893, authorizing the excavation of public waterways, and providing for liens upon the tide lands belonging to the state which are filled in under the contract, does not violate the state constitution, § 9, art. 12, and § 5, art. 8, prohibiting the loaning of the credit of the state in aid of any individual, where the act does not make the state liable for the improvements, nor to discharge the lien, but provides for a sale at not less than the appraised value, and the purchasers were bound to pay for the improvements, since the only remedy of the excavation company is to purchase the land at the appraised value.

SAME—CONTRACTION OF STATE DEBT. Such act does not violate § 3 of art. 8 of the state constitution, prohibiting the contraction of a state debt except for objects especially designated, nor without submitting the same to a vote of the people, since the state is not made liable for the improvement and is under no obligations to discharge the lien, and the creation of such lien upon state lands to be paid by the purchaser is not the creation of a state debt within the meaning of the constitution.

SAME—SPECIAL PRIVILEGES—COLLECTION OF TOLLS—SEPARABLE PORTION OF ACT NOT INVALIDATING THE BALANCE. The provision of the act of 1893, relating to the excavation of public waterways, which creates liens upon the state tide lands filled in under the contract, cannot be claimed to be invalid or contrary to § 22, of art. 12, and § 12, of art. 1, of the constitution, prohibiting monopolies and the granting of special privileges to any citizen, by reason of that part of the act granting to the waterway company the exclusive right to control the waterway and collect tolls, since such provision is a separable part of the act, and, if it fails, it does not affect the portion relating to certificates and liens for the improvements.

SAME—TAKING PRIVATE PROPERTY FOR DEBTS OF PUBLIC CORPORA-
TIONS.   Said act is not contrary to § 15 of art. 11 of the state
constitution, providing that private property shall not be taken
or sold for the payment of debts of public or municipal corporations except in the manner provided for by law for the collection
of taxes, as the claim for liens for the work is not a debt of any
such corporation.

Appeal from a judgment of the superior court for King
county, Tallman, J., entered October 14, 1903, upon findings in favor of the plaintiff after a trial upon the merits
before the court without a jury, foreclosing the lien of a
waterway company for its improvement of tide lands. Affirmed.

Ballinger, Ronald & Battle, for appellant. The law
under which plaintiff secured its contract was unconstitutional, because it embraced more than one subject, and subjects not embraced in the title.   Cooley, Const. Lim. (5th
ed.), 96, 172, 178; 23 Am. & Eng. Enc. Law, 233, 234;
Percival v. Cowychee etc. District, 15 Wash. 480, 46 Pac.
1035; *People v. Parks,* 58 Cal. 624; *In re Breene,* 14 Colo.
401, 24 Pac. 3; *In re Blodgett,* 89 N. Y. 392; *Grand
Rapids v. Burlingame,* 93 Mich. 469, 53 N. W. 620; *Skinner v. Wilhelm,* 63 Mich. 571, 30 N. W. 311. The act
deprived appellant of his property without due process of
law, because: (1)   There is no provision for the giving
of notice or opportunity for hearing, to which an owner is
entitled.   *Hagar v. Reclamation Dist.,* 111 U. S. 701, 4
Sup. Ct. 663; *Zeigler v. South etc. R. Co.,* 58 Ala. 594;
Spencer v. Merchant, 125 U. S. 345, 8 Sup. Ct. 921; *Ames
v. Port Huron etc. Co.,* 11 Mich. 139, 83 Am. Dec. 731;
Chicago etc. R. Co. v. Minnesota, 134 U. S. 418, 10 Sup.
Ct. 467, 702; *Fallbrook Irr. etc. Co. v. Bradley,* 164 U. S.
112, 17 Sup. Ct. 56; *Bauman v. Ross,* 167 U. S. 548, 17

Sup. Ct. 966; *Davidson v. New Orleans*, 96 U. S. 97;
Missouri Pac. R. Co. v. State, 164 U. S. 403, 17 Sup. Ct.
130; *Paulsen v. Portland*, 149 U. S. 30, 13 Sup. Ct. 750;
Norwood v. Baker, 172 U. S. 269, 19 Sup. Ct. 187; *New
Whatcom v. Bellingham Bay Imp. Co.*, 16 Wash. 131, 47
Pac. 236; *Snohomish County v. Hayward*, 11 Wash. 429,
39 Pac. 652; *Skagit County v. Stiles*, 10 Wash. 388, 39
Pac. 116; *Askam v. King County*, 9 Wash. 1, 36 Pac.
1097; *Violett v. Alexandria*, 92 Va. 561, 23 S. E. 909, 53
Am. St. 825; *Stuart v. Palmer*, 74 N. Y. 191; *Santa Clara
County v. Southern Pac. R. Co.*, 18 Fed. 410; *Gamble v.
McCrady*, 75 N. C. 509.   (2) The method provided for
determining the amount which appellant's lands are to pay
is arbitrary, and not "due process of law." *Bradley v.
Fallbrook Irr. Dist.*, 68 Fed. 964; *Tide Water Co. v.
Coster*, 18 N. J. Eq. 518, 90 Am. Dec. 634; *Norwood v.
Baker, supra; Thomas v. Gain*, 35 Mich. 155; *Craig v.
Philadelphia*, 89 Pa. St. 265; *Sears v. Boston*, 173 Mass.
71, 53 N. E. 138; *Dexter v. Boston*, 176 Mass. 247, 57
N. E. 379, 79 Am. St. 306; *Hutcheson v. Starrie*, 92 Tex.
685, 51 S. W. 848, 71 Am. St. 884; *Adams v. Shelbyville*,
154 Ind. 467, 57 N. E. 114, 77 Am. St. 484; *McKee v.
Pendleton*, 154 Ind. 652, 57 N. E. 532; *Fay v. Springfield*,
94 Fed. 409; *Loeb v. Columbia Tp.*, 91 Fed. 37; *Charles
v. Marion*, 98 Fed. 166; *Cowley v. Spokane*, 99 Fed. 840.
(3) The act delegates legislative or judicial power, or
both, to the executive department. *People v. Parks, supra;
Territory ex rel. Kelly v. Stewart*, 1 Wash. 98, 23 Pac.
405, 8 L. R. A. 106; *State v. Womack*, 4 Wash. 19, 29
Pac. 939; *People's Railroad v. Memphis Railroad*, 77 U. S.
38; *Bank of U. S. v. Earle*, 13 Peters 595, 10 L. Ed. 311;
Owensboro & N. R. Co. v. Todd, 91 Ky. 175, 15 S. W.
56; *Winters v. Hughes*, 3 Utah, 433, 24 Pac. 761; *Maxwell
v. State*, 40 Md. 273; *Fogg v. Union Bank*, 1 Baxter

(Tenn.) 435; *Clark v. Port of Mobile,* 67 Ala. 217; *Shum-way v. Bennett,* 29 Mich. 463. (4) The act is for a private purpose; or, if for a public purpose, it is at the expense of private individuals, and hence void. *Loan Ass'n v. To-peka,* 20 Wall. 655, 22 L. Ed. 455; *Hanson v. Vernon,* 27 Iowa 28; *People v. Salem,* 20 Mich. 452; *Sharpless v. Mayor of Philadelphia,* 21 Pa. St. 147, 59 Am. Dec. 759; *Coster v. Tide Water Co.,* 18 N. J. Eq. 54; *Kean v. Driggs Drainage Co.,* 45 N. J. L. 91; *Wurts v. Hoagland,* 114 U. S. 606, 5 Sup. Ct. 1086; *Jarrott v. Moberly,* Fed. Cas. No. 7223; *Garland v. Board of Revenue,* 87 Ala. 223, 6 South. 402; *Whiting v. Sheboygan etc. R. Co.,* 25 Wis. 167; 20 Am. & Eng. Enc. Law (2d ed.), 1090.

Sachs & Hale, for respondents.

MOUNT, J.—This action was brought by respondents to foreclose certain liens on tide lands in the city of Seattle. The liens arose under the provisions of chapter 99 of the laws of 1893, page 241 (Bal. Code, §§ 4080-4089), entitled, "An act prescribing the ways in which waterways for the uses of navigation may be excavated by private contract, providing for liens upon tide and shore lands belonging to the state, granting rights-of-way across lands belonging to the state."

The complaint contains five causes of action, each cause being based upon a lien upon a separate tract of land. The complaint alleges, in substance, that on October 27, 1894, the state of Washington, by its duly authorized commissioner of public lands, entered into a written contract with Eugene Semple, for the excavation of a waterway and filling in certain tide lands described (a copy of the contract is attached to the complaint); that, after the execution of the contract, Semple, for a valuable consideration, assigned and transferred the said contract, and all his

rights therein, to respondent Seattle & Lake Washington
Waterway Company, so that said company became substituted for the said Semple in the contract for all purposes; that the contract was entered into after due proceedings by advertisement and otherwise, in full compliance with the provisions of the laws of the state, which
proceedings are fully set out; that the respondent waterway company began the work of excavating the waterway
and filling in the tide lands, according to the contract,
prior to the dates of the certificates sued upon, and had
filled in and raised above hightide, in full compliance with
the contract, the tide lands upon which it is sought to foreclose the liens herein; that, on the dates of the certificates,
the commissioner of public lands issued to the waterway
company the certificates described, and which are attached to and made a part of the complaint, and which
contain a description of the lands improved, and the cost
of the improvements; that these certificates were filed in
the office of the auditor of King county immediately after
their execution, and were duly recorded, under the provisions of § 4 of the act above referred to; that, by the
filing of said certificates, the waterway company acquired
a lien upon the said lands for the amount due, and to
become due, upon the said certificates, under the provisions of said act; that afterwards the waterway company,
for value, sold, assigned, and transferred and delivered
to respondent Morris & Whitehead, Bankers, a corporation,
the said certificates and all right, title, and interest therein; that, subsequent to the making of the contract above
mentioned between the state of Washington and Eugene
Semple, and subsequent to the assignment thereof by Semple to the Seattle & Lake Washington Waterway Company,
the appellant acquired from the state of Washington the
tide lands upon which liens are sought to be enforced;

that the deed from the state, for the lands described in
the complaint, contained the following provision: "Subject, however, to any lien or liens that may arise or be
created in consequence of, or pursuant to, the provisions
of the act of the legislature of the state of Washington,
entitled, 'An act prescribing the ways in which waterways for the uses of navigation may be excavated by private contract, providing for liens upon tide or shore lands
belonging to the state, granting rights-of-way across lands
belonging to the state,' approved March 9, 1893;" that
certain installments on the certificates are long past due
and unpaid. The prayer is for a foreclosure of the
liens.

Defendant Hofius appeared, and disclaimed any interest in the lands. Appellant Seattle Dock Company appeared, and filed a general demurrer to the complaint,
which demurrer was overruled. It then filed an answer,
denying certain allegations, and pleaded six affirmative
defenses, substantially as follows: (1) That, under the
act of the legislature of the state, approved March 26,
1890, the owners of uplands in front of which these tide
lands are situated, or the improvers thereof, duly applied
for the purchase of the same, which applications were allowed and the contracts of purchase from the state issued
and executed, to all of which the appellant, by mesne conveyances, has become the owner; that the said act of 1893,
referred to in the complaint, is unreasonable and contrary to the federal and state constitutions in certain respects set forth in said defense, and that its passage was
an exercise of power prohibited by the fourteenth amendment to the federal constitution. (2) The contract set
forth was not in conformity with the act, but was contrary
thereto, in respects set forth in said defense, and that said
contract was the taking, or attempting to take, defend-

ant's property without just compensation, and is the depriving of defendant of its property without due process of law, contrary to the federal and state constitutions, and that, prior to the filling in of said lands, the defendant forbade the Seattle & Lake Washington Waterway Company from filling in the same. (3) That the certificates issued, and attempted to be foreclosed, are null and void in that the land commissioner had no jurisdiction to issue the same. (4) That the lots, included within the description set forth in the contract, of tide lands which the contractor was to fill were owned by many and divers persons; that the contractor has entered into contracts with certain of these owners, whereby said owners' lots and tracts should not be filled under the contract but should be exempt therefrom. (5) That the contractor has contracted with other owners of lots, included within said description of tide lands, by which said contractor agreed to fill, and is now filling said owners' lands, in manner and upon terms as agreed upon with said owners, and different from the manner and terms mentioned in the contract with the state. (6) That the contractor did not comply with the terms and conditions of the contract with reference to bulkheads, but violated the same, and constructed bulkheads in a manner different from, and of a different material from, that provided in the contract, which manner of construction and materials used were inferior in every respect to the manner of construction and materials prescribed.

The plaintiff demurred to these affirmative separate defenses, on the ground that none of them stated facts sufficient to constitute a defense. These demurrers were sustained, and defendant refused to plead further. Upon a trial of the issues made by the denials of defendant, the facts were stipulated, and the court entered a decree foreclosing the liens for the amount prayed in the complaint.

The appellant assigns error upon the orders of the trial court denying the demurrer to the complaint, and in sustaining the demurrers of the plaintiff to the affirmative defenses of the defendant. It is first urged that the act creating the liens is void because it embraces more than one subject, as shown both by the title and by the act itself. The title of the act is as follows, "An act prescribing the ways in which waterways for the uses of navigation may be excavated by private contract, providing for liens upon tide and shore lands belonging to the state, granting rights-of-way across lands belonging to the state." This title is no doubt broad enough to include three separate, independent subjects of legislation, but, when we come to examine the act itself, we find that the real subject or purpose of the act is the excavation of public waterways by private contract. The liens and rights-of-way provided for are merely incidental to the main subject, and are special only to this class of contracts. They are ends or means to the accomplishment of the main purpose of the act, and are not independent subjects. The act is therefore not void upon the ground urged.

It is next argued, that there is nothing in the title of the act indicating the powers conferred upon the land commissioner; that power is conferred upon the land commissioner to incumber private property with liens for the filling in of such property, against the owner's will. In the first place, we do not think the act is capable of the construction which appellant seeks to place upon it. The act intends, no doubt, to give a lien for filling in lands owned by the state on March 9, 1893, where a contract has been entered into while the state was owner of the land, but the act does not give a lien upon lands where

the contract is entered into after the state has parted with
its title thereto. But, if the act is susceptible of the construction placed upon it by appellant, it is not necessary
to the validity of it that the powers and duties of the land
commissioner shall be stated in the title. The office of the
title is to call attention to the subject matter of the act,
which must be looked to for a full description of the
powers and duties conferred. *Lancey v. King County,* 15
Wash. 9, 45 Pac. 645, 34 L. R. A. 817. It is not required that the title of the act shall be a complete index
to the act.

Appellant next insists that the act is in conflict with
§ 3, art. 1 of the state constitution, and the fourteenth
amendment to the constitution of the United States, which
declare that no person shall be deprived of property without due process of law. It is argued that this act deprives
appellant of its property without due process of law in
four particulars, viz.: (1) It does not afford the owner
any notice or opportunity to be heard touching the improvements; (2) the method provided by the act for determining the amount which appellant's lands are to pay
is arbitrary, and contrary to the constitutional provision
above named; (3) the act is a delegation of legislative
and judicial power to a branch of the executive department; (4) the act is an excess of legislative power and is
for a private purpose, or, if for a public purpose, then
it imposes burdens upon a small locality for the benefit
of the whole public. One hundred and sixty pages of
appellant's brief are taken up in discussing these four
propositions. The general principles laid down and discussed, and the authorities cited in the brief, are no doubt
correct, when applied to a state of facts where the state
itself is not the owner of the land; but, in this case, it is
conceded that the state was the owner of all the tide lands

in controversy at the time the act was passed, and at the
time the contract to fill the same was entered into. This
being true, the state could enter into any kind of a contract for filling the lands, at any price, and upon any
terms. It could also designate some officer to accept the
work, when such officer should deem it completed according to the contract. It could afterwards sell the land, and
the purchaser would take subject to all the terms and
conditions of the contract, and this is what the state did.
At the time the act was passed and the waterway contract
entered into, the state was the sole and exclusive owner
of the lands. Appellant had no interest in any of them.
Appellant's grantors had only a preference right to purchase. They had no vested or other interest. *Allen v.
Forrest,* 8 Wash. 700, 36 Pac. 971, 24 L. R. A. 606;
Mississippi Valley Trust Co. v. Hofius, 20 Wash. 272,
55 Pac. 54. They were, therefore, entitled to no notice
except such as is provided by the act or the contract.
When they purchased the land from the state, they took
with notice of the contract, and all the terms and conditions thereof. The commissioner of public lands is made
the judge of when the contractor is entitled to a certificate, and, in the absence of fraud, his decision is conclusive upon the appellant, as it would be upon the state if
the state were still the owner. *Scholpp v. Forrest,* 11
Wash. 640, 40 Pac. 133; *Mississippi Valley Trust Co. v.
Hofius, supra.* For these reasons there is no question of
due process of law or want of notice in the case.

It is next argued that the act is in violation of § 9 of
art. 12, and of § 5, of art. 8 of the state constitution, which
declares that, "The credit of the state shall not in any
manner be given or loaned to or in aid of any individual,
association, company, or corporation." We are unable

to see that this act in any manner gives the credit of the state to the enterprise. It is true that certain tide lands are authorized to be filled in, and at a stated price, but the state is not bound to pay even this price. The lands were to be appraised and not sold for less than the appraised price, but the purchasers of these lands were required to take notice of the lien created by the cost of filling the same, and were bound to pay for the improvements. So that no aid or credit was given by the state directly or indirectly to the waterway company. The state was not even liable to discharge the lien. It fixed the price of the land without the improvements, and any person qualified to purchase was at liberty to do so. It is argued that the certificates of liens have the state's land back of them, but this is only true after the state has sold the lands, and then the purchaser takes with notice of the lien and the improvements, which he impliedly, at least, agrees to discharge. If preference right purchasers did not see fit to pay the state the appraised value of the land, and, in addition thereto, pay the waterway company for the improvements, they were under no obligation to purchase. In the event that the state did not sell the land, the only remedy of the waterway company was to purchase the land from the state at the appraised price before the expiration of the lien. While it may have been an advantage to the waterway company to be able to purchase at the appraised price in case preference right purchasers did not do so, we fail to see that the credit of the state was thereby loaned or in any manner given to the waterway company.

It is next argued that the act is in violation of § 3 of art. 8 of the state constitution, which provides that, "No debts shall hereafter be contracted by or on behalf of the state, unless such debts shall be authorized by law for some single work or object to be distinctly specified therein.

. . . No such law shall take effect until it shall at a general election have been submitted to the people and have received a majority of all the votes cast for and against it at such election," etc. It is clear from what we have said above that this is not a debt created or contracted by or on behalf of the state. By the terms of the act and the contract, the state is not liable for any improvements upon the lands. Nor are the state's lands liable therefor while they remain the property of the state. The lands become liable only after the state has parted with all its interest. The purchaser from the state takes the title with notice, and agrees to pay the claim of the waterway company for improvements. If this claim may be said to be a debt, it is not such a debt as is meant by the provision named.

It is next argued that the act is contrary to § 12 of art. 1, which declares that, "No law shall be passed granting to any citizen, class of citizens or corporation other than municipal privileges or immunities which upon the same terms shall not equally belong to all citizens or corporations;" and § 22 of art. 12, which declares that monopolies shall not be allowed in this state. It is said that, because the act allows the respondent waterway company to erect locks in the waterway, and to exercise exclusive control thereof, and collect toll for its own private gain, this is a special privilege and a monopoly. Even if this contention is correct, it does not affect this case, because this is a separable part of the act, and, if this part fails, the portion relating to the certificates would not necessarily fail. Hence, it is unnecessary in this case to decide this question.

Appellant further claims that the act is contrary to § 15 of art. 11, which provides that private property shall not be taken or sold for the payment of corporate debts of any public or municipal corporation except in the mode provided by law for the levy and collection of taxes. As we have seen above, this is not a debt of any public or municipal corporation. It is no debt at all, until some one purchases the land, and thereby assumes it, and agrees to pay for the improvements which the state, as owner, has permitted the waterway company to place upon the lands. It then, and for that reason, becomes a debt of the purchaser. Hence this provision of the constitution is not violated.

The remaining questions presented by appellant are, that the contract is not in conformity with the act in a number of respects, and that the commissioner of public lands had no jurisdiction to issue the certificates sued on, because the certificates are not in conformity with the act. All these questions were settled by this court in *Scholpp v. Forrest,* 11 Wash. 640, 40 Pac. 133, and *Mississipp Valley Trust Co. v. Hofius,* 20 Wash. 272, 55 Pac. 54. We shall therefore not notice them further.

There is no error in the record, and the judgment is affirmed.

Fullerton, C. J., and Hadley, Anders, and Dunbar, JJ., concur.

[No. 5142. Decided August 3, 1904.]

PATRICK KANE *et al., Appellants*, v. ELIZABETH KANE, *Respondent.*[1]

VENUE—DIVORCE—STIPULATION FOR TRIAL IN ANOTHER COUNTY—LEGISLATIVE CHANGE OF DISTRICT. A stipulation between the parties to a divorce suit to try the case in another county of the same judicial district, the same judge presiding, amounts to a change of venue, and such judge does not lose jurisdiction to try the case in such county pursuant to the stipulation, by a subsequent legislative change putting that county in a separate district and appointing another presiding judge for the county in which the suit was originally commenced.

SAME—CONSENT TO CHANGE. A recital in a statement of facts that defendants to a cross-complaint had stipulated that the action might be tried in another county, sufficiently shows their consent to the change of venue, although the written stipulation therefor was originally made between the other parties and before said cross-defendants had been made parties.

DIVORCE—JURISDICTION—RESIDENCE OF PLAINTIFF WITHIN STATE FOR ONE YEAR—CONSOLIDATION OF ACTIONS. Where the husband and wife commenced independent actions for a divorce, and it was stipulated that the two actions should be tried as one, the action should not be dismissed for want of jurisdiction because the wife's suit was commenced before she had been a resident of the state for one year, when the husband was duly qualified by residence to bring his action, and the wife had resided in the state one year before filing a cross-complaint in that suit, and the trial was had upon the issues raised by the pleadings in the husband's suit, the wife's action being in effect abandoned.

TRIAL—MOTION FOR NONSUIT IN EQUITY—WAIVER. Appellants' challenge to the sufficiency of respondent's testimony and motion to dismiss an action for divorce are waived by proceeding to introduce evidence in their own behalf, instead of standing upon the challenge and motion.

TRIAL—REOPENING CASE—DISCRETION. It is not an abuse of discretion to allow appellant to reopen her case after a challenge to the sufficiency of her evidence was made, where the additional evidence consisted of a formal introduction of pleadings in the case.

[1]Reported in 77 Pac. 842.

APPEAL — STATEMENT OF FACTS — CERTIFICATE — ALL THE EVI-
DENCE. In an equity case triable *de novo* on appeal, where it appears from the record that all of the evidence has not been sent
up, it is not sufficient that the lower court certifies the statement
of facts to contain all the material evidence, but the certificate
must be that it contains all the facts which the parties have
agreed to be material, in order to secure a review of the evidence
on appeal.

DIVORCE — CANCELLATION OF FRAUDULENT CONVEYANCES — LIEN FOR
AMOUNT AWARDED WIFE. Where, in an action for a divorce, a
certain sum is awarded the wife as permanent alimony, and certain conveyances by the husband are canceled as a fraud upon
her, it is proper to declare a lien on the property in her favor for
the amount due.

COSTS — TAXATION. A cost bill should not be struck out because
it was served before it was filed and before the judgment was
filed, no prejudice appearing.

Appeal from a judgment of the superior court for Douglas county, Neal, J., entered October 21, 1903, upon findings in favor of the defendant, granting a divorce upon a
cross-complaint, after a trial on the merits before the
court without a jury. Affirmed.

Martin & Grant, for appellant Patrick Kane.

H. N. Martin, for appellant James L. Kane.

Alfred E. Barnes, Geo. A. Latimer, and *Alfred M. Craven,* for respondent.

HADLEY, J.—This is an action for divorce, involving
also the adjustment of property interests. On or about
the 1st day of October, 1901, Patrick Kane and Elizabeth
Kane became husband and wife. Thereafter, on March
31, 1902, the wife filed a complaint in the superior court
of Douglas county, asking for a divorce from the husband.
That action not having been brought on for trial, the husband thereafter, on the 15th day of November, 1902,
filed a complaint in the same court asking for divorce from

the wife. The wife then filed an answer and cross-complaint to the husband's complaint, demanding a divorce, together with alimony, attorney's fees, and a division of the property; also, that certain alleged fraudulent conveyances of the husband and his grantee should be declared void. By leave of court, the wife made Patrick J. Kane, Jr., and James L. Kane parties defendant to the cross-complaint. Said defendants are sons of the husband, and the cross-complaint alleges that they are fraudulent grantees for the purpose of defeating the rights of the wife in the property conveyed.

In the action brought by the husband, issues, as tendered by the complaint and cross-complaint, were joined by the several parties aforesaid. It was stipulated between the husband and wife that the separate actions for divorce should be consolidated and tried as one action, but the issues were really made up under the title of, and within, the case brought by the husband. The husband charged the wife with cruel treatment, and with other unbecoming conduct. The wife made like charges against the husband, and also charged that he broke into her trunk and took from her, without her consent, and appropriated to his own use, the sum of $1,800 in money, the same being her sole and separate property.

By stipulation, and for the convenience of the parties, the cause was transferred to Lincoln county for trial, where it was afterwards tried. The trial was by the court without a jury. Findings of facts and conclusions of law were made, and a decree was entered thereon, by the terms of which the wife was granted a divorce upon her cross-complaint, and was awarded $1,200 as permanent alimony, together with $250 as counsel fees. It is also provided that she shall recover from her husband the further sum of $1,800, which the court fixes as her just and equitable

portion of the property involved. The court found that
the husband had taken and appropriated the $1,800, which
was the wife's separate property when the two were married, and the item of $1,800 mentioned in the decree was
evidently based upon the theory that the money had become commingled with the husband's property, and that
a just division of the property interests required that
special account should be taken of that money. This,
doubtless, accounts for the statement of said sum as a
separate item in the decree. The decree also provides
that the wife shall have a specific lien for the total of said
several amounts, and for costs, upon the undivided half
of certain described real estate. It is also declared that
certain specified deeds and conveyances of said real estate
are null and void, as against the wife, and the same are
cancelled and set aside. The conveyances referred to are
three deeds, executed by said husband, Patrick Kane, to
his son, Patrick J. Kane, Jr., and, also, three deeds made
by the latter, and executed two days later than the others,
purporting to convey the same real estate to his brother,
James L. Kane. At the trial the cross-complaint was dismissed as to Patrick J. Kane, Jr., evidently on the theory
that he has no present real, or even apparent, interest in
the property, since he has conveyed it to said James L.
Kane. From the decree the said husband, Patrick Kane,
and said James L. Kane have separately appealed.

It is assigned that the court erred in overruling the
motion for a new trial, and in entering judgment, for the
reason that it had jurisdiction neither of the subject matter nor of the persons of the litigants. In support of the
contention on the question of jurisdiction it is argued that,
at the time the stipulation was made to try the cause in
Lincoln county, said county was in the same judicial district with Douglas county, and that Judge Neal, who was

the judge in Lincoln county, was also judge in Douglas county, but that, by an act of the legislature which took effect thereafter and before the trial of the cause, a new judicial district was created, whereby said counties were placed in separate districts. A new presiding judge was appointed for the district which includes Douglas county, and, at the time of the trial, Judge Neal was not the presiding judge of the superior court of that county. It is therefore urged that, since this action was brought in Douglas county, the judge of the superior court of Lincoln county, not being also the judge in Douglas county, had not jurisdiction to try it. We believe the change of districts did not affect the matter of jurisdiction. If no change had been made, Judge Neal, when trying the cause in Lincoln county, would have tried it as the superior court of that county, and not of Douglas county. The stipulation between the parties, to all intents and purposes, effected a change of venue to Lincoln county. It is, however, contended in behalf of appellant James L. Kane, that he never consented that the cause be tried in Lincoln county, the above mentioned stipulation for the transfer having been made before he was even made a party to the cross-complaint. The statement of facts proposed by appellants, and certified by the court, contains the following recital:

"This cause came on for trial on the 13th day of July, 1903, at 10 o'clock A. M., before C. H. Neal, Judge, it having been stipulated by the attorneys representing the plaintiff and defendant, as well as defendants to cross-complaint, that the same might be tried at Davenport, Lincoln county, Washington, before the above named judge."

The above statement, certified in the record, sufficiently shows the consent of appellant James L. Kane to try the case in Lincoln county.

It is further contended that the court had not jurisdiction, for the reason that, when the action brought by the wife Elizabeth Kane was commenced, she had been a resident of this state but about five or six months. It is true, jurisdiction could not have been conferred by that complaint, since she had not resided in this state one year. But it is not disputed that the husband, Patrick Kane, had been a continuous resident of this state for many years prior to the time he filed his complaint, and was then a resident of Douglas county. He was therefore competent, under the law, to institute an action for divorce. The wife, as the defendant to the husband's complaint, had the right to defend against it, even by way of cross-complaint, and the cross-complaint shown in the record was also filed after she had been a resident of this state for more than one year. While there was a stipulation in terms declaring that the two actions should be tried as one, yet the pleadings show that the action brought by the wife was, to all intents and purposes, abandoned. Jurisdiction was full and complete in the action that was tried.

It is urged that the court erred in refusing to sustain the challenge interposed by appellants to the evidence, when respondent, Elizabeth Kane, rested her case in chief, and in refusing to dismiss the case. It is not necessary that we should discuss the evidence, or pass upon its sufficiency, as it stood when the challenge and motions to dismiss were made, for the reason that appellants proceeded at once to the introduction of evidence on their own behalf, and did not stand upon their challenge and motion to dismiss. This court held, in *Scoland v. Scoland*, 4 Wash. 118, 29 Pac. 930, that, in an action for divorce, although the court may have erred in denying a motion to dismiss at the close of the plaintiff's testimony, yet the error was cured by the defendants thereafter proceeding with the case.

It was held that in equity one must stand upon his motion
to dismiss, if he would reap advantage from it. It had
been previously so held in *Cattell v. Fergusson,* 3 Wash.
541, 28 Pac. 750, which case was followed in the one first
above cited. Under that rule appellants must be held to
have waived the motion by proceeding to introduce their
own evidence.

It is further insisted that error was committed in permitting respondent to reopen her case, after the challenge
to the sufficiency of her evidence was made. We think
the court did not abuse its discretion in reopening the
case. Appellants were not prejudiced thereby. The additional evidence consisted of a formal introduction as evidence of the answers of Patrick J. Kane, Jr., and James
L. Kane, to the cross-complaint, which were already in
the case in the form of pleadings.

It is contended by appellants that certain of the material
findings of facts, as made by the court, are not supported
by the evidence. But it is urged by respondent that, under the record, this court would not, in any event, be justified in disturbing these findings, for the reason that it is
apparent from the record that all the evidence is not here.
The certificate of the court first recites that it contains
all the evidence, whereas it is apparent that said recital
is erroneous, as the depositions of four persons are shown
to have been read in evidence, and much time was consumed by objections to questions therein. The record
discloses only the names of the several persons whose
depositions were read, the numbers of the several interrogatories challenged by objections, the objections thereto,
and the rulings thereon. The deposition evidence itself
does not, however, appear in the record. The action is
triable *de novo* here, and this court must have all the
evidence before it which was before the court below, in

order to so try it. *Enos v. Wilcox,* 3 Wash. 44, 28 Pac.
364; *Cadwell v. First Nat. Bank,* 3 Wash. 188, 28 Pac.
365; *Kirby v. Collins,* 6 Wash. 297, 32 Pac. 1060;
State ex rel. Van Name v. Board of Directors, 14 Wash.
222, 44 Pac. 270. It is true, the judge's certificate makes
the further recital that the statement contains all the material evidence; but it being manifest that it does not
contain all the evidence, it becomes necessary, under
§ 5060, Bal. Code, that it shall recite that it contains all
the facts which the parties have agreed to be all that are
material. *Nickeus v. Lewis County,* 23 Wash. 125, 62 Pac.
763. The certificate is lacking in said particular. It
being manifest, therefore, that all the evidence which was
before the trial court is not before us, we cannot, in the
absence of agreement between the parties, try the case
de novo with a view to making new findings. We have,
however, read the evidence that is in the record, and we
may say that, standing alone, we think it justifies the
findings made by the court, both upon the divorce issue
and upon the money and property features of the case.
There is much evidence in the record that is here, but an
analytical discussion of it would require much space, and
we believe it would not serve any useful purpose, in view
of its conflicting nature. If we were required to make
findings in the case, we should be disposed, from the evidence before us, to adopt the findings of the trial court,
who heard and saw all the witnesses testify. The findings
will, therefore, not be disturbed.

The conclusions of law are not inconsistent with the
findings. The provisions of the decree as to alimony,
attorney's fees, and division of the property, are not unreasonable under the record showing. The cancellation of
the conveyances, as having been intended by the parties

thereto to be in fraud of respondent's rights, is sustained by the findings, and the lien declared thereon properly and logically follows.

Appellant Patrick Kane complains that the court denied his motion to strike the respondent's cost bill. The point urged seems to be that the cost bill was served the day before it was filed, and before the judgment was filed, it being claimed that, for said reasons, it was not a cost bill. Said appellant directs attention to no statute or ruling of court which requires that a cost bill shall necessarily be filed before it is served, or that it cannot be served before the judgment is filed. It is admitted that the court considered the cost bill, allowing some items and disallowing others. No specific items are pointed out, and no prejudice to said appellant's rights appears. The judgment is affirmed.

MOUNT, ANDERS, and DUNBAR, JJ., concur.

[No. 5173.   Decided August 3, 1904.]

C. H. BARTLETT *et al.*, *Appellants*, v. THE BRITISH AMERICA ASSURANCE COMPANY, *Respondent.*[1]

INSURANCE—POLICY—CONDITIONS—VACANCY OF BUILDING FOR MORE THAN TEN DAYS—ABSENCE OF CONSENT—REPRESENTATIONS. There can be no recovery under a policy of fire insurance which provides that the same should be void if the building was unoccupied and so remained for ten days without the company's consent, where the building was vacant at the time the policy was issued and so remained for more than ten days without the knowledge of the company; and the fact that no inquiries or representations were made upon the subject does not change the rule, or in any way estop the company.

Appeal from a judgment of the superior court for Yakima county, Rudkin, J., entered July 20, 1903, dismissing

[1]Reported in 77 Pac. 812.

on the merits an action to recover insurance upon a loss
by fire, after a trial before the court, a jury being waived.
Affirmed.

Whitson & Parker, for appellants.

Graves & Englehart, for respondent.

HADLEY, J.—On March 28, 1902, appellants were the
owners of a dwelling house in North Yakima, and on
said date the respondent issued its policy of insurance upon
said house in the sum of $400, whereby it undertook to
insure against loss or damage by fire, for a period of three
years from said date. The house was unoccupied at the
time the policy was issued, a fact unknown to respondent,
and it also appears that appellants had no actual knowledge that it was vacant. No representations were made
by appellants upon that subject, when their application
was made or when the policy was issued, and no information thereon seems to have been asked by respondent.
The policy contained the following provision: "This entire policy, unless otherwise provided by agreement indorsed hereon or added hereto, shall be void . . . if
a building herein described, whether intended for occupancy by owner or tenant, be or become vacant or unoccupied and so remain for ten days." No agreement was
made for an extension of time for the house to remain
vacant. It remained unoccupied until the 5th day of May,
1902, when it was destroyed by fire. Demand for payment was made by appellants, and refused by respondent.
This suit was brought to recover the amount mentioned
in the policy. Respondent interposed the defense that
the house had remained vacant for a period of more than
ten days without its permission, in violation of the terms
of the above quoted provision in the policy, and it brought
into court for the use of appellants the amount of pre-

mium paid. The cause was tried by the court without a
jury, the jury being waived. The trial resulted in a judgment dismissing the action. The plaintiffs have appealed.

The only question to be examined is whether appellants
are precluded from recovery by reason of the said provision in the policy. It is the position of appellants that,
inasmuch as the house was vacant when the policy was
issued, respondent therefore waived that provision in the
contract. It would seem that respondent should not be
charged with having waived the question of occupancy
when it had not even knowledge that the building was unoccupied. But appellants urge that, since no information
was asked upon that subject and no representations were
made, said requirement was therefore waived. We think,
under the terms of the policy, it was wholly immaterial
to respondent whether the building was vacant or occupied at the time the policy was issued. In either case it
undertook to bind itself for a period of ten days. The contract provided that the policy should become void, if the
building should then be, or should thereafter become, vacant
and should so remain for ten days. It will be observed that
the policy did not require that the property should be
then *occupied,* but rather that, if it was then *unoccupied*
and *remained* so for ten days without respondent's consent, it should become void. The contract by its terms,
was undoubtedly good against loss which might have occurred within ten days, but not for loss occurring after
that time, unless respondent had consented to an extension of the period of vacancy. The said provision of the
contract seems to be plain and unambiguous, and the
facts bring this case squarely within it, thus rendering
the policy void. The following authorities are directly
in point: *England v. Westchester Fire Ins. Co.,* 81 Wis.

583, 51 N. W. 954, 29 Am. St. 917; *Connecticut Fire
Ins. Co. v. Tilley*, 88 Va. 1024, 14 S. E. 851, 29 Am. St.
770; *Thomas v. Hartford Fire Ins. Co.*, 21 Ky. L. 914,
53 S. W. 297.

Appellants cite authorities to the point that an insurance company is estopped from asserting the invalidity
of its policy at the time it was issued, for the violation
of any of the provisions of the policy, if, at the time it
was issued, such violation was known to the company or
its agent. Such authorities are not pertinent here for the
reason that the insurance company in this case does not
seek to claim that its policy was, for any reason, void at
the time it was issued. It admits that the policy was
binding at the beginning, and remained so until rendered
void by appellants' failure to comply with a plain and
mandatory condition. Moreover, the violation of the condition was not known to respondent when it issued the
policy, and could not have been known, since it could not
foresee that appellants would permit the property to remain vacant for more than ten days. Appellants insist
that, by respondent's failure to inquire as to the vacancy,
it occupies the same position in law as if it had inquired
and ascertained the truth. It matters not to the respondent, however, what was the fact upon that subject. It
was willing to insure the property, even though vacant,
for a period of ten days, but for no longer time without its
permission. It so provided in its contract. Appellants
are chargeable with knowledge of the provision, and also
that their property was vacant. They were therefore
bound to know that the policy would become void after
ten days, if the property still remained vacant. We think
that, under the contract and attending facts, the judgment
was right, and it is affirmed.

MOUNT, ANDERS, and DUNBAR, JJ., concur.

[No. 5173. Decided August 3, 1904.]

Eliza A. Hill, *Appellant,* v. J. N. Gardner, *Sheriff, et al., Respondents.*[1]

APPEAL—NOTICE—PROOF OF SERVICE—ACCEPTANCE. Service of notice of appeal upon sureties on a redelivery bond is sufficiently shown by an acceptance of service by them, witnessed by an attorney of the supreme court, and by an affidavit of due service.

TRIAL—NONSUIT OVERRULED—DISMISSAL. In an action tried before the court without a jury in which the court orally refuses to grant a nonsuit, whereupon the case is argued without the introduction of any evidence, the court is not precluded by the ruling on the motion for nonsuit from finding for the defendant and dismissing the action.

COMMUNITY PROPERTY—EVIDENCE—SUFFICIENCY—WIFE'S SEPARATE ESTATE. A finding that a team of horses was community property will not be disturbed where the only evidence that the same was the separate property of the wife was that of the husband, to the effect that, thirty years before, she had received $1,000 from her father and had kept the money separate, tracing it through various investments, where the wife was present in court and failed to offer herself as a witness, and the husband's testimony was not wholly consistent.

EXECUTION—REDELIVERY BOND—VALUE OF PROPERTY—ALLEGATION OF CLAIMANT—ESTOPPEL. In an action to compel the delivery of property levied upon by a sheriff, in which the claimant alleges the value to be $300, the claimant and the sureties are bound thereby and cannot complain that judgment for defendant was entered for $300 as the value of the property, although the only evidence of value made it appear to be less than $300.

SAME—ORIGINAL AMOUNT DUE ON THE ATTACHMENT—JUDGMENT FOR VALUE—PRESUMED LESS THAN SUM DUE. Upon a judgment against a third party claimant of attached property, for $300 as the value of the property, where there is nothing to show the amount due under the attachment, it will be presumed in aid of the judgment that it was not a less sum, as required by Bal. Code, § 5266.

SAME—RETURN OF PROPERTY—JUDGMENT IN ALTERNATIVE FOR RETURN OR VALUE OF PROPERTY. Upon an action for the redelivery

[1]Reported in 77 Pac. 808.

34-35 WASH.

of attached property, it is error for the judgment to fail to provide in the alternative for the return of the property or its value.

INTEREST—JUDGMENT FOR REDELIVERY OF PROPERTY—INTEREST PRIOR TO DATE OF JUDGMENT. In an action for the redelivery of attached property there is no authority for the recovery of interest prior to the date of the judgment.

Appeal from a judgment of the superior court for Lincoln county, Neal, J., entered January 12, 1904, upon findings in favor of the defendant, dismissing on the merits an action to compel the delivery of personal property, after a trial before the court without a jury. Modified.

Martin & Grant, for appellant.

Myers & Warren, for respondents.

HADLEY, J.—This is an action to compel the delivery of personal property levied upon by the sheriff. The appellant, Eliza A. Hill, is the claimant. In pursuance of § 5262, Bal. Code, she filed an affidavit, which alleges, that the respondent Parrish commenced an action against E. Hill, and caused a writ of attachment to issue therein, which writ was delivered to respondent Gardner, as sheriff, and that the latter was directed to immediately levy upon the property of said E. Hill; that, under said writ of attachment, said sheriff levied upon and took possession of four horses, which are described in the affidavit; that said property was and is the sole and separate property of said Eliza A. Hill, and that no one else had or has any right to the possession thereof; that said E. Hill had neither any interest therein nor right of possession thereto. The value of the property is laid at $300, and it is alleged that a demand was made upon the sheriff and said Parrish for its delivery to said claimant, which was refused. The claimant, Eliza A. Hill, is the wife of said

E. Hill. The cause was tried before the court without a
jury, and resulted in a finding by the court that the property was the community property of the husband and wife,
and judgment was entered against the claimant, from
which she has appealed.

Respondents moved to dismiss the appeal, for the alleged reason that the notice of appeal was not served upon
the sureties upon the redelivery bond. The record shows
a service purporting to have been acknowledged in writing
by the sureties themselves. Their signatures to the acceptance of service are witnessed by the signature of H. N.
Martin, an attorney of this court, and the counsel for
appellant. We also find in the record an affidavit of said
Martin, showing due service made by him upon the bondsmen. The service is sufficiently shown, and the motion to
dismiss the appeal is denied.

It is argued that the court erred in finding that the
property levied upon was, at the time of the levy, the
community property of appellant and her husband, and
was not the separate property of appellant. The only
witnesses offered in behalf of appellant upon the question
of ownership were her son and husband. The former
simply testified, in a general way, that he had always
understood that the horses belonged to his mother, and
that he had always heard them referred to in the family
as her property. The husband testified that about thirty
years ago the appellant received about $1,000 from her
father, and that she has since kept that money separately
invested. He undertook to trace the investment of the
money down to and including the horses in question,
following it through a number of investments, sales, and
reinvestments. At the close of the testimony for appellant, respondents moved for a nonsuit upon the ground

that appellant had failed to show that the property belonged to her separately.   The motion was denied, and
respondents introduced no evidence.   The case was then
argued, and the court announced that the matter would
be taken under advisement   The court must have changed
its mind as to the force of the testimony after the ruling
upon the motion for nonsuit, as no further evidence was
introduced.   The argument of counsel, however, followed
that ruling, and, doubtless, features of the testimony,
cross-examination of witnesses, and circumstances were
analyzed and emphasized by the argument to the extent
that the court felt impelled to find for respondents as
aforesaid.   Appellant complains that the court reversed
its own ruling upon the motion for a nonsuit.   We think,
under the circumstances, that it had a right to further
consider the evidence, and enter its findings thereon.   No
order or judgment had been entered upon the motion for
nonsuit.   There was simply a hasty oral announcement
that the motion would be denied.   The testimony of the
husband is not wholly consistent, even upon his theory,
and we are not prepared to say that the court, who saw
and heard him testify, observing his manner, was not
justified in disbelieving him.   A further circumstance is
shown by the record, which we think the court had a right
to consider, along with the spoken testimony and other
circumstances.   The appellant herself sat in the court
room during the examination of her son and husband, but
she did not offer herself as a witness.   It seems almost in-
credible that she should have owned these horses as the
result of a long series of investments of her separate property, received from her father; that she should have man-
aged the investments herself as the husband testified, and
yet not have offered herself as a witness upon the subject
when she sat in the court room and was able to testify.

Under the circumstances detailed by the husband, the appellant, of all persons, was the one who should have been able to tell the true story. We shall, therefore, not hold that the court should have found the horses to be her separate property. Property received by either spouse after marriage is prima facie community property. *Lemon v. Waterman,* 2 Wash. Ter. 485, 7 Pac. 899; *Yesler v. Hochstettler,* 4 Wash. 349, 30 Pac. 398; *Curry v. Catlin,* 9 Wash. 495, 37 Pac. 678, 39 Pac. 101; *Woodland Lumber Co. v. Link,* 16 Wash. 72, 47 Pac. 222. The finding that the property in question was the community property of appellant and her husband will therefore not be disturbed.

It is next complained that judgment was entered for $300 as the value of the property. The only evidence upon the subject of value was that of the husband who said, "I am not posted on the prices of horses now. They are probably worth $50 apiece." Under that statement the four horses were not worth to exceed $200. But, inasmuch as the appellant herself alleged in her affidavit that the value was $300, we think she is bound thereby and cannot now show a less value. The undertaking of herself and sureties also recited that if she should fail to make good her title she would return the property, "or pay its value as stated in said affidavit." Both appellant and the sureties have, therefore, fixed the value at $300, and cannot now be heard to dispute it.

It is contended that the court was not authorized to enter the kind of judgment which was entered. It is simply for the recovery of $300, as the value of the property, with interest thereon. Section 5266, Bal. Code, provides that the judgment shall be for the value, "or for such less amount as shall not exceed the amount due on the original execution or attachment." There is nothing in the record to show whether the amount due under the attachment was less or more than the value of the property; but, in aid of the judgment, it will be presumed that it was not a less sum.

It is further urged that the judgment does not provide in the alternative that appellant shall return the property or pay its value. Section 5262, *supra,* shows that such is her right, and § 5266, *supra,* must be construed in connection with the former one. In said particular we think the judgment was erroneous.

Further complaint is made of the judgment in that it provides for the recovery of six per cent interest per annum upon the amount of the judgment, from the date of the affidavit made by appellant when she sought possession of the property. The judgment was entered more than a year after said date, and there was thus added to the value of the property more than $18 as interest. We believe no authority exists in this special proceeding for the recovery of interest. The statute does not so provide. It merely contemplates the return of the property or the payment of its value, and that is all that the sureties undertook to do. This judgment is against them as well as against appellant. The only theory upon which interest could be allowed would be that it is in the nature of compensation, as damages for the detention of the property; but the statute does not provide for the adjustment of damages in this proceeding. We think it was error to include interest in the judgment, which accrued prior to its date.

It is therefore the order of this court that the judgment shall be modified, so as to eliminate the provision for recovery of interest prior to the date of the judgment, and so as to further provide, in the alternative, for the return of the property or the payment of its value. In all other respects the judgment shall remain as it now is. Appellant shall recover the costs of the appeal. The cause is remanded, with instructions to proceed as above indicated.

MOUNT, ANDERS, and DUNBAR, JJ., concur.

[No. 5049.   Decided August 3, 1904.]

RICE FISHERIES COMPANY et al., Respondents, v. PACIFIC REALTY COMPANY et al., Appellants.[1]

APPEAL—TIME FOR TAKING—MOTION FOR NEW TRIAL—SUSPENDING FINAL EFFECT OF JUDGMENT. Where, after judgment, a motion for a new trial is made and denied, the judgment is not of final effect until the motion is determined, and the time for taking an appeal begins to run from the date of the order denying the motion for new trial.

APPEAL—REVIEW—AFFIDAVITS How BROUGHT UP. Affidavits in support of a motion for a new trial will not be considered on appeal unless brought up in a bill of exceptions or statement of facts.

LANDLORD AND TENANT—RIGHTFULNESS OF POSSESSION—NOTICE TO QUIT—INSTRUCTIONS. In an action for damages to personal property located on certain premises, wherein the complaint alleges that defendant wrongfully took possession of the premises, it was not error to instruct that, if the relation of landlord and tenant existed between the parties, the latter would be entitled to ten days' notice in order to determine its rights of occupancy, since the fact bears on the rightfulness of the possession.

MALICIOUS INJURY TO PROPERTY — PLEADING AND PROOF — INSTRUCTIONS. In an action for injury to property, where the complaint charged that defendants acted maliciously, wantonly, and unlawfully, proof of a mere wrongful or unlawful injury was in support of the complaint, and it was not error to refuse to instruct that the burden was upon plaintiff to show malicious and wanton damage.

Reported in 77 Pac. 839.

New Trial—Misconduct of Juror—Poll of Jury—Change of Vote. A new trial should not be granted on the ground of improper conduct of the jury, nor because the jury was not immediately returned to the jury room after a poll showing that ten jurors had not agreed to the verdict, where, in a case tried by eleven jurors, it was found upon poll that nine agreed to the verdict and two voted in the negative, and a second poll resulted in the same vote, whereupon one of the two asked and received permission to change his vote, and upon the third poll ten agreed to the verdict, and where the time consumed was only sufficient for the doing of these things in consecutive order with no appreciable intermission.

Trial—Receiving Verdict—Instructions to Jury. Upon receiving a verdict in the absence of counsel pursuant to stipulation, where, upon a poll of the jury, at first but nine agree, it is not error for the court, in the absence of counsel, to repeat the instructions as to the number necessary to agree, and to grant a request of a juror to allow him to change his vote, in case a mistake was made.

Appeal from a judgment of the superior court for Whatcom county, Neterer, J., entered June 24, 1903, upon the verdict of a jury rendered in favor of the plaintiff for $500 damages for injury to personal property. Affirmed.

Kerr, McCord & Craven, for appellants.

Crites & Romaine, for respondents.

Hadley, J.—Respondents brought this suit against appellants to recover alleged damages for injury to personal property, and also to their business of salting and smoking fish. The complaint alleges that respondents were, on the 12th day of December, 1902, the joint owners, and that the respondent Rice Fisheries Company was in the possession, of certain frame buildings known as "Sutherland Fish Company's smoke houses," in the city of Fairhaven; that they were also the joint owners of a large amount of other personal property located in said smoke houses and on adjoining grounds, consisting of barrels, tierces, vats,

tanks, box shooks, half barrels, saltpeter, kits, pails, and
other personal property; that all of said property, including buildings, was of the value of $1,500; that on said
date the appellants, acting together, maliciously, wrongfully, unlawfully, and by force, took possession of all of
said property, and broke, damaged, destroyed, and converted it to their own use; that by reason of the destruction
of said property, respondents were also damaged in their
business. Damages were demanded in the sum of $2,000.
The answer is a general denial. A trial was had before the
court and a jury, resulting in a verdict for respondents
in the sum of $500. The court withdrew from the con-
sideration of the jury the issue as to damage to respondents' business, for the stated reason that there was no
evidence upon that subject. Appellants' motion for new
trial was denied, judgment was entered upon the verdict,
and this appeal is from the judgment.

Respondents moved to dismiss the appeal, for the alleged
reason that the notice of appeal was neither served nor filed
within the time limited by law. The judgment was entered on the 24th day of June, 1903, and the notice of
appeal was served and filed on the 3rd day of October,
1903. It is true the appeal was taken more than ninety
days after the date of the judgment, but the motion for
new trial, which was seasonably served and filed, was not
acted upon by the court until September 26, 1903. By the
terms of § 1, p. 285, Session Laws of 1903, judgment in
conformity with the verdict shall be entered immediately, as
was done in this case. It is, however, provided in the same
section that, if a motion for new trial shall be seasonably
filed, execution shall not issue upon the judgment until the
motion shall be determined. Construing said section in
connection with other statutory provisions, this court held

in *State ex rel. Payson v. Chapman,* ante, p. 64, 76 Pac. 525, that, when a motion for new trial has been filed within time, a judgment is not of final effect until the motion is determined, and that the time for taking an appeal begins to run from the date of the order denying the motion for new trial. This appeal was therefore taken within the time limited by law. The motion to dismiss the appeal is denied.

Respondents also move to strike from the transcript certain affidavits purporting to be in support of the motion for new trial, for the reason that the same are not embodied in a bill of exceptions or statement of facts. It has been frequently held by this court that such affidavits are in the nature of evidentiary matter and must be certified by the trial court as a part of the record, and as containing facts which were considered by the court below, in order to entitle them to consideration here. *Chevalier & Co. v. Wilson,* 30 Wash. 227, 70 Pac. 487; *Griggs v. MacLean,* 33 Wash. 244, 74 Pac. 360; *Shuey v. Holmes,* 27 Wash. 489, 67 Pac. 1096. The motion to strike the affidavits is granted.

It is assigned by appellants that the court erred in instructing the jury that, if they found that the relation of landlord and tenant existed between the Rice Fisheries Company and Pacific Realty Company, then the former company would be entitled to ten days' notice in order to determine its right of occupancy, and unless such notice was given it would have the right, under certain conditions, to recover. The theory upon which this instruction is assailed is that the question of the right of respondents to possession of the realty upon which the buildings in controversy were located is not an issue under the pleadings. We think it must be presumed, from the allegations of the

complaint, that the respondents' occupancy of the buildings
where they stood was at the time a rightful occupancy.   No
other theory would sustain the allegation that the appellants wrongfully took possession of the buildings.   If the
occupancy of the buildings, as they then stood, was rightful,
then it must follow that the occupancy of the ground upon
which they stood was also rightful.   Appellants' general
denial put that fact in issue.   Evidence upon the matter
of notice, or lack of notice, to quit was, therefore, competent as bearing upon the question of rightful or wrongful possession, and, correspondingly, upon the right or
wrong of appellants in taking possession and removing the
property from the lands.   The criticized instruction submitted the issue raised by that evidence, and, for the
reasons stated, was not erroneous.

Errors are urged upon the court's refusal to give several
requested instructions to the effect that the only theory
upon which respondents could recover was that appellants
maliciously and wantonly injured and destroyed the property, and that the burden was upon respondents to show
that it was so done.   It is true the complaint charges that
appellants acted maliciously, but it also charges them with
acting wrongfully and unlawfully.   Proof of a mere
wrongful or unlawful injury to the property was, therefore,
in support of the complaint, even though the element of
maliciousness were wanting.   If respondents' occupancy of
the buildings was at the time a rightful one by reason of
tenancy, then it was wrongful and unlawful for appellants
to forcibly remove the buildings and other property, even
though it was not done maliciously or wantonly, and for
resulting damage in such case appellants must be liable.
We think the court did not err in refusing the requested
instructions, and we believe the jury were fully and fairly
instructed as to the law of the case.

It is next assigned that error was committed in overruling the motion for new trial. So far as evidence in
support of the verdict is concerned, there was, we think,
testimony to sustain it, and the conflicting features having
been settled by the jury, we shall not disturb the verdict
on that ground. It is, however, claimed that a new trial
should have been granted for alleged irregularities occurring at the time the jury returned to the court to announce
their verdict. The affidavits having been stricken from
the record, our examination of this matter is confined to
what appears in the statement of facts, in a statement prepared by the judge himself, and designated "Supplemental
Statement," but attached to the original statement of facts
and certified with it. That statement shows that it was
agreed by counsel for both parties that when the jury
should agree upon a verdict the court should receive it in
the absence of respective counsel. After a time the jury
reported an agreement upon a verdict and, as they were
about to return to the court room, one of respondents'
attorneys entered the room, appellants' attorneys being
absent. After the jurors had taken their places in the
jury box, the court inquired if they had agreed upon a
verdict. The foreman replied in the affirmative, and
passed the verdict to the court. The clerk, by direction of
the court, read the verdict, and immediately afterwards
the court asked if it was the verdict of each one, to which
the response came, "It is," and possibly some juror said
"It is not." Thereupon the court ordered the jury polled,
as is customary in said court when a verdict is received in
the absence of attorneys in the case. On being polled,
nine jurors replied in the affirmative, and two in the
negative (the cause by consent having been tried by eleven
jurors). The court then ordered the jury polled again,

thinking a mistake might have been made by some juror.
The result was the same as before. The court then stated,
in substance, that the jury had no business to announce
that it had agreed upon a verdict when it had not so
agreed, adding, "This is no verdict," and further stating
that they had been plainly instructed that it was necessary
for ten to agree before they could return a verdict. The
court then turned to examine the statutes and about this
time, or possibly just as the second poll was being taken or
commenced—as to that the court is not positive—one juror
who had voted in the negative stated that he would like to
say a word, if it was proper to do so, or words to that
effect. Whereupon the court promptly informed him that
no statement was proper. About this time the same juror
asked if he could change his vote, to which the court replied
"If you have made a mistake," or words to that effect.
The court thereupon directed the jury to be polled again,
and, upon doing so, ten jurors responded in favor of the
verdict, the aforesaid juror voting "Yes," instead of "No,"
as theretofore, and one other juror at all times voting
"No." Thereupon the verdict was ordered filed in the
presence of the jury, and the jury were discharged. The
court further stated that the time consumed in the foregoing proceedings was only sufficient for the doing of the
things above enumerated, in their consecutive order, without any appreciable intermission. The court believes that,
after the first poll of the jury, some of the jurors sitting
next to the said juror who changed his vote said something
to him by way of whispering, prior to his asking permission to change his vote. This fact was not observed by the
court, but from sworn statements of other persons, he is
convinced that such is the fact.

Appellants contend that the law provides that, if upon
a poll a sufficient number of jurors do not assent to a ver-

dict, they shall be immediately sent back to the jury room.
The statute, § 5012, Bal. Code, says: "In case ten of the
jurors do not answer in the affirmative, the jury shall be
returned to the jury room for further deliberation." The
statute does not say they shall be *immediately* sent back to
the jury room, and there is nothing in the statute to prohibit more than one poll, if the court believes a mistake has
been made, or is informed by a juror that he desires to
change his vote. Each juror's vote must be directed by his
own conscience, and is not under the control or direction
of the other jurors. There seems to be no good reason,
therefore, why he may not change his vote in the presence
of the court and jury, under the circumstances shown in
this case, without having to go through the mere form of
going back to the jury room. There is not sufficient showing that any improper influences were brought to bear
upon the juror. The mere whispering of one juror to
another does not, of itself, show that he was even speaking
about the verdict. Whether a whispered conversation
about the verdict, under the circumstances shown here,
would constitute prejudicial error would depend upon
what was said, and since there is nothing in the record to
show what was said, no prejudice appears.

It is contended that the communication of the judge to
the jury in the manner aforesaid was in the nature of
instructions, and should have been made in the presence of
appellants or their attorneys. What was said by the court
was but a reiteration of what he had said as to the law in
his instructions, given before the retirement of the jury.
No new feature as to the law of the case was introduced.
He simply stated what he said in his instructions, that ten
jurors must agree before they could return a verdict, and
informed a juror who asked for his own information, that

he could change his vote if he had made a mistake. That
a mistake had been made seems evident, as it will be presumed, under the instructions given and without other
showing, that the foreman understood that there were ten
votes in the jury room for the verdict, or he would not have
reported that a verdict had been reached. Counsel must
know the possibility of such circumstances arising, and,
if they voluntarily consent for the court to receive a verdict
in their absence, that consent must carry with it the understanding that the court is at liberty to act as a reasonable
and sensible man in dealing with such simple emergencies
when they arise. He should not be left as though he were
dumb, without privilege to open his mouth, merely because
counsel have not happened to be in court. The orderly
dispatch of business will not permit that he shall be thus
narrowly restricted. The juror asked a plain question,
which it would have been his right to ask if counsel had
been present. The answer of the court was concise and
correct. No prejudice to appellants' rights could have
resulted therefrom. The case of *State v. Austin,* 6 Wis.
203, cited by appellants, was a criminal case. On the first
poll of the jury one juror answered, "I subscribed the verdict." The court directed that the question be put to the
juror again, and told him he must answer "Yes" or "No."
The juror replied, "Then I will never say 'Yes,' because
I subscribed it." He being further instructed by the court
as to his duties as a juror, the question was put to him a
third time, and he answered, "Yes." The supreme court
held that it was evident that such a doubt existed in the
juror's mind, which fact was made known to the court, as
made the reception of the verdict erroneous. The holding
was clearly right, particularly in a criminal case where
the element of reasonable doubt is always material. In

Farrell v. Hennesy, 21 Wis. 639, also cited by appellants, a juror stated that he consented to the verdict as a matter of accommodation, but that it was against his conscience. It was held that the court should have directed the jury to retire and reconsider their verdict. No such conditions as appeared in the Wisconsin cases are shown in the case at bar. As far as the record discloses, the juror acted voluntarily as his conscience and judgment directed, and with no attending coercive or unduly persuasive circumstances. It was not error to receive the verdict.

The judgment is affirmed.

MOUNT, ANDERS, and DUNBAR, JJ., concur.

[No. 4554.   Decided August 4, 1904.]

STELLA BIER, *Respondent, v.* A. A. HOSFORD *et al.,*
Appellants.[1]

MASTER AND SERVANT—NEGLIGENCE—ASSUMPTION OF RISK—APPARENT DANGER FROM UNGUARDED MANGLE IN LAUNDRY. In an action for personal injuries sustained by an operator of a five roll mangle in a laundry, by reason of the alleged removal of a guard, whereby plaintiff's hand was caught between the rolls, the plaintiff assumes the risks or is guilty of contributory negligence as a matter of law, where it appears that she is an intelligent woman of the age of 25 years, had been working on the machine in question as a feeder for three months, and it was obvious that she would suffer injury if she allowed her hands to be caught while running clothes through the machine, and she fully appreciated the danger, and it is error to refuse to grant a nonsuit.

SAME—OBEYING INSTRUCTIONS. A servant is not justified, in the presence of apparent danger, in putting life or limb in jeopardy by rushing the work unreasonably in obedience to orders of a fellow-servant, who was in charge of the work.

[1]Reported in 77 Pac. 867.

SAME—PLEADING—ASSUMPTION OF RISKS—NONSUIT.   While assumption of risks is an affirmative defense which must be pleaded,
still, when it appears by the plaintiff's evidence that he cannot
recover in any event by reason thereof, defendant is entitled to
a nonsuit.

Appeal from a judgment of the superior court for Spokane county, Richardson, J., entered July 10, 1902, upon
the verdict of a jury rendered in favor of the plaintiff for
$2,100 for injuries sustained by the operator of a mangle
in a laundry.   Reversed.

Post, Avery & Higgins, for appellants.

Shine & Winfree and W. F. Townsend, for respondent.

PER CURIAM.—Action brought in the superior court
of Spokane county, by plaintiff, Stella Bier, against A. A.
Hosford, J. T. O'Brien, and J. Anthony Smith, copartners doing business under the firm name and style
of "Washington Steam Laundry," defendants, to recover
damages for personal injuries.   Verdict was rendered and
judgment entered in plaintiff's favor for $2,100, and de-
fendants appeal.

It is alleged in the complaint, that the defendants
negligently and wilfully permitted a five roll mangle,
owned and operated by them, to be run and operated without its guard, and ordered plaintiff to work around and
upon, and to adjust the clothing for, and to feed the
clothing to, the said mangle, which was unsafe and insecure
and unprotected by any of the ordinary guards usually
maintained upon such mangles, and the said defendants
wilfully removed the guard from the said five roll mangle,
with a careless disregard for the safety of others, and
greatly increased the danger of working in and around
said mangle, which danger, if the said guard had been
allowed to remain upon the said mangle, would have been

very slight, or none at all; that, in order that the said
mangle should receive and turn out more work, the said
defendants strained and forced their servants and this
plaintiff to increased activity in a place carelessly and
wilfully made unsafe by the defendants; that said guard
was removed from the said mangle by defendants prior to
the time plaintiff commenced work at said laundry, and
she was not informed, and did not know, that part of
said machine was missing, and she had no knowledge of
machinery, and said mangle was so constructed that she
could not have seen, and did not see, any danger connected
therewith; that the said defendants well knew the dangerous condition of said mangle, and of the risks incident to
the work required upon and around, and in feeding, said
mangle, and this plaintiff had no knowledge or means of
knowledge thereof; that defendants had full knowledge
and notice of plaintiff's ignorance thereof, and did not
warn said plaintiff, nor impart said knowledge to her. It
is also alleged in the complaint that on November 27, 1901,
the plaintiff, without fault of her own, had her right hand
caught under the first roller of said mangle, and the same
was severely crushed between said roller and the heated
concave iron underneath, and that said hand was also
severely burned.

Appellants by their answer deny the material allegations
of the complaint, except that a portion of respondent's hand
was caught in the mangle, but they deny any knowledge
or information sufficient to form a belief regarding the
extent of such injuries. For an affirmative defense, it is
alleged, that the respondent was, at the time of the accident, and for a long time prior thereto, thoroughly familiar
with the machine operated by her; that she had been
advised of the dangers incident to the operation thereof;

that such dangers were apparent and obvious, which she thoroughly knew and understood; that she assumed whatever risk there was connected with the operation of said mangle; that, at the time of the accident, she was operating such mangle in a careless and negligent manner; and that said accident was caused by her own negligence. The reply denies the affirmative matter alleged in the answer.

At the conclusion of the evidence adduced in respondent's behalf at the trial, appellants moved in the lower court that this case be taken from the jury, and that judgment be rendered herein in their favor. The assignment of error predicated upon this ruling of the trial court presents the pivotal question in this controversy.

The record shows that the trial of this action began in the lower court on June 18, 1902. Respondent testified, that she was then twenty-five years of age; that in the latter part of June, 1901, she commenced to work for appellants at their steam laundry as an ironer; that a month or so thereafter she went to work as one of the feeders on the mangle described in her complaint; that she had worked in a laundry about one year, but that this was her first experience in working on mangles. This mangle was installed in the Washington Steam Laundry between five and six years prior to the trial. James Thierry, a former part owner in this laundry, and a witness for respondent, testified that a guard came with this mangle.

"Q. Describe that guard to the jury. A. That guard is a piece of iron about eight feet six inches long, and is bent at an angle, and square, and one side of it is four inches, and the other side is about an inch, or an inch and a quarter; I could not say exactly."

He testified further that this guard was intended to be placed between the operator and the first roller, that he thought the machine,

" . . . would be just as safe without the guard as
with the guard, and be easier to work on the mangle. Q. If
that guard were on could a person put his fingers into the
rollers? A. . . . I could not say if they would put
them in with the guard or not. . . . There probably
was three quarters of an inch between the plate and the
guard—that is, from the plate to the guard.   Q. How
far was that guard placed in front of the first roller? A.
That top of the guard comes close on the roller, and
the bottom of it would be probably between an inch and a
half and two inches from the roller."

The five metal rollers or cylinders, comprising a portion
of this mangle, were a trifle over eight inches in diameter.
When in operation, these cylinders, enwrapped in blankets
with an outside covering of cotton fabric, revolved toward
the feeders, and approached the concave iron underneath
sufficiently close to catch the clothes fed into the machine
and carry them through.   The cylinders were visible.
Whether the concave iron was partly or completely hidden
from view while the mangle was in operation does not definitely appear from the testimony.   The respondent, however, admitted that she knew of this hot iron.   She testified, "I thought it was necessary to have an iron to iron the
sheets."   The concave iron was bare.   These cylinders
and this iron were hot when the machine was in operation.
If the fingers should come in contact with the cylinders, the
covering thereon would prevent them from getting burned.
Between the persons feeding and the foremost cylinder was
a sheet iron apron, attached to the machine, on which the
goods were placed, then straightened out, and the wrinkles
removed therefrom.   The feeders stretched the goods out
upon this apron, and held them in position till caught by
the moving cylinder and carried over the concave iron.
The purpose of this guard, when placed between the feed-

ers and front cylinder, was to prevent the hands of the
feeders from coming in contact therewith.

Between seven and eight o'clock on the morning of November 27, 1901, one Mrs. Dick and respondent were feeding this mangle, respondent taking her position at the right
and Mrs. Dick at the left, in front of the machine. Mrs.
Gladden was forewoman of the laundry at the time. Respondent testifies, that Mrs. Dick had charge of this mangle
at that time; that respondent received her orders from Mrs.
Dick; that the laundry at that date was overcrowded with
work, and that she (respondent) was then under "hurry
up" orders from Mrs. Dick to push the work; that there
was no guard on this mangle at the time she was injured;
that she did not know there was any place for a guard on
such machine, or that a guard came with the mangle; that
while she was engaged in feeding the mangle, she "did not
see any danger;" that she did not know there was any danger in feeding without a guard.   On respondent's further
direct examination, she testified in response to questions
propounded to her as follows:

"Q.   What were you feeding to the mangle at the time
before this accident?   A.   I was feeding a round cloth;
it was made of canvas, and there was a hole in the middle,
and a cord drawn around the edge, and I was feeding that
through, and in some way my hand got caught in the cord
and was jerked through.   Q.   This round cloth you describe, Miss Bier, what is it used for if you know; have you
heard since then?   A.   I think for gambling tables.   Q.
The cloth that you describe had a hole in the middle, a
small hole?   A.   Yes, for chips.   Q.   To drop chips
through?   A.   I think that is what it is for.   .   .   .
Q.   Was this cord you speak of loose or tied?   A.   It
was tied, gathered up.   Q.   What material did you say
that cloth was made of?   A.   Made of something heavy;
I think it was canvas.   .   .   .   Q.   Is it harder or easier
to feed that cloth to the mangle or a plain, ordinary spread

or sheet? A. I think it is harder to feed a cloth of that
kind. . . . Q. I will ask you now, in placing that cloth
into the mangle and trying to keep it straight, to explain to
the jury if you can how your hand got caught, as you are
testifying? A. I don't know how it got caught, it went
in so quick. Q. Where did your hand go to? A. It
went inside, under the upper first roller."

On cross examination respondent testified concerning this
cord: "I believe it was tied or it would not have drawn
up," and further, that she did not see either of the proprietors at the laundry that morning, prior to the accident.

In *Walker v. McNeill,* 17 Wash. 590, 50 Pac. 521,
which was an action to recover compensation for personal
injuries, the following language appears in the opinion of
the court:

"It has already been determined that contributory negligence is a defense to be pleaded and proven in this state.
We view assumption of the risk of employment as of kindred nature. The better authorities seem to favor this
rule; and it is certainly on principle the natural and orderly method of pleading and proof."

This language would seem to imply that contributory negligence and assumption of risks of employment are matters
of defense, and must be separately pleaded. This court
held that it would not consider the question of assumption
of risks in the above cause on appeal, because that proposition was not urged and presented in the trial court. In
Ball v. Gussenhoven (Mont.), 74 Pac. 873, the court says
that, "The defenses of contributory negligence and assumption of risk are entirely inconsistent with each other, and
do not rest upon the same principles; and the existence
of one necessarily excludes the existence of the other;"
citing, Bailey, Master & Serv., § 938 *et seq.; Miner v. Connecticut etc. R. Co.,* 153 Mass. 398, 26 N. E. 994; *Texas &
Pac. R. Co. v. Bryant,* 8 Tex. Civ. App. 134, 27 S. W. 825;

Mundle v. Hill Mfg. Co., 86 Me. 400, 30 Atl. 16. While
these defenses may rest upon different principles, still we
are not prepared to hold unqualifiedly that "the existence
of one necessarily excludes the existence of the other." In
the opinions of the ablest courts and jurists there may be
found language which is proper and accurate, as applied
to the facts of the particular controversy under consideration, but is warped from its obvious meaning when applied
in a different connection, or to a dissimilar state of facts.
True, the text books and reports contain many cases wherein the servant suffering injuries was careful in the line
of his employment, but yet the rule that the employe assumed the risks of such employment was applied. Each
controversy must necessarily depend in a great measure on
its own particular facts.

The case of *Greef v. Brown*, 7 Kan. App. 394, 51 Pac.
926, was an action brought by a Miss Brown against Greef
Bros. to recover for injuries sustained while she was working at a mangle in a laundry. Her hand was caught between the cylinders and burned. "A guard board, designed by the manufacturer of the machine to protect operators, was in the building, but had not been used. Of
this guard board, and its use, defendant in error was wholly ignorant." The servant when injured was nearly seventeen years of age. The accident happened on the second
day of her employment at the mangle. The court, commenting on the facts, observed:

"She could not fail to see and understand the danger,
for the reason that all the elements of it were wide open before her. The very thing happened which she knew was
most likely to occur if she allowed her fingers to get between the cylinders, and no warning or caution could have
increased her knowledge of the danger or the necessity for
care. She therefore assumed the risk (*Luebke v. Berlin
Machine Works*, 88 Wis. 442, 60 N. W. Rep. 711 [43 Am.
St. 913,]) and was guilty of contributory negligence; for

the assumption of risk is a species of contributory negligence.   This being true, it could make no difference even if plaintiffs in error had neglected reasonable precaution."

We therefore think, under the facts presented by this record, that the doctrines of contributory negligence and assumption of risk are closely related.   See, also, *Luebke v. Berlin Machine Works, supra;* Black's Law & Prac. in Accident Cases, § 333.

"There are many classes of cases in which the courts have defined and fixed the standard of duty both in its application to the defendant and to the plaintiff.   In such cases, where the facts are undisputed or the inferences to be drawn from them are certain, the court should decide the question of plaintiff's contributory negligence as a matter of law.   As a general principle, it is only where the circumstances of the case are such that the standard and measure of duty are fixed and defined by law, and are the same under all circumstances; or where the facts are undisputed, and but one reasonable inference can be drawn from them, that the court can interpose and declare, as matter of law, that there is such contributory negligence, as will defeat the action of the plaintiff.   As a general proposition, a question of negligence is a question of fact, and must be submitted to the jury."   Black's Law & Prac. in Accident Cases, § 279.

See, also, *Christianson v. Pacific Bridge Co.,* 27 Wash. 582, 68 Pac. 191, and authorities cited; Remington's Notes on Wash. Rep. p. 218.

"Where an employe knows, or in the reasonable exercise of his faculties, should know, the dangers which surround him, he must be held to have assumed the risk." *McDannald v. Washington etc. R. Co.,* 31 Wash. 585, 72 Pac. 481.

In *Danuser v. Seller & Co.,* 24 Wash. 567, 64 Pac. 783, Judge Dunbar uses the following language:

"It is well established that the employer must furnish the employee with a safe place to work, but it is just as well established that the employee assumes the risk of apparent peril."

Where the danger is obvious and apparent, and the servant is ordered by the master to work in a given place, he cannot recover if injured.   It is the servant's duty to disobey orders of that nature.   *Christianson v. Pacific Bridge Co.*, *supra.*   In *Crooker v. Pacific Lounge etc. Co.*, 34 Wash. 191, 75 Pac. 632, cited by respondent's counsel, an instruction given by the trial court expressed in the following language was sustained by this court on appeal:

"A general rule of law is that a person working with a defective or unguarded machine, and without complaint, and knowing of the dangers of the same, assumes the danger of the defect or unguarded part; but there is no longer any doubt that, where an operator of machinery has expressly promised to repair a defect, the workman does not assume the risk of an injury caused thereby, within such a period of time after the promise as would be reasonably allowed for its performance; nor, indeed, is any express promise or assurance from the master necessary.   It is sufficient that the workman may reasonably infer that the matter will be attended to.   So you are instructed that if the plaintiff, at the time of his employment and at the time of the accident, saw the danger from the lack of the guard, and complained of the same to the foreman, and the foreman promised to put on a guard, and the plaintiff went to work, and continued at work, on the promise, and you further find that the danger was not so imminent and immediate that a reasonably prudent man would not go to work or continue at work on the saw, and that at the time of the accident the plaintiff was relying upon the foreman's promise to place on a guard, then you are instructed that the plaintiff did not assume the risk and danger of an injury resulting from the lack of a guard."

In the case at bar it is not pretended that appellants ever promised to place any guard upon this mangle, or that respondent ever complained in that regard.   She testified that she did not know that there was any place for a guard on this mangle. Whatever dangers there were in operating the machine in question were apparent and obvious, known, or should have been known, by this respondent as well as by the appellants. Again, in the *Crooker* case there was evidence tending to show that the plaintiff was exercising due care when he received the injuries of which he complained. The evidence in the action at bar discloses that the respondent is an intelligent woman, and was twenty-five years of age at the time of the accident; that she had been working on this mangle as a feeder about three months prior to the accident, which was a sufficient length of time to enable her to understand fully and appreciate the danger surrounding it. It was apparent and obvious that, if, while running clothes through the machine, she should allow her hand or fingers to get caught between the nearest revolving cylinder and the hot concave iron underneath, she would suffer an injury. The bare statement of this proposition is sufficient to demonstrate its verity, notwithstanding respondent's statement that she was not aware of such danger. Physical facts, apparent to individuals of the most ordinary understanding, particularly those things capable of sensation and touch, cannot be overcome or discredited by word of mouth. Courts and juries in such instances are not warranted in making erroneous deductions from known premises. *Groth v. Thomann,* 110 Wis. 488, 86 N. W. 178. Moreover, we think, aside from this statement of respondent, taking her testimony in its entirety with reference to the nature of her employment, and her description of this mangle and its movement while in operation, that she sufficiently understood and appreciated the risks and dangers to which she was constantly exposed while at work thereon without any guard being attached to this machine. Within the rule of law enunciated

in *Christianson v. Pacific Bridge Co., supra,* respondent
was not obliged, in the presence of apparent and obvious
danger, to obey the alleged directions of Mrs. Dick, her
fellow-servant and companion feeder at the mangle, to rush
the work unreasonably, thereby putting' life and limb in
jeopardy.   It would seem that, even if respondent was
rushed with her work as she claimed, this fact ought not
to have prevented her, in the absence of any guard, from
controlling her hand and fingers and watching the movements of the rollers, thus obviating this unfortunate accident.   *Truntle v. North Star Woolen-Mill Co.,* 57 Minn.
52, 58 N. W. 832.

We are of the opinion that the facts appearing in the
record bring this action within the reasoning of *Oleson v.
McMurray Cedar Lumber Co.,* 9 Wash. 502, 37 Pac. 679,
wherein this court held that a person employed to work
about dangerous machinery assumes the risk of all dangers
which are obvious, and cannot recover for injuries sustained, although the master failed to instruct the servant
regarding his duties connected with the operation of such
machinery, and the danger of his employment in that behalf.   This salutary doctrine enunciated in the *Oleson*
case has been reaffirmed by several subsequent decisions
of this court.   Remington's Notes on Wash. Rep., p. 258.

"The machine was dangerous only because there was
danger in working upon it; and if it was in fact dangerous,
it was immaterial that the danger might have been averted
by appliances protecting against it. . . .   If the plaintiff undertook the work knowing the danger, the defendants
are not liable, although they might have prevented the
danger by guarding against it."   *Gilbert v. Guild,* 144
Mass. 601, 12 N. E. 368.

Again, the same learned court in *Connolly v. Eldredge,*
160 Mass. 570, 36 N. E. 469, uses this significant language:

"The danger to fingers from two cylinders in contact
with each other, and seen to be revolving inwardly, is
obvious to any person of ordinary powers, and plainly was
understood by the plaintiff. *Crowley v. Pacific Mills,* 148
Mass. 228 [19 N. E. 344]. In *Patnode v. Warren Cotton
Mills,* 157 Mass. 283, 289 [32 N. E. 161, 34 Am. St.
275], it might have been found that the plaintiff could not
see the revolving rolls by which he was hurt. In the present case, if there had been no guard across the shelf of
the mangle, the plaintiff would have acted at her peril.
But the guard did not convert the mangle into a trap. It
manifestly was not intended to protect the hand except in
the ordinary use of the mangle, when clothes were slid
under the guard. The plaintiff was putting a cloth upon
the cylinder, above the guard. She saw, or might have
seen, all the elements of danger, including the distance
between the guard and the cylinder on that side. To appreciate them required no warning or instruction beyond
what is furnished by common experience."

It is true, as respondent's counsel contend, that this
court has frequently affirmed the proposition of law that
contributory negligence and assumption of risks are matters of defense, which must be alleged and proven like
other defenses. Still, when it plainly appears, from the
respondent's evidence introduced at the trial, that she cannot recover, in any event, by reason of her contributory
negligence, the court cannot ignore the presentation of the
facts appearing in the record, which become a part of the
case for all purposes, whether in support of the main action
or of one or more of the grounds of defense. In several
of our own decisions, cited above, the doctrine of assumed
risks was recognized and applied on defendant's motion
for a nonsuit. See, *Brown v. Tabor Mill Co.,* 22 Wash.
317, 60 Pac. 1126.

Photographs of this mangle from different positions
were introduced in evidence by appellants, to which re-

spondent's counsel refer as silent witnesses in their client's behalf. We are not prepared to say, from inspection of these several views, that the concave iron above noted was partially or wholly invisible. Still, this inspection would seem to strengthen our conclusion that, if respondent had simply exercised ordinary prudence and caution in feeding that particular cloth into this machine, her fingers would not have been caught in the manner of which she complains. The counsel for respondent assert in their printed argument that, "It is also true, that respondent's hand became entangled in a peculiar combination of goods which were tendered her for passage through the mangle." We have read the testimony appearing in the statement of facts very carefully, especially that portion adduced in respondent's behalf, and fail to discover the reason for such contention. We assume that counsel refer to the cloth used as a covering for a gambling table, with a hole in the center thereof, through which chips may be dropped. The evidence fails to show that the feeding of such cloths through the mangle is attended with any extraordinary danger. These coverings came into the laundry the same as other goods, were run through the mangle, and then ironed out smoothly. In view of the testimony of respondent to the effect that she did not know how her hand got caught, it went in so quickly, we fail to see the bearing of the evidence regarding this particular covering cloth, on the issues involved in the present controversy. *Shine v. Cocheco Mfg. Co.*, 173 Mass. 558, 54 N. E. 245. On the facts appearing in the record, we are of the opinion that the appellants' motion for a nonsuit should have been granted.

The judgment of the superior court is therefore reversed, and this cause is remanded, with directions to dismiss the action.

[No. 5043. Decided August 10, 1904.]

THE STATE OF WASHINGTON, *Respondent*, v. PAUL UNDERWOOD, *Appellant*.[1]

CONTINUANCE—CRIMINAL LAW—WITHDRAWAL OF ATTORNEY FIVE DAYS BEFORE TRIAL—DISCRETION. Where an attorney, employed to defend against a charge of murder, withdrew from the case on the fifth day before trial, and the defense was entrusted to three other attorneys, it appearing that the facts of the case were simple and readily accessible, it was not an abuse of discretion for the trial court to deny defendant's motion for a continuance upon the affidavits of his attorneys that it would be impossible for them to properly prepare for trial in the time remaining.

HOMICIDE—DIFFERENT DEGREES—VERDICT FOR LESSER DEGREE WHERE EVIDENCE SHOWED HIGHER DEGREE. Upon a trial for murder in the first degree in having caused the death of an infant by drowning, where the main issue was whether the death was caused by drowning or by an accidental overdose of chloroform, and there was sufficient evidence to support either theory, and the jury are instructed to find the defendant not guilty if they believe the death was caused by chloroform or entertain a reasonable doubt as to the drowning, a verdict of murder in the second degrée should not be set aside upon the theory that the jury must find the defendant guilty of the first degree or not at all, and accused cannot complain that he was found guilty of a lesser degree than the evidence warranted.

HOMICIDE—DEGREES OF OFFENSE—INSTRUCTIONS PROPER AS TO LESSER DEGREE ALTHOUGH EVIDENCE SHOWED FIRST DEGREE ONLY. In a prosecution for murder in the first degree by causing the death of an infant by drowning, in which there was evidence that the defendant was guilty as charged and also that the death was accidental, the contention being that he was guilty of murder in the first degree or not at all, it is not error to instruct the jury that they may find the defendant guilty in the second degree or of manslaughter, since the deliberation and premeditation necessary to constitute the first degree, under the statute, do not necessarily follow from the facts showing malice, and must be submitted to and found by the jury, and the charge necessarily includes, and warrants a finding of, the lesser degrees.

[1]Reported in 77 Pac. 863.

CRIMINAL LAW—EVIDENCE—EXPERTS—OPINION AS TO PROPER METHOD OF CONDUCTING POST MORTEM EXAMINATION. Where experts are asked hypothetical questions showing their ideas as to the proper method of conducting a post mortem examination to determine the cause of death, it is not error to sustain an objection to a question as to whether another course, omitting steps which they considered necessary, was a sufficient and thorough examination to determine the cause of death.

EVIDENCE — EXPERTS — HYPOTHETICAL QUESTION — EXAMINER'S THEORY OF CASE. A hypothetical question calling for the opinion of an expert witness and based upon a detailed statement of the testimony of different witnesses, is not objectionable, although such testimony is not entirely harmonious, where the jury had a right to find the facts as stated, it being sufficient, if the question fairly states such facts as present the examiner's theory of the case.

CRIMINAL LAW — EVIDENCE — GOOD CHARACTER — INSTRUCTIONS. Where evidence of defendant's good reputation was not questioned as being the best evidence thereof, and its bearing upon the question of defendant's guilt was properly explained by an instruction to the jury, it was not error to refuse an instruction that, where a witness testifies that he knows the defendant and his associates in the community in which he lives, and that his character has never been questioned, such character is good.

SAME—TRIAL—HARMLESS ERROR IN INSTRUCTIONS. Erroneous instructions authorizing the jury to find the defendant guilty of murder in the first degree, could not have been prejudicial where the verdict was guilty of the second degree.

NEW TRIAL—MISCONDUCT OF JUROR—BIAS—CHARGE OF WILFULLY QUALIFYING. It is proper to deny a motion for new trial upon the ground of misconduct of the jury, upon affidavits showing prejudice by one of the jurors, and that he had wilfully qualified, where the charge is denied and is entirely overcome by other affidavits; and findings of the trial court in that respect reviewed and approved.

NEW TRIAL—NEWLY DISCOVERED EVIDENCE. A motion for a new trial upon the ground of newly discovered evidence is properly denied where the evidence is wholly cumulative.

Appeal from a judgment of the superior court for King county, Tallman, J., entered October 14, 1903, upon a trial and conviction of the crime of murder in the second degree. Affirmed.

Silas M. Shipley, E. E. Shields, and *T. D. Page,* for appellant, argued, *inter alia,* that it was error to deny the motion for a continuance. *State v. Brooks,* 39 La. Ann. 239, 1 South. 421; *State v. Collins,* 104 La. 629, 29 South. 180; *State v. Deschamps,* 41 La. Ann. 1051, 7 South. 133; *Bartel v. Tieman,* 55 Ind. 438; *Wray v. People,* 78 Ill. 212; *North v. People,* 139 Ill. 81, 28 N. E. 966; *State v. Lewis,* 74 Mo. 222. Under the evidence it was error to submit to the jury the question of guilt in a lesser degree than that charged. 1 Bishop, Crim. Proc. § 9; *State v. Craft,* 164 Mo. 631, 65 S. W. 280; *Smith v. United States,* 1 Wash. Ter. 262; 10 Enc. Plead. & Prac., 164; *State v. Stoeckwell,* 71 Mo. 559; *State v. Hollingsworth,* 156 Mo. 178, 56 S. W. 1087; *State v. Holloway,* 156 Mo. 222, 56 S. W. 734; *People v. Byrnes,* 30 Cal. 207; *Smith v. People,* 1 Col. 145; *State v. Calder,* 23 Mont. 504, 59 Pac. 903; 1 Bishop, Crim. Proc. (3d ed.), § 980; *Fertig v. State,* 100 Wis. 301, 75 N. W. 960; *Cornell v. State,* 104 Wis. 527, 80 N. W. 745; *People v. Turly,* 50 Cal. 469; *People v. Lee Gam,* 69 Cal. 552, 11 Pac. 183; *State v. Hopper,* 71 Mo. 425; *State v. Umble,* 115 Mo. 452, 22 S. W. 378; *People v. Chavez,* 103 Cal. 407, 37 Pac. 389; *People v. Chaves,* 122 Cal. 134, 54 Pac. 596; *Sparf v. United States,* 156 U. S. 51, 15 Sup. Ct. 273, 39 L. Ed. 343; *Davis v. United States,* 165 U. S. 373, 17 Sup. Ct. 360, 41 L. Ed. 750; *Andersen v. United States,* 170 U. S. 510, 18 Sup. Ct. 689, 42 L. Ed. 1116; *State v. Robinson,* 12 Wash. 349, 41 Pac. 51, 902; *State v. Fruge,* 106 La. 694, 31 South. 323; *People v. Huntington,* 138 Cal. 261, 70 Pac. 284; *Pugh v. State,* 114 Ga. 16, 39 S. E. 875; *Carr v. State* (Fla.), 34 South. 892; *Strong v. State,* 63 Neb. 440, 88 N. W. 772; *State v. Cole,* 63 Iowa 695, 17 N. W. 183; *State v. Mahan,* 68 Iowa 304, 20 N. W. 449, 27

N. W. 249; *State v. Munchrath,* 78 Iowa 268, 43 N. W.
211; *State v. Sterrett,* 80 Iowa 609, 45 N. W. 401; *State
v. Reed,* 162 Mo. 312, 62 S. W. 982; *Sanders v. State,* 113
Ga. 267, 38 S. E. 841. Under such instructions a convic-
tion should be reversed. *State v. Diller,* 170 Mo. 1, 70 S.
W. 139; *Gafford v. State,* 125 Ala. 1, 28 South. 406;
Futch v. State, 90 Ga. 472, 16 S. E. 102; *May v. State,* 94
Ga. 76, 20 S. E. 251; *McGrath v. State,* 35 Tex. Cr. Rep.
413, 34 S. W. 127; *Jarvis v. State,* 70 Ark. 613, 67
S. W. 76; *State v. Vinso,* 171 Mo. 576, 71 S. W. 1034;
New v. Territory, 12 Okla. 172, 70 Pac. 199; *State v.
Dixon,* 131 N. C. 808, 42 S. E. 944; *Strong v. State,* 63
Neb. 440, 88 N. W. 772; *Hall v. State,* 130 Ala. 45, 30
South. 422; *People v. McFarland,* 134 Cal. 618, 66 Pac.
865; *Johnson v. State,* 78 Miss. 627, 29 South. 515;
Rogers v. State (Miss.), 34 South. 320; *Flynn v. State,*
43 Tex. Cr. Rep. 407, 66 S. W. 551. It is error to
instruct as to manslaughter where there is no evidence to
support such a charge. *Johnson v. State,* 78 Miss. 627,
29 South. 515; *State v. Edwards,* 71 Mo. 312; *State v.
Wilson,* 86 Mo. 520; *Mackey v. Commonwealth,* 80 Ky.
345; *State v. Hanley,* 34 Minn. 430; *People v. Rogers,* 13
Abb. Prac. (N. S.) 370; *Green v. State,* 27 Tex. App.
244; *Henning v. State,* 24 Tex. App. 315. Where there
is but one question, as, for instance, that of identity, the
verdict should be guilty of murder in the first degree or
not guilty. *State v. Dixon,* 131 N. C. 808, 42 S. E. 944;
State v. Spivey, 132 N. C. 989, 43 S. E. 475; *State v.
Furgeson,* 162 Mo. 668, 63 S. W. 101; *Griffin v. State,* 113
Ga. 279, 38 S. E. 844; *State v. Meadows,* 156 Mo. 110, 56
S. W. 878; *State v. Lucey,* 24 Mont. 295, 61 Pac. 994;
Cannon v. State, 41 Tex. Cr. Rep. 467, 56 S. W. 351;
Hays v. State (Tex.), 57 S. W. 835; *State v. Rose,* 129

N. C. 575, 40 S. E. 83; *Hunnicutt v. State,* 114 Ga. 448, 40 S. E. 243; *Jordan v. State,* 117 Ga. 405, 43 S. E. 747.

W. T. Scott and *Elmer E. Todd,* for respondent, contended, *inter alia,* that it is not error to deny a continuance, if defendant is not prejudiced. *People v. Collins,* 75 Cal. 411, 17 Pac. 430; *State v. Reid,* 20 Iowa 413; *State v. Rhea,* 25 Kan. 576; *People v. Considine,* 105 Mich. 749, 63 N. W. 196; *Holland v. People,* 30 Colo. 94, 69 Pac. 519; *State v. Rice,* 7 Idaho 762, 66 Pac. 87; *State v. Baptiste,* 108 La. 586, 32 South. 461; *Simmons v. State,* 116 Ga. 583, 42 S. E. 779; *Rone v. Commonwealth* (Ky.), 70 S. W. 1042; *State v. Gilbreath,* 106 Tenn. 503, 62 S. W. 147; *State v. Madison,* 49 W. Va. 96, 38 S. E. 492; *Mayfield Lumber Co. v. Carver,* 27 Tex. Civ. App. 467, 66 S. W. 216; *Freeman v. State* (Miss.), 29 South. 75. Where the evidence would sustain a verdict of guilty in the first degree, a defendant cannot complain of a conviction of a lesser degree. *Commonwealth v. McPike,* 3 Cush. 181; *State v. Schieller,* 130 Mo. 510, 32 S. W. 976; *Briscoe v. State,* 37 Tex. Cr. Rep. 464, 36 S. W. 281; *Allen v. State,* 37 Ark. 433; *Brown v. State,* 31 Fla. 207, 12 South. 640; *Marshall v. State,* 32 Fla. 462, 14 South. 92; *Rolls v. State,* 52 Miss. 391; *Elliston v. State,* 10 Tex. App. 361; Bishop, Crim. Law, § 791; *Commonwealth v. Burke,* 14 Gray 100; *Commonwealth v. Creadon,* 162 Mass. 466, 38 N. E. 1119. It was for the jury to determine the degree of murder as well as the question of guilt. Bal. Code, §§ 6955, 6907; Const., art. 4, § 16; *Rhodes v. Commonwealth,* 48 Pa. St. 396; *Lane v. Commonwealth,* 59 Pa. St. 371; *Brown v. State,* 109 Ala. 70, 20 South. 103; *Jackson v. State,* 136 Ala. 88, 34 South. 188; *State v. Locklear,* 118 N. C. 1154, 24 S. E. 410; *State v. Gadberry,* 117 N. C. 811, 23 S. E. 477; *State v. Cunningham,* 111 Iowa

233, 82 N. W. 775; *State v. Crockett,* 39 Ore. 76, 65 Pac. 604. Defendant could not have been prejudiced by instructions as to manslaughter, having been convicted of a higher degree of homicide. *State v. Goddard,* 162 Mo. 198, 62 S. W. 697; *State v. McMullin,* 170 Mo. 608, 71 S. W. 221; *Johnson v. State,* 44 Tex. Cr. Rep. 332, 71 S. W. 25; *State v. Talbott,* 73 Mo. 347; *State v. Ellis,* 74 Mo. 207; *State v. Glahn,* 97 Mo. 679, 11 S. W. 260; *Territory v. Salazar,* 3 N. M. 210, 5 Pac. 462.

MOUNT, J.—Appellant was convicted of murder in the second degree, and appeals from a judgment entered thereon. The undisputed facts are substantially as follows: During the Month of May, 1902, appellant and his wife were living at Ballard, in King county. On the 15th day of May, 1902, a female child was born to them. On the last day of May, 1902, appellant disposed of all his household goods, and Mrs. Underwood and the baby spent the evening with Mrs. Hetzler, a neighbor. At about nine o'clock appellant came to the house of Mrs. Hetzler and, in company with his wife and baby, started for Seattle. The baby at that time was asleep and apparently well. The next morning, June 1, 1902, at about 6:30 o'clock, the baby was found dead on the tide flats, near the street car line leading to Seattle. The baby was tied inside of a sack, in the bottom of which was a stone weighing about ten pounds. The weight of the baby was about eight pounds. The body was carried to an undertaking establishment, where a post mortem examination was held on the next day, viz., June 2, 1902, when the doctors present concluded that death resulted from drowning. On June 1, defendant and wife left Seattle for Aberdeen, where their parents resided. On Tuesday, June 3, 1902, defendant heard that there was a warrant out for his arrest, and fled, but was afterwards arrested in the woods near Tokeland.

Defendant confessed that he had killed the child, but stated that the killing was done accidentally without criminal intent, and substantially as follows: That soon after leaving the house of Mrs. Hetzler, and while he and his wife were waiting for a street car on which to ride to Seattle, the child became sick and appeared in much distress; that, in order to relieve the suffering of the child, he administered chloroform which he happened to have in his pocket; that through inadvertence an overdose was given, from which the child died; that, being without friends and money, and not knowing what to do, defendant and his wife decided to dispose of the body by dropping it into the bay; that thereupon defendant went back to the house where they had lived, which was but a short distance away, and procured a sack and a rock, and placed the baby in the sack with the rock, and dropped sack and all into the bay, where it was found.

On a trial before a jury, the defendant was found guilty of murder in the second degree. Other facts necessary to an understanding of the questions discussed will be stated hereafter. Appellant assigns errors as follows: (1) In overruling appellant's motion for a continuance; (2) that the evidence is insufficient to support the verdict of murder in the second degree; (3) in submitting to the jury the question of appellant's guilt of any crime other than murder in the first degree; (4) in ruling on the admissibility of evidence; (5) in refusing to grant a new trial, because of misconduct of a juror, and of newly discovered evidence. We shall consider these assignments in the order stated.

(1) Soon after appellant's arrest, his father employed M. K. Snell, an attorney of Tacoma, to defend the accused. Snell accepted the employment, and was relied upon by

appellant to defend the case and procure witnessess. Defendant's father and mother, being poor people, sold and mortgaged all the property they had to raise money to pay Mr. Snell his fee. Three hundred and sixty-five dollars was paid thereon. Soon after the arrest of the defendant, he was arraigned in open court, entered a plea of not guilty, and the case was set down to be tried on September 22, 1902. On September 14, appellant's father employed E. E. Shields, an attorney of Aberdeen, to assist Mr. Snell in the trial of the case. On September 16th Mr. Snell notified appellant's father that he would withdraw from the case, and turned over to Mr. Shields all the papers and memoranda he had in the case, and thereafter also returned $250 of the money paid thereon. On the 18th Snell filed his withdrawal with the clerk, and on the same day the present attorneys appeared and filed a motion for a continuance of the trial for one month, upon the grounds that Mr. Snell had withdrawn from the case, and that thirty days would be necessary for counsel to prepare for the trial. This motion was supported by several affidavits, stating at length the employment and withdrawal of Mr. Snell, and that he had done nothing, and was of no assistance in finding witnesses for the defense, and that counsel then employed could not prepare, either upon the facts or law, in the short time remaining before the day set for the trial. The court, after hearing these affidavits and arguments by counsel, denied the motion on the same day it was filed. This ruling is the first error assigned.

This motion for a continuance was not based upon any statutory ground, but depended upon the discretionary power of the trial judge. This power will be reviewed and revised only for its abuse. It is true, so far as the affidavits show, that no fault attached to the appellant for the withdrawal of his principal attorney five days before the day set for the trial of the cause. It also appears, from the statements in the affidavit of the three attorneys representing appellant at the motion for a continuance, that it would be impossible for them to properly prepare for a trial of so much importance in so short a time as was remaining from the 18th to the 22d of September. This latter statement appears to be the principal one relied upon. The argument is made that appellant was entitled to a fair trial, and to be represented by counsel who were required to give their best ability to the interests of their client; that, in order to do this, they must have time to prepare themselves for the trial. But whether attorneys could possibly or properly prepare for the trial of the case in the three or four days left is a relative question, depending upon the circumstances of the particular case. It is claimed that many technical medical questions would arise, and that it was therefore necessary for defendant's counsel to prepare themselves upon that branch of the case, and particularly in reference to the symptoms and condition manifested upon a body which had met death by drowning. The facts in the case were few and very simple. It was not claimed that there were any absent witnesses. All who knew about the death of the child were at hand. The place where the child came to its death was within six miles of Seattle, where two of appellant's attorneys then resided, and on the line of a street car. Where the facts were so readily accessible, it seems that two or three days ought to be enough time to obtain them. It may be true, as counsel states, that it was necessary for counsel to inquire as to the symptoms of death by drowning and those caused by chloroform, in order to intelligently examine and cross-examine the expert witnesses thereon; but it seems to us that the time at the disposal of three competent attorneys was amply sufficient therefor. After reading all

the evidence and the whole record, we are convinced that
the trial court did not abuse its discretion in refusing a
continuance of the case upon the grounds stated.

(2) Appellant next insists that the evidence is not
sufficient to support the verdict of murder in the second
degree, because, under the evidence in the case, the defendant is guilty of murder in the first degree or is not guilty
at all. This contention is based upon the fact that there
is no direct evidence of deliberate or premeditated malice,
but that these elements of the crime depend upon circumstances. The main issue of fact was whether the child was
drowned or was killed by chloroform. The court instructed the jury that, if they entertained a reasonable
doubt that the child was drowned, or if they believed that
the child came to its death by chloroform, then they must
find the defendant not guilty. It is argued that the same
evidence which proved the death of the child by drowning
also proved deliberation and premeditation, and, since the
jury found that there was no deliberate and premeditated
malice, they must have found the defendant not guilty.
There was evidence to support a verdict of murder in the
first degree, and appellant cannot complain because he was
convicted of a lesser offense than the evidence warranted.
Appellant argues that the evidence shows that the child's
death did not result from drowning. It is true that the
defendant himself testified that the death was caused by an
overdose of chloroform. It is also true that some of the
physicians testified that, from certain symptoms, death
may have resulted from chloroform. There was also much
evidence that death resulted from drowning. This question was one entirely for the jury, and, from a careful
reading of the whole evidence, which need not be reviewed
here, we are of the opinion that there was ample evidence
that death resulted from drowning, and that therefore there

was evidence to support a verdict of either degree of murder.

(3) It is next assigned as error that the court submitted to the jury the question of murder in a lesser degree than the first. The court instructed the jury to the effect that: "Under this information and the laws of this state, the defendant can be convicted, if the evidence justifies it, of any one of three offenses. . . These offenses are murder in the first degree, murder in the second degree, and manslaughter." The court then proceeded to define each of these degrees of murder. It is argued that, because under the evidence but one of two verdicts could be returned, viz., guilty of murder in the first degree or not guilty, it was error to instruct the jury upon any other degrees of the crime charged. Many authorities are cited to the effect that, where there is no evidence which might authorize a verdict for a lower degree of the offense than that charged in the information, a charge defining other degrees should not be given. If we concede that these authorities state the correct general rule, they do not help appellant, because there was evidence of deliberation and premeditation. A charge of murder in the first degree contains all the elements or facts constituting murder in the second degree. The only difference, under the statute, between murder in the first degree and second degree is that in the former there must be deliberate and premeditated malice, while in the latter the killing must be done purposely and maliciously, but without deliberation and premeditation. The proof of deliberation and premeditation may, and frequently does, flow from the same circumstances as those which denote intent and malice, but one does not necessarily follow from the other. Where there are facts or circumstances from which intent and malice or deliberation and premeditation may be found, it is always the

duty of the court to submit such facts and circumstances to
the consideration of the jury under proper instructions. We
have seen above there were facts and circumstances from
which the jury may have found all the elements of murder
in the first degree, and the evidence was sufficient to support such a verdict. It follows that there is sufficient to
support one in a lesser degree. Furthermore, the question
under consideration was, we think, settled in *State v. Greer,*
11 Wash. 244, 39 Pac. 874, and *State v. Howard,* 33 Wash.
250, 74 Pac. 382. Questions of fact are purely questions
for the jury. Judges may not draw conclusions of facts
from other facts or circumstances. They must declare the
law and not comment on the facts. Const., art. 4, § 16.
If murder be charged, and the defendant plead guilty
thereto, a jury must be impaneled to hear testimony and
determine the degree thereof. § 6907, Bal. Code. From
these sections we think it clear that the jury, and not the
court, must determine the degree of murder of which a
defendant is guilty.

(4) When Dr. Powell, a witness on behalf of the defense, was on the stand, he was asked the following questions:

"Q. If an examination was held upon a body for the
purpose of ascertaining the cause of death, is it not necessary to take notes of the different steps, to measure the
parts examined, and, in a case where drowning is suspected, to examine microscopically the contents of the lungs
and stomach, to examine the brain, and all parts of the
body, before coming to a conclusion, and particularly
where a man's life is at stake, or murder is suspected?
A. It certainly was. Q. Now, in an examination such
as this one was, where the brain is not examined, the contents of the lungs are not microscopically treated, no test
is made to see what the fluid in the lungs and stomach is,
would you say that was a sufficient and thorough examination on which to base a conclusion as to the cause of death?"

An objection was sustained to this last question, on the ground that it called for a conclusion which the jury must draw. Other questions of this same kind were asked of other witnesses, and objections sustained thereto. These rulings are assigned as error. We think there was no reversible error in this, and that the position of counsel for respondent is correct where he says:

"The evidence was before the jury as to how the examination of the body of the child had been conducted. The previous question asked and answered by Dr. Powell indicated his idea of the requisites of such an examination, and the jury were required to judge whether the examination was conducted properly. Although great latitude is allowed in the examination of experts, it would seem wholly unnecessary for them, in a case like this, to characterize an examination in answer to a hypothetical question, especially when they had already detailed how such an examination should be conducted and what should be done."

The ruling of the court excluded no evidence which was not in fact before the jury.

A number of physicians were called as expert witnesses by the state, and to each of these witnesses the prosecuting attorney propounded a hypothetical question for the purpose of obtaining an opinion as to the cause of the child's death. A sample of these questions is as follows:

"I will ask you, doctor, to suppose the case of a child three weeks old, or thereabouts, was ordinarily healthy, was apparently well, was in its mother's arms at about nine o'clock on Saturday evening, and a little after, on the following Sunday morning at about 6:30 o'clock or thereabouts, the same child was found in a sack inclosed with a stone weighing about ten pounds, the child itself weighing between seven and eight pounds in life or immediately after death. The waters ebbed and flowed at the spot where the body of the child was found, to a depth of from three to five feet at high tide. The child was securely inclosed in the sack by a string tied around the top of the

sack or bag. When removed from the sack a frothy foam
was found in the nostrils and round about the mouth, and
some milk curds were found in the back part of the mouth.
The hands were rigid and closed or clenched. The left
hand was clasped, or grasping the garment, that was upon
the arm, by the fingers resting against the palm of the
hand. The child was removed from the sack and its
clothing removed, and a post mortem was held the following day. Whereupon the sternum was removed, and it was
found that the walls of the chest were expanded, and the
lungs filled the cavity of the chest so that some pressure
was exercised against the under side of the sternum or
breast bone. The right side of the heart was gorged with
blood. There was also some blood in the left side of the
heart. The veins throughout were gorged with blood. The
arteries were only slightly filled. The stomach was well
filled, or contained a watery fluid or milk curds. The
lungs were removed and slight incisions made in the outer
surface of the different lobes at different places. Immediately after the incisions were made a watery fluid would
come from the outer surface of the lungs. Upon squeezing
the nose a foam or froth would come from the nostrils.
The child was dead when found. In your opinion, if you
could form an opinion from these facts, what was the cause
of the death of that child?"

These questions were objected to upon the ground that
they assumed facts which were not established by the evidence, and included certain facts concerning which the
state's own witnesses were contradictory, and that these
questions, when the statements of the witnesses are conflicting, should state the facts most favorably to the oppos-
ing party, and not most favorably to the party propound-
ing the question. It is true that some of the witnesses for
the state were not entirely agreed as to the symptoms and
conditions of the child when it was taken from the sack
and examined. But all the conditions named in the hypothetical questions were testified to by different witnesses,

and were, therefore, facts which the jury had a right to
find and consider. We think the rule is fairly well settled
that, where the facts are in dispute, it is sufficient if a
hypothetical question fairly states such facts as present the
examiner's theory of the case. *Stearns v. Field,* 90 N. Y.
640; *Cowley v. People,* 83 N. Y.464, 38 Am. Rep. 464;
People v. Sessions, 58 Mich. 594, 26 N. W. 291; *Nave v.
Tucker,* 70 Ind. 15. It is for the jury to determine
whether the facts stated in such questions are true or
proven, and, if they are not true or not proven, it is the
duty of the jury to entirely disregard opinions based
thereon. The jury were so instructed in this case. There
was no error in the ruling.

Error is assigned upon the refusal of the court to give
an instruction requested relating to the good character of
the defendant. This instruction is quite long and involved,
but the substance of it is that, where a character witness
testifies that he knows the defendant and his associates in
the community in which he lives, and that he has never
heard defendant's character called in question, such character is good. This is no doubt the law, and in a proper
case should be given. In this case several witnesses stated
that they had known defendant for a long time, and knew
his associates, and that his reputation was good because
his character had never been questioned. This evidence
was submitted to the jury, and, so far as the record shows,
there is nothing to indicate that the prosecution questioned
that it was the best evidence of good character. Not being
questioned, and the court having submitted it to the jury
and said to them that evidence of previous good character
is competent, as tending to show that a defendant would
not be likely to commit the crime charged, if they found
that defendant had borne a good character among his neigh-
bors and acquaintances, after the jury had considered all

the evidence, including that bearing upon his previous
good character, or if they entertained a reasonable doubt,
they should acquit him. We think this was sufficient, and, ·
under the circumstances, it was not error to refuse the instruction requested.

Appellant argues that two other instructions are erroneous. These two instructions tell the jury that, if they find
certain enumerated facts to be true, "then their verdict
should be guilty of murder in the first degree," etc. It is
argued that these two instructions are inconsistent with the
facts, not supported by the evidence, and inconsistent with
the theories of both plaintiff and defendant. We do not
think these criticisms are well founded in fact. But even
if they are, they cannot avail appellant here. The jury
found the defendant guilty of murder in the second degree,
which was an acquittal of the higher degree. No possible
injury, therefore, could have resulted to the appellant from
giving these two instructions.

(5) Appellant argues that the court erred in refusing
to grant a new trial, first, upon the misconduct of the jury.
It appears that a juror by the name of Warson, upon his
voir dire examination, qualified himself as a juror and was
permitted to remain upon the jury. After a verdict had
been rendered, the appellant filed four affidavits, in which
it was stated, that the affiants in all of them were members
of a jury in a case on trial in another department of the
superior court of King county, on September 22, 1902,
while a jury was being obtained in this case; that said jury
was out all night on said night, considering their verdict;
that said juror Warson was also a member of said jury,
and out all night with affiants; that during the night of
the 22d of September, 1902, the jurors generally talked
over the facts in the Underwood case, and generally and
freely expressed their opinions respecting the defendant

Underwood for the killing of his child; that juror Warson
participated therein, and expressed his opinion to such an
extent that affiants were surprised when they learned that
he had qualified as a juror in the case. One of these
affiants also stated that in a conversation with Warson
some three or four days prior to the 22d of September,
when he said to Warson that he could not qualify as a
juror in the Underwood case, Warson replied, "Well, I
think I will qualify." Another of the affiants by the
name of Watton stated that, on the night of September
22, Warson said to him that he (Warson) had read all
about the killing of the Underwood child by the defendants, "that his mind was made up concerning the defendant's guilt, and all hell could not change it."

In answer to these affidavits Mr. Warson denied that he
made any of the statements attributed to him, denied that
he was acquainted with or knew the affiant Watton, or had
ever had any conversation with him about the Underwood
case, and denied that he heard any of the discussion or
opinions concerning the Underwood case by any of the
jurors on the night of September 22, or at any other time,
or that he was in any way biased, but alleged that he was
entirely qualified as a juror on the case. Another juror,
who was out with Mr. Warson on the said jury during the
night of September 22, testifies that there was no discussion of the Underwood case in his presence that night, or in
the presence of Warson to his knowledge, and he also testifies that he was closely associated with Warson on that
night, and that, if Warson had expressed any opinion, he
would have known it. Three other influential business
men make affidavit to the fact that they are intimately
acquainted with Warson, and had associated with him just
previous to the trial of the Underwood case, and that, if
said Warson had been biased in any way in the case, or had

an opinion, they would have known it; that they believed he had no opinion, and believed him to be a fair, impartial juror, unprejudiced in the case.

Appellant was no doubt entitled to a fair and impartial jury, and, if one of the jurors had made the statements above referred to, and had then wilfully qualified himself to sit on the jury, this would have been such misconduct as to give the appellant a new trial. It of course devolved upon the appellant to show the fact of misconduct, or at least to create in the mind of the court a well grounded suspicion that the fact may be true. The counter affidavits evidently convinced the lower court, as they convince us, that the charge was mistakenly or wrongfully made. We have gone carefully over all these affidavits, and it seems to us therefrom that the charge was entirely overcome by the answering affidavits on file.

It is finally argued that the court erred in denying a new trial on the ground of newly discovered evidence. This evidence consists, it is claimed, of a photograph of the dead child taken before the post mortem examination was held, which picture shows the open hand and closed eyes of the child; and also consists of the evidence of the undertaker Whitlock, to the effect that when he took the child out of the sack its eyes were closed and its hands were open. It was one of the main contentions of the appellant that closed eyes and open hands were symptoms of death by chloroform, and opposed to death by drowning. Much of the evidence for the ten days during which the trial lasted was devoted to this question. In other words, this evidence is wholly cumulative. The witness Whitlock was upon the witness stand and could have been examined upon these points if appellant had desired to do so. But, upon the ground that the evidence is cumulative, we think the lower court was justified in denying the motion.

Upon the whole record we are satisfied that the defendant had a fair trial, and that no substantial errors to his prejudice were made. The judgment is therefore affirmed.

FULLERTON, C. J., and HADLEY, ANDERS, and DUNBAR, JJ., concur.

[No. 4919   Decided August 24, 1904.]

THE STATE OF WASHINGTON, *Respondent*, v. C. W. IDE, *Appellant*.[1]

TAXATION—UNIFORMITY—POLL TAX EXEMPTING MALES OF CERTAIN AGES, FEMALES, AND MEMBERS OF VOLUNTEER FIRE COMPANIES—ACQUIESCENCE. Section 938, Bal. Code, providing that cities of the third class may levy upon and collect from every male inhabitant between certain ages, an annual street poll tax, but exempting therefrom members of volunteer fire companies, and city ordinances providing for the levy and collection of such a tax, and making the refusal to pay a misdemeanor, are unconstitutional and void, as in violation of art. 7, § 9, Const., requiring uniformity in taxation of persons and property; and long continued acquiescence therein cannot sanction the clear infraction of the law.

Appeal from a judgment of the superior court for Jefferson county, Hatch, J., entered July 24, 1903, upon a trial and conviction of the misdemeanor of refusing to pay a poll tax. Reversed.

Brinker, Coleman & Ballinger, for appellant.

A. W. Buddress, for respondent, contended, among other things, that Const., art. 7, § 9, applies only to property taxes. *Stull v. DeMattos,* 23 Wash. 71, 62 Pac. 451, 51 L. R. A. 892; *State v. Clark,* 30 Wash. 439, 71 Pac. 303. Under similiar provisions the same rule prevails elsewhere. *Denver City R. Co. v. Denver,* 21 Colo. 350, 41 Pac. 826; *Fairibault v. Misener,* 20 Minn. 396; *In Re*

[1]Reported in 77 Pac. 961.

Dassler, 35 Kan. 678, 12 Pac. 130; *Sawyer v. City of Alton,* 4 Ill. 126; *People v. Naglee,* 1 Cal. 232, 52 Am. Dec. 312; *Aurora v. McGannon,* 138 Mo. 38, 39 S. W. 469; Cooley, Const. Lim. (6th ed.), pp. 629, 630; Dillon, Mun. Corp. (4th ed.), §§ 762, 817; Tiedeman, Mun. Corp. §§ 260, 260a. The classification adopted was reasonable and valid. *Ex parte Smith and Keating,* 38 Cal. 702; *Rosenbloom v. State,* 64 Neb. 342, 89 N. W. 1053; *State v. Nichols,* 28 Wash. 631, 69 Pac. 372; *Seaboldt v. Northumberland County,* 187 Pa. St. 318, 41 Atl. 22; *Magoun v. Illinois Trust & Sav. Bank,* 170 U. S. 283, 18 Sup. Ct. 594; Cooley, Const. Lim. (6th ed.), 631. And the exemption of certain classes is not an unconstitutional grant of special privileges or immunities. *State v. Clark, supra; State v. Nichols, supra; Stull v. DeMattos, supra; Hall v. Burlingame,* 88 Mich. 438, 50 N. W. 289; *State v. Womble,* 112 N. C. 862, 17 S. E. 491; *Magoun v. Illinois Trust & Sav. Bank, supra.*

ANDERS, J.—On June 22, 1903, William Furlong filed a verified complaint in the police court of the city of Port Townsend, alleging, in substance, that he was, at said time, the city marshal and city street poll tax collector of the city of Port Townsend, a city of the third class, in the county of Jefferson and state of Washington, and that on said day one C. W. Ide, then and there being a male inhabitant of said city between the ages of twenty-one and fifty years, and not a member of any volunteer fire company of said city, nor a member of the militia of the state of Washington, did then and there commit the misdemeanor of failing and refusing to pay to said city street poll tax collector, on demand, his, the said defendant's, city annual street poll tax, for the year 1903, committed as follows: That the said city street poll tax collector did then and there per-

sonally demand of and from said defendant C. W. Ide, the
sum of two dollars for the payment by defendant to said
city and to its said street poll tax collector, the said city annual street poll tax for the year 1903, but said defendant
did then and there wilfully and unlawfully fail and refuse
to pay to said city street poll tax collector said sum of two
dollars for his city annual street poll tax of said city for the
year 1903, contrary to ordinance Number 675 of said city,
entitled "An ordinance imposing and levying an annual city
street poll tax for the year 1903, and providing for the collection thereof," approved June 3, 1903, and contrary to
ordinance number 639 of said city, entitled "An ordinance
to provide for the collection of a city street poll tax, and
making the refusal to pay the same a misdemeanor, and to
provide for the appointment of a tax collector and deputy,"
approved on May 3, 1899.

A warrant was issued on this complaint, and the defendant, having been arrested thereon and brought into court,
filed a demurrer to the complaint on the following grounds:
(1) That it appears upon the face of the complaint that defendant has not violated any law; (2) that said complaint
fails to state facts sufficient to constitute a crime or misdemeanor of any kind; (3) that said complaint does not
charge any offense against the laws of the state of Washington; (4) that said complaint does not charge defendant
with the commission of any crime or misdemeanor under
the ordinances of the city of Port Townsend.

The demurrer was overruled, and, on the hearing in the
police court, the defendant was convicted and fined, and
from the judgment he appealed to the superior court. The
demurrer was again argued and considered in the superior
court and was, by that court, overruled. Upon the trial in
the superior court, the defendant was convicted and fined

two dollars and costs, and it was thereupon adjudged that
he be imprisoned in the county jail until such fine and
costs be paid, unless otherwise discharged by law. From
this judgment and sentence the defendant has appealed
to this court.

Section 1, of ordinance No. 675, which is mentioned and
referred to by its title and date of approval, provides:
"That there be and hereby is imposed and levied an annual
city street poll tax upon each male inhabitant between the
ages of twenty-one and fifty years, residing in said city,
excepting any member of any volunteer fire company in
said city, the sum of two dollars, payable on demand between the first day of June, 1903, and the first day of September, 1903."   And section 2 provides, "That the poll
tax hereby imposed and levied shall be collected as provided by ordinance No. 639 of said city entitled 'An ordinance
to provide for the collection of a city street poll tax, and
making the refusal to pay the same a misdemeanor, and to
provide for the appointment of a tax collector and deputy,'
passed by the city council of said city on the 2nd day of
May, 1899, and approved on the 3rd day of May, 1899."

Ordinance No. 639, above mentioned and described, contains, besides others which it is not necessary to mention,
the following provisions:

"§ 1.   That it shall be the duty of the city marshal between the first day of May and the first day of September,
of each year, to collect all city street poll taxes levied or assessed by the city council, as herein provided, and shall
give to each person paying such city street poll tax a receipt therefor. . . . § 2.   That the said city marshal shall receive in full compensation for his services for
the collection of the said city street poll tax, under this ordinance, the sum of ten per centum upon all moneys so
collected.   § 3.   If any person liable for the city street
poll tax herein provided for, shall fail, refuse or neglect to

pay the same upon demand by the city marshal, the city marshal shall proceed to collect the same as herein provided. . . . § 5. That any person who shall fail, refuse or neglect to pay upon demand to the city marshal, or his deputy, the annual street poll tax, which shall have been levied or assessed by the city council of said city, or which may be hereafter levied or assessed by the city council of said city, shall be guilty of a misdemeanor, and upon conviction thereof shall be fined in any sum not exceeding twenty-five dollars, or be imprisoned not exceeding thirty days, or both such fine and imprisonment in the discretion of the court. § 6. That it shall be the duty of the city marshal to collect all the city street poll tax from every person liable therefor, and on the neglect or refusal of such person to pay the same, he shall collect the same by seizure and sale of any personal property owned by such person. The sale to be made after three days written notice of time and place of such sale to be posted in three of the most public places of said city before the day of sale. . . . § 13. The city marshal shall enforce the payment of the city street poll tax by any and all the modes herein provided in the name and at the cost of the city."

The constitution of the state (art. 11, § 10) provides, that the legislature shall, by general laws, provide for the incorporation, organization, and classification in proportion to population, of cities and towns; and it is conceded that Port Townsend is a city of the third class, duly organized and existing under and by virtue of a general law passed by the legislature in accordance with the mandate of the constitution. By that law (§ 938 of Bal. Code) the city council of such city is empowered:

"§ 7. To impose on and collect from every male inhabitant between the ages of twenty-one and fifty years an annual street poll tax not exceeding two dollars, and no other road poll tax shall be collected within the limits of such city: Provided, that any member of a volunteer fire company in such city shall be exempt from such tax. . . .

"§ 16. To impose fines, penalties and forfeitures for any

and all violations of ordinances, and for any breach or
violation of any ordinance to fix the penalty by fine or
imprisonment, or both, but no such fine shall exceed three
hundred dollars nor the term of such imprisonment exceed the term of three months."

If the provisions of section 938 of the Code, which we
have quoted, are not in conflict with the constitution of the
state, or of the United States, it can hardly be disputed
that the ordinances founded thereon, and numbered 675
and 639, are valid enactments of the city of Port Townsend.   And, if the ordinances in question are valid, we
think the averments of the complaint are sufficient to constitute an offense, and that the demurrer thereto was properly overruled.

But it is earnestly insisted by the learned counsel for the
appellant that the ordinances and statute providing for the
imposition and collection of this city street poll tax are,
each and all, violative of the constitution of the state, and
of the fourteenth amendment to the constitution of the
United States.

Before proceeding to the consideration of the objections
interposed by appellant to this poll tax law and these city
ordinances, we deem it proper to observe that it is settled
by the highest authority that a legislative enactment is
presumed to be constitutional and valid until the contrary
clearly appears.   In other words, the courts will presume
that an act regularly passed by the legislative body of the
government is a valid law, and will entertain no presump-
tions against its validity.   And, when the constitutionality of an act of the legislature is drawn in question, the
court will not declare it void unless its invalidity is so apparent as to leave no reasonable doubt upon the subject.
Cooley Const. Lim. (7th ed.), pp. 252-254, and cases cited;
id. p. 225; See, also, *Francis v. Atchison etc. R. Co.,* 19

Kans. 303-306. We have mentioned these well established rules because we believe that they should always be kept in mind when the court is called upon to declare invalid an act of the law-making body, a co-ordinate and independent part of the government.

The first and chief contention of appellant is that subdivision 7 of section 938 of the Code, above quoted, and the ordinances founded thereon, are unconstitutional and void for the reason that the tax attempted to be levied and collected under the ordinance, is levied and imposed upon males between the ages of twenty-one and fifty years, alone, and not upon females, nor upon males over the age of fifty years, nor upon males under the age of twenty-one years, nor upon the members of volunteer fire companies.

Although the sum involved in this case is small the question presented for our determination is one of great importance to the various municipalities of the third class throughout the state. This is the first time this precise question has been before this court for determination, and we find, upon investigation, that the decisions of other courts of last resort bearing directly upon the question are far from numerous.

It is true, we have several times had occasion to pass upon the validity of statutes and ordinances providing for the payment of license taxes, or fees, by persons engaged in certain occupations or callings and have held that such exactions, although imposed by the taxing power, are not taxes within the meaning of the constitution, or of the ordinary revenue laws. See, *Fleetwood v. Read,* 21 Wash. 548, 58 Pac. 665, 47 L. R. A. 205; *Stull v. De Mattos,* 23 Wash. 71, 62 Pac. 451, 51 L. R. A. 892; *Walla Walla v. Ferdon,* 21 Wash. 308, 57 Pac. 796. And in *State v. Clark,* 30 Wash. 439, 71 Pac. 20, we held that the inheritance tax law which exempts from its provisions sums below $10,000, when the estate passes to direct heirs and kindred, but grants no such exemption to collateral heirs or strangers to the blood who are devisees, and which does not require all classes of persons mentioned therein to pay taxes on the property received by them at a uniform rate, is not in conflict with the constitutional provisions requiring uniformity in the rate of assessment and taxation of property, for the reason that the so-called inheritance tax is only a charge upon the passing of the estate by succession and the privilege of the heirs or devisees to take it, and not a tax on property.

The tax in question is not a tax on property, but it is nevertheless a tax, under any proper definition of that term. It is a poll, or capitation, tax, and is so denominated both in the statute and the ordinances. It is levied for a public purpose, and is clearly a revenue measure. But its assessment is not governed by the general revenue law, or, strictly speaking, by § 2 of art. 7 of the state constitution, which declares that the legislature shall provide by law a uniform and equal rate of assessment and taxation on all property in the state according to its value in money.

It is settled law that the power of taxation is a legislative power, and an incident of sovereignty, and when the people adopt a constitution and thereby create a department of government upon which they confer the power to make laws, the power of taxation is conferred as a part of such general power. And, unless its power of taxation is limited by constitutional provisions, the state, by virtue of its sovereignty, has the power to tax all persons and property within its jurisdiction. Cooley, Taxation (2d ed.), pp. 4-5; (3d ed.), pp. 7, 8, 9, and cases cited. See, also, Judson, Taxation, § 431. Several of the state constitutions provide for the imposition of poll taxes, but such taxes are, it seems, prohibited by the constitutions of Ohio and Maryland. See, 1 Desty, Taxation, p. 296.

Our constitution does not expressly mention such taxation, and, as that instrument is not a grant of power, but a limitation of power inherent in the state, independent of that instrument, it follows that this tax must be declared valid, unless the legislature was indirectly and by necessary implication prohibited from authorizing it to be levied by some provision of the constitution.

While it is conceded by counsel for appellant that the legislature may, in the absence of constitutional restrictions, "confer upon a city almost supreme power over local taxation," yet they contend that the tax in question, by reason of its lack of uniformity, is repugnant to § 9 of art. 7 of our constitution, and therefore void. That section of art. 7 reads as follows:

"The legislature may vest the corporate authorities of cities, towns, and villages with power to make local improvements by special assessment, or by special taxation of property benefited. For all corporate purposes, all municipal corporations may be vested with authority to assess and collect taxes, and such taxes shall be uniform in respect to persons and property within the jurisdiction of the body levying the same."

Section 12 of art. 11, of the constitution, provides that,

"The legislature shall have no power to impose taxes upon . . . cities . . . or upon the inhabitants or property thereof, for . . . city . . . purposes, but may, by general laws, vest in the corporate authorities thereof the power to assess and collect taxes for such purposes."

These two provisions are the only ones relating to the vesting of the power of taxation in municipal corporations. And they clearly indicate, especially the latter, that the legislature may authorize the taxation, by cities, of persons,

as well as property, within their limits. Conceding, as
we must, that the legislature had the right to delegate to
cities of the third class the power to levy poll taxes on the
inhabitants thereof, the question naturally arises whether,
in this instance, they exercised the power in conformity
with the constitution. As we have seen, § 9 of art. 7 of the
constitution, empowers the legislature to vest all municipal
corporations with authority, for corporate purposes, to assess and collect taxes, such taxes to be uniform in respect
to persons and property within the jurisdiction of the body
levying the same. It is claimed by the learned counsel for
the respondent, as we understand his argument, that this
constitutional provision applies only to the taxation of
property, and that this court has so decided in several
cases. But counsel is in error, so far as the decisions of this
court are concerned. The cases referred to relate to license
taxes and the like, which are not deemed taxes, as that term
is ordinarily understood, and they are therefore not applicable to the case in hand.

The constitution says, in effect, that all municipal corporations may tax persons as well as property if authorized
so to do by the legislature, and we are not at liberty to construe that provision so as to eliminate, or give no effect to,
the words "as to persons," therein contained, which we
would be obliged to do in order to hold that it was the intention of the framers of that instrument that property
alone should be taxed by municipal corporations. All the
power possessed by cities and other municipal corporations
to tax either property or persons is conferred upon them
by the legislature, whose power, as we have already intimated, is practically, though perhaps not absolutely, unlimited in the absence of constitutional restrictions. And it
will be observed that the only restriction imposed by the
constitution upon the power of the legislature to vest mu-

nicipal corporations with the authority to tax persons and property is that "such taxes shall be uniform in respect to persons and property within the jurisdiction of the body levying the same." It is conceded by counsel for appellant that the uniformity rule in taxation usually prescribed by law does not preclude the legislature from selecting and classifying, in a proper and reasonable manner, the subjects of taxation, and that rule is so firmly established that the citation of cases in support of it is entirely unnecessary.

But it is claimed on behalf of the appellant that the rule of uniformity prescribed by the state constitution was, in this instance, wholly disregarded and ignored by the legislature in exempting from the tax all females, all males not within the designated ages, and members of volunteer fire companies, and that the classification of the persons to be taxed is arbitrary and unreasonable, because it is not based upon any "difference which bears a just and proper relation to the attempted classification." As to the right to classify subjects of taxation, this court, in *McDaniels v. Connelly Shoe Co.*, 30 Wash. 549, 71 Pac. 37, 60 L. R. A. 947, where the question of classification was under consideration, said, "It is true that the mere fact of classification is insufficient to relieve a statute from the reach of this clause of the constitution—that it must appear that the classification is made upon some reasonable and just difference between the persons affected and others, to warrant classification at all." And in *Gulf etc. R. Co. v. Ellis*, 165 U. S. 150, 17 Sup. Ct. 255, in which the question of the power of classification is elaborately discussed, the supreme court, respecting such power, observed, "That must always rest upon some difference which bears a reasonable and just relation to the act in respect to which the classification is proposed, and can never be made arbitrarily

and without any such basis." The classification made in
imposing this tax is based solely upon age and sex. It has
no relation to the property of the persons to be taxed, or to
their ability to pay. The persons selected to bear the
burden are under no greater obligations to pay for keeping
the streets in repair than others who are exempted from
the payment of the tax. Does such classification, then, rest
upon a reasonable difference between the persons taxed
and others who are not taxed? It has been stated by our
highest court that there is no precise application of the
rule of reasonableness of classification, and that there cannot be an exact exclusion or inclusion of persons and things.
Magoun v. Illinois etc. Bank, 170 U. S. 283, 18 Sup. Ct.
594.

Where exemptions from taxation are permissible, the
reasonableness of the classification of subjects must therefore be determined from the facts and circumstances appearing in each particular case. It is urged, on the part of
the respondent, that the statute under consideration ought
to be upheld because the people have acquiesced in it, and
these taxes have been levied and collected under it in cities
throughout the state ever since the organization of the state
government; and *City of Fairibault v. Misener,* 20 Minn.
396, is cited in support of that proposition. The constitution of Minnesota contained the following clause:
"All taxes to be raised in this state shall be as nearly equal
as may be." Pursuant to the authority given by its charter, the city of Fairibault, in each of the years 1872 and
1873, levied and assessed a poll tax of two dollars on every
qualified voter, except members of fire engine, hook and
ladder, and hose companies. The defendant, Misener, refused to pay the poll tax assessed against him for each of
those years, and an action was brought against him before
a justice of the peace to recover the same. The justice

rendered judgment in favor of the defendant, which, on appeal, was affirmed by the district court, and the plaintiff appealed to the supreme court. The principal question before the court in that case was whether the clause in the city charter exempting firemen from the payment of poll tax, was repugnant to the provision of the state constitution above set forth, and the court held that it was not. It seems apparent, from expressions in its opinion, that the decision of the court was largely influenced by the fact that a long continued acquiescence of the people in the statute under which the taxes in question had been collected, had established a legislative and popular construction of the constitution, which, in the opinion of the court, was entitled to great consideration. And it is true that, in case of doubt in the mind of the court as to the proper construction of any particular provision of the constitution, a contemporaneous interpretation, or the subsequent practical construction, of such provision is entitled to great weight. But, in the language of Judge Cooley,

"Acquiescence for no length of time can legalize a clear usurpation of power, where the people have plainly expressed their will in the constitution, and appointed judicial tribunals to enforce it. A power is frequently yielded to merely because it is claimed, and it may be exercised for a long period, in violation of the constitutional prohibition, without the mischief which the constitution was designed to guard against appearing, or without any one being sufficiently interested in the subject to raise the question; but these circumstances cannot be allowed to sanction a clear infraction of the constitution. We think we allow to contemporary and practical construction its full legitimate force, when we suffer it, where it is clear and uniform, to solve in its own favor the doubts which arise on reading the instrument to be construed." Cooley, Const. Lim. (7th ed.), pp. 106, 107.

See, *State ex rel. Chamberlain v. Daniel,* 17 Wash. 111,
49 Pac. 243.

The Minnesota case above cited is confidently relied on
by counsel for the respondent as supporting the ruling of
the trial court in this case, and it is, in fact, more nearly in
point than any other of the numerous cases cited. But,
conceding that decision to be correct under the constitution
and laws of Minnesota, it cannot be said to be entitled to
controlling influence here, for the reason that the general
constitutional provision there considered is materially different from the provision of our constitution, now before
us for interpretation, and which declares, as we have seen,
that taxes for corporate purposes "shall be equal and uniform in respect to persons and property within the jurisdiction of the body levying the same."

The tax attempted to be collected in this instance is not
uniform even as to the persons included in the classification
made by the legislature, for some persons in the general
class are exempted from the payment of the tax. It would
therefore seem clear that the section of the statute now
under consideration is repugnant to § 9 of art. 7 of the
constitution, and consequently void.

This conclusion is fully supported by the decision of the
supreme court of Illinois in *Hunsaker v. Wright,* 30 Ill.
146, wherein the constitutionality of a county tax levied
upon property within the limits of the city of Cairo was in
question, the provision of the constitution there interpreted
being in substance identical with § 9 of art. 7 of our constitution. The lower court in that case enjoined the collection of the tax, and its ruling was affirmed by the supreme
court. The constitution of that state declared that "The
General Assembly shall provide for levying a tax by valuation so that every person and corporation shall pay a tax in
proportion to the value of his or her property," and that,

"The corporate authorities of counties, . . . cities, towns and villages, may be vested with power to assess and collect taxes for corporate purposes, such taxes to be uniform in respect to persons and property within the jurisdiction of the body imposing the same." And with regard to those provisions, the court said:

"These provisions were manifestly inserted in the fundamental law, for the purpose of insuring equality in the levy and collection of the taxes to support the government, whether levied for state, county, or municipal purposes. The design was to impose an equal proportion of these burthens upon all persons within the limits of the district, or body imposing them. Under these provisions the legislature has no power to exempt, or release a person, or community of persons, from their proportionate share of these burthens. Not having such power themselves, they are unable to delegate such power to these inferior bodies."

See, also, to the same effect, Cooley, Taxation (2d ed.), pp. 25, 26. We have refrained from discussing the numerous cases cited by counsel upholding levies of taxes payable in labor on highways, for the reason that we have deemed such cases inapplicable to the case at bar. Though in the nature of a tax, such levies are, in general, referable to the police power.

"Neither in common speech nor in customary revenue legislation would a burden of this nature be understood as embraced in the term tax; and statutory provisions for assessment are not therefore applicable to it unless made so in express terms." Cooley, Taxation (2d ed.), p. 15.

Our conclusion is that both the ordinances for the violation of which appellant was tried and convicted, and the provision of the statute upon which they are founded, are unconstitutional and void, and the judgment and sentence is therefore reversed and the action dismissed.

HADLEY and MOUNT, JJ., concur.

FULLERTON, C. J., and DUNBAR, J., dissent.

[No. 4757. Decided September 21, 1904.]

CHARLES R. WILCOX, *Respondent,* v. JAMES HENRY,
Appellant.[1]

NUISANCE—SLAUGHTER HOUSE—SPECIAL INJURY—ENJOINED AT
SUIT OF OWNER OF A DWELLING.   The maintenance of a slaughter
house and stock pens adjacent to the residence section of a city,
and the suffering of the accumulation of offal, refuse, and decay-
ing matter, in the conduct of such business, is a public nuisance
that may be enjoined at the suit of the owner of a dwelling who
shows special injury by reason of nauseating and offensive smells
which taint the atmosphere and food in said house, rendering it
unfit for habitation and depreciating its market value.

SAME—INTERMITTENT INJURY. The fact that the nuisance was
intermittent and not continual is not ground for refusing equitable relief.

SAME—DECREE—CONSTRUCTION—SUPPRESSION OF BUSINESS. A
decree enjoining, as a public nuisance, the maintenance of a
slaughter house and restraining the defendant from conducting
the business "to the injury of the plaintiff and other residents,"
is not objectionable as a suppression of the entire business, the
evidence having shown that the objectionable features could be
obviated by the installation of deodorizing machines, since the
terms of the decree permit the conduct of the business if the
noxious odors are obviated so as not to injure or annoy the plaintiff.

Appeal from a judgment of the superior court for King
county, Tallman, J., entered July 20, 1903, upon findings
in favor of the plaintiff, after a trial before the court without a jury, enjoining the maintenance of a slaughter house
as a public nuisance. Affirmed.

James B. Murphy, for appellant.   The plaintiff cannot
maintain the action because the injury was not different in
kind from that suffered by the public at large.   *Carl v.
West Aberdeen Land & Imp. Co.,* 13 Wash. 616, 43 Pac.
890; *Jones v. St. Paul etc. R. Co.,* 16 Wash. 25, 47 Pac.

[1]Reported in 77 Pac. 1055.

226; *Griffith v. Holman*, 23 Wash. 347, 63 Pac. 239, 83
Am. St. 821, 54 L. R. A. 178; *Tacoma v. Bridges*, 25 Wash.
221, 65 Pac. 186; *Fidalgo Island Canning Co. v. Womer*,
29 Wash. 503, 69 Pac. 1121; *Grigsby v. Clear Lake Water
Co.*, 40 Cal. 396; *Jarvis v. Santa Clara etc. R. Co.*, 52 Cal.
438; *Payne v. McKinley*, 54 Cal. 532; *Bigley v. Nunan*,
53 Cal. 403; *Aram v. Schallenberger*, 41 Cal. 449; *Balt-
zeger v. Carolina Midland R. Co.*, 54 S. C. 242, 32 S. E.
358; *East St. Louis v. O'Flynn*, 119 Ill. 200, 10 N. E.
395; *Houck v. Wachter*, 34 Md. 265; *Thelan v. Farmer*,
30 Minn. 225, 30 N. W. 670; *Clark v. Chicago etc. R. Co.*,
70 Wis. 593, 36 N. W. 326; *Gundlach v. Hamm*, 62 Minn.
42, 64 N. W. 50. Under the evidence the injunction should
have named and been confined to the appliances necessary
to make the business inoffensive. *Ballentine v. Webb*, 84
Mich. 38, 47 N. W. 485; *Babcock v. New Jersey Stock
Yard Co.*, 20 N. J. Eq. 296; *Green v. Lake*, 54 Miss. 540,
28 Am. Rep. 378; *Canal Melting Co. v. Columbia Park*,
99 Ill. App. 215. Under the circumstances of this case, the
business ought not to be suppressed. *Huckenstein's Appeal*,
70 Pa. St. 102; *Tiede v. Schneidt*, 105 Wis. 470, 81 N. W.
826; *Eller v. Koehler*, 68 Ohio St. 51, 67 N. E. 89; *Riede-
man v. Mt. Morris etc. Co.*, 67 N. Y. Supp. 391; *Ballentine v. Webb, supra; Richards' Appeal*, 57 Pa. St. 105;
Green v. Lake, supra; Lambeau v. Lewinski, 47 Ill. App.
656. If the grievance can be remedied by science and skill,
a court of equity will go no further than to require those
things to be done. *Ballentine v. Webb, Green v. Lake,
Tiede v. Schneidt, supra; Trulock v. Merte*, 72 Iowa 510,
34 N. W. 307; *Richards v. Holt*, 61 Iowa 529, 16 N. W.
595; *Miller v. Edison etc. Co.*, 68 N. Y. Supp. 900; *Sei-
fried v. Hays*, 81 Ky. 377; *Minke v. Hopeman*, 87 Ill.
450; *Learned v. Hunt*, 63 Miss. 373; *McMenomy v. Baud*,
87 Cal. 134, 26 Pac. 795; *Fresno v. Fresno Canal etc. Co.*,

98 Cal. 179, 32 Pac. 943; *Callanan v. Gilman,* 107 N. Y. 360, 14 N. E. 264.

R. E. Ferree, J. L. Waller, and *R. W. Emmons,* for respondent, upon the point that defendant's business was both a public and a private nuisance, cited: Wood, Nuisances, 25; 2 Story, Eq. Jur., 225; *Morris v. Graham,* 16 Wash. 343, 47 Pac. 752, 58 Am. St. 33; *Georgetown v. Alexandria Canal Co.,* 12 Pet. 91; *Milhau v. Sharp,* 27 N. Y. 611, 84 Am. Dec. 814; *Wylie v. Elwood,* 134 Ill. 281, 23 Am. St. 676; *Lansing v. Smith,* 4 Wend. 9, 21 Am. Dec. 89; *Wesson v. Washburn Iron Works Co.,* 13 Allen 95, 90 Am. Dec. 186; *Norcross v. Thoms,* 51 Maine 503, 81 Am. Dec. 590; *People v. Gold Run etc. Co.,* 66 Cal. 155, 4 Pac. 1152; *White v. Flannigain,* 1 Md. 525, 54 Am. Dec. 668; *Whitfield v. Rogers,* 26 Miss. 84, 59 Am. Dec. 244; *Ankeny v. Fairview Milling Co.,* 10 Ore. 390.

MOUNT, J.—Respondent brought this action to restrain appellant from maintaining a nuisance. The nuisance complained of consisted of a slaughter house, rendering tanks, and stock pens, located in the city of Seattle, about a quarter of a mile distant from respondent's residence. On the trial of the case, the court made findings of fact in substance as follows: That respondent is the owner of certain lots and a dwelling house thereon, located on what is commonly known as "Beacon Hill," in the city of Seattle; that appellant is in possession of certain tide land lots of Elliott bay, lying immediately west of Beacon Hill, at the foot thereof, and about fifteen hundred feet in a southerly direction from respondent's dwelling; that appellant, at the time the action was begun, and for a long time before, was, and is now, operating and maintaining upon said tide land lots a slaughter house, stock pens, furnaces, vats, and other appliances for the manufacture of lard and tallow,

and for slaughtering large numbers of cattle, hogs, and
sheep; that the said slaughter house and stock pens are
kept in an unclean and filthy condition, and the appellant
suffers and allows the offal, filth, and animal refuse matter
to be collected, deposited, and remain in and about the
said premises, until the said matter becomes putrid and
decayed and fills the air with noxious and offensive odors;
that appellant also throws and deposits offal, filth, and
animal matter in the waters of Elliott bay, which said offal,
filth, and animal matter are, by the action of the winds
and tides, cast upon the shores and there decompose and
cause nauseating and offensive smells and odors; that these
nauseating, unwholesome, and offensive smells and odors
so taint the air and food, in and about respondent's said
dwelling house, that respondent's rest, and that of his
family, is disturbed at night and his said dwelling house is
thereby rendered unfit for habitation; that, by means of
the various acts and things done as above found, and by
reason of the location of said slaughter house and stock
yards with reference to the said Beacon Hill, appellant
pollutes and corrupts the atmosphere in and about the
homes of the people living on Beacon Hill, and thereby
deprives each and every of such homes and residents of
pure air; that thereby the comfort and peace of every resident of said Beacon Hill is destroyed, and said homes rendered less enjoyable, and the market value of the property
on said hill is, and has been, greatly depreciated; that said
Beacon Hill rises from one hundred and fifty to two hundred feet above the said slaughter house and stock pens of
appellant, is a beautiful place in which to live, is covered
with homes, and is thickly populated. The court concluded, that the said slaughter house and stock pens were
a public nuisance; that respondent suffered special injury
therefrom, and has no adequate remedy at law therefor,

and that respondent was entitled to an order restraining
the appellant from operating said slaughter house, and
from slaughtering animals, rendering offal, lard or tallow,
or depositing the offal or animal refuse matter in the
waters of Elliott bay to the injury of appellant; and a
decree was entered accordingly. From this decree defendant appeals.

It is first insisted by the appellant that the complaint
upon its face shows that the nuisance, if any exists, is a
public nuisance, and does not show that the respondent is
specially injured thereby; and, second, that, if respondent
was disturbed by noxious smells, such disturbance was intermittent and therefore not a cause for equitable relief.
The findings of fact, as above stated, follow very closely
the allegations of the complaint, and are in substance the
same. For that reason it is not necessary to set out the
complaint in more detail in this opinion. Section 3084,
Bal. Code, defines a public nuisance as follows:

"A public nuisance is one which affects equally the
rights of an entire community or neighborhood, although
the extent of the damage may be unequal."

And the next section, in enumerating such nuisances, provides that:

"It is a public nuisance, . . . (7) To erect, continue,
or use any building, or other place, for the exercise of any
trade, employment, or manufacture, which, by occasioning
noxious exhalations, offensive smells or otherwise is offensive or dangerous to the health of individuals or of the
public."

Section 3087 provides that:

"Every nuisance not included in the definition of section
3084 is private."

Section 3093 provides:

"A private person may maintain a civil action for a public nuisance, if it is specially injurious to himself, but not otherwise."

There can be no doubt that the nuisance alleged in the complaint, and shown by the evidence, is a public nuisance. The right of the respondent to restrain it, therefore, depends upon whether the allegations of the complaint and the facts proven show that respondent is specially injured thereby. The substance of the allegations of the complaint upon this point is that the filthy pens, the offal, and the refuse matter, made by appellant in the conduct of his business, cause obnoxious, nauseating, and offensive smells, which taint and corrupt the atmosphere and food in and about respondent's dwelling, so that said dwelling house is thereby rendered unfit for habitation, and the value of the property on Beacon Hill depreciated. These allegations, it seems to us, bring the case clearly within the rule of special injury. The rule upon this question is stated in Wood, Nuisances (3d ed.), at §§ 668, 669, as follows:

"The general doctrine is, and may be regarded as the well-settled rule in courts of law and equity, both in this country and England, that for damages arising from a purely public nuisance, that is, one whose effects are common to all, producing no special or particular damage to one, as distinguished from the rest of the public, there can be no redress except by indictment or information in equity at the suit of the attorney general or other proper public officer."

"By common injury is meant an injury of the same kind and character, and such as naturally and necessarily arises from a given cause, but not necessarily similar in degree, or equal in amount. If the injury is the same in kind to all, it is a common injury, although one may actually be injured or damaged more than another. To illustrate, we will take the case of a slaughter house erected upon a public street. To all who come within the sphere of its operation

or effects, it is a nuisance, and offends the senses by its
noxious smells. It is a common nuisance in such locality,
and in its general effects produces a common injury. But
to those living upon the street and within its immediate
sphere, it is both a common and a private nuisance. Common in its general effects, but private in its special effects
upon those living there. To the public generally it produces no injury except such as is common to all; but to
those owning property in its neighborhood, or residing
there, it produces a special injury, in that it detracts from
the enjoyment of their habitations, produces intolerable
physical discomforts, and diminishes the value of their
premises for the purposes to which they have been devoted."

See, also, *Ross v. Butler,* 19 N. J. Eq. 294, 19 Am. Dec.
654. In the case of *Ingersoll v. Rousseau, ante,* p. 92,
76 Pac. 513, which was a case where the nuisance complained of was a bawdy house located on a lot adjacent to
plaintiffs' residence, in discussing the question of special
injury, this court said:

"The respondents suffer, not only all the inconveniences
the general public suffers because of the maintenance of the
nuisance, but in addition thereto, they are compelled to
become witnesses to the boisterous and indecent conduct of
the inmates of the houses, and listeners to the loud and unseemly noises made by them and their dissolute companions.
The injury caused the respondents by these conditions is
clearly special, and different in kind from that suffered by
the general public, who are not compelled to be either such
witnesses or listeners."

We also held in that case that a private party may enjoin
a public nuisance by suit in equity, where such party
suffers a special injury. The legal principles involved in
that case are the same as those involved here, and must control. The complaint, we think, stated a cause of action.

To the point that the nuisance complained of was intermittent, and therefore not a cause for equitable relief,

appellant makes no argument, but cites the case of *Farrell v. New York Steam Co.,* 53 N. Y. Supp. 55. That case does not support the appellant. It was there held that the things complained of did not arise from the negligence of the defendants, and did not amount to a nuisance, and, for that reason, it was held that equity would not restrain the operation of defendants' steam plant. In the case at bar, the injury to respondent is caused by a nuisance, the result of negligence and carelessness on the part of the appellant.

"The fact that this nuisance is not continual, and that the injury is only occasional, furnishes no answer to the claim for an injunction." *Campbell v. Seaman,* 63 N. Y. 568, 583, 20 Am. Rep. 567.

The other questions presented by the appellant are to the effect that the findings, conclusions, and decree of the court are not in accordance with the evidence. This has necessitated a careful examination of all the testimony in the case, and we are satisfied therefrom that the findings, conclusions, and decree are justified, and are in accord with the preponderance of the evidence, the great weight of which is to the effect that the appellant's stock pens are permitted to become and remain in a filthy condition; that they are not cleaned regularly when in use, and emit noxious odors continually; that offal was frequently cast into the bay and floated to shore, or was deposited on the tide flats, and there became putrid. The appellant himself testified that offal was thrown into an open vat, and frequently remained there, sometimes for two or three days, until the vat was full enough, when it was finally cooked. It clearly appears that, when this stuff was cooking in this open vat, it emitted nauseating odors which could be detected more than a quarter of a mile away; that this odor was so great and offensive that respondent's dwelling was unfit for habitation.

It is true that there was evidence to the effect that these noxious odors might be dispensed with by cleanliness, and by the installation of deodorizing machines and appliances. During the progress of the trial, when this evidence was being introduced, the court continued the trial of the cause for six months to allow the appellant to install such machinery or appliances to render his slaughter house, etc., inoffensive. When the trial was resumed, at the end of this period, it was shown that effective deodorizers had not been installed, that there was little or no abatement of the nuisance, and the filth was allowed to accumulate and give off its offensive odors as before. In fact, the appellant manifested little regard for the rights of those living near his slaughter house.

Appellant also complains that the decree suppresses appellant's entire business, while the testimony shows that the offensive odors were emitted from an open tank in which offal was kept and cooked, and that the suppression of the use of this tank alone is all that was justified. It is true that the evidence shows that the most offensive odor, and the one most readily traced, was emitted from this tank when materials were being cooked in it. But the evidence also shows that there were other odors, such as those arising from heads and hides of animals which were permitted to become putrid, and from offal which was kept on hand for a time, and from the filthy stock pens and tallow rendering vats, and from refuse matter which was thrown into the bay. All these contributed to aggravate the nuisance. The evidence, we think, fairly shows that, by the installation of proper appliances and by constant care and cleanliness, all these odors may be obviated; but, until the appellant can and does suppress all these noxious odors, he certainly should not be permitted to operate his plant in that locality. The decree does not necessarily abolish appellant's business. It does restrain appellant from conducting the business, and from permitting others to conduct it, "to the injury of the plaintiff and other residents." If the appellant obviates all the noxious odors complained of, and thereby so conducts the business as not to injure or annoy the respondent, he is permitted under the decree to do so; otherwise the business should be suppressed.

The judgment appealed from accords with our views, and is affirmed.

FULLERTON, C. J., and DUNBAR and ANDERS, JJ., concur.

[No. 4965. Decided September 21, 1904.]

ALEXIA HALVERSON, *Respondent,* v. SEATTLE ELECTRIC COMPANY, *Appellant.*[1]

CARRIERS—NEGLIGENCE—SPEED OF STREET CAR—MOTORMAN AS EXPERT WITNESS. Upon an issue as to negligence in running a street car around a curve at a dangerous rate of speed, a motorman is qualified as an expert to answer questions as to what rate of speed would, in his opinion, be safe, where he testifies that he was familiar with the road throughout its entire length and knew the curve, that he had been a motorman on this line for six or seven months, and was familiar with the speed of cars; the matter of qualification resting largely in the discretion of the court.

DEATH—DAMAGES TO WIDOW—EVIDENCE—EARNING CAPACITY OF HUSBAND'S BUSINESS—STATEMENTS IRRESPECTIVE OF BOOKS—BEST EVIDENCE. In an action by a widow for damages for the death of her husband, where the wife had been associated with him in, and was familiar with the amount of, his business, as a photographer, it is competent, upon the subject of the damages, for the wife to testify that he was earning about $2,000 per year,

[1]Reported in 77 Pac. 1058.

without producing the books, her estimate being based thereon
and on her knowledge of the business, since the books, while the
best evidence of their contents, are only secondary evidence of
the income of the business.

CARRIERS—NEGLIGENCE—SPEED OF STREET CAR—EVIDENCE—EX-
PERIMENTS—SIMILARITY OF CONDITIONS—DISCRETION. Upon an
issue as to negligence in running a street car around a curve at
a dangerous rate of speed, it is not an abuse of discretion to
refuse to admit the result of experiments made with the same
car at a time when the conditions were different from those existing at the time of the accident, in that the time of day, the
load on the car, the load on the electric current, and the condition of the rails were different; and the fact that the conditions
were more favorable to the plaintiff than to the defendant does
not make such exclusion error, since the same was within the
sound discretion of the court, to be reviewed only for abuse.

APPEAL—REVIEW—COMMENT ON THE EVIDENCE—HARMLESS ER-
ROR. Unlawful comment upon the weight and value of evidence
which is excluded, made at the time of ruling upon an objection
thereto, is harmless.

CARRIERS—NEGLIGENCE—DUTY OF STREET CAR COMPANY TO PRO-
VIDE PASSENGERS WITH SEATS—INSTRUCTIONS. In an action against
a street car company for negligence in the running of its car, resulting in the death of a passenger who was standing upon the
platform, it is not error to instruct that it is the duty of a carrier
to furnish passengers with seats, and not negligence for the passenger to stand on the platform if all the seats were occupied,
the same principle with reference to seats applying to street cars
as to steam cars, and it not being negligence *per se* for a passenger to ride on the platform.

SAME—ASSUMPTION OF FACTS. Such an instruction is not erroneous as assuming that the deceased was compelled to stand on
the platform, especially where there was evidence that the seats
were all occupied and that there was but little standing room
inside.

CARRIERS—NEGLIGENCE—PASSENGER THROWN FROM STREET CAR—
FAILURE TO PROVIDE GUARDS. In an action against a street car
company for causing the death of a passenger who was thrown
from the car while rounding a curve, it is not error to instruct
the jury to the effect that the company would be liable for negligently failing to provide a guard or gate, and to refuse to instruct
that it was under no obligation to provide guards because not
required to do so by statute, where it appears that the failure to

provide a guard or gate was not the only element of negligence
complained of, but the accident was due thereto in connection
with negligence in running an overcrowded car around a curve
at a dangerous rate of speed while passengers were standing on
the platforms.

DAMAGES—DEATH OF HUSBAND—EXCESSIVE VERDICT. A verdict
for $20,000 for the death of plaintiff's husband will be held exces-
sive and reduced to $10,000, where it appears that his business as
a photographer, in which the wife was associated, produced a
net income of $2,000 per year, that she continued the business,
producing sufficient for her needs, and that there were no children
to support.

Appeal from a judgment of the superior court for King
county, Griffin, J., entered June 30, 1903, upon the verdict of a jury rendered in favor of the plaintiff, for
$20,000 damages for the death of plaintiff's husband,
occasioned by a fall from a street car. Affirmed on condition of remitting $10,000.

Struve, Hughes & McMicken, for appellant, to the point
that the motion of the car in passing around a curve does
not constitute negligence, and must be guarded against by
passengers, cited: *Moser v. South Covington etc. St. R.
Co.* (Ky.), 74 S. W. 1090; *Ayers v. Rochester R. Co.,*
156 N. Y. 104, 50 N. E. 960; *Hite v. Metropolitan St.
R. Co.,* 130 Mo. 132, 32 S. W. 33, 51 Am. St. 555; *Blakney v. Seattle Electric Co.,* 28 Wash. 608, 68 Pac. 1037.

Walter S. Fulton, Vince H. Faben, and *T. D. Page,* for
respondent.

Mount, J.—Plaintiff brought this action against defendant to recover damages for the death of her husband,
N. P. Halverson. She avers in her complaint, that on
the 26th day of December, 1902, the said N. P. Halverson became a passenger on one of defendant's cars running from the city of Seattle to Ballard; that the defendant failed and neglected to provide a gate or railing

around the platform of said car; and that defendant negligently permitted the said car to become overcrowded with passengers, so that the said N. P. Halverson was prevented from obtaining a seat, and was compelled to stand on the platform of said car.   She makes the following allegation of negligence:

"That at Stewart street and Western avenue, in the city of Seattle, on the line of defendant's road leading to Ballard, there is a sharp curve and turn; that when said car reached said point, to wit, at about 5:15 P. M. on said day, the motorman in charge of and propelling the same negligently and carelessly failed and neglected to slacken the speed of said car, and negligently and carelessly turned on a heavy current of electricity, without warning or notice to the said N. P. Halverson, and while the said N. P. Halverson was in all things exercising due care, thus negligently and carelessly causing said car to start forward violently and to run around said bend and curve rapidly and with a lurch and jerk, thereby throwing said N. P. Halverson from said car to the ground and inflicting upon the said N. P. Halverson mortal wounds, from which said mortal wounds the said N. P. Halverson languished and languishing died, in the city of Seattle, Washington, on the 27th day of December, 1902."

She further avers that the deceased was a photographer, having an established business in the town of Ballard, and was able to earn, and was earning, in the prosecution of his business, the sum of $2,000 per year.   Defendant, by its answer, put in issue the allegations of negligence, and those in relation to the earning capacity of the said deceased, and the damages suffered by plaintiff, and pleaded the following affirmative defense, to wit:

"That on the 26th day of December, 1902, the said N. P. Halverson boarded one of defendant's cars on Western avenue at or near its intersection with Pike street, which said car was bound to the town of Ballard; that

said N. P. Halverson entered said car in the front vestibule thereof, and remained standing near the step of said
car; that he failed and refused to occupy a seat vacant in
said vestibule, but carelessly and negligently stood near
the step of said car, smoking a cigar, and without holding
to any of the bars or rods placed there for that purpose;
and while said car was proceeding along one of the curves
in the track, rendered necessary by the irregularity of the
street, said N. P. Halverson fell from said car to the street
and received injuries from which he subsequently died,
and this defendant avers that the injuries and damage, if
any, sustained by the plaintiff, were caused and contributed to by the aforesaid negligent acts of the said N. P.
Halverson."

The foregoing affirmative defense was put in issue by the
reply.

The undisputed facts developed on the trial of the cause
are as follows: The plaintiff's husband, N. P. Halverson,
had, for about three years, been engaged with his wife in
conducting a photograph gallery, in the town of Ballard.
Defendant owned and operated a street railway line between the city of Seattle and Ballard, which line, as it
leaves the city, runs along Western avenue, starting at the
foot of Columbia street and extending northerly toward
Ballard. After reaching Pike street there is a grade of
about six per cent to Stewart street, the hill terminating
at Virginia street, about one block further on. About
5:15 o'clock P. M., on the 26th day of December, 1902,
the said N. P. Halverson offered himself as a passenger
on one of the defendant's cars, at the intersection of Pike
street with Western avenue. At this time the seats within
the body of the car were filled, and persons were standing
in the car, although there was standing room therein for
more. Said Halverson was smoking, and boarded the
front platform or vestibule of the car. There is no evi-

dence showing the motive of said Halverson in entering the vestibule, except as above stated.

The car was about forty-two feet long, and had a vestibule at each end. These vestibules were exactly alike. They were entirely cut off from the body of the car by a partition running from side to side. Immediately in front of this partition was a seat, running crosswise the entire width of the car and facing the front. This seat was seven feet nine inches long, capable of holding five or six persons. Within the vestibule, and in the extreme front of the car, were the motor box and brake, between which stood the motorman. The vestibule was entered at the opening on either side thereof. Halverson entered the front vestibule at the entrance or opening on the east side, the car facing north. At the time he entered, four persons were sitting on the seat in the vestibule, two women and two men, the women being on the end where Halverson entered. Two or three men were also standing in the vestibule. Halverson stood at the entrance where he boarded the car, with his back to the street and facing the vestibule. He remained in that position until he fell from the car. He had a package in one arm, and was smoking a cigar.

From Pike street to Stewart street the distance is a little more than a block. At the intersection of Stewart street, Western avenue, along which the car was running, changes its direction northerly, and at this point the tracks of defendant's line curve to conform to the direction of the avenue. This requires a double or compound curve, both being curves of large radius. After leaving Pike street, the car proceeded up the hill to Stewart street, and, while passing through the curves, the said Halverson, at the further curve, fell from the car to the street, striking his head and receiving injuries from which he died the following day.

The photograph business conducted by plaintiff and her husband yielded an income of about $2,000 a year. Halverson had been in the photograph business for about ten years, in Chicago, Seattle, and Ballard, which covered the period of his married life, and the accumulations of those years consisted of a small building on leased land, used as a photograph gallery (in which they also lived), together with the photographer's equipment and supplies. Plaintiff and her husband had no children.

At the close of all the testimony, the defendant challenged the sufficiency of the evidence to entitle the plaintiff to recover. This challenge was denied, and exception taken. The case was then submitted to a jury, which returned a verdict in favor of plaintiff for $20,000. A motion for new trial was denied, and judgment entered upon the verdict. Defendant appeals.

Appellant first insists that the court erred in overruling objection to questions propounded by respondent to the witness J. R. Dickson, as follows:

"Q. At what rate of speed, in your opinion and judgment, ought a car to be run into that curve in order to be operated with safety to passengers on it, basing your answer upon your experience as a motorman upon that road?"

"Q. You may state whether, in your judgment and opinion, based upon your experience as a motorman upon that road, a car with safety to passengers can be run into that curve at a rate of speed at from six to eight miles per hour."

These questions were objected to, upon the ground that the witness had not shown himself competent to testify. The witness had testified, that he was familiar with the road

throughout its entire length, and knew the curve; that he
had been a motorman over this same line for six or seven
months; that he was familiar with the speed of cars; and
that, in his judgment, the car was running through the
curves at the time of the accident at between seven and
eight miles per hour.   We think this evidence qualified
the witness to answer the questions.   There seems to be
no well defined rule by which to measure the qualifications
of an expert witness, and it rests largely in the discretion
of the trial court to determine them.   12 Am. & Eng. Enc.
Law (2d ed.), p. 427; *Traver v. Spokane Street R. Co.,*
25 Wash. 225, 65 Pac. 284.   Appellant argues other
grounds for the exclusion of these questions, but they
were not raised by the objection made at the time, and
for that reason we shall not consider them.   *Gustin v.
Jose,* 11 Wash. 348, 39 Pac. 687.

Appellant next contends that the court erred in permitting Mrs. Halverson to testify, over defendant's objection,
in respect to the income from their business, without producing the books.   After Mrs. Halverson had testified
that she was associated with her husband, had helped him
in the business, and was familiar with the amount of business he was doing, and knew what he was earning prior to
his death, she stated the amount at "about $2,000 per
year."   She thereupon testified as follows:

"Q. What did you base your estimates upon? A. On
the books. Q. And the amount of business that you took
in? A. Yes, sir. Q. And the receipts that you derived
from it—revenue? A. I kept the books."

Upon cross-examination she testified as follows:

"Q. Well, do you know what your total income was?
I suppose your books would show it, would they not?
A. My books will show. They will show it just to a
penny. Q. That is what I thought would probably be

the case.   But you don't know yourself just how much
you did take in—how much was the gross receipts of your
business ?   A. No, sir."

While the witness stated that she based her estimate upon
the books, yet it is clear, from her whole testimony, that
she meant she could not state the exact amount of earnings
of the business, but that the books would show exactly.
It is further clear that she based her estimate upon her
knowledge of the business derived from her association
therewith, and from the fact that she kept the books.   The
books, of course, are the best evidence of their contents,
but the contents of the books kept by the witness are not
necessarily the best evidence of the income of the business.
The witness might be heard to say that she had not entered
every item of income thereon, or that entries were incorrect
in certain particulars.   In other words, the books, being
private memoranda, are secondary evidence, and for that
reason the bookkeeper, or any other person with knowledge
of the income of the business, could be heard to state the
facts independent of the books.   *Cowdery v. McChesney,*
124 Cal. 363, 57 Pac. 221; *Elderkin v. Peterson,* 8 Wash.
674, 36 Pac. 1089.   It was therefore not error for the
court to refuse to strike the evidence of the witness.   Appellant also contends that the evidence in regard to the
earnings of the deceased prior to his death was incompetent; but, under the rule in *Walker v. McNeill,* 17
Wash. 582, 50 Pac. 518, and *Turner v. Great Northern
R. Co.,* 15 Wash. 213, 46 Pac. 243, 55 Am. St. 883, this
evidence, which tended to show his earning capacity and
income immediately prior to his death, was competent.

Appellant next contends that the court erred in refusing
to permit certain witnesses to testify to the results of experiments made by them in running the same car upon
which the accident occurred through the same curve.   The

witnesses showed that these experiments were made under
different conditions from those existing at the time of the
accident.   They were made at a different time of day,
when the electric current would have less load and, therefore, more power.   The experiments were also made with
no load upon the car, and upon a dry rail, while the car at
the time of the accident was heavily loaded with passengers
and the rails were wet.   It is argued by appellant that the
conditions existing when the experiments were made were
more favorable to the respondent than the conditions existing at the time of the accident, and that the court, therefore, should have permitted the results to be shown, notwithstanding the dissimilar conditions.   The general rule
as laid down by Mr. Freeman, in his note on page 375 to
Chicago etc. R. Co. v. Champion, reported in 53 Am. St.
Rep., at page 357, is as follows:

"There has been, until within recent years, some hesitation in receiving evidence of experiments or demonstrations; but the rule is now established that evidence of the
results of tests or experiments is admissible if based upon
conditions similar to those existing in the case on trial.
In all cases of this sort, very much must necessarily be
left to the discretion of the trial court, but the exercise
of its discretion will not be interfered with where it has
not been abused.   From the liability to misconception and
error, there can be no doubt that it is essential that the
experiments or demonstrations should be made under similar conditions and like circumstances.   When this is shown
as a foundation for the introduction of experiments as evidence, they ought to be admitted, and the court's exercise
of discretion in admitting them ought not to be interfered
with."

We have no doubt that this is the correct rule.   The fact
that the conditions are more favorable to the test, or less
favorable, ought not to change the rule that the experiments must be made under similar conditions and like cir-

cumstances. The similarity of the circumstances and conditions must be left to the sound discretion of the trial
court, and determined by him, subject to review only for
abuse. Where the conditions and circumstances are so
different or dissimilar as to probably bring about different
results, as they evidently were in this case, it is not an
abuse of discretion to exclude the results of the experiments.

In passing upon the question of the admissibility of the
evidence above referred to, the court said to counsel:

"I think that it already appears from the evidence that
the amount of power upon these cars, during the time of
climbing the hill, depends upon the number of cars that
are climbing other hills and the number on the road. It
seems to me that any tests that might be made would, on
that account, be dissimilar from the conditions that prevailed at the time, and I do not think it is within the
knowledge of any person to know where they were located,
whether upon grades or off grades, so that any test at any
other time would be of very little value, if any, in determining the operation of cars at one time or another."

Appellant now insists that this was a comment upon the
evidence. The evidence of tests was excluded, and the
statement of the court was made as his reason for excluding it. If the evidence had been admitted, and the court
had then made the statement, it would no doubt have been
a comment upon the weight of the evidence; but, where the
evidence was excluded, the remarks of the court were harmless. Furthermore, no exception was taken upon the ground
that the remarks of the court were a comment upon the evidence, and for that reason the point cannot be now made
here for the first time. 8 Enc. Plead. & Prac., p. 272.

Appellant also insists that the court erred in giving instructions Nos. 6 and 8. Number 6 is as follows:

"You are instructed that it is the duty and obligation of common carriers for hire to furnish passengers with seats for their accommodation, and if you believe from the evidence in this case that the defendant received the said N. P. Halverson as a passenger, the said N. P. Halverson thereby became entitled to a seat, and if he was prevented from obtaining a seat by reason of the car being overcrowded, you are instructed that it was not negligence for said N. P. Halverson to stand or be upon the platform of said car, providing you believe that in standing upon said platform the said N. P. Halverson was exercising ordinary care and prudence, and would have been safe from injury if said car had been run in a careful manner."

The substance of the above instruction is repeated in instruction No. 8.   It is first argued that there is no obligation to furnish passengers with seats upon ordinary street cars, and that the same rule does not apply to street cars as applies to steam railways; and, second, that the instruction assumes that there is evidence from which the jury might find that, owing to the crowded condition of the cars, the deceased was compelled to stand upon the platform. We cannot agree with either of these contentions of appellant.   The obligation of street car companies to furnish seats for their passengers rests upon the same principle as that of steam railways, viz., the accommodation and safety of their passengers.   No doubt swiftly moving steam railway trains are more dangerous to standing passengers than electric or other motor cars running less swiftly, and for that reason greater care is necessary upon steam railway trains.   But the principle is the same in both cases.   Both must care for the safety of their passengers.   It would not be negligence *per se* for a street car company to fail to furnish a seat to each of its passengers, but, where seats are not furnished, and passengers are permitted or required to stand upon cars, greater care is required in the operation

of its cars than where all are provided with seats.　Nor is
it negligence *per se* for a passenger to ride or stand upon
the platform of a car.　*Graham v. McNeill,* 20 Wash. 466,
55 Pac. 631, 72 Am. St. 121, 43 L. R. A. 300; *Thirteenth
etc. R. Co. v. Boudrou,* 92 Pa. St. 475, 37 Am. Rep. 707;
Cattano v. Metropolitan St. R. Co., 173 N. Y. 565, 66
N. E. 563.

We do not think the instructions are subject to the criticism that they assume that there was evidence from which
the jury might find that the deceased was compelled to
stand upon the car or the platform.　But, if they may be
said to assume such fact, the assumption was correct, because it appears that there was but little standing room
inside the car, and that the seat in front, which was seven
feet nine inches long, was occupied by four persons, and
two or three other passengers were standing on the platform; and, when deceased boarded the car, two women
were on the end of the seat next to where the deceased was,
and he made a remark, in substance, that he "did not want
to climb over ladies."

Appellant next contends that the court erred in giving
the following instruction:

"You are instructed that, if you believe from a preponderance of the evidence that the deceased, N. P. Halverson,
was permitted to ride by the defendant upon the platform
of defendant's car; that the defendant carelessly and negligently failed and neglected to provide and have on said car
a gate, railing or other protection around the platform
thereof, and that thereby said car was rendered an unsafe
and dangerous conveyance in that passengers on said platform were unprotected and liable to be thrown therefrom,
and you further believe that defendant permitted said car
to become overcrowded with passengers, and failed to provide said Halverson with a seat on said car, but permitted
him to be crowded and jostled by other passengers likewise
upon said platform, and if you further believe that said

car ran into said curve at a high rate of speed, without
warning or notice to said Halverson, that thereby said car
was caused to lurch and jerk as it went around said curve,
causing said Halverson to be thrown therefrom, and to receive injuries of which he died, then your verdict will be
for plaintiff," etc;

and in refusing to give the following instruction requested
by appellant:

"You are further instructed that there being no statute
or law of this state requiring street car companies to provide gates and have them closed on the front platform of its
cars, the fact, if you should so find, that at the place where
the said N. P. Halverson entered said car upon the front
platform there was no gate closed behind him, would not
constitute negligence upon the part of the defendant company."

This latter instruction is, no doubt, correct when applied
to a case where such is the only or principal negligence
complained of.   But in this case there were other elements
of negligence, the principal one of which was running the
car at a high rate of speed into a curve, while passengers
were permitted to stand, and were standing, and had no
means of knowing the danger, and were not warned to protect themselves against the danger of being thrown from
the car.   It may not be negligent of railway companies
to fail to provide railings or gates to prevent passengers
from falling or being thrown from the cars, where they
are run at the usual rate of speed upon straight or even
tracks, where no such protections are usually required;
but, when an unusual or high rate of speed is maintained
around curves, or over rough and uneven roads, then ordinary diligence requires such safeguards, even if they are
not required by positive statute.   For this reason, we think
the instruction requested would have been misleading, as
applied to the facts in this case, and we also think the

instruction given fairly stated the law applicable to the facts. Instruction No. 10 requested by appellant in reference to contributory negligence was given in substance, and it was therefore not error to refuse the one requested.

The next error complained of is that the court erred in overruling defendant's challenge to the sufficiency of the evidence. We have gone carefully over the whole of the evidence and, without extending this opinion by a discussion thereof, it is sufficient to say that there was enough in the case to warrant the jury in finding a verdict for the plaintiff.

Appellant contends further that the verdict of the jury is excessive. In this we agree. In cases of this kind, the plaintiff is entitled only to actual damages, as nearly as the same can be measured in money. It is difficult, of course, to measure in money the damages which the respondent sustained by the loss of her husband. She lost his society and comfort and the means of support which he provided. Society and comfort are largely sentimental, and incapable of accurate valuation. There were no children left for respondent to provide for. The means of support which the deceased provided were not large. The evidence shows that the only source of revenue was from their photograph business, conducted by both of them, the net income of which was $2,000 per year. Respondent continues the business, earning sufficient for her needs, but with what actual returns does not appear. For all the damages which respondent has suffered, we are satisfied that $10,000 is ample to reward her, and that $20,000 is so out of proportion to the actual damages as to show, upon its face, prejudice of the jury.

For this reason the judgment is reversed and remanded. unless, within thirty days from the date of the filing of this opinion, the respondent remits the excess of $10,000, in which event the judgment will stand affirmed. Appellant to recover costs of this appeal.

FULLERTON, C. J., and DUNBAR and ANDERS, JJ., concur.

[No. 4927. Decided September 21, 1904.]

CLIFFORD D. BEEBE *et al.*, *Respondents*, v. JOHN C. REDWARD *et al.*, *Appellants*.[1]

EVIDENCE—PAYMENT—RECEIPTS—SUFFICIENCY OF OBJECTIONS. An objection to the admission in evidence of receipts signed by judgment creditors acknowledging payment of their judgments, on the ground that such receipts did not show payment, is not sufficient to raise the point that there was no proof of execution or authentication, and the same will not be considered on appeal.

SAME—WRITINGS—INSPECTION AND COPY BEFORE TRIAL. The failure to offer an inspection and serve a copy of a writing, before trial, is not a valid objection to the writing as evidence, under Bal. Code, § 6048, since that section merely provides that such inspection and copy shall dispense with proof of execution and genuineness in case it is not denied by affidavit.

INDEMNITY—BUILDING CONTRACT—ACTION ON BOND—ACCRUAL—LIMITATIONS—DATE OF FIRST BREACH—DELAY IN COMPLETION OF BUILDING—BREACH WAIVED BY OWNER. Where an indemnity bond guaranteeing a building contract provided that actions thereon must be instituted within six months after the first breach of the contract, which called for the completion of the building in August, 1901, and the owner accepted the building upon its completion in December, 1901, the company cannot claim that the right of action accrued in August and was barred six months thereafter, since the owner waived that breach by accepting the building, and the surety cannot complain of the waiver of any breach of the contract or departure therefrom that does not operate to its prejudice.

SAME—MECHANICS' LIENS AS BREACH OF CONTRACT—WAIVER BY OWNER. Where an indemnity bond guarantees the performance

[1] Reported in 77 Pac. 1052.

of a building contract in which the contractor agrees to furnish all the material, the owner is not obliged to treat the filing of a mechanics' lien as a breach of the contract, and assume the burden of establishing the lien; but he may waive the same until it is established by a court of competent jurisdiction, in which case his right of action on the bond accrues at that time, and an action begun within the six months limited in the bond after the first lien is established by judgment is in time.

Appeal from a judgment of the superior court for King county, Bell, J., entered April 27, 1903, upon the verdict of a jury rendered in favor of the plaintiffs in an action upon an indemnity bond guaranteeing a building contract. Affirmed.

James B. Murphy, for appellant U. S. Fidelity & Guaranty Co.

E. H. Guie, for appellants Redward.

H. R. Clise, for respondents.

FULLERTON, C. J.—On May 24, 1901, the respondent Clifford D. Beebe entered into a contract with the appellant John C. Redward, by the terms of which Redward undertook to furnish all the necessary labor and materials and erect for the respondent a building, according to plans and specifications referred to in the contract, for the agreed price of $25,022. Shortly after the execution of the contract, the appellant Redward, as principal, and his co-appellant The United States Fidelity and Guaranty Company, as surety, executed and delivered to the respondent a bond in the sum of six thousand dollars, conditioned, among other things, that the contractor would well, truly, and faithfully comply with all the terms, covenants, and conditions of the contract on his part to be kept and performed according to its tenor and effect. After the execution of the contract and bond, Redward entered upon the work of constructing the building, substantially complet-

ing it about December 1, 1901, some three months later
than the time fixed in the contract for its completion.   On
the date last named, N. Clark & Sons filed a lien on the
building, to secure themselves for materials sold the contractor, and used in the construction of the building.   Later
on, two certain other liens were filed, one by the Robinson
Manufacturing Company, and the other by the Seattle
Lumber Copmany, each claiming balances due from Redward for materials furnished him for use in the construction of the building.

Foreclosure actions were thereafter begun on the several
liens, against which the respondents and the appellants
Redward unsuccessfully defended, the several claimants
recovering judgment of foreclosure against the property,
for the amount claimed by them, with costs of suit and
attorney's fees added, which judgments the respondents
paid in full.   The judgment in favor of N. Clark & Sons
was for the sum of $1,840.89, was entered June 30, 1902,
and was paid on July 2, 1902.   The judgment in favor of
the Robinson Manufacturing Company was for the sum of
$1,150, was entered on the 6th of November, 1902, and
was paid on December 5, 1902.   The judgment in favor of
the Seattle Lumber Company was for the sum of $1,038.38,
was entered on the 8th of October, 1902, and was paid December 10, 1902.   In addition to these sums, the respondents paid in each case the statutory appearance fee of
$2.00, and $50 to the attorneys employed by them to defend the actions.   At the time of the filing of the first lien,
the respondents had paid to the contractor all of the original contract price, except the sum of $280.   There was,
however, an amount owing for extra work and material.
This amount was in dispute between the respondents and
the contractor, but it was conceded by the respondents that
the amount aggregated at least $663.50.

This action was begun on December 16, 1902.   In their
complaint the respondents alleged that there was due them,
by reason of the matters above set forth, the sum of
$3,270.19, being the difference between the amount paid
on account of the construction of the building and the
contract price plus the value of the conceded extras.   To
the complaint the appellants answered separately.   They
put in issue the rendition and payment of the lien judgments set out in the complaint, and set up several affirmative defenses. One of those set up by the appellants Redward,
was the claim that the contractor Redward had performed
extra labor upon, and furnished extra material used in, the
construction of the building, to an amount aggregating
$1,676.50, which had not been paid or allowed to him by
the respondents.   The other appellant set up the same defense, contending however, that the reasonable value of the
extra work and material put on the building by the contractor more than exceeded the difference between the contract price and the amount actually paid to his account,
and the further defense that the action had not been begun
within the time prescribed by the terms of the bond.   Re-
plies were filed, putting in issue the new matter of the
answers, and a trial had before the court and a jury, resulting in a verdict and judgment in favor of the respondents
for the sum of $2,812.75 and the costs of the action.

The appellants Redward first assign that the court erred
in refusing to grant their motion for nonsuit, made at the
close of the plaintiffs' case.   The motion was based on the
ground that the respondents had failed to prove payment
by them of the judgments obtained by the lien claimants.
The proofs on this point consisted of a transcript of the
judgment roll, showing the commencement and prosecution
of the several actions, the judgments entered therein, and

a signed receipt from each of the judgment creditors acknowledging payment to them of the amounts of their respective judgments. It is objected that these receipts were incompetent to prove payment, because no proof was made of their authenticity or execution, and that they were not, before the trial, submitted to the apppellants for inspection, nor were the appellants, before the trial, served with a copy of the instruments or with notice that the respondents intended to read them in evidence, as required by the statute. But the receipts were objected to in the court below because they did not show payment, and not on the grounds here suggested, and we think the appellants cannot now urge these objections. By failing to object on the ground that the instruments were not duly authenticated, or shown to have been executed by the judgment creditors, the appellants admitted their genuineness, and they were properly admitted in evidence if competent for any purpose.

So, likewise, the failure to object on the ground that the writings were not submitted to inspection before the trial is a waiver of that objection. This objection is also unsound for the reason that the statute cited (§ 6048 Bal. Code) does not make it necessary that a writing, material as evidence, be offered to the other party for inspection and be served on him by copy prior to the trial, before it can be admitted in evidence. This section of the statute was intended to enable a party to ascertain, in advance of the trial, whether or not it will be necessary for him to prove the genuineness of his written evidence at the trial. If he offers the writings for the inspection of the other party, and delivers him a copy thereof, with notice that he intends to read the same in evidence at the trial, they may be so read without proof of their genuineness or execution, unless the other party, before the commencement of the trial, denies their genuineness by affidavit; but the statute was intended to afford an additional remedy; it was not intended as a denial of the right to put in evidence a writing in the manner prescribed by the general rules of evidence. It was proper, therefore, for the plaintiffs to offer these writings in evidence at the trial in the manner they did offer them, and the court did not err in admitting them over the objections urged. It may be well to say here, however, that we do not intend to assert that a receipt, acknowledging payment of money, is generally admissible as evidence of such payment as against strangers thereto; as to them, of course, it is but the hearsay declaration of the party who signed it. But where a receipt is admitted in evidence against such a stranger, without objection on that ground, it is, like other hearsay evidence so admitted, sufficient to support a finding based thereon. The motion for nonsuit was properly denied.

The next contention of these appellants is that the verdict of the jury, disallowing certain extras claimed by them, is not supported by the evidence. The appellants, as we have stated, claimed extras to the amount of $1,676.50. The respondents, in part in their pleadings, and in part at the time of the trial, admitted of this claim the sum of $827.50. The jury found that the appellants were entitled to something over two hundred dollars more than the amount admitted, but did not allow the full amount of the claim. The contention is that the full amount claimed should have been allowed, and that the verdict should be set aside because the jury did not so find. But while there was, doubtless, evidence sufficient to sustain the finding of the jury had they found for the appellants for the full amount claimed, the evidence was not of a conclusive nature; neither was it undisputed. It was, therefore, for the jury to find whether the claims were supported as a whole, or in part only, and, as they found the claims supported only in part, the finding is binding upon this court.

Passing to the assignments of error made by the appellant The United States Fidelity and Guaranty Company, we will notice first the contention that the action was not begun within the time fixed by the bond. The bond provided among other things "that any suits at law or proceedings in equity brought against this bond, to recover any claim hereunder, must be instituted within six months after the first breach of said contract." It is first contended that there was a breach of this provision of the bond in that the appellant Redward failed to complete the building before December 1, 1901, whereas the contract called for its completion on August 31, 1901; and, second, if there was not a breach because of this, there was such a breach when the appellant Redward suffered materialmen, furnishing material used in the construction of this building, to file liens thereon to secure payment for the material so furnished, and that, as one such lien was filed as early as December, 1901, the action, to have been in time, should have been commenced not later than six months from that date.

Concerning the first of these contentions, if it were true that there was a breach of the contract in the respect mentioned, it could not, in this action, be availed of by the appellants. The respondents make no complaint of this breach. They have accepted completion of the building on December 1, 1901, as performance of the contract, and cannot now claim a default because of the delay even though they were injured by it. The bond was given for the benefit of the respondents. Its purpose was to secure to them the faithful performance of the contract on the part of the contractor, and whatever they choose to accept as performance, is performance, as between themselves, on the one side, and the contractor and surety on the other. The surety, therefore, cannot complain of any breach of the contract which the owner waives, that does not operate to his prejudice. If the breach increases his liability, or causes him a loss in any manner, he can, of course, defend against such increased liability, and recoup such losses, and it may be that breaches of the contract having this effect would relieve him from his liability entirely, but he cannot escape liability by the mere showing that there has been a departure, in the performance, from the strict terms of the contract. To relieve on this ground there must be a showing, not only of departure from the terms of the contract, but that the position of the surety has been so changed thereby as to result in prejudice to him. In the case at bar there is no showing that the surety has been prejudiced by the failure to complete the building at the time stipulated in the contract, and, as the owners, for whose benefit the stipulation was inserted, make no complaint because thereof, the surety cannot plead it as a bar to the right of the·owners to recover for subsequent losses.

What we have said has been on the assumption that a breach of the contract, in the regard mentioned, has been shown by the proofs, but we think it may be questioned whether enough was proven to show a breach of the contract. It was made to appear that the time fixed in the contract for the completion of the building was August 31, 1901, and that the building was not completed until November, 30, 1901; but the obligation of the contractor to complete on the day named was subject to several contingencies expressly enumerated in the contract, and it was not shown that these contingencies did not happen. It would seem that it would be necessary to show that none of the conditions happened which would authorize the delay, before it could be said that the delay constituted a breach.

Concerning the second contention, we have held in another case that, where an owner let a contract for the erection of a building, by the terms of which the contractor undertook to furnish all the labor and material required for its construction, and gave a bond with sureties for the faithful performance of the contract, the owner might treat the filing of a lien on the property by a materialman as a breach of the covenants of the bond, and sue at once thereon. But we said he was not obligated to do so; that, by so doing, he took upon himself the burden of establishing, not only the technical sufficiency of the lien to create a charge upon his property, but the amount due thereon, as well; whereas, he could properly wait until the parties, who had personal knowledge of the facts, litigated these questions between themselves, and the sufficiency of the lien and the amount thereof became settled by the judgment of a court of competent jurisdiction, and could treat the rendition of the judgment as the breach of the covenant of the bond. The question last suggested was not strictly before the court in the case referred to, but it seems to us now, after further consideration, that the conclusion was a just one. There may seem to be, as a first impression, some inconsistency in saying that the same act may, or may not, be a breach of a written covenant, as the party affected wills it, but the explanation rests in the fact that the owner may waive such breaches of the covenants of the contract on the part of the contractor as he chooses. A mechanic's or materialman's lien, although duly executed and recorded, does not prove itself. It is, at most, only a tentative charge against the property it purports to bind, and is liable to be defeated for lack of technical sufficiency, as well as by showing that the indebtedness, or some considerable part thereof, is not owing. The owner may, therefore, waive the apparent breach of the contract caused by the mere filing of the lien, and insist that a covenant such as the one now before us is broken only when the lien is made a fixed and determinate charge against his property, by the judgment of a court of competent jurisdiction. The present action was begun within six months after the time the earliest of the liens here in question was put into judgment, and we hold it to have been commenced in time to comply with the terms of the bond.

In the course of the trial the appellant sought to show other acts which it claimed to be breaches of the contract on the part of the contractor, but against which the owner made no complaint, either against the contractor or the surety. It was denied the right, and complains of such denial. What we said above applies here. The surety cannot insist that anything constitutes a breach which the owner does not insist upon, unless he shows that the breach operated in some manner to his prejudice. As to the matters here complained of, there is no pretense that they operated in any manner to the prejudice of the surety, and hence they cannot avail it as a defense.

There is no error in the record, and the judgment will stand affirmed.

MOUNT, DUNBAR, and ANDERS, JJ., concur.

[No. 4656.   Decided September 21, 1904.]

CATHERINE A. FRAZIER, *Appellant,* v. J. J. WILSON *et al.,*
Respondents.[1]

TIDE LANDS—CONTRACT TO PURCHASE—CANCELLATION—RECORD
OF BOARD OF LAND COMMISSIONERS.   It is not necessary that the
record show a formal declaration by the board of state land commissioners that a contract for the purchase of oyster lands is canceled for default in payment, where notice having been given, the
contract is stamped "canceled" after default for a year and nine
months, and thereafter, upon contest with a subsequent applicant, the board awards a contract and deed to such subsequent
applicant, since the action of the board upon the contest is a
sufficient declaration of cancellation.

SAME—FRAUD IN CANCELLATION OF CONTRACT—SUBSEQUENT PUR-
CHASER AS TRUSTEE.   In an action seeking to hold a purchaser
of oyster lands from the state as a trustee of a former applicant therefor, upon the allegation of fraud and collusion in
securing the cancellation of the plaintiff's application, a nonsuit
is properly granted, where it appears that the plaintiff was in
default in making her deferred payments, that she received a
notice to pay or her contract would be canceled, and paying no
attention thereto, the contract was stamped "canceled," whereupon,
as claimed, she filed another application, but no files thereof could
be found in the office of the state land commissioner, and, after
a contest, the land was awarded by the board to the subsequent
applicant, there being no evidence of fraud on the part of the
purchaser, or that the officers were in any way interested in his
contract, and the face of the record showing that the land was
open for sale at the time he applied therefor.

Appeal from a judgment of the superior court for Thurston county, Linn, J., entered September 9, 1902, upon
granting a motion for a nonsuit, at the close of plaintiff's
case, at a trial before the court without a jury.   Affirmed.

J. W. Robinson, for appellant.

Troy & Falknor, for respondents.

[1]Reported in 77 Pac. 1064.

PER CURIAM.—This action was brought for the purpose of having a deed to certain oyster lands, held by Wilson, one of the respondents, declared to be in trust for the benefit of appellant, Catherine A. Frazier. The complaint alleges, collusion and fraud, on the part of said Wilson and the officers and clerks in the office of Robert Bridges, former state land commissioner, to deprive this plaintiff of the land and to give it to Wilson; that the said officers had an interest in Wilson's application; and that the original contract of Mrs. Frazier had never been legally canceled, and was still in full force and effect. Each of the defendants demurred to the complaint, which demurrers were sustained. The plaintiff elected to stand upon her complaint as to the land commissioner, and in due time filed an amended complaint as to defendants Wilson and wife. The defendants Wilson answered, denying the material allegations of the complaint, and setting up various affirmative defenses which we deem it unnecessary to discuss.

The case went to trial, and the evidence disclosed that, on the 13th of February, 1896, the state of Washington, through the office of the commissioner of public lands, issued to appellant a contract for the sale of certain oyster or tide lands in Thurston county, containing about twelve acres, in consideration of the payment of the following sums: $3.95 on the day of the execution of the contract, the receipt whereof was duly acknowledged; $3.95 principal, and $.07 interest, on March 1, 1896; $3.95 principal, and $.64 interest, on March 1, 1897; $3.95 principal, and $.32 interest, on March 1, 1898. It was further provided in said contract as follows:

"And the said second party covenants and agrees to pay said principal sum and interest as above specified at the rate of eight per cent per annum in gold coin of the United States at the office of the state treasurer at the capital of said state, and that she will pay all taxes and assessments of every kind that may be levied or assessed on said land and premises, and that if said second party shall fail to pay any of the sums above specified, either of principal, interest, taxes or assessments, when the same shall become due and for six months thereafter, she will, on demand of the board of state land commissioners or other authorized officer of the state, quietly and peaceably surrender the possession of the above described land and premises and every part thereof; and upon failure to pay as above specified, all rights of said purchaser under this contract may, at the election of said board of state land commissioners acting for the state of Washington, and without notice to said purchaser, be declared forfeited and when so declared forfeited, and thereupon, the state shall be released from all obligation to convey said land; and all payments theretofore made on this contract and any and all improvements made on said land, or any part thereof, shall thereupon be forfeited to and belong to said state of Washington."

It is admitted in appellant's brief that none of the deferred payments were made. On September 1, 1897, the land department sent a notice to Mrs. Frazier notifying her of her delinquency. No response was received by the land department, and, on November 17, 1897, the contract was marked "canceled," with a rubber stamp, but the minutes of the board of state land commissioners fail to disclose an order canceling said contract. On or about the 1st of December, 1898, Mrs. Frazier tendered to the state land commissioner the amount due under her contract, and demanded a deed; whereupon the officer in charge informed her that he could not receive her money, for the reason that her contract had been canceled; that she could make a new application, and that there was no other application on file; and gave her blanks to fill out. She took the blanks home, and claims to have returned a couple of days thereafter, and filed them. These files appear to have disappeared completely. However, the number given would indicate the filing to have been in February, 1899. On December 31, 1898, James J. Wilson made application to purchase the tide or oyster lands covered by Mrs. Frazier's contract, together with other lands. On February 19, 1900, appellant made a reapplication to purchase, solely for the purpose of contesting Wilson's claim. The application of Wilson, covering about thirty-two acres, was referred to the board of oyster land commissioners, with a request to answer the following questions: (1) Is the land or any portion thereof a natural oyster bed? (2) If the land, or any part of it, is a natural oyster bed, is it necessary, in order to secure adequate protection to it, to retain it or any part of it in the public domain? (3) Whether the land, or any portion thereof, having been a natural oyster bed within ten years past, may reasonably be expected to again become such within ten years in the future. All these questions seem to have been answered by the commission in the affirmative. Indorsed upon the report is the following:

"Upon protest being made, and upon an investigation had, it appears to me the proper answer to these questions is, No; this applies to all three questions. Upon the matter being called to the attention of the board of oyster land commissioners, they admitted they might have made an error.   ROBERT BRIDGES, Commissioner."

Subsequently the board of state land commissioners awarded the land to Wilson, and dismissed Mrs. Frazier's contest. From this decision, she appealed to the superior court, but, before the appeal was perfected, a deed was issued to Wilson, which, as appellant claims, rendered it necessary to dismiss the appeal. The testimony is not very complimentary to the administration of the land commissioner's office, as it was conducted at that time, but there is no evidence to show that Wilson had any knowledge of any fraud, if fraud there was, committed in his behalf. On the contrary, the record showed on its face that the land was open to entry, and, although some evidence was introduced to the effect that certain officers in the land department had claimed to have an interest in the claim, Wilson himself was put upon the stand by the appellant, and testified that no one other than himself had any interest in the land. A motion for nonsuit was sustained at the close of plaintiff's testimony, and plaintiff appeals.

It will doubtless be conceded that, whenever the board of land commissioners orders a contract for the purchase of land canceled, it is the duty of the land commissioner to make a record of the action of the board. In this instance the only record seems to be the rubber stamp, "canceled," upon the book of contracts. The presumption of law is that the officer did his duty. The appellant had been in default for about a year and nine months, and the contract was undoubtedly forfeitable. The appellant cites, *State v. Frost,* 25 Wash. 134, 64 Pac. 902, and, *Washington Iron Works v. King County,* 20 Wash. 150, 54 Pac. 1004, in support of the theory that the contract created a vested right in the appellant which could not be taken from her except by due process of law. An examination of those cases will disclose the fact that they were cases involving the right of the state to tax lands held under a contract of purchase from the state, and in no sense of the word involved the point contended for here. In fact, we should hesitate a long time before announcing a rule that would so seriously handicap the land department of the state, in the administration of the affairs of that office, as to require an action by the state to be brought to cancel such contracts. At the time Wilson made his application to purchase, the records of the office showed that Mrs. Frazier's contract had been canceled on November 17, 1897, over a year previous, after she had been delinquent for almost a year and nine months. Section 18, Laws 1897, page 242, provides:

"The commissioner of public lands shall notify the purchaser of the land in each instance when payment on his contract is overdue, and that he is liable to forfeiture if payment is not made within six months from the time the same became due, unless the time be extended by the commissioner on a satisfactory showing as above provided."

The appellant admits that she received some sort of notice from the land commissioner, with reference to her delinquency, on or about September 1, 1897, and we think it is reasonable to assume that the notice she received is the notice provided for by the above section. It is not necessary that the board should formally declare a contract canceled. It seems to us that it is a sufficient declaration in that respect, after a person has been in default for more than six months, and where there is a contest pending between the original and a subsequent applicant, for the board to decide in favor of the subsequent applicant. Although in this instance Mrs. Frazier was not contesting Wilson's claim by virtue of her original application, if she had had any rights under her original contract, they ought to have been set up at that time, and the board given an opportunity to repudiate the so-called cancellation, if it had, as a matter of fact, been fraudulently made.

Under the circumstances, we think the judgment should be affirmed.

[No. 4751. Decided September 21, 1904.]

F. L. CHASE, *Respondent,* v. C. V. SMITH, *Appellant.*[1]

DAMAGES—MEASURE OF—BREACH OF CONTRACT TO PAINT HOUSES
—DISCHARGE. Where plaintiff contracted to paint defendant's
houses for a specified sum, and, after working five days, was discharged, it is error to instruct that the measure of his damages
is the profit he would have made on the contract in addition to
the reasonable value of the work already performed at the time
of the discharge, since he was entitled only to pay for the work
performed at the contract price, and to the profit he would have
made upon the balance of the contract.

SAME. Such an instruction is not cured by recalling the jury
and, after withdrawing the part allowing a quantum meruit for
the work performed, instructing that the recovery for that part
must be proportional to the completed work at the contract price,
since it still permitted additional recovery for the profits of the
entire contract.

Appeal from a judgment of the superior court for King
county, Griffin, J., entered February 13, 1903, upon the
verdict of a jury rendered in favor of the plaintiff, in an
action upon contract for services. Reversed.

Peters & Powell, for appellant.

Hawley & Huntley, for respondent.

PER CURIAM.—Action for breach of contract, brought
by F. L. Chase, plaintiff, against C. J. Smith, defendant,
in the superior court of King county. The cause was
tried to a jury, and verdict rendered in favor of plaintiff
for $302. The defendant in due time made and filed his
motion for a new trial, which was overruled, and judgment was entered on the verdict in the court below, from
which defendant appeals.

On the 29th day of January, 1902, respondent, who was
a painter, entered into a written agreement with appel-

[1]Reported in 77 Pac. 1069.

lant to paint twenty-two dwelling houses, in the city of
Seattle, then owned by the appellant. By the terms of
the contract, the owner was to furnish a part of the necessary material to do the work, the same being described in
a written itemized statement attached to the contract.
The work was to be begun on or before February 1st, provided the premises were turned over at that time, and to
be completed on or before April 10, 1902. Respondent
was to receive for this labor $1,210, payable at certain
specified times, as the work progressed. He started to
work on the property March 31, 1902. On April 4, 1902,
appellant refused to permit respondent to continue at
work thereon any longer, and thereupon advertised for further bids for such painting, and let a contract to complete
the same to a painter named A. A. Smith, who performed
the work at an additional cost of $1,643 for labor, and $260
additional for material, making a total of $1,903.

In the autumn of 1902, the respondent brought the
present action to recover for a breach of the original agreement. He alleged in his complaint, among other things,
that he was prevented by appellant from performing such
contract, claiming $370 damages for the wrongful dis-
charge, and, also, $250 for delay in turning over to re-
spondent the premises on which he was to commence work.
This latter item was eliminated from the case by the ruling of the trial court. The answer admitted the contract,
and that appellant discharged respondent from said work
on April 4, 1902, but denied that respondent suffered any
damage. In our opinion, the vital question arising on this
record is whether the trial court erred in giving certain
instructions to the jury with regard to the measure of
damages. The instruction of which appellant particularly
complains is as follows:

"If you find from a fair preponderance of the evidence in this case—that is, the greater weight of evidence, that the plaintiff would have made a profit provided he had been permitted by the defendant to carry out the contract in strict accordance with the plans and specifications and terms of the contract, then it is your duty to find in favor of the plaintiff and against the defendant for the amount of profit, if you so find, together with the value of the work which you find was done by the plaintiff under the contract. If the plaintiff has failed to prove to you by a fair preponderance of the evidence that he would have made a profit had he been permitted to carry out the terms of the contract, then it is your duty to return a verdict for the plaintiff only for the sum which you find—for the reasonable value of the work which you find was performed by the plaintiff under the contract. In other words, you cannot return a verdict for the plaintiff for profit unless you find from a fair preponderance of the evidence that had the plaintiff carried out the contract in accordance with its terms and the specifications that he would have made a profit."

The trial judge then proceeded to further instruct the jury, "that in any event in this case you must return a verdict in favor of plaintiff for the value of the work done and performed by him under the contract." Counsel for respondent here said, "May I just suggest another one in this last . . . instruction, which I assume was on the theory that the sum of these two should constitute their verdict, if they should find such?" And the court continued its instructions as follows: "In any case, if you find there was a profit, then the amount of profit, together with the work done, will constitute the verdict." After the jury had retired to deliberate upon their verdict, they were recalled and given the following additional instructions:

"Gentlemen, I wish to withdraw my instructions that I gave you, which went to the effect that your verdict in any event must be for the plaintiff for the reasonable value of the work done; I don't think that is a proper measure of damages. Your verdict must be for the plaintiff, in any event, for the value of work done, in a proportion which that work stands—completed work at the contract price, and not what the reasonable value of that work is. The other instructions in regard to finding for the plaintiff for the profits will remain as I gave them to you. The other instructions in regard to the finding for the plaintiff for the work done, the rule is, that the plaintiff in this case would be entitled to recover for the work in proportion which work bears to the completed work, that recovery being in proportion to the work done—that which the work bears to the contract price, and which is $1,210. You may retire."

We think that the learned trial court erred in giving the foregoing instruction regarding the measure of damages in actions of this kind; that the attempted correction, on the part of the court, failed to eliminate or correct the erroneous features thereof. Waiving the point as to all verbal criticisms which may be urged relative to the language used in such charge, we conceive this charge to be misleading and erroneous in substance. It gave the jury to understand that they could, if they believed respondent's evidence and adopted his theory in the present controversy, find the value of the work already performed at the contract price, and also the profits that would have accrued to him on the entire job under the contract, if appellant had not interfered and prevented performance as alleged. This is not the rule. The contractor was entitled to recover for the work performed at the contract rate, and such profit, if any, as he would have made on the balance of the work had he been allowed to complete it. The respondent is to be placed in the same condition that he would have been placed in, had he been permitted to proceed without interference. 2 Sedgwick, Damages (8th ed.), § 618; *Tennessee etc. R. Co. v. Danforth*, 112 Ala.

80, 20 South. 502; *Masterton v. Mayor of Brooklyn,* 7
Hill 61, 42 Am. Dec. 38.

The case of *Noyes v. Pugin,* 2 Wash. 655, 27 Pac. 548,
was an action upon a quantum meruit for services rendered. The language employed in the opinion must be
considered in connection with the facts of the case decided. Moreover, it is stated in that opinion that, "It
is difficult to perceive why the respondent in this case
should receive more compensation for the labor actually
performed by him than he would have received for the
same services had the contract not been broken by appellant." There is nothing in that opinion which conflicts
with the propositions of law advanced by Mr. Sedgwick.

While it may be conceded that, under the instructions
as corrected by the trial judge, the value of respondent's
labor already performed should be determined according
to the contract price, in the proportion that the same as
it then stood bears to the entire work which respondent
undertook to perform under the original agreement, it was
manifest error to give the jury to understand that they
might also allow profits on the entire contract. A recovery at the contract rate for the labor performed must
necessarily include the profit made by such labor, and it
was only for profits on the uncompleted portion of the
work that he was entitled to recover in addition, and then
only after a showing that he would have made such a
profit. *Tennessee etc. R. Co. v. Danforth, supra.* Owing
to the contradictory testimony appearing in the record, especially regarding the matter of profits, we are unable to
find any data by which we can segregate the legitimate
from the unlawful damages, so that we can give the respondent the choice to accept a definite sum or submit to
a retrial of the issues.

The judgment of the superior court is reversed, and the
cause remanded for a new trial.

[No. 4785. Decided September 21, 1904.]

NORTHWESTERN LUMBER COMPANY, *Appellant*, v. CITY
OF ABERDEEN, *Respondent*.[1]

LIMITATION OF ACTIONS — DIVERSION OF SPECIAL FUND FOR
LOCAL IMPROVEMENTS—ACCRUAL OF RIGHT OF ACTION. The right of
action against a city for the wrongful diversion of a special fund
provided for the payment of warrants, does not accrue until the
holder of the warrant has notice of the diversion.

MUNICIPAL CORPORATIONS—SPECIAL FUND FOR LOCAL IMPROVE-
MENTS—WRONGFUL DIVERSION BY CITY—COMPLAINT—SUFFICIENCY.
The complaint in an action brought by the holder of warrants
drawn upon a special fund for local improvements, for the wrongful diversion by the city of the special fund by the payment out
of their order of subsequent warrants, thereby exhausting the
fund, fails to state facts sufficient to constitute a cause of action,
when it fails to allege that the money diverted was sufficient to
pay all of the warrants drawn on the special fund which were
prior to the plaintiff's warrants, or that plaintiff was prejudiced
by being rightfully entitled to said money, or a portion thereof.

Appeal from a judgment of the superior court for Chehalis county, Irwin, J., entered March 23, 1903, upon sustaining a demurrer to the complaint in an action to recover on city warrants. Affirmed.

Green & Griffiths (Sidney Moor Heath, of counsel),
for appellant.

E. H. Fox, for respondent.

PER CURIAM.—This is an action brought in the superior
court of Chehalis county by Northwestern Lumber Company against the city of Aberdeen to recover on certain
street improvement warrants described in the complaint.
The defendant city demurred to such complaint on two
statutory grounds: "(1) That said amended complaint
does not state facts sufficient to constitute a cause of ac-

[1]Reported in 77 Pac. 1063.

tion.   (2) That the action has not been commenced within
the time limited by law." This demurrer was sustained
by order of the lower court. The plaintiff refused to further plead, electing to stand on its said complaint, and
the action was thereupon dismissed.   Plaintiff appeals.

The transcript shows that the complaint was filed in
the clerk's office of the court below on February 24, 1903.
Appellant alleges therein a contract to improve certain
streets in the city of Aberdeen in the year 1891, respondent's agreement to collect without neglect or delay each
of the warrants drawn on a special fund, in the order and
number of its isssuance, the performance of the work,
and the issuance of appellant's and other warrants upon
such special fund, some of them in April, some in May,
and others in July, 1891; that such warrants were presented for payment about these several dates, and endorsed by the treasurer of the city of Aberdeen, "not
paid for want of funds;" that thereafter the respondent
city collected large sums of money for the benefit of these
special funds.   It is further alleged, that respondent
wrongfully paid, contrary to the city ordinance and the
law in that regard, numerous other warrants subsequently
issued and numbered on the same funds, instead of using
such money to pay appellant's warrants then due; that,
ever since such payments, there has been and is no money
or fund except the city general fund with which to pay
any of appellant's warrants; that all sources of payment
from the property of the several assessment districts in
said city have been exhausted, and the land situated therein
is released from any and all liability on account of such
special assessments.   Other allegations are thus stated in
appellant's brief:

"In the complaint three causes of action are set forth,
each relating to a different fund, and the number, amount,

and date of wrongful payment of the subsequent warrants are respectively mentioned, and the prayer is for
judgment upon each cause of action for a sum not exceeding the amount diverted by defendant for the payment of
such subsequent warrants. . . . More particularly the
irregular payments are as follows: In the first cause of
action plaintiff's warrant dated April 16, 1891, is No.
524, for $75 and interest. Defendant paid Nos. 527, 528,
on November 7, 1891, and No. 526, September 28, 1891,
each for $75, and No. 529, September 10, 1892, and No.
530, June 1, 1892. In the second cause of action plaintiff's warrant dated May 14, 1891, is No. 569, for $479
and interest. Defendant paid warrant No. 571, November 18, 1891, for $116, but No. 570 was paid March 21,
1895, for $15. In the third cause of action plaintiff's
fourteen warrants, ranging from $30 to $108 in amounts
were dated July 9th, 1891, and are numbered 729, 730,
732, 734, 735, 741, 742, 743, 747, 754, 755, 764, 767 and
772. Defendant paid warrant No. 731, July 31st, and
Nos. 733, 736, 737 and 738 in December, 1891. But 739
was paid in November, 740 and 744 in September, 748
was paid November 7th, but 750, November 3rd, and 751
and 752, September 30th, while 753 was paid August 31st,
and 756, 757, 758, 759 and 760 were paid July 31st; 761
was paid November 3rd; 762 and 763, November 7th,
while warrant 765 was paid September 30th, 766, July
31, 770, November 7th, and 773, September 25th—all in
1891, and in amounts ranging from $25 to $160 per warrant."

It is further alleged:

"That thereafter defendant collected a large amount of
money from the owners of the land in said assessment district abutting upon said B street improved as aforesaid,
to wit, more than the sum of three hundred and seventy-
eight dollars, and while said funds collected as aforesaid
were in the city treasury and said warrant No. 524 held
and owned as aforesaid by plaintiff was due and payable
in the order of its issuance, said defendant instead of paying plaintiff's said warrant in the order of its issuance as

required by the ordinances of said city and the laws of the state of Washington, wrongfully and without authority paid out of said moneys other warrants issued against the same fund and numbered subsequently."

Then follows a description of warrants subsequently paid as above noted, described in the first cause of action. The second and third causes of action respectively contain, in substance, similar allegations, except as to the dates, the amounts collected and paid, the description of the warrants, and the special funds on which they were drawn. The appellant alleged that it had no knowledge nor information of the collection and payment of this money out of its regular order, until November 25, 1902.

Considering the above grounds of demurrer, in the inverse of the order above, we are of the opinion that this action was not barred at the time of its commencement by virtue of the three year statute of limitations, under the ruling of this court as announced in the case of *New York Security & Trust Co. v. Tacoma,* 30 Wash. 661, 71 Pac. 194. This court held in that case that the cause of action did not accrue until the holder of the warrant drawn against, and payable out of, a special fund, designated by the appellant city, had notice or knowledge of the wrongful diversion of such fund to its prejudice.

The proposition whether there are alleged in the complaint sufficient facts to constitute a cause of action presents the vital question in the case. This proposition is scarcely alluded to in the arguments of respective counsel in their briefs. Their arguments are chiefly directed towards the one question regarding the bar of the statute of limitations above mentioned. The complaint alleges a wrongful diversion of the special street improvement funds of respondent, and the payment, without authority, of moneys belonging to said funds, on warrants which were

issued against the same and subsequently numbered.   But
it fails to allege that there was sufficient money, belonging
to any of these special funds, diverted therefrom, to have
paid and satisfied the other warrants against the same
funds, issued in their regular order and prior in dates and
numbers to these warrants held by appellant; or that appellant, at the times of the alleged diversion of such funds,
was rightfully entitled to have such money, or any part
thereof, applied towards the payment and liquidation of
its warrants described in the complaint.   In other words,
the appellant was required to allege sufficient facts to show
that it was prejudiced by the payment of those subsequent
warrants out of their regular order, and that it had the
lawful right to insist that this money, or some portion
thereof, should have been applied towards the payment of
the warrants in question.   For aught that appears from
the complaint, this money was insufficient in amount to
have paid such prior outstanding paper, and the accrued
interest thereon.   If such were the case, appellant has no
just or legal cause of complaint in the present controversy.
The allegation that the city, wrongfully and without authority, paid out said moneys on warrants subsequently
issued and numbered against the same fund, is a mere conclusion of the pleader; it does not alter the logical deductions naturally flowing from other specific and controlling
allegations appearing in the complaint.   Phillips, Code
Pleading, § 346.   In the case of *New York Security &
Trust Co. v. Tacoma, supra,* the only question considered
by this court was that regarding the statute of limitations.
On examination of the record therein, we find that it fully
appeared that there had been sufficient money paid into the
special fund to satisfy all warrants issued prior to the one
held by respondent company, in the regular order in which
they were issued against the same fund; that the money

collected and paid by the city of Tacoma on the warrants issued subsequently to the one owned by such respondent, was properly and legally applicable to the payment of its warrant. In this case this fact does not appear.

The judgment of the lower court is clearly right, and must therefore be affirmed.

[No. 4924. Decided September 21, 1904.]

WASHINGTON STATE BANK OF ELLENSBURG, *Respondent*, v. GEORGE E. DICKSON *et al.*, *Appellants.*[1]

SPECIFIC PERFORMANCE—AGREEMENT TO CONVEY LAND—DEFENSES —TITLE OF DEFENDANT—EVIDENCE—SUFFICIENCY.   In an action to compel the specific performance of an agreement to convey an undivided half interest in certain real estate, the defendant refusing to convey on the claim that he owned only a one-fourth interest, there is sufficient evidence to warrant a finding that he was the owner of a one-half interest, where it appears that originally the property was purchased at receiver's sale on behalf of the defendant and three others, each to own a one-fourth interest, that two of the other purchasers failed to pay their shares, and the defendant and one other, in whose name the deed was taken, jointly advanced the payments, leased the property as joint owners, and represented to the plaintiff that the defendant owned a one-half interest, by which representations plaintiff was induced to enter into the contract.

SAME—CORPORATION AS PURCHASER—DEFENSE THAT OFFICER WAS NOT AUTHORIZED TO PURCHASE.   In an action by a banking corporation to compel the specific performance of a contract to convey land, there is sufficient evidence that the contract was authorized by the plaintiff where it appears that it was made by its cashier under directions of the trustees, and that the corporation assumed the burdens of the contract by assuming ownership and paying the installment of the price, and subsequently the trustees by a formal order duly ratified all of the acts.

SAME—SALE OF COMMUNITY PROPERTY—ACTS OF HUSBAND RATIFIED BY WIFE.   A specific performance of a contract to convey

[1]Reported in 77 Pac. 1067.

41-35 WASH.

community property, made by the husband, may be decreed, although not signed by the wife, where she was informed of the sale, gave full consent thereto, and joined in the execution of a deed prepared to consummate the sale.

Appeal from a judgment of the superior court for Kittitas county, Rudkin, J., entered April 30, 1903, upon findings in favor of the plaintiff after a trial on the merits before the court without a jury, in an action for the specific performance of a contract to convey real property.   Affirmed.

Kauffman & Frost and *Eugene E. Wager,* for appellants.

Graves & Englehart, for respondent.

FULLERTON, C. J.—The respondent, plaintiff below, brought this action against the appellants to compel them to convey to it an undivided one-half interest in certain real property situated in the city of Ellensburg. The property was known as "The Snipes bank building." The facts out of which the controversy arises are, in substance, these: On November 4, 1889, the property belonged to the estate of Ben. E. Snipes & Company, an insolvent copartnership, which was then in the hands of a receiver appointed by the superior court of Kittitas county. The property had theretofore been ordered sold by the superior court, and the receiver had advertised it for sale—the sale to take place on the day above named. In anticipation of the sale, the appellants George E. Dickson and Frank N. McCandless, together with one E. E. Wager and one C. V. Warner, entered into an agreement for the purchase of the property. While the terms of the agreement are not very clear, it seems that Dickson was to bid the property in at the sale in his own name, and that each of the others was to have a one-fourth interest therein on the payment of

one-fourth of the purchase price. Pursuant to the agreement, Dickson bid on the property at the sale under the
title of "G. E. Dickson, Agent," and the same was struck
off to him for the sum of $10,350. The sale was confirmed
by the court on the 24th of November, at which time the
court made an order directing the receiver to issue a deed
to the property to "G. E. Dickson, trustee." The deed
was made by the receiver in due time, but was held by him
without delivery, pending the payment of the purchase
price, for a period of nearly three years thereafter, the
final payment being made and the deed delivered to Dickson after this controversy arose. Such portion of the purchase price of the property as was paid at the time of the
sale was paid by Dickson and McCandless, the former
paying $2,000 and the latter $2,707.26. Neither Wager
nor Warner paid any part of the purchase price, and they
subsequently withdrew from the agreement, with the consent of, or at least without objection on the part of, the
other parties. Dickson and McCandless continued thereafter to claim the property in equal shares, leasing the
same to the respondent, after its incorporation in 1902, by
a joint lease executed by themselves and their wives. On
September 25, 1902, one C. W. Johnsone, acting on behalf
of the respondent and for its benefit, entered into an agreement with McCandless for the purchase of his undivided
half interest in the property. The purchase price agreed
upon was $6,750, of which $1,000 was paid at the time,
and the balance agreed to be paid on the delivery of a
deed to the premises, showing perfect title, which was not
to be delivered later than October 5, 1902. At the time
the agreement was entered into, a memorandum thereof
was made by McCandless and delivered to Johnsone, to
the following effect:

"Ellensburg, Wash., Sept. 25, 1902.

"Received of C. W. Johnsone One Thousand Dollars ($1,000) part payment on one undivided one-half interest in and to the bank building known as "The Snipes bank building," situated on the corner of Pearl and Fourth streets, in Ellensburg, Wash.   The full purchase price of said one undivided half interest being $6,750, the remaining $5,750 to be paid by said C. W. Johnsone to Frank N. McCandless or order, on delivery to said C. W. Johnsone or order, of a good and sufficient deed of warranty, showing perfect title to said property.   Said deed to be executed and delivered by not later than October 5, 1902. (Signed)   Frank N. McCandless."

Some months later the appellants McCandless and wife executed a deed to the respondent for an undivided one-half interest in the property, but, pending the proceedings had to procure the delivery of the deed from the receiver to Dickson, the appellant Frank N. McCandless refused to proceed further with the matter, and announced that he would not deliver the deed he and his wife had executed, or permit a conveyance of his interests in the property to be made to the respondent by the holder of the legal title.   Dickson, also, pending the negotiations, refused to recognize the claim of McCandless to a one-half interest in the property, claiming that McCandless had at most nothing more than a one-fourth interest therein.

The respondent thereupon instituted this action.   In its complaint it set up, substantially, the foregoing facts, and prayed that it be declared to be the owner of an undivided one-half interest in the property in question, and that the appellants be compelled to convey such interest to it.   To the complaint the appellants answered separately; such answers consisting of a denial of the allegations of the complaint, and a separate defense to the effect that the contract was not enforceable because of the statute of

frauds. The court adjudged the respondent to have a
valid contract for the conveyance to it of an undivided
one-half interest in the property, and entered a decree accordingly. The parties appealed separately, and filed
separate briefs; the questions suggested, however, are in
the main the same, and will be discusssed without reference to the party raising the question.

It is first contended that the court erred in finding that
the appellants McCandless had an undivided one-half interest in the property in question, but the evidence supporting
the finding, it seems to us, does not leave the question in
doubt. It is true, Dickson testified that the original agreement for the purchase of the property, entered into by the
four persons above named, by which each was to acquire
only a quarter interest in the property, was to become
effective only in case the property was purchased for
$8,000 or less, and that it was to belong to a Mr. Treman,
if it cost more than that sum, yet this statement is not
borne out by any of the other parties to the contract, and
one of them testified that he had never before heard of it.
Against this are his admissions, shown by unimpeached
witnesses, made prior to the commencement of this action
and when it was evidently not in contemplation, to the
effect that McCandless did have an undivided one-half
interest in it. In the lease of the property made to the
respondent, as we stated before, both Dickson and Mc-
Candless joined, as if equal owners, and it was then assumed by all of the parties that they owned equal interests.
Moreover, it was because of these statements on the part
of Dickson and McCandless that the respondents were induced to enter into the contract for the purchase of Mc-
Candless' interest, and good faith would hardly permit
them now to successfully deny that he had such an interest.

It is next said that the respondent failed to show that
Johnsone was authorized to make a contract in its behalf,
for the purchase of the property, at the time he contracted
for the interest of the McCandless.' The evidence on this
point shows, that the respondent was a banking concern,
and that Johnsone was its cashier; that the trustees of the
corporation, although they had made no formal order to
that effect which was spread upon the minutes of their
meetings, had directed Johnsone to procure the property
for the use of the bank, and that he was acting pursuant
to such directions when he made the contract with McCandless; and that the bank at once took the benefits and assumed the burdens of the contract, by assuming ownership
of the interest acquired by the contract, and by paying the
installment of the purchase price.   Moreover, it was further shown that the board of trustees, by a formal order
which was duly recorded in their minutes, subsequently
ratified all of the acts of the cashier, had in the matter pursuant to their informal directions.   The formal ratification was had, it is true, after the appellants had repudiated
the contract, and after the commencement of this action,
but we think it was, nevertheless, when taken in connection
with what had preceded it, sufficient to show that the contract was the contract of the bank.   Unauthorized acts of
a person purporting to act on behalf of a corporation become binding upon the corporation whenever they are duly
ratified by it.   Such a ratification is equivalent to a precedent authorization, and cures any defect in the original
appointment.   In other words, it makes the acts of the
purported agent the acts of the corporation from the beginning.   10 Cyc. 1083, D, and cases cited.   This being
true, the bank could, of course, maintain this action.

Lastly, it is said that the interest of Frank N. McCandless acquired in the property by his purchase, was the com-

munity property of himself and wife, and that the contract sought to be enforced is void because it was not signed by the wife. But it is not the rule in this state that a contract for the sale of community real property must be signed by the wife in order to be binding upon her. We have held it enough if the contract, when made by the husband, had the sanction and approval of the wife, or if it was subsequently ratified by her. *Mudgett v. Clay,* 5 Wash. 103, 31 Pac. 424; *Konnerup v. Frandsen,* 8 Wash. 551, 36 Pac. 493; *Payne v. Still,* 10 Wash. 433, 38 Pac. 994; *Boston Clothing Co. v. Solberg,* 28 Wash. 262, 68 Pac. 715. Here there was both a previous authorization and a subsequent ratification. McCandless himself testified that he had talked the matter over with his wife prior to entering into the contract, and that it was entered into with her knowledge and full consent; and it will be remembered that she joined with her husband in a deed of the premises to the respondent. This was sufficient to bind her interest, under the authorities above cited.

The judgment is affirmed.

MOUNT, DUNBAR, and ANDERS, JJ., concur.

[No. 4902. Decided September 21, 1904.]

OUDIN & BERGMAN FIRE CLAY MINING AND MANUFACTURING COMPANY, *Appellant,* v. GEORGE E. COLE, RECEIVER, *Respondent.*[1]

RECEIVERS—ALLOWANCE FOR ATTORNEYS' FEES. An allowance of $150 for services of a receiver's attorney is sustained by the evidence, where they extended over a considerable period, during which the receiver constantly sought advice and, from an examination of the record, the allowance seems reasonable.

[1]Reported in 77 Pac. 1066.

SAME—ALLOWANCE TO MANAGER. Upon closing up a receivership an allowance of five dollars per day agreed to be paid to an expert brick and pottery manufacturer, as superintendent of the works, was proper, where it appears that his employment was justified by the increased production under his supervision, and that high wages were necessary.

Appeal from an order of the superior court of Spokane county, Kennan, J., entered June 6, 1903, allowing attorney's fees and other disbursements, after a hearing upon a receiver's final account. Affirmed.

W. J. Thayer, for appellant.

P. F. Quinn, for respondent.

PER CURIAM.—In the year 1900 Martin L. Bergman and others, as plaintiffs, began an action against Charles P. Oudin and others, as defendants, and asked, among other things, for the appointment of a receiver over the business and property of the appellant, a corporation. Pursuant to the request the court appointed as such receiver one A. P. Curry, who served until his death, which occurred about June 1st, 1901. On June 10, following, the respondent, Geo. E. Cole, was appointed to succeed him. Cole acted as receiver from that date until March 3, 1903, when he was discharged by the court, after the termination of the action between Bergman and Oudin above mentioned. In his final account as such receiver he showed that he had employed Bergman from about May 15, 1902, until the close of the receivership, as a sort of general manager over the work of manufacturing pottery, at a salary of $5 per day. This item the court allowed at the hearing. The court also allowed the receiver, for his services as such, the sum of $1,000; and for his attorney, the sum of $150. Exceptions were taken to the allowance of the items allowed Bergman and the attorney, which exceptions the court overruled, after a hearing had thereon. This appeal is from the order of allowance.

The first contention of the appellant is that the receiver maintained himself in office by a corrupt agreement with Bergman. It contends that the receiver employed Bergman at an exorbitant salary, in order to induce him not to settle his differences with Oudin so that the receivership, and his consequent appointment as receiver, might be prolonged indefinitely, and, for that reason, neither he nor Bergman ought to be allowed anything for their services. A further objection to the account of Bergman is that it is at least double the amount usually paid for like services. The objection to the claim of the attorney was that there was no evidence that he had performed any service.

Taking up the objections in the reverse order from that above stated, it appears that it was stipulated that the court should fix the amount to be allowed the attorney, without calling expert evidence as to the value of the services rendered; that the attorney thereupon made a general statement of the services he had rendered, and the court allowed the amount he claimed. It is true, this statement did not go into particulars, but the record of the receiver's doings was before the court, and was a proper matter to be examined in connection with the statement of the attorney. When these are examined, the allowance does not seem unreasonable. The services extended over a considerable period of time, and the receiver was in constant need of, and as constantly sought, the advice of his counsel.

The allowance to Bergman is supported by the receiver's statement to the effect that Bergman was an expert in the line of work that he was required to perform, and that the increased production of the plant when under his supervision more than justified his employment at the wages allowed him. The business in which the corporation was engaged, that of manufacturing pottery, required a man as manager who was skilled in the business. Such men, the receiver states, were not plentiful, and the necessities of the occasion required the payment of high wages. On the whole record we think the court properly allowed this item.

On the question whether or not there was a corrupt agreement between the receiver and Bergman, we are content also to accept the conclusion of the trial court. While the evidence on the question was conflicting, we cannot say, after a careful perusal of the record, that the trial court did not decide in favor of its preponderance.

The judgment should be affirmed, and it is so ordered.

[No. 4855. Decided September 21, 1904.]

CHARLES JAMES, *Respondent*, v. LE ROY JAMES, *Appellant*.[1]

APPEAL—DECISION. Upon a trial *de novo* on appeal, the judgment of the lower court may be sustained on other grounds than those adopted by the trial judge.

ADOPTION—REQUISITES—RECORDING AGREEMENT UNDER LAWS OF FOREIGN STATE—DESCENT AND DISTRIBUTION. An adoption in the state of Iowa by a written agreement which is not recorded, as required by the laws of that state, is invalid under the decisions in that state, and such an agreement of adoption, unaccompanied by due proof of recording in Iowa, is insufficient to show any interest in real estate under the law of descent and distribution.

EVIDENCE—RECORDING—CERTIFICATE OF OFFICER—FOREIGN RECORD. A certificate of the official keeper of a record in another state endorsed upon the back of an instrument required to be recorded in such state, is not sufficient to prove the fact of the recording of such instrument.

Appeal from a judgment of the superior court for Spokane county, Richardson, J., entered July 9, 1903, upon findings in favor of the plaintiff, after a trial on the merits

[1]Reported in 77 Pac. 1080.

before the court without a jury, in an action for partition. Affirmed.

Hartson & Holloway, for appellant.

Nash & Nash and *James Dawson*, for respondent.

FULLERTON, C. J.—This is an action for partition of real property. In his complaint the respondent, who was plaintiff below, alleges that he is the owner in fee of an undivided seven-tenths interest in the east half of the southwest quarter, and lots 3 and 4, of section 30, in township 24 north, of range 44 east, of the Willamette Meridian; that Bertha James, Mabel E. James, and Walter W. James, are the owners in fee of the remaining three-tenths interest, and that it is to the best interest of all of said owners that the property be partitioned between them. He then alleges that the appellant, Le Roy James, claims some interest in the property as the heir at law of Margaret James, the deceased wife of the plaintiff, who died leaving a community interest therein, but that "said Le Roy James is in no way related . . . to Margaret James, deceased, . . . and has no right, title, or interest of any name or nature in or to the property . . ." The prayer of the complaint was that the defendant Le Roy James be adjudged to be without interest in the property, and that it be partitioned between the plaintiff and defendants other than Le Roy James.

To the complaint Le Roy James answered, setting up that he had been adopted by the plaintiff and his wife, in the state of Iowa, in the month of March, 1888, by virtue of which he became an heir at law of Margaret James, since deceased. The answer was put in issue by a reply. On the issues thus made, a trial was had before the court without a jury, and resulted in a finding and judgment to the effect that the appellant had no interest in the property described in the complaint, and was not entitled to share in its partition.

The trial court rested its decision on a judgment rendered in the superior court of Spokane county, in an action in which the respondent was plaintiff and the appellant was one of the defendants, wherein the title to the property was quieted in the respondent against any claim or interest of the appellant. The appellant attacks this judgment, we think successfully, but, as the action is one triable *de novo* in this court, the judgment can be rested on other grounds, if such can be found in the record. We think there is another such ground. The appellant failed to prove that he had any interest in the property sought to be partitioned. His right therein, if any, rested on the claim that he was adopted by the respondent and his then wife, Margaret, in the state of Iowa in 1888, but the proofs fail to show a valid adoption under the laws of that state.

The statute of Iowa in force at the time of the purported adoption, as shown by the record, provided that the act of adoption should be evidenced by an instrument in writing, signed by the parties consenting to the adoption, and the parties or party adopting the child, which instrument should state, among other things, the names of the parents of the child, if known, and should be acknowledged by all the parties thereto in the same manner as deeds affecting real estate are required to be acknowledged, and should be recorded in the recorder's office in the county where the person adopting resides. It was further provided, that upon the acknowledgment, execution and filing for record of such instrument, the rights, duties, and relations of the parties arose.

To prove the adoption in the case before us, the appellant introduced a written instrument, substantially com-

plying with the foregoing requisites of the statute (with
the exception that it did not state the name of one of the
parents of the child, nor that this parent's name was unknown), but there was no proof that it was recorded in
the recorder's office of the county where the persons adopting the child resided. That the failure to record the instrument of adoption is fatal to the legality of the proceedings has been repeatedly held by the supreme court of
Iowa, while construing the very statute invoked by the appellant here. In *Tyler v. Reynolds,* 53 Iowa 146, 4 N. W.
902, this language was used:

"The right of inheritance is purely a statutory right,
and is, therefore, arbitrary, absolute and unconditional.
Nevertheless the provisions of the statute must prevail,
although to do so in some instances is inconsistent with
our views as to what constitutes natural rights or justice
and equity. Therefore, a child by adoption cannot inherit
from the parent by adoption unless the act of adoption has
been done in strict accord with the statute. The statutory
conditions and terms are that the written instrument must
be executed, signed, acknowledged and filed for record.
When this is done the act is complete. If the named requisites are not done, then the act is not complete, and the
child cannot inherit from the parent by adoption.

"The filing for record is just as important in a statutory
sense as the execution or acknowledgment; one may be dispensed with as well as the other, for the right depends
solely on the statute. There is no room for construction
unless we eliminate words from the written law, and this
we are not authorized to do. . . . The statute cannot be
regarded as directory, because a right is thereby declared
which did not previously exist. The descent of property
was thereby changed; to be done, however, only upon a
compliance with the terms and conditions declared. . .
In the case at bar the instrument was incomplete until filed
for record between the parties. No rights were acquired
until this was done, and neither was bound until then.
Before this was done Philo Reynolds died, and no one had

the power and authority to do what he failed to do, or to do what was required to be done to render the instrument valid or obligatory. Upon his death his natural heirs inherited; their rights became vested, and could not be prejudiced by filing the instrument for record after that time."

To the same effect are: *Gill v. Sullivan*, 55 Iowa, 341, 7 N W. 586; *Shearer v. Weaver*, 56 Iowa 578, 9 N. W. 907; and *McCollister v. Yard*, 90 Iowa 621, 57 N. W. 447.

What effect an omission such as we have above pointed out would have upon the legality of the proceedings, the highest court of the state seems not to have determined directly. It can be inferred, however, from what has been said by it in passing upon the question of the necessity of recording the instrument, that it would regard this as such an essential of the statute as to render its omission fatal. But, without determining this, we are compelled to hold the attempted adoption invalid because the instrument of adoption was not recorded. The adoption to be valid here must be valid in Iowa, and, as the highest court of that state has held that attempts similar to this are invalid under its laws, it must follow that this attempt is invalid also.

It may be argued that the endorsement on the back of the instrument was *prima facie* evidence that it was recorded, under the rule of the cases of *Garneau v. Port Blakely Mill Co.*, 8 Wash. 467, 36 Pac. 463, and *Peters v. Gay*, 9 Wash. 383, 37 Pac. 325; but the recital endorsed on this instrument is not a formal certificate over the hand and seal of the officer, as were the certificates in the cases cited; it is more in the nature of that found in *Jewett v. Darlington*, 1 Wash. Ter. 601, which was held not to be evidence of anything. Moreover, the certificate would not have been sufficient to prove the recording of the instrument had it been as full as the certificates mentioned in the cases from this state above cited. A record from a public office of a sister state is not admissible in evidence, on the mere certificate of the keeper of the record, over his hand and official seal. Only records from the public offices of this state, or of the United States, are so admissible. Records from public offices of sister states, other than courts, must be certified in accordance with the United States statutes, to be admissible in evidence in the courts of this state.

As we find no reversible error in the record, the judgment will stand affirmed.

MOUNT, DUNBAR, and ANDERS, JJ., concur.

[No. 4856. Decided September 21, 1904.]

CHARLES JAMES, *Respondent*, v. LE ROY JAMES, *Appellant*.[1]

APPEAL—NOTICE—SUFFICIENCY. A notice of appeal reciting that the party "had appealed," instead of that the party "appeals," as provided by Bal. Code, § 6503, is sufficient to effect the appeal, in view of Pierce's Code, § 1066, providing that no appeal shall be dismissed for defects in the notice.

APPEAL—BRIEFS—ASSIGNMENT OF ERRORS. An appeal will not be dismissed for failure to assign errors, where the only question presented is whether the complaint states a cause of action, and that is clearly stated in the brief.

PLEADINGS—DEMURRER—LEGAL CAPACITY TO SUE—ACTION TO QUIET TITLE—WAIVER OF DEFECT. In an action brought by a surviving husband to quiet his title to community real estate, in which it appears from the complaint that one of the defendants claims an interest as an heir of the deceased wife, in and to her undivided one-half of the estate, an objection that the other heirs and not the plaintiff are the persons interested, relates to the capacity of the plaintiff to sue, and is waived unless raised by special demurrer on that ground, a general demurrer not being sufficient.

[1]Reported in 77 Pac. 1082.

ADOPTION—VALIDITY—FALSE REPRESENTATIONS—LAWS OF FOREIGN STATE. An adoption of a child in the state of Iowa, induced by the false representations of the child's father that its mother was dead, does not render the adoption illegal, in the absence of proof of the laws of Iowa to that effect, since the rules in this state would then apply, and they do not so provide.

SAME—CONSENT OF THE MOTHER. Under the laws of this state the consent of the mother to the adoption of a child is necessary only when she is living with her husband or has the custody of the child, and a complaint alleging merely that an adoption was without the consent of the mother is, therefore, insufficient to show the invalidity of the adoption.

Appeal from a judgment of the superior court for Spokane county, Kennan, J., entered June 4, 1903, in favor of the plaintiff, upon overruling a demurrer to the complaint, in an action to quiet title. Reversed.

Hartson & Holloway, for appellant.

Nash & Nash, for respondent.

FULLERTON, C. J.—The respondent, as plaintiff in the court below, brought this action against Nathan O'Dell, Emma O'Dell, Margaret A. James, Le Roy James, Bertha James, Mabel E. James, and Walter W. James, as defendants, to quiet title in himself to certain real property situated in the county of Spokane. Le Roy James appeals from a judgment quieting title against his interests.

The respondent moves to dismiss this appeal, assigning as reasons therefor that the notice given is insufficient to effect an appeal, and that the opening brief contains no assignment of errors. That part of the notice to which objection is made is as follows: "You will please take notice that the defendant Le Roy James has appealed," etc., from the judgment entered. The argument is that a notice that a party "has appealed" from a judgment is not a notice that he "appeals" from that judgment, and hence there is no notice of appeal in the record. If the statute relating to the giving of the notice to appeal stood alone, doubtless the objection urged would be sound, inasmuch as that statute provides that a party desiring to appeal from a judgment or order of the superior court may serve on the prevailing party a written notice "that he appeals from such judgment or order." Bal. Code, § 6503. But the legislature later enacted that "no appeal shall be dismissed for any informality or defect in the notice of appeal, . . ." Laws 1899, p. 79; Pierce's Code, § 1066. And since then we have held that the words, "intends to appeal," "will appeal," or "give notice of their application to appeal," are equivalent to and have the same effect as, the more direct phraseology of the statute—that is, each will effect an appeal. *Ranahan v. Gibbons*, 23 Wash. 255, 62 Pac. 773; *In re Murphy's Estate*, 26 Wash. 222, 66 Pac. 424; *Brown v. Calloway*, 34 Wash. 175, 75 Pac. 630. And of course if the phrases above cited are sufficient to effect the appeal, the words "has appealed" will likewise perform the same office. Neither is the second objection well taken. The only question presented by the record or discussed in the brief is the question, does the complaint state facts sufficient to constitute a cause of action? and this is clearly stated in the brief. The fact that it was not formally assigned as the error relied upon, is not material.

In his complaint the respondent alleged, that he was the owner in fee of the land above mentioned; that he acquired the same under and by virtue of the homestead laws of the United States; that in 1888, the time he settled upon the same and filed his right of homestead, he was a married man; that his wife was then living with him, and that she continued to live with him and reside upon the land, until her death in February, 1891; that at the time of her

death she left surviving her, and as her heirs at law, Emma
O'Dell, Margaret A. James, Bertha James, Mabel E.
James, and Walter W. James, children of herself and the
respondent, some of whom were then and now are minors,
and that said children continued to reside with him upon
the land, from the time of their mother's death until he
proved up on the same and obtained a patent therefor from
the United States, in 1894; that Le Roy James, the appellant, is not the son of the respondent nor of his deceased
wife, but that his name was formerly Charles Le Roy Rumbaugh, and is no kin or relation to the respondent or his
deceased wife, but plaintiff alleges the facts to be in regard
to Le Roy James:

"That in the state of Iowa, in the county of Jasper, one
Newton Melville Rumbaugh, the father of said Charles
Le Roy Rumbaugh, herein called Le Roy James, represented to the plaintiff and his deceased wife Margaret, that
he was a widower and that the mother of said boy was dead
at the time aforesaid, to wit, in March, 1888, and requested
the said plaintiff and his said wife, now deceased, to adopt
the said Charles Le Roy Rumbaugh, and that the said
plaintiff and his said wife, relying upon the representations
of said Newton Melville Rumbaugh, that his wife, the
mother of said boy, was then dead, did adopt, under the
laws of the state of Iowa, the said Charles Le Roy Rumbaugh, under the name of Le Roy James, into his family,
but the said plaintiff alleges that in truth and in fact the
mother of said boy was not dead, as was represented by the
said father, Newton Melville Rumbaugh, but was still living, and plaintiff alleges that the whole adoption under
the said laws was illegal and was void and of no effect and
conferred no rights whatever upon the said boy in regard
to the property of the said plaintiff herein, and if plaintiff
had known that the said mother of said boy was living or
in existence, he would not have adopted said child as aforesaid. That in the fall of said year, 1888, during the month
of September, the said plaintiff, with his said wife and

children, left the state of Iowa and emigrated to the then
territory of Washington, bringing said Le Roy James with
them as a part of said family; and that in October of that
year he filed his homestead on said land in question, as
set forth in paragraph two of said complaint.

"Plaintiff further alleges that the said Le Roy James
continued to live in the family of said plaintiff until he became a wayward and at last incorrigible, and some time in
the month of October, 1893, upon an examination had by
the authorities of Spokane, he was committed to the state
reform school at Chehalis, Washington, as being an incorrigible boy, and he remained there for something like two
years in said institution for the reformation of wayward
boys, when the mother of said boy, who appeared to be
then living in Whatcom, Washington, appeared at said
state reform school, and demanded said Le Roy James,
claiming him as her son, and finally took him from said
reform school, and to her home in said Whatcom, Washington, where he was for a year or more. That said plaintiff alleges that he was entirely ignorant of her whereabouts and supposed that said boy had no mother and supposed that the representations of the father made at the
time of the adoption were true as therein stated. That
after the mother had taken charge and control of said boy,
as aforesaid, she informed the plaintiff of her identity as
the mother of said boy claiming the right and the custody
of him, and the said plaintiff then and there offered, and
did, relinquish all claim and right to the custody and control of said child, and plaintiff avers that he had had no
charge or control over the said boy since said time, and
avers that he has no right or claim to the said boy or the
custody of him. Plaintiff further alleges that he never
took any steps in the territory of Washington, or in the
state of Washington, to adopt said boy into his family
except in the state of Iowa, as aforesaid. Plaintiff further
alleges that the said adoption of the said boy in the state
of Iowa, as aforesaid, in consequence of the false and
fraudulent representations of the father of said boy in regard to the death of the said mother, was void under the
laws of the state of Iowa and that said boy acquired no

rights to property or otherwise by virtue of the said adoption, even in the state of Iowa. Plaintiff further alleges that said boy has no rights of property, either as the heir of plaintiff, or of his deceased wife in the state of Iowa, in the territory of Washington, or in the state of Washington. That the laws governing the adoption of children are not at all similar in the state of Iowa or the territory of Washington or state of Washington. That a different mode and a different tribunal is resorted to for adoption and even if the adoption of the said boy was in any way legal in the state of Iowa it has no force or effect in the territory of Washington, or the state of Washington."

The respondent further alleges that the defendants are claiming some right or interest in, or title to the property, but that they have no such right or interest, and he prays that his title to the premises be quieted. To the complaint the defendant Le Roy James filed a general demurrer, which the trial court overruled. He thereupon refused to plead further, and judgment was entered against him in accordance with the prayer of the complaint.

The appellant first contends that the allegations of the complaint, in reference to the manner title was acquired to the real property in question, show that the heirs at law of the deceased wife of the appellant have an interest in an undivided half of the property, under the rule of the case of *Ahern v. Ahern,* 31 Wash. 334, 71 Pac. 1023, and, as the respondent's interests are confined to the other undivided half, it is of no concern to him who claim to be heirs at law of the first. But this, it seems to us, is only another way of saying that the respondent has no legal capacity to sue, and to that objection it is a sufficient answer to say that appellant did not demur to the complaint on that ground. The demurrer filed, as we have said, was a general demurrer, one going to the sufficiency of the complaint to state a cause of action, and such a demurrer does not raise the question of the capacity of the plaintiff to maintain the action. The want of legal capacity to sue is made a special ground of demurrer by the statute, and, to raise it by demurrer, it must be pointed out specially.

The question then turns on the allegations concerning the adoption of the appellant. The respondent, it will be noticed, after alleging that he did adopt the appellant into his family under the laws of the state of Iowa, avers that such adoption was void and of no effect because of certain matters which he particularizes. But it seems to us that none of these could avoid the adoption proceedings. That the father of the boy, at the time of the adoption, made false statements concerning the death of the mother, or that the respondent would not have adopted the boy had he known that the mother was living, or that the boy afterwards became incorrigible and was sent to the reform school and was subsequently taken therefrom by his natural mother, or that the plaintiff did not subsequently, in the territory or state of Washington, take steps to adopt the boy, does not render the adoption had in Iowa illegal, in so far as we are informed as to the laws of that state. True, the appellant alleges in many places in his complaint that the adoption was void under the laws of Iowa, but this is only his conclusion from the facts alleged. He does not set out the laws of that state showing wherein they render the adoption void and of no effect, and this court must apply to the facts the rules of law of this state, and applying such rules we do not find the facts sufficient to avoid the adoption.

We have not overlooked the contention of the plaintiff to the effect that the consent of the mother is a prerequisite to a valid adoption under the laws of this state, and that the complaint sufficiently shows that there was no consent of the mother to the adoption of the appellant. But consent of the mother of a child to its adoption by another is only necessary when she is living with her husband, or has custody and control of her child; her consent is not necessary when she is living separate and apart from her husband, and the husband has the charge and control of the child. The complaint does not negative this condition, or show that the mother's consent was necessary.

As, under the laws of this state, an adopted child is the legal heir of his adopters to the same extent he would be if born to them in lawful wedlock, the appellant, under the facts shown by the complaint, is the lawful heir of the deceased wife of the appellant, and as such has an interest in the property in suit. *Ahern v. Ahern, supra.* The court therefor erred in overruling his demurrer to the complaint.

The judgment appealed from will be reversed, and the cause remanded, with instructions to sustain the demurrer to the complaint, with leave to the respondent to amend, if he so desires.

MOUNT, DUNBAR, and ANDERS, JJ., concur.

[No. 4982. Decided September 21, 1904.]

WOODMAN MATTHEWS, *Respondent,* v. BELFAST MANUFACTURING COMPANY, *Appellant.*[1]

EMINENT DOMAIN—WATERWAYS—LOGGING—CONDEMNING RIGHT TO USE STREAM FOR FLOATING LOGS. A private corporation which is not a boom company is not entitled to exercise the right of eminent domain against a lower riparian owner for the purpose of facilitating the floating of logs down a stream by means of dams and artificial freshets, which damage the lower proprietor and interfere with his use of the stream.

WATERS—NAVIGATION—FLOATING LOGS—NUISANCES — DAMS — ARTIFICIAL FRESHETS—INJUNCTION. The floating of logs down a

[1]Reported in 77 Pac. 1046.

stream by means of dams and artificial freshets at a time of the
year when it is not navigable in its natural state, is an abuse of
the right of navigation, for which an injunction will lie at the
suit of riparian owners injured thereby.

SAME—INJUNCTION—TERMS OF.   In such a case an injunction
is not too sweeping where it permits the defendant to use its
dam for lawful purposes.

SAME — DEFENSES — IMPROPER USE OF STREAM.   An action to
enjoin the defendant's abuse of the rights of navigation, by the
use of dams and the creation of artificial freshets in a logging
stream, will not be defeated by the fact that the plaintiff, also,
maintains a dam for the same purpose, where the evidence shows
that his use thereof is reasonable and proper, and his dam is not
a nuisance.

Appeal from a judgment of the superior court for Skagit
county, Joiner, J., entered July 17, 1903, upon findings
in favor of the plaintiff, after a trial on the merits before
the court without a jury, enjoining the obstruction and
unlawful use of a logging stream. Affirmed.

Million & Houser, for appellant.
Smith & Brawley and *Carr & Preston,* for respondent.

FULLERTON, C. J.—The appellant and respondent each
own timber lands in Skagit county, through which the east
fork of the Samish river flows; the lands of the appellant
being higher up the stream than those of the respondent,
although the lands abut upon each other. The Samish
river is an unmeandered stream, having an average width
between banks of some fifty feet, and during the wet season
of the year is capable of floating such mill timber as grows
upon its banks, and in its immediate vicinity. In the dry
season it is not navigable without artificial aids, having at
such time a depth of less than two feet in many places. The
respondent, some years prior to the commencement of this
action, had been engaged in logging on his own premises,

and had constructed a dam across the river on his own lands some distance below the lands of the appellant. This dam he has kept up ever since, maintaining therein, as he says, suitable gates through which logs pass unobstructed during the time of the year when the stream is high enough to float them.

In the summer of 1903, the appellant began logging off of its own lands. To facilitate the work it constructed a dam across the river about one and one-half miles above the respondent's dam. This dam it used, not only to retain logs until they were ready to be sent down the river, but, also, to create a storage basin for water, by means of which it could cause splashes, or artificial freshets, in the stream, and thus drive logs down the same after it became too shallow to float them in its natural state. The appellant operated in this manner: It would put into the bed of the river as many logs as could be readily driven; then it would open the gates of its own dam, and drive the logs down the stream as far as the dam of the respondent; from there, by repeated splashes from both dams, it would drive them to the deep waters of Bellingham Bay, into which the Samish river flows. In these operations the appellant found it necessary to use the respondent's dam, and it took possession of the same against the consent, and over the protest, of the respondent, and used it as if it were its own property. The appellant, also without the consent and against the will of the respondent, made such use of the respondent's land bordering the stream as it found necessary and convenient in order to drive its logs. The artificial freshets or splashes, created by means of the dams, drove the logs down the stream in lots or jams, which tore down and washed away the river's banks, forming a river bed out of what was before tillable land.

The respondent instituted this action to enjoin the appellant from using his property in the manner stated, and from floating logs down the stream across his property by means of artificial freshets and splashes, alleging, in his complaint, substantially the foregoing facts.

To the complaint the appellant answered, denying all its material allegations, and, by way of cross-complaint, alleged that it had gone to great expense to prepare for logging its premises, and that, if stopped by the court, would suffer irreparable injury; further alleging that it had instituted condemnation proceedings against respondent, for the purpose of acquiring the right to use the stream by means of splash dams therein, where necessary. It also alleged that the dam of respondent was an obstruction to navigation in the stream, and therefore a nuisance. It prayed for relief appropriate to matters set up in its answer. The new matter in the answer was put in issue by a reply, and a trial had before the court, resulting in a permanent injunction against the appellant, enjoining it from operating either of the splash dams mentioned, and from in any manner interfering with the possession or use of the respondent's land. There was a claim for damages made by the respondent for injuries already accrued, but the amount of the damages, if any, the court expressly refused to find, leaving the question as to the amount open to a determination by a jury, in an action to be brought for that purpose. This appeal is from that judgment.

The first contention on the part of the appellant, namely, that it has the right to condemn a right of way along the stream over the respondent's land for a logging way, is determined against it by the case of *Healy Lumber Co. v. Morris*, 33 Wash. 490, 74 Pac. 681. It was there held that the

statute attempting to confer upon the owner of timber lands
the power to condemn a right of way for a logging road
and lumbering purposes was in contravention of the state
constitution, and therefore void. As there is no such right
independent of the constitution and statute, it is plain that
the appellant's action to condemn can avail it nothing, and
its plea that it has brought such an action does not require
the court to await its result before restraining it from
making an unlawful use of the respondent's property. It
is true, this court has upheld the statute relating to the
organization of boom companies, which had for its object
the improvement of streams, such as the one in question,
so as to make them floatable for logs at all seasons of the
year, but that statute does not aid the appellant. The
appellant is not organized as a boom company. It does
not purpose improving the stream for the use of the public,
and engaging in the business of transporting logs down it
for the public, but seeks to acquire the right for its own private benefit, to the exclusion of every one else. This it
cannot do by the exercise of the right of eminent domain.
It has no power to exercise such a right. *Healy Lumber
Co. v. Morris, supra.*

The next contention is that the court erred in enjoining
the appellant from floating logs down the stream by means
of artificial freshets and splashes. The argument is that
the stream is a navigable one, and that it has the right to
use it for the purpose of floating logs, and is liable only
for a misuse or abuse of the privilege, and that the evidence
fails to show that there was any abuse or misuse in the
present case. The stream in question is undoubtedly navigable for floating logs for a part of the year, and during
that time the appellant, as well as others, may use it for
that purpose. But that is not the case before us. The

appellant was not attempting to float logs during the navigable season of the year, but was attempting to do so when the stream, in its natural state, would not float them. It sought to remedy this by creating unnatural conditions—by the creation of artificial freshets—which conditions damaged and destroyed the respondent's property. This was an abuse of the right of navigation, and for that an injunction would properly lie. *Watkinson v. McCoy*, 23 Wash. 372, 63 Pac. 245; *Monroe Mill Co. v. Menzel, ante,* p. 487.

It is next said that the injunction is too sweeping, in that it prohibits the appellant from operating its dam for any purpose, but a reading of the context of the judgment clearly shows that all that was meant was that the appellant should not operate it to float logs down the stream by means of artificial freshets and splashes, and not that it could not use it for such other purposes as it might find convenient in the conduct of its business.

It is further contended that the respondent is not entitled to relief because his dam is an obstruction to navigation, and he ought not to be allowed to complain of the appellant so long as he was making a misuse of the stream. But if this were a sufficient reason for denying the respondent the right to relief, we fail to find that the contention is supported by the evidence. An officer of the appellant did testify that logs could not be floated down the stream without making use of the respondent's dam, but he was speaking of floating logs by means of freshets and splashes, and not of floating when the stream would convey them in its natural state. On the other hand, the respondent testified that his dam did not obstruct the river, that he had constructed in it gates through which logs and other timber products could pass whenever the stream was capable of floating them. We think, therefore, that the evidence was insufficient to warrant the court in declaring the dam a nuisance, and ordering its removal. In order to successfully market logs by the use of a stream of this character, dams and booms are necessary; in fact, such streams can hardly be used for navigating logs without them. Being necessary, their use is lawful when reasonably exercised, and it is only when the right is misused or abused that other navigators can complain of them as obstructions. We do not wish, however, to be understood as foreclosing the appellant's right to complain, should the dam prove to be an obstruction, when an actual test under normal conditions is made. Should it then prove to be a nuisance, the appellant, or any one injured by it, may have it corrected by an action brought for that purpose.

As we find no substantial error in the record, the judgment appealed from will stand affirmed.

MOUNT, DUNBAR, AND ANDERS, JJ., concur.

[No. 4922. Decided September 21, 1904.]

A. R. BYRKETT et al., Appellants, v. JAMES E. GARDNER, Respondent.[1]

FORCIBLE ENTRY AND DETAINER—NOTICE TO QUIT—FARMING LEASE—DEFAULT IN PERFORMANCE—SPECIFYING CONDITIONS BROKEN. Where a farm lease provided that the land should be farmed in a certain specified manner, the lease containing many stipulations with reference to the lessee's performance, a notice to quit, requiring in the alternative the performance of the conditions and covenants of the lease or a surrender of the premises, which recites many of the covenants and states that the tenant has failed to keep "each and all" of the covenants mentioned, is too indefinite and uncertain to support an action of forcible entry and detainer, under Bal. Code § 5527, subd. 4, since a notice

[1]Reported in 77 Pac. 1048.

thereunder must specify with particularity the default so as to
give the tenant an opportunity to exercise his right of choice.

SAME.   Where the landlord is complaining that the general
performance is not up to the standard of excellence called for by
the covenant to farm in a husbandlike manner, such a notice reciting that fact generally is not sufficient to start the machinery
of the statute of forcible entry and detainer.

SAME—RENT DUE.   Such a notice is not sufficient as showing
nonpayment of rent, under Bal. Code, § 5527, subd. 3, where there
is the same indefiniteness with reference to the rent that is due,
and there is no chance for the lessee to save the forfeiture by
payment within ten days.

SAME—WASTE.   Such a notice does not show waste, within
subd. 5, of the same section, by the mere failure to farm the
lands in a husbandlike manner or keep fences in repair, since
waste is an act of destruction by the tenant.

Appeal from a judgment of the superior court for Klickitat county, A. L. Miller, J., entered August 19, 1903, upon
sustaining a demurrer to the complaint, dismissing an
action of forcible entry and detainer. Affirmed.

Huntington & Wilson, for appellants.

A. A. Jayne and *Bennett & Sinnott,* for respondent.

FULLERTON, C. J.—In January, 1901, the appellants
leased to the respondent a portion of their ranch situated in
Klickitat county, for a term of four years, commencing on
the 1st day of February, 1901. Among the conditions of
the lease, to be kept and performed on the part of the
respondent, were the following:

"1st.   To cultivate all of said premises in a good and
husbandlike manner, in such crops, fruits, and vegetables
as may be mutually agreed upon. 2nd.   To provide feed
for, feed, milk, and care for in all respects all the milk
cows, and to provide feed for, feed, and care for all the
stock now on said ranch and the increase thereof and at the
expiration of the first year of this lease, return them to the
parties of the first part, in good condition. To put in

repair and keep in repair all tools, farming implements,
machinery, and dairy supplies and at the expiration of the
first year of this lease return them to the parties of the first
part in good condition, natural wear excepted. To make
butter from said cows and to deliver to the parties of the
first part one-half thereof wrapped in two pound rolls with
the brand paper of said ranch. To deliver in the barns
upon said ranch or other buildings thereon one-half of all
crops grown upon said premises over and above that necessary for feed for the stock thereon, baled when hay, and in
proper packages for shipment. When crops raised on the
premises included in the one year term of this lease require
sacks for shipping each party is to furnish his own one-half
of said sacks. To repair all fences and build all new ones
necessary for the protection of crops on said premises, out
of materials provided by parties of the first part. To haul
out and distribute all manure upon said ranch. To furnish
one-half the labor for laying drain pipes, tiles, etc., for
drainage and irrigation of lands, included in the four years
term of this lease. To furnish one-half the hogs kept upon
said premises, provide feed for them, butcher and market
them and pay the first parties one-half of the price they
bring. To take said cattle to Trout Lake, about May 1st,
and keep them there until about October 1st. 3rd. To
plant, cultivate, pick, pack, box, and ship all berries raised
upon said premises and after deducting the cost of the
boxes and of picking, and packing, to divide the residue
of the proceeds of the sale thereof equally with the first
named parties. 4th. To plant, cultivate, pick, pack, box,
crate, or otherwise provide for shipment, and ship all
melons, vegetables, etc., grown upon the lands covered by
the four years term of this lease, and pay over to the parties
of the first part one-third of the gross proceeds of the sale
thereof. 5th. To at the earliest date possible, set out the
ground heretofore farmed to strawberries, in strawberries,
and also so much of the peach orchard as may be pulled out
for that purpose, and to keep all of said lands and the lands
now set to strawberries, in strawberries during the continuance of this lease. To replant said lands in strawber-

ries at the expiration of three years of life and bearing. To can, jelly, jam or make into wine all berries and vegetables when it is found advantageous to both parties hereto."

On the 21st day of May, 1903, the lessors served on the lessee a notice which after reciting the execution of the lease above mentioned proceeded as follows:

"To James E. Gardner; In and by the lease above mentioned, you covenanted and agreed, among other things: 'To cultivate all of said premises in a good and husbandlike manner in such crops, fruits, and vegetables as may be mutually agreed upon. To repair all fences and build all new ones necessary for the protection of crops on said premises, out of material provided by the parties of the first part. To plant, cultivate, pick, pack, box, and ship all berries raised upon said premises, and after deducting the cost of the boxes and of picking and packing, to divide the residue of the proceeds of the sale thereof equally with the first named parties. To plant, cultivate, pick, pack, box, crate, or otherwise provide for shipment and ship all melons, vegetables, etc., grown upon the lands covered by the four years term of this lease and pay over to the parties of the first part one-third of the gross proceeds of the sale thereof. To at the earliest date possible set out the ground heretofore farmed to strawberries, in strawberries, and also so much of the peach orchard as may be pulled out for that purpose, and to keep all of said lands and the lands now set to strawberries in strawberries during the continuance of this lease. To replant said lands in strawberries at the expiration of three years of life and bearing. That in case any controversies arise as to the meaning of this lease, or as to the faithful performance thereof by either party, S. C. Ziegler shall be the arbitrator between us to settle said controversy, whose decision shall be final.'

"Immediately upon the execution of said lease, it was mutually agreed by you and by us, the said A. R. Byrkett and Clara Byrkett, that you should cultivate to melons and other vegetables all of said land so leased for the term of four years, except such as had been and were to be cultivated to strawberries and blackberries. Subsequently to the execution of the written agreement of lease, it was further mutually agreed by you and by us, the said A. R. Byrkett and Clara Byrkett, that the proceeds of all crops sold outside of the state of Washington, and which were raised upon said lands leased to you for the term of four years, as aforesaid, should be deposited in the Bank of Butler & Company of Hood River, Oregon, to the credit of Byrkett and Gardner. You are hereby notified that we, the said A. R. Byrkett and Clara Byrkett, are now and at all times since the execution of said lease have been prepared, ready, and willing to provide, and have provided material for the fences necessary for the protection of crops grown upon said leased premises. You have failed to keep and perform each and all of the covenants and agreements hereinbefore mentioned. You are hereby notified to keep and perform each and all of the agreements and covenants contained in said written lease and said subsequent agreements hereinbefore specifically mentioned, or surrender the possession of said property. And if you fail so to keep and perform said covenants and agreements or surrender possession of said premises within ten days after the service of this notice upon you, we, the said A. R. Byrkett and Clara Byrkett will commence an action against you for the unlawful detainer of said premises."

Later on, the precise date not being shown by the transcript, the appellants began an action of unlawful detainer. In their complaint, for a first cause of action, they set forth the lease above mentioned and alleged that the respondent had failed to keep and perform its conditions, specifying certain acts and omissions of the respondent as constituting breaches thereof. They further alleged the service of the notice above recited on the respondent, his failure to comply with the terms of the lease after such notice, and his failure to quit and surrender possession of the premises within ten days from the date of such service. For a second cause of action, the appellants repeated the

allegations of their first cause, and added an allegation as
to the rental value of the premises, alleging that the rental
value thereof was two thousand dollars per annum. The
demand of the complaint was for a forfeiture of the lease,
the restitution of the premises to the appellants, and for
the rental value of the premises from February 1, 1901, at
the rate of two thousand dollars per annum.

The respondent interposed a general demurrer to each of
the causes of action set out in the complaint, which the
trial court sustained. The appellants thereupon refused
to plead further, whereupon the court entered a judgment
dismissing their action. This appeal is from that judgment.

The statute of forcible entry and detainer (§ 5527, Bal.
Code) provides that a tenant of real property is guilty of
unlawful detainer:

"(3). When he continues in possession in person or by
subtenant after a default in the payment of any rent and
after a notice in writing requiring in the alternative the
payment of the rent or the surrender of the detained premises, served (in manner hereafter in this chapter provided)
in behalf of the person entitled to the rent upon the person owing the same, shall have remained uncomplied with
for the period of three days after service thereof. Such
notice may be served at any time after the rent becomes
due; or

"(4). When he continues in possession in person or by
subtenant after a neglect or failure to keep or perform any
other condition or covenant of the lease or agreement under
which the property is held, including any covenant not to
assign or sublet, than one for the payment of rent, and after
notice in writing requiring in the alternative the performance of such condition or covenant or the surrender
of the property, served (in the manner provided in this
chapter) upon him, and if there be a subtenant in actual
possession of the premises, also upon such subtenant, shall
remain uncomplied with for ten days after service thereof.

Within ten days after the service of such notice the tenant, or any subtenant in actual occupation of the premises, or any mortagee of the term, or other person interested in its continuance, may perform such condition or covenant, and thereby save the lease from such forfeiture; or

"(5). When he commits or permits waste upon the demised premises, or when he sets up or carries on therein or thereon any unlawful business, or when he erects, suffers, permits, or maintains on or about said premises any nuisance, and remains in possession after service (in manner in this chapter provided) of three days' notice to quit upon him."

When the nature of the case is considered, it is at once apparent that, in so far as the action is founded on the fourth subdivision of the statute quoted, the case turns on the sufficiency of the notice to quit. If the breaches of the conditions of the lease, upon which the lessors rely to work its forfeiture, are recited in the notice in terms too general, or too indefinite and uncertain, to inform the lessee of the acts or omissions constituting the breach, so that he can have no opportunity to correct the acts or supply the omissions, it is plain that no sufficient complaint of unlawful detainer can be founded thereon. The notice cannot be aided by particularity in the complaint. The lessee is given, by the statute, the alternative of complying with the conditions and covenants of the lease, or quitting the premises, and in order to give him the opportunity to exercise his right of choice, the notice must specify with particularity the conditions and covenants which he has failed to keep or perform; a general recital of the conditions and covenants of the lease, followed by the statement that the lessee has failed to keep "each and all" of such conditions and covenants, cannot be sufficient.

Tested by these rules, the notice served on the respondent will not support an action of unlawful detainer under the fourth subdivision cited. It specifies no particular default.

It does not point out any act which the lessee could perform within the specified time and thus prevent a forfeiture. It is, indeed, but a general recital of the conditions of the lease, and a claim that a breach has been made in the performance of each and every condition. As it is elsewhere in the complaint made clearly to appear, the appellants are not complaining so much of the failure to perform any particular condition, as they are complaining that the general performance of the conditions did not reach the standard of excellence that, in their opinions, it ought to have reached. Inasmuch as the lessee agreed to perform the several conditions of the lease in a good and husbandlike manner, doubtless a failure to so perform would be such a breach of the conditions and covenants of the lease as to authorize this form of remedy. But a notice reciting that fact generally is not sufficient to put in motion the machinery of the statute. The notice must point out the defects with such particularity that the court can say there is reasonable grounds for believing there has been a breach of the conditions of the lease. The facts constituting the breach must be stated; the lessor cannot be both suitor and judge.

Considered, therefore, with reference to the causes for declaring a forfeiture of a lease provided for in the fourth subdivision of the statute above quoted, the notice is, as we say, insufficient upon which to found the action of unlawful detainer. The appellants, however, contend that the notice shows both a nonpayment of rent, and the commission of waste on the demised premises, on the part of the lessee, and that the notice is good under the third and fifth subdivisions of the statute above quoted. It may, we think, be doubted whether the failure to perform conditions such as those mentioned in the lease can be said to be not paying rent as that term is used in the statute, but conceding it to be so, there is the same indefiniteness with reference to that clause that there is with reference to the others. It cannot be ascertained how much the lessors claimed to be due, whether it was ten, or ten thousand dollars, and there was no possible chance for the lessee to save a forfeiture by the payment of the rent within the ten days allowed by the statute. To claim a breach for the non-payment of rent, the notice must specify the amount claimed to be due, so that it can be paid and a forfeiture abated, if the party owing the rent so desires it. The option is with the lessee, and the notice must be sufficiently definite to enable him to avail himself of it.

The acts recited in the notice do not constitute waste. Waste is some act which tends to the destruction of the tenement. To fail to farm lands in a good and husband-like manner or to keep in repair fences thereon, is not waste, however much it may lessen the income derived from the land.

The judgment appealed from is affirmed.

MOUNT, DUNBAR, and ANDERS, JJ., concur.

[No. 4718. Decided September 21, 1904.]

THOMAS H. McCLEARY, *Respondent,* v. J. E. WILLIS, *Appellant.*[1]

BROKERS—COMMISSIONS—ACTION TO RECOVER SHARE OF—AGREE-MENT TO DIVIDE IN CONSIDERATION OF ASSISTANCE IN MAKING SALE —FINDING PURCHASER—DISCLOSING NAME—PLEADINGS—EVIDENCE —SUFFICIENCY. In an action brought by one broker against an-other to recover one-half of the commission received by the de-fendant upon effecting a sale of real estate, agreed to be paid to the plaintiff if he would find a purchaser and assist in making the sale, a demurrer to the complaint and to the evidence for the reason that it was not alleged or proved that the plaintiff had in-

[1]Reported in 77 Pac. 1073.

troduced the purchaser or disclosed his name, is properly overruled, since that was not essential where it appears that the
agreement was to divide commissions for "assisting" in making
the sale, and plaintiff found the purchaser, showed the property
to him, endeavored to make the sale, and was the procuring cause
in effecting the sale afterwards made by the defendant.

PLEADINGS—AMENDMENT.   Where originally the complaint
had alleged defendant's agency in 1900, a trial amendment to
state the same fact was proper, under Bal. Code, § 4953.

COSTS.   Error will not be presumed in the allowance of costs
for witness fees and copies of documents where the record fails
to show that appellant suffered any prejudice.

Appeal from a judgment of the superior court for Lewis
county, Irwin, J., entered December 5, 1902, upon the
verdict of a jury rendered in favor of plaintiff in an action
for a broker's commission. Affirmed.

J. E. Willis and *Millett & Harmon,* for appellant.

Forney & Ponder, for respondent.

PER CURIAM.—Action to recover compensation for services rendered as a broker, brought by Thomas H. Mc-
Cleary against J. E. Willis in the superior court of Lewis
county. The cause came on for trial before the lower court
and a jury. A verdict was rendered in plaintiff's favor for
$150. The defendant in due time filed his motion for a
new trial on statutory grounds. This motion was overruled "upon condition that plaintiff remit the amount of
said verdict in excess of $143.75." Plaintiff consenting,
judgment for the amount last named, with interest from
said date, and costs, was entered on the 5th day of December, 1902. Defendant appeals from this judgment. The
complaint, omitting title of cause, is as follows:

"The plaintiff complains of the defendant, and for cause
of action alleges: (1) That the plaintiff now is, and at
all times herein mentioned was, engaged in the real estate
business in Centralia, Lewis county, Washington. (2)

That defendant during the years 1900, 1901, and 1902 was the agent for the United Trust Limited for the sale of a tract of land known as the Hoss place, near Centralia, Lewis county, Washington, being the north half of the Sidney S. Ford donation land claim. That defendant on or about the month of September, 1900, agreed with the plaintiff that if plaintiff would assist defendant in finding a purchaser for said tract of land he, defendant, would pay to plaintiff one half of the commissions he would receive from making a sale of said premises. (3) That the plaintiff, relying upon said agreement, did thereupon assist the defendant in procuring a purchaser for said land, to wit, one C. A. Ives and his wife, Katie Ives, who on, to wit, the 22nd day of May, 1902, purchased the premises aforesaid. (4) Plaintiff avers, according to his best knowledge, information and belief that defendant, on to wit, the 22nd day of May, 1902, received a large sum of money as commission for said sale of said land, to wit, the sum of seven hundred and fifty dollars. (5) That defendant neglects and refuses to pay to plaintiff one half of said commission or any sum, and there is now due and owing plaintiff from the defendant by reason of said agreement the sum of three hundred and seventy-five dollars, with interest thereon from and after May 22, 1902. Wherefore plaintiff prays for judgment against the defendant for the sum of three hundred and seventy-five dollars, with interest thereon at the legal rate from and after May 22, 1902, and for his costs herein."

Appellant made his motion in the lower court to require respondent to make paragraph two of the above complaint more definite and certain, in order "to show the time and place of making the agreement alleged to have taken place between the plaintiff and defendant," and to show whether said agreement was a "verbal agreement or in writing." This motion was overruled, and appellant excepted. The amended answer of appellant denies each and every allegation in paragraphs two and three of the complaint,

". . . except that he admits that said C. A. Ives and his wife, Katie Ives, have entered into a contract to purchase the premises described in paragraph two of plaintiff's complaint. That said defendant further admits and alleges that, since the service upon plaintiff of the original answer in this cause, to wit, on the 29th day of July, 1902, the United Trust Limited, a corporation, has conveyed by deed the lands and premises referred to and described in plaintiff's complaint at said paragraph two, to the said C. A. Ives, and his wife, Katie Ives."

This answer further denies each and every allegation in paragraph four of the above complaint, except appellant admits that he received two hundred eighty-seven and 50-100 dollars commission in negotiating such sale, that he refuses to pay respondent any part thereof, and denies all indebtedness to him on account of the aforesaid transaction. There is certain matter alleged in what purports to be appellant's further defense, which relates to his version of the above transaction. This matter is evidentiary in character, and pertinent to appellant's denials of the allegations in the complaint. The reply puts in issue the allegations of affirmative matter contained in this answer.

The real estate mentioned in the complaint is situated a few miles from Centralia, in Lewis county. Appellant is an attorney at law, and was located, at the above times, at Chehalis. Some time prior to the alleged transactions in the complaint, appellant, as the attorney of the United Trust Company, Limited, foreclosed a mortgage on this realty and obtained the title thereto for this company. Appellant, having been called as a witness for respondent, testified: "I only had this land for sale in this way: when I got a purchaser I was to submit the offer. I could not make any contract." Respondent's testimony tended to show that, some time during the summer of 1900, appellant and respondent had their first conversation with reference to the sale of the above realty, using this language:

"Well, first I met Mr. Willis in Chehalis, I think on the street. I told him I thought I could assist him in finding a purchaser for the old Hoss place. Mr. Willis said if I would he would divide the commissions with me. I told him, 'All right,' I would do it, and, after some further talk about the matter, we parted."

He further testified that Willis fixed the price at $5,400; that witness took several parties out to see this place at different times; that some time in November, 1901, Allen Ives, father of C. A. Ives, came to witness' house, told respondent that his son Charley, who was then living in California, intended to come to Lewis county, and, "he wanted me to bo on the lookout for a place for him. I then told him about the Hoss place, being the best place I know of for the money. I told him his son could buy it for $5,400." Thereafter Allen Ives came to the office of respondent several different times to talk about this place. He wanted witness to show the son this property when he arrived. When the son, C. A. Ives, arrived, respondent procured a rig, with which he took young Ives and a companion out to see this realty. Ives said he liked the place better than any that he had yet seen, and that he thought he would take it at the price of $5,400, if he could get satisfactory terms on payments. Respondent also testified that he told Mr. Ives that the attorney in Chehalis would fix such terms, and that he would go and see him, that respondent thought he told Ives the name of the attorney was Mr. Willis. In continuation of respondent's testimony, he said:

"Well, we started on back, and Mr. Ives said, 'I have seen a place advertised in the newspaper, near Seattle, that looks cheap on paper, I will go up and see that, and in the meantime you go to Chehalis, and get the best terms on

that place. You may say to him that I will make a substantial payment on the place and secure the rest.' I told
him, 'All right.' . . . I came right to Chehalis to see
Mr. Willis, I told him about having a buyer for the 'Hoss
place' and I thought surely we would be able to make a sale.
Q. Did you tell Mr. Willis who the buyer was? A. I
think not, I don't remember that anything was said about
that. Willis picked up a letter, which he said was from
McMaster & Birrell of Portland, to the effect that the price
of this land had been raised to $5,500—net to the owner,
and that we would have to sell it for $5,800 or possibly for
$5,750 so that we could make a commission of $300, or
any way $250, out of the sale. . . . I told Mr. Willis
that I was sorry that the raise had been made in the price
of the land, as it might knock out the sale, but that I would
go back and do everything I could and Mr. Willis said all
right. I told Allen Ives the next morning about the raise
in the price of the land, did not see C. A. Ives till after
he bought the land. He came to Chehalis the next day, I
think with his father, and bought the place from Mr.
Willis."

This was about February 12, 1902. It was admitted at
the trial that, at or about this date, C. A. and Katie Ives
entered into a written contract to purchase this land of
the United Trust Company, Limited, for the consideration
of $5,750. Appellant admitted that he received $287.50
commission for negotiating this sale, as alleged in the
answer. Respondent, on being recalled in his own behalf,
swore that, at the time of the above conversation with Willis, when he learned about the raise in the price of the land,
Willis said, "that if we made $300, he would divide it with
me, and I should get $150, and he the same; or if we made
$250, then we would get $125 each." The foregoing statement comprises substantially respondent's version of the
transaction, as the same appears in the record. At the trial,
when respondent rested, appellant demurred to the com-

plaint and the evidence, and moved to dismiss the action
for the following reasons:

"(1)   Because it appears upon the face of the plaintiff's
complaint that the complaint does not state facts sufficient
to constitute a cause of action, inasmuch as it does not appear that the plaintiff communicated to the defendant
knowledge of his negotiations for the sale of the premises.
(2) That the defendant challenges the sufficiency of the
evidence adduced by plaintiff at the time plaintiff rested
his cause, inasmuch as the plaintiff has failed to prove that
defendant at any time mentioned in the complaint, or at
all, was the agent of the United Trust, Limited, and because said evidence does not show that plaintiff in any
manner assisted defendant in making a sale of the premises
described in plaintiff's complaint."

The lower court overruled the demurrer and motion to dismiss, and appellant excepted.

On nearly all of the material points involved, the testimony of appellant and his witnesses is in direct conflict
with the evidence adduced in behalf of respondent.   It is
admitted, however, that Allen Ives and his son's attention
was first directed to this land by respondent.   Both of
these parties testified that respondent represented himself
as the sole agent for the sale of this land; that they first
learned through assessor Guin that Mr. Willis had the
handling of it.   Appellant testified, that during the summer of 1900, and about January 1902, respondent asked
appellant what there would be in it, or words to that effect,
if he found a purchaser for this Hoss place; that appellant
answered, if respondent would bring a purchaser to his office who made an acceptable offer, appellant "would do
the fair thing" by him.   Mr. Allen Ives testified concerning the alleged conversation between respondent and himself, while his son was in Seattle, as follows:

"I went to his office and was told he had gone to Chehalis, and would not be back until night; and I went to

his house again the next morning, and asked him what he had done. He said he hadn't done anything, but that he had gone to Chehalis, and while there had telephoned to Portland to these parties, and that they had risen on their price to $5,800, and seven per cent on back payment, instead of six per cent. And I said 'I will throw the whole thing aside.' "

Respondent denied, in rebuttal, that he told either Allen or C. A. Ives that he telegraphed or telephoned to Portland while in Chehalis. During the progress of the trial, the court below allowed respondent, on his verbal motion, to amend his complaint, so that it might appear by allegation that appellant was the agent of the United Trust Company in the year 1900, as well as during the years 1901 and 1902, as this pleading originally stood. Appellant excepted. After hearing the evidence and arguments of counsel, the cause was submitted to the jury under instructions of the trial court, and a verdict returned as above mentioned.

It is assigned that the lower court erred in overruling appellant's demurrer to the complaint and the evidence, and in refusing to dismiss the action. In support of the contention that the complaint does not state facts sufficient to constitute a cause of action, appellant's counsel in their brief make the following quotation from the opinion delivered by this court in *Penter v. Staight*, 1 Wash. 365, 25 Pac. 469.

"This was an action for a real estate agent's commission, and the complaint alleges that certain property was placed in the hands of plaintiffs by defendant for sale at a certain price, and the plaintiffs undertook to use their best efforts to find a purchaser at the price named, for which, they being successful, they were to receive the usual commission, alleged to be five per cent; and to charge the defendant, the complaint also alleged that plaintiffs had found a purchaser at the price named, and completed the bargain with the purchaser for the sale of the same. But there was no allegation that the plaintiffs had ever communicated knowledge of their action to the defendant, or that he had carried out the arrangement they had made for the sale, or had refused to carry it out after notice of the arrangement; and in these particulars, at least, it was fatally wanting."

Section 401, Pierce's Code; § 4931, Bal. Code, provides that, "In the construction of a pleading, for the purpose of determining its effect, its allegations shall be liberally construed, with a view to substantial justice between the parties." It is significant, in this connection, that appellant's objections to the complaint were first urged at the trial; that while he did, in the lower court, make a motion to require respondent to state whether the alleged contract of employment was in writing or verbal, no motion was interposed requiring respondent to state the terms of such employment more definitely than they were stated in the first instance. The dissimilarity between the allegations found in the complaint in the case of *Penter v. Staight, supra,* and the complaint in the present controversy is significant. In the *Penter* case, the action in part was founded upon a contract to pay a commission to plaintiffs, as brokers, for making a sale of the owner's real estate, at the instance of the latter party. The complaint therein was not only defective for failure to allege want of knowledge on the part of the owner, regarding the brokers' acts in the premises, but there were no substantive allegations in the pleading showing that defendant had carried out the arrangement the brokers had made for the sale of the real estate involved in such controversy, "or had refused to carry it out after notice of the arrangement." We think, under favor of this rule of liberal interpretation, that the complaint states sufficient facts to show a liability, on the part of appellant, to respondent, in consideration of services rendered by McCleary to Willis; that, under such contract of employment, as alleged, the respondent was to assist appellant in procuring a purchaser for the above real estate; that having rendered such assistance to appellant, respondent was entitled to remuneration for his services.

The vital question in this whole controversy is whether there was competent evidence to sustain the verdict of the jury. In this connection we make the following quotation from appellant's brief:

"To be frank, it is upon the testimony of the respondent himself, not upon the testimony of any other witness, that we ask this court to reverse the judgment of the court below. Certainly the respondent's own evidence does not show that he 'produced' a buyer 'ready and willing' to buy the property. Nor does it show that he 'communicated' to appellant 'knowledge' of his dealings with Ives."

In the case of *Bertelson v. Hoffman, ante* p. 459, 77 Pac. 801, which was an action to recover a broker's commission from the owner of the real estate, wherein the sale was not consummated because the owner refused to comply with his part of the contract made with his broker, this court held that the mere withholding of the intended purchaser's name from the owner, on the part of the broker, did not prejudice the plaintiff in that action, as the owner did not request that the identity of the purchaser be made known to him; and that it did not appear that the owner suffered any damage or injury by reason of such concealment. *Butler v. Kennard,* 23 Neb. 357, 36 N. W. 579, was an action brought by the broker, Butler, against Kennard, the owner, to recover a commission where the sale was com-

pleted between the owner and the purchaser. The following language occurs in the opinion of the court:

"It is a well established rule in this, as well as other,
states, that where a broker is employed to sell real estate,
it is not necessary that the whole contract should be completed alone by him, in order to entitle him to his commission. But if, through his instrumentality, the purchaser and owner are brought in contact, and a sale is
made through the instrumentality of the agent, he is entitled to his compensation; and this without reference to
whether the owner, at the time the sale was perfected, had
knowledge of the fact that he was making the sale, through
such instrumentality."

The question in such cases is whether the broker was the
procuring cause in bringing about the sale between the
owner and customer. *Lloyd v. Matthews,* 51 N. Y. 124;
Lunney v. Healcy, 56 Neb. 313, 76 N. W. 558, 44 L. R. A.
593, and note.

It must be borne in mind that, under respondent's allegations and proofs, he did not undertake to procure a purchaser for the sale of this realty, but only to assist in so
doing; that this action at bar is based on a special contract
of employment entered into between an agent or a representative of the owner (the Trust Company) and this respondent, who is only suing the agent, Willis, for one-half of the
commission received by him from the United Trust Company. In its essence, this is a controversy between brokers
or agents, over a division of commissions received by one
of these parties to this transaction. The jury evidently,
by its verdict, affirmed that Mr. McCleary was the procuring cause in producing a purchaser for this land, and that
he assisted in finding a purchaser or purchasers therefor.
We believe there is competent evidence in the record to
sustain such finding, and that the appellant, having re-

ceived the fruits of respondent's labors, should respond in
accordance with the contract as alleged.   It does not lie
with appellant to deny that he was the authorized agent
or representative of the United Trust Company for the
purposes of selling this land.   The company, by contracting
with, and conveying this real estate to, Ives, ratified all the
acts of appellant as its agent in the above transaction.   The
fact that appellant communicated with certain financial
agents of this company in Portland, Oregon, is a matter
of no significance, as far as the rights of respondent are
concerned in this controversy.   The Ives' could not arbitrarily have put an end to respondent's contract of employment, and then go ahead and make an agreement for
the purchase of this land with appellant, to the prejudice
of respondent, whose acts at that time had become, and
were, an integral part of the foregoing transaction.   Both
father and son swore that assessor Guin told the elder Ives
about appellant having this realty for sale as agent, which
was the first time that either the father or son had ever
heard the name of Mr. Willis mentioned in connection with
this real estate.   If this be true, in the light of the testimony in respondent's behalf, we think that there was sufficient evidence to show that respondent did assist appellant
in making a sale of such land, and therefore was entitled
to recover, under the contract of employment set forth in
the complaint.

The trial court committed no error in assessing the
amount of respondent's recovery.   It was consistent with
his proofs.   The granting of leave to amend the complaint
at the trial, to which we have heretofore referred, was perfectly proper under § 4953, Bal. Code.

The appellant contends that the lower court erred in
giving certain instructions to the jury, and in refusing to

instruct as requested by appellant. The instructions given, of which appellant complains, are in accord with our conclusions heretofore declared with regard to the sufficiency of respondent's allegations, and the evidence adduced in support thereof. The request refused was properly denied; that part embraced in the language following: "and unless the person claiming the commission finds such a purchaser, and communicates the fact to the other party at the time, he cannot recover," is objectionable, and contrary to the legal principles heretofore announced in this opinion.

Appellant further complains that the lower court erred in allowing two items in respondent's cost bill to be taxed against him—$4.80 for attendance and mileage of D. B. Rees, witness for respondent, subpœnaed but not called upon to testify at the trial, and $3 for copies of documents. Error will not be presumed; it must appear affirmatively. From the meager showing appearing in the transcript, we are not prepared to hold that appellant suffered any prejudice by reason of such ruling with respect to the taxation of these items of costs. *Ivall v. Willis,* 17 Wash. 647, 50 Pac. 467; *New Whatcom v. Bellingham Bay Imp. Co.,* 16 Wash. 135, 47 Pac. 236.

No reversible error appearing in the record, the judgment of the superior court must be affirmed, and it is so ordered.

[No. 4761. Decided September 21, 1904.]

HUGH McCONAGHY, *Appellant,* v. ALVA C. CLARK, *Respondent.*[1]

CONTRACTS — VALIDITY — CONSTRUCTION — CARRYING UNITED STATES MAIL—SUBSTITUTION OF CONTRACTORS—CONSENT AND APPROVAL OF GOVERNMENT—FAILURE OF PROOF—NONSUIT. In an action for damages for breach of a contract to substitute the defendant for the plaintiff in a sub-contract for carrying the United States mail, a nonsuit is properly granted on the ground that the complaint fails to state sufficient facts, and that the proof was insufficient, where it is not alleged or proved that the original contractor consented to the substitution or that the postmaster general authorized and approved the same, it appearing from the contract that such consent and approval were necessary.

Appeal from a judgment of the superior court for King county, Morris, J., entered March 30, 1903, upon granting a nonsuit at a trial before the court and a jury, dismissing an action upon contract. Affirmed.

Frank B. Wiestling and *William Martin,* for appellant.

Greene & Griffiths, for respondent.

PER CURIAM.—Plaintiff, Hugh McConaghy, sued defendant, Alva C. Clark, for breach of contract in the superior court of King county. At the trial the plaintiff was nonsuited. Thereupon in due time he made and filed his motion for a new trial, which was overruled. Judgment was entered in the lower court dismissing the action, and plaintiff appeals.

The cause of action, as alleged in the amended complaint, is predicated upon the following written agreement, entered into between the parties, to wit:

[1]Reported in 77 Pac. 1084.

"SUBSTITUTION OF A. C. CLARK, FOR HUGH McCONAGHY.

"Whereas Alfred Parker of London, Kentucky, did on the second (2nd) day of February, 1901, release one Hugh McConaghy from his obligations and liabilities on a certain United States mail service subcontract, dated July 2, 1898, for route No. 471,001. And whereas, the said Alfred Parker is desirous of substituting one A. C. Clark of King county, state of Washington, for, and in the place of said Hugh McConaghy. Now, therefore, the said Alfred Parker does hereby substitute the said A. C. Clark, for said Hugh McConaghy as party of the second part in said contract, and for value received, the said A. C. Clark does hereby substitute himself for, and in the place of said Hugh McConaghy, under said contract, as party of the second part. And the said Clark does hereby, for value received, agree faithfully on his part to perform each and all of the obligations and promises contained in said contract of July 2, 1898, on the part of the party of the second part, and said subcontract of said date is hereby referred to and embodied in, and made a part of this contract. And the said Alfred Parker, for value received, does hereby agree with the said A. C. Clark, that he will carry out with him his obligations in said contract, of July 2, 1898, to all intents and purposes as if the said Clark were the said McConaghy."

It is alleged in such complaint, that the parties to this written instrument

". . . made a mutual mistake regarding the recital therein contained, wherein it was stated that Alfred Parker did, on the 2nd day of February, 1901, release said Hugh McConaghy from his obligations and liabilities on a certain U. S. mail service subcontract dated July 2, 1898, for route No. 471,001, which said instrument is the same as exhibit 'A' herein referred to . . . in that said parties thereto both then and there well understood that said Hugh McConaghy had not, at that time, been so released by the said Alfred Parker."

It was further alleged that both of said parties (appellant and respondent) well know that appellant was still under

his obligations and liabilities contained in exhibit "A," and
that appellant had not been released therefrom. The
exhibit "A" referred to was the subcontract for transporting the mail on route No. 471,001, entered into between
Alfred Parker and Hugh McConaghy on July 2, 1898,
which was annexed to the complaint, and also referred to in
the agreement between McConaghy and Clark, above set
forth. There is a recital in this exhibit to the effect that
the original contract for transporting the mail on route No.
471,001 was executed between the United States, by the
postmaster general, and Alfred Parker, and that conditional permission was obtained to sublet the same to appellant McConaghy. Appellant further alleged, that he performed all and singular his obligations, promises, and
duties to be by him performed under the agreement between him and respondent Clark; that respondent totally
failed to carry out or perform any of the obligations, covenants, and promises to be performed by him, and especially

". . . failed, refused, and neglected to substitute
himself for and in place of said Hugh McConaghy under
the said contract herein referred to, to wit, exhibit 'A,' as
party of the second part therein, and the defendant totally
failed, refused, and neglected faithfully, or at all, on his
part, to perform any of the obligations and promises contained in said exhibit 'A,' to be performed by the said
defendant, the party of the second part therein, and the
defendant refused to assume any of the obligations of the
plaintiff under said exhibit 'A,' by reason of such neglect
and refusal on the part of the defendant to enter into said
contract with said Parker and to carry out with said
Parker the obligations thereunder of the plaintiff, the
plaintiff was compelled to continue the performance of his
obligations to said Parker, whereby the plaintiff has suffered damages at the hands of the said defendant in the
sum of six hundred dollars ($600), no part of which has
been paid."

Appellant prayed judgment for said amount, together
with his costs and disbursements. Respondent in the court
below demurred to this amended complaint, alleging,
among other grounds, that it "does not state facts sufficient
to constitute a cause of action." This demurrer came on
for hearing before Hon. W. R. Bell, one of the judges of
said superior court, and was overruled. The respondent,
for answer to the complaint, denied all the material allegations thereof, except the allegation that he signed the paper
writing therein set forth. The first affirmative defense
charges that appellant procured the signing of the above
contract by false representations. The second affirmative
defense is as follows:

"Further answering said amended complaint, this defendant alleges that the said agreement referred to in paragraph two of plaintiff's complaint, and all negotiations
with respect thereto between plaintiff and defendant, were
conditioned upon the approval of said Parker mentioned
therein, and of the government of the United States and
of the postmaster general thereof, and that the approval of
said Parker or of said government and of said postmaster
general was never obtained, and that this defendant never
qualified or became competent to act as mail carrier in accordance with the laws of the United States and postoffice
requirements, and that plaintiff continued uninterruptedly,
ever since before said agreement mentioned in paragraph
two aforesaid was signed until after the commencement of
this action, to perform the terms, conditions and requirements and to do the work referred to and required in said
agreement between plaintiff and said Parker, and to receive
the usual and contractual compensation for his services."

The reply is in the following words and figures, omitting
the title of the action:

"Comes now the plaintiff, and by his attorney, Frank B.
Wiestling, and for reply to the so-called answer or further
answer to the complaint, as amended, alleges as follows:
(1) He denies each and every allegation contained on

pages one, two, three, and four thereof, and especially denies that he has received any compensation since the 20th day of April, 1901, for the services mentioned on page four of said further answer to the amended complaint. Wherefore plaintiff demands judgment as is contained in his amended complaint."

The cause came on for trial before the superior court, with Hon. George E. Morris as the presiding judge thereof, and a jury. At the conclusion of the evidence in appellant's behalf, on motion of respondent's counsel, a nonsuit was granted upon the following grounds:

"(1) That the complaint does not state facts sufficient to constitute a cause of action; (2) that there is no evidence in the case showing any contractual relation between the plaintiff and the defendant; (3) that there is no evidence in the case that Mr. Parker consented to this alleged agreement of substitution; and (4) there is no testimony at all of any damage having been suffered by this plaintiff."

From an inspection of the pleadings filed by appellant, it is difficult to ascertain the nature of the issues tendered by him, with any degree of accuracy or precision. Under the ruling made by this court in *Shephard v. Gove,* 26 Wash. 452, Judge Morris had the legal right to pass upon, and determine, the sufficiency of this amended complaint at the trial, on the ground that it did not state facts sufficient to constitute a cause of action, notwithstanding the previous ruling of Judge Bell overruling the demurrer to such complaint. This pleading seems to be wanting in material averments, in that it fails to allege that Alfred Parker, the original contractor with the United States government concerning this mail service, ever consented to the substitution of respondent Clark in place of appellant McConaghy, with the approval of the postmaster general, representing the United States. It was necessary for appellant to allege and show, not only that this substitu-

tion was made with the consent and approval of Parker;
but that such change was authorized and recognized by the
postoffice department of the general government, or that
Parker and the general government were ready and willing
to accept such substitution.   This conclusion is strength-
ened when we consider the provisions of the above exhibit
"A," and the document thereto attached, designated as,
"principal requirements of the United States for transporting the mails," on the routes of the character and kind
named in the contract upon which the present action is
founded.   It appears that, from the contract between
Parker and appellant, it was necessary for Parker to first
obtain, from the postmaster general, conditional permission to sublet the same to appellant, which language plainly
implies that such permission was to be thus obtained before the subletting contract to appellant became effectual.
There is also a provision in these requirements, that, "This
service is subject in all respects to the approval of the
postmaster general."   Wherefore, it is evident that even
Parker himself could not have made such substitution complete without the consent of the postmaster general.   The
transportation of the mails is one of responsibility.   In
many respects it is both a personal and public trust.   It
involves important duties towards the general government,
and it is necessary that the head of the postoffice department should know the party or parties who are engaged
in such service.   A subcontractor cannot, during the life
of his contract for the transportation of the mails, change,
at his own instance, his contractual relations with regard
to such service; he must have the consent of his superiors.

The record discloses that the greater portion of the testimony was directed towards the alleged mistake in the recital contained in the above contract regarding the release
of appellant "from his obligations and liabilities" on the

subcontract between him and Parker. It appears that the
trial judge was very liberally inclined towards appellant,
in allowing him to put in his evidence, not only with regard
to such mistake, but also with reference to the alleged substitution of respondent for appellant in the mail service
sub-contract with Parker. Conceding, for the purposes of
this controversy, that the proofs adduced by appellant at
the trial, when considered in connection with respondent's
answer, showed prima facie that there was a mistake in that
respect, still we are of the opinion that there was a failure
of proof as to the alleged substitution of respondent for
appellant in the matter of this alleged subcontract. Much
of the testimony regarding this feature of the transaction
was hearsay in character, and indirect in its tendency.
There is no testimony that the postmaster general, acting
in behalf of the United States, conditionally or otherwise
approved this alleged substitution. The appellant's evidence only tended to show that Parker was willing to make
the change, provided the necessary contract and bond therefor were forthcoming; that respondent was aware of some
negotiations, the true nature of which does not appear,
between Parker and appellant relating to such substitution, but that the same was not consummated for some
reason not apparent from the evidence, or from any showing made in the record. The testimony leaves us in the
dark as to whether this alleged failure was owing to the
acts or defaults of respondent, or whether it was occasioned
by circumstances over which both the appellant and respondent had no control.

The further contention of appellant that, under the
showing made at the trial, he was at least entitled to recover nominal damages, is untenable for the reasons hereinbefore stated.

No reversible error appearing in the record, the judgment of the superior court must be affirmed.

[No. 4918. Decided September 21, 1904.]

H. W. BONNE *et al.*, *Respondents*, v. SECURITY SAVINGS SOCIETY, *Appellant.*[1]

PLEADINGS—COMPLAINT—OBJECTION AT THE TRIAL. An objection to a complaint made for the first time at the trial that it fails to state a cause of action, is too late to take advantage of technical defects that are capable of being cured by amendment.

DEDICATION—PLATS. An alley fourteen feet wide between two adjoining plats of additions to a city, which is as definitely marked on the plats and described in the dedications as any of the streets which are wholly within either plat, is dedicated to the public use by the parties dedicating the plats of which it forms a part.

APPEAL—REVIEW—HARMLESS ERROR. Rulings on the admission of evidence in a cause triable *de novo* on appeal are harmless.

Appeal from a judgment of the superior court for Spokane county, Kennan, J., entered April 4, 1903, upon findings in favor of the plaintiff after a trial on the merits before the court without a jury, enjoining the obstruction of a public alley. Affirmed.

P. C. Shine and *W. L. Husbands,* for appellants.

Merritt & Merritt, for respondents.

PER CURIAM.—In October, 1879, Samuel G. Havermale and wife platted the southeast quarter of the southeast quarter of section 18, in township 25 north, of range 43 east of the Willamette Meridian, into lots and blocks, calling the same Havermale's addition to Spokane Falls. In December, 1881, J. N. Glover and others platted the southwest quarter of the southeast quarter of the section mentioned into like lots and blocks, calling the same the Resur-

[1]This case has not yet been reported in the Pacific Reporter.—REP.

vey and Addition to Spokane Falls. The plats, as recorded and as marked upon the ground, showed an alleyway some 14 feet 6 inches in width between the most westerly tier of lots in the Havermale addition, and the most easterly tier in the Resurvey and Addition. The streets of the two additions, while they conformed one to the other, and paralleled each other in their north and south courses, making the alleyway of uniform width throughout, did not run parallel with the dividing line between the tracts so platted. The variation was such that the dividing line, when compared with the course of the alley, ran diagonally across it—that is, on the south end of the tracts, it was at the southeast corner of the most easterly tier of blocks in the Resurvey and Addition, while at the north end, it was at the northwest corner of the most westerly tier of blocks in the Havermale addition. This left a strip lying between lot 1, in block 17, of the Resurvey and Addition, and the dividing line between the two additions, of some 5.40 feet in width at its north end and about five feet at its south end. It is this tract that is in dispute in this action. The respondent is the owner of lot 1, in block 17, and claims the strip to be a part of the alleyway, and for the use of the public, while the appellant contends that it was never dedicated as an alleyway, and that it is the owner of it, by virtue of a tax title and a quitclaim deed from the dedicators of the Resurvey and Addition. The appellant sought to enclose the tract, and this action was begun to enjoin it from so doing. The trial court found that the tract had been dedicated to the public as an alleyway, and entered a decree accordingly.

The appellant first complains that the complaint fails to state facts sufficient to constitute a cause of action. The complaint consisted of three causes of action, each of which was separately stated. To it the appellant took issue by answer, both by denying its affirmative allegations, and pleading new matter in defense thereto. At the trial, when the respondents commenced the introduction of evidence, it, for the first time, made the objection. This, as we have repeatedly held, was too late to take advantage of any technical defect in the complaint; there must be a defect in substance, incapable of being cured by amendment, before courts will hold the complaint bad, when the objection to it is raised on the trial for the first time. The objections urged by the appellant against the sufficiency of the complaint before us are not matters of substance. At most they are but technical defects and omissions which can be cured by amendment, and will now, inasmuch as they were not suggested in time, be deemed corrected by amendment.

On the facts of the case, we think the evidence abundantly justifies the court's conclusion that the land in dispute was dedicated to the public use by the persons platting the subdivision of which it forms a part. This alleyway was just as definitely marked on the recorded plat as were any of the streets or alleyways shown thereon, and was just as definitely described in articles of dedication. It would seem that this could not be held to remain the private property of the dedicators, without holding every street and alley in the entire addition to be such. Manifestly such a holding would be absurd.

The appellant has raised numerous questions going to the admission and exclusion of evidence. Owing to the fact that the case was tried by the court without a jury below, and is triable de novo here, many of these objections are not pertinent, but such as seem to be we have examined, and do not find that they require a reversal of the case. To discuss them further, or to discuss other objections raised, would only unduly extend this opinion with no practical benefit.

Judgment affirmed.

[No. 4946. Decided June 30, 1904.]

CATHERINE BALL *et al.*, *Respondents*, v. JACKSON O'KEEFE *et al.*, *Appellants*.[1]

Appeal from a judgment of the superior court for Asotin county, C. F. Miller, J., entered June 18, 1903.   Affirmed.

Sturdevant & Bailey, for appellants.

M. M. Godman and *E. O'Neill*, for respondents.

PER CURIAM.—The statement of facts filed in this cause was stricken at the hearing because the same was not settled and certified in the manner prescribed by the statute, but the cause was retained for further examination on the suggestion that there was possibly a question made by the record not dependent on the statement of facts.   We are convinced, however, after such examination, that no question is presented by the record which can be reviewed without a consideration of facts shown at the trial, and that there is nothing before the court for review.   The judgment will therefore stand affirmed.

———

[No. 5178. Decided July 5, 1904.]

FLORENCE WOODS, *Respondent*, v. WASHINGTON MATCH COMPANY, *Appellant*.

Appeal from a judgment of the superior court for Pierce county, Snell, J., entered October 19, 1904.   Affirmed.

H. E. Foster, for appellant.

James J. Anderson, for respondent.

PER CURIAM.—By a written stipulation of counsel for the respective parties in this cause, it is agreed that the disposition of the appeal herein shall be controlled by the decision in *Mulholland v. Washington Match Company* [*ante*, p. 315, 77 Pac. 497]. The decision in said cause was filed July 5, 1904, and, on the authority thereof, the judgment in this cause is affirmed.

[1]Reported in 77 Pac. 382.

[No. 5177.   Decided July 5, 1904.]

ROBERT W. DICK, *Respondent*, v. WASHINGTON MATCH COMPANY,
Appellant.

Appeal from a judgment of the superior court for Pierce county,
Snell, J., entered October 19, 1904.   Affirmed.

H. E. Foster, for appellant.

James J. Anderson, for respondent.

PER CURIAM.—By a written stipulation of counsel for the respective parties in this cause, it is agreed that the disposition of
the appeal herein shall be controlled by the decision in *Mulholland v. Washington Match Company* [*ante*, p. 315, 77 Pac. 497].
The decision in said cause was filed July 5, 1904, and, on the
authority thereof, the judgment in this cause is affirmed.

———————

[No. 5012.   Decided August 5, 1904.]

SEATTLE & LAKE WASHINGTON WATERWAY COMPANY *et al.*, *Respondents*, v. CANNEL COAL COMPANY, *Appellant*, *and* THE
CITY OF SEATTLE, *Defendant.*

Appeal from a judgment of the superior court for King county,
Tallman, J., entered October 14, 1903.   Affirmed.

Ballinger, Ronald & Battle, for appellant.

Sachs & Hale, for respondents.

PER CURIAM.—This case is in all respects the same as, and is
controlled by, the case of *Seattle & Lake Washington Waterway
Company v. Seattle Dock Company* [*ante*, p. 503, 77 Pac. 845],
decided July 26, 1904.   For the reasons given in that case, the
judgment appealed from will stand affirmed.

[No. 4912.   Decided September 21, 1904.]

CHARLES R. WILCOX, *Respondent*, v. THOMAS CARSTENS *et al*,
Appellants.

Appeal from a judgment of the superior court for King county,
Tallman, J., entered July 20, 1903.   Affirmed.

Humphries & Bostwick, for appellants.

R. E. Ferree, J. D. Waller, and *R. W. Emmons*, for respondents.

PER CURIAM.—This case is not materially different from No.
4757, *Wilcox v. Henry ante*, p. 591], just decided.   For the reasons announced therein, the judgment in this case is affirmed.

INDEX

ABANDOMENT:

— Of employment. See ATTORNEY AND CLIENT, 1.

ABATEMENT:

— Of nuisance. See NUISANCE, 5–7.
— Of tax. See TAXATION, 5.

1. ABATEMENT—ACTIONS—INJURY TO PERSON—DEATH—SURVIVAL. Bal. Code, § 5695, read in connection with other parts of the act, was not intended to provide that "all other causes of action" survive to the personal representatives, but relates only to causes of action which the law had provided should survive; hence an action by a widow to recover damages for the mutilation of the body of her deceased husband, being an injury to the person, abates upon her death. *Jones v. Miller* 499

2. SAME—APPEAL—ABATEMENT BY DEATH—COSTS—DISMISSAL. Where the cause of action abates by the death of the party, the executor cannot be substituted and the cause retained on appeal for the purpose of determining the question of costs. *Id* 499

3. SAME—SUBSTITUTION OF PARTY ON APPEAL. Where a cause of action abates by the death of a party, an executor cannot be substituted for the purpose of continuing the action in his individual interest affected by the same wrong. *Id* 499

ABUTTING OWNERS:

— Damages by change of grade. See MUNICIPAL CORPORATIONS, 4.
— Estoppel as to local assessments. See MUNICIPAL CORPORATIONS, 7, 8.
— Of tide lands, charged with liens for improvements. See CONSTITUTIONAL LAW, 3–8.

ACCIDENT:

— Alighting from street car. See CARRIERS, 12.
— Attempt to board street car. See CARRIERS, 13.
— Breaking of swamp hook. See MASTER AND SERVANT, 2–4.
— Fall from street car on curve. See CARRIERS, 15–19.

ACCIDENT—Continued.

— Mangle in laundry. See Master and Servant, 5.
— Moving train on ferry boat. See Carriers, 7-10.
— Report of, confidential. See Discovery, 1.
— Slide in gravel pit. See Master and Servant, 1.

ACTIONS:

See Abatement; Limitation of Actions; Parties.
— Accrual. See Indemnity, 4, 5.
— Commencement. See Damages, 3.
— Consolidation of. See Divorce, 1.
— Dismissal, after overruling nonsuit. See Trial, 1.

ACTION ON THE CASE:

— Damages from overflow. See Limitation of Actions, 2, 3.
— For wrong. See Torts, 1.

ADJOURNMENT:

— Of hearing, promise of notice. See Municipal Corporations, 5, 6.

ADOPTION:

1. Adoption—Requisites—Recording Agreement Under Laws of Foreign State—Descent and Distribution. An adoption in the state of Iowa by a written agreement which is not recorded, as required by the laws of that state, is invalid under the decisions in that state, and such an agreement of adoption, unaccompanied by due proof of recording in Iowa, is insufficient to show any interest in real estate under the law of descent and distribution. *James v. James*.. 65

2. Adoption—Validity—False Representations—Laws of Foreign State. An adoption of a child in the state of Iowa, induced by the false representations of the child's father that its mother was dead, does not render the adoption illegal, in the absence of proof of the laws of Iowa to that effect, since the rules in this state would then apply, and they do not so provide. *James v. James*... 655

3. Same—Consent of the Mother. Under the laws of this state the consent of the mother to the adoption of a child is necessary only when she is living with her husband or has the custody of the child, and a complaint alleging merely that an adoption was without the consent of the mother is, therefore, insufficient to show the invalidity of the adoption. *Id.*........... 655

ADVERSE POSSESSION:

1. ADVERSE POSSESSION—PAYMENT OF TAXES—SEVEN YEAR LIMITATION—COLOR OF TITLE—PAPER TITLE ESSENTIAL. Bal. Code, §§ 5503-5504, providing for the obtaining of title to vacant land by the payment of taxes under color of title for seven years, has no application unless the payment is supported by actual paper title. *Hesser v. Siepmann* 14

2. ADVERSE POSSESSION—PLEADING—COMPLAINT—HOSTILE CLAIM SHOWN. A complaint alleging actual, open, notorious, and adverse possession, under color of title and claim of right, is not insufficient as failing to show hostile or exclusive possession. *Id.*.. 14

3. ADVERSE POSSESSION—CLAIM OF RIGHT—SUFFICIENCY WITHOUT COLOR OF TITLE. Where a deed of a lot excepted the west twenty feet thereof, upon the erroneous supposition that said west twenty feet extended into the adjoining street, and the grantee took possession up to the line of the street, including the excepted portion, supposing it to be the land purchased, there was sufficient claim of right to support a title by ten years' adverse possession without any color of title thereto, since such possession under claim of right is sufficient without color of title. *Id.* 14

4. ADVERSE POSSESSION—COLOR OF TITLE—PLEADING. An answer pleading title by adverse possession is not demurrable for failure to allege "color of title," where it is averred that defendants held under a warranty deed from the owner. *Jones v. Herrick* 434

AFFIDAVITS:

— How brought up. See APPEAL AND ERROR, 23, 24. Review of. See CERTIORARI, 2.

ALIBI:

See CRIMINAL LAW, 4.

AMENDMENT:

See PLEADINGS, 1-3.

APPEAL AND ERROR:

I. NATURE AND JURISDICTION.

II. DECISIONS REVIEWABLE.
— Amount in controversy. See CERTIORARI, 1.
— Costs, not subject of. See ABATEMENT, 2.

1. APPEAL—DISMISSAL— COSTS. An appeal involving only a question of costs will be dismissed on motion. *Lamona v. Odessa State Bank* 113

APPEAL AND ERROR—Continued.

2. Appeal — Final Orders — Vacation of Judgment for Fraud. An order vacating a judgment and granting a new trial, for fraud, made upon petition under Bal. Code, § 5153, must be treated as a proceeding in the original cause, and is not appealable, since it is not a final order and is reviewable on appeal from the final judgment in the case. *Post v. Spokane* 114

3. Appeal—When Lies—Amount in Controversy—Tender by Defendants Reducing Amount. In an action to recover $300, in which the defendants tendered and brought into court the sum of $270, no appeal lies to the supreme court, since the amount in controversy is less than $200. *Stewart v. Hanna* 148

4. Appeal — Jurisdiction — Amount in Controversy — Value of Personal Property Found by Jury. In an action for the recovery of the possession of personal property, the value of the property in controversy, determining the jurisdiction of the supreme court on appeal, is the amount found by the court or jury, and not the amount claimed in the complaint. *Graves v. Thompson* 282

5. Same—Value of Personal Property—Damages for Detention. Upon an appeal from a judgment in favor of defendant in an action for the recovery of the possession of personal property, and for damages for its detention, alleged in the sum of $475, the value of the property as found by the court or jury, and not the damages alleged, is the amount in controversy, and where the value fixed is $200, the appeal will be dismissed. *Id.* . 282

III. PRESERVATION OF GROUNDS.

— Statement of facts. See Appeal and Error, 18-24.

6. Appeal—Trial—Instructions—Exceptions. Error can not be predicated upon instructions where no exceptions thereto were taken. *Dodds v. Gregson* ....:........................... 402

7. Appeal — Review — Motion for New Trial — Necessity of. Errors relating to rulings of the trial court during the progress of the trial can be reviewed upon appeal without a motion for a new trial. *Rowe v. Northport Smelting & Ref. Co* 101

8. Appeal—Waiver of Error—Motion for New Trial a Waiver of Motion for Judgment. Where a defendant against whom a verdict is rendered moves for judgment in his favor upon a special verdict, and also moves for a new trial, and the motion for judgment is denied, and that for a new trial is granted, the granting of the new trial determines any rights of the defendant on his motion for judgment, since he did not stand thereon. *McInnes v. Sutton* 384

APPEAL AND ERROR—Continued.

IV. PARTIES.

— Co-parties to be served. See APPEAL AND ERROR, 15.
— Withdrawal of. See APPEAL AND ERROR, 28.

9. APPEAL—PARTIES—WITNESSES NOT ENTITLED TO APPEAL—DISALLOWANCE OF COSTS. Witnesses for the defendant in a criminal case, whose fees were disallowed by the lower court, are not parties to the action, and cannot appeal from the order of the court disallowing their fees. *State v. Fair* 127

V. REQUISITES.

10. APPEAL—TIME FOR TAKING AND PROPOSING STATEMENT OF FACTS —JUDGMENT—WHEN FINAL—SUSPENDED BY MOTION FOR NEW TRIAL. The time for taking an appeal, and for proposing a statement of facts, begins to run from the time a motion for a new trial, seasonably made, is overruled, in an equity case as well as in law actions, since the judgment is not final until that time. *State ex rel. Payson v. Chapman* 64

11. APPEAL—TIME FOR TAKING—MOTION FOR NEW TRIAL—SUSPENDING FINAL EFFECT OF JUDGMENT. Where, after judgment, a motion for a new trial is made and denied, the judgment is not of final effect until the motion is determined, and the time for taking an appeal begins to run from the date of the order denying the motion for new trial. *Rice Fisheries Co. v. Pacific Realty Co* 535

12. APPEAL—NOTICE—SUFFICIENCY. A notice of appeal reciting that the party "had appealed," instead of that the party "appeals," as provided by Bal. Code, § 6503, is sufficient to effect the appeal, in view of Pierce's Code, § 1066, providing that no appeal shall be dismissed for defects in the notice. *James v. James* 655

13. APPEAL—NOTICE—PROOF OF SERVICE—ACCEPTANCE. Service of notice of appeal upon sureties on a redelivery bond is sufficiently shown by an acceptance of service by them, witnessed by an attorney of the supreme court, and by an affidavit of due service. *Hill v. Gardner* 529

14. APPEAL—NOTICE—PROOF OF SERVICE—SIGNATURE OF PARTY WITHOUT PROOF OF GENUINENESS. An appeal will not be dismissed because the only proof of service upon one of the co-parties not joining therein, and who had appeared in the action, was an admission of service over his own signature, without any proof of its genuineness, since the lower and appellate court must judicially notice the signature of any party that has appeared in the action. *Tischner v. Rutledge* 285

APPEAL AND ERROR—Continued.

15. Appeal—Notice—Service on Co-Parties—Dismissal. An appeal by one of two joint wrongdoers from a judgment against both of them must be dismissed where no notice of appeal was served upon the co-party, and no joinder was made in the subsequent appeal of such co-party. *Davis v. Tacoma R. & Power Co.* 203

16. Appeal — Dismissal — Bond — Supersedeas — Order Fixing Amount—Necessity. Upon an appeal from an order other than a judgment for the recovery of money, the amount of a bond to effect a stay of proceedings must be fixed by the court, and a bond given both as an appeal and supersedeas bond in the sum of $500, without any order of court fixing the amount, is insufficient to give jurisdiction of the appeal, and the appeal must be dismissed. *In re Estate of Drasdo*........................... 412

VI. EFFECT AND STAY.

— Insufficient supersedeas. See Appeal and Error, 16.

17. Appeal — Supersedeas — Injunction Against Obstruction of Highway. An injunction against the obstruction of a public highway by the locking of gates and the erection of fences cannot be superseded on appeal, since a supersedeas operates only upon orders or judgments commanding some act to be done, and does not reach a case of a forbidden act. *State ex rel. Flaherty v. Superior Court*............................... 200

VII. RECORD.

18. Appeal—Statement of Facts—Time for Filing—Extension. The time for filing a statement of facts may be extended by stipulation of the parties without any order of court, under Bal. Code, § 5062. *Dodds v. Gregson* 402

19. Same—Time for Certifying Statement of Facts. Bal. Code, § 5058, providing that there shall be no extension of time for filing a statement of facts beyond ninety days, limits the time for filing only, and not the time for its settlement by the court, for which no limit is prescribed. *Id.*............................. 402

20. Same—Notice of Settlement—Sufficiency—Appearance. A statement of facts will not be struck out for failure to give notice of the time of settlement of proposed amendments, where notice was once duly given, continuances taken, and later when both parties were in court the time was set for two days thereafter without objection on account of want of notice, and respondents' counsel appeared at the hearing, and many of his amendments were adopted. *Id.*............................. 402

APPEAL AND ERROR—Continued.

21.   APPEAL—STATEMENT OF FACTS—CERTIFYING AS PROPOSED—WITH-
DRAWAL FOR PURPOSE OF AMENDMENT. After a proposed statement
of facts has been filed, and no amendments proposed, the same
should be certified as proposed, and the superior court has no
power to permit the same to be withdrawn, on motion of the
party proposing the same, for the purpose of amending, refiling
and serving the same, although the time for filing and proposing
a statement has not expired. *State ex rel. Royal v. Linn......* 116

22.   APPEAL — STATEMENT OF FACTS — CERTIFICATE — ALL THE EVI-
DENCE. In an equity case triable *de novo* on appeal, where it appears from the record that all of the evidence has not been sent
up, it is not sufficient that the lower court certifies the statement
of facts to contain all the material evidence, but the certificate
must be that it contains all the facts which the parties have
agreed to be material, in order to secure a review of the evidence
on appeal. *Kane v. Kane*..................................... 517

23.   APPEAL—REVIEW—AFFIDAVITS HOW BROUGHT UP. Affidavits in
support of a motion for a new trial will not be considered on
appeal unless brought up in a bill of exceptions or statement of
facts. *Rice Fisheries Co. v. Pacific Realty Co*................... 535

24.   APPEAL—STATEMENT OF FACTS—AFFIDAVITS IDENTIFIED IN CER-
TIFICATE — HOW BROUGHT UP. Upon an appeal from an order
made after a hearing upon affidavits, a statement of facts will
not be struck out for the reason that it failed to incorporate
therein the affidavits, where, after amendments were proposed
to the statement, the court certified, upon notice, that the matter
was heard upon the affidavits, which were specifically referred
to and attached to the record, and that they constituted all the
evidence before the court. *Templeman v. Evans*................ 302

VIII. BRIEFS.

25.   APPEAL—BRIEFS—TITLE OF CASE—SUFFICIENCY. The appellants' brief will not be struck out on motion of the respondent
on account of error in the title of the case, where the notice of
appeal and appeal bond were correctly entitled and gave the
supreme court jurisdiction, and the respondent entitled its brief
in the same style and was not misled or prejudiced. *State v.
Lewis* 261

26.   APPEAL—BRIEFS—ASSIGNMENT OF ERRORS—SUFFICIENCY. A brief
will not be struck out because it contains no formal assignment
of errors, where it is clear that the only error alleged is the
sustaining of a demurrer to the complaint, and all the argument
is directed to that point. *McKenzie v. Royal Dairy*........... 390

APPEAL AND ERROR—Continued.

27. Appeal—Briefs—Assignment of Errors. An appeal will not be dismissed for failure to assign errors, where the only question presented is whether the complaint states a cause of action, and that is clearly stated in the brief. *James v. James* 65

IX. MOTIONS AND DISMISSAL.

See also, Appeal and Error, 1-5, 12-16, 27, 38.

28. Appeal—Dismissal—Withdrawal of Co-Party. An appeal will not be dismissed because one of the co-appellants withdrew his appeal. *State v. Lewis* 26ʻ

29. Appeal — Dismissal — Recognizing Validity of Judgment — Payment When Not Voluntary. An appeal will not be dismissed on the ground that the appellant recognized the validity of the judgment by making a partial payment, where it appears that, there being no supersedeas, the respondents issued garnishment proceedings under the judgment, and the payment was made thereunder, after a contest, since the same was not voluntary. *Dodds v. Gregson* 40

X. REVIEW.

See also, Appeal and Error, 1-5; 22-24, 40.
— Affidavits. See Certiorari, 2.
— Common law writs. See Taxation, 4.
— Discretion of lower court, review only for abuse. See Carriers, 19; Continuance, 1; Injunction, 1.
— Evidence, conflicting. See Community Property 1, 2; Criminal Law, 11; Divorce, 2; Trial, 7-9.
— Harmless error. See Evidence, 6; Trial 11.
— Presumption as to error. See Costs, 2

30. Appeal—Review. A case is to be determined upon appeal on the same theory on which it was tried in the court below. *Riverside Land Co. v. Pietsch* 210

31. Appeal—Review—Evidence on Trial de Novo. The erroneous admission of testimony is not ground for a reversal where on appeal there is a trial *de novo*. *Cooke v. Cain* 353

32. Appeal—Review—Harmless Error. Rulings on the admission of evidence in a cause triable *de novo* on appeal are harmless. *Bonne v. Security Savings Society* 696

33. Appeal—Review—Harmless Error. Where a judgment for defendants is based upon certain defenses, error in refusing to sustain a demurrer to certain other separate defenses of the defendants is not prejudicial. *Jones v. Herrick* 434

APPEAL AND ERROR—Continued.

34. Appeal and Error—Review—Special Verdict—Harmless Error on Another Branch of Case. Where a special finding establishes that the county authorities had no notice of defects in a bridge, and there is a general verdict for the county, error committed on another branch of the case is harmless, as the county would not be liable in any event. *Robe v. Snohomish County*... 475

35. Appeal—Review—Harmless Error—Instruction Not Pertinent. An instruction is not necessarily prejudicially erroneous because it includes an abstract error which is not pertinent to the balance of the instructions nor to any of the evidence, when it does not take any question of fact from the jury. *Foster v. Seattle Electric Co*.. 177

36. Appeal—Review—Comment on the Evidence—Harmless Error. Unlawful comment upon the weight and value of evidence which is excluded, made at the time of ruling upon an objection thereto, is harmless. *Halverson v. Seattle Electric Co*......... 600

37. Appeal—Review—Judgment—Vacation—Error of Law. Error of law cannot be corrected upon a petition to vacate a judgment, but only by an appeal from the judgment. *McInnes v. Sutton*... 384

XI. DECISION.

38. Appeal—Decision—Assignment of Errors—Dismissal—Costs. Where, in appellant's brief, no error is assigned as to one of two joint tort feasors, as to whom the action was dismissed upon its separate appearance, and no claim is made that the court erred in entering judgment in its favor, the appeal will be dismissed as to such defendant, with costs where a separate brief was filed. *McKenzie v. Royal Dairy*.......................... 390

39. Appeal—Costs. Upon dismissing a joint appeal, as to one of the respondents, and reversing the case as to the other, the appellant is allowed only one-half of his costs of the appeal. *Id*.... 390

40. Appeal—Decision. Upon a trial *de novo* on appeal, the judgment of the lower court may be sustained on other grounds than those adopted by the trial judge. *James v. James*............. 650

APPEARANCE:

— Waiver of defects. See Process, 1.

1. Trial—Appearance—Waiver of Special Appearance—Motion to Dismiss Action of Unlawful Detainer. Where a special appearance is made to quash a summons in unlawful detainer and the writ of restitution, for want of jurisdiction, and a motion is subsequently made to dismiss the action for the reason

APPEARANCE—CONTINUED.

that no summons has been issued or served, the motion to dismiss invokes the jurisdiction of the court on the merits, and waives the special appearance. *Teater v. King* 138

ARCHITECT:

— Certificate, withholding. See MECHANICS' LIENS, 1.

ARREST:

— Damages for. See TORTS, 1.

ASSESSMENT:

See TAXATION; MUNICIPAL CORPORATIONS, 5-9.

ASSIGNMENT FOR CREDITORS:

— Federal bankruptcy act, effect on state law. See IN-SOLVENCY, 1.

— Title of act, sufficiency. See STATUTES, 3.

1. ASSIGNMENT FOR CREDITORS — JUDGMENT OUTSIDE INSOLVENCY PROCEEDINGS—ENFORCEMENT—SUPPLEMENTAL PROCEEDINGS. An assignment for the benefit of creditors, not objected to, discharges the debtor, and may be set up to defeat supplemental proceedings upon a judgment obtained by a creditor pending the insolvency proceedings. *Jensen-King-Byrd Co. v. Williams* 161

ATTACHMENT:

— Third party claim. See EXECUTION, 1, 2.

ATTORNEY AND CLIENT:

— Admission to practice, relevancy of. See EVIDENCE. 3, 4.
— Compensation. See CHAMPERTY, 1, 2.
— Contract of employment. See PLEADING, 7.
— Fees for receiver's attorney. See RECEIVERS, 1.
— Withdrawal, ground for continuance. See CONTINUANCE, 1, 2.

1. ATTORNEY AND CLIENT — CONTRACT FOR SERVICES — ABANDONMENT—FAILURE TO PROSECUTE ACTION—TERMINATION OF EMPLOYMENT. In an action to recover for services performed by an attorney under a special agreement to receive seven per cent of the amount recovered for the defendant upon the final judgment in a condemnation proceeding instituted by a railroad company, in which it appears that a judgment for the defendant for $9,500 was reversed by the supreme court for error, and a

ATTORNEY AND CLIENT—Continued.

new trial ordered, and that the defendant repeatedly requested
the attorney to proceed with the case, but he failed to do so for
over ten years, giving as a reason that owing to the hard times
the company would abandon the suit if pressed, and that he
would thereby lose his fee, such refusal was a termination of the
employment, justifying the defendant in making any settlement
with the railroad company, and warranting a finding that nothing was due the attorney under the terms of his special contract
of employment. *Farwell v. Colman*............................ 308

2.   Attorney and Client — Removal of Attorney — Voluntary
Withdrawal—Notice—Continuance. Bal. Code, § 4771, providing for twenty days' notice of further proceedings upon the death
or removal of a party's attorney, does not apply to a voluntary
withdrawal by the attorney, since a twenty days' delay could
thereby be secured by collusion. *McInnes v. Sutton*............ 384

ATTORNEY GENERAL:
— Fees of. See State and State Officers, 1.

BAIL:
1.   Bail—Release of Sureties—Failure to Prosecute Within
Time Prescribed — Dismissal of Prosecution Without Presence of Defendant. Where the accused on being held to answer by a justice of the peace, gave a bail bond conditioned
for his presence in the superior court when required, and no
information was filed against him within thirty days and he
was not brought to trial within sixty days, pursuant to Bal.
Code, §§ 6910, 6911, and no cause for such delay is shown by
the state, the sureties are released; and it is error to enter
judgment on the bail bond and to deny the sureties' motion to
dismiss the prosecution because they fail to produce the defendant in court at the time the motion is made, especially when
the prosecution is subsequently dismissed upon a motion confessed by the state, showing that the state had no case against
the defendant. *State v. Lewis*................................ 261

BANKRUPTCY:
— Federal act. effect of. See Insolvency, i.

BANKS:
— Insolvent, receiving deposit. See Criminal Law, 6, 7.

BENEFICIAL ASSOCIATIONS:

— Statutes, title, sufficiency. See STATUTES, 2.

BENEFICIAL ASSOCIATIONS — STATUTES — CONSTRUCTION — CERTAINTY—REFERENCE TO MORTALITY TABLE—MINIMUM RATE. The act of 1901, p. 356, regulating beneficial societies by fixing a rate for assessments not lower than as indicated by the table designated "Fraternal Congress Mortality Table," is not objectionable as vague and uncertain, nor because the same belongs to the domain of evidence and ought to be subject to impeachment, since it is competent for the legislature to determine the rate by adopting such tables and incorporating them into the law. *State v. Fraternal Knights & Ladies* 338

BILL OF PARTICULARS:

See PLEADINGS, 4.

BONDS:

See APPEAL AND ERROR, 16, 17; INDEMNITY.

— Redelivery. See EXECUTION, 1, 2.

— Upon granting injunction. See INJUNCTION, 1, 2.

BOUNDARIES:

— Sufficiency of description. See PUBLIC LANDS, 2.

BRIDGES:

— Repair, injury to licensee. See RAILROADS, 1, 2.

1.   BRIDGES—NEGLIGENCE—COLLAPSE THROUGH DECAY OF TIMBERS—NOTICE OF DEFECT—DUTY OF COUNTY—INSTRUCTIONS. In an action against a county for personal injuries caused by the collapse of a bridge through the decay of timbers, an instruction commencing with the statement that the county cannot be held liable unless the authorities had been notified of the defect, is not prejudicial error, where the instructions as a whole properly state the duty of the authorities to exercise care to detect and guard against such defects, and that it was not necessary to prove actual notice, and properly defining constructive notice. *Robe v. Snohomish County* 475

BRIEFS:

See APPEAL AND ERROR, 25-27, 38.

BROKERS:

1. BROKERS—ACTION TO RECOVER COMMISSION—DISCLOSING IDENTITY OF PURCHASER—COMPLAINT—SUFFICIENCY. A complaint in an action to recover a real estate broker's commission is not demurrable because of failure to allege that the agent disclosed to the defendant the identity of the purchaser, where it does not appear that he refused to do so, or that the defendant made demand therefor, or suffered any injury from the fact of concealment. *Bertelson v. Hoffman*............................ 459

2. BROKERS—ACTION TO RECOVER COMMISSION—EVIDENCE—MATERIALITY OF OTHER DEALS. Where, in an action to recover commissions, plaintiff was asked on cross-examination what other property he had ever been asked to sell for defendant, besides that involved in the suit, an objection on the ground of immateriality was properly sustained. *Id.*......................... 459

3. SAME—VALUE OF LAND. Evidence that the actual value of property is $20,000, and its rental value $1,500, is not admissible as tending to show the improbability of an agreement to sell for $18,000, since the disparity is not sufficient to warrant this class of evidence. *Id* 459

4. SAME—CUSTOMARY COMMISSIONS—PLEADING AND PROOF—INSTRUCTIONS. It was proper to refuse to instruct that under the pleadings plaintiff could not recover unless the jury should find an express promise by defendant to pay the commission, where the allegations of the complaint are predicated upon both an express promise and an agreement to pay the usual and customary commission for like sales, and evidence was received in support thereof, it not appearing that defendant objected to the complaint on the ground that it alleged duplicate cause of action. *Id.* 459

5. BROKERS—COMMISSIONS—ACTION TO RECOVER SHARE OF—AGREEMENT TO DIVIDE IN CONSIDERATION OF ASSISTANCE IN MAKING SALE—FINDING PURCHASER— DISCLOSING NAME— PLEADINGS—EVIDENCE—SUFFICIENCY. In an action brought by one broker against another to recover one-half of the commission received by the defendant upon effecting a sale of real estate, agreed to be paid to the plaintiff if he would find a purchaser and assist in making the sale, a demurrer to the complaint and to the evidence for the reason that it was not alleged or proved that the plaintiff had introduced the purchaser or disclosed his name, is properly overruled, since that was not essential where it appears that the agreement was to divide commissions for "assisting" in making the sale, and plaintiff found the purchaser, showed the property

BROKERS—Continued.

to him, endeavored to make the sale, and was the procuring cause
in effecting the sale afterwards made by the defendant. *Mc-
Cleary v. Willis*... 676

·BUILDING:

— Contracts. See Indemnity, 1-5.
— Permit. See Mandamus, 2-4.

BURGLARY:

See Criminal Law, 8-11.

CARRIERS:

— Refund of freight charges, illegality of. See Contracts, 4, 5.

1.   Relation of Passenger and Carrier. To give rise to the relation of passenger and carrier, there must be the intent of the
former to become a passenger, and an implied or express acceptance of the latter, and one who attempts to board a starting car
from a position where he could not be seen by the company's employes, by the exercise of ordinary care on their part, is not a
passenger. *Foster v. Seattle Electric Co*...................... 17

2.   Carriers—Ejection of Passenger—Street Car Not Running
to End of Line—Payment of Additional Fare—Nonsuit. In an
action by a passenger for damages by reason of being ejected
from a street car, a nonsuit is properly ordered where it appears
that the plaintiff boarded a car that did not run to his destination, paid a five-cent fare, without stating his destination, and,
upon reaching the end of the run of that car, was told by the
superintendent, who was acting as motorman, to take the next
car, and that the conductor thereof would be told to pick him
up and carry him to his destination, since the minds of the
parties did not meet in a contract to carry him to such point for
one fare. *Braymer v. Seattle etc. R. Co*...................... 34

3.   Same—Contract of Carriage—Transfer Contrary to Custom.
The statement of the superintendent that he would tell the conductor of the next car to pick him up and carry him on was not
sufficient to create a contract to carry him without the payment
of another fare, there being no custom to transfer passengers
without an additional fare under such circumstances. *Id*...... 34

4.   Same—Promise of Employe. The fact that the superintendent testifies that he intended to so notify the next conductor, but
forgot to do so, does not create any obligation on the part of the
company to carry the passenger further without pay. *Id*........ 34

CARRIERS—Continued.

5. Same—Evidence—Disposition of Conductor Ejecting Passenger. In an action for forcibly ejecting a passenger from a street car, based entirely on the contract of carriage, evidence of the general character and disposition of the conductor who ejected the plaintiff is inadmissible, in the absence of allegations of incompetence. *Id* 346

6. Same—Evidence as to Car Schedules. In an action against a street car company for failing to carry a passenger to his destination, where there is no question as to the destination of a certain car boarded by plaintiff, and he made no inquiry as to the same, it is not error to strike out evidence relating to the car schedules of the defendant. *Id* 346

7. Carriers— Railroads— Negligence— Presumption From Accident to Passenger. The fact of an injury to a passenger on a railroad train does not alone raise a presumption of negligence in all cases regardless of the circumstances and nature of the accident. *Allen v. Northern Pac. R. Co* 221

8. Same—Sudden Lurch or Jerk as Evidence of Negligence. That an injury to a passenger was due to a sudden lurch or jerk imparted to a train is not prima facie proof of negligence, where it appears that the same was necessary to effect the movement of the train up an incline from a ferry boat. *Id* 221

9. Same—Obstruction Near Tracks—Necesssary Support for Railroad Ferry. That a passenger on a railroad train slowly moving from a ferry boat was injured while attempting to board the train by coming in contact with a post twenty-six inches from the car, is not prima facie proof of negligence when it appears that the post was a necessary support or appliance for the operation of the ferry as constructed. *Id* 221

10. Same—Injury to Passenger While Moving Train From Ferry Boat — Evidence of Negligence — Sufficiency. In an action against a railroad company brought by a passenger for personal injuries, there is no evidence of negligence upon the part of defendant warranting a submission of the case to the jury, where it appears that the plaintiff alighted from the train for the purpose of getting breakfast while it was being ferried across the Columbia river, as he was told that he could do, and upon learning that the train was being moved off the boat, he attempted to board the train while it was moving slowly, no warning being given to him that it was dangerous so to do, and while in such act, lost his balance by reason of a sudden lurch necessarily imparted to the train in moving it off the boat, bringing plaintiff

CARRIERS—Continued.

in contact with an upright twenty-six inches from the platform of
the car, which was a necessary support for the operation of the
boat; since there was no duty to warn and there is no presumption of negligence from an injury to a passenger under such circumstances (Hadley and Dunbar, JJ., dissenting). *Id* 22

11.   Same—Duty of Carrier to One Desiring to Become a Passenger. Street railway employes are not required to exercise the
highest degree of care in ascertaining whether a person desires
to become a passenger, hence it is not error to instruct that the
company is not liable to one injured in attempting to board a car,
if the conductor, by the exercise of ordinary care, could not have
seen him before starting the car. *Foster v. Seattle Electric Co.* . 1

12.   Carriers—Negligence—Injury to Passenger on Street Car—
Degree of Care Required of Company—Instructions. In an
action for personal injuries sustained by a passenger while
alighting from a street car, it is error to instruct that while the
company is not an insurer, the law calls upon it to do whatever
can be done to insure the protection of passengers, since the
company is only bound to exercise the highest degree of care
consistent with the practical conduct of its business, and such an
instruction is reversible error where it is the only one defining
the measure of defendant's duty to passengers. *Johnson v. Seattle Electric Co* 3

13.   Carriers—Negligence—Instructions—Duty Owed to Passengers—Highest Degree of Care Consistent With Practical Conduct of Business. In an action against a street railway company to recover damages for personal injuries, an instruction to
the effect that the company is not liable if it exercises towards
its passengers the highest degree of care consistent with the
practical conduct of its business, is a correct statement of defendant's legal duty. *Foster v. Seattle Electric Co* 1

14.   Same. While it is incorrect in giving such an instruction, to
further state that the conductor of the car should exercise the
highest degree of care "consistent with the proper discharge of
all the other duties of such employes," yet it is not prejudicial
error where there was no evidence to the effect that the injury
was caused by the fact that he was engaged in the performance
of any other duty. *Id* 177

15.   Carriers—Negligence—Duty of Street Car Company to Provide Passengers With Seats — Instructions. In an action
against a street car company for negligence in the running of its
car, resulting in the death of a passenger who was standing upon

CARRIERS—Continued.

the platform, it is not error to instruct that it is the duty of a carrier to furnish passengers with seats, and not negligence for the passengers to stand on the platform if all the seats were occupied, the same principle with reference to seats applying to street cars as to steam cars, and it not being negligence *per se* for a passenger to ride on the platform. *Halverson v. Seattle Electric Co*........... 600

16.   SAME—ASSUMPTION OF FACTS. Such an instruction is not erroneous as assuming that the deceased was compelled to stand on the platform, especially where there was evidence that the seats were all occupied and that there was but little standing room inside. *Id*.................. 600

17.   CARRIERS—NEGLIGENCE—PASSENGER THROWN FROM STREET CAR—FAILURE TO PROVIDE GUARDS. In an action against a street car company for causing the death of a passenger who was thrown from the car while rounding a curve, it is not error to instruct the jury to the effect that the company would be liable for negligently failing to provide a guard or gate and to refuse to instruct that it was under no obligation to provide guards because not required to do so by statute, where it appears that the failure to provide a guard or gate was not the only element of negligence complained of, but the accident was due thereto in connection with negligence in running an overcrowded car around a curve at a dangerous rate of speed while passengers were standing on the platforms. *Id*.. 600

18.   CARRIERS—NEGLIGENCE—SPEED OF STREET CAR—MOTORMAN AS EXPERT WITNESS. Upon an issue as to negligence in running a street car around a curve at a dangerous rate of speed, a motorman is qualified as an expert to answer questions as to what rate of speed would, in his opinion, be safe, where he testifies that he was familiar with the road throughout its entire length and knew the curve, that he had been a motorman on this line for six or seven months, and was familiar with the speed of cars; the matter of qualification resting largely in the discretion of the court. *Id*... 600

19.   CARRIERS—NEGLIGENCE—SPEED OF STREET CAR—EVIDENCE—EXPERIMENTS—SIMILARITY OF CONDITIONS—DISCRETION. Upon an issue as to negligence in running a street car around a curve at a dangerous rate of speed, it is not an abuse of discretion to refuse to admit the result of experiments made with the same car at a time when the conditions were different from those existing at the time of the accident, in that the time of day, the

CARRIERS—Continued.

load on the car, the load on the electric current, and the condition of the rails were different; and the fact that the conditions were more favorable to the plaintiff than to the defendant does not make such exclusion error, since the same was within the sound discretion of the court, to be reviewed only for abuse. *Id.* 600

CERTIORARI:

1. Certiorari—When Lies—Amount in Controversy Less Than $200. A writ of review will not lie to review a judgment from which no appeal lies because the amount in controversy is less than $200, and the fact that the judgment is not merely erroneous, but is void for want of jurisdiction, is immaterial. *State ex rel. Corbin v. Superior Court*........................... 201

2. Certiorari—Hearing—Affidavits Not Presented Below. Upon a hearing in the supreme court upon a writ of certiorari to review an order of the superior court, affidavits not presented below cannot be considered, as the supreme court is restricted to the record actually made in the lower court. *Swope v. Seattle*............. 69

CHAMPERTY:

1. Champerty—Attorney and Client—Agreement to Pay Costs and Prosecute for Contingent Fee. It is doubtful if the doctrine of champerty was ever in force in this state, and if it was, it was repealed by Bal. Code, § 5165, declaring that the compensation of attorneys shall be left to the parties, and hence an agreement whereby the attorney agrees to pay the costs and to prosecute a case for a percentage of the recovery is legal. *Smits v. Hogan*... 290

2. Same—Damages to Defendant by Reason of Champertous Agreement — Malice — Malicious Prosecution. In an action brought against an attorney for damages for maliciously inciting an insolvent person to prosecute an unfounded action against the plaintiff, and which was prosecuted under a champertous agreement, it is proper to instruct that the plaintiff must show malice and want of probable cause, as in an action for malicious prosecution, and the action is not maintainable as a claim for damages for champerty irrespective of malice, since the doctrine of champerty does not prevail in this state. *Id.*............. 290

CHATTEL MORTGAGES:

— Fraudulent. See Fraudulent Conveyances, 1, 2.

CITIES AND CITY OFFICERS:
See Municipal Corporations.

COLOR OF TITLE:
See Adverse Possession.

COMMUNITY PROPERTY:

— Sale by husband. See Specific Performance, 3.

1. Community Property—Evidence—Sufficiency—Wife's Separate Estate. A finding that a team of horses was community property will not be disturbed where the only evidence that the same was the separate property of the wife was that of the husband, to the effect that, thirty years before, she had received $1,000 from her father and had kept the money separate, tracing it through various investments, where the wife was present in court and failed to offer herself as a witness, and the husband's testimony was not wholly consistent. *Hill v. Gardner* 529

2. Same—Division of Property. Findings of the trial court, upon granting a divorce, that all of the property was community property, and making an equal division thereof, will not be disturbed on appeal, upon the claim of the wife that her separate earnings, accumulated before marriage, constituted the sole consideration for a certain part of the property, where the evidence showed that the same was purchased about one year after the marriage, that both parties were industrious and accumulated money, and there was not sufficient evidence to overcome the presumption that property acquired after marriage belonged to the community. *O'Sullivan v. O'Sullivan* 481

COMPROMISE:

— Induced by fraud. See Master and Servant, 8.

1. Compromise—Release of Damages Secured by Fraud—Parties not on Equal Footing—Question for Jury. In an action to recover for personal injuries sustained by an employe, whether the plaintiff was fraudulently misled and induced to sign a release of his damages is a question for the jury, where it appears that the company's physician told the plaintiff that his injury was slight and he would be well in a short time, but wrote a letter showing a serious injury, and when it appears that the plaintiff understood English imperfectly, and supposed he was signing a receipt for wages for the time he had lost, then paid to him, under a promise for future employment, and under the representations of the company's claim agent that it was such receipt, and

COMPROMISE—Continued.

that from long service he placed reliance in the defendant's agents
and physician; since the jury could reasonably find that the parties did not stand upon an equal footing, and that the plaintiff
was justified in placing confidence in the representations because
of his long established relations with the company. *Bjorklund
v. Seattle Electric Co*.. 439

2.   Same—Expressions of Opinion. In such a case it is for the
jury to say whether the physician's statements concerning the
extent of the plaintiff's injuries were mere expressions of opinion or statements of fact upon which the plaintiff had a right to
rely. *Id*.. 439

3.   Same—Surrender of Amount Paid on Settlement. It is not
necessary to return a sum received in a settlement induced by
fraud, before bringing action on the demand, but the same may
be credited thereon. *Id*...................................... 439

CONDEMNATION:
   See Eminent Domain.

CONSTITUTIONAL LAW:
   — Due process. See Taxation, 10.
   — Fixing compensation. See State and State Officers, 1.
   — Partial invalidity. See Taxation, 6.
   — Scienter. See Criminal Law, 1-3.
   — Uniformity of tax. See Taxation, 2, 11.

1.   Constitutional Law — Class Legislation — Equal Protection — Regulations Applying to New Corporations. Laws 1901,
p. 356, regulating new corporations to be thereafter authorized to do business, in this state, and making them a class unto
themselves, does not violate the constitution, art. 1, § 12, forbidding the granting of special privileges to any citizen or class;
nor does it violate art. 12, § 7, providing that no corporation
outside the limits of the state shall be allowed to transact business on more favorable conditions than those prescribed for
domestic corporations, where the law applies equally to all foreign and domestic corporations thereafter to be authorized to
transact business, since it is only necessary that the laws operate
alike upon all similarly situated. *State v. Fraternal Knights &
Ladies.* .... 33(

2.   Same—Constitutional Law—Due Process—Promise of Notice
of Hearing Objections. The fact that a property owner was
lulled into security by a promise of city officials to give him

CONSTITUTIONAL LAW—Continued.

notice of the time to be fixed for a hearing upon his objections to an assessment for local improvements does not deprive him of his property without due process of law, where he had no right to rely upon the promise. *Alexander v. Tacoma*.............. 366

3. Same — Constitutional Law — Due Process of Law — State Contract for Excavation of Tide Lands—Rights of Subsequent Purchasers. The act of 1893, authorizing the excavation of public waterways by private contract, and providing for liens upon the filled in tide lands belonging to the state, and which the state afterwards sells, does not violate the state and federal constitutions, in that, by the foreclosure of such liens, it deprives the subsequent purchasers from the state of their property without due process of law, since the state could make any contract with reference to filling up its tide lands, and subsequent purchasers take subject thereto, and are not entitled to notice or opportunity to be heard touching the improvements. *Seattle & Lake Washington Waterway Co. v. Seattle Dock Co*....................... 503

4. Same—Abutters on Tide Lands—Vested Rights. Abutters, with only a preference right to purchase tide lands, have no vested rights therein, and are not entitled to notice or opportunity to be heard respecting the improvement thereof, contracted for by the state while the state is still the owner. *Id*. 503

5. Same—Loaning Credit of State—State Not Liable for Improvements. The act of 1893, authorizing the excavation of public waterways, and providing for liens upon the tide lands belonging to the state which are filled in under the contract, does not violate the state constitution, § 9, art. 12, and § 5, art. 8, prohibiting the loaning of the credit of the state in aid of any individual, where the act does not make the state liable for the improvements, nor to discharge the lien, but provides for a sale at not less than the appraised value, and the purchasers were bound to pay for the improvements, since the only remedy of the excavation company is to purchase the land at the appraised value. *Id*. 503

6. Same—Contraction of State Debt. Such act does not violate § 3 of art. 8 of the state constitution, prohibiting the contraction of a state debt except for objects especially designated, nor without submitting the same to a vote of the people, since the state is not made liable for the improvement and is under no obligations to discharge the lien, and the creation of such lien upon state lands to be paid by the purchaser is not the creation of a state debt within the meaning of the constitution. *Id*.......... 503

7. SAME—SPECIAL PRIVILEGES—COLLECTION OF TOLLS—SEPARABLE PORTION OF ACT NOT INVALIDATING THE BALANCE. The provision of the act of 1893, relating to the excavation of public waterways, which creates liens upon the state tide lands filled in under the contract, cannot be claimed to be invalid or contrary to § 22, of art. 12, and § 12, of art. 1, of the constitution, prohibiting monopolies and the granting of special privileges to any citizen, by reason of that part of the act granting to the waterway company the exclusive right to control the waterway and collect tolls, since such provision is a separable part of the act, and, if it fails, it does not affect the portion relating to certificates and liens for the improvements. *Id*... 503

8. SAME—TAKING PRIVATE PROPERTY FOR DEBTS OF PUBLIC CORPORATIONS. Said act is not contrary to § 15 of art. 11 of the state constitution, providing that private property shall not be taken or sold for the payment of debts of public or municipal corporations except in the manner provided for by law for the collection of taxes, as the claim for liens for the work is not a debt of any such corporation. *Id*... 50

CONTINUANCE:

— Withdrawal of attorney. See ATTORNEY AND CLIENT, 2.

1. CONTINUANCE—CRIMINAL LAW—WITHDRAWAL OF ATTORNEY FIVE DAYS BEFORE TRIAL—DISCRETION. Where an attorney, employed to defend against a charge of murder, withdrew from the case on the fifth day before trial, and the defense was intrusted to three other attorneys, it appearing that the facts of the case were simple and readily accessible, it was not an abuse of discretion for the trial court to deny defendant's motion for a continuance upon the affidavits of his attorneys that it would be impossible for them to properly prepare for trial in the time remaining. *State v. Underwood*... 55

2. SAME—WITHDRAWAL AS GROUND FOR CONTINUANCE. When a case is regularly set for trial, the voluntary withdrawal of defendant's attorney is not ground for a continuance, and a judgment entered after hearing plaintiff's evidence is not irregularly entered, where no leave of court was obtained for such withdrawal, since the relation of attorney and client cannot be so severed as to effect the rights of others or to secure a delay of the trial. *McInnes v. Sutton*... 38

CONTRACTS:

— Abandonment of. See ATTORNEY AND CLIENT, 1.
— Carriage. See CARRIERS, 3, 4.
— Commissions. See BROKERS.
— Consideration. See GUARANTY, 2.
— Demurrage, extension. See SALES, 1.
— Employment, breach. See DAMAGES, 5.
— Improvement of tide lands. See PUBLIC LANDS, 4; STATE AND STATE OFFICERS, 2.
— Public lands, validity. See PUBLIC LANDS, 2, 3.
— Sales, construction. See SALES, 1.
— Substantial compliance. See MECHANICS' LIENS, 1.
— Tide Lands. See PUBLIC LANDS, 6.

1. CONTRACTS—CONSTRUCTION—AGREEMENT BETWEEN TENANTS IN COMMON. Where L and W were in joint possession of government land, and enter into an agreement defining their interests as owners of undivided halves, and whereby L agrees to hold possession as trustee in the interest of both, paying certain rent, and agrees to pay W $214 "as his part of the expense of erecting the dwelling" thereon, the natural import of the language is that L was paying the sum mentioned as L's part of the cost, and not that he was buying W's half interest therein. *Waring v. Loomis* 85

2. CONTRACTS—CONSTRUCTION—CITY ORDER—PAYABLE FROM CERTAIN FUND. An order, drawn upon a city by a contractor constructing water works, requesting payment of a certain sum "out of any moneys belonging to me, or that may hereafter be due me . . . on the water works contract, either in the twenty per cent reserve, or on account of money to be due me on account of final estimate," is payable only out of said reserve or final estimate, and not out of semimonthly payments falling due as the work progressed. *Dickerson v. Spokane* 414

3. CONTRACTS — VALIDITY — CONSTRUCTION — CARRYING UNITED STATES MAIL—SUBSTITUTION OF CONTRACTORS—CONSENT AND APPROVAL OF GOVERNMENT—FAILURE OF PROOF—NONSUIT. In an action for damages for breach of a contract to substitute the defendant for the plaintiff in a sub-contract for carrying the United States mail, a nonsuit is properly granted on the ground that the complaint fails to state sufficient facts, and that the proof was insufficient, where it is not alleged or proved that the original contractor consented to the substitution or that the postmaster general authorized and approved the same, it appearing from the contract that such consent and approval were necessary. *McConaghy v. Clark* 689

CONTRACTS—Continued.

4. Contracts—Evidence—Varying Writing by Parol—Legality—Agreement as to Refund on Freight Shipped. Where the purchaser of stone agreed in writing to pay the freight, and alleges an oral agreement whereby the vendor guaranteed that the same should not exceed thirty cents per cwt., agreeing to pay any excess, or to turn over to the purchaser any amount that the railroad company might refund, oral evidence will not be held admissible to vary the terms of the written agreement, as in the case of an illegal contract, on account of the illegality of such refund, where the illegality of the contract was not pleaded, and the evidence touching such illegality was meager, and fails to show any intent to violate the law, except by indulging in forced construction or innuendo. *Minnesota Sandstone Co. v. Clark*... 466

5. Same—Contracts—Illegal Part Separable. If such an agreement were illegal, plaintiff could still recover on the balance of the contract, since the consideration is legal and the illegal provision is separable from the rest of the contract. *Id*........... 4

6. Same—Construction of Contract—Oral Agreement Varying Terms of Writing. Where a written contract of sale provided that the purchaser will pay the freight charges "as agreed upon between you and I, the above price being f. o. b.," parol evdience of an oral agreement that the seller would pay any freight charges in excess of a certain rate is inadmissible, as contradicting the writing. *Id*........ 46

7. Same—Pleading and Proof—Original Consideration for Order When Inadmissible. In an action upon an order, drawn by a contractor upon a city, seeking to recover thereon and not on the original consideration, evidence showing that such consideration was labor or material furnished the contractor, making it a preferred claim, is inadmissible, although such consideration is alleged in the complaint, as plaintiff cannot assert that the order is payable otherwise than according to its terms. *Dickerson v. Spokane.* 41

CONTRIBUTORY NEGLIGENCE:

See Carrier, 15; Master and Servant, 5.

CORPORATIONS:

— Fraud of promoters. See Fraud, 1.
— Public, debts of. See Constitutional Law, 8.
— Regulation, conditions, class legislation. See Constitutional Law, 1.

CORPORATIONS—Continued.

— Stockholders, injunction against. See Prohibition, 1.
— Succeeding partnership, not same person. See Criminal Law, 6, 7.

COSTS:

— On appeal, divided. See Appeal and Error, 39.
— Subject of controversy. See Appeal and Error, 1.

1. Costs—Taxation. A cost bill should not be struck out because it was served before it was filed and before the judgment was filed, no prejudice appearing. *Kane v. Kane*.................. 517

2. Costs. Error will not be presumed in the allowance of costs for witness fees and copies of documents where the record fails to show that appellant suffered any prejudice. *McCleary v. Willis* 676

CO-TENANCY:

— As to public lands. See Public Lands, 1.
— Contracts between. See Contracts, 1.

COUNTIES AND COUNTY OFFICERS:

— Negligence. See Bridges, 1.
— Parties. See Mandamus, 4.

1. Counties and County Officers—Drainage Districts—Establishment—Petition Signed by County—Conflicting Duties of County Commissioners—Disqualification. A board of county commissioners cannot be permanently enjoined from entertaining a petition for the establishment of a drainage district, because the county and the chairman of the board, on behalf of the county, signed the petition praying for the establishment of the district, since a subsequent board could not be thereby disqualified; neither is the present board disqualified because the statute may have imposed conflicting duties upon the board, since the power to act is expressly conferred by the statute, and the members of the board, as individuals, are not interested in the result. *O'Connell v. Baker*.................................... 376

2. Counties—Warrants—Issuance. A county warrant is not "issued" until it is actually delivered to the person authorized to receive it, and the auditor's forgery of the payee's indorsement and a wrongful delivery do not discharge the duty to issue a warrant to the person entitled thereto (Fullerton, C. J., dissents). *American Bridge Co. v. Wheeler*.............................. 40

COUNTIES AND COUNTY OFFICERS—Continued.

3. Same—Duty to Issue Warrant Upon Claim Allowed by Commissioners—Mandamus. Since the allowance of a claim by the county commissioners has the force of a judgment, the auditor has no discretion, and his duty to issue a warrant therefor is ministerial and may be enforced by mandamus. *Id*.............. 40

4. Same—Mandamus to Compel Issuance of County Warrant—Wrongful Delivery by Predecessor—Action on Official Bond—Adequate Remedy at Law. Mandamus will lie to compel the county auditor to issue a warrant, when the former county auditor drew a warrant, forged the payee's name, and drew and misappropriated the funds; and the fact that the relator has a remedy on the official bond of the auditor will not preclude the remedy by mandamus, since the remedy on the bond is inadequate to compel the performance of the officer's duty, and a remedy by ordinary action will not defeat the right to mandamus, unless it is a remedy against the respondent in the mandamus proceedings (Fullerton, C. J., dissents). *Id*.................................. 40

COURTS:
— Jurisdiction as to excessive tax. See Taxation, 8.

CRIMINAL LAW:

I. INFORMATION AND DEFINITIONS.

— Information, failure to file. See Bail, 1. Time for filing. See Criminal Law, 14.

1. Criminal Law—Receiving Deposit After Insolvency of Bank—Defenses—Individual Liability of Officer. Const., art. 12, § 12, making officers of a bank individually responsible for receiving a deposit after knowledge that the bank was insolvent, does not preclude the legislature from passing a law making them criminally liable therefor. *State v. Oleson*................ 149

2. Criminal Law—Living Off Earnings of Prostitute—Scienter. Laws 1903, p. 320, § 2, making it a felony for any male person to accept or live off the earnings of a prostitute is not unconstitutional because it fails to require that the same be knowingly done. *State v. Zenner*............................ 249

3. Same—Information—Act Wilfully Committed—Knowledge. An information charging the crime of accepting the earnings of a prostitute is not insufficient for failure to allege that it was knowingly done, where it is alleged that the defendant wilfully committed the act. *Id*.............................. 249

CRIMINAL LAW—Continued.
II. EVIDENCE.

4. CRIMINAL LAW—EVIDENCE OF ALIBI—SUFFICIENCY. There is sufficient evidence to justify a conviction of robbery, where the defendant's evidence as to an alibi was contradicted by two witnesses who identified the defendant. *State v. Fair* 127

5. CRIMINAL LAW — ROBBERY— INFORMATION— VARIANCE— OWNERSHIP OF PROPERTY TAKEN. Under an information for robbery charging that the money taken was the property of M, there is no variance by proof that it belonged to a partnership of which M was a member, and that it was in his immediate and exclusive control, since Bal. Code, § 6944, so providing as to property stolen or fraudulently received, is applicable to robbery although robbery is not specifically mentioned. *Id* 127

6. SAME—INFORMATION—VARIANCE—NAME OF DEPOSITOR—CORPORATION SUCCEEDING PARTNERSHIP—IDEM SONANS. Under an information against a bank officer for receiving, after the insolvency of the bank, a deposit from the B. G. Co., a corporation, it is a fatal variance to prove a deposit by B. & S., a copartnership, consisting of the incorporators of the B. G. Co., which was not in existence at the time alleged, and the fact that the corporation was the successor of the copartnership does not bring the two names within the principle of *idem sonans*. *State v. Oleson* 149

7. SAME—NAME OF DEPOSITOR NECESSARY TO IDENTIFY DEPOSIT. The fact that the bank was insolvent at a particular time, and that a deposit of $113 was made at that time, does not identify the act of such deposit with certainty, without the name of the depositor, within the provision of Bal. Code, § 6846, respecting material variances. *Id* 149

8. CRIMINAL LAW—BURGLARY—EVIDENCE—COMPETENCY. Where, in a prosecution for burglary, a witness testified that he saw the defendant enter a stable and take away two saddles, and that he notified the police by phone, it is not reversible error to sustain an objection, on cross-examination, to the question why witness did not notify the owners of the stable. *State v. Detherage* 326

9. SAME—FLIGHT. Upon a witness' testifying that he saw defendant twenty-five miles from the place where the burglary was committed, and only eight hours thereafter, it is not error to permit the witness to answer the question, "Was defendant under arrest?" it not appearing that the witness was not qualified, and the

CRIMINAL LAW—CONTINUED.

primary purpose of the testimony being to show the fact of flight.
Id. 326

10.   SAME.   Where there is evidence that defendant committed a
burglary at 2 o'clock A. M., and upon being discovered, disappeared, and admits that he walked twenty-five miles by 10
o'clock of the same morning, without giving any reason therefor,
there was sufficient evidence of the flight of defendant to submit
the fact to the jury. Id..................................... 326

11.   BURGLARY—EVIDENCE—SUFFICIENCY—CONFESSION BY ANOTHER—
CONFLICTING EVIDENCE—NEW TRIAL. A conviction of burglary
will not be set aside as unwarranted by the evidence, because
another states positively that he and not the defendant committed the crime, where, upon cross-examination, the witness
was unable to state any of the surrounding circumstances, and
admitted having been convicted of a felony and having occupied the same cell with defendant, and his evidence was squarely
contradicted, since a new trial should not be awarded on conflicting evidence where there was evidence clearly sufficient to
warrant the verdict. Id..................................... 326

12.   CRIMINAL LAW—EVIDENCE—EXPERTS—OPINION AS TO PROPER
METHOD OF CONDUCTING POST MORTEM EXAMINATION. Where experts are asked hypothetical questions showing their ideas as to
the proper method of conducting a post mortem examination to
determine the cause of death, it is not error to sustain an objection to a question as to whether another course, omitting steps
which they considered necessary, was a sufficient and thorough
examination to determine the cause of death. State v. Underwood 558

13.   CRIMINAL LAW—EVIDENCE—GOOD CHARACTER—INSTRUCTIONS.
Where evidence of defendant's good reputation was not questioned as being the best evidence thereof, and its bearing upon
the question of defendant's guilt was properly explained by an
instruction to the jury it was not error to refuse an instruction
that, where a witness testifies that he knows the defendant and
his associates in the community in which he lives, and that his
character has never been questioned, such character is good.
Id............... 558

III.   TRIAL—INSTRUCTIONS.

14.   CRIMINAL LAW—INFORMATION—TIME FOR FILING—DISMISSAL
OF PROSECUTION AFTER THIRTY DAYS. Where the accused, after
being held to answer to the superior court by a justice of the

CRIMINAL LAW—Continued.

peace, gives a bail bond for his appearance, and no information is filed against him for thirty days, as required by Bal. Code, § 6910, the prosecution must be dismissed unless good cause for the delay is shown, and the burden of showing such cause is upon the state. *State v. Lewis*.............................. 261

15. Same—Trial—Harmless Error in Instructions. Erroneous instructions authorizing the jury to find the defendant guilty of murder in the first degree, could not have been prejudicial where the verdict was guilty of the second degree. *State v. Underwood* 558

16. Criminal Law—Trial—Failure of Defendant to Testify—Instructions. An instruction that no inference of guilt shall arise against the accused because of his failure to testify in his own behalf is not objectionable because the court states that the statute make it the duty of the judge to so instruct the jury. *State v. Detherage*... 326

17. Criminal Law—Trial—Instructions as to Fact of Flight. An instruction that evidence of flight of the accused may be considered in determining his guilt, is not objectionable as a comment on the evidence. *Id*.................................. 326

18. Same. Neither is such an instruction objectionable because it fails to explain that circumstances explaining the fact of flight may be considered, where there were no facts or circumstances to explain or excuse the flight. *Id*..................... 326

19. Homicide—Different Degrees—Verdict for Lesser Degree Where Evidence Showed Higher Degree. Upon a trial for murder in the first degree in having caused the death of an infant by drowning, where the main issue was whether the death was caused by drowning or by an accidental overdose of chloroform, and there was sufficient evidence to support either theory, and the jury are instructed to find the defendant not guilty if they believe the death was caused by chloroform or entertain a reasonable doubt as to the drowning, a verdict of murder in the second degree should not be set aside upon the theory that the jury must find the defendant guilty of the first degree or not at all and accused cannot complain that he was found guilty of a lesser degree than the evidence warranted. *State v. Underwood* 558

20. Homicide—Degrees of Offense—Instructions Proper as to Lesser Degree Although Evidence Showed First Degree Only. In a prosecution for murder in the first degree by causing the death of an infant by drowning, in which there was evidence that the defendant was guilty as charged and also that the death was accidental, the contention being that he was guilty of murder

CRIMINAL LAW—CONTINUED.

in the first degree or not at all, it is not error to instruct the jury that they may find the defendant guilty in the second degree or of manslaughter, since the deliberation and premeditation necessary to constitute the first degree, under the statute, do not necessarily follow from the facts showing malice, and must be submitted to and found by the jury, and the charge necessarily includes, and warrants a finding of, the lesser degrees. *Id...* 558

CUSTOM:

— Commissions, pleading and proof. See BROKERS, 4.

DAMAGES:

— For champertous agreement. See CHAMPERTY, 2.
— For death, earning capacity. See DEATH, 1.
— For detaining premises, instructions. See LANDLORD AND TENANT, 4.
— For detention, in replevin. See APPEAL AND ERROR, 5.
— For overflow of premises. See LIMITATION OF ACTIONS, 2, 3.
— For tortious injury. See TORTS, 1.
— Measure of, on breach of contract. See SALES, 1, 3.

1. MEASURE OF DAMAGES — MENTAL SUFFERING IRRESPECTIVE OF BODILY INJURY. A wrong having been committed by the defendant in ordering the plaintiff out of a public park where she had a right to be, it is proper to instruct that the jury, in estimating the damages, may consider the plaintiff's mental suffering, even though no bodily injury was inflicted. *Davis v. Tacoma R. & Power Co.* 203

2. DAMAGES — EVIDENCE — TESTIFYING TO AMOUNT IN MONEY — WHEN PERMISSIBLE. In an action by a riparian owner for damages caused by a boom company in floating logs down a stream, it is not prejudicial error to allow the plaintiff to testify to his damage in money, where the injury consisted in the depreciation of the value of the land and the destruction of personal property, and he testified as to the values and afterwards stated the sum total, which could have been arrived at by a mathematical calculation. *Ingram v. Wishkah Boom Co...* 191

3. SAME—DAMAGES SINCE COMMENCEMENT OF ACTION—INSTRUCTIONS WITHOUT EVIDENCE ON POINT. In an action for damages to plaintiffs' premises by fumes from a smelter, commenced by the service of a summons in August, in which the complaint was not filed until December, and in which there was no evidence as to the damage sustained from August to December, it is error to

DAMAGES—Continued.

instruct the jury to assess damages sustained during the two years next preceding December as the date of the commencement of the action, since the action was commenced when the summons was served. *Rowe v. Northport Smelting & Refining Co*........ 101

4. SAME—INSTRUCTIONS—WAIVER OF ERROR—SUFFICIENCY OF EXCEPTION. The objection to such an instruction is not waived by failing to object to a preliminary statement of the court that the date of filing the complaint would be considered as the date of commencing the action, where timely exception was taken to the instruction after retirement of the jury. *Id*................. 101

5. DAMAGES—MEASURE OF—BREACH OF CONTRACT TO PAINT HOUSES —DISCHARGE. Where plaintiff contracted to paint defendant's houses for a specified sum, and, after working five days, was discharged, it is error to instruct that the measure of his damages is the profit he would have made on the contract in addition to the reasonable value of the work already performed at the time of the discharge, since he was entitled only to pay for the work performed at the contract price, and to the profit he would have made upon the balance of the contract. *Chase v. Smith* 631

6. SAME. Such an instruction is not cured by recalling the jury and, after withdrawing the part allowing a quantum meruit for the work performed, instructing that the recovery for that part must be proportional to the completed work at the contract price, since it still permitted additional recovery for the profits of the entire contract. *Id*... 631

7. SAME — DAMAGES — EXCESSIVE VERDICT DUE TO PASSION OR PREJUDICE. In an action for personal indignities inflicted upon the plaintiff in being ordered from a public resort as a disreputable woman, in which it appears that it was due to a mistake of the defendant's employe, who immediately apologized therefor, and the defendant also openly apologized for the mistake, and the evidence showing actual damages is very meager, a verdict for the sum of $750 is not warranted, and is clearly the result of passion and prejudice, requiring a reversal. *Davis v. Tacoma R. & Power Co* 203

8. DAMAGES—DEATH OF HUSBAND—EXCESSIVE VERDICT. A verdict for $20,000 for the death of plaintiff's husband will be held excessive and reduced to $10,000, where it appears that his business as a photographer, in which the wife was associated, produced a net income of $2,000 per year, that she continued the business, producing sufficient for her needs, and that there were no children to support. *Halverson v. Seattle Electric Co*............ 600

DAMAGES—Continued.

9.   Damages — Excessive Verdict — Power of Trial Court to Remit Excess—New Trial.   Where the trial court was of the opinion that the damages for personal injuries awarded by the jury were excessive, it has power to require the plaintiff to remit the excessive amount or submit to a new trial.   *Bailey v. Cascade Timber Co* 295

10.   Damages—When Excessive.   Where $6,000 was awarded for personal injuries sustained in the fracture of the ulna and a dislocation of the head of the radius, resulting in limiting the turning motion of the forearm, but which did not destroy the usefulness of the arm or greatly lessen plaintiff's earning ability, a finding of the trial court that the verdict was excessive and should be reduced to $4,000 will be sustained.   *Id.* 295

DANGEROUS PREMISES:
— Negligence of agent of building.   See Negligence, 1-4.

DEATH:
— Abatement of action by.   See Abatement, 1-3.
— Excessive verdict for.   See Damages, 8.

1.   Death—Damages to Widow—Evidence—Earning Capacity of Husband's Business—Statements Irrespective of Books—Best Evidence.   In an action by a widow for damages for the death of her husband, where the wife had been associated with him in, and was familiar with the amount of, his business, as a photographer, it is competent, upon the subject of the damages, for the wife to testify that he was earning about $2,000 per year. without producing the books, her estimate being based thereon and on her knowledge of the business, since the books, while the best evidence of their contents, are only secondary evidence of the income of the business.   *Halverson v. Seattle Electric Co..*

DEDICATION:

1.   Dedication—Plats.   An alley fourteen feet wide between two adjoining plats of additions to a city, which is as definitely marked on the plats and described in the dedications as any of the streets which are wholly within either plat, is dedicated to the public use by the parties dedicating the plats of which it forms a part.   *Bonne v. Security Sav. Society* ....

DEED:
— As color of title.   See Adverse Possession, 3-4.

DEFAMATION OF CHARACTER:

See Libel and Slander, 1, 2.

— Measure of damages. See Damages, 1.

DEMAND:

— Before suit. See Municipal Corporations, 3.

DEMURRAGE:

— Modification of agreement for. See Sales, 1.

DEMURRER:

See Pleadings.

— Conclusions not admitted. See Mandamus, 4.

— Harmless error. See Appeal and Error, 33.

DEPARTURE:

See Pleadings, 7.

DESCENT AND DISTRIBUTION:

— Rights of adopted child. See Adoption, 1-3.

DISCOVERY:

— Of Facts. See Pleadings, 4.

1.   Discovery—Interrogatories—Accident Report—Confidential Communications. In an action against a railroad company for personal injuries to an employe, it is proper to strike out from interrogatories for a discovery, propounded to the defendant under Bal. Code, § 6009, one that compels the defendant to produce the accident report and confidential correspondence touching the case, since such communications are privileged. *Cully v. Northern Pac. R. Co* 241

2.   Same—Inspection of Papers. Doubted whether the production of documentary evidence can be enforced by interrogatories under Bal. Code, § 6009, in view of § 6047, making provision for their inspection. *Id* 241

3.   Same—Writings—Inspection and Copy Before Trial. The failure to offer an inspection and serve a copy of a writing, before trial, is not a valid objection to the writing as evidence, under Bal. Code, § 6048, since that section merely provides that such inspection and copy shall dispense with proof of execution and genuineness in case it is not denied by affidavit. *Beebe v. Redward* 615

CARRIERS—CONTINUED.

in contact with an upright twenty-six inches from the platform of
the car, which was a necessary support for the operation of the
boat; since there was no duty to warn and there is no presumption of negligence from an injury to a passenger under such circumstances (HADLEY and DUNBAR, JJ., dissenting). *Id*........ 221

11. SAME—DUTY OF CARRIER TO ONE DESIRING TO BECOME A PASSEN-
GER. Street railway employes are not required to exercise the
highest degree of care in ascertaining whether a person desires
to become a passenger, hence it is not error to instruct that the
company is not liable to one injured in attempting to board a car,
if the conductor, by the exercise of ordinary care, could not have
seen him before starting the car. *Foster v. Seattle Electric Co*.. 177

12. CARRIERS—NEGLIGENCE—INJURY TO PASSENGER ON STREET CAR—
DEGREE OF CARE REQUIRED OF COMPANY—INSTRUCTIONS. In an
action for personal injuries sustained by a passenger while
alighting from a street car, it is error to instruct that while the
company is not an insurer, the law calls upon it to do whatever
can be done to insure the protection of passengers, since the
company is only bound to exercise the highest degree of care
consistent with the practical conduct of its business, and such an
instruction is reversible error where it is the only one defining
the measure of defendant's duty to passengers. *Johnson v. Seattle Electric Co*... 382

13. CARRIERS—NEGLIGENCE—INSTRUCTIONS—DUTY OWED TO PASSEN-
GERS—HIGHEST DEGREE OF CARE CONSISTENT WITH PRACTICAL CON-
DUCT OF BUSINESS. In an action against a street railway company to recover damages for personal injuries, an instruction to
the effect that the company is not liable if it exercises towards
its passengers the highest degree of care consistent with the
practical conduct of its business, is a correct statement of defendant's legal duty. *Foster v. Seattle Electric Co*............. 177

14. SAME. While it is incorrect in giving such an instruction, to
further state that the conductor of the car should exercise the
highest degree of care "consistent with the proper discharge of
all the other duties of such employes," yet it is not prejudicial
error where there was no evidence to the effect that the injury
was caused by the fact that he was engaged in the performance
of any other duty. *Id*.. 177

15. CARRIERS—NEGLIGENCE—DUTY OF STREET CAR COMPANY TO PRO-
VIDE PASSENGERS WITH SEATS — INSTRUCTIONS. In an action
against a street car company for negligence in the running of its
car, resulting in the death of a passenger who was standing upon

EJECTMENT—Continued.

equitable estoppel, in that the land in question, being a hillside and valueless, the plaintiff induced the defendants to enter thereon and inclose, irrigate, and improve the same at great expense, under the oral representation that after ten years' possession the defendants would have title thereto, which improvement enhanced the value of plaintiff's other lands in the vicinity, the defendants can recover only on the theory of the equitable estoppel as alleged, and the allegations that the land was valueless when the defendants entered, and that its improvement enhanced the value of plaintiff's adjoining property, are material allegations, necessary to be shown as part of the oral contract for the sale of the property, by clear and satisfactory evidence, in order to take the case out of the statute of frauds. *Riverside Land Co. v. Pietsch* 210

2. Same—Instructions. Accordingly, in such a case, it is error to instruct that the only question for the jury is whether the plaintiff put the defendants in possession with the understanding aforesaid, thereby eliminating the said allegations as to nonvalue and enhancing the value of other lands, and requires a reversal and a new trial. *Id* 210

EMINENT DOMAIN:

1. Eminent Domain—Municipal Corporations—Public Purpose—Electric Light Plant. The city of Seattle is authorized to exercise the right of eminent domain for the purposes of an electric light plant, under Bal. Code, § 739, subd. 6 authorizing cities of the first class to appropriate property for corporate purposes, and subd. 15, authorizing it to erect and maintain plants for furnishing lights to the city or its inhabitants. *State ex rel Kent Lumber Co. v. Superior Court* 303

2. Same—Condemnation of Lands Outside City Limits. Such power may be exercised to appropriate lands outside of the city limits. *Id.* 303

3. Same—Ordinance Authorizing Condemnation. An ordinance condemning the land, providing for a proceeding in the superior court to appropriate it, and authorizing the corporation counsel to conduct the proceedings, is sufficient to confer authority upon the city to maintain the action. *Id.* 303

4. Eminent Domain—Waterways—Logging—Condemning Right to Use Stream for Floating Logs. A private corporation which is not a boom company is not entitled to exercise the right of eminent domain against the lower riparian owner for the purpose

EMINENT DOMAIN—Continued.

of facilitating the floating of logs down a stream by means of dams and artificial freshets, which damage the lower proprietor and interfere with his use of the stream. *Matthews v. Belfast Mfg. Co* 662

EQUITY:
— Practice in. See Trials, 4.

ESTOPPEL:
— Acquiesence in unlawful use of stream. See Waters, 3.
— By delay. See Rescission, 2.
— By judgment, sureties. See Execution, 1; Indemnity, 3.
— Local assessments. See Municipal Corporations, 8.
— Oral representations, title. See Ejectment, 1, 2.

EVIDENCE:
— Agent's authority to repair, sufficiency. See Negligence, 2-4.
— Alibi, sufficiency. See Criminal Law, 4.
— Authority to assign mail contract. See Contracts, 3.
— Broker's commissions, sufficiency. See Brokers, 5.
— Burglary, sufficiency. See Criminal Law, 11.
— Character of property. See Community Property, 1, 2.
— Confidential communications. See Discovery, 1.
— Consideration. See Contracts, 7.
— Cumulative. See New Trial, 3.
— Damages. See Damages, 2; Nuisance, 1-3.
— Degrees of offense. See Criminal Law, 15, 19, 20.
— Disposition of conductor, admissibility. See Carriers, 5, 6.
— Earning capacity of deceased. See Death, 1.
— Experiments. See Nuisance, 3; Carriers, 19.
— Experts. See Criminal Law, 12; Carriers, 18.
— Flight. See Criminal Law, 10.
— Fraud. See Compromise, 1; Fraudulent Conveyances, 1, 2.
— Good character. See Criminal Law, 13,
— Harmless Admission. See Appeal and Error, 31, 32.
— Inspection of copies. See Discovery, 2, 3.
— Lease, notice, sufficiency. See Landlord and Tenant, 1, 2.
— Negligence, slide in gravel pit. See Master and Servant, 1. Moving train on ferry. See Carriers, 10.
— Opinions. See Compromise, 2.
— Other transactions, materiality. See Brokers, 2.
— Parol. See Rescission, 1. To vary writing. See Contracts, 4-6.

EVIDENCE—Continued.

— Recording. See Records, 1.
— Robbery. See Criminal Law, 5.
— Signature, acceptance of service. See Appeal and Error, 13, 14.
— Title. See Specific Performance, 1.
— Values. See Execution, 2; Brokers, 3.
— Wanton damages. See Malicious Injury, 1.

1. Evidence—Letters—Competency—Authority of Agent. Although a letter not shown to be signed by an authorized agent might not be competent as an independent letter, it is admissible when referred to in a letter of the duly authorized agent, where both letters are offered as one. *Washington Iron Works v. McNaught* 10

2. Evidence — Experts — Hypothetical Question — Examiner's Theory of Case. A hypothetical question calling for the opinion of an expert witness and based upon a detailed statement of the testimony of different witnesses, is not objectionable, although such testimony is not entirely harmonious, where the jury had a right to find the facts as stated, it being sufficient, if the question fairly states such facts as present the examiner's theory of the case. *State v. Underwood* 558

3. Attorney and Client—Action for Services—Evidence—Relevancy of Improper Conduct in Securing Admission to Practice. In an action against an attorney for the alleged conversion of money and notes belonging to his client, in which it is alleged and admitted that he is duly admitted to practice in this state, it is prejudicial error to permit cross-examination suggesting that he had resorted to bribery in order to obtain his admission, since it is immaterial and irrelevant and would have the effect of arousing the passions of the jury. *Dodds v. Gregson* 402

4. Same—Evidence—Objection—Sufficiency. Where such cross-examination is objected to in the beginning and the court rules the same pertinent, further objection might increase the prejudice of the jury, and is not essential to secure a review of the ruling on appeal. *Id.* 402

5. Evidence—Payment—Receipts—Sufficiency of Objections. An objection to the admission in evidence of receipts signed by judgment creditors acknowledging payment of their judgments, on the ground that such receipts did not show payment, is not sufficient to raise the point that there was no proof of execution or authentication; and the same will not be considered on appeal. *Beebe v. Redward* 615

EVIDENCE—Continued.

6. Evidence—Admission of Answer Without the Complaint—Harmless Error. The admission in evidence of an answer to contradict the statement of the party verifying it, without introducing the complaint, is harmless where the only part of the answer read could not have been explained by anything in the complaint. *Ingram v. Wishkah Boom Co*.............. 191

EXCEPTIONS:
   See Appeal and Error, 6.

EXECUTION:
   — Sale, failure to comply with law. See Homesteads, 2, 3.

1. Execution—Redelivery Bond—Value of Property—Allegation of Claimant—Estoppel. In an action to compel the delivery of property levied upon by a sheriff, in which the claimant alleges the value to be $300, the claimant and the sureties are bound thereby and cannot complain that judgment for defendant was entered for $300 as the value of the property, although the only evidence of value made it appear to be less than $300. *Hill v. Gardner*.. 52

2. Same—Original Amount Due on the Attachment—Judgment for Value—Presumed Less Than Sum Due. Upon a judgment against a third party claimant of attached property, for $300 as the value of the property, where there is nothing to show the amount due under the attachment, it will be presumed in aid of the judgment that it was not a less sum, as required by Bal. Code, § 5266. *Id*.. 52

3. Same—Return of Property—Judgment in Alternative for Return or Value of Property. Upon an action for the redelivery of attached property, it is error for the judgment to fail to provide in the alternative for the return of the property or its value. *Id*. 52

EXECUTORS AND ADMINISTRATORS:
   — Survival of action. See Actions, 3.

EXEMPTIONS:
   See Homesteads; Taxation, 3.

FELLOW SERVANTS:
   See Master and Servant, 4, 6.

FLIGHT:

— As proof of guilt. See CRIMINAL LAW, 9, 10.

FORCIBLE ENTRY AND DETAINER:

See LANDLORD AND TENANT, 1, 2.

1. UNLAWFUL DETAINER—NOTICE TO QUIT—SUFFICIENCY OF TIME ALLOWED—MONTHLY RENTAL. Where rent was paid November 23d for one month in advance under a tenancy from month to month, a notice to quit on December 23d, served on December 2d, was in time. *Teater v. King*.................................. 138

2. SAME—DEFENSES. In an action of unlawful detainer against a subtenant, where the evidence tended to show that he was not guilty of the wrongful detention, it cannot be claimed that his rights in the premises can only be enforced in an equitable action. *Id*... 138

3. FORCIBLE ENTRY AND DETAINER—NOTICE TO QUIT—FARMING LEASE—DEFAULT IN PERFORMANCE—SPECIFYING CONDITIONS BROKEN. Where a farm lease provided that the land should be farmed in a certain specified manner, the lease containing many stipulations with reference to the lessee's performance, a notice to quit, requiring in the alternative the performance of the conditions and covenants of the lease or a surrender of the premises, which recites many of the covenants and states that the tenant has failed to keep "each and all" of the covenants mentioned, is too indefinite and uncertain to support an action of forcible entry and detainer, under Bal. Code § 5527, subd. 4, since a notice thereunder must specify with particularity the default so as to give the tenant an opportunity to exercise his right of choice. *Byrkett v. Gardner*... 668

4. SAME. Where the landlord is complaining that the general performance is not up to the standard of excellence called for by the covenant to farm in a husbandlike manner, such a notice reciting that fact generally is not sufficient to start the machinery of the statute of forcible entry and detainer. *Id*............... 668

5. SAME—RENT DUE. Such a notice is not sufficient as showing nonpayment of rent, under Bal. Code, § 5527, subd. 3, where there is the same indefiniteness with reference to the rent that is due, and there is no chance for the lessee to save the forfeiture by payment within ten days. *Id*.............................. 668

6. SAME—WASTE. Such a notice does not show waste, within subd. 5, of the same section, by the mere failure to farm the lands in a husbandlike manner or keep fences in repair, since waste is an act of destruction by the tenant. *Id*................. 668

FORECLOSURE:
— Of mortgage. See Mortgages, 1.
— Of tax lien. See Taxes, 10.

FOREIGN LAWS:
— As to adoption. See Adoption, 1-3.

FORGERY:
— Of warrant by auditor. See Counties, 2.

FRAUD:
— Delay in suing, estoppel. See Rescission, 2, 3.
— Evidence of, sufficiency. See Compromise, 1.
— In law, instructions. See Fraudulent Conveyances, 2.
— Upon government, contracts as to land. See Public Lands, 1, 3.

1. Fraud—By Corporation—Rescission of Sale of Stock—Duty of Purchaser to Investigate Representations—Truth Not at Hand. The purchaser of treasury stock from a corporation may rescind the sale for fraud where he relied upon false representations of the officers and promoters with regard to the ownership by the corporation of a device for manufacturing matches and the patents therefor, and a prospectus containing false representations as to the capacity of such machine, since the facts with reference to the existence of the machine and the patents therefor were not at hand, and the representations involved a special skilled knowledge, concerning which the plaintiff was not under obligations to investigate for himself. *Mulholland v. Washington Match Co*... 315

2. Same—Fraud in Cancellation of Contract—Subsequent Purchaser as Trustee. In an action seeking to hold a purchaser of oyster lands from the state as a trustee of a former applicant therefor, upon the allegation of fraud and collusion in securing the cancellation of the plaintiff's application, a nonsuit is properly granted, where it appears that the plaintiff was in default in making her deferred payments, that she received a notice to pay or her contract would be canceled, and paying no attention thereto, the contract was stamped "canceled," whereupon, as claimed, she filed another application, but no files thereof could be found in the office of the state land commissioner, and, after a contest, the land was awarded by the board to a subsequent applicant, there being no evidence of fraud on the part of the purchaser, or that the officers were in any way interested in his

FRAUD—Continued.

contract, and the face of the record showing that the land was open for sale at the time he applied therefor. *Frazier v. Wilson.* 625

FRAUDS, STATUTE OF:

— Oral representations as to possession of land. See Ejectment, 1, 2.

FRAUDULENT CONVEYANCES:

— Cancellation of, in action for divorce. See Divorce, 3.

1. Fraudulent Conveyances—Chattel Mortgage in Fraud of Creditors—Good Faith—Evidence—Sufficiency. Upon an issue as to whether a chattel mortgage given by a debtor was fraudulent and void as to attaching creditors, there is sufficient evidence to require the good faith of the transaction to be submitted to the jury, where it appears that the mortgage was given by the debtor to his brother when insolvent and on the brink of financial ruin, that the mortgage covered all his property, valued at from $3,000 to $4,000, while the debt secured was only $1,650, and that the debtor had repeatedly said that he owed his brother nothing. *Adams v. Dempsey* 80

2. Same—Fraud in Law—Instruction as to Facts Constituting Fraud. Upon an issue as to whether a conveyance was fraudulent as to creditors, it is proper to instruct that a debtor in failing circumstances, who transfers all his property to one creditor with a secret understanding to receive part of the proceeds or secure a benefit at the expense of other creditors, is guilty of a fraud upon his creditors; since such facts constitute fraud in law, and are more than mere evidence of fraud. *Id* 80

GUARANTY:

1. Guaranty—Extension of Time—Acceptance of Drafts. The acceptance of drafts extending the time for payment does not operate to discharge a guarantor, when they were drawn at his request or at the request of his agent, and for his benefit. *Washington Iron Works v. McNaught* 10

2. Guaranty—Consideration. There is sufficient consideration for a contract guaranteeing the payment for machinery sold and delivered on board of one of the purchaser's boats, where one dollar is the expressed consideration and the vendor refused to let the boat depart without payment of the balance due, and gave permission in consideration of the written guaranty. *Id*... 10

HIGHWAYS:

— Obstruction, injunction, stay on appeal. See APPEAL AND
ERROR, 17.

HOMESTEADS:

1. HOMESTEADS—EXEMPTIONS—OCCUPATION NOT ESSENTIAL AFTER
SELECTION. Where a homestead has been duly selected by recording the declaration under Laws 1895, p. 109, actual occupancy
of the same is not necessary to maintain the right to the homestead exemption. *Lewis v. Mauerman*........................ 156

2. SAME—EXECUTION SALE—FAILURE TO COMPLY WITH LAW RE-
SPECTING EXEMPTION—INCREASE OF EXEMPTION BY SUBSEQUENT LAW.
Where the law respecting the sale of homesteads was not complied with and no exemption at all allowed, an execution sale
of premises that have been duly selected as a homestead, cannot
be sustained on the theory that since the judgment was obtained
the exemption for a homestead was increased from $1,000 to
$2,000, and the premises were worth more than $1,000. *Id*...... 156

3. SAME—CONFIRMATION OF EXECUTION SALE—COLLATERAL AT-
TACK—HOMESTEAD CLAIM NOT CONCLUDED BY CONFIRMATION. An
action to recover possession of a homestead, sold under execution without complying with the law regulating such sales, is
not a collateral attack upon the confirmation of the sale, since
the only matter that can be determined on the confirmation is
the regularity of the proceedings concerning the sale, and the
same does not constitute an adjudication upon the question of
the homestead claim. *Id*.................................... 156

HOMICIDE:

See CRIMINAL LAW, 12, 19, 20.

HUSBAND AND WIFE:

See COMMUNITY PROPERTY; DIVORCE.
— Earning capacity, damages. See DEATH, 1.
— Sale by husband. See SPECIFIC PERFORMANCE, 3.

INDEMNITY:

1. INDEMNITY—BUILDING CONTRACT—AGREEMENT TO FURNISH ALL
MATERIALS—BREACH—FILING OF MECHANICS' LIEN—SUIT ON BOND
BEFORE DISCHARGE OF LIEN. Where an indemnity bond guarantees the faithful performance of a building contract in which the
contractors agree to furnish all the material for the building,
the failure of the contractors to pay for the materials furnished,

INDEMNITY—Continued.

resulting in the filing of a mechanics' lien, is a breach of the contract and the bond, entitling the owner to maintain a suit on the bond before the payment and discharge of the lien claim for materials. *Friend v. Ralston*.................................. 422

2. Same—Defenses—Failure to Pay Contractors—Credits for Balance Due Allowed on Claim Against Contractors. In an action upon a bond guaranteeing a building contract, in which the owner seeks to recover the amount of a judgment establishing a mechanics' lien for material furnished to the contractors, it is no defense that the plaintiff had refused to pay the contractors two small items for a balance due and for extras, where due credits were received therefor by the contractors and inured to the benefit of the surety on the bond, having been deducted from the amount of the plaintiff's claim. *Id*............................ 422

3. Same—Judgment Against Principal—Notice to the Surety to Defend—Estoppel. Where a surety company guaranteed, by its bond, the faithful performance of a building contract in which the contractors agreed to furnish all the material, and is given due notice to defend an action commenced by materialmen to foreclose a lien for material furnished to the contractors, a judgment obtained in good faith against the contractors, the principals in the bond, establishing the claim and foreclosing the lien, is binding upon the surety, to the same extent that it binds the contractors, and in an action on the bond estops the surety company from claiming that there was no breach of the contract. *Id.* 422

4. Indemnity—Building Contract—Action on Bond—Accrual—Limitations—Date of First Breach—Delay in Completion of Building—Breach Waived by Owner. Where an indemnity bond guaranteeing a building contract provided that actions thereon must be instituted within six months after the first breach of the contract, which called for the completion of the building in August, 1901, and the owner accepted the building upon its completion in December, 1901, the company cannot claim that the right of action accrued in August and was barred six months thereafter, since the owner waived that breach by accepting the building, and the surety cannot complain of the waiver of any breach of the contract or departure therefrom that does not operate to its prejudice. *Beebe v. Redward*...................... 615

5. Same—Mechanics' Liens as Breach of Contract—Waiver by Owner. Where an indemnity bond guarantees the performance of a building contract in which the contractor agrees to furnish

INDEMNITY—Continued.

all the material, the owner is not obliged to treat the filing of
a mechanics' lien as a breach of the contract, and assume the
burden of establishing the lien; but he may waive the same until
it is established by a court of competent jurisdiction, in which
case his right of action on the bond accrues at that time, and an
action begun within the six months limited in the bond after the
first lien is established by judgment is in time. *Id*............. 615

IDEM SONANS:

— Rule not applicable to different persons. See CRIMINAL
LAW, 7.

IMPROVEMENTS:

— Diversion of fund for. See MUNICIPAL CORPORATIONS, 9.
— Of tide lands. See CONSTITUTIONAL LAW, 3-8; STATE AND
STATE OFFICERS, 2.

INFORMATION:

See CRIMINAL LAW, 3, 5, 6, 14, 19, 20.

INJUNCTION:

— Against change of grade. See MUNICIPAL CORPORATIONS, 4.
— Against dam for floating logs. See WATERS, 7, 8.
— Against disorderly house. See NUISANCE, 7.
— Against slaughter house. See NUISANCE, 8, 9.
— Against threatened error. See PROHIBITION, 1.
— Superseding on appeal. See APPEAL AND ERROR, 17.

1.   INJUNCTION — BOND — REQUIRING NEW BOND — DISCRETION OF
LOWER COURT. Before an injunction can issue against the grading
of a street by a city, the plaintiff must be required to give a bond
as required by Bal. Code, § 5438, and if insufficient, a new bond
may be required, in the discretion of the court, to be exercised
legally, not arbitrarily. *Swope v. Seattle*.................... 69

2.   SAME—REQUIRING NEW BOND—SUFFICIENCY OF SHOWING—ABUSE
OF DISCRETION. Where abutting property was about to be materially damaged by the grading of a street, and plaintiffs' right to
an injunction seemed clear, and an injunction was granted
against such grading until compensation should be made for such
damage upon the plaintiffs' giving a bond for $100, it is an abuse
of discretion to require a further bond in the sum of $3,000, which
is more than the value of the property, upon the application of the
contractor, who did not deny any of the allegations of the plain-

INJUNCTION—Continued.

tiffs, but merely made a showing that he would be greatly damaged by the delay, neither the city nor its officers applying for any further bond. *Id*... 69

INSOLVENCY:

See Assignment for Creditors, 1.

1. Insolvency—Federal Bankruptcy Act—State Laws Not Suspended. The federal bankruptcy law, approved July 1, 1898, did not supersede or suspend the state insolvency law, in existence at that time, where no proceedings in bankruptcy were instituted. *Jensen-King-Byrd Co. v. Williams*...................... 161

INSTRUCTIONS:

See Appeal and Error, 35, 36; Brokers, 4; Bridges, 1; Carriers, 11-17; Criminal Law, 10, 15-18; Damages, 3, 5, 6; Ejectment, 1, 2; Landlord and Tenant, 4; Malicious Injury, 1; Trial, 5, 6, 10.

JURISDICTION:

— Erroneous exercise. See Prohibition, 1.

JURY:

— Misconduct. See New Trial, 1, 2.
— Passion or prejudice. See Damages.
— Poll, change of vote. See Trial, 10.

LANDLORD AND TENANT:

See Forcible Entry and Detainer.
— Agents' duty to repair. See Negligence, 1-4.
— Measure of damages on failure to rent. See Sales, 3.

1. Landlord and Tenant—Unlawful Detainer—Validity of Sublease—Evidence—Sufficiency—Question for Jury. In an action of unlawful detainer brought by a tenant of the whole premises against a subtenant of a part, there is sufficient evidence to require the submission to the jury of an issue as to whether defendant was rightfully in possession under a sublease prior to plaintiff's lease, where it appears that the owners originally leased to D for an indefinite period, and D subleased for two years, subject to the continuance of her own term, and the owners in writing recognized the sublease, and for a valuable consideration agreed to approve the same, and the evidence tended to show that plaintiff, who bought out D before the

LANDLORD AND TENANT—CONTINUED.

expiration of said two years, had knowledge at the time, of the sublease, and of the owner's recognition thereof. *Teater v. King* 138

2. SAME—OWNER'S RECOGNITION CONCLUSIVE. In such case, the plaintiff cannot raise the question of the validity of the original lease, nor of the owner's recognition of the sublease, when those questions are not raised by the owner. *Id.* 138

3. LANDLORD AND TENANT — LEASE — CONSTRUCTION — PERPETUAL RENEWALS. An intention to create a perpetual lease by a clause for perpetual renewals must be clear and unequivocal, and is not shown by reserving a monthly rental terminating at a certain time "with the privilege at the same rate and terms each year thereafter from year to year," where the lease contains only covenants applicable to a short fixed period without employing any terms of perpetuity. *Tischner v. Rutledge* 285

4. LANDLORD AND TENANT—RIGHTFULNESS OF POSSESSION—NOTICE TO QUIT—INSTRUCTIONS. In an action for damages to personal property located on certain premises, wherein the complaint alleges that defendant wrongfully took possession of the premises, it was not error to instruct that, if the relation of landlord and tenant existed between the parties the latter woud be entitled to ten days' notice in order to determine its rights of occupancy, since the fact bears on the rightfulness of the possession. *Rice Fisheries Co. v. Pacific Realty Co* 53

LACHES:

See RESCISSION.

LAW OF CASE:

— Negligence. See MASTER AND SERVANT, 3.

LEASE:

See LANDLORD AND TENANT.
— Performance of covenants. See FORCIBLE ENTRY AND DETAINER, 3-6.

LEGISLATURE:

— Discretionary power. See TAXATION, 1.
— Restrictions at extra session. See STATUTES, 1.

LIBEL AND SLANDER:

1. SLANDER—PERSONAL INDIGNITIES—DEFAMATION OF CHARACTER—PUBLIC RESORTS—RIGHT TO REMAIN AT—DAMAGES FOR EX-

LIBEL AND SLANDER—Continued.

cluding From—Words Not Actionable per se. Any person not belonging to a proscribed class who goes to a public pleasure resort or park, and is not guilty of improper conduct, may recover for personal indignities inflicted by an employe of the parties owning and in charge of the place, in being publicly ordered out in an insulting manner as an unfit and improper person, without showing that the language used was actionable *per se*, if any special damages were suffered. *Davis v. Tacoma R. & Power Co.* 203

2.   Same—Malice or Wilful Conduct. In such a case, it is not necessary for the plaintiff to show malice or a wanton or wilful wrong in order to recover actual damages, the same being material only to enhance the damages. *Id*.................... 203

LICENSE:

— Injury to licensee on bridge. See Railroads, 1, 2.

LIENS:

See Mechanics' Liens; Taxation.
— For alimony. See Divorce, 3.
— For improvements on tide lands. See Constitutional Law, 3-8; Public Lands, 4; Statutes, 3.
— Unrecorded, foreclosure. See Mortgages, 1.

LIMITATION OF ACTIONS:

1.   Limitation of Actions—Three-Year Limitation Upon Contracts Not in Writing—Construction of Statute. The limitation of Bal. Code, § 4800, subd. 3, for the commencement of actions upon a contract "or liability" express or implied which is not in writing, refers only to contractual liabilities. *Suter v. Wenatchee Water Power Co.*.................................... 1

2.   Same—Damage to Real Property by Overflow—When Not a Trespass. An action for damages to real property through an overflow caused by the defendant's negligent construction of an irrigating canal, lawfully built, but without sufficiently providing for carrying off the surplus water or controlling the flow, is not an action for trespass within the purview of the three-year limitation for actions for "trespass on real property," since the damages are consequential only, and not direct, as required to create trespass at common law; and such action is barred if not commenced within two years from the time the damage accrued. *Id.* 1

LIMITATION OF ACTIONS—Continued.

3.   Same. In such a case, even if the water was under control, negligently permitting it to escape would not create a forcible trespass, and the damages would be consequential, recoverable at common law in an action on the case only. *Id*................. 1

4.   Limitation of Actions — Diversion of Special Fund for Local Improvements—Accrual of Right of Action. The right of action against a city for the wrongful diversion of a special fund provided for the payment of warrants, does not accrue until the holder of the warrant has notice of the diversion. *Northwestern Lumber Co. v. Aberdeen*...................................... 636

LOGS AND LOGGING:

See Eminent Domain, 4; Waters, 1-8.

MALICE:

— In prosecution. See Champerty, 2.

— To enhance damages. See Libel and Slander, 2.

MALICIOUS INJURY:

1.   Malicious Injury to Property—Pleading and Proof—Instructions. In an action for injury to property, where the complaint charged that defendants acted maliciously, wantonly, and unlawfully, proof of a mere wrongful or unlawful injury was in support of the complaint, and it was not error to refuse to instruct that the burden was upon plaintiff to show malicious and wanton damage. *Rice Fisheries Co. v. Pacific Realty Co*........ 5

MALICIOUS PROSECUTION:

— Malice necessary. See Champerty, 2.

1.   Malicious Prosecution—Conviction of Plaintiff Admitted. An action for a malicious prosecution cannot be maintained where the plaintiffs were admittedly convicted of the offense charged against them. *McKenzie v. Royal Dairy*.............. 3

MANDAMUS:

— To compel issuance of warrant. See Counties, 3, 4.

1.   Mandamus — Parties — County Commissioners Proper Parties in Action Against Auditor. County commissioners may be proper but they are not necessary parties to a proceeding in mandamus against the county auditor to compel him to issue a warrant upon a claim allowed by the commissioners against the

MANDAMUS—Continued.

county, since the county may be affected by the result (Anders, J., dissents). *American Bridge Co. v. Wheeler*................ 40

2. Mandamus—When Lies—Issuance of Building Permit—Discretionary Powers of Building Inspector—Appeal to Board of Public Works—Decision by Quasi Judicial Body—No Writ to Compel Change of Judgment. Where a building inspector must hear protests against the issuance of building permits, and refer reasonable objections to the board of public works, and his decisions are binding until reversed, and an appeal may be taken therefrom to said board, which hears the matter upon evidence taken, mandamus will not lie to compel such officers to issue a building permit for a livery stable, after objections and a hearing duly had before said board, upon which the board refused the permit, since the inspector and board exercise discretion, and have determined the matter in a judicial capacity, and mandamus does not lie to compel a change of judgment. *Hester v. Thomson* 119

3. Same—Action by Board—Construction of Ordinance. In such a case it cannot be claimed that the board has not acted, under an ordinance suspending proceedings until the matter is "adjusted" by the board, since that signifies simply a determination by the board. *Id*.. 119

4. Same—Motion to Quash Writ—Demurrer—Conclusions Not Admitted. A motion to quash a writ of mandamus for want of sufficient facts performs the office of a demurrer, and only admits the facts stated, and not the conclusions drawn therefrom; and a conclusion that defendants acted capriciously and arbitrarily is unavailing in the absence of facts in the petition showing such action. *Id*.. 119

MASTER AND SERVANT:

1. Master and Servant—Negligence—Safe Place—Injury to Servant by Slide in Gravel Pit. An employe working in and about a gravel pit cannot recover for injuries received by reason of a slide, where there was no evidence of negligence on the part of the master in failing to discover the danger or to give warning thereof, since the rule that he must furnish a safe place in which to work has no application to that class of cases. *Cully v. Northern Pac. R. Co*.................................. 241

2. Master and Servant—Negligence—Safe Appliances—Instructions—Sufficiency. In an action for personal injuries sustained by an employe upon the breaking of a swamp hook,

MASTER AND SERVANT—Continued.

instructions sufficiently submit to the jury the question whether defendant furnished proper appliances, where the jury are told that the burden of proof as to whether defendant furnished a reasonably safe swamp hook was upon the plaintiff, and that the plaintiff could not recover unless that was shown to be the proximate cause of the injury. *Bailey v. Cascade Timber Co.*. 295

3.   SAME—SELECTION OF APPLIANCES—APPEAL—DECISION—LAW OF THE CASE. The supreme court having decided upon a former appeal that the removal of a heavy tank was not a mere ordinary detail of the work of a logging crew that could be delegated to fellow-servants of the plaintiff, the same becomes the law of the case and is conclusive. *Id*.................................. 295

4.   SAME—FELLOW-SERVANTS—DELEGATED DUTIES—IMMATERIAL BY WHOM DISCHARGED. The supreme court having decided upon a former appeal that a hook tender charged with the duty of selecting a proper swamp hook to be used in moving a heavy tank is not a fellow-servant, but a vice-principal with respect to such duties, it is immaterial whether that duty was discharged by him or by some other employe, as in either case it is a duty owed by the master. *Id*.................................. 295

5.   MASTER AND SERVANT—NEGLIGENCE—ASSUMPTION OF RISK—APPARENT DANGER FROM UNGUARDED MANGLE IN LAUNDRY. In an action for personal injuries sustained by an operator of a five roll mangle in a laundry, by reason of the alleged removal of a guard, whereby plaintiff's hand was caught between the rolls, the plaintiff assumes the risks or is guilty of contributory negligence as a matter of law, where it appears that she is an intelligent woman of the age of 25 years, had been working on the machine in question as a feeder for three months, and it was obvious that she would suffer injury if she allowed her hands to be caught while running clothes through the machine, and she fully appreciated the danger, and it is error to refuse to grant a nonsuit. *Bier v. Hosford*.................................. 54

6.   SAME—OBEYING INSTRUCTIONS. A servant is not justified, in the presence of apparent danger, in putting life or limb in jeopardy by rushing the work unreasonably in obedience to orders of a fellow-servant, who was in charge of the work. *Id*.. 54

7.   SAME—PLEADING—ASSUMPTION OF RISKS—NONSUIT. While assumption of risks is an affirmative defense which must be pleaded, still, when it appears by the plaintiff's evidence that he cannot recover in any event by reason thereof, defendant is entitled to a nonsuit. *Id*.................................. 54

MASTER AND SERVANT—Continued.

8. Master and Servant—Release Secured by Fraud—Servant's Continuance of Employment—Estoppel. Where a servant was induced, by an agreement for future employment and false representations respecting the extent of his injuries, to sign a release for personal injuries sustained through the negligence of the master, the fact that he shortly afterwards went back to work under representations of the master's claim agent and physician that his injuries were slight, and worked and received wages for about a year and a half, does not militate against his recovery for the injuries received. *Bjorklund v. Seattle Electric Co.* 439

MECHANICS' LIENS:
— Breach of building contract. See INDEMNITY, 1-5.

1. Mechanics' Liens — Foreclosure — Evidence—Sufficiency— Substantial Completion of Building—Acceptance by Owner— Architect's Certificate. An action to foreclose a mechanics' lien should not be dismissed, because it appears that it would take the trifling sum of $57 to complete a $3,850 building, where the record shows a substantial compliance with the contract, together with an offer on the part of the contractors to complete any work, and where the building was received and occupied, and the refusal of the architect to furnish the required certificate was whimsical. *Windham v. Independent Telephone Co.* 166

MORTGAGES:
—Redemption, necessity of proffer. See QUIETING TITLE, 1.

1. Mortgages—Foreclosure Sale—Purchaser Without Notice of Unrecorded Interests—Quieting Title—Pleading. An answer in an action to quiet title, pleading title in the defendants through a foreclosure sale, need not allege that the plaintiffs were parties to the foreclosure proceeding, where it is alleged that plaintiffs had no interest of record at the time, and that the purchaser had no notice of any such interest or claim, since he holds as an innocent purchaser for value as to outstanding unrecorded liens of which he has no notice. *Jones v. Herrick* 434

MUNICIPAL CORPORATIONS:
— Building permit, powers of board. See MANDAMUS, 2-4.
— Change of grade, bond. See INJUNCTION.
— City orders, construction. See CONTRACTS, 2. Consideration. See CONTRACTS, 7.

MUNICIPAL CORPORATIONS—Continued.

— Diversion of special fund. See LIMITATION OF ACTIONS, 4.

— Notice of assessment, promise of officers. See CONSTITUTIONAL LAW, 2.

— Ordinances, building permits, construction. See MANDAMUS, 2-4.

— Power to condemn lands. See EMINENT DOMAIN, 1-3.

— Toleration of bawdy house. See NUISANCE, 5.

1. MUNICIPAL CORPORATIONS—ORDER PAYABLE ACCORDING TO ITS TERMS — CITY COMPTROLLER'S ADMISSION. A city comptroller, upon filing an order on the city, drawn by a contractor, has no power to bind the city or create a liability beyond the terms of the order, by stating that it is all right and would be paid. *Dickerson v. Spokane* 414

2. MUNICIPAL CORPORATIONS—NUISANCE—LIABILITY OF TOWN FOR MAINTENANCE OF PESTHOUSE—RATIFICATION OF ACTS OF OFFICERS. In an action for damages for the establishment and maintenance of a nuisance on plaintiffs' premises, by converting one of their dwellings into a pest house for smallpox patients, a motion for a nonsuit, on the theory that the town was not responsible for the acts of its officers, is properly overruled, where there was sufficient evidence to warrant a finding that the health officer acted with the knowledge and authority of the town council and that his acts were ratified by the town. *Watson v. Town of Kent* 21

3. MUNICIPAL CORPORATIONS—ACTIONS—PRESENTING CLAIM FOR DAMAGES—WHEN NOT NECESSARY. In an action for damages for the wrongful act of a town through its qualified agents in establishing a nuisance on plaintiffs' premises, the presentation of a claim is not necessary before bringing suit against the town. *Id.* 21

4. MUNICIPAL CORPORATIONS—STREETS—GRADING—DAMAGE TO ABUTTING PROPERTY—INJUNCTION AGAINST GRADING. Where a city has let a contract and is about to change the grade of a street so as to damage abutting property in excess of the benefits, injunction is the proper remedy of the owner, and the city may be restrained until just compensation has been paid, as required by Const., art. 1, § 16. *Swope v. Seattle* 69

5. MUNICIPAL CORPORATIONS — LOCAL IMPROVEMENTS — ASSESSMENTS—HEARING ON OBJECTIONS—PROMISE OF CITY TO GIVE NOTICE OF ADJOURNMENT. Where proceedings are instituted before a city council to reassess property for local improvements and, pending a hearing thereon, adjournments are taken, and the city officials promise an objector to give notice of the time to be thereafter set for the hearing, the promise relates only to the pending pro-

MUNICIPAL CORPORATIONS—Continued.

ceeding, and not to a subsequent proceeding begun after the
abandonment of the first. *Alexander v. Tacoma* 366

6. Same—Indefinite Adjournment—Right to Rely on Promise
of Notice. A property owner objecting to proceedings to reassess
property has no right to rely upon an oral promise made by
city officials that he would be given notice of the time to be
thereafter set for hearing his objections, after the hearing had
been adjourned to an indefinite date. *Id* 366

7. Same—Objections to be Made Before City Council. Objections to assessment proceedings not going to the jurisdiction
must be made before the city council on the hearing pending
the confirmation of the proceedings. *Id* 366

8. Same—Objections Not Going to Jurisdiction—Waiver. Objections to a local improvement assessment, that it was made
without regard to benefits, that it exceeded the actual cost, that
it included the cost of future repairs, and exceeded the benefits,
do not go to the jurisdiction of the council to make a reassessment under the act of 1893, and are waived if not made before
the city council. *Id* 366

9. Municipal Corporations—Special Fund for Local Improvements—Wrongful Diversion by City—Complaint—Sufficiency.
The complaint in an action brought by the holder of warrants
drawn upon a special fund for local improvements, for the wrongful diversion by the city of the special fund by the payment out
of their order of subsequent warrants, thereby exhausting the
fund, fails to state facts sufficient to constitute a cause of action
when it fails to allege that the money diverted was sufficient to
pay all of the warrants drawn on the special fund which were
prior to the plaintiff's warrants, or that plaintiff was prejudiced
by being rightfully entitled to said money, or a portion thereof.
Northwestern Lumber Co. v. Aberdeen 636

MURDER:
See Criminal Law, 12, 19-20.

NAVIGABLE WATERS:
— For logging purposes. See Waters, 2-8.

NEGLIGENCE:
See Carriers; Master and Servant.
— Damages for, excessive. See Damages, 8-10.
— Driving logs, damage to land. See Waters, 1.

NEGLIGENCE—Continued.

— Decision on former appeal. See Master and Servant, 3.
— Railroad bridge. See Railroads, 1, 2.

1. Negligence—Dangerous Premises—Principal and Agent—Duty to Repair—Liability of Agent in Charge of Building—Owner a Nonresident. Agents in charge of a building, charged with the duty to make repairs, are liable for failure to keep the same in a safe condition, resulting in personal injuries to the child of a tenant, especially if the owner is a nonresident, or if service of process upon him is impossible. *Lough v. Davis & Co.*.. **449**

2. Same—Evidence of—Agents Authority—Implied From Conduct. In an action against an agent of a nonresident owner of a building, for damages sustained by the child of a tenant, through want of repairs, the fact that certain other repairs were authorized and paid for by the agent, who collected the rents and had funds that could be applied thereto, coupled with the fact that the owner was a nonresident or absent, is admissible to show that the agent had authority to make repairs, where the authority was not in writing, since it may be proved by parol and the agency implied from the conduct of the parties. *Id....* **449**

3. Same—Evidence of Agent's Authority—Sufficiency—Question for Jury. In an action against agents alleged to be charged with the duty to make repairs, brought on behalf of the child of a tenant to recover for injuries sustained by the breaking of a rotten railing on the second floor, a nonsuit is properly refused, where it appears that the agents, who collected the rents, ordered and paid for similar repairs, and personally supervised the same, apparently on their own authority, and the owner was a nonresident, or, at least, was never seen about the premises. *Id....* **449**

4. Dangerous Premises—Negligence—Agent Charged with Duty to Repair — Evidence of Authority — Sufficiency — Denial of Authority by Agent — Direction of Verdict. The fact that agents testify that they had no authority to make repairs to a building except where it was specially given, and that none was given to repair a railing and banister, which was necessary for the safety of the occupants, does not warrant a directed verdict for the defendants, where the agents made some repairs apparently on their own authority, and testified, as to their authority, that the owner did not want to spend any more money than absolutely necessary, and where the janitor, under their orders, made and oversaw many small repairs such as securing the guard rail in question. *Id.*.. **449**

NEW TRIAL:

— Necessity of motion. See APPEAL AND ERROR, 7.

— Practice in equity. See TRIAL, 4.

— Suspending judgment. See APPEAL AND ERROR, 10, 11.

— Waiver of error. See APPEAL AND ERROR, 8.

1. NEW TRIAL—MISCONDUCT OF JUROR—POLL OF JURY—CHANGE OF VOTE. A new trial should not be granted on the ground of improper conduct of the jury, nor because the jury was not immediately returned to the jury room after a poll showing that ten jurors had not agreed to the verdict, where, in a case tried by eleven jurors, it was found upon a poll that nine agreed to the verdict and two voted in the negative, and a second poll resulted in the same vote, whereupon one of the two asked and received permission to change his vote, and upon the third poll ten agreed to the verdict, and where the time consumed was only sufficient for the doing of these things in consecutive order with no appreciable intermission. *Rice Fisheries Co. v. Pacific Realty Co* 535

2. NEW TRIAL—MISCONDUCT OF JUROR—BIAS—CHARGE OF WILFULLY QUALIFYING. It is proper to deny a motion for new trial upon the ground of misconduct of the jury, upon affidavits showing prejudice by one of the jurors, and that he had wilfully qualified, where the charge is denied and is entirely overcome by other affidavits; and findings of the trial court in that respect reviewed and approved. *State v. Underwood* 558

3. NEW TRIAL—NEWLY DISCOVERED EVIDENCE. A motion for a new trial upon the ground of newly discovered evidence is properly denied where the evidence is wholly cumulative. *Id.* 558

NEW TRIAL—NEWLY DISCOVERED EVIDENCE—CREDIBILITY OF WITNESS. A new trial should not be granted for newly discovered evidence which merely goes to the credibility of the opposite party as a witness, rather than to the right of recovery. *Harvey v. Ivory* 397

NOTICE:

— Bona fide purchaser. See MORTGAGES, 1.

— Of adjournment of hearing. See MUNICIPAL CORPORATIONS, 5, 6.

— Of appeal. See APPEAL AND ERROR, 12-15.

— Of defect in bridge. See BRIDGES, 1.

— Of settlement of statement. See APPEAL AND ERROR, 18-20

— Of suit. See INDEMNITY, 3.

— Of tax. See TAXATION, 4, 10.

— Of withdrawal of attorney. See ATTORNEY AND CLIENT, 2.

— To quit. See FORCIBLE ENTRY AND DETAINER, 1, 3-6.

NUISANCES:

— Obstruction of stream. See WATERS, 5, 29.
— Pesthouse, damages. See MUNICIPAL CORPORATIONS, 2, 3.

1. NUISANCE — DAMAGES — FUMES FROM SMELTER — EVIDENCE OF CONDITIONS AT ANOTHER PLACE. In an action for damages to an orchard and vegetation caused by fumes from a smelter, evidence of the damage done in another place under different conditions, while subject to criticism, is not prejudicial error, when the witness states that the damage was similar to that done to the plaintiffs' property. *Rowe v. Northport S. & R. Co* 101

2. SAME. In such a case, where there was evidence that the smelter released sulphur on plaintiffs' farm two miles distant, it is competent to prove the release of sulphur in the immediate vicinity of the smelter, in corroboration. *Id* 101

3. SAME—EXPERT EVIDENCE OF EFFECT OF SULPHUR FUMES—EXPERIMENTS BEFORE JURY—COMPETENCY. It is error, in examining an expert witness as to the effect of sulphuric acid, to permit experiments to be made before the jury with some substance when there is no proof as to what the substance is, and none that the elements which combined to produce the experimental results were the same as combined to produce the injury to plaintiffs' farm, or that there was any similarity of conditions. *Id* 101

4. NUISANCE—ADJOINING PROPERTY—RIGHTS RUNNING WITH LAND —CONTINUING OFFENSE. In an action to enjoin a continuing nuisance upon adjoining premises, rendering plaintiffs' property unfit for residence purposes, it is immaterial that plaintiff purchased his property after the commencement of the nuisance, as the right of action existing in favor of plaintiffs' grantors runs with the land, and, also, is a continuing offense, and lapse of time bars recovery only for a completed offense. *Ingersoll v. Rousseau* 9

5. NUISANCE—ABATEMENT—DISORDERLY HOUSES—TOLERATION BY CITY NO DEFENSE. The fact that city officials tolerate the maintenance of bawdy houses is no defense to an action to abate the same as a nuisance specially injurious to adjoining property. *Id.* 9

6. SAME—ABATEMENT AT SUIT OF PRIVATE CITIZEN—SPECIAL INJURY. The owner of adjoining premises may sue to abate the maintenance of bawdy houses as a public nuisance specially injurious to his premises used for residence purposes, where the occupants are compelled to witness indecent conduct and listen to unseemly noises, the injury being special and different in kind from that suffered by the general public. *Id* 9

7. SAME—INJUNCTION TO ABATE DISORDERLY HOUSE—REMEDIES AT LAW—INADEQUACY. Injunction lies to abate the maintenance of a

NUISANCES—Continued.

bawdy house as a public nuisance specially injurious to plaintiffs'
adjoining property used for residence purposes, the common law
remedies of indictment and action on the case being inadequate,
and this rule has not been changed by statute in this state. *Id.*   92

8.   Nuisance—Slaughter House—Special Injury—Enjoined at
Suit of Owner of a Dwelling. The maintenance of a slaughter
house and stock pens adjacent to the residence section of a city,
and the suffering of the accumulation of offal, refuse, and decay-
ing matter, in the conduct of such business, is a public nuisance
that may be enjoined at the suit of the owner of a dwelling who
shows special injury by reason of nauseating and offensive smells
which taint the atmosphere and food in said house, rendering it
unfit for habitation and depreciating its market value. *Wilcox
v. Henry*   591

9.   Same—Intermittent Injury. The fact that the nuisance was
intermittent and not continual is not ground for refusing equitable relief. *Id*   591

0.   Same—Decree—Construction—Suppression of Business. A
decree enjoining, as a public nuisance, the maintenance of a
slaughter house and restraining the defendant from conducting
the business "to the injury of the plaintiff and other residents,"
is not objectionable as a suppression of the entire business, the
evidence having shown that the objectionable features could be
obviated by the installation of deodorizing machines, since the
terms of the decree permit the conduct of the business if the
noxious odors are obviated so as not to injure or annoy the plaintiff. *Id*   591

OFFICERS:
  — Certificate of. See Records, 1.
  — Power of city comptroller, admissions of. See Municipal
      Corporations, 1.
  — Ratification of acts of health officers. See Municipal Cor-
      porations, 2.
  — Record of canceled contract. See Public Lands, 6.

ORDERS:
  See Contracts, 2, 7; Municipal Corporations, 1.

PARENT AND CHILD:
  —See Adoption.

PARTIES:

— Capacity to sue. See PLEADINGS, 6.
— To foreclosure. See MORTGAGES, 1.
— To mandamus against county. See MANDAMUS, 4.
— Witnesses. See APPEAL AND ERROR, 9.

PAYMENT:

— Evidence of, sufficiency. See EVIDENCE, 5.
— Involuntary. See APPEAL AND ERROR, 29.

PERPETUITIES:

— Perpetual lease. See LANDLORD AND TENANT, 3.

PLATS:

See DEDICATION, 1.

PLEADINGS:

— As evidence, harmless error. See EVIDENCE, 6.
— Averments, when not inconsistent. See WATERS, 2.
— Complaints, sufficiency of. See ADOPTION, 3; ADVERSE POS-
    SESSION, 2; BROKERS, 1, 4, 5; CONTRACTS, 3, 7; MUNICIPAL
    CORPORATIONS, 3, 9; WATERS, 1, 3.
— Demurrer, conclusions. See MANDAMUS, 4.
— Interrogatories. See DISCOVERY, 3.
— Pleading and proof. See DAMAGES, 3; EJECTMENT, 1, 2.
— Title of defendant. See MORTGAGES, 1; REPLEVIN, 1, 2.

1. PLEADINGS—AMENDMENT. Where originally the complaint had
alleged defendant's agency in 1900, a trial amendment to state
the same fact was proper, under Bal. Code, § 4953. *McCleary
v. Willis* 676

2. PLEADINGS—AMENDMENT—MISTAKE IN ANSWER—NECESSITY OF
AFFIDAVITS AND NOTICE—SURPRISE. Where, after sustaining demurrers to defendants' affirmative defenses, an action based upon
a written contract went to trial upon issues raised by general
denials, it was not error to permit the defendants to file a trial
amendment setting up affirmatively an oral rescission of the
contract and the substitution of an oral agreement providing
a different consideration which was paid in full, without requiring an affidavit and notice to the plaintiff under Bal. Code, § 4953,
where it appeared by sworn statements of the defendants as
witnesses that a mistake was made in the first attempt to draw
the answer, and the plaintiff had early notice at the trial of the
defendants' claim and defense, and no continuance was asked
and no claim made that the plaintiff was surprised. *Cooke v.
Cain* 353

PLEADINGS—Continued.

3. Pleadings—Complaint—Objection at the Trial. An objection to a complaint made for the first time at the trial that it fails to state a cause of action, is too late to take advantage of technical defects that are capable of being cured by amendment. *Bonne v. Security Sav. Society* 696

4. Pleadings — Definiteness — Bill of Particulars — Unnecessary to Plead Evidence—Discovery of Facts. It is not error to refuse to require the complaint to be made more definite and certain or to refuse to require a bill of particulars, where the complaint pleads the ultimate facts, and the object was to require the plaintiff to plead his evidence, or to obtain a discovery of facts in possession of the plaintiff, since the remedy is by interrogatories served and answered before the trial. *Ingram v. Wishkah Boom Company* 191

5. Pleading—Demurrer—Waiver by Withdrawing—Objection to Any Evidence. The objection that the complaint does not state a cause of action, first raised by demurrer, is waived by the withdrawal of the demurrer and answering on the merits, and cannot be subsequently raised by an objection to any evidence. *Watson v. Town of Kent* 21

6. Pleadings—Demurrer—Legal Capacity to Sue—Action to Quiet Title—Waiver of Defect. In an action brought by a surviving husband to quiet his title to community real estate, in which it appears from the complaint that one of the defendants claims an interest as an heir of the deceased wife, in and to her undivided one-half of the estate, an objection that the other heirs and not the plaintiff are the persons interested, relates to the capacity of the plaintiff to sue, and is waived unless raised by special demurrer on that ground, a general demurrer not being sufficient. *James v. James* 655

7. Pleadings—Departure—Consistency of Complaint and Reply. Where a complaint alleges that a note for $400 belonging to the plaintiff came into the defendant's possession through his employment as the plaintiff's attorney, and alleges its conversion, and the answer sets up the defense that it was given to him in payment for his services, a reply admitting the allegations of the answer but averring that afterwards the defendant received other pay for his services and agreed to return the note, which he failed to do, is not inconsistent with the complaint, and a motion for judgment on the pleadings and an objection to any evidence on that account are properly overruled. *Dodds v. Gregson* 402

PRINCIPAL AND AGENT:

— Authority of agent to repair. See Negligence, 2-4.
— Authority of bank cashier, ratification. See Specific Performance, 2.
— Letter of agent. See Evidence, 1.

PRINCIPAL AND SURETY:

See Guaranty; Indemnity.
— Discharge of surety. See Bail.

PRIVILEGED COMMUNICATIONS:

See Discovery. 1.

PROCESS:

— Foreign judgment, proof. See Judgment, 1.

1. Process—Summons—Waiver of Defect by Appearance. A motion to quash the service of a summons for insufficiency in form is properly overruled, where defendant had already entered a full appearance in the action, and filed an answer to the complaint. *Mulholland v. Washington Match Co*.................. 31

2. Same—Requisites of Summons. The general statutes as to summons by publication are applicable to tax foreclosure proceedings under Laws, 1901, p. 383, § 1. *Williams v. Pittock*...... 2

3. Process—Summons—Date of First Publication. The requirement of the general statute that a summons for publication shall contain the date of the first publication is sufficiently complied with where immediately below the attorney's signature the "Date of the first publication" is stated. *Id*.................. 27

PROHIBITION:

1. Prohibition—Against Enforcement of Injunction—Equity Jurisdiction. Prohibition will not lie against the threatened enforcement of a temporary injunction issued in a suit brought against a corporation, enjoining the relators from acting as stockholders in a corporation, during the pendency of the action, where the relators intervened in that suit, moved to dissolve the injunction, and appealed from the decision; since a court of equity manifestly has jurisdiction of the subject-matter of the action, and the court acquired jurisdiction of the persons of the relators, and prohibition will not lie to prevent an erroneous exercise of conceded jurisdiction. *State ex rel. Fisher v. Kennan* 52

PROSTITUTION:

— Accepting earnings. See Criminal Law, 2. 3.

PUBLICATION:

— Of summons. See PROCESS, 3.

PUBLIC LANDS:

— Agreements respecting. See CONTRACTS, 1.
— Purchase of. See FRAUD, 2.
— Tide lands, liens on. See CONSTITUTIONAL LAW, 3-8.

1.   PUBLIC LANDS—POSSESSORY RIGHT OF SETTLERS AS CONSIDERATION FOR CONTRACT—SUFFICIENCY. Parties who have entered upon government land in good faith with the intent to lawfully acquire title to the property at some future time, are not trespassers, and may contract with reference to their right of possession, which is a sufficient consideration for mutual agreements respecting the same. *Waring v. Loomis*...................................... 85

2.   SAME—CONTRACTS RESPECTING POSSESSION OF—DESCRIPTION OF UNSURVEYED LANDS—SUFFICIENCY. A contract between parties in possession of unsurveyed public land sufficiently describes the premises, as between the parties, by referring to it as upon a certain creek and in their possession, where it was bounded by fences and the contour of certain bluffs, which formed a natural fence for a portion of the property. *Id*........................ 85

3.   PUBLIC LANDS—CONTRACT TO ACQUIRE TITLE FOR ANOTHER—VALIDITY—FRAUD ON GOVERNMENT—COMPLAINT SHOWING NO INTENT TO VIOLATE LAWS OF UNITED STATES. A contract between parties in the possession of government land, referred to as a "ranch," whereby one was to obtain a patent, if possible, and hold a half interest in trust, is not necessarily void as a fraud upon the United States, since there are various ways in which title can be secured to government land, even if agricultural in character, not inconsistent with a contract of that kind, and the presumption is that a lawful way was contemplated, especially where the complaint on such contract alleges that there was no intent to acquire the land in violation of the laws of the United States. *Id*...................................... 85

4.   TIDE LANDS—STATUTES—CONSTRUCTION OF ACT FOR EXCAVATION OF WATERWAYS—LIENS—CONSTITUTIONAL LAW—VESTED RIGHTS. Bal. Code, §§ 4080 *et seq.* providing for the excavation of public waterways by private contract, does not confer power upon the land commissioner to encumber private property with liens for filling in such property against the owner's will, but the same intends to give such liens only where the state was the owner of the tide lands when the contract was entered into. *Seattle & Lake Washington Waterway Co. v. Seattle Dock Co*............. 503

PUBLIC LANDS—CONTINUED.

5.   SAME—STATUTES—TITLE—SUFFICIENCY—POWERS OF LAND COM-
     MISSIONER. If such act gave such power, it would not be neces-
     sary to refer thereto in the title, as the title need not be a com-
     plete index to the act. *Id* 50

6.   TIDE LANDS—CONTRACT TO PURCHASE—CANCELLATION—RECORD
     OF BOARD OF LAND COMMISSIONERS. It is not necessary that the
     record show a formal declaration by the board of state land com-
     missioners that a contract for the purchase of oyster lands is can-
     celed for default in payment, where, notice having been given,
     the contract is stamped "canceled" after default for a year and
     nine months, and thereafter, upon contest with a subsequent ap-
     plicant, the board awards a contract and deed to such subsequent
     applicant, since the action of the board upon the contest is a
     sufficient declaration of cancellation. *Frazier v. Wilson* 62

PUBLIC RESORT:
     — Right to frequent. See LIBEL AND SLANDER, 1, 2.

QUANTUM MERUIT:
     — Instructions. See DAMAGES, 6.

QUIETING TITLE:
     See PLEADINGS, 6.

1.   QUIETING TITLE—RIGHT TO REDEEM FROM MORTGAGE—PROFFER OF
     REDEMPTION—BARRED BY LAPSE OF TIME. An action to quiet title,
     brought by one who only had the right to redeem from a mort-
     gage, must fail where, after foreclosure and sale to an innocent
     purchaser, the plaintiff made no proffer of redemption, and where
     the right to redeem was barred by lapse of time prior to the com-
     mencement of the action. *Jones v. Herrick* 434

RAILROADS:
     — Negligence, moving train on ferry boat. See CARRIERS, 7-10.

1.   RAILROADS—LICENSEE ON TRACK—BRIDGE MADE DANGEROUS BY
     REPAIRS—DUTY OF RAILROAD COMPANY. Although a railroad com-
     pany has permitted its bridge to be used as a thoroughfare by
     pedestrians, it is not liable to a person using the same for his
     own convenience, for injuries sustained by reason of a hole thirty
     inches wide left by the company while repairing the bridge, since
     such defect does not create a concealed danger, and the com-
     pany's liability to mere licensees is limited to avoiding wilful
     wrong and wanton carelessness. *McConkey v. Oregon R. & Nav.
     Co.* 55

RAILROADS—CONTINUED.

2. SAME—WALKING ON RAILROAD BRIDGE AT NIGHT—CONTRIBUTORY NEGLIGENCE. A licensee upon a railroad bridge who was injured by falling through a hole, was guilty of contributory negligence as a matter of law in undertaking to walk thereon in the night, where the ties were some inches apart and it was so dark that he could not see the ties or the hole. *Id*...................... 55

REAL PROPERTY:
— Rights running with land. See NUISANCES, 4.

RECEIVERS:

1. RECEIVERS—ALLOWANCE FOR ATTORNEYS' FEES. An allowance of $150 for services of a receiver's attorney is sustained by the evidence, where they extended over a considerable period, during which the receiver constantly sought advice and, from an examination of the record, the allowance seems reasonable. *Oudin & Bergman Fire Clay etc. Co. v. Cole*.......................... 647

2. SAME—ALLOWANCE TO MANAGER. Upon closing up a receivership an allowance of five dollars per day agreed to be paid to an expert brick and pottery manufacturer, as superintendent of the works, was proper, where it appears that his employment was justified by the increased production under his supervision, and that high wages were necessary. *Id*.......................... 647

RECEIVING DEPOSITS IN INSOLVENT BANK:
See CRIMINAL LAW, 1, 6, 7.

RECORDS:
— Of canceled contract. See PUBLIC LANDS, 6.

1. EVIDENCE—RECORDING—CERTIFICATE OF OFFICER—FOREIGN RECORD. A certificate of the official keeper of a record in another state endorsed upon the back of an instrument required to be recorded in such state, is not sufficient to prove the fact of the recording of such instrument. *James v. James*............... 650

RELEASE:
— Of damages. See COMPROMISE, 1-3.

REPLEVIN:
— Value of property, amount in controversy. See APPEAL AND ERROR, 4, 5.

1. REPLEVIN—PLEADINGS—ANSWER—DEFENDANT'S TITLE UNDER A GENERAL DENIAL. In an action of replevin the defendant may,

REPLEVIN—Continued.

under a general denial of plaintiff's title and right of possession, show title to the property in himself. *Harvey v. Ivory* 3

2. Replevin—Judgment for Return of Property—Relief to Defendant Without Proof of Title. Where plaintiff replevins and obtains possession of property, and fails at the trial to establish his title or right thereto, upon dismissal of the action the defendant is entitled to judgment for the return of the property, or its value if return cannot be had, without allegation or proof in support of such relief. *Id* 3

REPUTATION:

— Injury to. See Torts, 1.

RESCISSION:

— Of sale. See Fraud, 1.
— Of writing, by parol. See Pleadings, 2.

1. Evidence—Written Contract—Oral Rescission—Uncorroborated Testimony of a Party—Findings on Conflicting Evidence. It seems that the uncorroborated testimony of a party may establish that a written contract was orally rescinded, the only requirement being that the testimony be "clear, cogent and convincing," and a finding of a rescission based wholly on oral evidence will not be disturbed upon conflicting testimony, where a corroborating circumstance supports the finding and the trial court had the demeanor of the witnesses for a guide. *Cooke v. Cain* 35

2. Rescission—Fraud—Laches—Diligence in Bringing Suit. A delay of eighteen months in bringing an action for rescission of a sale of stock in a corporation on the ground of fraud will not estop the plaintiff, where the complaint alleged that the action was commenced within a reasonable time after the discovery of the fraud, and the plaintiff testified that he believed the representations to be true until one month before the commencement of the action. *Mulholland v. Washington Match Co.* 31

3. Rescission—Sale Induced by Fraud—Estoppel—Collateral Security Not Affecting Fraud in Original Contract. Where a purchase of treasury stock in a corporation was induced by fraud, the purchaser is not estopped to rescind the contract by the fact that afterwards certain other shares of stock were pledged as a guaranty, and other stock was put up as collateral, and that plaintiff had availed himself of the guaranty and collateral, since such guaranty and collateral do not affect the fraud in the original contract, or carry with it any estoppel. *Id.* 315

RIPARIAN RIGHTS:

See WATERS.

— Amount of injury. See DAMAGES, 2.

ROBBERY:

— See CRIMINAL LAW, 5.

SALES:

— Consideration. See GUARANTY, 2.
— Construction. See CONTRACTS, 4-6.
— Foreclosure, bona fide purchaser. See MORTGAGES, 1.
— Homestead, on execution. See HOMESTEAD, 3.
— Rescission for fraud. See FRAUD, 1, 3.

1. SALES—DELIVERY—DEMURRAGE ON DELAY. Nothing is due for delay in delivering machinery sold under a contract providing for $100 a day demurrage where, shortly before the day fixed, the contract was modified to include additional machinery and sixty days was given within which to manufacture the same, and the machinery was delivered in said time. *Washington Iron Works v. McNaught*.. 10

2. SALES—REFUSAL OF PURCHASER TO COMPLETE SALE—AGREEMENT TO RETIRE FROM BUSINESS AND FOR SACRIFICE SALE OF STOCK—PURCHASER'S COVENANT TO KEEP UP STOCK DURING SALE—BREACH—MEASURE OF DAMAGES. Upon the breach by defendant of a contract to purchase a stock of goods from the plaintiff, in which the defendant agreed to pay eighty-five per cent of the inventoried cost of the remaining stock after a sacrifice sale conducted under direction of the defendant, reducing the value thereof to $25,000, the defendant to keep up the stock during the sale, the measure of plaintiff's damages upon the defendant's refusal to take the remnant of the goods after the completion of the sacrifice sale, is the difference between the contract price and the value of the goods; hence it was proper to strike from the complaint claims for damage for loss of goods sold at the sacrifice sale, loss of customers by reason of failure to keep up the stock during the sale, and by reason of being unable to procure goods for the following trade, and loss to business reputation and financial credit. *Schott Co. v. Stone, Fisher & Lane* 252

3. SAME. In such a case, it is error to strike from the complaint a claim for damages by reason of the unsalable condition of the remaining stock, because not kept up during the sacrifice sale; since the same is based on the difference between the actual value of the remnant of the stock and the price agreed to be paid, and the court was not justified in striking it, although

SALES—CONTINUED.

it may have been pleaded on a different theory from the above.
Id. 2

4.   SAME—LEASE—REFUSAL OF TENANT TO ACCEPT—MEASURE OF
DAMAGES. In such a case the fact that the purchaser had also
agreed to rent the premises for a term at a certain rental,
does not change the rules ordinarily applicable to a breach
of contract for the sale of goods, or render the damages uncertain, since the measure of damages as to the lease is the
difference between the rental value and the amount agreed to
be paid. *Id.*.. 25

SLAUGHTER HOUSES:

— See NUISANCES, 8, 10.

SPECIFIC PERFORMANCE:

1.   SPECIFIC PERFORMANCE—AGREEMENT TO CONVEY LAND—DEFENSES
—TITLE OF DEFENDANT—EVIDENCE—SUFFICIENCY. In an action to
compel the specific performance of an agreement to convey an
undivided half interest in certain real estate, the defendant refusing to convey on the claim that he owned only a one-fourth
interest, there is sufficient evidence to warrant a finding that he
was the owner of a one-half interest, where it appears that
orginally the property was purchased at receiver's sale on behalf
of the defendant and three others, each to own a one-fourth
interest, that two of the other purchasers failed to pay their
shares, and the defendant and one other, in whose name the deed
was taken, jointly advanced the payments, leased the property
as joint owners, and represented to the plaintiff that the defendant owned a one-half interest, by which representations plaintiff
was induced to enter into the contract. *Washington State Bank
v. Dickson*.. 64

2.   SAME—CORPORATION AS PURCHASER—DEFENSE THAT OFFICER
WAS NOT AUTHORIZED TO PURCHASE. In an action by a banking
corporation to compel the specific performance of a contract to
convey land, there is sufficient evidence that the contract was
authorized by the plaintiff where it appears that it was made by
its cashier under directions of the trustees, and that the corporation assumed the burdens of the contract by assuming ownership
and paying the installment of the price, and subsequently the
trustees by a formal order duly ratified all of the acts. *Id.*...... 64

3.   SAME—SALE OF COMMUNITY PROPERTY—ACTS OF HUSBAND RATI-
FIED BY WIFE. A specific performance of a contract to convey
community property, made by the husband, may be decreed,

SPECIFIC PERFORMANCE—Continued.

although not signed by the wife, where she was informed of the
sale, gave full consent thereto, and joined in the execution of a
deed prepared to consummate the sale. *Id*.................... 641

STATEMENT OF FACTS:

See APPEAL AND ERROR, 18-24.

STATE AND STATE OFFICERS:

— Connivance at sale of poisonous milk. See TORTS, 1.
— Debt of state. See CONSTITUTIONAL LAW, 6.
— Loaning credit. See CONSTITUTIONAL LAW, 5.

1. STATE OFFICERS — ATTORNEY GENERAL — SALARY — TERRITORIAL
LAW ALLOWING FEES—REPEAL. Territorial Laws, 1887-8, providing that the attorney general shall receive an annual salary of
$1,800, and the further sum of ten per cent on all money collected
upon legal process instituted to enforce claims due the territory,
is repugnant to Const., art. 3, § 21, providing that he shall receive
an annual salary of $2,000, which may be increased by the
legislature, but shall never exceed $3,500, since it is clearly the
intent of the constitution that the whole compensation of the
executive officers should be fixeed by salary, as distinguished
from the fee system. *State ex rel. Stratton v. Maynard*........ 168

2. SAME—DECISION OF COMMISSIONER OF PUBLIC LANDS. In the
absence of fraud, the decision of the commissioner of public lands
upon the right of the contractor, excavating a public waterway
under the act of 1893, to a certificate, is as conclusive upon subsequent purchasers as it would be upon the state, if the state were
still the owner. *Seattle & Lake Wash. Waterway Co. v. Seattle
Dock Co* 503

STATUTES:

— Certainty, reference to mortality tables. See BENEFICIAL
    ASSOCIATIONS, 1.
— Title, sufficiency. See PUBLIC LANDS, 5.

1. STATUTES — ENACTMENT — LEGISLATURE — EXTRA SESSION—RE-
STRICTING LEGISLATIVE ACTION—CRIMINAL LAW—VALIDITY OF SAV-
ING CLAUSE FOR PENDING PROSECUTIONS. Const., art. 3, § 7, authorizing the governor to call an extra session of the legislature for a
particular purpose, which shall be stated in the call, does not
restrict legislative action at such session to that purpose, nor has
the governor power to do so, hence the legislature had power to
enact Laws Ex. Sess. 1901, p. 13, saving pending criminal prosecutions in cases of repeal, at the extra session called for the pur-

STATUTES—CONTINUED.

pose of amending the law relating to capital punishment. *State
v. Fair* 1

2.   STATUTES — TITLE — BENEFICIAL ASSOCIATIONS — REGULATION—
PRESCRIBING MINIMUM RATE. Laws 1901, p. 356, entitled "an act
regulating fraternal beneficiary societies," does not violate the
constitutional prohibition against a bill's embracing more than
one subject, by reason of the inclusion of § 12, p. 362, which
fixes a minimum rate for insurance by all such associations
thereafter authorized to transact business in this state, since
"regulation" is broad enough to include said section. *State v.
Fraternal Knights & Ladies*...................................

3.   SAME—STATUTES—TITLE. Section 15 of the insolvency act
[Laws 1890, p. 88] entitled "An act to secure creditors a just
division of the estate of debtors who conveyed to assignee for
the benefit of creditors," is not unconstitutional as embracing
more than one subject since it embraces but one subject, which
is sufficiently expressed in the title. *Jensen-King-Byrd Co. v.
Williams* 16

4.   STATUTES— TITLE — SUFFICIENCY — EXCAVATION OF WATERWAYS
AND PROVISION FOR LIENS. The title to Laws 1893, p. 241 (Bal.
Code, § 4080), the main purpose of which is to provide for the
excavation of public waterways by private contract, which is specified in the title, is broad enough to include a provision for liens
for the work performed, as that is merely incidental to the main
subject and a means of accomplishing the main purpose, and the
act is not objectionable as embracing more than one subject,
although the title also embraces the subject of such liens and the
granting of rights-of-way across the lands, and might have been
included in three separate acts. *Seattle & Lake Washington
Waterway Co. v. Seattle Dock Co*.............................. 50

STREET RAILWAYS:
    — Negligence of. See CARRIERS.

SUPERSEDEAS:
    See APPEAL AND ERROR, 16, 17.

SUPPLEMENTAL PROCEEDINGS:
    — Defenses. See ASSIGNMENT FOR CREDITORS, 1.

SURETIES:
    See PRINCIPAL AND SURETY.

TAXATION:

— Of costs. See Costs, 1.

— Judgment, vacation, tender of tax. See Judgment, 2.

— Payment, for seven years. See Adverse Possession, 1.

— Summons. See Process, 2.

1. TAXATION—EXPEDIENCY OF METHOD—DISCRETION OF LEGISLATURE. The power to impose and the method of collecting taxes, rests in the discretion of the legislature, and the expediency thereof will not be questioned by the courts. *Nathan v. Spokane County*.... 26

2. SAME—MIGRATORY STOCK TAX—UNIFORMITY—DIFFERENT METH- ODS OF ASSESSMENT. The "migratory stock tax" (Laws 1899, p. 295, § 12) upon goods brought into the state after the time for as- sessing property, to be sold in a place of business temporarily oc- cupied, is not unconstitutional on account of making distinctions as to the manner of assessments, since there is uniformity in the rate and basis of valuation. *Id*................................. 26

3. SAME—ASSESSMENT OF PROPERTY TAXED IN ANOTHER STATE. Where property is otherwise taxable it is not exempt because it may have been taxed for the same year in another state. *Id*. 26

4. SAME—VALUATION—NO PROVISION FOR EQUALIZATION—NOTICE— DUE PROCESS OF LAW—HEARING BEFORE ASSESSOR—REVIEW BY COMMON LAW REMEDIES. Laws 1899, p. 295, § 12, providing for a tax upon stocks of goods temporarily brought into the state for sale, is not unconstitutional as a taking of property without due process of law, in that it fails to provide for notice of the tax, or for any hearing before the board of equalization, since it is made the duty of the owner to notify the taxing officers, and the law provides for a hearing before the assessor, who acts in a judicial capacity in fixing the valuation, and the common law remedies may be invoked to review his decision. *Id*.................... 26

5. SAME—PROVISO AUTHORIZING ABATEMENT OF PART OF TAX. The proviso added to the "migratory stock tax" law of 1899, authoriz- ing an abatement or deduction from the next regular assessment corresponding to the portion of the year that the goods were in this state, is unconstitutional, since such discrimination is un- equal, the property must be taxed in proportion to its value, and no person can be released or discharged from any share of his tax. *Id*.......... 26

6. SAME — PARTIAL UNCONSTITUTIONALITY OF ACT NOT AFFECTING OTHER PORTIONS. The unconstitutionality of the proviso added to the "migratory stock tax" law, authorizing an abatement or de- duction of a portion of the tax, does not affect the validity of other portions of the section, since the balance is distinct and separable and complete in itself. *Id*......................... 26

TAXATION—Continued.

7.   Taxation — Assessment — Omitted Property — Duty of Assessor—Unauthorized Order of Commissioners.   The county
assessor may, on his own motion, enter for assessment on the
list of the current year, any property omitted from the list of
any preceding year, and the fact that the county commissioners
made an unauthorized order that he do so, does not affect the
validity of such an assessment, or show that the assessor did
not exercise his own discretion in the matter. *Phillips v. Thurston County* 187

8.   Same — Excessive Assessment — Validity — Jurisdiction of
Court to Restrain Collection.   Where the assessor adds to
the current assessment, personal property omitted in the preceding year, in a grossly excessive amount, or makes an assessment based upon property not owned by the party or not subject to taxation, the same is void, and the courts have jurisdiction to inquire into the propriety thereof, and to set aside the
excess, or restrain its collection. *Id*.......................... 187

9.   Same—Tender of Tax Justly Due—Bringing Tender Into
Court—Estate Already in Court.   In such a case a tender of
the amount of the tax due, made before suit and renewed in
the complaint, need not be brought into court, where the property assessed belonged to an estate in the process of administration then under the control of the same court, at least, not
without a specific objection on that ground. *Id*................. 187

10.   Taxation—Foreclosure of Lien—Notice—Summons by Publication—Name of Owner—Due Process of Law.   A summons
by publication in a tax certificate foreclosure against nonresident owners need not name or be addressed to the real owner
of the property, in order to constitute due process of law, and
is sufficient under the statute if directed to the person in whose
name the property was assessed, and to all persons, unknown,
if any, having an interest in the property; since the proceeding
is *in rem*, and the owner is bound to take notice of the tax and
all steps towards its collection. *Williams v. Pittock*............ 271

11.   Taxation—Uniformity—Poll Tax Exempting Males of Certain Ages, Females, and Members of Volunteer Fire Companies—
Acquiescence.   Section 938, Bal. Code, providing that cities of
the third class may levy upon and collect from every male inhabitant between certain ages, an annual street poll tax, but exempting therefrom members of volunteer fire companies, and city
ordinances providing for the levy and collection of such a tax
and making the refusal to pay a misdemeanor, are unconstitutional and void, as in violation of art. 7, § 9, Const., requiring

TAXATION—Continued.

uniformity in taxation of persons and property; and long continued acquiescence therein cannot sanction the clear infraction of the law. *State v. Ide*...................................... 576

TENDER:

— Of amount received in settlement induced by fraud. See COMPROMISE, 3.
— Of redemption. See QUIETING TITLE, 1.
— Of tax. See JUDGMENT, 2; TAXATION, 9.
— Reducing amount in controversy. See APPEAL AND ERROR, 3.

TIDE LANDS:

— Excavation of. See CONSTITUTIONAL LAW, 3-8; PUBLIC LANDS, 4-6; STATE AND STATE OFFICERS, 2.

TOLLS:

— Special privileges. See CONSTITUTIONAL LAW, 7.

TORTS:

— Ordering from public resort. See DAMAGES, 1.

. TORTIOUS INJURY—DAMAGES—SALE OF POISONOUS MILK—CONNIVANCE OF STATE DAIRY COMMISSIONER—INJURY BY PROSECUTION AND DAMAGE TO BUSINESS AND REPUTATION. In an action for damages by reason of the sale of poisonous milk to the plaintiffs, resulting in their arrest and prosecution for innocently reselling the same, thereby injuring their reputation and business, the complaint states a cause of action against the state dairy commissioner, as one of the defendants, where it alleges that he was a stockholder in the defendant corporation making the sale, and engaged in selling supplies to it, and to further his own interest connived at the poisoning of the milk, and afterwards caused the arrest and prosecution of the plaintiffs for using and reselling the same, since he would be a joint tort feasor. *McKenzie v. Royal Dairy*...................................... 390

TRESPASS:

— Damages from overflow. See LIMITATION OF ACTIONS, 2, 3.
— On banks of streams. See WATERS, 6.

TRIAL:

See APPEAL AND ERROR, 6-8, 30-36; CRIMINAL LAW, 14-20; EVIDENCE; JUDGMENTS; NEW TRIAL; PLEADINGS.
— Appearance. See APPEARANCE; CONTINUANCE, 1, 2.

TRIAL—Continued.

— Continuance. See Continuance.
— Exceptions. See Damages, 4.
— Inspection of papers. See Discovery, 2, 3.
— Jury, polling. See New Trial, 1.
— Nonsuit, pleading. See Master and Servant, 7.
— Objections to evidence. See Evidence, 4, 5.
— Question for jury. See Compromise, 1; Fraudulent Conveyances, 1; Landlord and Tenant, 1; Negligence, 3.
— Theory of trial. See Appeal and Error, 30.
— Verdict, excessive. See Damages, 7-10.
— Verdict, power to remit excess. See Damages, 9.

1.   Trial—Nonsuit Overruled—Dismissal. In an action tried before the court without a jury in which the court orally refuses to grant a nonsuit, whereupon the case is argued without the introduction of any evidence, the court is not precluded by the ruling on the motion for nonsuit from finding for the defendant and dismissing the action. *Hill v. Gardner* 529

2.   Trial—Motion for Nonsuit in Equity—Waiver. Appellants' challenge to the sufficiency of respondent's testimony and motion to dismiss an action for divorce are waived by proceeding to introduce evidence in their own behalf, instead of standing upon the challenge and motion. *Kane v. Kane* 517

3.   Trial—Reopening Case—Discretion. It is not an abuse of discretion to allow appellant to reopen her case after a challenge to the sufficiency of her evidence was made, where the additional evidence consisted of a formal introduction of pleadings in the case. *Id* 517

4.   Trial—New Trial—Practice in Equity. The practice upon entering judgment and the right to move for a new trial is the same in equity as in cases tried before a jury. *State ex rel. Payson v. Chapman* 64

5.   Trial—Instructions. Instructions which are not justified by any evidence are properly refused. *Washington Iron Works v. McNaught* 10

6.   Trial—Instructions—Comment on Evidence. It is not reversible error to state the issues raised by the pleadings, although there may have been no evidence offered as to some of them, where the jury is properly instructed to base their findings entirely upon the evidence. *Lough v. Davis & Co.* 449

7.   Trial—Verdict—Conflicting Evidence. The verdict of a jury will not be disturbed upon conflicting testimony, when supported by substantial evidence. *Bertelson v. Hoffman* 459
       Dodds v. Gregson 402

TRIAL—Continued.

8. TRIAL—VERDICT—WHEN NOT DISTURBED. A verdict will not be disturbed where there is substantial evidence in support of all the issues, and there is nothing to indicate that it was the result of passion or prejudice. *Ingram v. Wishkah Boom Co.* 191

9. TRIAL—VERDICT—CONFLICTING EVIDENCE. The verdict of the jury will not be disturbed upon conflicting evidence where there is testimony which, if true, is sufficient to justify it, and the trial court passed upon its sufficiency in refusing a new trial. *State v. Fair* 127

0. TRIAL—RECEIVING VERDICT—INSTRUCTIONS TO JURY. Upon receiving a verdict in the absence of counsel pursuant to stipulation, where, upon a poll of the jury, at first but nine agree, it is not error for the court, in the absence of counsel, to repeat the instructions as to the number necessary to agree, and to grant a request of a juror to allow him to change his vote, in case a mistake was made. *Rice Fisheries Co. v. Pacific Realty Co.* 535

1. TRIAL—VERDICT—FAILURE TO ASSESS AMOUNT—NO DISPUTED QUESTION OF FACT. Where a verdict is returned without assessment of the amount of the recovery, but there was no disputed question of fact and the amount is known, the irregularity does not require a reversal, since the court could either direct a verdict or discharge the jury and enter the judgment. *Casety v. Jamison* 478

TRUSTS:

See FRAUD, 7.

UNLAWFUL DETAINER:

See FORCIBLE ENTRY AND DETAINER.

VARIANCE:

See PLEADINGS.

VENDOR AND PURCHASER:

See BROKERS; SPECIFIC PERFORMANCE.

VENUE:

1. VENUE—DIVORCE—STIPULATION FOR TRIAL IN ANOTHER COUNTY—LEGISLATIVE CHANGE OF DISTRICT. A stipulation between the parties to a divorce suit to try the case in another county of the same judicial district, the same judge presiding, amounts to a change of venue, and such judge does not lose jurisdiction to try the case in such county pursuant to the stipulation, by a subse-

VENUE—Continued.

quent legislative change putting that county in a separate district and appointing another presiding judge for the county in which the suit was originally commenced. *Kane v. Kane* 51

2. Same—Consent to Change. A recital in a statement of facts that defendants to a cross-complaint had stipulated that the action might be tried in another county, sufficiently shows their consent to the change of venue, although the written stipulation therefor was originally made between the other parties and before said cross-defendants had been made parties. *Id* 51

WAIVER:

— Of breach of building contract. See Indemnity, 4, 5.
— Of demurrer. See Pleadings, 5.
— Of error. See Appeal and Error, 8.
— Of motion for nonsuit. See Trial, 2.
— Of objections to assessments. See Municipal Corporations, 7, 8.
— Of objections to complaint. See Pleadings, 6.
— Of special appearance. See Appearance, 1.

WARRANTS:

— Issuance of. See Counties, 2-4.

WASTE:

— What is. See Forcible Entry and Detainer, 6.

WATERS:

— Excavation of waterways. See Constitutional Law, 3-8.
— Condemnation of waterway, riparian rights See Eminent Domain, 4.

1. Waters—Riparian Rights—Overflow in Floating Logs in Unusual Manner — Negligence Not Essential — Complaint — Sufficiency. A complaint by a riparian owner against a logging company using the stream for floating and driving logs need not allege negligence on the part of the defendant, where it is alleged that the defendant created log jams and by dams and artificial freshet floated the logs and overflowed plaintiff's premises, since these acts are wrongful and an abuse of the right of navigation. *Ingram v. Wishkah Boom Co* 191

2. Waters—Stream Navigable for Shingle Bolts—Pleadings—Complaint to Enjoin Obstruction—Averments Not Inconsistent. An averment in a complaint that a stream is navigable for shingle bolts is not negatived by another averment that plaintiff

WATERS—Continued.

had constructed a dam for the purpose of furnishing a sufficient
supply of water to conveniently and rapidly float shingle bolts
and other timber products down said stream; and it was not
error to admit evidence supporting such a complaint. *Monroe
Mill Co. v. Menzel*... 487

3.   SAME—RIPARIAN RIGHTS—ACQUIESCENCE IN UNLAWFUL USE OF
STREAM—ESTOPPEL—PLEADINGS—SUFFICIENCY OF COMPLAINT. Averments in a complaint that plaintiff cleared a stream of obstructions on defendant's land, in order to facilitate the floating of
shingle bolts, that defendant acquiesced therein, assisted in clean-
ing out such obstructions, and thereafter used the benefits therefrom, and the flow of water as furnished by a dam constructed
by plaintiff for a period of two years, are not sufficient to plead
an estoppel against defendant's objecting to the interference by
plaintiff with the natural flow of the stream; but such failure to
show an estoppel does not defeat the plaintiff's action for an injunction, where by other averments it appears that the stream is
navigable and defendant threatens to obstruct the same. *Id*.... 487

4.   SAME—NAVIGABILITY OF STREAM—FRESHETS—LOWER RIPARIAN
RIGHTS. A stream which in its natural state is capable of floating shingle bolts after heavy rains and during freshets which
occur with periodic regularity in the spring and fall of each
year, without the storage of water by a dam, is a navigable
stream for that purpose, and plaintiff is entitled to use it as such
across the lands of a lower riparian proprietor, and interference
with such right will be enjoined. *Id*.......................... 487

5.   SAME — OBSTRUCTIONS — DETENTION AND RELEASE OF WATER —
OVERFLOW. The maintenance of a dam and the detention of the
water in a stream which is navigable for the purpose of floating
shingle bolts, and the release of the water at irregular intervals,
causing the stream to overflow and wash the lands of a lower
riparian proprietor, and obstructing his navigation thereof, is
such an interference with the natural flow of the water as will
be enjoined. *Id*.. 487

6.   SAME—RIGHT TO BANKS OF UNMEANDERED STREAM. One who
makes use of an unmeandered stream for driving timber is not
entitled to go upon the banks of a riparian owner unless the
land owner consents, or until the right to their use has been
acquired in a lawful way. *Id*.................................. 487

7.   WATERS—NAVIGATION—FLOATING LOGS—NUISANCES—DAMS—
ARTIFICIAL FRESHETS—INJUNCTION. The floating of logs down a
stream by means of dams and artificial freshets at a time of the
year when it is not navigable in its natural state, is an abuse of

WATERS—Continued.

the right of navig. on, for which an injunction will lie at the suit of riparian owners injured thereby. *Matthews v. Belfast Mfg. Co*.............. 66

8.   Same—Injunction—Terms of. In such a case an injunction is not too sweeping where it permits the defendant to use its dam for lawful purposes. *Id*................................... 66

9.   Same — Defenses — Improper Use of Stream. An action to enjoin the defendant's abuse of the rights of navigation, by the use of dams and the creation of artificial freshets in a logging stream, will not be defeated by the fact that the plaintiff also maintains a dam for the same purpose, where the evidence shows that his use thereof is reasonable and proper, and his dam is not a nuisance. *Id*.. 66

WITNESSES:

— Disallowance of fees, parties to appeal. See Appeal and Error, 9.

Ex. a. C.C.
12/9/04.

4784 616

Lightning Source UK Ltd.
Milton Keynes UK
UKHW020206091118
331957UK00012B/1673/P

9 780260 67